Y0-BSQ-308

ACTS OF THE APOSTLES

ACTS OF THE APOSTLES

Expository and Homiletical
Commentary

by
David Thomas

KREGEL PUBLICATIONS
Grand Rapids, Mi. 49501

Acts of the Apostles by David Thomas.
Published in 1980 by Kregel Publications
a division of Kregel, Inc. All rights reserved.

Library of Congress Cataloging in Publication Data

Thomas, David, 1813-1894.
    Acts of the Apostles.

    Reprint of the 1870 ed. published by R.D.
Dickinson, London, under title: Homiletic Com-
mentary on the Acts of the Apostles.
    1. Bible. N.T. Acts—Commentaries. I. Title.
(BS2625.T43   1980   226'.607   79-2543
ISBN 0-8254-3810-1

Printed in the United States of America

Contents

vi / Contents

viii / Contents

Preface

THIS book is for the most part made up of homiletic sketches which appeared from month to month in the "Homilist," during a period of five years. Though they are the productions of one author for one purpose, they were written by various scribes at various times, under various conditions and moods. Hence they vary in length, vigour, and finish. They are now gathered together and shaped into a volume, in obedience to the urgent and oft-repeated requests of the numerous readers of the "Homilist." Those who read them in that serial will find that here they have undergone some modifications and received considerable additions. They have here added to them Emendative Renderings, Exegetical Remarks, and the various readings of the three most celebrated MSS. of the original Greek text.

The aim of the author in this work is that for which, as a homiletical writer, he has been labouring for years, namely, the promotion of *expository* preaching: the preaching which St Chrysostom describes as that in which "God speaks much and man little." Profound and growing is the author's conviction that this mode of preaching is at once the most legitimate, powerful, and indispensable. Whence come the ideas necessary to work out the spiritual regeneration of mankind? Are they born of the human brain? No. The thoughts of the greatest of human thinkers are, like their authors, imperfect and frail. None of them are solar rays; they fall as cold moonbeams upon the minds of their contemporaries. God's ideas are the only soul-vivifying forces in our fallen world: and these ideas are contained in the histories, the metaphors, the conversations, discourses, gospels, and epistles of His Holy Book. It is only as they are brought out of the text and flashed into souls that men are spiritually and really helped. This is the work of *true* preaching. No man deserves the name of preacher who does not so critically and inductively study the Scriptures as to reach those ideas, bring them out, and so arrange them as to commend them to every man's intellect, conscience, and heart, as the quickening thoughts of God. For well nigh five hundred years, alas! this kind of preaching has fallen into desuetude. Out of the ten thousand preachers in Christendom there are but few expositors. Men take isolated passages, attach to them their own theological notions, and call the work preaching. Texts are used as mere instruments on which to hang some piece of theological patchwork, a flimsy, tawdry rag, which is called a sermon. An awful outrage this upon the Holy Book, a grim trifling with the realities of eternity! The sentences of God's Book should not be used as pegs on which to exhibit man's thoughts, but rather as seminal substances out of which, by culturing effort, he may bring out trees of life whose fruit shall be for the healing of the nations. Why is expository preaching so rare in these days? Not because it cannot be rendered of all preachings the most attractive and profitable to the hearer, but because it requires on the preacher's part a scholarship which he is too lazy to acquire, an inductive study of the Holy Word which his self-indulgence forbids. A distinguished American scholar and divine, in suggesting to his late charge the principles on which they should select a pastor, says, "Do not choose a man who always preaches upon insulated texts. I care not how powerful and eloquent he may be in handling them. The effect of his power and eloquence will be to banish a taste for the Word of God, and substitute the preacher in its place."

The author, in glancing over some portions of the work now lying before him, discovers sundry mistakes and blemishes. As, however, they do not touch any vital truth, he will leave the reader to find them out for himself, and will not catalogue the *errata*. The next edition may reach a higher perfection. Whilst the ablest reader will discover the most blemishes, he will be the most merciful in his treatment of the author: for he will appreciate the difficulties in producing a work involving so much mental labour of various kinds—interpretation, invention, generalisation, grouping, and illustration. As the greatest sinners are the severest judges, so the smallest men are the most heartless critics. "The man," says Shenstone, "who fails in writing a work himself, becomes often a morose critic. The weak and insipid white wine makes at last the best vinegar."

With all its faults, the author entertains the hope that the commentary will be of some service. There is no other work exactly like it, and it takes an unoccupied place in homiletic literature. The most similar to it, but transcending it in many respects, is that edited by Dr Lange, a most valuable production on account of its scholarly renderings and exegetical explanations, but imperfect in its homiletical department. Its "Homiletical Hints," it is true, abound with many striking, suggestive, and beautiful thoughts, but they have often no logical arrangement, and sometimes but little vital connexion with the truths contained in the passage under review.

The author would here record his obligations to those authors from whom he has received great assistance. Amongst those the names of Conybeare and Howson, Alford, C. J. Vaughan, Neander, Baumgarten, Barnes, Stier, Livermore, Lange, Bengel, and J. W. Alexander of New York, stand pre-eminent.

It is the author's earnest hope that this work may be of some service to those who are engaged with him in the ministry of the Word. Those who derive benefit from it will, he is sure, treat it as the bee treats the flower, extract what they want without hurting the old stem, so that perchance it may blossom again, and exude some useful nectar.

David Thomas

Homiletical Commentary
on Acts of the Apostles

Part 1. The Church Among the Jews
Acts 1-8

Acts 1:1-5

THE UNIQUENESS OF CHRIST'S EARTHLY MINISTRY

" The former treatise have I made, O Theophilus, of all that Jesus began both to do and teach, until the day in which he was taken up, after that he through the Holy Ghost had given commandments[1] unto the apostles whom he had chosen: to whom also he showed himself alive after his passion by many infallible proofs, being seen of them forty days, and speaking of the things pertaining to the kingdom of God: and, being assembled together with them, commanded them that they should not depart from Jerusalem, but wait for the promise of the Father, which, saith he, ye have heard of me. For John truly baptized with water; but ye shall be baptized with the Holy Ghost not many days hence."

EMENDATIVE RENDERINGS.—(1.) Had given commandments to the apostles whom He had chosen through the Holy Ghost.—ALFORD.

EXEGETICAL REMARKS.—*" The former treatise have I made."* The former work was by general consent his Gospel, the Gospel according to Luke.

" O Theophilus." Who this Theophilus was, to whom he inscribes this and his former production, is not known. We have only here the mere mention of his name. From the fact, however, that Luke made him his dedicatee, we may infer the probability that he was a friend of the writer, a man of some social distinction, and a Christian of eminence. The etymology of his name indicates that he was a friend of God. Who Theophilus was, however, is a matter of little importance; the substance of the book that is dedicated to him is what is vital and momentous, that is, the deeds and doctrines of Christ.

"All." This word is not to be understood as literal, but relative. It does not designate the whole of what Christ did actually do and teach on earth; it would have taken ponderous folios to have recorded all this: but it means all that came within the plan of the writer in his history.

" *That Jesus began both to do and teach.*" Now, from the arrangement of these words in the original Greek, two things are plain which escape the English reader : First, there is an emphasis on the verb "*began;*" secondly, there is none on the word "*Jesus.*" The contrast is not that the former treatise related what *Jesus* began, and this relates what some other person or persons continued ; but it is that the former treatise related what Jesus *began* to do and to teach : and this relates what He, the same Jesus, *continued* to do and to teach. And thus we have won already a position of some importance for the understanding of what is to follow. It is to be a continuation or second part of the acts and teachings of the Lord, as that former treatise was a beginning or first part. So that it has rather unfortunately been called " *The Acts of the Apostles,*" being rather "the second part of the Gospel," or the " latter," or second treatise of St Luke.—ALFORD.

" *The day in which he was taken up.*" "The day" refers to the day of ascension, which is here expressed as being " taken up," or, as some express it, " taken back" into heaven ; and it is here said that this ascension took place " after" He had, by the Holy Ghost, qualified His disciples to represent Him on the earth, and carry on His cause when He was gone.

" *After he through the Holy Ghost had given commandments unto the apostles whom he had chosen.*" As this phrase in the original stands between the verbs *commanded* and *chose*, the passage may mean either that He chose the apostles through the Holy Spirit, or that He gave them the commission of the Holy Ghost. As both ideas are true, it is of no vital matter which idea is intended to be conveyed.

" *To whom also he showed himself alive after his passion by many infallible proofs.*" Christ seems to have made *ten* distinct appearances of Himself to His disciples after His resurrection from the dead. The first was to Mary Magdalene, recorded in Mark xvi. and John xx. : the second was to Cleophas and another of the disciples on the way to Emmaus, (Mark xvi. 12 ; Luke xxiv. 13–32 :) the third was to Simon Peter, (Luke xxiv. 33–35 ; 1 Cor. xv. 5 :) the fourth was in the evening of the same day to the eleven, in the absence of Thomas, and at Jerusalem, (Luke xxiv. 36–43 ; John xx. 19–25 :) the fifth, when, " eight days afterwards," He appeared to the eleven at Jerusalem, Thomas being present, (Mark xvi. 14 ; John xx. 26–29 ; 1 Cor. xv. 6 :) the sixth, when He appeared to all, or part of, the women who had first visited the sepulchre, and sent a command by them to the disciples to depart unto Galilee, (Matt. xxviii. 1–10 :) the seventh, when he appeared to the apostles, and probably to the whole body of disciples, on a certain mountain in Galilee, (1 Cor. xv. 6 :) on the eighth He appeared to certain of his disciples while fishing on the lake of Galilee, (John xxi. 1–24 :) the ninth, when He appeared to James, "the Lord's brother," in Galilee, (1 Cor. xv. 7 :) the tenth, on the morning of His ascension, when He appeared to the apostles assembled in Jerusalem, (Luke xxiv. 43–51 ; Acts i. 4–8.)

" *The promise of the Father.*" This promise was given not only in the Old Testament, as in Joel iii. 7 ; Zach. ii. 10, but also in the teaching of Christ, Luke xxiv. 49 ; John xiv. 16, xv. 26, xvi. 7-13 ; and compare Matt. x. 20, and John xx. 22.

" *For John truly baptized with water]: but ye shall be baptized with the Holy Ghost.*" " *As* John baptized with water, *so* ye shall be baptized," &c. " *Though* John baptized with water, *yet* ye must be baptized," &c. The extraordinary influences of the Holy Spirit are repeatedly described both in the language and the types of the Old Testament, as *poured* on the recipient. Thus the standing symbol of official gifts and graces is the rite of unction or anointing, as described or referred to in the Law, (Lev. viii. 12,) the Psalms, (cxxxiii. 2,) the Prophets, (Isa. lxi. 1,) and the Gospel, (Luke iv. 18.) The official inspiration of Moses was extended to the seventy elders by being *put upon them*, (Num.

xi. 17, xxv. 13, xxix.,) and the highest spiritual gifts are promised in that exquisite expression, " until the Spirit be *poured upon us* from on high," (Isa. xxxii. 15.) This effusion is the very thing for which they are here told to wait ; and, therefore, when they heard it called a baptism, whatever may have been the primary usage of the word, they must have seen its Christian sense to be compatible with such an application, particularly as they must ,have known it to be used in Hellenistic Greek to signify a mode of washing where immersion was excluded, such as that of tables or couches, and the customary pouring of water on the hands before eating, as still practised in the East. (See Mark vii. 4-8 ; Luke xi. 38.) With their fixed Old Testament associations, when assured that they were soon to be *baptized with the Holy Ghost*, they would naturally think, not of something into which they were to go down, but of something to be *poured upon them from on high.* The indefinite expression, *Holy Spirit*, might, without absurdity, be taken as parallel to *water* in the first clause, each then denoting a baptismal element or fluid.—ALEXANDER.

HOMILETICS.—The paragraph before us reveals two facts which mark off the *ministry of Christ on earth from that of any other :*—

I. THAT HIS MINISTRY ON EARTH WAS ORIGINAL.

He *" began."* His ministry here was the *beginning* of a work which earth had never witnessed before ; something absolutely *new.* His *works* were original. What He did here He did in His *own* strength. The most brilliant deeds the holiest men of past times performed, were wrought not in their own strength, but in the strength of Heaven. They were organs ; nothing more. Not so with His works : what He did He did in His own name, and by His own might as a God. His *teaching* was original. The doctrines He proclaimed, He derived not from others, or from any source out of Himself. "He was the truth." The doctrines He enunciated went out from Him as living streams from a fountain of life. His *life* was original. Such a life was never lived on this earth before ; so blending the weak with the strong, the fleeting with the eternal, the human with the Divine, and in all so absolutely true and pure. His entire history was the *beginning* of a something that earth had never seen or felt before. It was a new fountain opened up on earth's parched desert, a new light kindled in earth's dark sky. He *began* a new river of spiritual influence, a new system of government, a new race of men. He *began*, He did not *finish.*

His ministry was initiatory. What He did here was only introductory. Luke's idea, probably, might have been, that his Gospel was the commencement of a life which was now developed in that history of the apostles which he was now about to write. This is a view taken by certain eminent modern critics, and it is a view that harmonises with the facts of the case. When Christ *corporeally* left the world, His work did not cease. His spirit was still here. " I am with you always, even unto the end of the world." In spirit He abode with the apostles, He lived in them, and wrought through them. "His spirit was manifested in their mortal bodies." Before His ascension, He lived and wrought in *one* human body, that which was born in Bethlehem and expired upon the cross. After his ascension, He lived and wrought in *many* human bodies. His inspired apostles were, in a sense, multiplied Christs. He was in them. They were conscious of His presence and His power, and they ascribed their triumph to his strength. " Thanks be to God who always causeth us to triumph in Christ." So that this Acts of the Apostles is but a chapter in the earthly biography of the Son of God. The following remarks of Baumgarten illustrate and confirm the view, that the history in the ACTS OF THE APOSTLES is but the history of Christ in His disciples :—" He it is who appoints the twelve witnesses, (i. 24,) who, after He himself has received the Spirit, sends Him down from on high on His Church, (ii. 33 ;) who adds to His Church in Jerusalem, (ii. 47 ;) He, too, during the first days of the Church, is ever near His people Israel, to bless them in turning them away from their iniquities. He it is who works miracles, both of healing and destruction, in testimony to His apostles' preaching, (iii. 6, 10, 30 ; ix. 34; xiii. 11 ; xiv. 3 ; xix. 13 ;) to His dying martyr, Stephen, He reveals Himself standing at the right hand of God, (vii. 55, 56 ;) His angel speaks unto Philip, (viii. 26 ;) it is His Spirit that caught him away, (viii. 39 ;) He appears to Saul of Tarsus, (xix. 5, 27 ; xxii. 8, 26 ;) His hand established the first church among the Gentiles, (xi. 27 ;) His angel delivers St Peter, (xii. 7, 11, 17 ;) His angel strikes the hostile Herod, (xii. 23 ;) He again it is who appears to St Paul in the temple, and commits to him the conversion of the Gentiles, (xxii. 17, 21 ;) to Him the apostles and brethren address themselves on the occasion of the first mission to the Gentiles, (xiii. 2, v. 47 ;) to Him are the infant churches commended, (xiv. 23 ;) His Spirit prevents the apostolic missionaries from preaching in Bithynia, (xvi. 7 ;) He calls them by the voice of the man of Macedonia into Europe, (xvi. 10;) He opens the heart of Lydia and effects the conversion in Europe, (xvi. 14 ;) He comforts and encourages Paul at Corinth, (xviii. 9, 10 ;) He strengthens him in prison, and informs him of his journey to Rome, (xxiii. 11.) These interventions of Jesus, so numerous, express, and decisive, are a sufficient warrant for our regarding His ascension as essentially His really setting on His throne. We are, therefore, fully justified in ascribing all to His influence, even in those instances where, without any express mention of His name, we are referred to the invisible world. In this way, therefore, we must consider the conversion of the Samaritans by miracles, (viii. 6–12 ;) the restoration of Tabitha, (ix. 36–42 ;) the vision of St Peter, (x. 10–16.) And in like manner in those passages, also, where the Holy Ghost is spoken of as the efficient cause, (as *e.g.* xiii. 2,) we must bring before our minds the Lord Himself; for the Holy Spirit is the Spirit of Jesus, (xvi. 6, 7 ;) and also, in every mention of the name of God, as at xxvii. 23, we are to understand the person of Jesus, for, from i. 22, iv. 30, we learn that God works by Him," (29.)

Moreover, the passage teaches :—

II. THAT HIS MINISTRY ON EARTH WAS POSTHUMOUS.

" Until the day in which He was taken up, after that He through the Holy Ghost had given commandments unto the apostles whom He had chosen." *Christ did not leave the world before He had made effective arrangements for the working out of the grand purpose of His mission.* Whatever Christ did, He did *through the Divine Spirit.* Divinity was the breath of His every word, and the pulse of His every act. Thus, after He had passed through the agonies of death, and been buried in the grave, He appeared again amongst men, and exercised His personal ministry for about forty days. The words of Luke here suggest two things.

First, *That His personal ministry " after His passion," was an undoubted reality.* " To whom also He showed Himself alive after His passion by many infallible proofs, being seen of them forty days, and speaking of the things pertaining to the kingdom of God." We offer the following remarks on these appearances :—

(1.) *They were in themselves " infallible proofs."* We might challenge, with the utmost confidence, the most shrewd and intelligent enemies of Christianity to produce any fact in history so well attested as these appearances attest the fact of Christ's resurrection. They took place not only in the evening, but in the morning, and in the full blaze of day, at *ten* different times. They were not made to one or two individuals, but to several, and even to hundreds. Those appearances were not shadowy and intangible ; He appeared in a veritable corporeity. Thomas *felt* His wounded side ; He ate and drank with His disciples, and talked to their conscience and their hearts.

(2.) *The witnesses of these appearances were indisposed to believe in the fact of His resurrection.* The disciples to whom He showed Himself expected that He would establish a visible kingdom upon the earth. When He died their hopes for the hour were entirely dissipated ; black disappointment had enshrouded their spirits ; they never supposed that He would rise again. " For as yet they knew not the scripture, that he must rise again from the dead," (John xx. 9.) Hence Thomas said, " Except I shall see," &c. In fact, they were so incredulous on this subject, that they regarded the first information they received as entirely fabulous. " Their words seemed to them as idle tales, and they believed them not," (Luke xxiv. 11.)

(3.) *Though the witnesses were indisposed to believe in the fact of His resurrection, they were thoroughly convinced.* Not one of the witnesses ever seem to have doubted the fact ; it was universally admitted ; they proclaimed it publicly at Jerusalem, and before the very Sanhedrim they thundered out their conviction on the point. Peter, for example, standing up, said, " Whom God," &c., (Acts ii. 24–32.) His appearances, then, were " infallible proofs."

> " Twice twenty days he sojourn'd here on earth,
> And show'd himself alive to chosen witnesses,
> By proofs so strong, that the most slow-assenting
> Had not a scruple left. This having done,
> He mounted up to heaven. Methinks I see him
> Climb the aerial heights, and glide along
> Athwart the severing clouds."—BLAIR.

Secondly : *His personal ministry, after His passion, was confined to His disciples.* Before His death He spoke to Scribes, Pharisees, Sadducees, Herodians, to promiscuous crowds. But we have not an instance of His speaking to any after His death but His disciples. He confined His attention to the men between whom and Himself there was a vital spiritual connection. Henceforth He would deal with the unconverted world, not directly, but through the medium of His disciples.

Observe here :—

(1.) The grand subject of His ministry amongst them was the *kingdom of God.* " The things pertaining to the kingdom of God" were the grand themes of His discourse. The discoveries of science, the speculations of philosophy, the politics of nations—such subjects as these, which agitated the outward world, were not touched upon in His loftiest converse with His disciples. " Things" of a higher type ; things that underlie and regulate the universe ; things, compared with which the greatest realties of earth are but as passing shadows ; things that restore polluted spirits to holiness, disordered spirits to harmony, apostate spirits to God—were the things of His ministry, the things pertaining to His kingdom ; a kingdom that "is not meat or drink, but righteousness, and peace, and joy, in the Holy Ghost." Before His death, in many a living sentence and striking parable, He taught much about this "kingdom of God." Death had not changed His views, or modified His feelings in relation to this grand subject. Observe :—

(2.) The grand endeavour of His ministry amongst men was to *prepare them to become His propagandists.* He was going to leave His cause in their hands. The diffusion of the knowledge of Himself, His ideas and purposes, was now to depend upon their agency. For a work of such awful magnitude and responsibility, they required special direction, training, and encouragement. To qualify them for this grand mission was the great purpose of His ministry amongst them during these " forty days."

He did this in various ways :—

(*a.*) By giving them distinct impressions of the work He required them to discharge, (Matt. xxviii. 19–20 ; Mark xvi. 15–16.)

(*b.*) By giving them an immovable conviction of the fact of His resurrection. Such a conviction was an indispensable qualification. Doubts on this subject would render them utterly powerless in their mission. This conviction He gave by many "infallible proofs." These apostles *never* after questioned this fact.

(*c.*) By preparing them for the reception of their great Helper, the Holy Spirit. He commanded them to wait for the promise of the Father. This Helper the Father had promised, (Joel iii. 1; Zech. ii. 10.) This Helper John the Baptist had predicted, and his spiritually purifying work he had symbolised by his baptism in the Jordan. "John truly baptized with water, but ye shall be baptized with the Holy Ghost." This Helper was to come in an extraordinary plenitude of influence, after His departure. "It is expedient for you that I go away," &c. For this Spirit He bids them now "wait" in Jerusalem—"wait" in holy thought, and earnest prayer, and rapt devotion, so as to be prepared for the celestial visitant.

What a ministry was Christ's! Absolutely original. The holiest ministries of the greatest of God's servants have all been borrowed. He "began" the work for Himself. He laid the foundation-stone of a superstructure which He is now carrying on, and which, when He has finished, will fill the universe with wonder and praise. His ministry was initiatory. He personally resumed it after death, and He carries it on now. Through the long line of ages do you find any other teacher rising from his grave to resume his work? No. Death puts an end to our ministry here. We can do nothing for the world when we are gone. Mortality seals our lips for ever. But His work goes on here, and advances among the children of men. He is preaching through all the good. "Lo, I am with you always," &c. Purify, enlighten, and raise up in ever-augmenting numbers, O Christ, men through whom Thou shalt breathe Thy Heavenly Spirit, and speak Thy quickening words to souls dead in trespasses and sin.

Acts 1:6-8

CHRIST'S LAST WORDS TO HIS DISCIPLES

" *When they therefore were come together, they asked of him,*[1] *saying, Lord, wilt thou at this time restore*[2] *again the kingdom to Israel? And he said unto them, It is not for you*[3] *to know the times or the seasons, which the Father hath put in his own power.*[4] *But ye shall receive power, after that the Holy Ghost is come upon you:*[5] *and ye shall be witnesses unto me*[6] *both in Jerusalem, and in all Judea, and in Samaria, and unto the uttermost part of the earth.*"

EMENDATIVE RENDERINGS — (1.) They therefore came together and asked him. —ALFORD. (2.) Art thou restoring? (3.) It is not yours. (4.) Authority.— ALFORD. (5.) The Holy Ghost coming upon you.—ALEXANDER. (6.) My witnesses.—LANGE.

"EXEGETICAL REMARKS.—*"Lord wilt thou at this time,"* &c.—Their question seems to have taken for granted that the kingdom would be restored in some form or other. Prophecy justified them in this belief. See Isa. i. 26, ix. 7; Jer. xxiii. 6, xxxiii. 15, 17; Dan. vii. 13, 14; Hos. iii. 4, 5; Amos ix. 10; Zech. ix. 9. What they wanted to know was, would the restoration take place at *this time?*

"It is not for you," &c. It is not your business.

"Times and seasons," χρόνοι and καιροὶ, spaces and points, as some understand. The terms are evidently not synonymous, but generic and specific terms. "The one denoting intervals and periods; the other points and junctures, like era and epoch in modern English."

"Ye shall receive power." — This means that ye shall receive strength, moral strength—strength of principle and purpose.

"Ye shall be witnesses unto me both in Jerusalem, and in all Judea, and in Samaria, and unto the uttermost part of the earth."—The Greek word μάρτος, translated "witness," has given us the word "martyr." Because the men who were the faithful witnesses of the facts of Christ's history were exposed to suffering and death, martyr and witness became almost synonymous. The word here, however, is not to be regarded as meaning martyr, but must be taken in its modern popular acceptation.

HOMILETICS.—Frequent were the interviews which the Heavenly Teacher had with His disciples previous to His death, and to those interviews we are indebted for much of His most elevated teaching. Rivers of truth, reflecting on their pellucid bosoms the brightest things of the upper heavens, and bearing life in their course, rose out of those delightful interviews. Some nine or ten times, too, He met them after His death; but here is the *final* interview. The best things on earth must come to a close. Here closes the earthly history of the Great Son of God. The divine drama is over; the curtain falls, and the Great Actor quits the world in chariots of clouds. The place of this final meeting was the Mount of Olives—a mount hard by the Holy City, lying to the east—a scene over which He had often passed, and where, before His death, He had often mingled with His disciples. The passage before us gives us His last words; and His last words were words of *correction, encouragement, direction,* and *benediction.*

I. His last word were words of CORRECTION. The old prejudice, strange to say, of the disciples, came up on this hallowed occasion. "They asked of him, saying, Lord, wilt thou at this time restore again the kingdom to Israel?" The meaning is—Tell us if Thou art restoring. By the restoring, they meant making Israel the triumphant and the ruling power, the imperial mistress of the world. This had been the brilliant dream of their ancestors for ages, and it haunted them now. Their question indicated the working of several wrong elements in them:—(1.) *Materialism.* Notwithstanding the spirituality of the teaching they had received from their Master, their notions of dominion were associated with material conquests, material thrones, and crowns, with all the pomp and pageantry of earthly kingdoms.

That empire of truth and love which Christ came to establish over human souls, compared with which all earthly kingdoms were but as passing shadows, had not yet penetrated them with its transcendent glory. (2.) *Prejudice.* Such a temporal dominion they had been taught in their childhood to anticipate. The idea they had not reached by conviction, but by tradition ; and, without examination, they had allowed it to grow with their growth. The three years' teaching of Christ, which bore directly against such temporal ideas of dignity and dominion, had failed to shatter this old prejudice. It comes up now in their final meeting with their Master. (3.) *Ambition,* too, is seen at work in this question. They undoubtedly had an eye to temporal elevation. Probably they expected to be the leading ministers in such a kingdom, and to share its brilliant honours and immunities. (4.) *Curiosity.* They were prying into that which lay out of their province. They should have directed their curiosity, not to kingdoms, but to duties.

Now Christ directs words of *correction* to this morally mistaken state of mind. " It is not for you to know the times." Christ in His reply does not touch the question of empire itself. He does not say that there shall be no restoration of the kingdom, He leaves their errors on that subject to be corrected by that enlightening Spirit who was about to descend, and whom he bade them await at Jerusalem.

First : *His words served to check the spirit of idle curiosity concerning the future.* Virtually, Christ says, " Let the future alone, it is a realm impenetrable to your vision. The future is to reveal itself in history, not to be ascertained by human inquiry. Your duty is with the present, out of which the future grows. Let the present be holy, and the future will be bright." Would that modern prophet-mongers would listen to this reproof !

Secondly : *His words served as a ground for unbounded trust.* " The Father hath put in his own authority." All futurities are in the jurisdiction of a Father, who has the tenderest interest in us, and the most affectionate regard for us. It is love that hides the future. Were He to withdraw the veil, and make bare to us the events that are on their march, our social arrangements would be shattered, our free agency destroyed, and all our powers of action paralysed. A Father manages the awful future, and a Father's loving hand hath woven the veil that conceals it from mortal gaze.

II. His last words were words of ENCOURAGEMENT. " But ye shall receive power." The power here promised was of two kinds :—

First : *Miraculous.* The Spirit that descended on them on the day of Pentecost enabled them to work mighty marvels. " Signs and wonders " followed them in working out their apostolic mission.

Secondly : *Moral.* The *moral* power with which they were endued

—the power that made them brave, faithful, magnanimous, self-sacrificing, and successful in their mission, was, for many reasons, greater than the *miraculous*.

Both kinds of power, however, came to them with the advent of that Holy Ghost which Christ now promised, and which was just at hand. Hence this, His last word of *encouragement*, was exquisitely opportune. The reproof which He had dealt them in reply to their inquiry concerning the restoration of the kingdom, would be felt by them as caustic and severe. This promise of power comes as a healing balm. The power He promises infinitely transcends the political power of kingdoms ; before it, the might of the Cæsars is feebleness. It was a power to change the heart of kings, to regulate the springs of empire, to mould the governments of the world. The advent of this power would supply His absence, and its operations would deepen upon the heart of the world the impressions of His doctrine, widen the range of His influence, and work His wise and heavenly purposes to a triumphant issue. This power would build up His kingdom in the world. A kingdom, His, far sublimer than that which loomed in the vision of the disciples now. The old, gorgeous, theocratic kingdom of Israel was but a faint type of His. The grandest earthly dynasties are shadows to it. Napoleon Bonaparte, in a conversation with General Bertrand a little before his death, said, " Alexander, Cæsar, Charlemagne, and I have founded empires ; but on what have we rested the creations of our genius ? Upon *force*. No one but Jesus has founded an empire on *love ;* and at this moment millions of men would die for Him. It was not a day, nor a battle, that won the victory over the world for the Christian religion. No ! it was a long war, a fight of three centuries, begun by the apostles and continued by their successors and the Christian generations that followed. In that war all the kings and powers of the earth were on one side ; and on the other side I see no army, but a mysterious force, and a few men scattered here and there through all parts of the world, who had no rallying point but their faith in the mysteries of the Cross. I die before my time, and my body will be put into the ground to become the food of worms. Such is the fate of the Great Napoleon ! What an abyss between my deep wretchedness and Christ's eternal kingdom, proclaimed, loved, adored, and spreading through the world." Was that dying ? Was it not rather to live ? This " mysterious force," of which the conqueror of Europe speaks, we are accustomed to call " the power of God."

III. His last words were words of DIRECTION. " Ye shall be witnesses unto me both in Jerusalem," &c. The words of *direction* which Christ here gives, point to three things.

First : *The nature of their ministry.* They were to be " witnesses ;" they were to declare what they had actually seen, and heard, and felt in relation to Christ. Hence their preaching at first was little more than an honest and fervid declaration of *facts* concerning Christ which had been demonstrated to them. (Chap. ii. 22–36 ; iii. 12–33 ; iv. 8–12 ; v. 29–32.) These men left all the theorising about these facts for the weaker, but more pretentious, men of later ages.

Secondly : *The universality of their ministry.* They were not to confine their labours to any district, or tribe, or nation ; they were to go to the "uttermost parts of the earth." The wide world, including Jew and Gentile, and all the races of man, was their field. "They were to go into all the world," &c. Christ's philanthropy embraces universal man.

Thirdly : *The method of their ministry.* They were to "begin in Jerusalem, then proceed through all Judea, then through Samaria, then through the uttermost parts of the earth." They followed this order. They began in Jerusalem ; the great Pentecostal work started there. They seem to have remained working in this city for nearly eight years. The martyrdom of Stephen was the means of drawing them forth into various parts of Judea, and into Samaria. (Chap. viii.) Afterwards they proceeded to the "uttermost parts of the earth." During the apostolic age, the gospel was preached throughout most of the known world. (Rom. x. 18 ; Col. i. 6–23.) In this method of propagating the Gospel, we discover two things :—

(1.) Unexampled mercy. Offering mercy first to His greatest enemies.

(2.) Consummate policy. It was for reasons most wise, which we have elsewhere explained, that Christ instituted this method.* Well would it have been for Christianity if the Church, in her missionary efforts, had practically observed this policy.

IV. His last words were words of BENEDICTION. We gather this, not from the text, but from the account which Luke gives in his gospel. "And he led them out as far as to Bethany, and he lifted up his hands, and blessed them," (Luke xxiv. 50.) "He lifted up his hands," an attitude expressive of sentiments most inspiring and uplifting. "He blessed them." In what sweet words did He pour out His parting benediction. What were the valedictory utterances of this great Friend of sinners ? They are not recorded ; perhaps they are wisely and mercifully omitted from the sacred page.

---

* See "Homilist," vol. v. p. 32, first series.

Acts 1:9-11

THE ASCENSION OF CHRIST AN ILLUSTRATION OF HIS FINAL ADVENT

" *And when he had spoken*[1] *these things, while they beheld,*[2] *he was taken up; and a cloud received him out of their sight. And while they looked steadfastly*[3] *toward heaven as he went up, behold, two men stood by them in white apparel;*[4] *which also said, Ye men of Galilee, why stand ye gazing up into heaven ? this same Jesus, which is taken up from you into heaven, shall so come in like manner as ye have seen him go into heaven.*"

EMENDATIVE RENDERINGS.—(1.) Having spoken. (2.) They beholding. (3.) They were gazing. (4.) White garments.

EXEGETICAL REMARKS.—"*And when he had spoken these things.*" Immediately after the ascension took place, which is more minutely described here than in any other place. " The description is divided into two parts : at first, the Lord is raised in a visible manner, the eyes of the apostles could follow Him for a time as He went up : then a cloud (probably a bright cloud, Matt. xvii. 5.) coming down, received and removed Him from the sight of the disciples, (ὑπὲλ αβεν.")—LANGE.

" *Out of their sight.*" They were undoubtedly looking intensely. This distinguishes the case from every other like it : not only from the fabled apotheosis of Hercules amidst the smoke of his own funeral pile, and that of Romulus during an eclipse, with the addition, in both cases, of a preternatural and fearful storm ; but also from the fiery translation of Elijah, (2 Kings ii. 11,) the difference between which and our Lord's ascension has been thought to prefigure that between the spirit of the old economy, or of the law and gospel."

" *This same Jesus which is taken up from you into heaven, shall so come in like manner as ye have seen him go into heaven.*" " The Greek phrase ὃν τρόπον," says a modern critic, " never indicates mere certainty or vague resemblance : but wherever it occurs in the New Testament, denotes identity of mode or manner," (Matt. xxiii. 37 ; Luke xiii. 34 ; Acts vii. 28 ; 2 Tim. iii. 8.) Some regard the advent here predicted by these " two men," as referring to Christ's coming in the destruction of Jerusalem : others as referring to His coming by His Spirit on the day of Pentecost : and others, to His coming in the last judgment to settle the condition of humanity for ever. We leave others to canvass the merits of these views, whilst we adopt the last as the most generally received, and, we think, the best sustained.

HOMILETICS.—As His last words were falling, in all their celestial melody and significance, upon their ears, and as they were gazing in rapt attention at Him, He disappears. The words of the " two men who stood by them in white apparel," as they were gazing intently on their ascending Master, justify us in looking at Christ's ascension *in order to illustrate His final advent.*

I. He ascended in His ACTUAL PERSONALITY. So will He descend. " He was taken up." It was not some shadowy form of Him, some apparition, some spectral outline of Him, that they saw ascend heavenward; it was He *Himself*, their veritable Friend, Redeemer, Lord; He whom they had followed three years; with whom they had often mingled in closest fellowship; whom they had seen die upon the cross; and whose living words were now vibrating upon their ear and heart. After this His person was no more seen on earth. No one ever saw Him afterwards in Galilee, Jerusalem, or any other of the scenes of His favourite resort. He now, at Bethany, left the world, nor has the world ever seen His person since.

Now this "*same Jesus*" is to come at last. These heavenly messengers said these words, no doubt, to comfort those who now beheld the dearest Object of their hearts depart. This *same* Jesus shall come; the same loving Brother, tried Friend, and mighty Lord, will be seen at last coming "in the clouds of heaven;" He, the Son of Man, (Matt. xvi. 27,) before whose dread tribunal all must at last appear. "We must all stand before the judgment-seat of Christ," (2 Cor. v. 10.) To this the good in all ages have been encouraged to look. "Their conversation has been in heaven, from whence also they have looked for the Saviour, the Lord Jesus Christ," (Phil. iii. 20; Col. iii. 3, 4; Tit. ii. 3.) Blessed truth this. That which divests the future judgment of its terror; that which makes it tolerable for men to look at; that which may make it even an object of delightful anticipation, is, that the "*same* Jesus" will appear, and conduct its sublime transactions, as He who wept in tender sympathy over Jerusalem, and died in love upon the cross. "I know that my Redeemer liveth," (Job xix. 25.)

II. He ascended VERY UNEXPECTEDLY. So He will descend. The language gives the idea that they were struck with surprise. "While they beheld, He was taken up." With wondering souls they stood and looked steadfastly toward heaven as He went up. Though He had often told them that it was expedient for Him to go away, His words had not the power on their hearts to make them expect His departure. They knew not that this was the *last* meeting. Perhaps as His lovely aspects and heavenly thoughts were thrilling their hearts with ecstacy, they hoped for many meetings more; but in a moment, when they thought not, they saw Him mysteriously ascend.

In "like manner" He will unexpectedly appear in judgment. "As in the days that were before the flood they were eating and drinking, marrying and giving in marriage, until the day that Noah entered into the ark, and knew not until the flood came, and took them all away; so shall also the coming of the Son of Man be." "The day of the Lord will come as a thief in the night." That such a day will dawn, is revealed with great clearness and frequency; but *when* it will dawn, in what year of the world's history, still less in what month or week, is known to the Father only. It will take the world by surprise. The generation that will be here then, will be pursuing their ordinary avocations. Some will be navigating the deep, and some cultivating the soil; some busy at their manufactories, and others engaged in commerce; some taken up in politics, and others in literature and religion; some in one clime of earth and sphere of life, and some in others, but all busy; and thus, while all the abounding myriads the world over are plying their faculties with the spirit of their avocations strong upon them, the harbinger of the dread crisis will startle the living and waken the dead with his blast, and on the awful heavens will be seen "the Son of Man coming with great glory."

III. He ascended in a MYSTERIOUS GRANDEUR. So will He descend. Two things show this:—

First, *The receiving cloud.* "A cloud received him out of their sight." What kind of a cloud was it? Was it a dark thunder-cloud, like that with which the Almighty robed Himself on Sinai? or was it a cloud luminous with unearthly rays, like that which overhung the Messiah on the Mount of Transfiguration? or was it a mystic cloud, like that which guided and guarded the Israelites in their pilgrimage? Who knows? This we know, that clouds are emblems of grandeur. Thus Jehovah is said to make "the clouds His chariots, and to ride upon the wings of the wind." Scripture represents Christ as returning in clouds to judge the world, (Matt. xxiii. 40, xxvi. 4; Mark xiii. 26; Rev. i. 7; Dan. vii. 13.) The other circumstance which shows the mysterious grandeur is—

Secondly, *The attendants.* "Two men stood by them in white apparel." Who were those men? Were they angels in human form, like the strangers who appeared at the resurrection? It may be, that the same two angels who rolled away the stone, and appeared at His open sepulchre, were present now. Or were they the "two men" Moses and Elijah, who had appeared at the Transfiguration, and talked about the decease He was to accomplish at Jerusalem? Did the great legislator and the great reformer of Israelitish times, appear now to witness His departure, and to welcome Him to heaven? Perhaps so. Whoever they were, they were glorified beings sent to do honour to Christ. In like manner, also, He will come with glorified attendance. "He will come with all his holy angels." "He shall come to be glorified in his saints, and to be admired in all them that believe."

Acts 1:12-14

THE FIRST PRAYER MEETING AFTER CHRIST'S ASCENSION

Then returned they unto Jerusalem from the mount called Olivet, which is from Jerusalem a sabbath-day's journey.[1] And when they were come in, they went up into an upper room, where abode both Peter[2] and James, and John, and Andrew, Philip, and Thomas, Bartholomew, and Matthew, James the son [3] of Alpheus, and Simon Zelotes, and Judas the ([3]) brother of James. These all continued with one accord in prayer and supplication, with the women, and Mary the mother of Jesus, and with his brethren."

EMENDATIVE RENDERINGS.—(1.) Which is nigh unto Jerusalem, being a Sabbath-day's journey. (2.) They went up into the upper-room chamber, where they were sojourning, namely, Peter, &c. (3.) The words " son " and " brother " are not in the original.

EXEGETICAL REMARKS. — " *The Mount called Olivet,*" τὸ ὄρος των ἐλαιῶν. The exact expression, " the Mount of Olives," occurs in the Old Testament, in Zech. xiv. 4, only ; in the other places of the Old Testament in which it is referred to, the form employed is the "ascent of the Olives," (2 Samuel xv. 30,) or simply "the Mount," (Neh. viii. 15,) "the mount facing Jerusalem," (1 Kings xi. 7,) or " the mountain which is on the east side of the city," (Ezek. xi. 23.) In the New Testament, three forms of the word occur. 1. The usual one, "the Mount of Olives," (τὸ ὄρος των ἐλαιῶν.) 2. By St Luke twice, (xix. 29, xxi. 37), "the Mount called Elaiôn," (τὸ ὄ. τὸ καλ. ἐλαιών,) as well as in this place.—Dr W. SMITH.

"*A sabbath-day's journey.*" A distance of seven stadia or furlongs, making a little less than one of our miles. The measure is supposed to have been borrowed from the space between the people and the ark, when they passed over Jordan, (Joshua iii. 4.) The Sabbath-day's journey means a short distance. The space they had to walk, therefore, from Bethany, the eastern side of Olivet, to Jerusalem, was short ; yet, with what thoughts and feelings they trod that mile, we are not told.

Imagination may suggest much that may be touching though not true.

" *An upper room.*" " Upper rooms were a kind of domestic chapels in every house. There they assembled to read the law and to transact religious affairs."—VITRINGA.

" *They continued.*" The Greek verb here used, strictly denotes personal attendance, sticking close to anything or person, particularly that of a superior ; and it is then transferred to perseverance in duty, such as that of public worship, and particularly of prayer.

" *Mary the mother of Jesus.*" This is the last time her name is mentioned in the holy book, and she is not mentioned with any idolatrous homage, but spoken of simply as one of the disciples of Christ. What became of her afterwards is not known. One old tradition says she died early in Jerusalem, and another says she accompanied John to Ephesus, and lived to an advanced age.

" *With his brethren.*" Or his brothers. Who were they? They were probably those who had accompanied the mother of Jesus on different occasions, as recorded in the gospels. See John ii. 12 ; Matthew xii. 46–50 ; Mark iii. 31–35 ; Luke viii. 19–21.

HOMILETICS.—There are three things in this first prayer-meeting of the disciples, after Christ's departure to heaven, that claim special attention—its *scene*, its *attendance*, and its *spirit*.

I. The SCENE of this first prayer-meeting. " They went up into an upper room " chamber. This was the scene of their devotion. " Upper " does not mean a room above the lower floor, much less a garret or inferior apartment, but one comparatively spacious—reserved both in Greek and Jewish houses for the use of guests, or for unusual occasions. It is not likely that this room was in the Temple. The probability is that it was the chamber where our Lord ate the Passover, and where the apostles appear to have assembled on the evening of the resurrection ; it was a room, therefore, full of hallowed associations to them.

Now, in immediately returning to Jerusalem, they showed—

First, Their *obedience to Christ*. Their Master had commanded them to tarry at Jerusalem until they should receive the promise of their Father. In promptly retiring thither, therefore, they were acting in loyalty to His will.

Secondly, Their *fearless faith*, too, was seen in this. Jerusalem was the home of those who insulted, persecuted, tortured, murdered their Master. Every street was filled with those who execrated the name of Jesus of Nazareth. It was nobly courageous, therefore, for those poor disciples to hold their first meeting there, now that their great Protector and Lord had left them.

II. The ATTENDANCE at this first prayer-meeting. There "abode both Peter, and James, and John," &c. The word "abode" does not mean that this room was their permanent residence, but was the place where they were waiting the advent of the Spirit. The remarks of Dr Alexander upon this apostolic roll are so intelligent and discriminative that we invite attention to them.*

---

* " We have then a catalogue of the apostles, introduced, as some suppose, because they were now re-assembled and re-organised after their dispersion, (Matt. xxvi. 56 ; Mark xiv. 50.) But besides that, they had several times met since that defection, (Matt. xxviii. 16 ; Mark xvi. 14 ; Luke xxiv. 36 ; John xx. 19-26 ; xxiv. 14.) A distinct enumeration of their names would have been natural, not to say necessary, as an introduction to the apostolic history. This is the fourth list contained in the New Testament, (compare Matt. x. 2-4 ; Mark iii. 16-19 ; Luke vi. 14-16,) and in some points different from all the rest. Although no two of these catalogues agree precisely in the order of the names, they may all be divided into three quarterions, which are never interchanged, and the leading names of which are the same in all. Thus, the first is always Peter, the fifth Philip, the ninth James, the son of Alphæus, and the twelfth Judas Iscariot. Another difference is, that Matthew and Luke's Gospels give the names in pairs, or two and two, while Mark enumerates them singly, and the list before us follows both these methods one after the other. A third distinction is, that this list adds no titles or description to the leading names, but only to those near the end. *Both Peter*, like a similar expression in ver. 8, means not only Peter, but the others also. This, with his uniform position at the head of the list, marks distinctly his priority, not as a superior in rank and office, but as a representative and spokesman of the rest, like the foreman of a jury, or the chairman of a large committee. This priority, which often incidentally appears throughout the gospel history, (*e.g.*, Matt. xv. 15, xvi. 16, 17-24, xviii. 21, xix. 27 ; Mark x. 28, xi. 21 ; Luke viii. 45, xii. 41, xviii. 28, xxii. 32, 33 ; John vi. 68, xiii. 24,) so far from amounting to a primacy or permanent superiority, was less an advantage to himself than a convenience to his brethren, and indeed, occasioned some of his most serious errors and severest trials. (See Matt. xvi. 16-22, xxvi. 33, 51, 58 ; Mark viii. 32, xiv. 29, 47, 54, 66 ; Luke xxii. 34, 50, 55 ; John xiii. 8, 36, 37, xviii. 10, 11, 16.) It is now a very general belief that the affecting scene in John xxi. 15-17, was Peter's restoration to the apostleship, from which he had fallen for a time by the denial of his Master ; the three questions and injunctions there recorded corresponding to his three acts of apostasy. Be this as it may, we find him here resuming the position which he occupied before, and is to occupy throughout a large part of the present history. The

The roll of names here given reminds us of :—

First, *The sociality of Christ's system.* What brought them together? A community of feeling and purpose awakened by One in whom all their hearts centred. If you would unite men in social affection, you must get them to love supremely your common object. Souls can never be brought into close sympathetic contact, but by means of objects which they love in common. Christianity alone supplies an object that all hearts can love supremely; and, therefore, of all systems in the world it is the most social. The roll reminds us of :—

Secondly, *The triumph of grace.* These disciples had all been scattered by the crucifixion. That event so shocked and shattered their faith, that they all forsook Him and fled; but here we find them restored again to Christian feeling and fellowship. There are here some persons whose presence on this occasion delights us much. Peter, who thrice denied his Master, is here, and in his right mind. Incredulous Thomas, too, who resolved not to believe, has had his faith established and is present. Mary, the mother of Jesus, is here.

other names are all familiar from the Gospels. *James* and *John,* the sons of Zebedee, and sons of thunder, early called to be disciples and apostles, (Matt. iv. 21, x. 2 ; Mark i. 19, 29, iii. 17 ; Luke v. 10, vi. 14,) and, with Peter, frequently distinguished from the rest as confidential servants and companions of our Saviour, (Matt. xvii. 1; Mark v. 37, ix. 2, xiii. 3 ; Luke viii. 51,) while John was admitted to a still more intimate and tender friendship, (John xiii. 23, xix. 26, xxi. 7, 20.) Traits of their character appear in Mark x. 35-41 ; Luke ix. 52-56. *Andrew,* the brother of Simon Peter, and placed next to him by Mark, but here postponed to the two sons of Zebedee. On one or two occasions in the Gospel history, we find him incidentally referred to, as attending on the Master and conversing with him, (Matt. iv. 18, vi. 8, xii. 22.) The same thing may be said of *Philip,* his townsman and associate, (Matt. x. 3 ; Mark iii. 18; Luke vi. 14 ; John i. 14-44, vi. 5-7, xii. 21, 22, xiv. 8, 9.) It is worthy of remark, that these two apostles are known only by Greek names, though, according to the custom of the age, they may have had Hebrew ones besides. *Thomas,* elsewhere surnamed *Didymus,* (the twin,) a Greek translation of his Armenic name. He also appears now and then in close attendance on his Master, and peculiarly devoted to Him, although chiefly remembered for refusing to believe that Christ was risen from the dead until assured of it by ocular inspection, (John xi. 16, xiv. 5, xx. 24–29, xxi. 2.) *Bartholomew* is commonly supposed to be the same with the *Nathanael* of John's Gospel, chiefly because it seems improbable that one so highly honoured by the Saviour, and so intimately known to the apostles, should be excluded from their number, while a person otherwise unknown was admitted to it. (See John i. 46–50, xxi. 2.) *Matthew,* the publican, also called Levi, and the son of Alphæus, whose vocation and first intercourse with Christ are recorded by himself and others. (See Matt. ix. 9, x. 3 ; Mark ii. 14, iii. 18 ; Luke v. 27–29, vi. 15.) *James of Alphæus, i.e.,* as is commonly supposed, his son; while, on the other hand, *Judas of James* is no less generally understood to mean his brother, although some assume the same ellipsis in both places, and make Jude the son of a James otherwise unknown. By comparing the Evangelists, it seems that Jude, or Judas not Iscariot, was also called Lebbæus, or Thaddæus. (See Matt. x. 3 ; Mark iii. 18 ; Luke vi. 16 ; John xiv. 22.) Between James and John, appears the name of *Simon,* surnamed here *Zelotes,* in reference either to his ardent temper, or to his previous connection with the party of the Zealots, whose fanatical zeal ultimately caused the downfall of the Jewish State, and of whose organised existence there are traces even in the book before us. *Zelotes* seems to be the Greek translation, as *Canaanites* is the Greek form of an Armenic name denoting Zealot. The Greek word for *Canaanite* is altogether different. The meaning of *Canaite* (inhabitant of Cana) rests upon another reading. (See Matt. x. 4; Mark iii. 18 ; Luke vi. 15.)"

A sword had pierced her heart, and she had passed through unknown agonies of soul. Other women, too, are mentioned ; their names are not given. Perhaps some of the wives of the Apostles were here, for some of them were married. (Matt. viii. 14 ; 1 Cor. ix. 5.) Mary Magdalene, and other women who were last at His cross, and earliest at His grave, were in all probability present. Christianity has raised woman to her present position in the civilised world, and woman has ever proved the most ardent and loyal in her love to the system that has made her what she is. This little assembly truly demonstrates the triumphant power of grace. This roll reminds us of :—

Thirdly, *The ravages of sin.* We discover, in looking at the list, that there is one of the apostles absent. Where is Judas ? He was present at the Passover with all the other names here given—present, perhaps, in this very same upper room. But where is he now ? There is a Judas here, it is true, but it is not Judas Iscariot. Where is he ? We know the sad story of this miserable man, and his absence on this occasion preaches a terrible homily concerning the ravages of sin.

III. The SPIRIT of this first prayer-meeting : "These all continued with one accord in prayer and supplication." These words teach us that there was a spirit of *union* and *perseverance* in their prayers.

First, There was a spirit of *union* : "They continued with one accord." They were not only assembled together in the same place, and for the same purpose, but there was a great unanimity of sentiment amongst them. They agreed in the blessings they sought, and in the mode of seeking them. A common desire ruled them all.

Secondly, There was a spirit of *perseverance* in the prayers : "they continued." The parable of the unjust judge is a striking illustration of the importance of *perseverance* in prayer.

Would that all prayer-meetings agreed in their unanimity and perseverance with this, the first prayer-meeting after Christ's ascension. We must go back to apostolic times for our models of devotion.

Acts 1:15-26

THE FIRST ECCLESIASTICAL MEETING FOR BUSINESS ; A MODEL CHURCH-MEETING

" And in those days Peter stood up in the midst of the disciples, and said, (the number of names together[1] were about an hundred and twenty,) [2] Men and brethren, this scripture must needs have been fulfilled, which the Holy Ghost by the mouth of David spake before concerning Judas, which was

*guide*³ *to them that took Jesus. For he was numbered with us, and had obtained part of this ministry.*⁴ *Now this man purchased a field with the reward of iniquity; and falling headlong, he burst asunder in the midst, and all his bowels gushed out. And it was known unto all the dwellers at Jerusalem; insomuch as that field is called in their proper tongue, Aceldama, that is to say, The field of blood. For it is written in the book of Psalms,*⁵ *Let his habitation be desolate, and let no man dwell therein : and his bishop-rick let another take. Wherefore of these men which have companied with us all the time that the Lord Jesus went in and out among us, beginning from the baptism of John, unto that same day that he was taken up from us, must one be ordained to be a witness*⁶ *with us of his resurrection. And they appointed two,*⁷ *Joseph called Barsabas, who was surnamed Justus, and Matthias. And they prayed, and said, Thou, Lord, which knowest the hearts of all men, shew whether of these two thou hast chosen, that he may take part of this ministry and apostleship, from which Judas by transgres-sion fell,*⁸ *that he might go to his own place. And they gave forth their lots ;*⁹ *and the lot fell upon Matthias ; and he was numbered with the eleven apostles."*

EMENDATIVE RENDERINGS.—(1.) There‾was a crowd of names together.—ALX. (2.) Brethren. (3.) Judas who turned guide.—WILLS. (4.) Shared the allotment of this ministry. (5.) It has been written in the book of Psalms. (6.) Must one become a witness.—ALFORD. (7.) And they set forth two.—WILLS. (8.) Passed away (9.) Cast lots for them.

EXEGETICAL REMARKS.—*" In those days."* In some period between the ascension of Christ and the day of Pentecost. Probably it took place on the very eve of that ever-memorable day.

" The number of names together were an hundred and twenty." Whether names here is synonymous with persons, or merely implies the registration of an organisation, or whether the hundred and twenty is used as a sacred number, or to designate a definite multitude or an indefinite crowd, are questions that have been raised and discussed with very different results. We see no reason to object to the authorised version in this case, and we take the words therefore as they stand—conveying the idea that there were a hundred and twenty individuals present.

" This scripture must needs have been fulfilled, which the Holy Ghost by the mouth of David spake before concern-ing Judas." This passage to which Peter refers is generally supposed to be that recorded in Psalm xli. 9. We believe this to be a mistake, though it is expressly applied to Judas by our Saviour :—" He that eateth bread with me hath lifted up

his heel against me," (John xiii. 18.) The psalm referred to is that quoted in the 20th verse :—" For it is written in the Book of Psalms," (Psalm lxix. 25; cxix. 8.) Peter, in quoting the Psalms assumes that they were well known to his auditory, and avows that they were the utterances of the Holy Ghost, by the mouth of David. He does not say that any scripture predicting such a *fall* as that of Judas, must needs be fulfilled, but that the scripture predicting the ruin of such a sinner must be accomplished.

" A guide to them that took Jesus." Referring undoubtedly to the course which the betrayer took in the garden of Gethsemane, (John xviii. 2–23.)

"He was numbered with us, and had obtained part of this ministry." He helped with us to make up that sig-nificant and sacred number, twelve, which is now broken and must be restored. The ministry referred to was that of the apostleship.

" Now this man purchased a field with the reward of iniquity." Matthew says, "the chief priests bought with the money the potter's field, to bury strangers in." There is no contra-diction, inasmuch as in the Scriptures

a man is said to do that which he causes or occasions to be done, (Gen. xlii. 38 ; Rom. xiv. 15.) Judas was the means of the field being bought : he furnished the money.

"*Falling headlong, he burst asunder in the midst, and all his bowels gushed out.*" Matthew says, "he hanged himself." There is no contradiction here either. Matthew merely relates the act of suicide. Peter, in his speech, states what occurred to the suspended body : that it fell down and was dashed to pieces.

"*Aceldama.*" A word composed of two Syro-Chaldaic words, and means literally "The field of blood."

"*It is written in the book of Psalms,*" &c. The words are a combination of Psalm lxix. 25, and cix. 8 ; and their original reference was to David and to Ahitophel and his fellow-conspirators against David. The Apostle points to them as an apt illustration of the case of David.

"*Bishoprick.*" Charge or office, as in the margin.

"*Wherefore of the men which have companied with us all the time that the Lord Jesus went in and out among us, beginning from the baptism of John, unto that same day that he was taken up from us, must one be ordained to be a witness with us of his resurrection.*" Probably Peter refers to the seventy disciples, (Luke x. 1, 2.) These seventy Christ himself had despatched on a missionary tour at a very early stage of His public ministry, soon after His baptism by John. Peter's principle was this : That the new apostle should be elected from the number of those who were intimate with the Son of God, their Great Master : a principle this that ought ever to be observed. He only is qualified for the highest office in the church whose alliance with Christ is the most cordial and intimate.

"*And they appointed two, Joseph, called Barsabas, who was surnamed Justus, and Matthias.*" The word "appointed" must be regarded as meaning merely setting up as candidates ; and in this we think the voice of the whole Church assembled was taken. Two of the best men were selected from amongst the number who were considered the most eligible for such a momentous office. There seems to have been perfect unanimity in the nomination of these two as candidates. But why two rather than any larger number ? Probably the claims of those two above all the rest were so distinguishing as to confine them to that number.

"*And they prayed and said, Thou, Lord,*" &c. Here we have the first example of prayer offered to Jesus Christ, and it recognises both His omniscience and supremacy.

"*And they gave forth their lots, and the lot fell upon Matthias, and he was numbered with the eleven apostles.*" Two questions start here : (1.) What were the lots ? The expression "they gave forth their *lots*," does not mean the same as the expression, "they gave forth their *votes.*" The lot was something more than a *vote*, it was an old method of reaching a decision. According to Grotius, they proceeded thus : "They put their lots into two urns, one of which contained the names of Joseph and Matthias, and the other a blank, and the word apostle. In drawing these out of the urns, the blank came up with the name of Joseph, and the lot on which was written the word apostle came up with the name of Matthias. Thus their decision was reached and their prayer answered. The use of the lot is elsewhere spoken of in the Scriptures, (Josh. xviii. 1–10 ; 1 Sam. xiv. 41–42 ; Prov. xvi. 33, xvii. 18.)—LIVERMORE. Another question started is : (2.) Who gave the lots ? Did the whole asssembly, the hundred and twenty, or did the eleven apostles only ? There is no way of reaching a certainty on this point : although our impression is that the whole were engaged in it. Christianity recognises the individual, and demands his agency in all that concerns its interests. "While the Lord remained with the Apostles, they employed no lots ; neither did they subsequently employ them after the coming of the Holy Ghost, chap. x. 19, xvi. 6, &c. : but in this single intermediate period, and in this peculiar affair, they very fitly adopted the lot."—BENGEL.

HOMILETICS.—This paragraph chronicles the *first* meeting of the Christian Church ever held for the transaction of mere business, and we shall look at it as a *model* church-meeting.

I. IT WAS A MEETING TO TRANSACT BUSINESS OF VERY GRAVE IMPORTANCE. The business was nothing less than the *election* of an apostle—the election of one to fill the post which Judas desecrated and deserted—one, to use the language of Peter, who should " *be a witness with us of his resurrection.*" The resurrection of Christ is the key-stone of the Christian system ; it presupposes His life and death, and demonstrates the Divinity of His nature and His message.* Hence it was evermore the salient and constant theme in apostolic preaching. Of all the important men in the world, none so important as those who could bear witness to this fact from their own personal observation and knowledge. To be able to do so was necessary to constitute an apostle. The fact was so extraordinary in its nature, and clashed so mightily with the popular prejudices, that no one in that age would be qualified with the necessary heroism to proclaim it, who had not been deeply convinced of it by the irresistible evidence of his own senses. Hence the first Christian propagandists were witnesses of Christ's resurrection. To appoint one of these was the business of this meeting.

II. IT WAS A MEETING IN WHICH THE ASSEMBLED MEMBERS HAD A DUTY TO FULFIL. " A hundred and twenty," we are told, were assembled on this occasion. Probably this number comprehended all the disciples of Christ in and about Jerusalem. Now each individual in this multitude, male and female, had their duty to fulfil in this meeting. They were called on to exercise their best judgment, and to give their conscientious vote in the election of candidates. The candidates were set up, mark you, not merely by the existing apostles, but by the whole body of the disciples assembled. The appointment of ministers is not the right of an individual, however distinguished in Church or State, nor of a community of ministers, but of the assembled Church.

III. IT WAS A MEETING COMPETENT IN ITSELF TO DISCHARGE THE BUSINESS. All the power for business was in the room that contained these " hundred and twenty." They sought no counsel from any body of men external to themselves, nor would they have received any dictation from any person or society outside, however dignified in authority. The power of a Church for its own business is in itself, inspired and guided by Christ its Head.

---

* Christ's resurrection is called by Augustine, *the peculiar faith of Christians :* by Tertullian, *the model of our hope, the key to our tomb :* by Calvin, *the chief head in the gospel :* by P. Martyr, *the clasp uniting all the articles :* by Melancthon, *the especial voice of the Church.*

IV. It was a meeting superintended by the ablest of its members. Peter took the management, and for many reasons he was the most competent man. "He stood up in the midst of the disciples." Peter!—He had once grievously fallen: but having truly repented of his heinous offence, and been restored to the apostolate in the most solemn manner by Christ, when he dined with Him on the Galilean shore after His resurrection—is here, with renewed and heightened zeal, the leader of the young Church. With his wonted boldness, he stands up in the midst of the disciples, and begins his speech. His conduct on this occasion shows that he was the man to direct affairs.

Observe, First, *His sketch of the miserable man who had once occupied the vacant post.* He reminds them of Judas's crime. The description of the man's fearful delinquency is remarkably *mild.* He speaks of Judas as *a guide to them that took Jesus.* Probably, Peter's memory of his own fall was too vivid to allow him to express himself in harsher terms of Judas.

He saw in the betrayal of Judas an illustration of an old scripture. "*This scripture must needs have been fulfilled, which the Holy Ghost, by the mouth of David, spake before concerning Judas.*" He does not say that any scripture predicting such a fall "must needs" be fulfilled, but that the scripture predicting the ruin of such a servant "must needs" be accomplished. Punishment *must needs* follow crime.

He reminds them of the office which Judas once held. "*He was numbered with us, and had obtained part of this ministry.*" How great his fall! He then proceeds to describe his terrible end. "*Now this man purchased a field with the reward of iniquity; and falling headlong, he burst asunder in the midst, and all his bowels gushed out.*" "*Falling headlong!*" Striking retribution this! The very plot of ground which he bought with the price of blood, was to be strewn with his mangled frame, and dyed with his gore. Physically, as well as spiritually, he went to his own place. The accursed body fell on an accursed spot.

The terrible end of this Judas was a notorious fact. "*And it was known unto all the dwellers at Jerusalem; insomuch as that field is called in their proper tongue, Aceldama, that is to say, The field of blood.*" The fact that the body of the betrayer was dashed to pieces on the spot which he had purchased with the money for which he had sold the Son of God to an excruciating death, had a significance so terrible as to give it a wide circulation, and make the spot memorable through all time.

Observe, Secondly, *His counsel as to their present duty.* "*Wherefore of these men which have companied with us all the time that the Lord Jesus went in and out among us, beginning from the baptism of John, unto that same day that he was taken up from us, must one be ordained to be a witness with us of his resurrection.*" In his direction he indicates two things: (1.) The work to which the man is to be appointed;—he is to be a witness to us of His resurrection. (2.) The class from which he is to be appointed;—he is to be selected from "these men which have companied with us," &c. "*Of these men,*" &c. Peter's principle was this,—that the new apostles should be elected from the number of those who were most intimate with the great Master,—a principle this that ought ever to be observed. He only is qualified for the highest office in the Church whose alliance with Christ is the most vital and intimate. Yes; of those men, and only of those.

V. IT WAS A MEETING IN WHICH THEY ENGAGED IN UNITED PRAYER TO HEAVEN FOR DIRECTION. After the nomination you have this prayer: "Thou, Lord, which knowest the hearts of all men, show whether of these two thou hast chosen." This prayer implies:

First, A recognition of Divine omniscience. "Thou knowest the hearts of all men;" a deep impression of God's acquaintance with all hearts is essential to sincere and earnest devotion. This prayer implies:

Secondly, A desire to have their choice regulated by the Divine— "Show whether of these two thou hast chosen." As if they had said, "Thy choice shall be ours, we desire only to vote for him whom Thou hast ordained for the office. Thy will be done." This is the spirit of all true prayer. Their prayer to Him attests their faith in His Godhead.

Thus ends the meeting. Matthias is elected to take the place of Judas, and complete the apostolic circle. Twelve was a venerated number. As the number of the sons of Jacob and the tribes of Israel, Jesus had chosen twelve. These disciples felt that they were not complete without this magic *twelve,* and for this they held this church-meeting, and gained their object by counsel, prayer, and lots. Though Judas is gone, his place is filled, and the apostolate number is complete.

CONCLUSION.—Would that all "church-meetings," in subsequent times had ever been ruled by this model! Gathered not for trivial but important business; recognising the right of every member to a voice in its deliberations;—holding the power to transact all its affairs independently of any external authority—having always the ablest men to preside over its transactions; and conducting the whole in the spirit of united prayer.

Acts 2:1-13

PENTECOST (NO. I.)—A NEW MANIFESTATION OF THE DIVINE SPIRIT

" *And when the day of Pentecost was fully come, they were all with one accord*[1] *in one place. And suddenly there came a sound from heaven as of a rushing mighty wind, and it filled all the house where they were sitting. And there appeared unto them cloven tongues like as of fire, and it sat upon each of them. And they were all filled with the Holy Ghost, and began to speak with other tongues, as the Spirit gave them utterance. And there were dwelling at Jerusalem Jews, devout men, out of every nation under heaven. Now when this was noised abroad,*[2] *the multitude came together, and were confounded, because that every man heard them speak in his own language. And they were all amazed*[3] *and marvelled, saying one to another, Behold, are not all these which speak Galileans? And how hear we every man in our own tongue, wherein we were born? Parthians, and Medes, and Elamites, and the dwellers in Mesopotamia, and in Judea, and Cappadocia, in Pontus, and Asia, Phyrgia, and Pamphylia, in Egypt, and in the parts of Libya about Cyrene, and strangers of Rome, Jews and proselytes,*[4] *Cretes and Arabians, we do hear them speak in our tongues the wonderful works of God. And they were all amazed, and were in doubt, saying one to another, What meaneth this? Others mocking said, These men are full of new*[5] *wine.*"

EMENDATIVE RENDERINGS.—(1.) Together. (2.) Now when this sound was heard.
(3.) They were amazed. (4.) And Romans sojourning, both Jews and proselytes.
(5.) Sweet.—WILLS.

EXEGETICAL REMARKS.—" *The day of Pentecost was fully come.*" Fully come means fulfilled. The PENTECOST is a modern name for one of the stated Jewish festivals, from the Greek πεντηκοστη, fiftieth; the day of the feast being fixed in the law to take place on the fiftieth day after the second of Passover, or after the revolution of seven complete weeks. Its more proper name was " the feast of weeks," or " the feast of harvest." It had a twofold import with the Jews, physical and historical ; it was, in the first place, a festival of thanksgiving for the first-fruits of the harvest. The Jews on this day presented offerings of the first-fruits of the harvest. The offering consisted in two loaves of unleavened bread, (three pints of meal each,) and various domestic animals, (Lev. xxiii. 15–21; Deut. xvi. 9, 10.)

It was one of the three great festivals in which all the males were required to appear before the Lord, (Exod. xxxiv. 22, 23.) It is called the "feast of harvest," and "the feast of first-fruits." It was a great national harvest-home. But it was more than this : it had a reference to the giving of the law on Mount Sinai, which was fifty days after the exodus from Egypt. The giving of the law was one of the most wonderful epochs in the history of the Jews, which was a history of wonders, and its commemoration was an exercise most proper and important.

" *In one place.*" Was this place the "upper room" mentioned in Acts i. 13 ? Perhaps so. No one knows of its precise locality. Many expositors, and of late Olshausen, Baumgarten, and Lange, suppose that the house where the disciples met belonged to the temple; that it was one of the thirty rooms in the adjoining buildings of the temple, mentioned by Josephus, and which he calls οἶκους.

"*And suddenly there came a sound from heaven as of a rushing mighty wind, and it filled all the house where they were sitting.*" The sound came "suddenly;" the atmosphere does not pass at once from the serene to the tempestuous, but it was thus now, for the moment before a profound quiet reigned around them. The suddenness indicates the supernatural.

"*It was of a rushing mighty wind.*" The sound was powerful. The language expresses a violent commotion in the air. The sound is from heaven. It does not sweep horizontally through the room, but comes directly down with a sudden rush, and startling roar.

"*And there appeared unto them.*" Who were the "them ?" Not an indiscriminate multitude, nor even the select apostles, but the whole hundred and twenty referred to in the preceding chapter. These disciples had met together in obedience to the command of their Master: they felt His absence deeply : they earnestly looked to heaven for help : they were thoroughly united, "of one accord :" they prayed and waited for the promised Comforter, and now He came.

"*Cloven tongues like as of fire.*" The word "cloven" designates—not the division of the tongues themselves, but their distribution amongst the people. It means that one flame, in the form of a tongue, rested upon each. The tongue was not fire, but like fire.

"*And they were all filled with the Holy Ghost.*" The Eternal Spirit not only entered them, but filled them, and filled not one of them, but all the disciples.

"*Began to speak with other tongues.*"

There was nothing extraordinary in this, taken by itself ; what was extraordinary in the matter was, that the Christians, in consequence of the gift of the Spirit, spoke with other tongues, (ἑτέραις γλώσσαις.) This can primarily signify nothing else to our minds than that, by the influence of the Spirit, the tongues of the disciples were essentially changed, or that, whereas before they had been organs of the flesh, they were now become instruments of the Holy Ghost.—BAUMGARTEN.

"*Now when this was noised abroad.*" Now when this sound was heard. "This" what ? Not the voice of the language, but the "rushing mighty wind," &c. Like an earthquake the phenomenon arrested the attention of the surrounding population.

"*The multitude came together and were confounded,*" &c. The astonishment of the people is expressed by various terms in the context : "*confounded,*" "*amazed,*" "*marvelled.*"

"*Behold are not all these which speak Galileans? And how hear we every man in our own tongue, wherein we were born,*" &c. The cause of the wonder was that the disciples spoke in tongues understood by so many people of different languages.

"*Parthians and Medes,*" &c. This list of fifteen countries from which people were present, is, upon the whole, systematically arranged, proceeding from the north-east to the west, then turning to the south, and concluding with the west ; but in single instances the order is not followed with scholastic strictness. The four first names comprehended the east, lands beyond the Euphrates, into which the Israelites were driven by the Assyrian and Babylonish captivities. Then Judea is suddenly named where we would least expect it, because it forms the transition to the Asiatic districts.—LANGE.

HOMILETICS.—Though we cannot, with Schaff, regard this day of Pentecost as the birthday of the Church—for the Church was born centuries before this—we are bound to regard it as the grand crowning period in the development of the Divine plan of human redemption. Periods in the working out of this Divine plan of mercy mark the history of upwards of four thousand years, one period leading to another.

From Adam to Abraham, from Abraham to Moses, and from Moses to Christ, and now from the advent of Christ to this day of Pentecost. To this last all the others pointed, and in it they are all crowned with glory. Even Christ Himself frequently pointed to this advent of the Spirit. He taught His disciples that it was expedient for Him to depart that the Spirit might come. The mission of the Spirit was the burden of His departing discourses before His death and after His resurrection. He bade them tarry in Jerusalem until they should receive this promise of the Father. The time had now arrived. "The day of Pentecost was fully come," and as this festival was being celebrated at Jerusalem by the Jews, who were gathered together from all parts of the civilised world, this wonderful advent of the Spirit took place. This epoch, this advent of the Spirit, according to the account given in this chapter, was characterised by three things :—*A new manifestation of the Divine Spirit; A new style of religious ministry ; and, A new development of social life.* The first is the subject of that part of the history now before us.

A NEW MANIFESTATION OF THE DIVINE SPIRIT.

We are not to suppose that this was the first time that the Divine Spirit visited this world. He strove with the antediluvians, He inspired the old prophets, He dwelt in the old saints. David, who, by his transgression, had dispelled the Divine visitant from his heart, prays, "Restore unto me the joy of Thy salvation, and uphold me with Thy free Spirit." He was with the apostles before this. "Ye know Him," said Christ, "for He dwelleth with you and shall be in you." But He never came in such a demonstration of power, and plenitude of influence as now. Before, He had distilled as the dew, now He comes down as a shower ; before, He had gleamed as the first rays of morning, now He appears in the brightness of noon. There are three things here observable in His advent : His action *upon* the disciples ; His action *in* the disciples ; and His action *through* the disciples.

I. HIS ACTION UPON THE DISCIPLES.

First, *Upon their ear.* "There came a sound as of a rushing mighty wind," &c. Wind, an emblem of the Spirit :—(1) invisible ; (2) mysterious ; (3) powerful ; (4) refreshing. The great epochs of history are usually preceded or accompanied by extraordinary phenomena in nature. "Thunders and lightnings, and the voice of the trumpet exceeding loud," accompanied the promulgation of the law on Sinai. A strange star careering in the heavens attended the birth of the Son of God. The darkening sun, the rending rocks, and the quaking earth, marked the wonderful death of the world's Redeemer ; and now this sudden, violent, heaven-sent noise, as a wind in the fury of tempest, marked the advent of the Divine Spirit. Here is the action :

Secondly, *Upon their eye.* " And there appeared unto them cloven tongues like as of fire, and it sat upon each of them : "—"Fire" is (1) purifying ; (2) consuming ; (3) transmuting ; (4) diffusive.

Perhaps these supernatural appeals to the ear and the eye in the rushing wind and the distributed tongues of fire, were intended to express the relation of the Divine Spirit :—(1) To *life*—wind or air is vital, it is the breath of life ; (2) to *speech*—" the tongues " would indicate that the Spirit had to give men new utterances ; (3) to *purity* —" fire " would indicate that the Spirit had to consume all the corruptions of the soul. The baptism of the Spirit is the baptism of fire.

II. HIS ACTION IN THE DISCIPLES.

" They were filled with the Holy Ghost." The Holy Ghost entered their spiritual natures, *filled* them with Divine thoughts and emotions. Now were realised to the experience the promises that Christ made to them. " The Spirit of truth shall testify of me, and ye also shall bear witness," (John xv. 26, 27.) Again : " It is not ye that speak, but the Spirit of your Father which is in you," (Matt. x. 20.) The Spirit now so took possession of their souls, that they henceforth spoke His thoughts, throbbed with His sympathies, and acted out His will. He filled them. They had no thoughts but His, or such as agreed with His ; no feelings but such as glowed with His inspiration ; no will but His. They were now the consecrated temples of the Holy Ghost, workers that were to become mighty through God. Nothing but the Divine can really fill the soul. Without God there will be a boundless vacuum within.

III. HIS ACTION THROUGH THE DISCIPLES.

Three things are observable concerning their speech :

First, *The speech followed their Divine inspiration.* It was not until *after* the Spirit had entered them, filled them, purified them with His holy fire, given them the right thoughts and feelings, that the speech came. Better be dumb, than speak out the thoughts of a soul unrenewed by the Spirit. It would be well for the race if the tongues of the unrenewed were sealed in silence. It is when the Spirit comes into us, fills us with its purifying and vivifying influence, that we want speech, and we shall have it. The old dialect will not do to express the new life. A divinely-filled soul must break forth in divine language. " They spoke as the Spirit gave them utterance." Each spoke with the tongue which the Spirit gave at the time, not each with all the tongues.

Secondly, *The speech unquestionably was miraculous.* These disciples spake out the wonderful things which the Spirit gave them, not in their vernacular, but in a language or a dialect with which before they were perfectly unacquainted. Language is a wonderful art in itself. Words are at once the necessary media by which we form our thoughts, and the arbitrary signs by which we convey them to our fellow-men. Hence a new language is never attained but by long, systematic, and often trying labour. The coming *at once* into the possession of a new language is as great a miracle as if we came into possession of a new limb. This was the miracle now. These men got a new language at once, through which they could pour forth the Divine things that now came into them. The miraculousness of the gift was felt by all that heard them, and all that heard them understood. "*Now when this was noised abroad, the multitude came together, and were confounded, because that every man heard them speak in his own language. And they were all amazed, and marvelled, saying one to another, Behold, are not all these which speak Galileans?*"

Thirdly, *The speech was unspeakably useful.* It served to impress the multitude with the divinity of the system with which the disciples were identified, and it enabled the disciples at once to proclaim the Gospel to the multitude assembled from every part of the world. Without the miraculous gift of tongues, the disciples would have had to spend years in obtaining such a knowledge, even of one language, as to have enabled them to preach in it, and in the natural order of things, ages would have rolled away before the Gospel could have spread beyond the boundaries of Judea. Now, through these tongues, they spoke the Gospel to representatives from all parts of the known world, and who, after the grand festival was over, would return to their countries and radiate through their own spheres the wonderful intelligence. Chrysostom has said that the different tongues pointed out as a map what land each should visit and occupy as the scene of his labours in converting the world. Our Lord prophesied that before the close of the generation in which He lived, "*This Gospel of the kingdom should be preached in all the world for a witness unto all nations;*" and Paul tells us in Rom. x. 18, that the sound of the Gospel "*went into all the earth, and their words unto the ends of the world.*" This gift of tongues alone explains this world-wide diffusion of the Gospel.

Fourthly, *The speech was profoundly religious.* This wonderful faculty of speech was given, not to declare any of the weak things of the human spirit, still less anything wicked, but to declare "*the wonderful works of God.*" Their *speech* and their *subject* were both wonderful. Heaven gave them a wonderful medium to reveal a wonderful thing. What were the works they spoke of? We rest assured that they were works connected with the redemption of the world in the mission of Christ, and the advent of the Spirit. Oh, come the day when the languages which God has given man, instead of being as now the vehicle of the erroneous in thought, the impure in feeling, the depraved in purpose, shall convey to men the purest thoughts and the holiest feelings concerning the "*wonderful works of God!*"

Acts 2:14-21

PENTECOST (NO. II.)—A NEW STYLE OF RELIGIOUS MINISTRY

" But Peter, standing up with the eleven, lifted up his voice, and said unto them, Ye men of Judea, and all ye that dwell at Jerusalem, be this known unto you, and hearken to my words: for these are not drunken, as ye suppose, seeing it is but the third hour of the day. But this is that which was spoken by the prophet Joel; And it shall come to pass in the last days, saith God, I will pour out of my Spirit upon all flesh: and your sons and your daughters shall prophesy, and your young men shall see visions, and your old men shall dream dreams: and on my servants and on my handmaidens I will pour out in those days of my Spirit; and they shall prophesy: and I will show¹ wonders in heaven above, and signs in the earth beneath; blood, and fire, and vapour² of smoke: the sun shall be turned into darkness, and the moon into blood, before that great and notable day of the Lord come: and it shall come to pass, that whosoever shall call on the name of the Lord shall be saved."

EMENDATIVE RENDERINGS.—(1.) Give.   (2.) Cloud.

EXEGETICAL REMARKS. — *" Be this known unto you."* It has been remarked that Peter here bespeaks attention with the skill and grace not unlike that with which Brutus, in Shakespeare, attempts to justify the death of Cæsar : "Hear me for my cause, and be silent that you may hear."

" The third hour of the day." The " third hour " of the Jews would answer to our nine o'clock in the morning. The improbability of this would appear, perhaps, from two circumstances. It was the hour of morning-worship and sacrifice, and it was a regular practice with the Jews not to eat or drink anything until after the third hour of the day. So established was this custom, that Paul tells us that it was not usual even for drunkards to become drunken in the daytime. " They that are drunken, become drunken in the night."

" Spoken by the prophet Joel," &c. This passage is found in Joel ii. 28–32, and Peter quotes it not with verbal accuracy either from the Hebrew or Septuagint, but with substantial faithfulness. Peter here identifies the "last days" with that period which had now commenced. In quoting the passages, the apostolic orator seems to take it for granted that his auditory would understand that the "last days" meant the day of the Messiah, and that they regarded Joel as an undoubted authority.

HOMILETICS.—We have said that this grand epoch was characterised by three things: *A new manifestation of the Divine Spirit; A new style of religious ministry; and, A new development of social life.* The first characteristic engaged our attention in the last section, and is developed in the first thirteen verses of the chapter. To the second, which is displayed from verses 14–37, we must now give ourselves.

A NEW STYLE OF RELIGIOUS MINISTRY.

" But Peter, standing up with the eleven, lifted up his voice," &c.

The sermon of Peter on this occasion is something strikingly fresh in the history of preaching. There had been religious preaching before :—Moses preached, Joshua preached, prophets preached, John the Baptist preached, Christ preached, but this preaching of Peter was, in many respects, a new thing in the earth. (1.) The *occasion* was new. The spiritual excitement of the disciples, produced by Divine influence, and leading to strange thoughts and miraculous utterances, which was the occasion of Peter's discourse, was something thoroughly new in the mental history of the world. (2.) The *substance* of his sermon was new. It was not a prophetic or a present, but a *historic* Christ,—a Christ who had been here and wrought miracles, had been crucified, had been buried, had risen from the dead to the throne of the universe. No one had ever preached Christ in this form before. It was Peter's honour to commence a new, but a permanent, form of religious ministry. (3.) The *impression* of his sermon was new. He convicted the multitude of having put to death their Messiah. This sermon worked a new and terrible feeling in human souls. "When they heard this, they were pricked in their heart."

Now, in analysing so much of the discourse as we have recorded— for "*in many other words*" did he speak to them—we find it consist of three distinct parts :—*A statement for refuting the charge of the scoffer ; An argument for convicting the hearts of the hardened ;* and, *An address for directing the conduct of the awakened.* In this sketch we must confine our attention to the first.

I. HERE IS A STATEMENT FOR REFUTING THE CHARGE OF THE SCOFFER.

The charge of the scoffer was, that the wonderful excitement and the miraculous speech of the disciples were the result of intoxication. "Others mocking said, These men are full of new (γλεύκους, *sweet*) wine." They, in the spirit of derision, ascribed the Divine thing to wickedness, as the Pharisees before had done, when they ascribed the miracles of Christ to Beelzebub. Detestable as is ever the spirit of ridicule and derision, and frivolous and impious as were the expressions of these empty mockers, their conduct gave occasion to this ever-memorable discourse of Peter. "But Peter, standing up with the eleven, lifted up his voice, and said unto them, Ye men of Judea, and all ye that dwell at Jerusalem, be this known unto you, and hearken to my words : for these are not drunken, as ye suppose, seeing it is but the third hour of the day." How true is this verse to all we know of Peter ! How prompt his zeal ! Though "the eleven" may have stood forth with him, he is the spokesman. No sooner does the impious aspersion of the scoffer fall on his ear, than his warm temper is up, and he is prompt to crush the upas in the germ. Nor does he speak in a whisper, or with bated breath ; but "he lifted up his voice," raised it, perhaps, to its highest notes, so that the vast multitudes might hear his refutation of the calumny. He spoke not to the few scoffers, but to the men of Judea, and to all that dwelt at Jerusalem, whether they were Jews or proselytes. But his exordium shows that strong as was his zeal, it was, in this case, tempered by judgment. There is great rhetorical tact in his opening words. *"Be this known unto you, and hearken to my words."* His refutation consists of two parts, the negative and the positive. Let us notice each.

First, *The negative.* *"For these are not drunken, as ye suppose, seeing it is but the third hour of the day."* This negative part, consisting of one short sentence, includes, it has been said, three distinguishable points :—*A categorical denial.* "These men are *not* drunken." It is a libel. *An intimation of the groundlessness of the charge.* "As ye suppose." Intimating that it was a mere empty assumption, not a belief built on evidence. *A suggestion of high improbability.* "Seeing it is but the third hour of the day." An able critic thus paraphrases the sentence :—"As to the charge of drunkenness, it refutes itself; for unless you mean to class us with the lowest revellers and debauchees, which all who see us see to be absurd, it is inconceivable that all of us should be already drunk at this early hour of the day." Methinks I see Peter, directing, by his looks and his finger, the attention of his audience to the excited disciples on whom the Spirit of God had descended ; and, with amazement mingled with holy indignation, exclaiming with emphasis, *"These are not drunken."* Their radiant looks, their stately bearing, show that they are more like seraphs than drunkards. Let us notice now—

Secondly, *The positive part of the defence.* He now gives them the explanation of the phenomenon. He tells them that, so far from having to be ascribed to intoxicating drinks, it was the effect of Divine inspiration. "This is that which was spoken by the prophet Joel ; and it shall come to pass in the last days, saith God, I will pour out of my Spirit upon all flesh." The days of the Messiah are indeed the last days of the world. No other dispensation of mercy will succeed them. The passage teaches four things in relation to these "last days," the first of which had now dawned :—

(1.) *It teaches that these "last days" would be connected with an extraordinary effusion of the Spirit.* "I will pour out of my Spirit upon all flesh," &c. The inspiration of the Spirit in these days would not be limited to any particular *class of persons*—not limited to *sex ;* "Your sons and your daughters shall prophesy." Not limited to *age ;* "Your young men shall see visions, and your old men shall dream dreams." The Spirit of the Lord enables men to see visions, and to speak out Divine things by prophecy. "They tell out what they see." Oh ! for more of this Spirit in the Church now—a Spirit enabling all to see the true thing, and to speak it out !

(2.) *It teaches that these "last days" would be connected with.*

prodigious revolutions. " And I will show wonders in heaven above, and signs in the earth beneath; blood, and fire, and vapour of smoke," &c. These words may perhaps be properly regarded as a highly poetic representation of that revolution in governments, churches, and all other human institutions, which would inevitably follow the working out of the divine ideas and spiritual influences of these last days, (Isa. xiii. 10, xxxiv. 4.)

(3.) *It teaches that these " last days" would be succeeded by a notable day.* " Before that great and notable day of the Lord come." " That notable day " refers most probably to the destruction of Jerusalem by Titus. That was, indeed, a day of judgment to the Jewish people. " Their sun was turned into darkness and their moon into blood." But there is another notable day of the Lord, which lies at the end of "these last days "—the day of universal judgment.

(4.) *It teaches that these " last days" would be connected with a possibility of salvation to all who seek it.* " And it shall come to pass, that whosoever shall call on the name of the Lord shall be saved." This is the most glorious characteristic of these "last days." Whosoever shall call—call in the true spirit of faith in Christ— "shall be saved." *Whosoever!* Thank Heaven for this *whosoever!*

Acts 2:22-36

PENTECOST (NO. II.)—A NEW STYLE OF RELIGIOUS MINISTRY

"Ye men of Israel, hear these words; Jesus of Nazareth, a man approved of God among you by miracles,[1] and wonders, and signs, which God did by him in the midst of you, as ye yourselves also know : him, being delivered by the determinate counsel and foreknowledge of God, ye have taken, and by wicked hands have crucified and slain ;[2] whom God hath raised up, having loosed the pains of death : because it was not possible that he should be holden of it. For David speaketh concerning him, I foresaw the Lord always before my face ; for he is on my right hand, that I should not be moved : therefore did my heart rejoice, and my tongue was glad ; moreover also, my flesh shall rest in hope : because thou wilt not leave my soul in hell,[3] neither wilt thou suffer thine Holy One to see corruption. Thou hast made known to me the ways of life : thou shalt make me full of joy with thy countenance. Men and brethren, let me freely speak unto you of the patriarch David, that he is both dead and buried, and his sepulchre is with us unto this day. Therefore being a prophet, and knowing that God had sworn with an oath to him, that of the fruit of his loins, according to the flesh, he would raise up Christ to sit on his throne ;[4] he, seeing this before, spake of the resurrection of Christ, that his[5] soul was not left in hell,[6] neither his flesh did see corruption. This Jesus hath God raised up, whereof we all are witnesses. Therefore being by the right hand of God exalted, and having

received of the Father the promise of the Holy Ghost, he hath shed forth this, which ye now see and hear. For David is not ascended into the heavens: but he saith himself, The Lord said unto my Lord, Sit thou on my right hand, until I make thy foes thy footstool. Therefore let all the house of Israel know assuredly, that God hath made that same Jesus, whom ye have crucified, both Lord and Christ."

EMENDATIVE RENDERINGS.—(1.) Mighty works.—LANGE. (2.) Ye by the hand of lawless men nailed up and slew.—ALFORD. (3.) The kingdom of the dead.—LANGE. (4.) He would set one upon his throne. (5.) He. (6.) The kingdom of the dead.

EXEGETICAL REMARKS. — " *Men of Israel.*" In this antique simplicity of address there is more earnestness than in our own day, when so many epithets of *nobility* and dignity are accumulated in titles.—BENGEL.

" *Jesus of Nazareth.*" He is the grand subject of all apostolic sermons, (chap. iii. 13.)

"*A man approved of God.*" The Greek word ἀποδεδειγμένον means more than approved ; it means authenticated, accredited ; it means He was shown to be that which He claimed to be. " *Miracles*" and " *wonders*" and " *signs*" attested His divine legation.

" *Determinate counsel.*" Determinate is not *determined*, in the moral sense of resolute, intrepid ; but *determined*, in the physical or proper sense of bounded, defined, settled, as opposed to what is vague, contingent, or indefinite. The dative may be either one of cause, *by the will*, or of rule and measure, *according to the will*, most probably the latter.—ALX.

" *Ye have taken*," &c., or as Alford renders it, " Ye by the hand of lawless men nailed up and slew." What God permitted they performed. God's eternal plan allows even the most wicked freedom of action.

" *Whom God hath raised up.*" He whom they crucified, God restored. The Greek verb ἀνίστημι, in its active tenses, always means to raise up, from what or to what is determined by the context.—ALX.

" *Having loosed the pains of death.*" Probably Peter used this term, meaning the *snares of death*—Ps. xviii. 5, where death is personified as a hunter. This expression is translated in the Septuagint, ὠδῖνας θανατου, pang of death, and Luke has followed them

(MEY)—Latin, *funes*, cords, bands ; but it is also used of the pangs of childbirth. *Pains*, out of which new life arose. Jesus in dying felt the pains of death. In death it is finished, and in consequence, after death there were no pains. A little after, His resurrection effected a loosing, not of the pains, but of the bonds which had caused the pain while He was dying.—CRITICAL ENGLISH TESTAMENT. Death is but a parturition struggle, giving birth to a higher life.

" *Because it was not possible that he should be holden of it.*" The remaining of Christ in the grave was an impossibility. It would imply unfaithfulness in the promises of Him who *cannot* lie, and in the plans of Him who *cannot* change.

" *For David speaketh concerning him*," &c. The words of David referred to are found in Ps. xvi. 11. The quotation, as is usual in the New Testament, is made from the Septuagint Greek, not from the Hebrew original. Because David was regarded by the Jews as a type of the Messiah, Peter here applies these words to Christ.

" *Therefore did my heart rejoice.*" " Therefore," on account of this assurance of divine protection. My tongue corresponds to my glory in Hebrew, and may be regarded as a very ancient exposition of that phrase, preserved in the Septuagint version, and according to which the tongue (*i.e.*, the faculty of speech) is regarded as the glory of the human frame, or as the instrument of the Divine praise.—ALX.

" *Because thou wilt not leave my soul in hell*," &c. *In hell*, or Hades, literally to the place of Hades. Hades is, as it were, the sepulchre of souls.

Hell is rendered Hades by the Septuagint. The (Hebrew verb) *forsake, leave in,* is found in Lev. xix. 10, Ps. xlix. 11, Job xxxix. 14. He was in Hades; he was not left in Hades. David's confidence is, *thou wilt* not leave my soul in hell, or Hades, *i.e.,* in the dark and unseen state. (The Greek ἄδης, Hades, means *unseen.*) This is all he says of it. But when the Lord speaks of it, He calls it not Hades, hell, but Paradise, (Luke xxiii. 43)—a consoling difference between Jewish and Christian ways of speaking.—C. E. T. From this the article of the Creed, "He descended into hell," is clearly deduced. Before His resurrection the soul of Christ was in hell (Hades); but it was not there before His death; therefore, upon or after His death, the soul of Christ descended into hell.—WEBSTER and WILKINSON.

"*Of the fruit of his loins according to the flesh.*" Several of the oldest manuscripts and latest critical editors omit the words, "according to the flesh would raise up Christ," so that the clause reads, "knowing that

God had sworn with an oath to him that of his loins (one) should sit upon his throne." Besides the external evidence in favour of this reading, it relieves the text from an enfeebling and embarrassing anticipation of what follows in the next verse.—ALX.

"*The Lord saith unto my Lord,*" Ps. cx. 1. Though the same word is used in Greek for "Lord" in both instances, yet, in the original Hebrew, it is, "*Jehovah* said unto my Lord," or *adoni,* a title of high honour and respect, and one form of which is sometimes used by the Jews instead of the word *Jehovah,* which they feared to utter commonly. The expression is used by Peter, however it may have been originally employed, to describe the superiority which God gave His Son over His enemies, by raising Him up on high, and placing him at His right hand.

"*Thy foes thy footstool.*" It was sometimes the custom for conquerors, in ancient times, to put their foot on the neck of the vanquished, in token of their victory and power over them.—LIVERMORE.

HOMILETICS.—In illustrating this new order of religious ministry, we have already dwelt upon the first part of Peter's sermon—namely, his statement for refuting the charge of the scoffer. We now pass on to the second part—namely,

II. HIS ARGUMENT FOR CONVICTING THE HEARTS OF THE HARDENED GENERALLY. Peter passes from the groundless aspersions of the scoffer to deal more directly with the consciences of all. "Ye men of Israel, hear these words; Jesus of Nazareth, a man approved of God among you by miracles, and wonders, and signs, which God did by him in the midst of you, as ye yourselves also know," &c. He sets himself to the work of demonstrating that the Jesus of Nazareth, whom they had crucified, was the true Messiah, the Holy One, the Lord of David, &c. He knew that if he could establish this to their conviction, he would rouse their consciences into an agony of distress, and to this he gives himself; and his argument for the purpose, when closely examined, resolves itself into four facts :—

First, *That Jesus had wrought miracles before them while living.*

"Jesus of Nazareth," says Peter, "a man approved of God among you by miracles and signs," &c. As if the apostle had said, "Jesus of Nazareth, as you call Him with reproach and derision, did, as you well know, work miracles, wonders, and signs amongst you. You cannot deny these works; they were so numerous, so extraordinary, seen so frequently by thousands in open day, that the denial of them by you is impossible. These miracles were God's attestation of His Messiahship, they were what God did by Him in the midst of you, 'as ye yourselves also know.' He, that Nazarene, let me tell you, was a man from God, attested by the wonders you saw Him work." Another part of this argument is—

Secondly, *That His crucifixion by them was only the working out of the Divine plan.* "Him, being delivered by the determinate counsel and foreknowledge of God, ye have taken, and by wicked hands have crucified and slain." The apostle might have been prompted to make this wonderful statement to meet an objection that might possibly start in their minds against the fact of His Messiahship. They might have said: "How could He, whom we had the power to kill and to bury, be the Messiah? Would the Great Jehovah allow the Messiah, His Anointed One, to be thus crushed by mortals?" The objection would be natural, and the apostle's statement is equal to its triumphant refutation. He tells them that Jehovah delivered Him to them, "by His determinate counsel." He says virtually to them—" Your conduct towards Jesus of Nazareth, though free and terribly wicked, was the working out of the eternal plan of Heaven. Your conduct towards Him was the very conduct which Heaven determined you should be *permitted* to pursue towards the Messiah on this earth." So great is God that He can make His greatest enemies, in working out their most hostile rebellions against Him, work out, at the same time, His great plans. He makes them frustrate their own purposes, but fulfil His. Another part of his argument is—

Thirdly, *That His resurrection from the dead, which they could not deny, was a fact which accorded with their Scriptures.* "Whom God hath raised up," &c. He states this as a fact so generally admitted by them, as to require not one single word in evidence. Who there, on that occasion, could deny, or even question the fact? It had only just occurred within a few weeks. It was fresh in the minds of all; perhaps the one dominant thought, and the one prominent topic of conversation. He says, " whereof we all are witnesses.' They were now standing near the very spot where it took place. There was lying the open grave before them, where some had seen Him buried. It was unnecessary, therefore, for the apostle to spend one word in arguing the fact of His resurrection. He employs himself, therefore, in doing that which was required, and which was to the point—namely, to prove that the fact was in accordance with their own Scriptures. "Whom God hath raised up, having loosed the pains of death: because it was not possible that he should be holden of it. For David speaketh concerning him," &c.

In the quotation and use of this passage by the apostle, it is instructive to mark what he assumes, and what he attempts to prove.

(1.) *He assumes that the document which he quotes will be admitted by them as of Divine authority.* " For David speaketh," he says. He does not say a word to them as to who David was; there was no need for that ; no name in history was better known, no name gathered around it more loving and brilliant associations. Nor does he say a word as to the Divine authority of David's utterances. This would have been unnecessary. They regarded him as a man after God's own heart. They regarded him as inspired with the Spirit of God, as the consecrated organ of Heaven's thoughts to the world. There was nothing, therefore, debateable between him and his audience as to the Divine authority of the document he quotes.

(2.) *He takes for granted that the document refers to the resurrection of some one of distinguished excellence.* He is described as having " the Lord always before his face," " always on his right hand ;" as the " Holy One of God," who speaks with an exultant assurance of His own resurrection. " Therefore my heart was rejoiced, and my tongue was glad ; moreover, also, my flesh shall rest in hope." " My flesh, my body, shall go down to the grave in a joyful hope of resurrection." He speaks of His soul, also, as not being left in hell, (Hades, the world of separate souls.) He expresses the assurance that it would not continue for ever separate from the body. Nay, more, that the separation of His soul from the body would not be for long, not long enough for the body to " see corruption." " The ways of life " beyond the grave were clearly revealed to Him by Heaven, and He anticipates the full joy of Jehovah's countenance.

(3.) *He reasons that the resurrection of the Distinguished One predicted could not be David.* " Men and brethren, let me freely speak unto you of the patriarch David." As if the apostle had said—" Men and brethren, give me your indulgence. Hear with patience and candour what I have yet to say, let me freely speak unto you of the patriarch David, a man whom we all venerate, I as much as any of you ;—he is not risen from the dead. He is both dead and buried, and his sepulchre is with us unto this day. Yonder, on Mount Zion, with many of our great kings, his ashes sleep ; the sepulchre in which his illustrious son Solomon buried him, with such pomp and splendour, is known and honoured by us all. None of you believe that he is risen from the dead, for you regard him as sleeping there. His body has seen corruption, and his soul is yet in Hades. The resurrection, therefore, predicted in those passages I have quoted, and which you acknowledge to be divine, could not be his resurrection."

(4.) *He concludes that the resurrection predicted must have referred to Christ.* " Therefore, being a prophet, and knowing that God had sworn with an oath to him, that of the fruit of his loins, according to the flesh, he would raise up Christ to sit on his throne ;

he, seeing this before, spake of the resurrection of Christ, that His soul was not left in hell, neither His flesh did see corruption. This Jesus hath God raised up, whereof we all are witnesses."

His conclusion that the Messiah is the One whose resurrection is predicted, is supported by the description which he here gives of the patriarch David.

(*a*) David sustained the prophetic character. "Being a prophet." The Jews regarded David as one who had the Divine gift of prophecy, (2 Sam. xxiii. 2; Ps. xxii. 1, 8, 18, lxix. 21, 25.) Being a prophet, and especially a prophet of the Messiah, it was in accordance with his character to foretell such an event.

(*b*) David had the assurance that the Messiah would spring out of his loins. "Knowing that God had sworn with an oath to him that of the fruit of his loins, according to the flesh, he would raise up Christ to sit on his throne." God is in various places spoken of as having sworn to David, (Ps. lxxxix. 3, 4, 35, 36, cxxxii. 11.) David, therefore, had the most settled assurance that from his seed the Messiah would spring. The Jews understood this, (Matt. xii. 22, 23, xxi. 9, xxii. 42–45.) It is natural to suppose, therefore, that a man like David, who was a prophet, and who knew that the Messiah would descend from him, would, "seeing this before, speak of the resurrection of Christ," &c. Hence the conclusion of the apostle from the passage, that "this Jesus hath God raised up, whereof we all are witnesses."

Another, and the last point of his argument in proof of the Messiahship of Jesus, was—

Fourthly, *The extraordinary spiritual phenomena which they now beheld in the disciples of Jesus.* The miraculous utterances, and the wonderful deportment of the disciples, which now attracted the multitudes to whom Peter spoke, established the same conclusion. It was the only explanation of the phenomena which astonished all: "Therefore, being by the right hand of God exalted, and having received of the Father the promise of the Holy Ghost, he hath shed forth this, which ye now see and hear." Jesus of Nazareth, whom they have crucified, had not only risen from the dead, but had ascended into heaven, and was at the right hand of God, the Lord of David, and the Lord of all, and, according to His promise, had now sent down the Holy Spirit, filling the souls of His disciples with wondrous sentiments, and endowing them with miraculous speech. What they now saw and heard was a proof that He had ascended to heaven, and His ascension to heaven was a proof of His Messiahship. This is his argument for the Messiahship, which he proclaims as irresistible, and his audience felt it as such. "Therefore, let all the house of Israel know, assuredly, that God hath made that same Jesus, whom ye have crucified, both Lord and Christ." What a fact is this! Wonderful in itself, and especially wonderful in its bearing on the men to whom it was now proclaimed; and wonderful also for

Peter to declare to such an audience. What sublime intrepidity and invincible courage does he display in doing so! He, a poor fisherman, stands up before assembled thousands of his nation, and charges home upon them the enormous crime of crucifying the Messiah, their great hope as a people, whom David, their mightiest monarch, predicted and adored as Lord, and who had now ascended the throne of the universe. " God hath made that same Jesus, whom ye have crucified, both Lord and Christ."

Acts 2:37-40

PENTECOST (NO. II.)—A NEW STYLE OF RELIGIOUS MINISTRY

" *Now, when they heard this, they were pricked in their heart, and said unto Peter and to the rest of the apostles, Men and brethren, what shall we do ?* Then Peter said unto them, Repent, and be baptized every one of you in the name of Jesus Christ for the remission of sins, and ye shall receive the gift of the Holy Ghost. For the promise is unto you, and to your children, and to all that are afar off, even as many as the Lord our God shall call. And with many other words did he testify and exhort, saying, Save yourselves from this untoward generation.*"

EXEGETICAL REMARKS. — " *Were pricked.*" The word translated " were pricked" ($\kappa\alpha\tau\epsilon\nu\acute{v}\gamma\eta\sigma\alpha\nu$) is only used here, and nowhere else in the New Testament. It denotes, to penetrate as with a needle, to pierce as with a sharp instrument. It answers to our word "compunction." It expresses an agony of being, both *intense* and *sudden.*

" *What shall we do ?* " The compunction they felt roused the will. What shall we do ? Something must be done ; tell us what, and we shall attempt it. All this is implied.

" *Repent.*" This is his answer to their appeal. The word "repent," which, etymologically and at first, meant after-thought and reflection, means in the New Testament sense a moral change of mind—a thorough revolution in character. This revolution implies great internal effort on man's part. It is not a something imparted from without, it is something produced within. It implies profound reflection upon our con-

duct, renunciation of the evil connected with it, and a determination in future to pursue a holier course.

" *Be baptized.*" If the baptism here is a baptism of water, in those two things we find, first, an internal effort involving a renunciation of evil ; and the second, an external effort involving the expression of that renunciation. Peter does not explain to these men what baptism was. They, being Jews, knew its meaning well. They knew it as revealed in the Levitical system ; they knew it as it had been just applied to them by John the Baptist on the banks of the Jordan ; and by the disciples of Jesus, who baptized even more than John. They knew that it was a symbol of spiritual cleansing. The language of Peter, perhaps, taken as a whole, would mean, " be cleansed from your sins within by repentance, and symbolically express that cleansing by being baptized in the name of Jesus." Some, however, think that the reference is not to baptism by water, but to the moral cleansing of the soul, and that Peter means nothing more than " repent and be clean in heart."

" *Remission of sins.*" " The first Greek noun,"says Alexander, "(αφεσιν,) derived from a verb, (αφιημι,) which means, to let go, is applied by Plutarch to divorce ; by Demosthenes to legal discharge from the obligation of a bond ; by Plato to the emancipation of a slave, and to exemption from

punishment : which last is its constant use in the New Testament. The whole phrase, *to* (or towards) *remission of sins,* describes this as the end to which the question of the multitude had reference, and which, therefore, must be contemplated also in the answer."

" *With many other words did he testify.*" The whole sermon is not here, but a mere abstract or summary.

We now come to the last part of this memorable sermon, where he solemnly and practically deals with those whom his arguments had convicted of their terrible guilt.

III. An Exhortation to the Awakened.

" Now, when they heard this, they were pricked in their heart, and said unto Peter and to the rest of the apostles, Men and brethren, What shall we do ?" They had been convicted of an act—(1.) *Most guilty.* They had murdered the kindest, the holiest, the greatest of beings that ever appeared on earth—the Messiah, the Son of God, the Prince of life. What ingratitude, what injustice, what impiety, what rebellion, were involved in their act ! The sense of their guilt pierced them now with the agony of *remorse* and *foreboding.* They had been convicted of an act—(2.) *Most irreparable.* What they had done could not be undone. If they had merely inflicted corporal sufferings upon Him, those sufferings might have been healed, and they might have restored Him ; but they had killed Him. He was gone from them for ever. They could make no reparation. They had stained themselves with a guilt that all the water of oceans could not cleanse. Hence their exclamation, " What shall we do ? What shall we do ? our moral anguish is intolerable, and our apprehensions are most terrible ; our moral heavens are black with clouds that threaten a terrible tempest."

Now to this appeal, Peter, with characteristic promptness, responds. Though the convicted hearers appeal not only to Peter, but to the " rest of the apostles," Peter is the spokesman ; and here is his address :—" Then Peter said unto them, Repent, and be baptized every one of you in the name of Jesus Christ for the remission of sins, and ye shall receive the gift of the Holy Ghost. For the promise is unto you and to your children, and to all that are afar off, even as many as the Lord our God shall call."

In this exhortation of his, three things are observable.

First, *He directs them to the only blessings that could meet their case.* These blessings are the remission of sins, and the gift of the Holy Ghost, which means *Divine pardon* and *Divine influence.* They needed *remission of sins.* To remission or freedom from punishment he directs them, as one who directs shipwrecked mariners, struggling in the billows and about to sink, to the approaching life-boat bounding on the crested waves. But they needed not only Divine pardon, but Divine influence ; not only the remission of sins, but the *gift of the Holy Ghost.* They would require this Spirit after the remission to remove all the sad effects of sin from their nature, to guide them rightly in their future course, strengthening them evermore to resist the wrong and pursue the right. These two things, the Divine pardon and the Divine Spirit, are essential to the salvation of our fallen world. To these, therefore, Peter directs his sin-convicted hearers.

Secondly, *He directs them to the course of conduct essential to the attainment of those blessings.* He knew that those blessings would not come to them except they, as moral agents, exerted those powers with which they were endowed in a way suitable to the end ; and hence he directs them to repentance and baptism. "Repent, and be baptized," &c.

John the Baptist had predicted, in connexion with Christ's mission, a baptism of the Spirit. "I indeed," said John, "baptize you with water ; but one mightier than I cometh, the latchet of whose shoes I am not worthy to unloose : he shall baptize you with the Holy Ghost and with fire." And Jesus Himself, just before He left the world, promised this baptism of the Spirit. "For John truly baptized with water ; but ye shall be baptized with the Holy Ghost not many days hence." This baptism of the Spirit—a baptism that cleanses the soul from all moral impurities—is, after all, the essential thing ; a baptism this, of which water-baptism is at the best but a symbol, and without which it is but an impious sham.

Thirdly, *He directs them to the gracious promise of Heaven to encourage them in the course of conduct required.* "For the promise is unto you, and to your children, and to all that are afar off, *even* as many as the Lord our God shall call." The promise he here points to, is that which he held forth to the multitude in the preceding verse, the promise of the Holy Ghost. This promise he had referred to in the introduction of his discourse, when he quoted the words of Joel : "I will pour out of my Spirit upon all flesh," &c. This promise he assures them was for *them* and their *posterity,* "you and your children." To *you,* bad as you are,—you that spat in His face, you that derided Him, you that plaited the crown of thorns, you that placed it on His bleeding brow, you that put on Him the purple robe of mock royalty, you that rent the heavens with the cry "Away with Him, away with Him," you that railed at Him when He hung upon the cross, you that gave Him gall to quench His burning thirst— the promise is to *you.* "*Every one of you.*" "What a blessed 'every one of you' is here," says Bunyan. "To your *children.*" To your posterity down to the latest period of time, it shall echo on the ear and shine on the face of "the last of Adam's race." To those *here,* and to those *everywhere.* "To those that are afar off." Not only to

Jews who were scattered in different countries, but to Gentiles also. To men on every zone of the globe. " *To all that the Lord our God shall call.*" And whom does He not call? His words are gone out to all the earth. His call in the Gospel is to all. Blessed promise this. It is a rainbow that encircles the world. It reflects the rays of the upper heavens, and heralds universal sunshine for the race.

Such is the substance of the apostle's wonderful sermon. We say substance, for the whole is not here. We are told that " with many other words did he testify and exhort, saying, save yourselves from this untoward generation." *Be saved* from the sins of a crooked generation.

Does not this *new order of religious ministry,* now inaugurated by Peter, stand in sublime and censuring contrast to much of the ministry that is called " Evangelical" in these days? It has none of the dogmas that form the staple ministry of many pulpits now. There is nothing here about the election of some and the reprobation of others. Nothing here about the final perseverance of the saints, nothing here about a forensic justification. No theory of the atonement is propounded here. Nothing is here about the moral ability or inability of the sinner. No metaphysical theologisings of any kind are here. CHRIST, in His relation to the men and women, the good and bad, who stood before him, was the grand theme of Peter's discourse. As a speaker he steps forth with a distinct object in view, namely, the awakening the souls of the multitude to a true sense of their sin, and he employs an argument most philosophically suited to gain his end ; it was an argument to convince them that they had murdered their Messiah. He understands the subject thoroughly; he feels it profoundly ; and he speaks it with all earnestness and point. There is no attempt to be smart or quaint, elegant or grand, in his speech. Such things, with ranting declamations, and oratorical flourishes, suit the hollow-hearted, but are ever revolting to a soul in genuine earnestness. His words were few, clear, direct, arranged with logical skill, and uttered with a voice intoned by the Spirit of the living God.

Acts 2:41-47

PENTECOST (NO. III.)—A NEW DEVELOPMENT OF SOCIAL LIFE

" *Then they that gladly received his word were baptized : and the same day there were added unto them about three thousand souls. And they continued steadfastly in the apostles' doctrine and fellowship, and in breaking of bread, and in prayers. And fear came upon every soul : and many wonders and signs were done by the apostles. And all that believed were together, and had all things common ; and sold their possessions and goods, and parted them to all men, as every man had need.   And they, continuing daily with one accord in the temple, and breaking bread from house to house, did eat their meat with gladness aud singleness of heart, praising God, and having favour with all the people.   And the Lord added to the church daily such as should be saved."* [1]

EMENDATIVE RENDERINGS.—(1.) The Lord brought together daily more that were in the way of salvation.—ALF.

EXEGETICAL REMARKS.—*"And breaking bread."* Whether this refers to the Eucharist, (the Lord's Supper,) or the *agapœ*, (love-feasts,) or their common social meal, is a question still in dispute amongst critics. The name, however, of this service, "the breaking of bread," inclines us to believe that the Lord's Supper is meant ; for it is said " Jesus took bread, and blessed it, and *brake it."* And with His disciples, whom He joined on their way to Emmaus, He was known to them by the *" breaking of bread."* " The bread of the Hebrew," says a modern expositor. "was made commonly into cakes, thin, hard, and brittle, so that it was broken instead of being cut. Hence, to denote intimacy or friendship, the phrase ' to break bread together,' would be very expressive, in the same way as the Greeks denoted it, by ' drinking together,' (συμπόσιον.) " It has been supposed that the Lord's Supper was observed once a week by the early Christians, (Matt. xxvi. 26 ; Luke xxiv. 30 ; Acts xx. 7 ; 1 Cor. xi. 23.) The whole of this 42d verse may be regarded as a summary description of the young Church. It had apostolic teaching, mutual communion, and common prayer. *"And fear came upon every soul."* For God was present among them. (So Herod and all Jerusalem with him were troubled at the birth of Jesus, Matt. ii.) This fear withheld persecutors from breaking out against the new Christians before the time was come.—(C. E. T.)

HOMILETICS.—Two of the features which characterised this day of Pentecost, namely, a new manifestation of the Divine Spirit, and a new order of religious ministry, have already engaged our attention. We now proceed to notice the last, which is—

A NEW DEVELOPMENT OF SOCIAL LIFE

" Then they that gladly received his word were baptized : and the same day there were added unto them about three thousand souls." As the result of Peter's wonderful sermon, a form of society rises which had never appeared on earth before. New forces act upon the social natures of men, and bring them together from new feelings, and for new engagements, and new purposes. There is a *new* society before us. *New*, at least, in many respects. The εκκλησια receives new elements, throbs with new impulses, assumes new proportions, sets itself to new functions, and exerts new influences upon the world.

The passage presents several things in relation to this *new* society.

I. THE INCORPORATING PRINCIPLE OF THIS NEW SOCIETY. What was it that brought those " three thousand souls " into close fellowship with themselves, and with the existing body of Christ's disciples ? What was the magnet that drew together and centralised into a loving unity these souls, which a few hours before were so discordant and antagonistic ? The answer is at hand.

First, The apostle's " *word*." It was that sermon of Peter's that did the work, the sermon which demonstrated to their conviction the Messiahship of Him whom they, by wicked hands, had " crucified and slain."

Secondly, The apostle's word " *received*." This word, had it not been received, would have died away in silence, without any effect. They *received* it. They were convinced of its truth, and accepted it as a Divine reality.

Thirdly, The apostle's word received " *gladly*." " Then they that gladly received his word," &c. They gladly received his word, for whilst his word convinced them of their enormous wickedness, it also assured them of God's readiness to pardon and to save. This word thus received, then, was the uniting power that broke down all social barriers, and made their profoundest sympathies mingle and run in one direction. The Messiahship of Christ, which Peter's word now demonstrated, is the rock-truth on which the Church of God is built. " Upon this rock," says Christ, " I will build my church, and the gates of hell shall not prevail against it."* Observe—

II. The introductive ceremony to this new society. " They were baptized." Baptism we regard as a *symbolical* ordinance—an ordinance designed to express a twofold truth of vital moment— *the moral pollution of humanity, and the necessity of an extraneous influence in order to cleanse its stains away.* These truths, these sinners felt under Peter's mighty sermon ; and, as a most seeming and proper thing, they were admitted into communion with the disciples by an impressive symbolic declaration of them. As to the *mode* in which they were baptized, this is a trifle that is only interesting to those religionists who live upon such rites. When it is remembered that Jerusalem had only the fountain of Siloam to supply its population with water, and that its supplies were always scanty —that " the three thousand " were baptized in one day which had passed its noon before the operation had commenced, and that the thousands of course included both sexes—it requires a larger amount of credulity than we profess to have to believe that they were all immersed in water. However, what matters it ? The mode of the act is nothing, the spirit is everything. Observe—

III. The unremitting services of this new society.
" They continued steadfastly in the apostles' doctrine and fellowship, and in breaking of bread, and in prayers." The day of Pentecost is over, the incorporation of these thousands into the Church has taken place, and Luke continues now to give a history of their subsequent life. " They were," he says, " continuing steadfastly in

* See my Homiletic Commentary *in loco*.

the apostles' doctrine and fellowship, and in breaking of bread, and in prayers."

First, They were *persevering;* for such is the meaning of this word "steadfastly," in *the* teaching. The word "doctrine" does not mean the thing taught, but the act of teaching. They were constant in their attendance on the teaching of the apostles. After Peter's great sermon he had much more to say; and after their conversion, they had much more to learn. This new society was a society of *students.* They "inquired" in the house of the Lord. They regularly attended *the* teaching, as distinguished from all other teachings of men, and as designating, perhaps, the highest teaching of the apostles. What teaching was theirs? What a privilege to study in the apostolic college.

Secondly, They were persevering in *the* fellowship. They appreciated the communion of saints. Meetings for mutual counsel, exhortations, and spiritual intercourse, they constantly attended. They regarded themselves as members of a brotherhood whose rules they were bound to obey, and whose interests they were bound to promote. In this fellowship, like the saints of old, they " *spake often one to another."* They considered one another *"to provoke unto love and to good works,"* They exhorted " *one another daily."* They endeavoured to " *edify one another,"* and, perhaps, they confessed their " *faults one to another."* There is a blessed fellowship in the true Church.

Thirdly, They were persevering in *the* breaking of bread. "And in breaking of bread." They attended to the dying command of their Master.

Fourthly, They were persevering in *the* prayers. *The* prayers here designate, we think, certain services for prayer which were recognised amongst them—prayer-meetings or prayer-services. They were a praying community. Thus much for their services. "The whole," to use the language of another, "may be summed up as consisting in apostolical teaching, mutual communion, and common prayer." Observe—

IV. THE DISTINGUISHING SPIRIT OF THIS NEW SOCIETY.

The spirit that animated the converts who formed this new brotherhood of souls was distinguished—

First, *By reverence.* "Fear came upon every soul." Whilst they were profoundly happy, there was no frivolous hilarity in their natures, a reverential awe had settled on their being. The cause of this reverence is expressed in the words, " many wonders and signs were done by the apostles." They felt that God was near, that His hand was on them. (φόβος !) A deep feeling of solemnity and wondrous awe pervaded their minds ; like the old patriarch, who, roused from his dream, felt " how awful is this place." The spirit was distinguished—

Secondly, *By generosity.* "And all that believed were together, and had all things common : and sold their possessions and goods, and parted them to all men, as every man had need." They were *together ;* not, perhaps, locally, for no house could contain the multitude, but spiritually. They were one in spirit, they were together in soul. What one felt, all felt. They wept with those that wept ; they rejoiced with those that rejoiced. Like Christ and His apostles they had all things common ; they put their property into a common stock, " and sold their possessions and goods, and parted them to all men, as every man had need." Here is generosity. Selfishness has no place in this *new* community. The new commandment is supreme. The benevolence which inspired them was a benevolence that *made sacrifices.* "They sold their possessions and goods." The love of property in them gave way to the love of man. The law of social Christianity enjoins the strong to bear the infirmities of the weak, the rich to help the poor, and all to bear each other's burden, and so fulfil the law of Christ.

This benevolence adjusted itself to the occasion. The circumstances of the persons assembled on this occasion required such an effort as this. Many of them came from distant regions, and who had come unprepared to settle down in Jerusalem, and many of them, too, of the poorer classes of society, who had not themselves the means of subsistence. The benevolence of those who had property, therefore, was called out to meet the case. There is no reason to regard the community of goods here—a state of things rising up to meet a crisis—as a *precedent* binding on future times. The terms of the narrative authorise not an application so universal. The Gospel everywhere recognises the distinction of the rich and the poor ; and the diversity in the instincts and habits of mankind would render a community of property, as a permanent and lasting institution, an impossibility. The spirit was distinguished—

Thirdly, *By gladness.* "Did eat their meat with gladness." Their hearts exulted with joy. The rich were happy, for their benevolence was gratified in giving. The poor were happy, for their hearts glowed with gratitude in receiving. All were happy in themselves, happy with each other, because they were happy in God. The spirit was distinguished

Fourthly, *By simplicity of spirit.* There was " singleness of heart." There was no pride, no ostentation, no self-seeking, no hypocrisy amongst them ; but all were exquisitely child-like in spirit. All were transparent, they saw each other's souls, and in each other trusted. The spirit was distinguished—

Fifthly, *By religiousness.* " Praising God." This is not so much a particular in description as a pregnant summary of the whole. As if the historian had said, " in all they praised God ; whether they ate or drank, whatsoever they did, they did all to His glory." Worship is not a particular service, but a spirit that inspires all services. Observe—

V. THE BLESSED CONDITION OF THIS NEW SOCIETY.

First, Their *influence was great.* " They had favour with all the people." Favour, not with a class—not with priests, Pharisees, Sadducees—but with (τὸν λαὸν) all the people. Their spirit and conduct commanded the esteem of the people around them.

Secondly, Their *growth was constant.* They were not a declining community, nor a stationary one. They were *daily* increasing.

Thirdly, Their *accession was divine.* " The *Lord* added daily." He only can add true men to the Church.

Fourthly, Their *salvation was promising.* " Such as should be *saved,*" or rather such as were in the way of salvation. The word σωζομένους means persons in the way of deliverance, as the Israelites were in respect of temporal safety when they marched out of Egypt.

Acts 3:1-10

THE MIRACLE AT THE BEAUTIFUL GATE.—(NO. I.) A FACT

" *Now Peter and John went up together into the temple at the hour of prayer, being the ninth hour. And a certain man, lame from his mother's womb, was carried, whom they laid daily at the gate of the temple which is called Beautiful, to ask alms of them that entered into the temple ; who, seeing Peter and John about to go into the temple, asked an alms. And Peter, fastening his eyes upon him with John, said, Look on us. And he gave heed unto them, expecting to receive something of them. Then Peter said, Silver and gold have I none; but such as I have give I thee : In the name of Jesus Christ of Nazareth rise up and walk. And he took him by the right hand, and lifted him up ; and immediately his feet and ancle bones received strength. And he, leaping up, stood, and walked, and entered with them into the temple, walking, and leaping, and praising God. And all the people saw him walking and praising God : and they knew that it was he which sat for alms at the Beautiful gate of the temple : and they were filled with wonder and amazement at that which had happened unto him.*

EMENDATIVE RENDERINGS.—And he looked on them attentively, expecting to receive something of them.—G. V. LECHLER, D.D., and K. GEROK.

EXEGETICAL REMARKS. — Observe here four things :—First, the instrumental authors of the miracle : " *Now when Peter and John,*" &c. In these verses we have the record of the first apostolic miracle. This is recorded for reasons that will hereafter appear. We are not to suppose that the circumstances recorded in this chapter follow immediately the events of the preceding one. Luke does not appear at all times to chronicle events in their chronological order. No one can tell how soon or how long after Pentecost the events of this chapter occurred. " Peter and John went up together." " There is something," says a modern expositor, " striking in the mutual relations of Peter and John, as they may be traced in the history. After their joint mission to prepare for the last Passover, (Luke xxii. 8,) they seem to have been inseparable, notwithstanding the marked difference in their character and conduct. Peter alone denied His Master; John alone continued with Him to the last. See John xviii. 15, 19, 26. Of Peter's fall, John would seem to have been the only apostolic witness. Yet we find them still together at the sepulchre, and in Galilee after the resurrection, (John xx. 2, xxi. 7.) It is an observation of Chrysostom, that Peter's question, (John xxi. 21,) ' *Lord, what shall this man do ?* ' was prompted rather by affection than by curiosity."

Observe, secondly, the season of the miracle :—

" *The hour of prayer.*" The hour of prayer, Lightfoot informs us, is the same in the Hebrew code. The examples of David, Daniel, Peter, as well as the authority of the Talmuds, teach us that the Jews had three hours for prayer daily; the third hour, nine o'clock in the morning; the sixth, twelve o'clock; and the ninth, three o'clock in the afternoon. These disciples of Christ did not give up the temple at once, they worshipped in the temple as they were wont.

Observe, thirdly, the subject of the miracle :—

" *And a certain man lame from his mother's womb.*" In the next chapter, in the 22d verse, we are told that he was above *forty years* old; upwards of forty years, therefore, he had lived a cripple. His lameness was not the result of accident or disease, or some infirmity that had come upon him after a period of physical perfection, but was a constitutional defect; he was born a cripple.

Observe, fourthly, the scene of the miracle :—

" *At the gate of the temple which is called Beautiful.*" Some suppose this was the gate called Nicanoe, which led to the court of the Gentiles, to the court of the women. Others suppose that it was the gate to the eastern entrance of the temple, commonly called Susan or Sushan; th the common and the more supposition. Josephus says gates, nine of them were ev overlaid with gold and silver, likewise the posts and the lintels. But one, without the temple, made of Corinthian brass, did much exceed in glory those that were overlaid with gold and silver." At that gate began the inner temple, as distinguished by Josephus from the outer temple. This being the most frequented gate of the temple, and in the vicinity of Solomon's porch, the cripple was placed there as the best position for appealing for charity to the passing crowd. *He asked alms of them that entered into the temple.* The position of this lame man at the gate of the temple implies, both on behalf of himself and those who carried him thither, that—(1.) *His condition was such as to give him a claim upon the charity of others.* So it verily was. Such cases as his demand our compassion and our aid. They are means which God has appointed for the practical development of our benevolence. (2.) *That the exercises of piety are favourable to the display of benevolence.* Why was he carried to the gate of the *temple* ? Not merely because of the multitudes that passed to and fro; other positions, such as the public streets and commercial thoroughfares, might have been selected were this the only reason. He felt, undoubtedly, that the men who approached God in worship were above all men disposed to help his suffering children. Piety is the fountain of philanthropy.

Observe, fifthly, the method of performing the miracle :—

" *And Peter fastening his eyes upon him with John, said, Look on us.*" It would seem that Peter and John both fastened their eyes on this man— threw their glance right into his. The eye, when it is the organ of a great living thought, is a mighty organ. A divine electricity often streams through it. They fastened their eyes on him, that he might fasten his eyes on them, so that a kind of spiritual contact might take place, that they might connect him with the divine that was in them.

"*Then Peter said, silver and gold have I none.*" The poor man having had his attention arrested, expected that he should receive from them what he desired—alms; but in this he was disappointed by the declaration of Peter, "*Silver and gold have I none.*" As if he had said, "Money I have none ; I am poor in this world ; but such as I have—the power that God has given me to help others—I will employ on your behalf." It is recorded that Thomas Aquinas, who was highly esteemed by Pope Innocent IV., going one day into the Pope's chamber, where they were reckoning large sums of money, the Pope said to him, "You see that the Church is no longer in an age in which she can say, ' silver and gold have I none.'" "True, holy father," said Aquinas ; "neither can she say, ' Rise up and walk.'" A Church may be secularly rich, and morally poor. A man like Peter may be without money, and yet have God with him, and in him, to work His will.

"*In the name of Jesus Christ of Nazareth, rise up and walk.*" They wrought their miracle in the name of Jesus of Nazareth. The apostolic miracles were all performed in the name of Christ, according to His own command and promise, (Mark xvi. 17, 18 ; John xiv. 12 ; Acts ix. 34, ix. 40, x. 28, xiv. 9, xvi. 18.) "*In the name,*" that is by the delegated power, "of Jesus of Nazareth." "Jesus of Nazareth," an allusion to the contempt with which that name was popularly regarded. "*Rise up and walk.*" The man might have said, "You have mocked me ; I cannot move a limb ; I have never walked a step." Peter's command implied that *faith* and *volition* were required on the part of the cripple.

"*And he took him by the right hand, and lifted him up.*" "In this, as in many of our Saviour's miracles," says a modern expositor, "the healing word was attended by an outward touch or gesture, serving to connect the miraculous effect with the person by whom it was produced, (Matt. viii. 15, ix. 25, xiv. 31, xx. 34.) Such was the order or method with which the miracle was wrought. The simple and minute account of the successive steps gives to the whole narrative a living reality."

Observe, sixthly, the reality of this miracle.

"*And immediately his feet and ancle bones received strength. And he, leaping up, stood, and walked,*" &c. Two circumstances here show the indubitableness of the miracle :—(1.) *The effect upon the man himself.* The poor cripple who had never used his limbs for forty years, and who did not seek their restoration, "stood and walked, and entered with them into the temple, walking and leaping, and praising God." Though the cure was well-nigh instantaneous, yet there is a great gradation observed. First, Strength came into "*his feet and ancle bones ;*" then he leaped up ; then stood ; then walked ; then entered the temple. The man's frame bounded with new energy, his soul was flooded with divine joy and praise, and his limbs were agile and blithe, expressing these emotions. Who can describe—nay, who can imagine—the man's feelings ! Then, (2.) *The effect upon the people themselves.* "*All the people saw him walking and praising God.*" The miracle was *public;* it was not wrought in a corner, it was almost in the height of day, and before the eye of the multitude. The subject of the miracle was well known. "They knew that it was he which sat for alms at the Beautiful gate of the temple." Many had seen him lie there, year after year, a helpless cripple at the gate. The people, therefore, were "filled with wonder and amazement." They were struck with astonishment. The whole neighbourhood felt the shock ; Jerusalem was awe-struck.

HOMILETICS.—The miracle here recorded may be said to extend in its particulars and influences to the 22d verse of the next chapter. The whole of the passage brings the miracle under our notice in three aspects :—As a *fact,* a *text,* and an *epoch.* The first eleven verses of this chapter presents it to us in the first aspect, and to this aspect we now give our attention.

The exquisite simplicity with which it is stated, and the minute details specified, show—as plainly as anything can show—that it has nothing of the parabolic or mythical about it. It is a FACT. If there be history in any writing, these verses are a history. In the fact we see three things, which are very significant and suggestive.

I. POOR MEN BECOMING THE ORGANS OF OMNIPOTENCE.

Peter and John were the *instrumental* authors of the miracle. They were two of the apostles who, in mental character, were the most dissimilar. John seems to have been calm, retiring, intuitional, living not so much in the scientific forms or historical details of truth, as in the transcendental region of its spiritual elements. Peter, on the other hand, was restless, forward, and somewhat dogmatic. Albeit, no two of the apostles seem more intimately allied. They were on the Mount of Transfiguration together; they prepared the last Passover, and were in the Garden of Gethsemane together; they were together, also, at the sepulchre on the morning of the resurrection; and here we find them together "going up into the temple," &c. Though John knew Peter's defects and crimes, yet he seemed so to love him as to elect him as his companion; and Peter loved him in return. As a rule, natural diversities of mental temperament are favourable to the closest friendship. In them there is a supplementing of mutual deficiencies, and a dovetailing into each other. Natural diversities, where there is moral purity, are aids to social harmony. God worked a wonder by these men now. He often makes men mighty: Moses, Elijah, and the apostles are examples.

Another thing which we discover in this fact is—

II. A WRETCHED CRIPPLE MADE THE OCCASION OF GREAT GOOD.

Thoughtful men have often asked the question, Why, under the government of a benevolent God, should such cases as this of the poor lame man occur? Why should the Great One send men into the world, sometimes without the use of their limbs, cripples? sometimes without the use of their eyes, blind? sometimes without the use of their reason, idiots?

Three facts may go a great way towards the obviation of the difficulty:

First, *That persons who come into the world in this state, being unconscious of physical perfection, feel not their condition as others.* Men who have never seen, know nothing of the blessedness of vision; men who have never had the use of their limbs, know nothing of the pleasures of healthful exercise of the limbs; men without reason, know nothing of the high delights of intellectual action. Hence persons of constitutional defect in form, organ, or limb, often display a peace of mind, and often a joy, at which others wonder. The subjects, therefore, of constitutional defects feel not their loss as we are too prone to imagine.

Another fact which may contribute to the removal of the difficulty is—

Secondly, *Such cases of organic imperfection serve by contrast to reveal the wonderful goodness of God.* In the material world, those parts of the earth that have been shattered by earthquakes, that lie in black desolation for the want of sun, that thunder in hideous chaos, serve to set off in more striking and soul-inspiring aspects the beauty and the order that reign everywhere but with such few exceptions. It is so with the human world in those cases of constitutional defects. A hunchback here, a blind man there, a cripple in another place, and an idiot there in the crowded walks of life, only serve to set off the goodness of God in the millions of men and women that are perfect. These are a few dark strokes which the Great Artist employs to set off the picture of the world in more striking aspects of beauty—a few of the rougher notes which the Great Musician uses to swell the chorus of universal order.

Another fact which contributes to the disposal of this difficulty is—

Thirdly, *They serve to inspire the physically perfect with gratitude to heaven.* In the poor idiot, who stares vacantly at you, God says, " Be thankful to me for the light of reason." In the poor blind man, groping his way in darkness, God says, " Be thankful to me for that eye that gives you a bright world." In the poor cripple, that lies helpless by the wayside, God says to the passing crowd, " Be thankful to me for those agile limbs that carry you about." The blind, the idiotic, the crippled, the deformed, are sacrifices for the public good. They are God's homilies to the millions, demanding gratitude to Him for perfection in faculty and limb. Who can tell the spiritual good that this poor cripple accomplished, as he lay daily at the gate of the temple, observed by the hundreds that passed to and fro for worship?

Fourthly, *They afford scope and stimulus for the exercise of benevolence.* Were all men equal in every respect, it is obvious there would be no object to awaken charity, and no field for its display.

This fact also shows us another thing—

III. CHRISTIANITY TRANSCENDING HUMAN ASPIRATIONS.

This poor man wanted alms—" silver and gold;" but in the name of Christ he received physical vigour and power to use his limbs, blessings which he had never ventured to expect. Thus it is ever : Christianity gives man *"more* than he can ask or think." " Eye hath not seen, ear hath not heard," &c.

Acts 3:11-26

THE MIRACLE AT THE BEAUTIFUL GATE.—(NO. II.) A TEXT

"*And as the lame man which was healed held Peter and John, all the people ran together unto them in the porch that is called Solomon's, greatly wondering. And when Peter saw it, he answered unto the people, Ye men of Israel, why marvel ye at this? or why look ye so earnestly on us, as though by our own power or holiness we had made this man to walk? The God of Abraham, and of Isaac, and of Jacob, the God of our fathers, hath glorified his Son Jesus; whom ye delivered up, and denied him in the presence of Pilate, when he was determined to let him go. But ye denied the Holy One and the Just, and desired a murderer to be granted unto you; and killed the Prince of life, whom God hath raised from the dead; whereof we are witnesses. And his name, through faith in his name, hath made this man strong, whom ye see and know: yea, the faith which is by him hath given him this perfect soundness in the presence of you all. And now, brethren, I wot that through ignorance ye did it, as did also your rulers. But those things, which God before had shewed by the mouth of all his prophets, that Christ should suffer,[1] he hath so fulfilled. Repent ye therefore, and be converted, that your sins may be blotted out, when the times of refreshing shall come from the presence of the Lord; and he shall send Jesus Christ, which before was preached unto you:[2] whom the heavens must receive until the times of restitution of all things, which God hath spoken by the mouth of all his holy prophets since the world began. For Moses truly said unto the fathers,[3] A prophet shall the Lord your God raise up unto you of your brethren, like unto me; him shall ye hear in all things whatsoever he shall say unto you. And it shall come to pass, that every soul, which will not hear that prophet, shall be destroyed from among the people. Yea, and all the prophets from Samuel, and those that follow after, as many as have spoken, have likewise foretold of these days. Ye are the children of the prophets, and of the covenant which God made with our fathers, saying unto Abraham, And in thy seed shall all the kindreds of the earth be blessed. Unto you first, God, having raised up his Son Jesus, sent him to bless you, in turning away every one of you from his iniquities.*"

EMENDATIVE RENDERINGS.—(1.) By the mouths of all the prophets that his Christ should suffer.—ALF. (2.) That the times of refreshing come from the presence of the Lord, and that He may send Him who was before appointed your Messiah, even Jesus.—ALF. (3.) Moses has said.—LECHLER and GEROK.

EXEGETICAL REMARKS.—"*And as the lame man which was healed held Peter and John.*" The healed cripple held them, either because he was perhaps fearful of a relapse, or, which is more probable, because of his intense gratitude to them for the deliverance and restoration which they had brought him.

"*All the people ran together unto them in the porch that is called Solomon's, greatly wondering.*" All felt convinced that a great miracle had been performed. "There are," says Livermore, "particulars which make the cure of the cripple a strong proof of the miraculous power of the apostles, and exclude the possibility of deception. The man had been lame from his birth. He had been known for forty years as an invalid, and been brought daily to his place to beg at one of the most crowded thoroughfares of the temple. He asked not to be cured, but begged money ; and there could have been no collusion between him and his benefactors. He was suddenly and entirely restored, so as immediately to stand, leap, and walk, as if he had always enjoyed the exercise of his limbs. The cure was done in a public place, and the people were witnesses of it. They were convinced that it was a miracle. They manifested all the natural signs of astonishment, and after listening to the address of Peter, became converts to the Christian faith in great numbers, (Acts iv. 4.) It would be credulity of the grossest kind to believe, against all proof or probability, that the apostles in this case practised any deception or fraud. It would be to take up the saying of one of old, 'It is impossible ; therefore I believe.'"

"*And when Peter saw it.*" Saw what ? The concourse of the people, and their immense amazement.

"*He answered unto the people.*" He seizes this occasion in order to preach to them the religion of Christ.

"*Ye men of Israel, why marvel ye at this ? or why look ye so earnestly on us, as though by our own power or holiness we had made this man to walk ?*" He does not address them as a tumultuous mob, but as a religious assembly. "*Men of Israel, why marvel ye at this?*" He does not intend to express censure because of their astonishment, for that was natural, but because of their ascribing the deed to them, as the primal authors. "*Why look ye so earnestly on us, as though by our own power or holiness we had made this man to walk ?*" Lightfoot says that such a conceit walked among the nation, that extraordinary holiness might attain to miraculous workings. The apostles emphatically disclaim the glory of such an amazing deed.

"*The God of our fathers hath glorified his Son Jesus.*" The word translated *Son* is not the one commonly so rendered, ($vi\acute{o}s$,) but another, ($\pi a\hat{i}s$,) used both for son and servant, (Matt. viii. 6, 8, 13, xiv. 2 ; Luke xii. 45, &c.) Peter means to say that the God of their fathers wrought this miracle through them, not merely for the benefit of the lame man, but for the honour and glory of that Jesus whom they delivered up, denied, preferred a murderer in his stead, and murdered him at last.

"*And his name, through faith in his name, hath made this man strong, whom ye see and know ; yea, the faith which is by him hath given him this perfect soundness in the presence of you all.*" The Rev. Hilkiah Bedford Hall, M.A., gives the following rendering of this verse, which we think makes the meaning clearer :—" And through faith in his name hath made this man strong, whom ye see and know. His name, and the faith which is by him, hath given him this perfect soundness in the presence of you all." Here he propounds the cause of the miracle— faith in the name of Christ. Christ's name is Himself.

"*And now, brethren, I wot that through ignorance ye did it, as did also your rulers.*" "*I wot,*" old English for " I know," from the Anglo-Saxon *witan,* to see, to know ; from which comes our word "*wit.*" The apostle extenuates their guilt in the same way that Christ did upon the cross, "Father, forgive them, they know not what they do." Though their ignorance was a mitigation of their guilt, it was no justification, for they had the means of knowing better.

"*Repent ye, therefore, and be converted.*" These two words mean pretty well the same thing, namely, moral revolution. It means, change your heart and conduct.

"*That your sins may be blotted out.*" Blotted out, erased, cancelled. The metaphor occurs several times elsewhere—Ps. li. 9, cix. 14 ; Isa. xliii. 25 ; Jer. xviii. 23 ; Col. ii. 14.

"*When the times of refreshing shall come.*" A better rendering, perhaps, would be, " in order that the times of refreshing may come." "*Times of refreshing*"—literally, " breathing again "—would come to them as the result of their repentance and remission.

"*From the presence of the Lord.*" Rendered by Bloomfield as a Hebrew circumlocution for " by God's providence."

"*And he shall send Jesus Christ, which before was preached unto you.*" This is connected with the preceding clause, and means "*that he may* send Jesus Christ." Most probably the reference is to Christ's spiritual advent ; to those who are converted and forgiven ; Christ ever comes to such.

"*Whom the heavens must receive.*" They expected that the Messiah would dwell and reign on the earth. Peter assures them that it was necessary for Him to have been received into heaven. During the process of the world's spiritual renovation He will remain unseen.

" *Until the times of restitution of all things, which God hath spoken by the mouth of his holy prophets since the world began.*" The "*all things*" to be restored are the things which God has spoken by His prophets of old. Humanity has lost many precious things : truth, holiness, liberty, usefulness, perfect joy. These will be restored one day.

HOMILETICS.—Having looked at this miracle as a *fact*, we proceed now to look at it as a TEXT. Peter, inspired with the spirit of his mission as an apostle of the new religion, seized this marvel as a *subject* for a gospel discourse. It is a law of mind to look at all outward things through its dominant sentiments, and to subordinate all outward things to its dominant purposes. The apostles were full of thoughts pertaining to Christ, and they looked at the universe and all passing events through this medium. In treating this miracle as a subject of discourse, he does three things :—He traces it to its true Author ;—he connects it with the name of Christ ;—he develops the Christian plan of restitution.

I. HE TRACES THE MIRACLE TO ITS TRUE AUTHOR. He does this :—

First, *Negatively.* He disclaims for himself and his colleague the authorship. "When Peter saw it, he answered unto the people, Ye men of Israel, why marvel ye at this ? or why look ye so earnestly on us, as though by our own power or holiness we had made this man to walk ?" The people were marvelling. That was natural, for it was a great wonder ; but they seemed to marvel, not merely at the fact, but at the means by which they thought that fact was produced. They considered that these poor apostles did it by their " own power or holiness." Peter at once seeks to correct the false impression, and to sweep the thought from their minds. This prompt disclaimer of the authorship of the miracle by the apostles, is a remarkable demonstration of their *honesty.* Had they taken the credit of this marvellous achievement, their social power would have become regnant at once ; the people would have gathered around them by millions, followed them as heroes, worshipped them as gods. To the ambitious instincts which they had within them, in common with all men, this might have been a temptation ; nor was there any difficulty in their obtaining universal credit for this work. The people seem at once to have ascribed the deed to them ; there was no difficulty in the way to this honour. They looked with devout wonder at them, so that Peter said, " *Why look ye so earnestly on us ?* " Every eye looked with mingled awe and amazement at them, and every heart trembled with a strange reverence in their presence. For the apostles, therefore, under such circumstances, to disclaim at the outset the authorship of the miracle, is a proof of their honesty, a proof whose strength will increase in our estimate as we compare it with the ordinary conduct of mankind. But in tracing the miracle to its Author, he advances from the negative to *the positive*.

Secondly, *Positively*. He affirms at once who the real Author was. " The God of Abraham, and of Isaac, and of Jacob, the God of our fathers, hath glorified his Son Jesus ; whom ye delivered up, and denied him in the presence of Pilate, when he was determined to let him go." He shows—

(1.) That *their* God had wrought the miracle. It was not *a* god, believed in by some other peoples and nations ; it was *the* God *they* believed in, *their* God, " The God of Abraham, and of Isaac, and of Jacob."

(2.) That *their* God had wrought the miracle in order to *glorify His Son*. The miracle was not wrought for its own sake—not merely to restore a wretched invalid. It had an ulterior purpose. It was to confer honour on His Son, to furnish an additional attestation of the Messiahship of Him whom they had put to death as a malefactor.

II. HE CONNECTS THE MIRACLE WITH THE NAME OF CHRIST. " And his name, through faith in his name, hath made this man strong, whom ye see and know ; yea, the faith which is by him hath given him this perfect soundness in the presence of you all." In this verse the apostle seems to hit the philosophy, so to speak, of the miracle. God was the Author of it, they were the instruments ; and they became the instruments because of their faith in the name of Christ ;—the name of Christ means Christ Himself. These apostles had unbounded faith in Jesus, as the true Messiah—the Saviour of the world—and because of this faith they were invested with the power to perform works that should demonstrate to the world the divine authority of Him in whose service they were engaged. The effects which, in consequence of their faith, they were enabled to produce upon the bodies of men, were only faint types of the sublime results which faith in Christ will enable its possessor to produce upon the spirits of mankind. Spiritual works are the " greater works."

Now this Jesus, through faith in whom this miracle was performed, Peter takes the opportunity of bringing prominently under their notice, so as to work upon their hearts the profoundest impressions concerning Him. He presents Him to them in three ways :—

First, *In the titles that belong to Him*. He describes Him as the *Son of God*, having a relation to the Eternal, unique in all that is close and tender ; as the " *Holy One and the Just;* " attributes these, which the consciences of Judas who betrayed Him, and Pilate who condemned Him, were bound to ascribe to Him ; and as the " *Prince of Life,*" the Leader, the Chief, the Captain of life.

Secondly, *In the history of their conduct.* He sketches their treatment of Him. This he does in a kind of graduated method, until he reaches the terrible crisis of murder.

(1.) They "delivered Him up." They abandoned Him to His enemies ; " He came to His own, and His own received Him not," they rejected Him.

(2.) They "denied" Him in the presence of Pilate, denied His Messiahship in the presence of a heathen ruler. This indignity they offered to their Messiah before the face of a scoffer at their religion, and a tyrant of their country.

(3.) They did this when Pilate was determined " to let Him go." Though this heathen ruler was so convinced of His innocence, that he was determined to release Him, their clamour overbore his judgment, and thwarted his wish.

(4.) They desired " a murderer" to be granted unto them. They not only demanded the condemnation of the innocent, but preferred the murderer Barabbas to the Prince of Life.

(5.) They killed Him. "And killed the Prince of Life." Here is the climax of folly and impiety ; the top-stone in hell's grand edifice of crime. He presents Him to them—

Thirdly, *In His relation to God.*

(1.) God had glorified Him ; " He hath glorified His Son Jesus."

(2.) He raised Him from the dead. " Whom God hath raised from the dead, whereof we are witnesses." They killed the Prince of Life, but He raised Him from the grave. His resurrection from the dead was a fact too obvious, too patent, for them to question—" whereof we are witnesses."

(3.) He overruled their conduct towards Him. " And now, brethren, I wot that through ignorance ye did it, as did also your rulers. But those things, which God before hath showed by the mouth of all his prophets, that Christ should suffer, he hath so fulfilled."

Observe—(*a*) It was the purpose of the Eternal Father that Christ should suffer. " *God hath before shewed by the mouth of all his holy prophets, that Christ should suffer.*" " All his prophets" means not literally all, but the general voice of prophecy. The old Testament prophets may be regarded as an official corporation—a grand representative body, and their utterances, therefore, are rather the voice of one than of many. The ruling reference of all is to the Messiah, His birth, His works, His sufferings, His death, (Is. liii. 3–10 ; Dan. ix. 26.)

Observe—(*b*) That this conduct of the Jewish people, in relation to Christ, was overruled for the working out of this grand purpose. " He hath so fulfilled," or fulfilled so. The sufferings which He eternally purposed were inflicted not directly by Himself, not by the agency of holy intelligences, but by the wicked conduct of wicked men. "The Son of man goeth, as it is written of him, but woe unto that man by whom the Son of man is betrayed." "Him being delivered by the determinate counsel." So perfect is the control which the great Monarch of the universe has over His creatures, that He makes the greatest rebels His servants to work out His grandest plans.

Observe—(c) The wicked Jew, in thus working out the Divine purpose, was ignorant of what he was doing. "And now, brethren, I wot that through ignorance ye did it, as did also your rulers." Peter admits their ignorance for one of two purposes, either to extenuate their guilt, or to impress them with the fact, that, contrary to both their knowledge and their design, their very wickedness was the working out of an eternal plan. The former idea, though it has some passages to recommend it, (Luke xxxiii. 34; 1 Tim. i. 13; 1 Cor. ii. 8,) is inadmissible, from the fact that Peter includes the rulers in his charge of ignorance. "Also your rulers." The rulers, the most enlightened and the best Biblically instructed of the nation and the times, were certainly not ignorant of what they were doing. The latter, therefore, is the probable idea. This ignorance does not extenuate their guilt, but rather adds to it a crushing sense of their own folly and helplessness. In treating this miracle—

III. HE DEVELOPS THE CHRISTIAN PLAN OF RESTITUTION. "Repent ye, therefore, and be converted, that your sins may be blotted out, when the times of refreshing shall come from the presence of the Lord; and He shall send Jesus Christ, which before was preached unto you: whom the heaven must receive until the times of the restitution of all things, which God hath spoken by the mouth of all His holy prophets since the world began." *This passage may be regarded as presenting the Christian plan for effecting the moral restitution of the world,* and it suggests the following thoughts in relation to that plan :—

First, *It aims at a thorough spiritual reformation as a necessary condition.* This spiritual reformation is here represented as including three things—

(1.) *A change of heart;* "Repent ye, therefore, and be converted."

(2.) *Forgiveness of sins;* "That your sins may be blotted out."

(3.) *Invigoration of being;* "When the times of refreshing shall come," &c. All these things are included in that great spiritual reformation which Christianity aims to accomplish in our world.

Another thought suggested here concerning the Christian plan of restitution is—

Secondly, *That it is ever under the direction of the Great God.* "From the presence of the Lord," *i.e.,* by the providence of the Lord.

Observe here—(1.) *That the invigorating influence of the scheme is from God.* The times of refreshing are from *His presence.*

(2.) *That the Chief Agent of the scheme is from God.* " He shall send Jesus Christ."

(3.) *That the revelation of the scheme is from God.* " Which God hath spoken by the mouth of all His holy prophets since the world began."

Another thought still suggested concerning the Christian plan of restitution is—

Thirdly, *That it shall realise its end before the final advent of Christ.* " Whom the heavens must receive until the times of the restitution of all things." *Christ is now in heaven.* He is there as the monarch of the creation, the representative of humanity, the object of universal wonder and worship. Though in heaven, His work proceeds on earth. His system is slowly but gradually advancing. When the work is accomplished, He will come again, and not before. Pre-millennialism is a delusion.*

Another thought suggested concerning the Christian plan of restitution is—

Fourthly, *That it is the grand burden of prophetic truth.* " Which God hath spoken by the mouth of all His holy prophets since the world began."

(1.) Observe the cases of prophetic references to Christ which the apostle adduces. The first case is Moses. " For Moses truly said unto the fathers, A prophet shall the Lord your God raise up unto you of your brethren, like unto me ; him shall ye hear in all things whatsoever he shall say unto you. And it shall come to pass, that every soul, which will not hear that prophet, shall be destroyed from among the people." This passage is found in Deut. xviii. 15–19. The quotation is made with scarcely any variation from the Septuagint version. The resemblance between Christ and Moses as prophets, mediators, legislators, and founders of new dispensations, is so strikingly obvious that it forms the basis of many a popular sermon. Samuel is mentioned. " Yea, and all the prophets from Samuel, and those that follow after." Moses and Samuel are the most distinguished names in the history of the Jewish nation—the strongest human centres in Jewish association. But these men are simply mentioned here as samples and references. He says, " all the prophets." We may not be able always to trace references to Christ in the writings of each prophet ; yet in the majority of the prophetic books there are notes of hope struck from the harp of future ages, flashes of light from that bright day of Christ which Abraham saw afar.

(2.) Observe the reason for the adduction of these references. " Ye are the children of the prophets and of the covenant which God made with our fathers, saying unto Abraham, And in thy seed shall

* See " Homilist," vol. v., p. 260.

all the kindreds of the earth be blessed." "Children," a phrase not indicative of physical descent, but of spiritual relationship. They were the pupils, the disciples of the prophets. They inherited the writings; they were their acknowledged authorities in all cases of faith and practice. They were the children of the covenant; they were admitted to all its privileges, a party in the compact in which the Lord should be their God and they His people. He states their close spiritual relation to the prophets and to the covenant, it would seem, as a reason for his prophetic reference, and truly a good reason too. Prophecy was their Bible; the acknowledged rule of their present, and the bright hope of their future.

Another idea suggested in relation to the Christian plan of restitution is—

Fifthly, *That its merciful mission was first to be presented to the Jews.* "Unto you first God, having raised up his Son Jesus, sent him to bless you, in turning away every one of you from his iniquities." Observe—(1.) *Christ was sent to bless, not to curse.* Justly might we have expected malediction to have been His mission. Observe—(2.) *Christ was sent to bless with the greatest blessing.* "Turning away every one of you from his iniquities." Iniquity is the greatest curse; to turn men from that is the greatest boon. Observe—(3.) *Christ was sent to bless with the greatest blessing the greatest sinners first.* You first—" beginning at Jerusalem."*

Acts 4:1-22

THE MIRACLE AT THE BEAUTIFUL GATE—(NO. III.) AN EPOCH

" And as they spake unto the people, the priests, and the captain of the temple, and the Sadducees, came upon them, being grieved that they taught the people, and preached through Jesus the resurrection from the dead. And they laid hands on them, and put them in hold unto the next day: for it was now eventide. Howbeit many of them which heard the word believed; and the number of the men was about five thousand. And it came to pass on the morrow, that their rulers, and elders, and scribes, and Annas the high priest, and Caiaphas, and John, and Alexander, and as many as were of the kindred of the high priest, were gathered together at Jerusalem. And when they had set them in the midst, they asked, By what power, or by what name, have ye done this? Then Peter, filled with the Holy Ghost, said unto them, Ye rulers of the people, and elders of Israel, if we this day be examined of the good deed done to the impotent man, by what means he is made whole; be it known unto you all, and to all the people of Israel, that by the name of Jesus Christ of Nazareth, whom ye crucified, whom God

* See " Homilist," vol. iv., New Series, p. 377.

raised from the dead, even by him doth this man stand here before you whole. This is the stone which was set at nought of you builders, which is become the head of the corner. Neither is there salvation in any other : for there is none other name under heaven given among men, whereby we must be saved. Now, when they saw the boldness of Peter and John, and perceived that they were unlearned and ignorant men, they marvelled ; and they took knowledge of them that they had been with Jesus. And beholding the man which was healed standing with them, they could say nothing against it. But when they had commanded them to go aside out of the council, they conferred among themselves, saying, What shall we do to these men ? for that indeed a notable miracle hath been done by them is manifest to all them that dwell in Jerusalem ; and we cannot deny it. But that it spread no further among the people, let us straitly threaten them, that they speak henceforth to no man in this name. And they called them, and commanded them not to speak at all, nor teach in the name of Jesus. But Peter and John answered and said unto them, whether it be right in the sight of God to hearken unto you more than unto God, judge ye. For we cannot but speak the things which we have seen and heard. So, when they had further threatened them, they let them go, finding nothing how they might punish them, because of the people, for all men glorified God for that which was done. For the man was above forty years old on whom this miracle of healing was showed."

Exegetical Remarks.—"*And as they spake.*" "But whilst they spake to the people," would perhaps be a more correct rendering. This is the continuation of the narrative commenced in the last chapter. This should not have been the commencement of a new chapter.

"*The priests, and the captain of the temple, and the Sadducees, came upon them, being grieved,*" &c. "The interference of the hierarchy against the apostles (in which the Jewish and priestly commander on duty of the Levitical guard of the temple was at the service of the priests and Sadducees) had a twofold motive. The Sadducees were annoyed, because the apostles, in testifying of the resurrection of Jesus, testified along with it of the resurrection in general ; this was a thorn in their side. The priests also could not endure that the apostles should teach the multitude, without possessing encroachment on the privileges of the Levitical priesthood. The Sadducean motive is stated, but it did not work exclusively, at least in the whole transaction before the council it was not brought forward at all."—G. V. Lechler and K. Gerok.

"*And they laid hands on them, and put them in hold unto the next day, for it was now eventide.*" They were arrested, not as a punishment, for they had not been legally tried, but for safe keeping until the next day, when they would be brought before their judges and be tried for their conduct.

"*Howbeit, many of them which heard the word believed, and the number of the men was about five thousand.*" Persecutors may imprison the apostles of truth, but they cannot imprison truth. While Peter and John were bound, their cause advances, and obtains five thousand new adherents.

"*And it came to pass on the morrow.*" They only rested the previous evening. No time is lost in bringing them to judgment.

"*That their rulers, and elders, and scribes, and Annas the high priest, and Caiaphas, and John, and Alexander, and as many as were of the kindred of the high priest, were gathered together at Jerusalem.*" A solemn and formal meeting of the Sanhedrim is called, (5, 6.) In no other way could the matter be decided. For essentially the question to be decided was the grave one, whether the apostles were, to be regarded as prophets of God, or as seducers to idolatry. This, however, was a question which it belonged to the Sanhedrim to decide.— BAUMGARTEN.

The Sanhedrim consisted of about seventy members, and before them the apostles were now brought. Some of their names are here mentioned. "Annas the high priest, and Caiaphas, and John, and Alexander, and as many as were of the kindred of the high priest." Though Caiaphas was actually the high priest, yet it is probable that Annas, on account of his having occupied that position for a considerable time and by reason of his age, and the fact of his having had several of his sons in that lofty position, was now called upon to act in that capacity, and sat as president of the court. The form in which the Sanhedrim sat was that of a semicircle ; the president, the high priest, at the head. Now the apostles were set in the "midst" of them, that is, in the area, surrounded by the seats of the members.

"*And when they had set them in the midst, they asked, By what power or by what name have ye done this ?*" The question of the judges—(1.) implies that they believed in the miracle as a fact ; indeed, there was no gainsaying it ; there was the cripple of forty years in the full possession of his health, and the full use of all his limbs and faculties : (2.) implies their suspicion that some improper means had been employed in its performance. The Jews believed that miracles could be performed by magic arts, incantations, and diabolic agencies.

"*Then Peter, filled with the Holy Ghost, said unto them, Ye rulers of the people, and elders of Israel,*" &c. Peter had now fulfilled in his own experience the promise of his great Master : "But when they shall lead you, and deliver you up, take no thought beforehand what ye shall speak, neither do ye premeditate; but whatsoever shall be given you in that hour, that speak ye, for it is not ye that speak, but the Holy Ghost." He was filled with the Spirit—thoroughly spiritualised, elevated into the circle of spiritual ideas and influences.

"*Be it known unto you all, and to all the people of Israel*"—the rulers, priests, scribes, pharisees, all—mark this—"*That by the name of Jesus Christ of Nazareth, whom ye crucified, whom God raised from the dead, even by him doth this man stand here before you whole.*"

"*This is the stone which was set at nought of you builders, which is become the head of the corner.*" This is a quotation from Ps. cxviii. 22, and applied by way of illustration to himself by Jesus, Matt. xxi. 42, as it is also here by Peter. They were the professed builders of the great temple of human virtue, and the essential stone of that temple they had rejected ; but that essential stone, despite their rejection, had now become the chief of the building.

"*Now, when they saw the boldness of Peter and John, and perceived that they were unlearned and ignorant men, they marvelled ; and they took knowledge of them, that they had been with Jesus. And beholding the man which was healed standing with them, they could say nothing against it.*" Several things are specified in these words, which silenced the judges : *Boldness*, or the freedom of their speech. *Ignorance*, that is, in the estimation of their judges, not being versed in Rabbinic lore, or trained to courtly manners. Their recollection that they had seen them with Jesus Himself, and the healed cripple standing at their side.

"*Let us straitly threaten them, that they speak henceforth to no man in this name.*" This is the result of their judicial investigations. They could not deny the miracle, they admitted it ; and they had been evidently deeply impressed with the address of Peter ; but they dreaded the spread of the new religion amongst those over whom they held supreme jurisdiction, and therefore they resolved if possible to prevent them speaking any more in the name of Jesus. "*And they called them, and commanded them not to speak at all, nor teach, in the name of Jesus.*" In a solemn and formal assembly, they agree together to put forth all the influence of their high office and authority to stop the preaching of the apostles.

"*But Peter and John answered and said unto them, Whether it be right in the sight of God to hearken unto you more than unto God, judge ye.*" Here is an appeal to the reason and con-science of the judges, and a declaration of their moral impossibility to desist from the work in which they were engaged.

HOMILETICS.—This first miracle, wrought by the apostles within the precincts of the temple, we have already noticed as a *fact*, and as a *text*. We have now to consider it as an EPOCH. The discourse which Peter delivered upon it as a text woke impulses and started efforts both amongst the adherents and opponents of the new religion, that introduced, in some respects, a new order of things. It led to the first assault ˌupon the Christian Church; it brought the new faith into violent conflict with the formalism of the Pharisee, the infidelity of the Sadducee, and the craft of priestly rule; and thus demonstrated its power to battle successfully with all the evils it is missioned to destroy. In looking at it as an epoch, we discover two things :—*A new impulse to the world's antagonism to Christianity,* and *a new demonstration of God's power in Christianity.*

I. A NEW IMPULSE TO THE WORLD'S ANTAGONISM TO CHRISTIANITY.

Observe two things—First, The *representatives* of the antagonism. Who were those who now stood forward as the representatives of the world against the Church—as the defenders of the false in theory, and the corrupt in practice? The first verse answers the question : " The priests, and the captain of the temple, and the Sadducees." The first represent religion, the second government, the third scepticism. Here you have, therefore, religion, politics, and infidelity, coming forth to crush the young Church. The hostile sections of a wicked world are ever ready to merge their differences in an attack upon the divinely pure and good. Pilate and Herod become friends in their endeavour to crush the Divine. Observe—

Secondly, The *reason* of this antagonism. What roused this opposition? The second verse furnishes the reply : "Being grieved that they taught the people, and preached through Jesus the resurrection from the dead." Bengel and others see different motives at work in these assailants. The priests were "grieved," because these apostles should presume to teach, and thus arrogate their peculiar office. The captain of the temple was "grieved," because social tranquillity was disturbed and the public peace in danger. The Sadducees were "grieved," because they proclaimed a resurrection of the dead, a dogma which they repudiated. Wicked men hate truth for different reasons, and according to their passions·and interests. Observe—

Thirdly, The *development* of this antagonism. The persecutors do three things :

(1.) They *imprison* the apostles. " And they laid hands on them,

and put them in hold unto the next day : for it was now even-tide."
It would seem that it was too late in the day to hold a court in order
formally to try their conduct. It was, perhaps, if not unlawful, in-
convenient to assemble the Sanhedrim at such a late hour in the day.
They were, therefore, put in safe keeping until the morning. So
strong had the feeling of hostility to the teachings of these apostles,
and dread of their influence, grown in all classes, that they could not
wait until the morning. Their endurance was exhausted ; and they
seized the apostles at once, dragged them from their sphere of influence, deprived them of their liberty, and confined them in prison
during the night.

(2.) They *arraigned* the apostles. "And it came to pass on the
morrow, that their rulers, and elders, and scribes, and Annas the high
priest," &c. The word "rulers" is, perhaps, to be taken in a generic
sense, comprehending both the elders and the scribes—the one class
distinguished by the dignity of age, and the other by that of occupation as transcribers and interpreters of the Jewish law. "*By what
power, or by what name, have ye done this ?*" The question assumes
their belief in the miracle. The fact that a miracle had been wrought
in the man was beyond all dispute. Their question was, with what
power they did it. The conclusion which they undoubtedly sought
to reach was, that it was by some diabolical influence. Probably they
expected that the two poor unlearned Galileans would be intimidated
by such a question, as they stood in the presence of such an august assembly. Though this question is all that they are reported to have
addressed to the apostles, it is probable that much more was said on
the occasion. Peter's reply, which we shall notice in the sequel,
seems to have silenced and confounded them.

(3.) They *threatened* the apostles. "And they called them, and
commanded them not to speak at all, nor teach, in the name of Jesus."
Their command, we may rest assured, was enforced by many a terrible threat. Imprisonment, torture, and death, were, in all probability, held forth to their view as the results of disobedience.

Such, in brief is the reported antagonism which Peter's discourse
upon this miracle awoke against himself and colleague. It was
strong in its spirit, but futile in its efforts. In sooth, all endeavours
to crush truth are vain, fruitless, and self-confounding.

> "Truth, crush'd to earth, shall rise again ;
> The eternal years of God are hers.
> While Error, wounded, writhes in pain,
> And dies amidst her worshippers."

II. A NEW DEMONSTRATION OF GOD'S POWER IN CHRISTIANITY.
The fierce opposition, instead of retarding the progress of Christianity,
quickens its speed ; instead of enfeebling its energy, evolves its victorious powers. We see its power here—
First, *In multiplying its adherents.* "Howbeit many of them
which heard the word believed ; and the number of the men was

about five thousand." "Howbeit;"—*notwithstanding* the persecution, the Divine cause advanced. Though the clouds gather and thicken into blackness, the sun rises. The tides flow, though the force of the mightiest tempest bears against them ; and God's truth moves on to universal empire, though earth and hell combine against it. "Howbeit;"—aye, and not only despite the persecution did many which heard the word believe, but perhaps *because* of it. Persecution does two things which give an impulse to the cause of the Christian martyr. It presents on the one side such a hideous manifestation of evil as produces a social recoil, and on the other such an exhibition of Christian goodness in the spirit and conduct of the sufferers as awakens social sympathy and admiration. As the aromatic plant sends forth its sweetest odours by pressure, so the Christian character gains charm by its suffering. As the stars can only shine in the night, so the brightest virtues can only shine in trial. In this way the blood of the martyr has often been the seed of the Church. We see its power here—

Secondly, *In strengthening its advocates.* With what a sublime power did it invest the apostles on this occasion ? A power which enabled them heroically to expound their cause, thoroughly confound their enemies, and invincibly pursue their mission. They *heroically* expound their cause. They stand as prisoners in the midst of this august assembly—the great council of the nation—and the question is put to them, "By what power, or by what name, have ye done this?" and instead of being overawed or intimidated, Peter stands forth, "filled with the Holy Ghost," and addresses them with a heroism more than human. "Ye rulers of the people, and elders of Israel." In this short address, he states three things that were adapted, and undoubtedly intended, to awaken within them the profoundest moral concern :

(1.) That the said miracle was wrought by Him whom they had crucified. "*Jesus Christ of Nazareth,*" a name which ye despise, and whom ye crucified, is the name of Him by whom this wonder is effected.

(2.) That He whom they had crucified had become pre-eminent in the universe. "This is the stone which was set at nought of you builders, which is become the head of the corner." Peter borrows his words from Ps. cxviii. 22. They were the professed builders of the great temple of religion, but the chief stone for the building they had rejected. This was their folly and their crime. What they had rejected, God had honoured. Observe—(*a*) That men in their enterprises often reject the Divine. (*b*) That though they reject the Divine, the Divine shall be honoured at last to their confusion. (*c*) That He whom they had crucified was the only One that could save them. "Neither is there salvation in any other." They needed salvation. Salvation could be obtained through Christ *exclusively.* Such is the substance of Peter's address to this august assembly, his judges. It contains no word of apology, no hint of conciliation. He does not crouch as a menial before his master, or as a culprit before the administrators of justice. Nay, he offers no word of defence for himself; but with a clearness that could not be mistaken, and a directness that could not be evaded, he charges on them, his judges, the greatest crime that had ever been committed. In that court he stands clothed with the power of God. We see its power—

Thirdly, *In confounding its enemies.* Four effects seem to have been produced upon the enemies:

First, *They were astonished.* "Now when they saw the boldness of Peter and John, and perceived that they were unlearned and ignorant men, they marvelled; and they took knowledge of them that they had been with Jesus." They marvelled at the "boldness," that is, the *fluency* or ready utterance of these men; for such is the meaning of the word translated "boldness." It is true they were brave in speaking such things on such an occasion; but the fluent way in which such men on this occasion spoke struck their hearers with amazement. Instead of a nervous hesitancy in their speech, there was a bold flow of language. Two things would heighten their astonishment.

(*a*) The intellectual and social position of the men. "They perceived that they were unlearned and ignorant men." An unhappy translation this, (αγράμματοί,) *illiterate,* uneducated in that Rabbinical knowledge which the Jews regarded as the most important; (ἰδιῶται,) men in a private station, without professional knowledge.* These men had the instincts of the pedant. Pedants in every age consider those illiterate that do not know exactly that branch of learning in which they pride themselves. The linguist regards that man as illiterate who understands not the language he does, though he may know a hundred times as much of God's universe as he. Peter and John were not up in Rabbinical law, but they had a far deeper knowledge of the government of God than the most learned of the Rabbis. The men who delivered such speeches, and wrote such letters as did Peter and John, were no illiterate men. They had not received, it is true, the education of sophists and casuists, but they had received the teachings of Christ. The word "ignorant" should have been rendered "common men," "laymen." The astonishment was, that those apostles, who had never graduated in their schools, and who sustained no office in their institutions, but were private men, should speak with such fluency and force. The other thing that heightened their astonishment was—(*b*) The connection of the men with Christ. "They took knowledge of them that they had been with Jesus." They recognised them as those who had been with Jesus, as His companions and disciples. This would only heighten their astonishment; for how could they understand that men who had been the companions of Jesus of Nazareth, the carpenter's

* Webster and Wilkinson.

son, the blasphemer, the malefactor who had been crucified as a public offender, could speak in this way?

Secondly, *They were silenced.* "And beholding the man which was healed standing with them, they could say nothing against it." Facts are stubborn things. There was the man who had been a cripple for forty years standing side by side with the apostles, vigorous in body and with full use of limb. There was the fact in all its reality before them. What could they say? There was no denying it! The way to silence the enemies of Christianity is not by endeavouring to expose the fallacy of their objections, and logically involve them in absurdity, nor by declaiming with a pious horror against their infidelities, but by presenting to them the triumphs that Christianity has achieved. *Show them the facts.* Show them the morally blind who have been made to see, the deaf to hear, the lame to walk; show them the moral cripples that have been restored. This will silence them.

Thirdly, *They were perplexed.* They felt that something must be done to prevent the influence of these apostles spreading, and thus undermining their authority and shaking the conventional faith. "But when they had commanded them to go aside out of the council, they conferred among themselves, saying, What shall we do to these men? for that indeed a notable miracle hath been done by them is manifest to all them that dwell in Jerusalem; and we cannot deny it. But that it spread no further among the people, let us straitly threaten them, that they speak henceforth to no man in this name. And they called them, and commanded them not to speak at all, nor teach, in the name of Jesus." Everything recorded in these words shows their perplexity. They were at their wits' end. (1.) They command the apostles "to go aside out of the council." (2.) They then confer "among themselves" as to what is to be done. (3.) They then resolve to "threaten them." (4.) They then command them "not to speak at all, nor teach, in the name of Jesus." What a humiliating position for the great council of the nation to be placed in! What a sight! Seventy at least of a nation's magnates and magistrates confounded by two poor men whom they considered illiterate and ignorant! It is heaven's eternal law that the men who perversely struggle against the truth shall involve themselves in inextricable bewilderments.

Fourthly, *They were thwarted.* "But Peter and John answered and said unto them, Whether it be right in the sight of God." The address of Peter and John at this point involves three grand truths—

(1.) That the will of God is the imperial rule of life. The rule is "to obey God rather than man," in any capacity, or under any circumstance—man, either as a parent, a prince, monarch, or emperor. God's will is above the united will of nations, hierarchies, or worlds.

(2.) That universal conscience gives its sanction to the supreme law. "Judge ye." The apostle felt that his judges, one-sided, prejudiced, and corrupt as they were, had still within them that conscience that would compel them to the truth that God was to be obeyed rather than man. How beautifully Socrates is supposed to express this : "You, O Athenians, I embrace and love ; but I will obey God more than you."

(3.) That gospel truth, when truly felt in the soul, is an irrepressible force. "We cannot but speak the things which we have seen and heard." Men may repress mathematical doctrines, and truths of natural and abstract science, but such is the relation of gospel truth to the profoundest sympathies of the human heart, to the most vital interests of the human soul, that when they are truly felt, they must find utterance. "Necessity is laid upon me," says Paul.

The Sanhedrim, having heard this address of wondrous point and power, felt themselves powerless in their endeavour to crush the apostles. "So when they had further threatened them, they let them go, finding nothing how they might punish them, because of the people ; for all men glorified God for that which was done." They could not *punish* them, either because their consciences had been so touched by the address that they were self-prevented, or because the people were so thoroughly in sympathy with their work, that they were afraid to punish lest they should awaken public indignation. The latter reason is assigned ; perhaps both operated. Anyhow, the Sanhedrim was so far thwarted. Truth ever has, and always will, thwart the purposes of its opponents.

In conclusion, two remarkable things should be noticed before closing this section of apostolic history.

First, *The wonderful improvement in the character of Peter.* A few weeks before this, we find this Peter close to the spot in which he now stood, and in the hearing of the very men whom he now confronted, with a base cowardice, denying all knowledge of the Son of God ; but now he is invincible. The enemies of Christ he looks in the eye, he addresses, he charges with crime, with a courage that is unconquerable and majestic. How this change—this rapid improvement ? He has been thrown upon his own resources ; he has been studying the Scriptures in the light of Christ's history ; he has been earnest in prayer ; and he has received the Holy Ghost. His present position shows the truth of what Christ had taught, that "it was expedient for him that he should go away." The other remarkable thing which deserves notice here, is—

Secondly, *The difference in the effect of Peter's discourse on this occasion to that which took place under his sermon on the day of Pentecost.* Under his discourse on the day of Pentecost, which occurred just before, multitudes were pricked to the heart, and thousands were converted to God ; but no such effect as this seems to have taken place under the discourses which he delivered to the Sanhedrim. The same facts are stated, the same truths are brought forth, with the same burning fervour and unflinching fidelity, and yet there is no record of one conversion. There is wonder and perplexity, and that is all—no repentance. Why the difference? May not the cause be found in the different character of the audiences?

Acts 4:23-37

CHRISTIAN SOCIALISM

" *And being let go, they went to their own company, and reported all that the chief priests and elders had said unto them. And when they heard that, they lifted up their voice to God with one accord, and said, Lord, thou art God, which hast made heaven, and earth, and the sea, and all that in them is; who by the mouth of thy servant David hast said,*[1] *Why did the heathen rage, and the people imagine vain things ? The kings of the earth stood up, and the rulers were gathered together against the Lord, and against his Christ. For of a truth against thy holy child Jesus, whom thou hast anointed, both Herod and Pontius Pilate, with the Gentiles, and the people of Israel, were gathered together,*[2] *for to do whatsoever thy hand and thy counsel determined before to be done. And now, Lord, behold their threatenings : and grant unto thy servants, that with all boldness they may speak thy word, by stretching forth thine hand to heal ; and that signs and wonders may be done by the name of thy holy child Jesus. And when they had prayed, the place was shaken where they were assembled together ; and they were all filled with the Holy Ghost, and they spake the word of God with boldness. And the multitude of them that believed were of one heart and of one soul : neither said any of them that ought of the things which he possessed was his own ; but they had all things common. And with great power gave the apostles witness of the resurrection of the Lord Jesus : and great grace was upon them all. Neither was there any among them that lacked : for as many as were possessors of lands or houses sold them, and brought the prices of the things that were sold, and laid them down at the apostles' feet : and distribution was made unto every man according as he had need. And Joses, who by the apostles was surnamed Barnabas, (which is being interpreted, The son of consolation,) a Levite, and of the country of Cyprus, having land, sold it, and brought the money, and laid it at the apostles' feet.*"

EMENDATIVE RENDERINGS.—(1.) Who by the mouth of our father David hast said. —ALF. (2.) Gathered together in this city.

EXEGETICAL REMARKS.—" *Their own company.*" πρὸς τοὺς ἰλίους. There is nothing answering to " *company*" in the Greek. Who were their own ? Most probably their fellow-disciples, who had now increased to many thousands—a goodly fellowship. " *To their own*" they reported all that the chief priests and elders, that is the great council of the nation, had said unto them.

" *And when they heard that, they*

lifted up their voice to God with one accord." They were all religiously excited, and all joined in holy worship. Who led the devotions of the multitude we are not told.

" *Thy servant David."* The Greek word here translated " *servant,"* is the same as that rendered in chap. iii., verse 13, " *son."* Wiclif reads " *our father David,"* which reading is adopted by Alford.

" *Why did the heathen rage?"* This is from Psalm ii., which has no superscription, but it is, however, identified with David as the author. φρυασσω,—rage, originally signifies the wild snorting of a spirited and unmanageable horse. It is here figuratively employed, to represent the wild fury of Christ's enemies. Baumgarten supposes that the whole Church on this occasion sung this second psalm of David's, applying it to their present circumstances.

" *Holy child Jesus."* " *Child* " is from the same Greek word as that translated " *son,"* iii. 13 ; and " *servant,"* iv. 25.

" *And when they had prayed, the place was shaken where they were assembled together."* This was a direct reply to their prayer. Bengel understands the shaking of the place as a symbol of the approaching agitation, which would penetrate everywhere through the gospel. Baumgarten understands it as a sign that the will of God has power over the continuance of visible things.

" *And the multitude of them that believed were of one heart and of one soul ; neither said any of them that aught of the things which he possessed was his own, but they had all things common."* Here is a beautiful picture of unity. They were one. What one felt, all felt. What one purposed, all purposed. What one had, all had. They had all things in common. They testified their love to one another by yielding up their property for the common weal. The ideas of private property were lost in a common love. The property of each was at the service of all.

" *And Joses, who by the apostles was surnamed Barnabas, (which is being interpreted, the son of consolation,) a Levite, and of the country of Cyprus, having land, sold it, and brought the money, and laid it at the apostles' feet."* This Joses who is thus so particularly described by Luke, is by common consent regarded as Barnabas, who subsequently became the companion of Paul. His generosity is given as a specimen of that of others, not because it was greater, but probably because he was destined to become so well known in apostolic labour.

The community of goods here represented must not be regarded as a social regulation, or a settled article in the polity of the first churches, but was the spontaneous expression of the new, fresh, loving, relationships into which they were brought.

HOMILETICS.—Here we have a specimen of *Christian socialism.* The narrative gives us such a view of it as throws the secular thing called by that name into contempt, and reveals the lamentable imperfection connected even with the highest form of spiritual fellowship now existing on this earth. From it we learn that the socialism which these first Christians enjoyed was *attractive, religious,* and *amalgamating.* It was—

I. ATTRACTIVE. No sooner were the two apostles free, than they returned at once, as if drawn by a magnetic force, to their chosen society. "And being let go, they went to their own company." They " *went to their own."* There were two things that made " *their own"* people attractive to them, and which are always found in connection with true Christian socialism—

First, *Responsive listening.* They had something to say, and they felt that in that brotherhood they should have responsive listeners. They wanted to report all that the chief priests and elders had said unto them. Whether they wished to "report" this to awaken the congratulations of their brethren on account of their triumphs, or to get their counsels on account of their difficulties, or both, we have no data to determine with certainty. We know this, however, that there is a law of mind which urges a man to communicate that to others to which he attaches some great importance, and the more pressing the thing is in its nature, the more forcible is that law. It is also a law to seek the most responsive listeners to such communications. To the men who will give us the most cordial listening, we go with the thing we have to say, rather than to those who are hostile or even indifferent. Hence, naturally, these apostles went to "*their own*" to report that to which they attached such moment. There they knew they would have open ears and receptive hearts. True Christian socialism involves this responsive listening. There the speaking brother, whose heart is full, will find an audience all candour and love. Such a thing as this is not found in secular socialism. There you have the cavilling and the captious. Nor is it often found, alas, in the fellowship of Churches. There is too frequently the prejudice that deafens the ear and closes the heart.

The other thing which made their "own company" attractive to them, and which is always found in true Christian socialism, was—

Secondly, *Sympathetic co-operation.* So strong is our social nature, that we instinctively crave the sympathy of others to enable us to bear our burdens and discharge our mission. Without this the strongest of us are weak either to endure or to toil. Without the breeze of social sympathy, the sails of our spirits would collapse in the voyage of duty. Peter and John had been engaged in a severe struggle, had also suffered much; and naturally did their hearts turn to that circle which was in thorough sympathy with their sentiments and aims. All the while they were battling with the Sanhedrim, and the night they spent in prison, they knew that their "own company" were thinking of and praying for them, and to their fellowship they hastened the moment they were "*let go.*" In true Christian socialism there is always a deep genuine sympathy in all with everything connected with the cause of God and truth. There is a weeping with those that weep, a rejoicing with those that rejoice. What one feels in fact, the other feels in sympathy.

Thus the Christian socialism of these early times was an *attractive* thing. Kindred souls flowed to it as rivers to the sea. What circle on earth is more attractive to kindred spirits than the circle in which there is—(1.) a common object of supreme affection; (2.) a common class of dominant thoughts; (3.) a common cause engrossing the chief activities of being? This is the ideal of Christian fellowship. Would it were realized on earth, and that every church were a true home of love.

From the narrative we learn that the socialism of these first Christians was—

II. RELIGIOUS. "And when they heard that, they lifted up their voice to God," &c. This whole passage, which extends through several verses, shows that a *profound religiousness* pervaded every member of that "company." Godliness was the vital air that fanned the lungs of their spiritual being. "They were filled with the Holy Ghost." God was the grand fact in their consciousness, the one centre in their hearts. In their horizon He stood as the one majestic object to which they traced all the beauty and the goodness they beheld. Their religiousness here comes out in two forms—that of *ascription,* and that of *supplication.*

First, *Ascription.* There is here their recognition of several things.

(1.) *There is their recognition of His authority.* "And when they heard that, they lifted up their voice to God with one accord, and said, Lord, thou art God." The word here rendered "*Lord,*" is Δέσποτα not Κύριε. From it our English word "despot" is taken, and it stands for authority that is absolute. Deeply did this company now feel the absoluteness of the Divine control.

(2.) *There is their recognition of His creatorship.* "Thou art God, which hast made heaven, and earth, and the sea, and all that in them is." They felt Him to be not merely the Sovereign Lord o all things, but the Almighty Maker.

(3.) *There is their recognition of His revelation.* "Who by the mouth of thy servant David hast said, Why did the heathen rage, and the people imagine vain things?" This quotation, which is from the second Psalm, shows their conviction that David there spoke not by his own wisdom, or of himself, but by the inspiration of God concerning the great Messiah. What David said on this point was Divine revelation concerning the opposition of worldly authorities to the Lord and His Christ. The words contain several things concerning the hostility of worldly men to Christ:

(a) *Furiousness.* "The heathen rage." The word ἐφρύαξαν, designates, as we have said, the neighing or snorting of highly-excited horses—horses excited somewhat like the pawing prancing war-horse in the Book of Job. It is metaphorically used, to represent the noise and fury of insolent and overbearing men, and well designates the furious temper and the insolence of Christ's enemies towards Him.

(b) *Vanity.* They "imagine vain things." Those who aspire to thwart the plans of Christ, to crush Christianity, live in a region of mad dreams. They are agents of consummate folly, and must fall victims to their own delusions.

(c) *Combination.* "The kings of the earth stood up, and the rulers were gathered together." They were banded together against

Christ. Ungodly men, that differ widely in other things, are *one* in their antagonism to Christ.

(4.) *There is their recognition of His predestination.* They regarded Herod, Pontius Pilate, the Gentiles, the people of Israel, and all the enemies of Christ, as wicked agents blindly and unconsciously working out the eternal plans of Heaven. " For of a truth against thy holy child Jesus, whom thou hast anointed, both Herod, and Pontius Pilate, with the Gentiles, and the people of Israel, were gathered together." He who sees the end from the beginning conducts the government of the universe after a preconcerted plan, so vast that it comprehends alike things of the greatest magnitude and minuteness. Nothing can ever occur that is not in that plan, and the most hellish spirit can do no more than contribute his part towards it. How great is God ! He maketh His enemies do His work.

Their religiousness comes out, not only in their *ascription*, but,

Secondly, *In their supplication.* " And now, Lord, behold their threatenings : and grant unto thy servants, that with all boldness they may speak thy word, by stretching forth thine hand to heal ; and that signs and wonders may be done by the name of thy holy child Jesus." Mark—

(1.) *The substance of their prayer.*

They invoked—(*a*) *Personal protection.* " Behold their threatenings." The threatenings refer to those contained in the 17th and 21st verses of the chapter—threatenings addressed by the rulers to the apostles. The meaning of the invocation, " Behold their threatenings," is " Guard those who are the objects of those threatenings, and thus frustrate the evil designs of our enemies."

They invoked—(*b*) *The power of spiritual usefulness.* " That with all boldness they may speak thy word." Though they pray for personal protection, it is only as a means to discharge their official functions. They wanted their lives preserved, not because they dreaded the death of martyrdom, not because of themselves, but because they had a paramount desire to be successful promoters of the new religion.

They invoked—(*c*) *Miraculous interposition.* " By stretching forth thine hand to heal ; and that signs and wonders may be done by the name of thy holy child Jesus." The meaning is, " Enable us to work miracles in the name of Christ, that we may be more successful in spreading abroad His knowledge." This power Christ had promised, (Mark xvi. 17, 18,) and they had an authority, therefore, to seek it.

Such is the beautiful prayer, the spirit of which is this, " Deliver us from our enemies, and grant us miraculous power, not for our own gratification or aggrandisement, but in order that we may speak the word of God with greater fluency and force." Mark,

(2.) *The success of their prayer.* " And when they had prayed, the place was shaken where they were assembled together; and they were filled with the Holy Ghost, and they spoke the word of God with boldness."

In the answer there was

(1.) A *miraculous sign.* "The place was shaken where they were assembled together." Perhaps they were in the same as that in which they were assembled on the day of Pentecost, (chap. ii. 2,) of which this scene was a partial repetition. The sign here given of God's presence was familiar to the saints of the Old Testament, (Exod. xix. 18; Ps. lxviii. 8.) "The special presence of the Holy Ghost is accompanied with a sign to the senses—an earthquake as before, with, probably, the appearance of flame. Both phenomena are mentioned by Virgil as marks of Divine favour. Coincidences between the facts of revelation and the opinions and superstitions of the heathen world, occur too frequently to be accounted for by the supposition that they are accidental. Such resemblances seem to admit one of two solutions: either that God condescended to use methods which men had already without authority supposed Him to use, or that men *had* an authority for so believing, viz., a tradition which was derived to them from a distant age, through some unknown channel. The former hypothesis seems better to account for the appearance of the star to the Magi; the latter will apply to the present passage, to chap. ii. 3, 19, and to the Gentile anticipations of the incarnation." *

In the answer there was

(2.) *The impartation of Divine power.* They were all "filled." The remarks made on the effusion of the Spirit on the day of Pentecost are applicable here.† The power which they sought to preach the gospel, came. "They spake the word of God with boldness."

Such, then, are the forms of *ascription* and *supplication* in which their religiousness was expressed on this occasion.

A feature in their devotions worth noticing is—*their thorough unity.* They were all "with one accord." Some have asked, How could it have been with one accord? Did they all use these words as a part of a liturgy which they had amongst them? or did they all receive a special inspiration prompting in all hearts the same aspirations, thoughts, and words? or did one inspired voice lead the devotions, and express the common thought and desire of all? It scarcely matters; sufficient is it for us to know that there was perfect unity in the worship.

From the narrative we learn the Christian socialism of the first Christians was—

III. AMALGAMATING. "And the multitude of them that believed

---

* Webster and Wilkinson.
† See "Homilist," vol. iii., Third Series, p. 69.

were of *one* heart and of one soul: neither said any of them that ought of the things which he possessed was his own; but they had all things common." The inspired writers had not that dread of repetition in their productions which belong to modern authors. The community of goods here recorded, Luke has stated before in the previous chapter. He repeats it, perhaps, in order that we may dwell on the extraordinary state of Christian society at that time, or in order to show that however tumultuous and violent were the rage of their enemies, there was a blessed peace and a sensible security amongst themselves. Outward tempests produced no ripple on the stream of their new affection. God was in the midst of them, and they rejoiced. Four thoughts are suggested in relation to the amalgamating force :

First, *It was most hearty and practical.* The thorough *unity* of soul expressed itself in the surrender of every member's worldly possessions for the common good. The definition of friendship ascribed to Aristotle by Diogenes Laertius, which stated that it consists in one soul residing in two bodies, is actualised here. They were of " one soul," and all the members of the body united in acting out the common volition. " Neither said any of them that ought of the things which he possessed was his own." What was once their private property they call no more their own, they regard it as the common possession of the brotherhood. The rising tide of brotherly affection bore away from their hearts that love of gain which is a power in all unconverted men, and which has grown into a passion in this age, making mammon the God of the world. This surrender of personal interest was not only the expression of thorough unity, but the best method of preserving it. It is the narrow and the mean that disorganise society, and bring all the members of the social system into conflict and confusion.

Secondly, *It consisted with a diversity of position and service.* "As many as were possessors of lands or houses sold them, and brought the prices of the things that were sold, and laid them down at the apostles' feet : and distribution was made unto every man according as he had need." The name of one is especially mentioned who did this, " Joses, who by the apostles was surnamed Barnabas, (which is, being interpreted, The son of consolation,) a Levite, and of the country of Cyprus, having land, sold it, and brought the money, and laid it at the apostles' feet." He is singled out here because he was a man of distinction, and was to play an important part in the history of the future of the young Church. These verses show a diversity of position and service in that social circle that was so united in soul.

The apostles were both the spiritual and economical heads of that community. Material bodies may get so thoroughly amalgamated as to lose all their *individual peculiarities*, and be fused into one common mass. Not so with souls. Minds, however closely welded together by social love, will retain for ever their individuality of being, position, and mission. Though the body is moved by one soul, the eye is still the eye, and the hand the hand. Social unity is not at all the uniformity of a regiment moving with one step and attired in the same garb, but rather like the variety of landscape, each object clad in its own costume and bending to the breeze according to its own structure and style. It is not the sound of one monotonous note, but the echo of all the varying notes of being, brought into sweetest harmony.

Thirdly, *It was produced by the gracious favour of Heaven.* "Great grace was upon them all." Grace means favour, (John i. 16;) and the favour here may mean either the favour with which they were regarded by men, or the favour which they had received from God. Grace was upon them all in the two senses; the latter is the idea most probably here. The grace or love of God was the cause of that love and liberality which existed amongst them. We must feel God's love towards us before we can feel true love to our brethren. Piety is the parent of philanthropy. God's grace it is that brings souls into loving harmony. No social contracts, no code of rules, no uniformity of belief can do it; it must be the love of God, consuming our native selfishness, and opening those Divine fountains of sympathy within us which sin has sealed. Let this great grace come upon all the Churches now, and a holy unity will exist amongst them.

Such is the Christian socialism which we have in this narrative. In what a sublime contrast does it stand to all the socialism of the world. Would that there were on one spot of this earth a circle, however small, where it was perfectly and fully unfolded. Who would not admire it—what heart would not feel its attractions! It would be the heavenly Jerusalem in miniature. It would be an Eden in the world's social desert.

> "Behold, how good and how pleasant it is
> For brethren to dwell together in unity!
> It is like the precious ointment upon the head,
> That ran down upon the beard, *even* Aaron's beard :
> That went down to the skirts of his garments ;
> As the dew of Hermon,
> And as the dew that descended upon the mountains of Zion :
> For there the Lord commanded the blessing,
> *Even* life for evermore."

Acts 5:1-11

ANANIAS AND SAPPHIRA—THE MORAL ENORMITY OF RELIGIOUS PRETENSIONS.

" *But a certain man named Ananias, with Sapphira his wife, sold a possession, and kept back part of the price, his wife also being privy to it, and brought a certain part, and laid it at the apostles' feet. But Peter said, Ananias, why hath Satan filled thine heart to lie to the Holy Ghost, and to keep back part of the price of the land? Whiles it remained, was it not thine own? and after it was sold, was it not in thine own power? why hast thou conceived this thing in thine heart? thou hast not lied unto men, but unto God. And Ananias, hearing these words, fell down, and gave up the ghost: and great fear came on all them that heard these things. And the young men arose, wound him up, and carried him out, and buried him. And it was about the space of three hours after, when his wife, not knowing what was done, came in. And Peter answered unto her, Tell me whether ye sold the land for so much? And she said, Yea, for so much. And Peter said unto her, How is it that ye have agreed together to tempt the Spirit of the Lord? behold, the feet of them which have buried thy husband are at the door, and shall carry thee out. Then fell she down straightway at his feet, and yielded up the ghost: and the young men came in, and found her dead, and carrying her forth, buried her by her husband. And great fear came upon all the church, and upon as many as heard these things.*"

EXEGETICAL REMARKS.—" *Ananias and Sapphira his wife.*" All that is known of these two persons is what is recorded in this sad story. Their conduct stands in contrast to the example of Barnabas and others, who sold their estates, and brought the money daily to the apostles' feet.

" *Sold a possession, and kept back part of the price.*" The estate which they sold is stated in the third verse to be "land." The price which they obtained, instead of handing it over to the apostles, as Barnabas and others did, they "*kept back*"—literally, they set apart, purloined, (Titus ii. 10.)

" *Why hath Satan filled thy heart to lie to the Holy Ghost?*" Peter, who is here again the representative and spokesman of the Twelve, detects the fraud, reproves it, and traces it to its source. " Satan is a Hebrew word, meaning an adversary or opponent, whether in war (1 Kings v. 4) or liti-

gation, (Ps. cix. 6,) often applied to human enemies, but in one place to an angel, (Num. xxii. 22,) and with the article, (2 Sam. xxiv. 1,) or as a proper name without it, (1 Chron. xxi. 1,) to the Evil Spirit, or the Prince of fallen angels, as the adversary and accuser of mankind, (Job i. 7, ii. 2, Zech. iii. 1, 2 ; compare Rev. xii. 9, 10.) In this sense and application it is nearly equivalent to the Greek Διάβολος, (Rev. xii. 9, xx. 2,) and Latin *Diabolus*, meaning slanderer, informer, false accuser ; to which the English *Devil* may be easily traced back, through the intermediate forms of the French (*Diable*) and Italian, (*Diavolo*.) As the same being is the *tempter* of our race from the beginning, (2 Cor. xi. 3,) the name *Satan* sometimes has that special meaning, (Matt. iv. 10, xvi. 23 ; Mark viii. 33,) and is so used here."
—ALEXANDER.

" *Whiles it remained, was it not thine*"

own ?" He had not been compelled to sell his land. There was no rule in the Church requiring him to do so. Nor, after selling it, was he compelled to give a whole, or any part of it, to the apostles. His freedom in relation to his property was in no way interfered with by the Church. There was no *ab extra* restraint.

" *Thou hast not lied unto men, but unto God.*" He had committed a lie, not in language, but in conduct. He had acted a moral falsehood. This lie had been, not unto men, but unto God. It was, of course, intended to deceive men ; but, inasmuch as it had relation to God's cause, it was a lie unto Him. It was a lie in His sight ; it was a sacrilegious fraud. They professed to be the organs of the Divine Spirit, but they acted as the agents of Satan.

" *And Ananias, hearing these words, fell down, and gave up the ghost.*" Did his death occur in accordance with Peter's desire ? Baumgarten rightly says, that in his words there is not contained any expression of his own will. Or did the remorse and alarms of conscience which Peter's words evoked within him strike him to the ground ? Whatever was the proximate cause, it was undoubtedly divine visitation. It was a bolt from the hands of insulted justice.

" *And great fear came on all them that heard these things.*" So terrible was this judgment, in order to guard the first operations of the Holy Spirit, before the admixture of that poison which is always most prejudicial to the operations of divine power on mankind, and to secure a reverence for the apostolic authority, which was so important as an external governing power for the development of the primitive Church, until it had advanced to an independent steadfastness and maturity in the faith.— NEANDER.

" *And it was about the space of three*

hours after, when his wife, not knowing what was done, came in." Bloomfield suggests that it was at the next prayer-time, as the intervals were of three hours. The conjecture is probable. How she had remained three long hours ignorant of the terrible fate that had befallen her husband we are not told. Various causes might be suggested, but where Scripture is silent, it behoves us to be mute.

" *And Peter answered unto her, Tell me whether ye sold the land for so much ? And she said, Yea, for so much.*" Here is an acknowledgment of her husband's criminal act, and of her own guilty participation in the deed.

" *Then Peter said unto her, How is it that ye have agreed together to tempt the Spirit of the Lord ?*" It is plain that this preconcert or conspiracy was viewed by the apostle as a serious aggravation of the sin committed ; not only because each was bound to hinder or dissuade, instead of helping and encouraging the other, but because this previous agreement showed the sin to be deliberate and presumptuous, and cut off all excuse or palliation that might otherwise have been derived from haste, ignorance, or inconsideration. The sin itself is here described as that of tempting God— *i.e.*, trying His patience, or putting to the test, and thereby impiously questioning, not merely His omniscience, but His veracity and power to punish. —ALEXANDER.

" *Behold, the feet of them which have buried thy husband are at the door, and shall carry thee out.*" Melancholy union in death, as there was guilty partnership in life ! Others of the early Church fell martyrs to the cause of truth, and their names were honoured ; but Ananias and Sapphira died . victims to their own base passions and hypocrisy, and are enrolled for ever with the company of Judas, the traitor.—LIVERMORE.

HOMILETICS.—Providential events are commentaries on biblical statements ; and as such, they are often introduced into the sacred page. Facts are everywhere recorded in the divine volume to illustrate principles. An extraordinary fact of Providence is here recorded to set forth great moral truths. The one great subject set forth in this narrative is *the enormity of religious pretensions.*

In this case of religious pretension we discover several things.

I. THE SIN-GENERATING POWER OF AVARICE. The lust of money was in this case the cause of the sacrilegious fraud and falsehood Ananias and Sapphira here perpetrated. And what a crime was theirs. (1.) It was an insult to the Holy Ghost ; (2.) It was committed deliberately (ver. 4) ; (3.) It was preconcerted by a wedded pair. They "agreed together." It was a deception practised on the Church. The love of money—the root of all evil—was the spring of all its wickedness. Achan, Judas, Demas, are, with this Ananias and Sapphira, among the many examples which history furnishes of the wickedness of avarice.

II. AN UNDUE ATTENTION TO PUBLIC SENTIMENT. The young Church had adopted the principle of having " all things in common." No member was to hold any private property. All money was to be thrown into the common stock ; this was the common practice. Ananias and Sapphira, without any heart-sympathy with this system, professed to adopt it, because it was popular ; they did not act from themselves, but from others ; they wished to appear as good as their brethren, and they did that outwardly for which their inner hearts had no respect. This prompted their hypocritical action.

In this case of religious pretension we discover :—

III. A SPIRITUAL CONNEXION WITH THE EVIL ONE. " Why hath Satan filled thy heart," said Peter, "to lie to the Holy Ghost ? " Satan can enter the heart ; can inject his thoughts into the spirit ; and his thoughts always prompt men to deception. " He is a liar," and the father of lies.

In this case of religious pretension we discover :—

IV. RELIGIOUS CONTRIBUTIONS REGARDED AS A CRIME. " While it remained, was it not thine own ? and after it was sold, was it not in thine own power ? " &c. There was no necessity for them to give it. God does not want our property, except as it expresses the loving loyalty of the spirit to Him. A thousand times better is it to hold your property with the iron hand of a miser, than to give it, if the heart goes not with it. Propertywhen given to pacify conscience, or for an ostentatious display, or with the idea of its returning back with interest, is an insult to Omniscience. There are often great sins in great contributions.

In this case of religious pretension we discover :—

V. A DELIBERATE ATTEMPT TO IMPOSE UPON GOD AND HIS CHURCH. " How is it that ye have agreed to tempt the Spirit of the

Lord ?" Hypocritical conduct is "a lie unto God," as well as unto man. God detects it, and is not deceived. Poor man, however, is often deluded by such pretensions.

In this case of religious deception we discover :—

VI. A SOLEMN DISPLAY OF THE DIVINE DISPLEASURE. "Ananias, hearing the words of Peter, fell down and gave up the ghost." After this Peter speaks to the wife. "Behold, the feet of them which have buried thy husband are at the door, and shall carry thee out. Then she fell down straightway," &c. How did Peter detect their hypocrisy? Perhaps by their appearance ; guilt shows itself in the face. Or perhaps by the inspiration of heaven. It was God, however, that took away their life—Peter's volition could not do it. Their death was sudden and public. It impressed the whole Church with fear. "And great fear came upon all the Church, and upon as many as heard these things." The following general truths may be inferred from this narrative :—

First, *That social benevolence is the law of Christianity.* The new Church had all things in common. Though we do not hold the obligation of social benevolence in *this form* now, the spirit it expressed must be regarded as ever binding. Christianity commands us to "bear one another's burdens, and so fulfil the law of Christ."

Secondly, *That the tendency of depravity is to counterfeit goodness.* Ananias and Sapphira were selfish to the very core, yet they mimicked benevolence. Sin necessarily tends to hypocrisy ; goodness never ! It is the sinner is the hypocrite, not the saint.

Thirdly, *That Satan's influence upon man, however great, is no palliation of man's crime.* Though Satan put it into their thoughts, the act was theirs ; Heaven held them responsible. Satan cannot *force* us to sin.

Fourthly, *That hypocrisy must one day be unmasked and punished.* The hypocrisy of Ananias and Sapphira very speedily met with an exposure and a retribution. Though a retribution does not always come as quickly, it comes as certainly. "The hidden things of darkness will assuredly be brought to light."

Acts 5:12-16

PHASES OF THE YOUNG CHURCH

" And by the hands of the apostles were many signs and wonders wrought among the people ; (and they were all with one accord in Solomon's porch. And of the rest durst no man join himself to them ; but the people magnified them. And believers were the more added to the Lord, multitudes both of

men and women ;) insomuch that they brought forth the sick into the streets, and laid them on beds and couches, that at least the shadow of Peter passing by might overshadow some of them. There came also a multitude out of the cities round about Jerusalem, bringing sick folks, and them which were vexed with unclean spirits : and they were healed every one."

EXEGETICAL REMARKS.—*"And by the hands of the apostles were many signs and wonders wrought among the people."* As the impression made by the events of Pentecost was strengthened and maintained by a succession of miraculous performances, (ii. 43,) so now the effect of the tremendous judgment upon Ananias and Sapphira was continued or increased in the same manner. —ALEX. The kind of miracles is specified in the succeeding verse.

"And they were all with one accord in Solomon's porch." This was not probably built by Solomon, but stood where his portico had done, and upon the same foundation. It was on the east of the temple, and overhung a very deep valley, from which a wall of immense stones had been built up to support it. It afforded a sheltered way in stormy weather ; and from hints in the New Testament, we infer that it was a much-frequented place," (John x. 23.) This—one of the most capacious and public places in Jerusalem—was the scene where the growing numbers of disciples assembled. *"And of the rest durst no man join himself to them."* The *"rest"* here does not, I presume, mean the remainder of the unconverted generally, but those who felt themselves to be of the same class as Ananias and Sapphira—avaricious in heart. None of the avaricious from sinister motives were prompted to join the Christian community.

"They brought forth the sick into the streets, and laid them on beds and couches, that at the least the shadow of Peter passing by might overshadow some of them." The sick of all classes were brought into the street, or, as it is in the margin, in every street. The rich and poor were there. Those on beds and those on couches. The latter were the small mattresses of the poor. It is not said that Peter's shadow effected the cure. The woman in the gospel was cured, not by the hem of Jesus' garment, but by the exertion of His miraculous power And those diseased multitudes out of the cities round about Jerusalem were now healed, not by Peter's shadow, but by the power of Almighty God working through him. "In order that these miracles of healing might extend to all who sought them, and yet be visibly connected with the persons who performed them, it pleased God that their shadow should, in this case, answer the same purpose with the words and gestures used on other occasions."—ALEX.

HOMILETICS.—The verses before us present the young Church in two aspects,—as *an organ of restorative power*, and *as an institution differently affecting different men.*

I. AS AN ORGAN OF RESTORATIVE POWER. We are told in the twelfth verse that " by the hands of the apostles many signs and wonders were wrought among the people." And in the sixteenth verse *the restorative character* of all their works is distinctly stated : *"And they were healed every one."* It is true that the works here recorded by the apostles were miraculous and material, but they may be fairly regarded as *specimens and symbols of those spiritual works which the true Church has ever been, and still is, constantly performing for the moral restoration of mankind.*

Two remarks are suggested concerning this restoration—

First, *It was manifestly divine.* The " many signs and wonders ' which the apostles wrought among the people were beyond all controversy divine, and were felt by those who were the subjects and spectators to be so. So little did the people regard them as the effects of the natural power of the apostles, that they seemed to consider that the very *shadow of Peter* would be enough to accomplish them. Luke does not say that any were healed by Peter's shadow ; he merely states what was in the mind of the people on the subject. There was no doubt anywhere as to the divinity of the works. The *moral* power in the Church to restore souls is also incontrovertibly divine. No man, however exalted his piety, extensive his attainments, brilliant his talents, mighty his logic, and overwhelming his eloquence, can restore one lost soul.

Another remark suggested concerning this restorative work is—

Secondly, *It was very extensive.* Great were the crowds of "sick folks," of both sexes, of all ages, and social grades, now brought to Solomon's porch on this occasion " from every street." They were in different circumstances and afflicted with different diseases. Some were even " vexed with unclean spirits," but the healing power was equal to all. " And they were healed *every one.*" So it is with the *morally* healing power in the Church. It is equal to every case, " a balm for every wound."

The other aspect in which the verses present the young Church is—

II. AS AN INSTITUTION DIFFERENTLY AFFECTING DIFFERENT MEN. The Church which met there " with one accord in Solomon's porch," was an institution effecting very different results in the population around.

First, *In some it produced a revulsion.* " And of the rest durst no man join himself to them." The " rest," that class of avaricious men to whom Ananias had belonged. They were so alarmed at the judgment that had come down upon Ananias and Sapphira, that they recoiled with terror, and dared not unite themselves to the fellowship of the disciples. A Church whose discipline is so severely pure, which will not tolerate untruthfulness, dishonesty, or selfishness in any form, is sure to keep aloof the multitudes of the carnal, the mercenary, and the false. Would that the discipline of the Church were now of such an exalted character as would draw a broad line of demarcation between her and the ungodly world. Good discipline in the Church is a pruning-knife lopping off the corrupt branches, a strong wind blowing away the chaff.

Secondly, *In some it awakened admiration.* "But the people magnified them." The multitudes, the general body of the people, felt a high respect and admiration for a community where such purity was displayed as that which appeared in the doom which befell Ananias and Sapphira. Incorruptible sincerity, and high spiritual purity, will always command the honour and respect of the unsophisticated multitudes. The common people heard Christ gladly, because He spoke the true thing in the true spirit. And the common people will always honour the Church for what is pure and noble in the life of her members.

Thirdly, *In some it effected a conversion.* "And believers were the more added to the Lord, multitudes both of men and women." Many saw in the case of Ananias and Sapphira, and in the miracles the apostles wrought, the hand of God; they believed, turned to the Lord, and identified themselves with His disciples.

Thus the young Church produced different effects amongst men ; some it frightened off ; from some it won respect ; and amongst others it won converts. All this it has ever done, and still does in proportion to the amount of divine purity and truth which it displays in its ministries and deportment.

Acts 5:17-33

THE ACTIVITY AND BAFFLEMENT OF PERSECUTORS

" *Then the high priest rose up, and all they that were were with him, (which is the sect of the Sadducees,) and were filled with indignation, and laid their hands on the apostles, and put them in the common prison. But the angel[1] of the Lord by night opened the prison-doors, and brought them forth, and said, Go, stand and speak in the temple to the people all the words of this life. And when they had heard that, they entered into the temple early in the morning,[2] and taught. But the high priest came, and they that were with him, and called the council together, and all the senate of the children of Israel, and sent to the prison to have them brought. But when the officers came, and found them not in the prison, they returned, and told, Saying, The prison truly found we shut with all safety, and the keepers standing without before the doors : but, when we had opened, we found no man within. Now, when the high priest, and the captain of the temple, and the chief priests, heard these things, they doubted of[3] them whereunto this would grow. Then came one and told them, saying, Behold, the men whom ye put in prison are standing in the temple, and teaching the people. Then went the captain with the officers, and brought them without violence : (for they feared the people, lest they should have been stoned :) And when they had brought them, they set them before the council : and the high priest asked them, saying, Did not we straitly command you, that ye should not teach in this name ? and, behold, ye have filled Jerusalem with your doctrine, and intend to bring this man's blood upon us. Then Peter and the other apostles answered and said, We ought to obey God rather than men. The God of our fathers raised up Jesus, whom ye slew, and hanged on a tree: Him hath God exalted with his right hand to be a Prince and a Saviour, for to give repentance to Israel, and forgiveness of sins. And we are his witnesses of these things; and so is also the Holy Ghost, whom God hath given to them that obey him. When they heard that, they were cut to the heart, and took counsel to slay them."*

EMENDATIVE RENDERINGS.—(1.) An angel. (2.) At the break of day. (3.) Doubted concerning.—ALF.

EXEGETICAL REMARKS.—*" Then the high priest rose up."* Probably Caiaphas, the chief agent in the crucifixion of their blessed Master.

" And all they that were with him, (which is the sect of the Sadducees,) and were filled with indignation." The Sadducees were a Jewish sect, often mentioned in the New Testament. According to Jewish tradition, its founder was Zadok, a disciple of Antigonus, who was president of the Jewish Sanhedrim, and lived about B.C. 260. Perhaps this Zadok was the high priest of Solomon's reign, and his descendants may have originated the sect. The Sadducees seem to have been closely connected with the priesthood. They taught that there were no future rewards or punishments appointed unto men, and consequently no world of retribution, and no angels or spirits, and no resurrection, (Matt. xxii. 23; Acts xxiii. 8.) The doctrine of these sceptical materialists was received by few, though such as did embrace it were commonly persons of wealth and dignity. As a sect, however, they had no influence over the people. It has been thought that the Sadducees received only the Pentateuch, but there is no real foundation for such a charge.—EADIE. It is not said that the high priest himself belonged to this sect. All that is meant is, that this sect zealously joined him in this persecution.

" And laid their hands on the apostles, and put them in the common prison." The apostles are arrested and imprisoned in order that they might be arraigned and formally tried. The prison was the common one, that is, the public one.

" The angel of the Lord by night opened the prison doors, and brought them forth." That this is a mere poetical oriental idea for the release of the apostles by the jailer or the guards, is amongst the absurdest of sceptical suggestions. Nor is there any authority for the idea that their deliverance was effected in a natural way, with the crash of a thunderbolt or the vibrations of an earthquake. An angel of the Lord did it,—did it perhaps without noise, silently in the silence of the night.

" And said, Go, stand and speak in the temple to the people all the words of this life." The order of the angel was, that they should stand free and undismayed, (σταθέντες,) and preach openly in the temple to the people; τὰ ῥήματα τῆς ζωῆς ταύτης, are the words which relate to this life—the blessed life in Christ and by Christ. By adopting the supposition (by no means necessary) of an hypallage, the idea " words of life" arises, which appears less suitable to Luke and to that early time.—L. and G.

" And when they heard that, they entered into the temple early in the morning, and taught." They were not disobedient to the heavenly vision, but promptly at the break of day they entered the temple, and taught concerning all the words of this life.

" But when the high priest came, and they that were with him, and called the council together, and all the senate of the children of Israel." The senate literally means the eldership, and stands no doubt for the elders of Israel in general, who were invited to be present on this important occasion.

" The prison truly found we shut with all safety, and the keepers standing without before the doors: but when we had opened, we found no man within." This was the intelligence which the officers—the men who attended to execute the commands of

the Sanhedrim—brought back to their masters. The word "*without*" (εξω) is omitted in the oldest manuscripts and latest critical editions.

"*Whereunto this would grow.*" They knew that their authority was disregarded. The doctrines of the apostles were gaining ground, and all their efforts were of no avail. Perplexity, mingled with alarm, agitated their spirits.

"*And when they had brought them, they set them before the council: and the high priest asked them, saying, Did not we straitly command you, that ye should not teach in this name? and, behold, ye have filled Jerusalem with your doctrine, and intend to bring this man's blood upon us.*" Having been brought by the captain and officers, "without violence, for they feared the people," before the Sanhedrim, the high priest reminds them of an injunction which had been laid upon them before. (Chap. iv. 18.)

"*Then Peter and the other apostles answered and said, We ought to obey God rather than men.*" Their address, extending to ver. 32, contains facts and statements which they had before made. It is another confession of the same faith.

"*When they heard that, they were cut to the heart, and took counsel to slay them.*" Διεπρίοντο signifies literally, they were sawn through: *dissecabantur* (Vulg.) *findebantur,*—they were cut to the heart, they were moved with hot displeasure; so that the idea to make away with the men suggested itself to many of the members. On this they consulted with one another, though secretly, for we cannot suppose a formal and open consultation until the apostles were removed. (Ver. 34.)

HOMILETICS.—The subject of our last section was the " Phases of the young Church." We looked upon the Church as the organ of restorative power, and as an institution differently affecting different men. In some it produced a revulsion, in some it awakened admiration, and in some it effected conversion. Such various effects the Church in all ages has produced. It has never been uniform in its influence upon external society. It is a characteristic of moral forces, that their results are seldom uniform. The verses now under notice lead us to consider *the arrest and imprisonment of the apostles, their deliverance and commission,* and *their arraignment and defence.*

I. THEIR ARREST AND IMPRISONMENT. " Then the high priest," &c. This new attack upon the Church, the language teaches, was not only preceded, but occasioned, by the things described in verses 12-16. It was after the disciples were multiplied, and the people impressed by the miracles, that this new persecution arose. The apostles' success fanned into furious flame the indignation of their persecutors. Our success always makes the hell of envy burn hotter in the breast of our enemies. The " high priest" is particularly mentioned as the leader of this new assault, and the Sadducees are mentioned as following. He was not a Sadducee, but the Sadducees sympathised and moved with him in this attack. They were one with Annas, Caiaphas, and all the Pharisees, in their antagonism to the *new* religion. Two things are to be observed—

First, *The feeling of the persecutors.* What was the feeling that moved them to this attack ? " Indignation." High priest and Sadducees and all were filled with this. The Greek word does not necessarily mean a malignant passion, but a strong affection either of love or anger. Here, of course, it means the latter ; it is malignity. The success of Peter and his associates inflamed with indignation all the factions in the great council of the nation. All hearts throbbed with the same passion, and answered to the same persecuting call. The other thing to be observed here is—

Secondly, *The conduct of the persecutors.* They " laid their hands on the apostles," that is, they caused them to be arrested. Not only Peter and John, but most probably the twelve. They were stopped in their work, taken into custody, and put in the " common prison." A public prison is of all social scenes the most revolting and disreputable. In this hideous and degrading cell, where the worst of characters were incarcerated, these twelve apostles were confined. Thus, as ever, bigotry shows the weakness of its opinions, and the malignity of its aims, by substituting force for argument, might for right.

The words lead us to consider—

II. THEIR DELIVERANCE AND COMMISSION.

First, *Their deliverance.* "But the angel of the Lord by night opened the prison doors, and brought them forth." On a former occasion they were delivered from prison (chap. iv. 21) by the timid and apprehensive policy of their oppressors. Here, they are delivered by a direct messenger from heaven. An " angel of the Lord." Some messenger from heaven came in the stillness of the night and liberated these apostles of the new faith. Prison walls, iron gates, and massive chains, are nothing to the touch of an angel. This miraculous rescue was adapted to rebuke their persecutors, and to rouse amongst the people the strongest emotions of reverence and of wonder. Observe—

Secondly, *Their commission.* The angel who miraculously wrought their deliverance gave them this commission :—" Go, stand and speak in the temple to the people all the words of this life."

Observe—(1.) The *subject* of this commission. " The words of this life." A summary and sublime description this of the whole Gospel—" The words of this life." The Gospel is a record of " words" that *generate, nurture, develop,* and *perfect* the true life of humanity.

(2.) The *scene* of this commission. " In the temple." " Go, stand and speak in the temple." Go to the place where the people assemble in largest concourse, the most public of all public places, and where old prejudice will rouse the strongest opposition, and there stand and speak " all the words of this life." The commission is to preach not a partial, but a whole Gospel—not a few words, but " *all ;*" and not to any particular class of men, but to the whole body of the people assembled in the most public place.

(3.) The *execution* of the commission. " And when they heard that, they entered into the temple early in the morning, and taught."

They were not disobedient to the heavenly vision. They " conferred not with flesh and blood," but set themselves at once to work out the angelic behest, " *early in the morning.*" As the first gray beams of the opening day fell on Moriah's brow, and as the people began to assemble, they were there to meet them. The commission they received in the night, when the angel brought them forth, led them to watch the first dawn of the morning with new interest, in order to fulfil the heavenly injunction. They were delivered from prison for this purpose. They were not brought forth from the cell in order that they might retire to solitude or to rest, but that they might preach the Gospel.

Now, we find that the *deliverance* and the *commission* of these apostles had a twofold effect upon their enemies :

(*a*) *It confounded them with disappointment.* The previous night the rulers of the nation had committed the apostles, as they supposed, to safe custody, intending to have them arraigned in their presence, in order to make out such a charge as would legally terminate their ministry. The plans of this august assembly were formed, and their dread determinations perhaps fixed. The morning comes. They meet in all the ceremony of office. The first thing they do is to despatch officers to the prison in order to conduct the culprits to their bar. They wait. The officers return ; but they have no prisoners in their charge. And here is the message delivered to the council :—" The prison truly found we shut with all safety, and the keepers standing without before the doors : but when we had opened, we found no man within." What miserable victims of disappointment these magnates must have felt themselves ! What a dark and chilling shadow was thrown upon the dignity of their state and the pomp of their office ! The wicked work in the dark, and Providence makes them the victims of their own plots.

But whilst the Sanhedrim were confounded with disappointment, the subordinate officers also must have been terribly surprised when they went to the prison, found the door " shut with all safety," saw " the keepers standing without before the doors," all things indicating that the prisoners were safe within, but when they entered the dreary precincts there was not a man to be found. The angel had done no injury to the building, no violence to the gaolers. The whole appeared just as it had on the previous night.

Another effect of the deliverance and commission of the apostles upon their enemies was—(*b*) *They were filled with apprehension.* " They doubted of them whereunto this would grow." The council was thrown into the utmost perplexity. " They were," says Dr Alexander, " wholly at a loss, and knew not what to think of, or what to expect from them." The words do not so much express their wonder at what had happened, as their fear at what would be the issue of the whole—the terrible bearing upon themselves. And well might they fear. Their authority was disregarded. Heaven had thwarted their plans by a miracle. The new religion was rapidly progressing, and their efforts to stem the advancing tide were utterly abortive.

The passage leads us to consider—

III. THEIR ARRAIGNMENT AND DEFENCE

First, *Their arraignment.* Intelligence comes to the Sanhedrim as to where the apostles were, and as to what they were doing. "Then came one and told them, saying, Behold, the men whom ye put in prison are standing in the temple, and teaching the people." This intelligence would heighten the apprehensions of the council. It was alarming that they should have been delivered from the prison, but still more alarming that they should be found at the work of preaching again. Upon this information, "the captain with the officers" went forth at once, "and brought them without violence: for they feared the people, lest they should have been stoned." Such was the popular regard for the apostles that the men sent to arrest them were afraid, not merely of bodily injury, but of being denounced as untrue to the theocracy and the law of Moses. They are now before the Sanhedrim, and the high priest, the president of the court, addresses them in these words: "Did not we straitly command you that ye should not teach in this name? and, behold, ye have filled Jerusalem with your doctrine, and intend to bring this man's blood upon us." This language is most significant. It expresses—

(1.) Their mortification at the disregard to their authority: "Did not we straitly command you that ye should not teach in this name?" They had so commanded them in the strongest and most unequivocal terms, (Acts iv. 17-21.) But the apostles, with a sublime heroism, set their mandates at defiance. This must have wounded their official pride, and filled them with chagrin and vexation. This language expresses—

(2.) An assumed contempt for the founder of the new faith. They do not mention any of the distinguishing titles of the Messiah. They only say "*this name*"—"*this man's blood.*" Though the suppression of a name may sometimes be reverential, rather than contemptuous, it is evidently not so here. They, in the heat of their indignation, would have the apostles to suppose that His name was unworthy their mention. The contempt, however, I think, was assumed, for their very antagonism shows that they had a deep faith in the mystic grandeur of His character. This language expresses—

(3.) Their reluctant testimony to the progress of Christianity. "Behold, ye have filled Jerusalem with your doctrine." A stronger testimony than this to the zeal of the apostles, and to the growth of their cause, could scarcely have been given. It was given by the most intelligent men in Jerusalem—men who knew the prevailing feeling and the general character of the population well—men, too, who would have ignored and denied the fact if they could. Circumstances wrested it from their reluctant lips. Their language expresses—

(4.) The foreboding of a terrible retribution : "And intend to bring this man's blood upon us." To "bring blood upon the head" is a peculiar Hebrew idiom ; meaning to make one answer for the murder or the death of another. There was conscience in this. They felt that they were implicated in the horrid crime of the crucifixion of Christ ; and that which they once dared in the fury of their rage, when they cried, "Let his blood be upon us," they now deprecated as the direst of judgments.

Secondly, *Their defence.* How did the apostles answer this address of the high priest, who spoke in the name of the Sanhedrim ? Here are their words :—" Then Peter and the other apostles answered and said," &c. In this defence, which Peter delivers not only for himself but also for his brother apostles, we have several things worthy of note :

(1.) Here is one of the grandest of principles : " We ought to obey God rather than men." This principle he had enunciated before. (See notes on chap. iv. 19, 20.)

(2.) Here is one of the most wonderful of facts : " The God of our fathers raised up Jesus." This is the great crowning fact of Christianity. It is the corner-stone in the great temple of Gospel truth.*

(3.) Here is one of the most appalling of crimes : " Whom ye slew and hanged on a tree." Here he charges, as he had more than once done before, the crime of crucifixion home upon them. What superiority to the fear of man, what inflexible fidelity to truth, what more than human heroism, are exhibited by Peter as he stands before the most august assembly of the land, and charges them with the greatest crime ever perpetrated under heaven !

(4.) Here we have the most glorious of communications : " Him hath God exalted with his right hand," &c. Here observe—(*a*) That Christ is exalted to the highest dignity—"the right hand of God." (*b*) That He is exalted to the highest dignity for the sublimest functions—" to be a Prince and a Saviour." (*c*) That in these functions He has to communicate to the world the greatest of blessings—" repentance" and " forgiveness of sins."

(5.) Here we have the most exalted of missions. " And we are his witnesses of these things ; and so is also the Holy Ghost, whom God hath given to them that obey him." The apostles here regarded themselves as witnesses of the greatest realities—" these things "— the great things of the Gospel ; and as fellow-workers with the great Spirit Himself. " So is also the Holy Ghost."

(6.) Here we have the most intense exasperation. " They were cut to the heart. No doubt remorse mingled with their indignation, and gave intensity to their rage.

---

* See " Homily on the Resurrection of Christ," Third Series, vol. i. p. 19.

Acts 5:34-42

THE SPEECH OF GAMALIEL AT THE SANHEDRIM: GOOD ORATORY

" *Then stood there up one in the council, a Pharisee, named Gamaliel, a doctor of the law, had in reputation among all the people, and commanded to put the apostles forth a little space ; and said unto them, Ye men of Israel, take heed to yourselves what ye intend to do as touching these men. For before these days rose up Theudas, boasting himself to be somebody ; to whom a number of men, about four hundred, joined themselves : who was slain ; and all, as many as obeyed him, were scattered, and brought to nought. After this man rose up Judas of Galilee, in the days of the taxing,*[1] *and drew away much people after him : he also perished ; and all, even as many as obeyed him, were dispersed. And now I say unto you, Refrain from these men, and let them alone : for if this counsel or this work be of men, it will come to nought : but if it be*[2] *of God, ye cannot overthrow it, lest haply ye be found even to fight against God. And to him they agreed: and when they had called the apostles, and beaten them, they commanded that they should not speak in the name of Jesus, and let them go. And they departed from the presence of the council, rejoicing that they were counted worthy to suffer shame for his name.*[3] *And daily in the temple, and in every house, they ceased not to teach and preach Jesus Christ.*"

EMENDATIVE RENDERINGS.—(1.) Enrolment. (2.) If it is. (3.) They departed rejoicing from the presence of the council, because they were counted worthy to suffer shame for the name—viz., of Christ.—ALF.

EXEGETICAL REMARKS.—The sanguinary termination of the Sanhedrim was thwarted for the time by the oratory of Gamaliel.
" *Then stood there up one in the council, a Pharisee, named Gamaliel, a doctor of the law, had in reputation among all the people, and commanded to put the apostles forth a little space.*" *Gamaliel,* an old and honourable name in the tribe of Manasseh, (Num. i. 10, ii. 20.) There is no reason for disputing the identity of this man with the Gamaliel of the Talmud, a grandson of the famous Hillel, and a son of Simon, (supposed by some to be the Simeon of Luke ii. 25,) himself so eminent for wisdom, and especially for moderation, that his death is represented in the Jewish books as the departure of true Pharisaism from Israel. Nor is there any ground for

doubt that this was the Gamaliel at whose feet Saul of Tarsus sat.—ALEX.
" *Before these days rose up Theudas.*" This was a name quite common among the Jews. Of this man nothing more is known than is here recorded. Josephus (Antiq., b. xx. chap. v.) mentions one Theudas, in the time of Fadus, the procurator of Judea, in the reign of the Emperor Claudius, (A.D. 45, or 46,) who persuaded a great part of the people to take their effects with him and follow him to the river Jordan. Fadus, however, came suddedly upon them, and slew many of them. Theudas was taken alive and conveyed to Jerusalem, and there beheaded. But this occurred at least ten or fifteen years after this discourse of Gamaliel. Many efforts have been made to reconcile Luke and Josephus, on the supposition that they refer to

the same man. Lightfoot supposed that Josephus had made an error in chronology. But there is no reason to suppose that there is reference to the same event; and the fact that Josephus has not recorded the insurrection referred to by Gamaliel, does not militate at all against the account in the Acts. For—(1.) Luke, for anything that appears to the contrary, is quite as credible an historian as Josephus. (2.) The name Theudas was a common name among the Jews; and there is no improbability that there were two leaders of an insurrection of that name. If it is improbable, the improbability would affect Josephus's credit as much as that of Luke. (3.) It is altogether improbable that Gamaliel should refer to a case which was not well authenticated; and that Luke should record a speech of this kind unless it was delivered when it would be so easy to detect the error. (4.) Josephus has recorded many instances of insurrection and revolt. He has represented the country as in an unsettled state, and by no means professes to give an account of all that occurred. Thus he says, (Antiq. xvii., x. 4,) that there were "at this time ten thousand other disorders in Judea," and (p. 8) that "Judea was full of robberies." When this Theudas lived cannot be ascertained; but as Gamaliel mentions him before Judas of Galilee, it is probable that he lived not far from the time that our Saviour was born; at a time when many false prophets appeared, claiming to be the Messiah. *"Boasting himself to be somebody."* Claiming to be an eminent prophet probably, or the Messiah. *"Obeyed him."* The word used here is the one commonly used to denote belief. As many as believed on him, or gave credit to his pretensions.—BARNES.

"After this man rose up Judas of Galilee, in the days of the taxing." After Archelaus (Matt. ii. 22) was deposed from the government, and Judea was reduced to a Roman province, in the reign of Augustus, a census or enrolment, called "taxing" in the text, was taken by Quirinus, or Cyrenius, president of Syria, to which Judea was attached. Josephus says, "that the Jews were at first surprised at the name of a census, but that, by the persuasion of Joazer, the high priest, they generally acquiesced in it. However, Judas Gaulanitis, associating to himself Sadduc, a Pharisee, excited the people to rebellion; told them that an assessment would introduce downright slavery, and persuaded them to assert their liberty. The people heard the discourses with incredible pleasure. And it is impossible to represent the rods the nation has suffered, which were owing to these men." In another place, the same writer says, "Judas, the Galilean, was the leader of the fourth sect. In all other points they hold the same sentiments with the Pharisees. But they have an invincible affection for liberty, and acknowledge God alone their Lord and Governor. From this time the nation became infected with the distemper; and Gessius Floms, by abusing his power when he was president, threw them into despair, and provoked them to rebel against the Romans." Elsewhere he says that Judas told the people "they had a mean spirit if they could endure to pay tribute to the Romans, and acknowledge mortal men for their lords, after God had been their King," (Matt. xxii. 17–24; Luke xiii. 1, 2.) This revolt was the beginning of difficulties, which were never entirely quieted until the city and nation of the Jews were destroyed in the great war of Titus. Josephus gives no account of the fate of Judas, but it is recorded in the text. His principles, however, were imbibed and carried out by the faction called Zealots, mentioned in the history of the Jewish war. "The taxing" or enrolment here spoken of was subsequent about twelve years to that related in Luke ii. 2. Judas is called by Josephus, not only the Galilean, as by Gamaliel in the text, but also Gaulanitis, the Gaulanite, as above, because he is said to have been a native of Gamala, a city belonging to Gaulanitis, which was included in Galilee.—LIVERMORE.

HOMILETICS.—We have four things in this narrative that are worth looking at :—Good oratory neutralised by a corrupt audience ; culpable indifference justifying itself by plausible logic ; a test by which the divinity of Christianity is established ; and an example of the unconquerable spirit of genuine religion. Here we have—

I. GOOD ORATORY NEUTRALISED BY A CORRUPT AUDIENCE. The storm of opposition to the apostles was raging furiously in the Sanhedrim, when one, the most illustrious, of their number stands up to moderate its violence. We have his address here, and in it there are several things which show its power.

First, *The ability and position of the speaker :* " A Pharisee, named Gamaliel, a doctor of the law, had in reputation among all the people." The name Gamaliel was an old historic name, honourable in Israel. Some suppose him to be the son of Simeon, who took Jesus in his arms in the temple, and the grandson of Hillel, both famous Jewish doctors. The exalted title of *Rabban* was conferred on him on account of his great wisdom and reputation. He had been at one time the president of the Sanhedrim, and at his feet the great apostle of the Gentiles studied. A most popular man in the state, too, was he. "He was had in reputation among all the people." Such high character and reputation would give weight to his oratory. The speech of a man whose ability has not yet been recognised, and whose reputation has yet to be made, would not carry with it half the power, in an audience, as words falling from the lips of him who has won a "high reputation among all the people." The force of a speech on the minds of hearers is greatly regulated by the place the speaker holds in their judgment and esteem. Gamaliel's speech, therefore, would have this advantage. Another thing here which would give power to his speech is—

Secondly, *The course he recommended.* Had he urged on their acceptance some abstruse proposition, or recommended to them a course of action involving great difficulties and dangers, one need not have wondered at the ineffectiveness of his address ; but the course he recommended was most reasonable and most easy : "Refrain from these men, and let them alone." A most common-sense course to pursue under the circumstances. There is yet another thing which shows the power of his oratory—

Thirdly, *The argument he employed :* "If this counsel or this work be of men, it will come to naught ; but if it be of God, ye cannot overthrow it." His argument was—

(1.) If the movement was *undivine*, opposition was *unnecessary;* it would come to naught of itself. In support of this he does two things —he gives facts and he states a principle. The facts are two : one referring to Theudas, the other to Judas of Galilee. Gamaliel wished the Sanhedrim to understand, that if the cause of the apostles was undivine and merely human, it would perish just like this Theudas and

Judas. His doctrine is, *that the human would perish, the divine flourish.* " If this counsel or this work be of men, it will come to naught; but if it be of God, ye cannot overthrow it." The argument is *ad hominem,* and designed to show that his hearers, on their own principles, were bound to take the course he recommended. They professed to regard the new religion as an undivine thing. They need not therefore go to the trouble of opposing it; on their own view of it, it would soon die.

Another part of the argument is—(2.) If the movement was *of God,* opposition would be *futile and impious.* " If it be of God, ye *cannot* overthrow it ; lest haply ye be found even to fight against God." Attempts to crush the cause of God are as futile as attempts to roll back the tides of ocean, or reverse the course of planets—worse than futile, it is fighting against God—a mad and impious battling against the Infinite. Another thing which shows the power of his oratory is—

Fourthly, *The impression he produced :* " And to him they agreed." Their judgments went with him. They could not but see the reasonableness of the course he recommended, and feel the force of the arguments he employed.

So far Gamaliel's speech seems powerful, and one might have thought that he would have gained his end, and brought his audience practically to his conclusions. But no ; they pursued their course of persecution. " When they had called the apostles, and beaten them, they commanded that they should not speak in the name of Jesus, and let them go." Now the question is, What rendered this man's oratory so ineffective ? It was the *character of his audience.* Prejudice warped their judgment, and malice inspired their hearts. So it ever is. What boots a good speaker or a good speech, if the minds of the hearers are pre-occupied with hostile opinions and feelings ? The eloquence of a discourse greatly depends upon the mind of the auditory. Hence what is felt to be eloquence in one *audience,* would not be in another. He is the most eloquent man in his sphere who echoes the views and advocates the wishes of his audience. The man who propounds opinions not agreeing with the general views of his listeners, though he reasons with the logic of Aristotle, and declaims with the power of Demosthenes, will not be felt to be eloquent. Paul himself was a babbler at Athens. This fact is fraught with lessons both to hearers and to speakers. Let hearers who would benefit from the discourses of the men they hear, free their minds from prejudices, and listen with candour ; and let speakers despise that eloquence that comes rather from the low tastes, and narrow views, and sectarian sympathies of a spiritually-degraded audience, than from the true thoughts and honest arguments and noble motives of a speaker inspired with the truth of God.

Here we have—

II. CULPABLE INDIFFERENCE JUSTIFYING ITSELF BY PLAUSIBLE

LOGIC. The course of *non-intervention* which this orator recommends to the Sanhedrim may, perhaps, in some aspects, admit of justification. On the ground, for example, of *statesmanship*, the policy he recommends might be defended. Earthly rulers have no right to interfere with the religious opinions and movements of the people, so long as there is no infringement of the rights of others. Free thought and action in spiritual matters is the inalienable right of every man ; the empire of conscience is sacred to God. Men are permitted to step into it for purposes of argument, but not to legislate or coerce. Or supposing that Gamaliel believed that the cause which the apostles were enthusiastically promoting was not *divine,* a mere superstition or imposture, the policy he recommends might be justified on the ground of *social philosophy.* The way to give an impulse and a social power to error is to persecute its votaries. Many an error which would have died at its birth has been nursed into power by harshness and cruelty. Storms of persecution have nursed the absurdest systems into empires, and so they ever will. They are the breath that the devil breathes to inspire and strengthen his own.

But looking at the conduct of Gamaliel and the policy he recommends here in a broad human light, he develops a most reprehensible moral indifference—

(1.) Because, as a man, he was morally bound to satisfy himself whether the apostles' cause was that of man or of God. He was not justified in allowing it to remain an hypothesis. By an honest investigation he should have satisfied himself on the question before he presumed to give any advice.

(2.) Because he had abundant evidence to satisfy himself on the question. The marvels that Jesus of Nazareth had wrought must have been known to him, as a member of the great council of the nation. The miracles of His death and resurrection too, and the wonders of the Pentecost, which had just occurred, were present to his mind ; a thousand voices had told him that the work was the work of God.

(3.) Because, if it was the work of God, it was his bounden obligation to go heart and soul into it. We cannot, therefore, but regard his argument as formulated to apologise for his indifference. In this respect Gamaliel is the type of a large class in every age. Their policy is to allow things to take their course, and settle themselves. They will not concern themselves with the truth or falsehood of things, in order to shape their conduct in relation to them. They allow the whole to remain an hypothesis; it is all "*if.*" This is a state as criminal as it is perilous. It is the duty of every man to whom Christianity presents itself to settle at once, in his own mind, the question of its divinity. Of all questions it is the most vital and urgent, and it should not be left a moment in doubt.

Here we have—

III. A TEST BY WHICH THE DIVINITY OF CHRISTIANITY IS ESTABLISHED. The rule is, that what is divine will flourish. "If it be of God, ye cannot overthrow it." We accept this rule, and by it we prepare to test the claims of Christianity to divinity. "Since the Gospel," to use the language of another, "has not been overthrown, but has gone on conquering and to conquer, from age to age, and was never so great a power as at this day, we infer, conversely to the proposition of Gamaliel, that it is of God, and never can be over-thrown. It is true that false systems of religion have spread far and wide, and flourished long in the earth. But they have often relied upon the sword for their extension and perpetuity. They have, too, made a compromise with the passions, and not demanded the pure morals of the Christian system. They have also fallen into perver-sions and corruptions, from which they could not recover, being destitute of the conservative and self-recuperative energy of the Gos-pel. Our holy faith has been attacked by every species of foe, open and concealed; by the arm of the persecutor, and the argument of the philosopher; by the doubts of the ignorant, and the sneers of the witty. But it has come forth brighter and purer from every furnace in which it has been tried. It still lives; it prevails by moral suasion; it fills the world. Cities and empires rise and fall, but this kingdom endureth throughout all generations.

IV. AN EXAMPLE OF THE UNCONQUERABLE SPIRIT OF GENUINE RELIGION. This we have in the conduct of the apostles. "And when they had beaten them, they commanded that they should not speak in the name of Jesus, and let them go. And they departed from the presence of the council, rejoicing that they were counted worthy to suffer shame for His name. And daily in the temple, and in every house, they ceased not to teach and preach Jesus Christ." Observe two things—

First, *Their exultation in ignominious suffering:* "They were beaten." The word here used, which properly means flaying, denotes the severest kind of scourging. It was a punishment regarded as peculiarly disgraceful, ($\tau\iota\mu\omega\rho\iota\alpha$ $\alpha\iota\sigma\chi\iota\sigma\tau\eta$, as Josephus calls it.) The usual number of lashes was thirty-nine, (2 Cor. xi. 24.) Thus dis-honoured, and with bleeding wounds, they left the council, not dejected by grief, not saddened in spirit, but *rejoicing that they were counted worthy.* The ignominy they counted honour. This is an experience which can scarcely be explained to those who have it not. The following things may help to account for this sublime feeling:—

(1.) A consciousness of rectitude.

(2.) A supreme affection for Christ. It is the law of love to rejoice in suffering for its object.

(3.) A recollection that their Master suffered in the same way. He was scourged and reviled.

(4.) A fresh assurance of their genuine interest in Christ. He had told them that they should thus suffer, Matt. v. 11, 12, x. 17–22. Such things as these enabled them to glory in tribulation. Observe—

Secondly, *Their invincibility in prohibited labour :* Though charged with awful threats by the council not to speak in the name of Jesus, they marched forward in their mission with indomitable heroism. "And daily in the temple, and in every house, they ceased not to teach and preach Jesus Christ." No power on earth could break down their holy purpose. They set all human authority at defiance.

Acts 6:1-7

THE FIRST ELECTION OF DEACONS

" *And in those days, when the number of the disciples was multiplied,*[1] *there arose a murmuring of the Grecians*[2] *against the Hebrews, because their widows were neglected in the daily ministration. Then the twelve called the multitude of the disciples unto them, and said, It is not reason*[3] *that we should leave the word of God, and serve tables. Wherefore, brethren, look ye out among you seven men of honest report, full of the Holy Ghost and wisdom, whom we may appoint over this business. But we will give ourselves continually to prayer, and to the ministry of the word. And the saying pleased the whole multitude : and they chose Stephen, a man full of faith and of the Holy Ghost, and Philip, and Prochorus, and Nicanor, and Timon, and Parmenas, and Nicholas a proselyte of Antioch ; whom they set before the apostles ; and when they had prayed, they laid their hands on them. And the word of God increased ; and the number of the disciples multiplied in Jerusalem greatly ; and a great company*[4] *of the priests were obedient to the faith."*

EMENDATIVE RENDERINGS.—(1.) Multiplying. (2.) Grecian Jews. (3.) Our pleasure (4.) Multitude.

EXEGETICAL REMARKS.—"*In those days.*" There are but few points in the chronology of the Acts can be ascertained with certainty. But the expression " *those days* " is likely to refer to the preceding verse, while the apostles were daily engaged in the temple and in every house preaching the gospel, and when the disciples, as stated in this verse, were as a consequence " *multiplied.*"

" *There arose a murmuring of the Grecians against the Hebrews.*" By the " *Grecians* " is meant the Hel-

lenists, or Grecian Jews. They were Hebrews in descent and religion, but Grecians in their country and in their language. Some of these had now become members of the new Church, and they found fault with the Hebrews (genuine Jews) because they overlooked, as they thought, the claims of their widows in the daily ministration or distribution of Church charities. This is the first dissension within the Church.

" *Then the twelve called the multitude of the disciples unto them, and said.*"

Matthias having been elected (i. 26) the number of the apostolate was now complete. And these twelve, in consequence of this dispute, assembled the whole multitude of the disciples together.

"*It is not reason that we should leave the word of God and serve tables.*" For "*reason*" Alford reads "our pleasure;" Alexander, "not pleasing;" L. and G., "not agreeable." The meaning undoubtedly is, it is not right or proper. "Serve tables," a figurative representation of attention to secular affairs; here refers to the temporalities of the Church.

"*Wherefore, brethren, look ye out among you.*" They did not elect the required officers themselves, they appealed to the Church, and not to a section, but the whole. Nor did they dictate in the least what selection should be made. They described the kind of men required, that was all.

"*Seven men of honest report, full of the Holy Ghost and wisdom.*" Whether seven, rather than any other number, was mentioned arbitrarily, or as a matter of convenience, or because of its sacred associations, are matters scarcely worth inquiring into, as no certainty can be reached. The character, rather than the number of the men, is the important matter, and that is given—"*Honest report,*" men whose integrity had been well certified, and "*full of the Holy Ghost,*" filled with inspirations of the divine "*wisdom*" —men of practical sagacity, equal to all the emergencies of their office.

"*Whom we may appoint over this business.*" The business of taking care of the widows, and all the financial matters of the Church.

"*But we will give ourselves continually to prayer, and to the ministry of the word.*" Here they indicate their own work, which is of a purely spiritual character—devotional and didactic.

"*And the saying pleased the whole multitude.*" It was customary among the Jews for three persons to be appointed by each synagogue to oversee the secular concerns of the body, and to provide for the poor. Hence the proposition of the apostles would

coincide in some measure with their former usages, and prove the more acceptable. It is worthy of remark that all the names proposed and specified in this fifth verse are Greek names, and were probably selected from the Grecian members of the Church—the Hellenists, in order to silence their complaints. Were this really the case, it shows a generous spirit of conciliation on the part of the Christians.

"*And when they had prayed, they laid their hands on them.*" The imposition of hands is a natural symbol of transfer or communication, whether of guilt, as in the sacrificial ritual, (Lev. ii. 2, viii. 13,) or of blessing, (Gen. xlviii. 14; Mat. xix. 13.) In the New Testament, we find it accompanying certain signal gifts, as that of bodily healing, (Mat. ix. 18; Mark vi. 5, vii. 32, viii. 23, xvi. 18; Luke, iv. 40, xiii. 13,) that of the Holy Spirit, (Acts viii. 17, xix. 6,) and in one case both together, (Acts ix. 17.) In the case before us, it denotes not only delegation of authority, but also the collation of the special gifts required for its exercise. This might seem to render doubtful the propriety of using it in modern ordinations, where no extraordinary gifts are thus imparted; but even when performed by the apostles it was only as a sign, without intrinsic efficacy of its own.—ALEX. The following remarks on this election of deacons by an excellent writer, are worthy of quotation :—" The individuals appointed and set apart above are usually called *deacons,* from the Greek word to 'serve,' ver. 2 ; and the duties of those thus designated among us somewhat resemble the office of the seven in the text, in their oversight of the temporals of the Church. But it is utterly in vain to draw, as many sects of Christians attempt to do, precedents for one or another form of ecclesiastical organisation and government from these early usages of the Christian Church. The regulations then adopted sprang up with the exigencies of the times, like the growth of nature herself. There was no rigid system, no formal arrangements. The spiritual life of the believers took such outward forms as were needful to express and cherish itself; but there was no forcing, no iron bed of uniformity. If a particular mode of government, gradation of officers, and fabric of laws and rules, were essential to the existence and prosperity of the Church, we should have naturally looked for them in the Acts of the Apostles. Since we do not find them here; since as many inferences can be drawn from apostolic usages, and plausibility, too, in some measure, as there are modes of church government in the world; we cannot but come to the irresistible conclusion, that the more simple, natural, and well adapted to human wants, any modes are, the more nearly they correspond in spirit, if not in letter, to the administration of the primitive and apostolic age."

HOMILETICS.—A terrible evil is referred to in the first verse, in most respects a worse evil than had hitherto happened to the first Church, namely, DISSSENSION WITHIN. Hitherto, there had been furious storms without, but the utmost concord within. They "were of one heart and of one soul." The parties now contending were Hellenists and Hebrews.

The *subject* of contention was the neglect of widows "in the daily ministration." It was said, perhaps, by some, that there was something like favouritism in the distribution of the charities of the Church, and that the widows of the Hellenist Christians were *overlooked.* Whether this was a fact or not, there must have been a great liability to it in that new communion. The native Jews or the Hebrews would, of course, be far the most numerous, and the ties of country and language would give them a special interest in each other, and this might have led to a partiality in the distribution of the Church's temporal favours.

The *expression* of discontent was a "murmuring," a suppressed grumble. This is a form which social discontent frequently takes, and it is for many reasons the most vile and pernicious. The Church member who speaks out his discontent audibly, fully, frankly, is a noble character compared with him who goes about murmuring, groaning, whispering out his miserable spirit.

This first dissension within the Church was the immediate occasion for the election of a new class of officers called "deacons." This passage gives us an account of their election, and leads us to consider *the reason of their election, the method of their election, the qualification for their election, and the usefulness of their election.*

I. THE REASON OF THEIR ELECTION. Two things make plain the reason why this office was now called into existence, and they are here referred to.

First, *The temporal necessities of the poor members of the Church.* There were many poor in that new and large community; many who were dependent, perhaps almost entirely, for their support on the public funds. "*Widows*" are especially mentioned here, and they, as a rule, in all communities are the most abject, and the most deserving of aid. The Bible especially commends them to the compassion of the benevolent. " Pure religion and undefiled before God and the Father is this, To visit the fatherless and widows in their affliction, and to keep himself unspotted from the world." It is the duty of the Church to attend to the *temporal* as well as the spiritual necessities of its members. In this, Christ left us an example. *The Gospel is more a record of His beneficent acts than of His doctrinal ideas.*

Secondly, *The absorbing work of the Gospel ministry.* This the " twelve apostles " referred to as a reason. " It is not reason—not agreeable, right or proper—that we should leave the Word of God, and serve tables." " Serve tables," figuratively expresses the temporal administration that was necessary ; and may include not only the distribution of the funds of the Church among its poorer members, but the entire management of all its temporalities. Up to this time it seems that the apostles had attended to this—they had looked to the poor, they had attended to the widows. But their spiritual work now was becoming too absorbing, and they felt that it was neither right nor proper that they should in any way neglect the spiritual for the temporal. Hence the election of deacons. They were elected not to *rule*, as some arrogant modern deacons fancy. Their work was a *subordinate* one, merely to take care of the finances, as the almoners of the public bounty. Nor were they elected to *preach*, as some modern deacons also think. All who are qualified to preach, should preach, and all *should pray ;* but preaching is no more the office of deacons than of any private member.

II. THE METHOD OF THEIR ELECTION. In their election the Church and the apostles had their different parts to fulfil.

First, *The Church had its part.* The multitude of the disciples were called together. The aggregate body assembled in order to act in their corporate capacity. They had first to look out for " seven men," the most suitable for the work amongst them. They were to make inquiries, and use their best judgment in discovering the most eligible persons. Having discovered them, they were then to choose them. Each one was to exercise his best judgment, and conscientiously give his vote.

Secondly, *The apostles had their part.* What did the apostles do in the matter ?

(1.) They *originated* the election. The suggestion for new officers came from them, not from the members ; and they, not the members, called the Church together for the purpose.

(2.) They *directed* the election. Though they did not perhaps formally nominate the men for the office, they did that which was more important and equally influential, *described the character of the men,* held up to the multitude their moral portraits, and said, " We want men like this picture." " Seven men of honest report, full of the Holy Ghost and wisdom."

(3.) They *confirmed* the election. The men the Church elected, Stephen, Philip, Prochorus, &c., they " set before the apostles." What for ? That the apostles might ordain them. Had they not been up to the apostles' idea, answered to the qualifications they had laid down, would they have ordained them ? I trow not. They undoubtedly had the veto—the power of accepting or rejecting the choice of the Church. The apostles in this case, however, accepted that choice. " And when they had prayed, they laid their hands on them." Amongst the Jews it was customary, as we have seen, to lay hands on the heads of any persons who were set apart for any particular office.

III. THE QUALIFICATION FOR THEIR ELECTION. There are three qualifications stated here :

First, *Unblemished reputation.* " Men of honest report," that is, men universally regarded as men of integrity, whose characters were above suspicion, whose reputation stood before the world without a stain.

Secondly, *Eminent godliness.* " Full of the Holy Ghost." Full of the thoughts and purposes of the Gospel ; under the domination of Christianity.

Thirdly, *Practical sagacity.* " Wisdom." They were to be men who had an aptitude for the work ; who could distinguish between the merits of cases ; administer the charities with judgment and equity. Paul more fully describes these qualifications, (1 Tim. iii.)

IV. THE RESULT OF THEIR ELECTION. " And the word of God increased ; and the number of the disciples multiplied in Jerusalem greatly ; and a great company of the priests were obedient to the faith." " It seems," says Dr Alexander, " to be implied, though not explicitly affirmed, that this effect was promoted by the measure just before described—the ordination of the seven almoners or deacons." It may have operated thus in several ways :

First, *By quelling the spirit of contention.* This spirit would, of course, act as an obstruction to the advancement of the Church.

Secondly, *By the augmented agency of the Church.* Seven noble men set to work.

Thirdly, *By enabling the apostles to give themselves entirely to preaching the Gospel.* In this way the election contributed to the extension of the Church.

It is said that " a great company of the priests were obedient to the faith." This is stated as something remarkable.

Acts 6:8-15

STEPHEN (I.)—HIS ACCUSATION

" *And Stephen, full of faith and power, did great wonders and miracles among the people. Then there arose certain of the synagogue, which is called the synagogue of the Libertines, and Cyrenians, and Alexandrians, and of them of Cilicia and of Asia, disputing with Stephen. And they were not able to resist the wisdom and the spirit by which he spake. Then they suborned[1] men, which said, We have heard him speak blasphemous words against Moses, and against God. And they stirred up the people, and the elders, and the scribes, and came upon him, and caught him, and brought him to the council, and set up false witnesses, which said, This man ceaseth not to speak blasphemous words against this holy place, and the law : for we have heard him say, that this Jesus of Nazareth shall destroy this place, and shall change the customs which Moses delivered us. And all that sat in the council, looking steadfastly on him, saw his face as it had been the face of an angel.*"

EMENDATIVE RENDERING.—(1.) Instigated.—L. and G.

EXEGETICAL REMARKS.—"*And Stephen, full of faith and power, did great wonders and miracles among the people.*" Here we have Stephen, the first-named deacon, commencing a wonderful history. He was full of faith ; or, as some read, grace and power. His natural power was not only great—the power of mind and character—but he had preternatural endowments. He worked wonders and miracles—prodigies and signs.

"*Then there arose certain of the synagogue, which is called the synagogue of the Libertines,*" &c. The number of synagogues, or Jewish places of worship, was very great in Jerusalem, and variously recorded by the Talmuds as being four and five hundred. As Jews from every part of the then known world resorted to the holy city at the festivals, they had synagogues for their own use, designated by the names of the countries from which they came ; and in them the Greek language, to which they were habituated, was used, and their particular wants more regarded. According to some authors, the various classes here enumerated constituted one party, with a synagogue in

common. But the better view is, that the Jews from each nation had their peculiar place of worship ; one belonging to the Cyrenians, and another to the Cilicians. "*Libertines.*" There has been much discussion among critics as to who these Libertines were—whether they take their name from their civil condition, or from the country they were supposed to inhabit, a country in Africa, called Libertum, near Carthage. Roman slaves, who had obtained their freedom, were called *Libertii*, and their posterity *Libertini*. The "*Cyrenians*" take their name from the place they lived in, mentioned in chap. ii. 10. The "*Alexandrians*" were the inhabitants of Alexandria, a city of Egypt, situated on the Nile, built by Alexander the Great in the fourth century B.C., and originally peopled by colonies of Greeks and Jews. "*Cilicia,*" a province of Asia Minor, bound on the south by the Mediterranean Sea, east by Syria, north and west by Cappadocia, Lycaonia, Itauria, and Pamphylia.

"*And they were not able to resist the wisdom and the spirit by which he spake.*" His oratory, divinely inspired as it was, was felt to be resistless by all these varied and opposing classes.

" *Then they suborned men, which said, we have heard him speak blasphemous words against Moses, and against God.*" The word " *suborned*" means " instigate." They, those persons with whom he had argued and whose conclusions they could not resist, procured witnesses not to fabricate utter falsehoods, but to put a false construction on what was really said.

" *And all that sat in the council, looking steadfastly on him, saw his face as it had been the face of an angel.*" In the history of David it has been remarked that he is four times compared by others to *an angel*, (or *the angel of God*,) but always in reference to intellectual or moral qualities—his goodness, (1 Sam. xxix. 9,) or his wisdom, (2 Sam. xiv. 17, xx. 19-27.) An analogous comparison to that before us, but still stronger, is the one addressed by Jacob to Esau, (Gen. xxxiii. 10,) "I have seen thy face, as though I had seen the face of God, and thou wast pleased with me." Professor Lechler says, "that at that moment, not only the soul of Stephen was full of the Holy Ghost, but also his countenance shone with a miraculous light, the focus of which was in the soul." That this was the case I have no doubt, because the soul and the body do generally clasp into each other and harmonize.

HOMILETICS.—This portion of Holy Scripture leads us to consider THE ACCUSATION OF STEPHEN. Stephen was one of the seven newly-elected deacons, and his *character* is summarily described in the eighth verse : " And Stephen, full of faith and power, did great wonders and miracles among the people." In the next chapter he is described as a man " being full of the Holy Ghost." All that is recorded of him shows that he was a man of distinguished excellence, and a chosen organ of divine thought and power. He was not only the first Christian martyr, but the first miracle-worker beyond the apostolic circle. Against this man of distinguished goodness and power we have here an *accusation ;* and we have something concerning the *authors*, the *spirit*, the *subject*, and the *weakness* of the accusation.

I. THE AUTHORS OF THE ACCUSATION. Who were they ? " The Libertines, and Cyrenians, and Alexandrians." These different classes of Jews who had synagogues in the Holy City, disputed with Stephen, and became his accusers. It is not said what was the subject of their disputation, but we may well conjecture that the Messiahship of Jesus was their great theme. Observe—

First, *That moral perversity is common to men of every race, clime, and tongue.* All these men, differing widely in *many* respects, agreed in their antagonism to the true and divine.

Secondly, *That theological controversy often irritates rather than convinces.* It did so now.

II. THE SPIRIT OF THE ACCUSATION. What roused the antagonism of these different classes of Jews against this lonely man, this humble follower of Jesus ? The tenth verse answers the question : " And they were not able to resist the wisdom and the spirit by which he spake." Hostility to a truth which they felt an utter incapability to

deny, was the feeling that inspired their breasts on this occasion.
They could not *resist* the wisdom and the spirit by which he spoke.
An unpopular truth was forced upon them, despite of all their learn-
ing and logic, by the overwhelming arguments of one man.

First, *This mortified their pride.* Nothing makes the soul more
furious than to wound its pride.

Secondly, *This struck at their cherished prejudices.*

III. The subject of the accusation. "We have heard him
speak blasphemous words against Moses and against God;" and again,
in the thirteenth verse, " This man ceaseth not to speak blasphemous
words against this holy place and the law;" and again, in the
fourteenth verse, " We have heard him say, that this Jesus of Nazareth
shall destroy this place, and change the customs which Moses delivered us." The charge here preferred, would be considered by the
council of the nation as involving a crime of all crimes the most
heinous, a crime sufficient to wake the vengeance of the nation against
the perpetrator. Blasphemous words against Moses and against God,
and against the holy place and against the law, a threat to destroy
Jerusalem and change the customs of the Jewish nation ! What to
the Jewish mind could be a greater enormity ? This was the charge.
Whether well-founded or not will appear as we proceed :—

IV. The weakness of the accusation. Two things here, show
the utter futility of the charge :

First, *The mode of procuring witnesses.* "Then they suborned
men," &c., (ver. 11.) They got men to swear falsehood—to perjure
themselves. Alas ! that there should be men found, to whom pelf
is more precious than principle ; men who will sell truth for gain !
The very fact, however, that witnesses were thus procured, indicates
the utter groundlessness of the charge. Facts require no such
support.

Secondly, *The appearance of the accused before the council.*
" The face of an angel." That face, beaming with an incorruptible
honesty, with an invincible courage, was in itself a mighty refutation
of the charge. (a) The face is the mirror of the soul. (b) Christianity makes the soul angelic. Its great thoughts, holy emotions,
and lofty purposes, transfigure the countenance into lofty beauty.

Acts 7:1-53

STEPHEN (II.)—HIS DEFENCE

" *Then said the high priest, Are these things so ?   And he said, Men, brethren, and fathers, hearken ; The God of glory appeared unto our father Abraham, when he was in Mesopotamia, before he dwelt in Charran, and said unto him, Get thee out of thy country, and from thy kindred, and come into the land which I shall show thee.   Then came he out of the land of the Chaldeans, and dwelt in Charran : and from thence, when his father was dead, he removed him into this land, wherein ye now dwell," &c.*

EXEGETICAL REMARKS. — As Stephen's defence occupies fifty-two verses of this chapter, and is for the most part a mere statement of a well-known history, it is scarcely necessary to print the whole. As Dr C. J. Vaughan has given such a brief paraphrase of the whole as obviates the necessity of any exegetical remarks, and represents, we think, with remarkable accuracy, the spirit, scope, and point of Stephen's argument, we cannot do better than to quote his words.

" You charge me with disparaging the local character of our religion. You say that I speak of this temple as destined to an overthrow predicted by my Master. Let me remind you then how far, and how far only, the faith of our fathers is bound up with local conditions. The original home and cradle of our race was not Palestine, but Mesopotamia, in the far East, on the other side of the great river, the river Euphrates. It was there that the voice of God was first heard calling to fallen man. The God of glory appeared unto our father Abraham, when he was in Mesopotamia, before he even dwelt in Haran: before even that first migration which landed him not in Canaan but in a temporary resting-place. Hence in due season He removed him by the same Divine call, into this land in which ye now dwell. But how did he enter it ? As an owner? As a conqueror ? As a sovereign ? Nay, he possessed not in it land enough to set his foot on. And yet the promises were all his even then : and the Divine favour and protection : and the Divine communion and friendship. Judge ye, therefore, how far God's blessing is local ! Judge ye, even in this first and greatest example, how far God is a respecter either of place or form ! And that independence of place which was first exemplified in Abraham, was indicated no less in the prediction of his children's fortunes. In a strange land should they sojourn for centuries, and yet be God's people and God's chosen still. See how that prophecy was fulfilled : by what sins, through what sufferings, of man : by what providences and what interpositions on the part of God. Behold the young brother sold as a slave by foes of his own household : see him carried into a remote and unfriendly land : him the best and noblest of the sons of Israel : see him cast out of his father's home as one despised and forsaken, and yet, through vicissitudes as strange as they were sudden, raised to the pinnacle of greatness, while his father's sons bowed down to him. Does the thought occur to you, that in the varying fortunes of Joseph may have been prefigured the suffering and glory of a later and a mightier One ? May not your own hands be red with the blood of a brother after the flesh, who is also after the spirit of your Lord and your Judge ?

" Trace then yet onward the course of the national history and see the whole family of Israel seeking refuge out of Canaan : see generation after generation toiling on in Egyptian bondage : excluded from the land of promise, yet losing thereby no one mark of their ancestral privilege : still recognised, in heaven if not upon earth, as God's people, beloved for the father's sake. And yet, all this time, nothing was theirs in Canaan but a burying-place, and century after century was wheeling its slow course over their exile. Mark then how the national fortunes were sunk to their lowest level : the very permission to live sought in vain for their sons from their oppressors : when at last he arose, guarded by God's special providence from a threatened similar fate, who was to be first the deliverer from bondage, and then (under God) the founder of a new dispensation.

"And observe when he came, late in time and mature in age : came with thoughts and words of kindness, seeking to reconcile or to avenge his brethren : how he was received and dealt with. Who made thee (it was said to him) a ruler and a judge over us ? If he whom you so much reverence was once thus despised and rejected of his countrymen, may it not perhaps have been so with One whom God sent to supersede him ? Can you urge as an argument against the mission of Jesus, that general reproach and rejection, which would have been equally fatal to the authority of Moses ? For forty years he was in exile : a double exile : not from Canaan only, but from Egypt also. At last his call came : came once more, not in the land of promise, but in the wilderness : came too on the ground not of a new, but an old relationship : not as to the founder of a new religion, but as to the inheritor of a patriarchal covenant. Forget not Abraham in Moses ! Never allow yourselves to date from Sinai a possession which was yours from Mesopotamia and from Haran ! In your zeal for a Levitical law, lose not sight of a patriarchal promise ! The God who appeared to Moses in the burning bush of Horeb was already the God of his fathers, the God of Abraham, and the God of Isaac, and the God of Jacob !

"This Moses whom your ancestors refused, the same did God send to be their ruler and their deliverer. He brought them out. And do I disparage his high mission by declaring that he was neither the first nor the last of God's messengers : that his dispensation came in but by the way, between the patriarchal and the Messianic ? Listen to his own words. A prophet (he said) shall the Lord your God raise up unto you of your brethren, like unto me : Him shall ye hear. He himself pointed the eye of faith onward to One who should come : like himself, as to the human nature: yet greater than himself, in proportion as the forerunner is less than the foreannounced, the servant of one nation than the Lord of all. I then am but echoing the voice of Moses, when I declare that the customs which he delivered were not designed to be indestructible or final.

"This is that Moses : and how did you receive him ? He was with the Church in the wilderness : with him was the angel of the Divine Presence : to him were delivered those living oracles by which God communicated with His people : how did you treat him ? Again and again you thrust him from you, and in your hearts turned back again into Egypt : little did you think then of that pleasant land which you would now make the whole of your inheritance and of your hope : yea, in the very wilderness you committed idolatry, and drew down upon you, before you entered Canaan, the threat of a second exile, of a national dispersion.

"You charge me with blasphemy against the temple. What have I said of it ? I have said, it may be, that the temple was no more God's first or God's last dwelling-place below, than the dispensation of Moses was either God's earliest or God's latest revelation. I have said that before the temple was a tabernacle : a tabernacle fashioned under Divine direction : and exhibiting in solemn type realities which have their place in heaven. That was the centre of the Divine Presence with Israel at the time when Joshua conquered, and through all the generations from

Joshua to David. Does that consist with the idolatry of this temple, as though without it God's presence would be impossible? Nay, have not your own prophets declared that no temple made with hands can contain or enclose God? that heaven is His throne and earth is His footstool, and the very house which you build for Him already His handywork? But with what hope can I urge upon you suggestions of reason or arguments of revelation? There is in you a tradition of resistance to the divine and the spiritual. Ye do always resist the Holy Ghost; as your father's did, so do ye. As they did to the servants, so have ye done to the Master: they slew the heralds of the Just One, and ye have been now His betrayers and murderers. O blessed and privileged —knew ye but your happiness—above all nations! possessors of a law in the promulgation of which, on Mount Sinai, the very principalities and powers in heavenly places exercised a solemn and terrific office! and yet not keeping it: trifling ever with God's day of visitation, until at last your house is left unto you desolate!"

Sceptics have made a great deal of a discrepancy between the account which Stephen gives of the burying-place bought by Abraham, and that which is given by Moses. Moses says that the burying-place was at Mamre or Hebron, not at Sychem, and that it was bought by him of the Hittite; Jacob, not Abraham, being the purchaser of the ground at Shechem. Such a discrepancy as this in truth is an argument for the truth of the Scriptures. Things shape themselves so differently to different men, that no two, if they are honest, would give exactly the same description of them. When two witnesses in a court of justice give an account of the same thing in the same words, there is at once a suspicion of falsehood. To account, however, for this discrepancy, some critics say that Abraham was introduced by some transcriber without authority, and that the true nominative is *"he,"* referring to Jacob in the 15th verse, who is the last mentioned. But the matter is scarcely worth discussion. See Livermore, Alexander, Baumgarten, Barnes on the Passage.

HOMILETICS.—We have here THE DEFENCE OF STEPHEN. "Then said the high priest, Are these things so?" And he said, "Men, brethren, and fathers, hearken," &c. The defence extends from verses 2–53. Were we to analyse this defence, we should discover in it many precious things, but our space will only allow us to give a very general view of it. Two things are to be observed—the *source* and *point* of argument in his defence.

I. THE SOURCE OF HIS ARGUMENT. He draws his argument *exclusively* from the sacred history of the Jews—a source they all professed to hold, both his accusers and his judges, in profound reverence. He did not go into abstract reasoning, nor quote questionable authorities, but took the document whose authority was acknowledged. In doing this he secured their attention in two ways.

First, *By giving them to understand that his faith in that history was as strong as theirs.* The Sanhedrim would feel that they and the accused agreed in their belief of facts, the most vital in their creed, and the most hallowed in their associations.

Secondly, *By giving them to understand how thoroughly conversant he was with their history.* He had not been indifferent to that history, he had studied it attentively, he esteemed his knowledge of it as the most precious of his attainments. Hence he gives, with that condensation and consecutiveness which are always proofs of a thoroughness of knowledge, the great salient facts of their sacred story.

II. THE POINT OF HIS ARGUMENT. The point of his argument was this, *that all God's dealings with His chosen people pointed to those very changes which he was accused of having promoted.* This position he makes good by showing—

First, *That the external condition of the Church had undergone repeated changes.* (1.) There was a change under Abraham, (ver. 2-8.) (2.) There was a change under Joseph, (ver. 9-16.) (3.) There was a change under Moses, (ver. 17-44.) (4.) There was a change under David, (ver. 45, 46.)

Secondly, *That the present external state of the Church had no existence before Solomon ;* and that even this was intended from the beginning to be temporary. "Solomon built him an house. Howbeit the Most High dwelleth not in temples made with hands ; as saith the prophets, Heaven is my throne, and earth is my footstool : what house will ye build me ? saith the Lord : or what is the place of my rest ? Hath not my hand made all these things?"

III. THE APPLICATION OF HIS ARGUMENT. "Ye stiff-necked and uncircumcised in heart and ears, ye do always resist the Holy Ghost : as your fathers did, so do ye. Which of the prophets have not your fathers persecuted ? and they have slain them which showed before of the coming of the Just One ; of whom ye have been now the betrayers and murderers : who have received the law by the disposition of angels, and have not kept it." This appeal evidently starts from an interruption in his argument. Probably the Sanhedrim having discovered and felt the strong bearing of his argument became clamorous and violent, and ended his masterly historical defence. This interruption, instead of subduing him, rouses the divinity of his manhood, and he hurls his thunders directly at them, "Ye stiff-necked and uncircumcised in heart and ears," &c. Mark two things—

First, *The vile character he gives them ;* "Stiff-necked," contumacious, rebellious, "uncircumcised," unsacred, impure.

Secondly, *The crimes he charges upon them.* Resistance to the Holy Ghost ; the persecuting conduct of their fathers, and the betrayal and murder of the Son of God.

Thus ended the defence of Stephen. He had discharged his conscience, he had done his work, and now the crown of martyrdom awaited him.

Acts 7:54-60

STEPHEN (III.)—HIS MARTYRDOM

" *When they heard these things, they were cut to the heart, and they gnashed on him with their teeth. But he, being full of the Holy Ghost, looked up steadfastly into heaven, and saw the glory of God, and Jesus standing on the right hand of God ; and said, Behold, I see the heavens opened, and the Son of man standing on the right hand of God. Then they cried out with a loud voice, and stopped their ears, and ran upon him with one accord, and cast him out of the city, and stoned him : and the witnesses laid down their clothes at a young man's feet, whose name was Saul. And they stoned Stephen, calling upon God, and saying, Lord Jesus, receive my spirit. And he kneeled down, and cried with a loud voice, Lord, lay not this sin to their charge. And when he had said this he fell asleep.*"

EXEGETICAL REMARKS.—" *They were cut to the heart.*" "Sawn asunder in their hearts" is the exact expression. Their rage and self-exasperation were intense. "As a chained dog, says one, bites him who unchains it, so the ungodly cannot endure the conduct of them who would rescue them."

" *He being full of the Holy Ghost.*" The expression implies not that he became so now, but that he had been so before, that he was habitually filled with the divine.

"*Looked up steadfastly into heaven.*" He looked into the spiritual scene whither the Saviour had ascended.

"*And saw the glory of God.*" Some brilliant light like the Shekinah, the well-known symbol of the Divine Presence.

" *And Jesus standing on the right hand of God.*" "Right hand" the post of honour and power co-equal. "Standing" not sitting, standing as if watching him, ready to welcome him to his heaven.

" *And said, Behold I see the heavens opened.*" What he saw he describes, he proclaims in the ears of his enemies.

" *Then they cried out with a loud voice.*" They shouted in an agony of rage. Some understand that they called upon him to be silent, and to utter to them no more such things.

" *And stopped their ears.*" They did this not only to express their unwillingness to hear what he was saying, but to express their abhorrence of his words.

"*Ran upon him with one accord.*" They made a fierce, spontaneous, and simultaneous rush upon him.

" *And cast him out of the city, and stoned him.*" The blasphemer in the wilderness was stoned without the camp, (Lev. xxiv. 14,) and the same form was observed in the case of Naboth, (1 Kings xxi. 13.) In the case of an idolater, the law explicitly requires, "that the hands of the witnesses shall be first upon him to put him to death, and afterwards the hands of all the people," (Deut. xvii. 7.) This law was designed, no doubt, to regulate the zeal of informers and accusers, by requiring them to act so conspicuous a part in the execution of the sentence founded by their testimony.—ALEXANDER.

" *And the witnesses laid down their clothes at a young man's feet.*" This they did to facilitate the hurling of the large stones. The upper garments, their flowing robes would have been a great incumbrance in this diabolic work.

" *Whose name was Saul.*" Wonderful fact that the same man as Paul the aged mentioned in Philemon v. 8. An educated, moral, reflecting young man, well acquainted with the letter of God's law, but still in heart, as he confessed, a "persecutor," "blasphemer," and "injurious."

"*And they stoned Stephen, calling upon God, and saying, Lord Jesus, receive my spirit.*" Some omit the word God, (for it is not in the original,) and render these words, "And they stoned Stephen, calling and saying, Lord Jesus, receive my spirit." This is an improvement. "This prayer of Stephen is not only a direct imitation of our Lord's upon the cross, (Luke xxiii. 46,) but a further proof that he addressed Him as a divine person, since he here asks the Son precisely what the Son there asks of the Father."

"*And he kneeled down, and cried with a loud voice, Lord, lay not this sin to their charge.*" Amid the uproar of enraged yells and shouts, and the clash of cutting, crushing stones, he kneels down and prays for his enemies. "Lay not this sin to their charge." Was that prayer heard? In the case of Saul it was. Augustine said that, "If Stephen had not prayed, the Church would not have had St Paul."

"*And when he had said this, he fell asleep.*" Our word "cemetery" is borrowed from the same Greek term which is here employed to express the death of Stephen, and means literally a sleeping-place, a place of slumber and repose.

HOMILETICS.—One can scarcely read this deeply interesting narrative without being struck with three very extraordinary things :—

First, *The professed patrons of religion engaged in banishing it from the world.* The persons engaged in the martyrdom of Stephen were, "The chief council of the nation," &c. What gives a peculiar enormity to this crime is, that it was done in the name of religion.

Secondly, *The most eminent future apostle of Christianity an accessory to the martyrdom of one of its most eminent disciples.* Perhaps Saul was one of the agents of the Jewish council, for the witnesses who, according to custom, had to cast the first stone, laid their garments at his feet. We read of him afterwards. "And Saul yet breathing out threatenings," &c. (Acts ix. 1.) This teaches—

(1.) How the conscience may be perverted. Saul was a Pharisee of the Pharisees. He thought he was doing God service. An action is not essentially right because the author *believes* it to be so.

(2.) How concealed the spirituality of the law may be from the most diligent student. Paul knew the letter of the law, but he had not as yet learnt the alphabet of its spirit. "The letter killeth," &c.

(3.) How sovereign and almighty is the grace of God. Christ selected this Saul to become His great apostle to the ages. Perhaps the martyrdom of Stephen was one of the causative elements in his conversion. "He is able of these stones to raise up children unto Abraham," &c.

Thirdly, *The most useful man of his time allowed to be stoned out of the world as a blasphemer!* This is very extraordinary. Why should it be? Ah why!

Stephen appears before us in two very opposite lights—as a *victim* and as a *victor*. Though he was crushed yet he conquered. We may look at this portion of his history as illustrating "*the dark and bright side of piety.*"

We observe—

I. The dark side of piety. You here have Stephen in a most lamentable position. The nation opposed to him, and he dying under a shower of stones. The world has ever hated vital Christianity. It lives under its frowns and curses, and often is subject to the utmost indignity and even fatal violence. "The world hateth you," &c. There were two causes which led to this result.

First, *He had obtained convictions which clashed with the prejudices and worldly interests of his contemporaries.* These convictions referred to Christ.

Secondly, *He exerted himself faithfully to declare those convictions.* "Ye stiff-necked," &c. Had he kept them to himself, compromised them, or endeavoured to tone them down to the corrupt spirit of his age, he would have avoided such an end as this. But he was *true* to the *true* thing in him ; he flashed his convictions on the rotten spirit of his age, and thus set it on fire with wrath. Thus it will always be. The true man must have the frown of the world.

We observe—

II. The bright side of piety. Piety looked upon from the world's side of things is rather a miserable object,—but not so when viewed from the spiritual side.

First, *His being was in vital connexion with God.* "Filled with the Holy Ghost." God was in him. This does not mean anything miraculous. We are commanded to be "filled with the spirit ; " that is, to have God's thoughts and disposition, &c. Paul in suffering had this, and said, "We glory in tribulation," &c. Filled with God, as the Holiest of all with the Shekinah, the loving child with his parent, the body with the soul.

Secondly, *He had a glorious vision of heaven.* "He looked up steadfastly to heaven and saw the glory of God," &c. Having God within him, everything without was full of the Divinity. "The heavens opened," &c. If God be in thee, the material will withdraw its curtains, and the spiritual universe will beam forth. A true inner light will brighten the outward universe into glory.

Thirdly, *His spirit was invested with the sublimest magnanimity.* His enemies were "cut to the heart," they were exasperated, they "stopped their ears," they "gnashed their teeth." But how calm is he ! He is the conqueror. He can pity them, and pray for them. "Lord, lay not this sin to their charge," &c.

Fourthly, *He had a delightful departare from the world.*

(1.) He commended his spirit to Christ. "Lord Jesus, receive my spirit." This prayer implies (*a*) consciousness that he had a *spirit.* He felt now that his tortured, dying body was not himself, but that *he* was spirit. (*b*) A belief that that spirit would *survive* his expiring body. Though my body is going to its dust, I shall be. (*c*)

Unbounded faith in Christ to take care of his spirit. What is meant by committing the spirit to Christ? Does it mean the giving up of our *personality*, or the power of our *free* action? Neither, emphatically neither. The Ego of man can never be absorbed, the voluntary agency of man never destroyed. I cannot take care of my departing spirit. Thou *canst* and Thou *wilt*.

(2.) He fell asleep. "When he had said this he fell asleep." A beautiful idea of death this, implying two things—

(*a*) *A welcome rest.* Sleep is refreshing rest to the labourer. The work of a Christian here is hard work; the work of cultivation, building, battling, voyaging. His death is a sweet rest.

(*b*) *An anticipated rising.* We give ourselves to sleep in the full hope of rising in the morning, and to go forth to the joys and duties of life with new zest and energy.

Acts 8:2

STEPHEN (IV.)—HIS FUNERAL

"And devout men carried Stephen to his burial, and made great lamentation over him."

EXEGETICAL REMARKS.—For the sake of biographic completeness we insert this verse here, and take the first verse of the chapter, which begins a second part of apostolic history, for our next section.

"*And devout men carried Stephen to his burial.*" Some render this: "But devout men buried Stephen," Δέ after συνεκόμισαν expresses a contrast between the piety of these individuals and the excited passions of the mass of the people.—L. and G. Whilst some were mad with rage, there were others with a calm and religious sympathy with the martyr, if not with his cause. These were the devout men, the ἄνδρες εὐλαβεῖς. These were probably the foreign Jews who witnessed the effusion of the Spirit on the day of Pentecost. Two objections have been urged against their being considered disciples of Christ:—(1.) The high improbability of their being allowed by the infuriated persecutors to have performed this act had they been known Christians; (2.) The epithet applied to them is nowhere else applied to Christians.

"*And made great lamentation over him.*" *Lamentation*, literally *beating*, in allusion to the ancient practice of beating the breast as a sign of mourning. (Analogous, both in etymology and usage, is the Latin *planctus*, from *plango*.) *Over*, not merely in the figurative sense of about, concerning, but in the literal and local sense, implying that they mourned while standing (or hanging) over the dead body.—ALEX. This demonstration of feeling, when the public mind was turned against the Christians, would doubtless increase the exasperation of the Sanhedrim. At the same time it corroborates the opinion that the proceedings which resulted in the death of Stephen, though conducted according to the forms of the Jewish law, were illegal and violent. Had his death been the execution of the capital sentence of a competent tribunal, the authority which pronounced it could and would have prevented the public honours of his funeral. Subsequently, however, the Roman government of the time seems to have authorised or connived at the punishment of Christians by imprisonment, if not by death.—WEBSTER and WILKINSON.

HOMILETICS.—We have here a *highly-honoured* funeral. Three things will show this :—

I. *Not all men that die* ARE BURIED. The bones of many are left to bleach in the open winds, or rot in the depths of ocean. Some are consumed by fire, some are devoured by wild beasts, and some are thrown into the rivers, and left to the mercy of the elements, and the ravenous beasts of prey. God alone knows how many of the human race moulder into dust unshrouded, uncoffined, and unknelled. Stephen had a sepulchre.

II. *Not all that are buried* ARE LAMENTED. The death of many is felt to be a deliverance, and this often where there is the mimicry of sorrow and the pageantry of mourning. Who could lament the death of the tyrant, the oppressor, the persecutor, the churl, or the heartless miser ? The lives, alas, that many live here are so thoroughly cold, selfish, ill-tempered, that they fail to awaken any sympathy in their circle, and their death is felt to be a blessed relief. Few sights are more sad to a thoughtful mind than to witness a deceased father, mother, master, committed to the earth, with their relations around the grave, but with no tear in the eye, no regret in the heart. Their lives had won no love, and their death could draw no tear.

III. *Not all that are lamented* ARE LAMENTED BY THE DEVOUT. There is often the sorrow of the wordling and the selfish, because of the secular loss experienced. A politician who has served the temporal interests of his country, a merchant on whose transactions numbers are dependent, the companion who has ministered to the gratification of others, will be lamented, but not by *devout* men, as such.

Now Stephen was not only buried and lamented, but lamented by *devout* men. Why was this? The following reasons may be suggested :—

First, *He had embodied their ideal of man.* They felt they carried the corpse of one that approached their idea of what a man ought to be. They had witnessed his self-sacrificing labours, heard his noble defence for the truth, and observed the sublime spirit with which he met his martyrdom. They felt they were burying a *man*—not a merchant, not an artist, not a priest, &c.—but a *man*. Well might the devout weep over the death of a *man!*

Secondly, *His martyrdom had revealed the iniquity of their age.* The moral obliquity, injustice, and heartless cruelty which their countrymen displayed in his persecution, must have filled them with inexpressible grief.

Thirdly, *His departure was a grievous loss to the cause of godliness and humanity.* His zealous efforts and his earnest prayers were over. No wonder that these devout men lamented Stephen's death.

Part 2. The Church in its Passage from the Jews to the Gentiles

Acts 8-12

Acts 8:1-4

THE PERSECUTION AFTER STEPHEN, AND THE CONSEQUENT
SCATTERING OF THE CHRISTIANS

" *And Saul was consenting unto his death. And at that time there was a great persecution against the church which was at Jerusalem; and they were all scattered abroad throughout the regions of Judea and Samaria, except the apostles. And devout men carried Stephen to his burial, and made great lamentation over him. As for Saul, he made havoc of the church, entering into every house, and haling men and women committed them to prison. Therefore they that were scattered abroad went every where preaching the word.*"

EXEGETICAL REMARKS.—This chapter begins a new period in the history of the apostles. Up to this point we have had the history of the undivided mother Church of Jerusalem. We have now to look at that Church scattered, and its various parts working in the common cause, endeavouring to bear the Gospel to the ends of the earth.

" *And Saul was consenting unto his death.*" Some read: Saul had pleasure in the execution. Tischendorf places this sentence at the conclusion of the seventh chapter. And perhaps it would have been better there. Saul had pleasure in the slaughter of Stephen. " *Consenting* " is too feeble. It is a very strong word, expressive of hearty approval and thorough sympathy. It is the word by which the same apostle describes the worst sign of the heathen world in its lowest degradation :—" *Who, knowing well the sentence of God, that they who do such things are worthy of death, not only do them but even consent unto (have pleasure in) them that do them.*" In this sense it is written here, that *Saul was consenting unto (taking pleasure in) the murder of* the holy Stephen.—DR J. C. VAUGHAN.

" *And at that time.*" Literally, *in that day.* It was on the very day of Stephen's death and burial, and probably in consequence of it, that the persecution arose.

" *There was a great persecution against the church which was at Jerusalem.*" The " great persecution" was a violent and general attack upon the Church. Hitherto the rulers were the persecutors. Now the people were maddened with the spirit of their masters. Stephen's martyrdom, instead of allaying the appetite for blood, made it more intensely ravenous.

" *They were all scattered abroad.*" πάντες διεσπάρησαν must not be taken as meaning literally *all*, but meaning *many* or *most.* For it is said, " except the apostles ;" they remained. There is a tradition that the apostles were ordered to continue in Judea for twelve years.

" *As for Saul he made havoc of the Church.*" He laid waste to the Church, (ἐλυμαίνετο)—ravaged it as a beast of prey.

" *Entering into every house.*" Every house where he expected to find a disciple of Christ. None would be exempt from his violence. Neither sex nor age, refinement nor influence, would offer protection against his ravages. "*Haling men and women committed them to prison.*" He dragged them violently forth, and thrust them into prison. It is obvious that Saul had the hierarchy on his side, for otherwise he would not have ventured to force himself into private houses, nor would the prisoners be at his command. "*Therefore they that were scattered abroad went everywhere preaching the word.*" The persecution leads to the dispersion, and the dispersion increases the power and widens the empire of the persecuted cause.

HOMILETICS.—These verses bring under our attention three remarkable sights—sights fraught with instruction and encouragement :—

I. A MAN WHO BECAME THE GREATEST APOSTLE OF CHRISTIANITY ACTING AS ITS MOST MALIGNANT FOE.

First, *He was an accomplice in the martyrdom of Stephen.* He "was consenting (*rejoicing in*) unto his death." In chap. vii. ver. 58, it is said the murderers "laid down their clothes at a young man's feet, whose name was Saul." Afterwards he gives a most touching account of the fact himself : "And when the blood of thy martyr Stephen was shed, I also was standing by, and consenting unto his death," &c., Acts xxii. 20. He was therefore virtually guilty of the martyrdom of Stephen, &c.

Secondly, *He was an infuriate leader in the general persecution.* "As for Saul, he made havoc of the Church, entering into every house, and haling men and women committed them to prison." The word "made havoc" is commonly applied to wild beasts, such as wolves, &c., and denotes the devastation they commit. Paul, after his conversion, frequently refers to this, Acts xxi. 10, Gal. i. 6.

Now, the fact that this man became the greatest apostle, demonstrates two thing : First, The greatness of his conversion ; Secondly, The power of the gospel. These two subjects will receive further illustration as we proceed. Thirdly, The infinitude of mercy. Here we have :—

II. MEN RISING ABOVE THE MOST POWERFULLY HOSTILE CIRCUMSTANCES. This is here exemplified in "the apostles" remaining in Jerusalem, and "the devout men" who carried Stephen to the grave.

Mark—First, "*The apostles" stood calmly in the scene where their lives were in the most imminent danger.* "At that time there was a great persecution against the Church which was at Jerusalem." Jerusalem was on fire against the Christians at that moment ; the blood of persecution flushed the face and boiled in the veins of the city. Yet they *stood* with death before them. And more, *They thus maintained their ground while most of their own fellow disciples fled.* Thus they not only overcame the power of danger, but did it against strong social influence.

Secondly, "*The devout men" discharged a duty most exciting to the rage of their enemies.* They did not merely stand, but they did something,—a something that tended to heighten the fury of their persecutors. What did they do ? " Carried Stephen to his burial, and made great lamentation over him." Away, then, with the dogma that man is the creature of circumstances. He is only so as he loses his manhood. Here we have :—

III. THE MOST INTOLERANT PERSECUTION FURTHERING THE CAUSE OF TRUTH. " They that were scattered abroad went everywhere preaching the word :" evangelising. This has been so often the case that it has become a proverb : " The blood of the martyrs is the seed of the Church." The wind of persecution often fans the torch of truth. There is not much difficulty in seeing how persecution does this.

First, *It throws the persecuted more entirely upon their God.*

Secondly, *It enables them to furnish in their lives a nobler manifestation of Christianity to the world ;*—more earnest, more united, more devout.

Thirdly, *It awakens general sympathy amongst men on their behalf, and thus disposes them to attend to their teachings.*

Acts 8:5-8

PHILIP'S MINISTRY IN SAMARIA

" Then Philip went down to the city of Samaria, and preached Christ unto them. And the people with one accord gave heed unto those things which Philip spake, hearing and seeing[1] the miracles which he did. For unclean spirits, crying with loud voice, came out of many that were possessed with them : and many taken with palsies, and that were lamed, were healed. And there was great joy in that city."

EMENDATIVE RENDERING.—(1.) When they heard them, and saw.

EXEGETICAL REMARKS. — " *Then Philip.*" This is not the apostle Philip, but that Philip who, together with Stephen, was one of the seven chosen in the sixth chapter to assist the apostles in the daily distribution. He is called in the twenty-first chapter Philip the Evangelist, " who was one of the seven."

" *Went down to the city of Samaria,*" A city in Samaria. There is no article in the Greek. The metropolis of Samaria was at this time called " Sebastle," having been re-built by Herod the Great. If this had been meant, it would have been εἰς πόλιν Σαμάρειαν. The work assigned to Philip in Jerusalem was finished, as the dispersion put an end to the primitive community of goods and daily distribution. We may mark the providence of God in sending a Hellenistic Jew to a people who from national antipathy would have been unlikely to attend to a *native* of Judea.—WEBSTER and WILKINSON.

"*And preached Christ,*"—that is, the Messiah. The grand question was whether the Messiah had really appeared? This, no doubt, he endeavoured to demonstrate.

"*And the people with one accord gave heed unto those things which Philip spake.*" Christ Himself had prepared the way in Samaria for the reception of the Gospel. He had made the fields white to the harvest, (John iv. 31-38.) Where could he have got a better reception than where his master preached? Samaria, says Baumgarten, furnished the bridge between Jerusalem and the world—a bridge, we may add, over which to convey the Gospel from the mother Church to universal man.

"*For unclean spirits,*" &c. The nominative case : the accusative must be understood after τῶν ἐχόντων, *who were possessed with.* It is worth remarking, that Luke, in the Acts, in speaking of the possessed, never employs the term *demons,* (δαιμόνια,) which he himself in his Gospel has used more frequently than the other Evangelists. Hence we may infer that the power of possession was feebler after the death of Christ, (1 John iii. 8 ; Col. ii. 15 ; Heb. ii. 14.)—BENGEL, C. E. T.

"*And there was great joy in that city.*" The joy arose not only from the amount of relief which Philip afforded to the sick and the wretched, but also from the good news from heaven which he proclaimed.

HOMILETICS.—These words lead us to consider *suggestions arising from the scene,* the *subject,* the *reception,* the *attestation,* and the *influence,* of Philip's ministry.

I. Suggestions arising from THE SCENE of his ministry. "The city of Samaria." In his selection of this as the *scene* of his labours we discover :—

First, *His practical sagacity.* Christ had been there, and He had prepared the way.

Secondly, *His obedience to Christ.* Christ commanded it, (Acts i. 8.)

Thirdly, *His largeness of soul.* They were a people hostile to his own, by political and religious prejudices.

Fourthly, *His intrepidity of conduct.* He was doing that which would put him directly against the Jews. Even the disciples at one time wanted Christ to bring down fire from heaven on these Samaritans, (Luke ix. 21.)

II. Suggestions arising from THE SUBJECT of his ministry. "Preached *Christ* unto them." (1.) He preached Christ, *not Moses.* (2.) He preached Christ, *not creed.* The living Christ, the anointed of God, the Saviour of the world. Perhaps he showed Christ to the Samaritan in the two aspects in which all preachers should show Him : —

First, *As the great burden of the past promises which God had made to the world.* No doubt he proved to them that He was the Messiah which their scriptures led them to expect. This is what we have to do: show "Him of whom Moses and the prophets did write."

Secondly, *As the great foundation of all future hopes which God hath given to the world.* His the "only name given," &c. The only Saviour. No one else to look forward to.

III. Suggestions arising from THE RECEPTION of his ministry. "The people with one accord gave heed to those things which Philip spake." They yielded proper attention to what he said. What would be proper attention to a theme like this?

First, *Profoundly reverential.* It is a divine communication.

Secondly, *Devoutly grateful.* Infinite love is displayed in the message.

Thirdly, *Earnestly practical.* Demanding most strenuous personal application.

IV. Suggestions arising from THE ATTESTATION of his ministry. The miracles which he did: "For many taken with palsies," &c. His wonders were :—

First, *Illustrations of the benign glories of his ministry.*

Secondly, *Powers to impress the divinity of his ministry.*

V. Suggestions arising from THE INFLUENCE of his ministry. "There was great joy in that city." They had been partly prepared for this by Christ's conversation with the woman of Samaria. *The gospel brings joy to a people.* It is "glad tidings of great joy." It is a "joyful sound."

"There was never found," says Bacon, "in any age of the world, either philosophy, or sect, or law, or discipline, which could so highly exalt the public good as the Christian faith."

Acts 8:9-24

SIMON MAGUS, OR THE ESSENCE AND CURE OF WRONG-HEARTEDNESS

" *But there was a certain man, called Simon, which beforetime in the same city used sorcery, and bewitched the people of Samaria, giving out that himself was some great one : to whom they all gave heed, from the least to the greatest, saying, This man is the great power of God.* [1] *And to him they had regard, because that of long time he had bewitched them with sorceries. But when they believed Philip preaching the things concerning the kingdom of God, and the name of Jesus Christ, they were baptized, both men and women. Then Simon himself believed also : and when he was baptized, he continued with Philip, and wondered, beholding the miracles and signs which were done. Now when the apostles which were at Jerusalem heard that Samaria had received the word of God, they sent unto them Peter and John : who, when they were come down, prayed for them, that they might receive the Holy Ghost : (for as yet he was fallen upon none of them : only they were baptized in the name of the Lord Jesus.) Then laid they their hands on them, and they received the Holy Ghost. And when Simon saw that through laying on of the apostles' hands the Holy Ghost was given, he offered them money, saying, Give me also this power, that on whomsoever I lay hands, he may receive the Holy Ghost. But Peter said unto him, Thy money perish with thee, because thou hast thought that the gift of God[2] may he purchased with money. Thou hast neither part nor lot in this matter : for thy heart is not right in the sight of God. Repent therefore of this thy wickedness, and pray God, if perhaps the thought of thine heart may be forgiven thee. For I perceive that thou art in the gall of bitterness, and in the bond of iniquity. Then answered Simon, and said, Pray ye to the Lord for me, that none of these things which ye have spoken come upon me."*

EMENDATIVE RENDERINGS.—(1.) The power of God, which is called great. (2.) Thou thoughtest to acquire the gift of God.

EXEGETICAL REMARKS.—*"Bewitched the people of Samaria."* The Samaritans, indeed, received no part of the Old Testament but the Pentateuch: yet they were more susceptible than the proper Jews to superficial religious impressions and foreign influences, and, of course, also to all sorts of superstition and fanaticism ; and they expected from the Messiah the general restoration and consummation of all things. They were thrown into great excitement by Simon, one of those wandering Goëtæ to whom the door was then opened by the general longing after something higher, and by the prevailing receptivity for the secret wisdom of the East ; and who with their deceitful arts presented the same contrast to the apostles and evangelists, as did the Egyptian sorcerers to Moses and his divinely-wrought miracles. This Simon, who received from the Church fathers the surname Magus, the magician, and was regarded by them as the patriarch of all heretics, especially of the Gnostics, gave himself out for a higher being, and on account of his sorceries, including perhaps astrology, necromancy, exorcism by formulas of the Græco-oriental theosophy, &c., was gazed upon by old and young as an emanation or incarnation of Deity.—SCHAFF.

" This man is the great power of God." This is literally, says Alford, in all our oldest MSS., "the power of God which is called great." Such was the impression that this man made. Here is another illustration of the prevalency of human belief and the doctrine of divine incarnation. These Samaritans saw God in this Simon.

Some of the early writers regard Simon as the head of the Gnostics and the father of all heresies.

" Bewitched." This unfortunate translation was made at a period when witchcraft was a part of the popular, and even religious belief. The same word is translated "wondered" in the thirteenth verse, in relation to the emotion felt by Simon for the miracles of Philip, and should have been rendered in the same way in this verse. He astonished the people of Samaria, or made them wonder.—LIVERMORE.

" Then Simon himself believed also." His belief, of course, was a feigned faith. Philip's wonders had thrown his into the shade, and the credulous, superstitious multitudes had left him for Philip. His popularity, like all popularity, urged him to go with the populace. Hence he professed to believe and was baptized. The works of Philip astonished him as much as his works astonished the people. Philip had no power to read the heart, otherwise he would have checked the cheat of this impostor. Why did this man join the followers of Philip ? Was it to hide the shame of his own desertion and defeat ? or was it from a wish to know the power of Philip's miraculous performances ? or was it, as we have already intimated, to retain his popularity ? Perhaps all these considerations had their influence upon him.

" Now when the apostles which were at Jerusalem heard that Samaria had received the word of God, they sent unto them Peter and John." Why did the success of Philip's ministry at Samaria prompt the college of apostles at

Jerusalem to send a deputation thither ? Not—to use the language of Alexander—as has been variously imagined, because Philip was only a deacon, for he was more, as we have seen, or because they were jealous or suspicious of him, or because they doubted the sincerity or depth of the Samaritan conversions, or to show that the apostles, though this work began without them, still retained their old position ; but because they were the constituted organisers of the Church, and as such not only authorised, but bound, to enter every open door, whoever might have opened it.

"*That they might receive the Holy Ghost : for as yet he was fallen upon none of them.*" Does "the Holy Ghost" here mean the spiritual influence, or the miraculous endowment ? If the former, then we must suppose that those whom Philip baptized were either not converted, or if converted, were converted without the Spirit's influence. It is, we think, the Spirit as a miraculous endowment that is here referred to, else how could Simon see it, (ver. 18,) and why did the juggler wish to purchase it ?

"*Then laid they their hands on them, and they received the Holy Ghost.*" There is no reason to believe that there was any particular virtue in imposition of hands, except as a sign or token. It was a custom, not an essential. Jesus put His hands upon the children He blessed. The apostles laid their hands upon the seven deacons, when they were set apart for their office. The act was symbolical of a blessing invoked and conferred, (Matt. xix. 15 ; Acts vi. 6.)

"*He offered them money, saying, Give me also this power, that on whomsoever I lay hands, he may receive the Holy Ghost.*" Though Simon had formally identified himself with Christianity, he knew nothing of its spirit ; he regarded it only as a species of sorcery superior to his own, and which he desired to attain in order to enrich his exchequer. The term *Simony*, which means trading in sacred things and in ecclesiastical offices, is derived from this mercenary Simon, who now

desired to purchase the sacred for secular ends.

"*Thy money perish with thee.*" Is this language a prediction, a denunciation, or an imprecation ? An imprecation we think. An anathema, says Bengel, of the person and the thing.

"*Thou hast neither part nor lot in this matter.*" Thou hast neither share nor inheritance in the blessings of the Gospel. "This matter," literally, in this word.

"*Thy heart is not right in the sight of God.*" Thy heart is not straight, but crooked and insincere ; the very core of thy being is wrong in the sight of God.

"*Repent therefore of this thy wickedness, and pray God.*" Repentance should come first ; we may then seek gifts of grace. However abandoned a man may be, he ought nevertheless to pray himself, and not depend on the intercession of others, (ver. 24.)— V. G. For Θεοῦ, God, read Κυρίου, the Lord.—Tisch., Alf., C. E. T. Some think that the force of the doubt falls on Simon's penitence and prayers, not on the forgiveness of sin which the penitent should hope for. Others think that Peter indicates that the forgiveness is doubtful, because of the high grade of guilt.

"*For I perceive that thou art in the gall of bitterness, and in the bond of iniquity.*" The original order of the sentence is, says Alexander, "for in the gall of bitterness and the bond of iniquity I see thee being." Sin is a bitter thing and an enslaving thing.

"*Then answered Simon, and said, Pray ye to the Lord for me, that none of these things which ye have spoken come upon me.*" This request was prompted by a dread of punishment, not from a desire to be delivered from sin. What became of Simon, we are not informed, as the narrative ends abruptly here. "Tradition represents him as having persevered in his iniquity, and classes him amongst the heresiarchs of the apostolic age. Some regard him as the founder of the Simonians of the second century, who held a mixture of Jewish and Samaritan opinions, with certain oriental theosophic notions ; while others deny all connexion, even in the names." " The poetical fancies," says Neander, "of Christian antiquity, which make Peter the representative of the principle of simple faith in revelation, and Simon the representative of the magical and theosophic (speculative) tendency in the human mind, have important truths for their basis."

HOMILETICS.—The short sketch of the history of Simon Magus, as presented in these words, reminds us:—

First, *That men in every age of the world have been prone to deify great wickedness.* Simon was a sorcerer or juggler ; he obtained his livelihood by imposing on the credulity of the ignorant.

Secondly, *That great wickedness, to answer its end, has often identified itself with religion.* These Samaritans were visited by a servant of Christ—a man of principle and understanding. He preached to them the truths of Christianity. " They believed," &c. The sorcerer saw that his power was being undermined. In order, therefore, to maintain his reputation, he adopted the new system which the people had embraced: "he was baptized," &c.

But all this for sinister purposes. This is the most revolting but common embodiment of iniquity. It bows at the shrine of God in order to aggrandise self. The blackest deeds ever committed have been performed in the name of religion : in its name the noble army of martyrs bled, the Son of God himself was put to death.

Thirdly, *That true religion exposes all such imposture.* When this man came to the apostle, " Saying," &c., Peter saw through the action into the motive, and said, " Thy money perish with thee," &c. The tendency of the truth of God is to strip hypocrisy of its mask. We take Simon as the representative of *wrong-heartedness.* In relation to which observe :—

I. THE ESSENCE OF WRONG-HEARTEDNESS. " Thy heart is not right in the sight of God." We make two remarks :—

First, *That covetousness is its essence.* " He offered them money." Money was his god. The spirit of mercenariness was his inspiration. This man was covetous. And in relation to this, we observe :—

(1.) It is opposed to mental improvement. It seems impossible that even the intellectual faculties can reach their perfect development, while the mind is under the supreme command of covetousness. It necessarily blinds the eye and limits the horizon. Christ said, " My judgment is just, because I do not mine own will," &c. Benevolence elevates the mind, gives vastness to the view, and places every object in the full light of heaven.

(2.) It is condemned by moral consciousness. There is a principle within us which is an infallible indicator of the health of the soul. This principle has ever condemned covetousness. The selfish man wears out his own self-respect, and stands before himself, as well as before his God, a wretched man.

(3.) It is condemned by the verdict of society. Society may flatter, but cannot respect, a covetous man. Hence men, who would gain applause, assume the features and speak the language of benevolence. As error must adopt the form of truth to win faith, so selfishness must attire itself in benevolence to win love. God made us to approve of each other, but since we cannot approve of covetousness, it follows that covetousness is a wrong state of the heart.

(4.) It is incompatible with moral order. This requires oneness —mutual attraction. But selfishness substitutes repulsion—drives planet from planet, and all planets from God, the central orb.

(5.) It is denounced by Scripture. Covetousness is declared to be idolatry, against which, as the most revolting form of depravity, the most awful curses and heaviest judgments are denounced.

Secondly, *That ruin is its tendency.* This is no constitutional infirmity, claiming palliation, but a disease of the heart. As in physics, so in morals ; if the *heart* be wrong, the most serious consequences are imminent. The text reminds us of three evils :—(1.) It involves the greatest sacrifice. " Thy money perish with thee." Peter took it for granted that *he* would perish. Thy hopes, friendships, money, houses, &c., will also perish. " Thy sons come to honour and thou knowest it not." A good man's money lives in its consequences. (2.) It precludes an interest in religion. " Thou hast neither part nor lot," &c., *i.e.*, in Christianity, with its glorious doctrines, promises. and provisions. It is no more to thee than if it had never been, and all the past portion of thy existence is a blank, so far as the realising of thy destiny is concerned. (3.) It necessitates great personal wretchedness. Two figures are employed to designate it. " Gall of bitterness ! " " Bonds of iniquity ! " Covetousness is at once a *bitter* and a *slavish* life.

II. The cure of wrong-heartedness. Observe :—
First, *The cure prescribed.* (1.) *Repentance.* " Repent, therefore, of this thy wickedness." What is repentance ? A change of character,—not a mere change of thoughts, feelings, or habits ; but a *change* in its controlling disposition. It is such a radical change as to be represented by a " resurrection," a " new birth," a creation. (2.) *Prayer.* " Pray God." The spirit of prayer is conscious dependence on God, and this lies at the very root of religion. (3.) *Forgiveness.* " If perhaps the thought of thine heart be forgiven thee." Covetousness is a sin against God, and for that sin the sinner must be forgiven or damned. Repentance and prayer are essential to pardon.

Secondly, *The cure ignored.* Simon did not attend to the heavenly prescription. He did not repent of his sin, though he deplored the threatened consequences. He did not pray for himself, but he asked Peter to pray for him, and to pray, not that his heart might be changed, but that the consequence of his sin might be averted. Observe two evils ever prevalent in connexion with false religion :—(1.) *Selfishness.* " That none of these things which ye have spoken come upon me." To avoid misery is the leading idea in the religion of millions. (2.) *Proxyism.* "Pray *for me.*" He does not pray for himself. The tendency to trust to others in religious matters is the foundation of all ecclesiastical imposture, and the great curse of the world.

Acts 8:25-40

PHILIP AND THE EUNUCH : A WONDERFUL MEETING

"*And they, when they had testified and preached the word of the Lord, returned to Jerusalem, and preached the gospel in many villages of the Samaritans. And the angel*[1] *of the Lord spake unto Philip, saying, Arise, and go toward the south, unto the way that goeth down from Jerusalem unto Gaza, which is desert. And he arose and went ; and, behold, a man of Ethiopia, an Eunuch of great authority under Candace, queen of the Ethiopians, who had the charge of all her treasure, and had come to Jerusalem for to worship, was returning, and sitting in his chariot, read Esaias the prophet. Then the Spirit said unto Philip, Go near, and join thyself to this chariot. And Philip ran thither to him, and heard him read the prophet Esaias, and said, Understandest thou what thou readest ? And he said, How can I, except some man should guide me ? And he desired Philip that he would come up and sit with him. The place of the scripture which he read was this, He was led as a sheep to the slaughter ; and like a lamb dumb before his shearer, so opened he not his mouth : in his humiliation his judgment was taken away : and who shall declare his generation ? for his life is taken from the earth. And the Eunuch answered Philip, and said, I pray thee, of whom speaketh the prophet this ? of himself, or of some other man ? Then Philip opened his mouth, and began at the same scripture, and preached unto him Jesus. And as they went on their way, they came unto a certain water : and the Eunuch said, See, here is water ; what doth hinder me to be baptized ? And Philip said, If thou believest with all thine heart, thou mayest. And he answered and said, I believe that Jesus Christ is the Son of God.*[2] *And he commanded the chariot to stand still : and they went down both into the water, both Philip and the Eunuch ; and he baptized him. And when they were come up out of the water, the Spirit of the Lord caught away Philip, that the Eunuch saw him no more : and he went on his way rejoicing. But Philip was found at Azotus : and passing through, he preached in all the cities, till he came to Cæsarea.*"

EMENDATIVE RENDERINGS.—(1.) An angel. (2.) This verse should be altogether omitted.

EXEGETICAL REMARKS.—"*And they, when they had testified and preached the word of the Lord, returned to Jerusalem, and preached the gospel in many villages of the Samaritans.*" (Peter and John) when they had preached, (in the city where Philip's labours had been so richly blessed,) returned . . . . and preached in many villages of the Samaritans—embracing the opportunity of their journey back to Jerusalem to fulfil their Lord's commission to the whole region of Samaria. In returning, these two apostles must have felt that the two nations which had been most obstinately at variance for ages were now, to some extent, united by the spirit of Christianity into a brotherhood of love.

"*And the angel of the Lord spake unto Philip.*" Properly, "an angel." How the communication was made we are not told. By an external voice, or by an internal suggestion.

"*Saying, Arise, go towards the south, unto the way that goeth down from Jerusalem unto Gaza, which is desert.*" The direction he was to take was south from Samaria. Gaza was one of the five chief cities of the Philistines. There was a road across Mount Hebron, which Philip might have taken without going to Jerusalem.

"*And he arose and went.*" It was no doubt painful to leave a scene of labour where his ministry met with so much acceptance, and to go whither he knew not alone. His call was something like that of Abraham's, who went out not knowing whither.

"*And, behold, a man of Ethiopia.*" This man is here described pretty fully. He is from Ethiopia—from the high land of the south of Egypt, and now comprehends Nubia, Cordofan, and Abyssinia. He was a eunuch. Eunuchs were generally employed for confidential offices in the East, and are sometimes still. He was of "great authority under Candace," the family name of the queens of Upper Egypt, like Pharaoh, Cæsar, &c.

"*He had the charge of all her treasures.*" The office of treasurer was one of the highest in rank. He was a lord chamberlain of the royal household, a councillor of state.

"*He had come to Jerusalem for to worship.*" Far away in his African home he had learnt to know that the God of Israel was the true God, and the worship of Jehovah was the true religion. It is evident from this that he was a Hellenist, or a foreign Jew from birth, or a proselyte from heathenism to the Jew's religion.

"*Was returning, and sitting in his chariot, read Esaias the prophet.*" He was returning to his own country by the way of Egypt. He was reading at the time when Philip first caught sight of him.

"*Then the Spirit said unto Philip, Go near, and join thyself to this chariot.*" Philip heard him reading aloud —reading perhaps to his charioteer— and the inner voice of the Spirit bade him approach the chariot.

"*Understandest thou what thou readest?*" To one so engaged in reading God's holy word, Philip's question would not be considered rude. The form of the original interrogation, says Alexander, seems to anticipate a negative answer, as if he had said, "You surely do not know what you are reading?"

"*And he said, How can I, except some man guide me.*" Beautiful expression at once of humility and docility. The invitation to Philip which immediately followed, "Come up, and sit with me," being but the natural expression of this.

"*The place of the scripture which he read was this, He was led as a sheep to the slaughter,*" &c. One cannot but wonder that this, of all predictions of the Messiah's sufferings in the Old Testament the most striking, should have been that which the Eunuch was reading before Philip joined him. He could hardly fail to have heard at Jerusalem of the sufferings and the death of Jesus, and of the existence of a continually-increasing party who acknowledged Him to be the Messiah. But his question to Philip, whether the prophet in this passage meant himself, or some other man, clearly shows that he had not the least idea of any connexion between the prediction and those facts. —P. C. The words are difficult and ambiguous. Taken from the Septuagint version of the Old Testament, they differ in some respects from the Hebrew original, and therefore also from our authorised translation. Even as they here stand, some would render them differently.—VAUGHAN.

"*Then Philip opened his mouth, and began at the same scripture, and preached unto him Jesus.*" The Eunuch's question was answered by Philip's sermon on Christ. He showed to him the glorious burden of the prophecy he was reading, and interpreted in the light of Christ's wonderful life.

" *And as they went on their way, they came unto a certain water : and the Eunuch said, See here is water ; what doth hinder me to be baptized ?*" It is natural to suppose that Philip, in preaching Jesus, had mentioned the ordinance of baptism, had quoted perhaps to him the well-known promise, *He that believeth and is baptized shall be saved :* and in growing confidence of his new faith, the Ethiopian would fain satisfy at once the outward as well as the inward condition of salvation. When, if not now, could he hope for either a Christian teacher or a Christian baptist ?—VAUGHAN.

" *And Philip said, If thou believest with all thine heart, thou mayest. And he answered and said, I believe that Jesus Christ is the Son of God.*" This verse is not genuine.—TISCH., ALF. Dean Alford, in his Greek Testament, says, on this interpolation, that "the insertion appears to have been made to *suit the formularies of the baptismal liturgies,*" it being considered strange that the Eunuch should have been baptized without some such confession." And Webster and Wilkinson, no mean authorities, remark, that " this verse is wanting in the best manuscripts, and is generally regarded as an interpolation. Its insertion in the text marks the progress made in the importance attached to forms of profession in the administration of the sacraments."

" *And he commanded the chariot to stand still : and they went down both into the water, both Philip and the Eunuch ; and he baptized him.*" The following remarks on this passage by Dr Alexander, are so scholarly, fair, and pertinent, that we cannot refrain from quoting them :—"The expression in the first clause shows that he was not driving it himself, but, as might have been expected from his rank, was accompanied by one or more domestics. That they went down *into the water,* can prove nothing as to its extent or depth. Without insisting, as some writers have done, that the Greek phrase (εἰς τὸ ὕδωρ) may mean nothing more than to the water's edge ; its stronger sense is fully satisfied, if we suppose that they stood in it, which in any language would be

naturally expressed by saying, *they went into it.* That the phrase does not necessarily imply submersion is moreover clear from the consideration that such an inference would prove too much for those who draw it, namely, that the baptizer must himself be totally immersed. For not only is there no distinction made, but it is twice said expressly, in two different forms, as if to preclude all doubt and ambiguity, that *both* (ἀμφοτεροι) *went down into the water,* both (ὅ τε) *Philip and the Eunuch.* If the verb and preposition necessarily imply immersion, they imply it equally in either case. If they do not necessarily imply it in the one, there can be no such necessary implication in the other. This is not used as an argument to prove that there was no immersion here, but simply to prevent an unfair use of the expression, as conclusively proving that there was."

" *And when they were come up out of the water, the Spirit of the Lord caught away Philip, that the Eunuch saw him no more : and he went on his way rejoicing. But Philip was found at Azotus ; and passing through, he preached in all the cities, till he came to Cæsarea.*" Some see no reason for supposing that the separation was effected in any miraculous way. The minds of both were no doubt full and elevated with divine thoughts. Each felt it his glorious mission to proclaim the gospel. The Ethiopian hurried on his way, and Philip hastened to prosecute his glorious mission. Azotus is the Greek or Latin form of Ashdod, one of the five capitals of the Philistines. Here Philip seems to have resumed his missionary labours, either because, as some suppose, he was transported thither through the air, or because the country between Ashdod and the place where he had left the Eunuch was a wilderness, affording no opportunity of preaching. — ALEX. Henceforth we lose sight of zealous and honoured Philip, as by and by we shall lose sight even of Peter. As the chariot of the Gospel rolls on, other agents are raised up, each suited to his work. But " he that soweth and he that reapeth shall rejoice together."—P. C.

HOMILETICS.—Here we have a most memorable and influential meeting :—

I. IT WAS A MEETING OF REMARKABLE MEN. Each stood out amongst his contemporaries as a marked man. They were not of the millions that are lost in the crowd and that flow with the stream. One was distinguished by his high political position, the other by his adherence to a new faith, and his advocacy of doctrines that clashed with the general opinions of his age. We read of Philip in subsequent parts of this book. His history may thus be summed up. He was a practical believer in Christ; he was honoured by the Church in being elected as one of the seven deacons ; he was called by the Spirit to be an evangelist to go from place to place preaching the Gospel, and he was endowed with the power of working miracles. The Eunuch, we are told, was a man of " great authority under Candace, queen of the Ethiopians." He was chamberlain of her household, entrusted with all her treasures, and, perhaps, her secrets too. He was the greatest man in the kingdom. The fact that he had been to Jerusalem to worship, and was found reading in his chariot the Hebrew scriptures, shows that he was a Jew, either by birth or by proselytism, probably the latter. The Jews, from all parts of the world, were in ancient times accustomed to attend the religious feasts at Jerusalem. These were the two men that now met ; confessedly, no ordinary men. In appearance and in worldly possession they greatly differed. Philip was poor, without wealth, social status, or political power, under a hot sun prosecuting his journey on the dusty roads on foot. The great divine ideas with which his soul was charged, helped no doubt to bear him on and make his journey light. The Eunuch was an affluent man, high in office, and great in his country's esteem ; he was wending his way homeward, not on foot, but in a chariot, provided with all that the civilisation of his age could supply to make his journey pleasant. These were the men that met. It was—

II. IT WAS A MEETING BROUGHT ABOUT BY EXTRAORDINARY CIRCUMSTANCES. The circumstances that brought these two remarkable men together, not merely in body, but in soul, are so extraordinary as to give something of a romantic character to the event. It was—
First, *The direction of Philip to Gaza.* What induced Philip to go to Gaza, one of the five old Philistine cities, whose gates the famous Samson once bore away, and which was now " desert ?" The twenty-sixth verse answers the question : " And the angel of the Lord spake unto Philip, saying, Arise, and go towards the south, unto the way that goeth down from Jerusalem unto Gaza, which is desert." He did not decide on the journey by his own reasoning, nor by the advice of a fellow man, but a messenger from heaven came to him, " an angel of the Lord." Who or what the messenger was, a celestial

intelligence or an inward suggestion by the Divine Spirit, is an open question. One thing is clear, that the direction came from God, and Philip felt it to be so, and hence at once obeyed the mandate. He was not disobedient to the heavenly voice. He was directed this way most probably for the very purpose of meeting this Lord Chamberlain, to instruct him in the gospel, in order that he might become an influential preacher to the sable sons of Ethiopia.

Another extraordinary circumstance which brought about this meeting was—

Secondly, *The occupation of the Eunuch in his chariot.* " He was reading Esaias the prophet." Most likely the version of Scripture he was reading from was the Greek or Septuagint, a translation of the Scriptures which was made in Egypt for the special use of the Jews in Alexandria and throughout Egypt, and which was in general circulation. Why was he reading it? Was it to relieve the tedium of the journey? If so, he could not have done anything better. The Bible, as a literary production, has charms to interest that transcend the highest efforts of human genius. Travellers on long journeys would find it far more interesting, to say nothing else, than the trash they purchase on railway stalls. Or was it for the purpose of intellectual culture? Did he wish to give vigour to his intellect, and buoyancy to his imagination? He could not do better than to read the Scriptures. No book on earth furnishes such helps to mental development as the Bible. Or was it to store his mind with the knowledge of the true principles of social order and political government? If so, he adopted the wisest course. Or was it in obedience to the Jewish Rabbis, who directed that " when any one was going on a journey, and had not a companion, he should study the law?" Or was it because he had just heard in Jerusalem so much about the crucifixion and the resurrection of Christ, and also the wonders of the Pentecost, that he was determined to search the Scriptures in order to see whether He was the true Messiah or not? Whatever might have been his particular reasons I know not. It is with the fact we have to do ; inasmuch as it was that which brought him into contact with Philip. The narrative gives the impression that had not Philip seen this Eunuch with the Scriptures in his hand, and heard him read, he might have passed him by, and there would have been no meeting. The Bible was the magnet that drew the heart of the Evangelist to the Chamberlain.

The other extraordinary circumstance which brought about this meeting was—

Thirdly, *The strange impulse that prompted Philip to join the chariot.* " Then the Spirit said unto Philip, go near, and join thyself to this chariot." The impulse to join the Eunuch in his chariot is here ascribed to the Spirit, that is, the Spirit of God. The reading of the Bible perhaps first attracted Philip's attention, and the Spirit started the impulse to join him. In truth, without a divine impulse, it is scarcely likely that a poor pedestrian like Philip would have ventured to have rushed to this nobleman, and have asked the question, " Understandest thou what thou readest ? " There is something more than human in this boldness.

Such are the circumstances that brought about this meeting. They are not fortuitous occurrences or accidental coincidences. There is a divinity in them. God is in all history, originating the good and controlling the bad. It was—

III. IT WAS A MEETING TURNED TO RARE SPIRITUAL ACCOUNT. Coming together, what did they do ? Discuss politics or converse on the common-place topics of the day ? No ! They commence an earnest talk about God's Scriptures. Philip said, " Understandest thou what thou readest ? And he said, How can I, except some man should guide me ? And he desired Philip that he would come up and sit with him." Two things now took place :—

First, *The Eunuch was enlightened by Philip.* Two things are necessary in order for one man spiritually to enlighten another :—

(1.) There must be on the part of one a disposition to receive knowledge. This the Eunuch now possessed. He said, " How can I, except some man should guide me ? And he desired Philip that he would come up and sit with him." He felt his ignorance, and confessed it. In the bosom of this swarthy man there was a strong desire for more light ; hence he seized this opportunity. Had he not had this disposition, Philip's expositions, if listened to, would have been of no service whatever. A consciousness of ignorance is the alphabet to knowledge.

(2.) There must be on the part of the other a power to impart knowledge. Philip had this. He knew Christ ; and knowing Christ, he could explain the passage which the Eunuch seems to have been reading, but which he could not understand. The question which the Eunuch raised on the passage was not whether it was the word of God or not, but to whom did the words refer. " I pray thee, of whom speaketh the prophet thus ? of himself, or of some other man? " Just the question this on which Philip was at home, and to which he was prepared at once to give a full answer. He " opened his mouth, and began at the same scripture, and preached unto him Jesus." He showed, perhaps, how exactly the history of Jesus answered to the prophet's description, and how He was indeed the Messiah of the Old Testament. The biography of Jesus is the key to interpret the writings of the prophets. He "*preached unto him Jesus.*" He did not preach a *creed*, but *Christ* as the Son of God and the Saviour of the world. His sermon is not reported. We have nothing more than his text, and his grand theme—Jesus. This seems to have solved the moral questions of the Eunuch, to have satisfied the cravings of his nature, and to have effected the salvation of his soul ; for " he went on his way rejoicing."

Secondly, *The Eunuch was baptized by Philip.* "And as they went on their way, they came unto a certain water : and the Eunuch said, See, here is water ; what doth hinder me to be baptized?" There is nothing, as we have seen, in these verses (36–39) to show certain things about baptism that are held with earnestness by a certain body of Christians. The passage does not teach—(1.) That baptism is an obligation. There is no proof that Philip enjoined baptism on the Eunuch, or that he said a word about it ; indeed it seems that the sudden sight of water suggested the thought to the Eunuch's mind. Being a proselyte to the Jewish faith, and having been baptized when he joined that religion, he perhaps thought that now he was joining a new religion he should be baptized again. We do not say—for we believe otherwise—that baptism is not a duty for some ; all we say is, that these verses do not teach it. The passage does not teach—(2.) That baptism is to be performed by immersion. We do not say that immersion is not the right way ; we say there is nothing in this passage to teach it. (*a*) The reference to the water does not teach it. "Certain water." Travellers have visited this spot in order to see whether there was sufficient water for immersion, and not one has discovered such. (*b*) The words employed do not teach it. "And they went down both into the water. . . . And when they were come up out of the water." The preposition εἰς, here translated *into*, is translated in other parts of the Bible many hundred times *to ;* and the preposition ἐκ, *out of*, is translated *from* nearly two hundred times in other places. So all that the words mean is, that they went to the water and came from it ; and they apply to Philip as well as to the Eunuch. If they mean dipping to the Eunuch, they mean dipping to Philip; but they mean no such thing. The passage does not teach—(3.) That baptism is only for believers. It is very true here that Philip is reported to have said, "If thou believest with all thine heart, thou mayest," and the Eunuch to have replied, "I believe that Jesus Christ is the Son of God ;" but this passage is an interpolation—it is not in the original Scriptures.

So much for the baptismal reference of the passage, which leaves the question of baptism, as to its mode and subject, open to be settled, if settled at all, by other passages. It was—

IV. IT WAS A MEETING WHOSE TERMINATION WAS SUBLIMELY HAPPY. All meetings on earth have their termination, some end in sorrow.

First, *It was happy to Philip.* "The Spirit of the Lord caught away Philip, that the Eunuch saw him no more." The Spirit that had suggested to Philip to meet the Eunuch and to speak to him, now suggested his departure. "He was *caught away.*" There is no need of supposing, as some have entertained, that he was borne away in the air by miraculous agency ; all that is meant is, that he was strongly impelled by the Spirit. Such powerful impulses were awakened within him that he could not but go. Such impulses he required no doubt to effect his separation, for his connexion with the Eunuch had become close and strong. He was directed to Azotus, the Greek name for the city of Ashdod, about thirty miles from Gaza ; and thence he proceeded and preached in all the cities until he came to Cæsarea. He had fulfilled his mission with the Eunuch, and he proceeded by divine impulse to work out the divine will in relation to others. Thus moving away by the influence of God, Philip must have felt sublimely happy.

Secondly, *It was happy to the Eunuch.* "He went on his way rejoicing." And well he might rejoice. The Bible had become a new book to him. A divine light had fallen on its pages that gave it a meaning he never understood before, a charm he never felt before. He had found Him—Him of whom Moses and the prophets did write. "*Rejoicing,*" for he was full of love to that Jesus whom Philip preached to him ; "*rejoicing,*" for he felt that he had a wonderful blessing to impart to his sable countrymen.

Thus they parted, the one to go home in stately pomp, to be welcomed by his countrymen with marks of honour and distinction, the other to go as a poor evangelist into strange regions, to deliver a message which would rouse against him obloquy and persecution. Thus they parted, never again perhaps to meet on this earth, but both anticipating a joyous meeting in the holy heavens above.

CONCLUSION.—The subject suggests a lesson to those of you who have not yet experimentally understood the meaning of God's Holy Scriptures. Study them, as did the Eunuch, with an earnest heart and an inquiring mind. If you do so, God will send to you some Philip, who shall give that for which your natures crave. It suggests a lesson to those who experimentally know Jesus. Go and preach Christ to men as Philip did.

Acts 9:1-19

THE CONVERSION OF SAUL

" *And Saul, yet breathing out threatenings and slaughter against the disciples of the Lord, went unto the high priest, and desired of him letters to Damascus, to the synagogues, that if he found any of this way, whether they were men or women, he might bring them bound unto Jerusalem. And as he journeyed, he came near Damascus : and suddenly there shined round about him a light from heaven: and he fell to the earth, and heard a voice saying unto him, Saul, Saul, why persecutest thou me ? And he said, Who art thou, Lord ? And the Lord said, I am Jesus, whom thou perse- cutest: it is hard* [1] *for thee to kick against the pricks. And he trembling and astonished said, Lord, what wilt thou have me to do ? And the Lord said unto him, Arise, and go into the city, and it shall be told thee what thou must do. And the men which journeyed with him stood speechless, hearing a voice, but seeing no man. And Saul arose from the earth ; and when his eyes were opened, he saw no man : but they led him by the hand, and brought him into Damascus. And he was three days without sight, and neither did eat nor drink. And there was a certain disciple at Damascus, named Ananias ; and to him said the Lord in a vision, Ananias. And he said, Behold, I am here, Lord. And the Lord said unto him, Arise, and go into the street which is called Straight, and enquire in the house of Judas for one called Saul, of Tarsus: for, behold, he prayeth, and hath seen in a vision a man named Ananias coming in, and putting his hand on him, that he might receive his sight. Then Ananias answered, Lord, I have heard by many of this man, how much evil he hath done to thy saints at Jerusalem ; and here he hath authority from the chief priests to bind all that call on thy name. But the Lord said unto him, Go thy way; for he is a chosen vessel unto me, to bear my name before the Gentiles,* [2] *and kings, and the chil- dren of Israel ; for I will show him how great things he must suffer for my name's sake. And Ananias went his way, and entered into the house ; and putting his hands on him, said, Brother Saul, the Lord, even Jesus, that ap- peared unto thee in the way as thou camest, hath sent me, that thou mightest receive thy sight, and be filled with the Holy Ghost. And immediately there fell from his eyes as it had been scales : and he received sight forthwith, and arose, and was baptized. And when he had received meat he was strength- ened. Then was Saul certain days with the disciples which were at Damas- cus.*

EMENDATIVE RENDERINGS.—(1.) From *"it is hard"* to the end of ver. 6 should be omitted. (2.) nations.

EXEGETICAL REMARKS.—*"And Saul, yet breathing out threatenings and slaughter against the disciples of the Lord, went unto the high priest."* Saul's conduct is here placed in con- trast to that of Philip. The one is engaged in destroying, the other in building up, the Church. The ex- pression ἐμπνέων ἀπειλῆς καί φόνου in- dicates this, which represents threat- ening and murder, as if they were his native air in which he breathed.— L. and G. The emphatic " yet " is in- tended to denote the remarkable fact that up to this moment his rage against the disciples burned as fiercely as ever.

"And desired of him letters to Da- mascus." The jurisdiction of the high priest extended to the Jews at Da-

mascus. The destruction of Chris- tians in Jerusalem was not sufficient to gratify the wrath of this persecu- tor. He must go to Damascus, the capital of Syria, the great highway between Eastern and Northern Asia, about a hundred and thirty miles north-east of Jerusalem, the most ancient city perhaps in the world.

"That if he found any of this way, whether they were men or women." "This way," the Christian way—a way the most abhorrent to the heart of Saul. His cruelty was indiscriminate and unsparing—men and women alike. *"Any,"* &c.

"And as he journeyed he came near Damascus ; and suddenly there shined round about him a light from heavn." In one of his own later narratives

of the event, he says that it was *at mid-day* that this light gleamed upon him, and that it was distinguishable even from the blaze of an eastern noon; it was *above the brightness of the sun.* His attention was to be arrested, and the Creator of light and of the sun knew how to do this effectually. —VAUGHAN.

"*And he fell to the earth, and heard a voice saying unto him, Saul, Saul, why persecutest thou me ?*" The voice, he tells us himself, was in the Hebrew tongue—a language with which he was familiar. Though he was ignorant of Jesus, Jesus knew him —knew his name, his purpose, his mission, and appeals to him. That Saul *saw* as well as *heard* this glorious speaker is expressly said by Ananias, (ver. 17; xxii. 14,) by Barnabas, (ix. 27,) and by himself, (xxvi. 16 ;) and in claiming apostleship, he explicitly states that he had "*seen* the Lord," (1 Cor. ix. 1 ; xv. 8,) which can refer only to this scene.—P. C.

"*And he said, Who art thou, Lord ? And the Lord said, I am Jesus, whom thou persecutest.*" The "I" and "thou" here are touchingly emphatic in the original, while the term "Jesus" is purposely chosen to convey to him the thrilling information that the hated name which he sought to hunt down—*the "Nazarene,"* as it is in chap. xxii. 8—was now speaking to him from the skies, "crowned with glory and honour," (see chap. xxvi. 9.)

"*It is hard for thee,*" &c. These words, up to the end of ver. 6, are not found in any Greek MS. in existence. They were put in here by Erasmus from the Latin version, having been first inserted from chaps. xxvi. 14, and xxii. 10. —ALF.

"*And the men which journeyed with him.*" In St Paul's own narratives of the event, in the 22d and 26th chapters, he says, "*When we were all fallen to the earth,*" and again, "*They that were with me saw indeed the light, and were afraid; but they heard not the voice of him that spake to me.*" These varieties,

for contradictions they are not, prove one thing : that the descriptions of the sacred writers are free and independent. They have one great mark of truth upon them, that they are not studied and servile : they do not echo each other's words, they tell each its own story ; there is none of that elaborate guarding and fencing of expressions, none of that careful reconciliation of statement with statement, which every court of justice regards with strong suspicion as a sure indication of design and falsehood. Easy would it have been for St Luke, the writer of this history, to compare the 9th chapter with the 22d and with the 26th, and to bring the three into a rigid verbal consistency. That he did not do so is a proof of his veracity, of his single-mindedness, of his confidence in the force of truth.— VAUGHAN.*

"*And he was three days without sight, neither did eat nor drink.*" Was this three days' fast of Saul a natural expression of his penitence and grief, or the means for the restoration of his sight, or the spontaneous effect of his abstraction from his ordinary thoughts and his absorption in the care of his salvation ? One thing is certain, that during these three days he passed through a wonderful experience.

"*And the Lord said unto him, Arise, and go into the street which is called Straight, and enquire in the house of Judas, for one called Saul of Tarsus : for behold he prayeth.*" These words addressed by Christ in vision to Ananias, one of his disciples at Damascus, are very remarkable. Not only is the name of the street given, but that of the proprietor of the house in which Saul was to be found. Christ knows our streets, their houses, and their inhabitants. Seek Saul out. Why ? "*Behold he prayeth.*"

"*And hath seen in a vision a man named Ananias coming in and putting his hand on him, that he might receive his sight.*" Saul sees in a vision the very man that is to minister to him,

---

* See also some admirable remarks on the discrepancies in the account of Saul's conversion, by Rev. Thomas Binney, in a work which we take this opportunity of recommending to our readers, entitled, "St Paul, his Life and Ministry."

and the very man that is to minister to him sees in a vision the very work which he is called upon to do. Christ has access to all minds and at all times.

"*Then Ananias answered, Lord I have heard by many of this man, how much evil he hath done to thy saints at Jerusalem.*" He seems to have felt as Moses (Ex. iii. 11, Jer. i. 6) when God spoke to him. He was diffident and doubtful. He had heard of Saul—heard of his diabolic persecution of the saints at Jerusalem, and of his commission to carry on the infernal work in Damascus.

"*But the Lord said unto him, Go thy way : for he is a chosen vessel unto me, to bear my name before the Gentiles, and kings, and the children of Israel.*" The circles of humanity to which Saul was to carry the name of Jesus are three : —1. ἔθνη : this cannot here denote nations in general, as the υἱοὶ Ἰσραήλ are afterwards expressly distinguished from them, but only the heathen nations ; 2. βασιλεῖς, ruling lords, princes ; 3. υἱοὶ Ἰσραήλ.—L. and G.

"*I will show him how great things he must suffer for my name's sake.*" The spirit of these words is : "Think no more of how much suffering he has caused on account of my name, for I am about to show him how much he shall suffer in his turn for my name's sake."

"*And Ananias went his way, and entered into the house.*" Encouraged by the assurance that the persecutor of the new religion had himself embraced it, he commences forthwith the execution of his commission. He goes to the house ; he finds Saul ; he puts his hand on him ; he addresses him, "*Brother Saul, the Lord, even Jesus, that appeared unto thee in the way as thou camest, hath sent me that thou mightest receive thy sight, and be filled with the Holy Ghost.*" The word "even" is not in the original, and is superfluous.

"*And immediately there fell from his eyes as it had been scales.*" The meaning is, that the recovery of his sight took place as if scales had dropped from the organ of vision. The restoration was instantaneous and supernatural.

"*And arose and was baptized.*" He was "*baptized*" to symbolise the change which the Spirit of God had effected in his moral character.

"*And when he had received meat, he was strengthened.*" He had fasted three days, and the prostration must have been considerable.

"*Then was Saul certain days with the disciples which were at Damascus.*" How long he continued at Damascus we are not told. The language is indefinite—"*some days.*" He had come on a mission of destruction, but his purposes were changed, and he was there as the helper of a cause he had intended to overthrow.

HOMILETICS.—The three greatest facts that have ever occurred in the history of God's redemptive providence, are—the advent of Christ, the Pentecostal dispensation, and the conversion of Saul of Tarsus. The first is confessedly pre-eminent. Christ's incarnation, teachings, miracles, sufferings, death, resurrection, ascension, constitute the grand central epoch in the history of our race : all things that have happened in the history of humanity before or since are reckoned from it, and are measured by it. The second stands next to it. The day of Pentecost was the culminating point in the system of redemption—introducing a new dispensation of the Divine Spirit, a new style of religious ministry, a new development of social life. The third, namely, the conversion of Saul of Tarsus, stands next in order, and has had nothing through all subsequent times, in Divine significance and power, comparable to it. The thirty years of his ministry, which according to Neander began between the years A.D.

30 and 40, threw the ideas of Jesus with a force into the heart of the world, that shattered old systems, and established everywhere those organisations called "churches," which have been multiplying ever since, and which are destined to work a moral revolution in the world. It has been said, obliterate from the world the influence of this man's thirty years' ministry, and you sweep all churches from the face of the earth, you quench the moral lights of the age, you give back Ephesus to Diana, Athens to Minerva, Paphos to Venus, Rome to all the gods of her Pantheon, and plunge the whole world once more into Pagan darkness and heathen dissoluteness.

We have now to consider the history of that event which changed this man, and endowed him with this tremendous power. In the history of his conversion, as recorded in this passage, he appears before us in three aspects—*as an enemy to the cause of Christ; as conquered by the revelation of Christ; as enlisted in the service of Christ.*

I. As an enemy to the cause of Christ. We learn from the account here given, that his enmity was *intense* and *practical*.

First, It was *intense*. "And Saul, yet breathing out threatenings," &c. The martyrdom of Stephen had, like the taste of blood to the beast of prey, heightened his ferocity ; and he was earnest in making "havoc of the Church." The very breath of his soul was malignity towards the disciples of the new religion. There was much in this man's caste of character that would give intensity and power to his enmity. *He was a man of strong intellect.* Intellect rules the feelings, both of love and anger. In those of feeble understanding the emotions will be feeble as compared with those who are endowed with strong powers of thought. He who has a great intellect will, if he loves, love intensely ; if he hates, will hate with passion. Whilst thought can quench the hottest flame of feeling, it can also fan a spark into fury. *He was a man of strong impulses.* There are natures whose susceptibility of feeling is very small, they are cold, phlegmatic, unimpassioned ; the fires of their natures are too weak to flame, they only smoulder and smoke. Not so with Saul. Feeling in him was a sea of fire, and its tides throbbed through every part of his nature. He did nothing without feeling. Feeling gave a force to every purpose, a flash to every look, an emphasis to every word, a resoluteness to every act. The love of such an emotional nature would be love worth the name ; the hatred of such a nature would be such as we might well tremble at. *He was a man of invincible conscientiousness.* If conscience give her sanctions to our feelings, their strength will reach their highest point. Whatever feeling, thought, or effort, conscience sanctions, it intensifies. Saul's conscience not only sanctioned, but enforced his enmity towards Christ. He considered he was "doing God's service," and regarded it as a sacred obligation to blot the name of Jesus from the earth.

Secondly, This enmity was *practical.* It did not live in feeling, however strong, nor expend itself in anathemas, however terrible. It took a practical form—the most determined. The passage before us records two things which he does on this occasion :—

(1.) He gets his persecuting plans *legalised."* He " went to the high priest, and desired of him letters to Damascus." The reason why Saul sought a commission to work out his malignant purposes against Christianity in this place was probably on account of the number of disciples who were there. Perhaps many of those who were converted on the day of Pentecost had come from Damascus, and returned earnest propagandists of the new faith. On all such, whether young or old, male or female, Saul was determined to wreak vengeance. Whoever "he found of this way, whether they were men or women," he was determined to "bring them bound unto Jerusalem."

(2.) He *prosecutes* his commission. "And as he journeyed, he came near Damascus." After the letters from the high priest were obtained, we are warranted to suppose that he lost no time, but commenced at once his journey. It was a difficult journey to prosecute in those times. Who can tell the route he took ? how did he travel ? Modern pictures represent him on horseback, but there is no authority for this. Who were his companions ? where did they rest on their way ? These inquiries remain unsettled. All we know is, that he all but completed the prosecution of his journey, and that a furious malignity towards the cause of Jesus was the all-dominant passion of his soul.

His enmity, which the verses before us indicate, is variously and forcibly expressed elsewhere in the Holy Word. We are told that he made "havoc of the Church," that he "shut up many saints in prison," and that he "compelled them to blaspheme." He is represented as invading the sanctuaries of domestic life—" entering into every house "—and ruthlessly tearing away those whom he committed to prison. He has described himself as a "blasphemer, a persecutor, and injurious." Such was Saul before his conversion.

We proceed to note him in another light in which he is presented to us in the passage.

II. AS CONQUERED BY THE REVELATION OF CHRIST. This man, just before he reaches the city, is struck to the earth, and thoroughly overcome. The animating malignity has left his spirit, his persecuting purposes are broken, new feelings rush into his soul, so powerful that they paralyse his physical energies. He " was three days without sight, neither did eat nor drink." There, just as he was entering Damascus, he lies prostrate on the ground, thoroughly conquered by an invisible power. Observe—

First, *The nature of the revelation that Christ made to Saul.* The revelation which brought this rebel to the dust, shook his soul with "trembling and astonishment," and made him pray earnestly to Him whose name he sought to blot from the memory of men, was twofold:—

(1.) A revelation by *symbol*. "Suddenly there shined round about him a light from heaven." This was not an ordinary flash of lightning. It was a supernatural interposition. It was probably that light denominated the Shekinah, in which the Almighty, in olden times, was wont to appear to men. Hence it is spoken of as the appearance of Christ himself elsewhere. Barnabas declared, when he brought Paul to the apostles at Jerusalem, how that "he had seen the Lord." The light was very bright. Paul himself says it was "above the brightness of the sun at mid-day." The sun at midday in that Eastern spot would have a brilliance unknown to us here in the temperate West. That light was the garment with which He clothed Himself. Those who were with Saul saw it, and fell to the ground in terror, (chap. xxvi. 4.) But Saul saw in that awful brilliancy what they beheld not—he saw Christ whom he was persecuting.

(2.) A revelation by *words*. He "heard a voice saying unto him, Saul, Saul, why persecutest thou me?" The words were in the Hebrew tongue, we are told elsewhere; the same language in which Christ, during His earthly life, spoke to Peter and to John, to the blind man at the walls of Jericho, and to the woman who washed His feet with her tears. The language is emphatic: "Saul, Saul." Jesus frequently used such repetitions in order to fix attention. "Martha, Martha," "Simon, Simon," "Jerusalem, Jerusalem." The language is most exciting. "Why persecutest thou Me?" "Whatever thou dost against my disciples thou dost against Me. I and my people are one. Why persecute Me? What injury have *I* done THEE? Thou hatest Me without a cause." Observe—

Secondly, *The effects of the revelation upon Saul.* The revelation did two things:—

(1.) Brought him into a *conscious contact* with Christ. "Who art thou, Lord?" The question implies that, as yet, he did not know who it was that had appeared and spoken. The word "Lord" here means nothing more than "Sir." As yet he was in the dark as to the Being who had appeared to him. He knew not who came in that brilliance, who spoke in those electric words! Jesus answers his question: "I am Jesus, whom thou persecutest." This reply must have made Saul feel that he was in contact with Jesus of Nazareth. "I am Jesus, whom thou persecutest." Now, for the first time, he saw Jesus with the eye of his conscience; he never forgot this sight. Contending for the validity of his own apostleship, in his letter to the Corinthians, he says, "Have I not seen Jesus Christ the Lord?" And again, in another place, he says, "Last of all, he was seen by me also, as one born out of due time." And again, referring, perhaps, to this very time, he says, "It pleased God to reveal His Son in me." This revelation—

(2.) Brought him to a *complete submission to the will* of Christ. "And he, trembling and astonished, said, Lord, what wilt thou have me to do?" His own will was overcome; the will of the Sanhedrim was nothing to him now—the will of Christ was everything. "Lord, what wilt *thou* have me to do?" As if he had said, "Something must be done, whatever thou teachest, I will do. Teach me what Thy will is!" The question indicates a thorough revolution in his soul—an unqualified submission to the will of Christ. This is religion. It is remarkable that Christ, in answer to his entreaty, did not give him a direct revelation of His will, but told him to go into the city to receive instruction. For three days he was alone, unable to see, unable to move, unable to eat or drink, on account of the moral convulsions he had experienced. During those three days his soul was turned in upon itself; it was the crisis of its history. It was the period when the vessel of his being took a new reckoning of the sea of life, and reversed its course; or, to change the figure, it was the period when the Divine Spirit, brooding over the chaos of his nature evolved a new creation.

The passage leads us to look upon Saul in another aspect:—

III. As enlisted in the service of Christ. In the 20th verse it is said, "And straightway he preached Christ in the synagogues, that He is the Son of God." What a change is this! How thorough, how wonderful, how rapidly accomplished! Here is a man turned right against his former self, and earnestly engaged in a cause which he had set his heart upon destroying. The passage presents to us *the messenger engaged to enlist him in this service.* Christ, as we have already stated, did not Himself *directly* tell him what to do in His cause. Ananias is selected for the purpose. All that we know of him is, that he was a Jew and a "disciple," and that he was regarded "as a devout man according to the law among all the Jews who dwelt there." There is no mention made of him in any of the Epistles. The narrative before us is to us the sum of his history, and invests him with an undying and ever-widening fame. As a messenger to Saul, he was (1.) *especially selected.* "The Lord in a vision" came to him; whether in his sleeping or waking hours is not known. In either case, his spiritual senses were open to recognise the divine in form and utterance. "Behold, I am here, Lord." He felt that the Lord was with him in reality. As a messenger to Saul, he was (2.) *especially directed.* "And the Lord said unto him, Arise, and go into the street which is called Straight, and inquire in the house of Judas for one called Saul of Tarsus." How minute the direction! The name of the street, called "Straight," a name which the street in that old city still retains. The "house of Judas." The house is still pointed out as the place where Paul lodged. The description of the man he was to visit—"Saul of Tarsus." Four things are observable here:—

First, The *reasons* assigned for the message received. The reasons are, that Saul was *praying*, and that he had received—perhaps in answer to his prayer—a vision of Ananias coming and "putting his hands on him, that he might receive his sight." Saul's prayer reached the heart of Christ, and the mission of Ananias was the answer.

Secondly, The *manner* in which the message was *first* received : " Lord, I have heard by many of this man, how much evil he hath done to thy saints at Jerusalem." From this, it would seem that reports of Saul's cruelty had reached Damascus, and that his fiendish persecutions were notorious. The disciples, perhaps, at Damascus, had heard that, like a raging beast of prey, he was on his way to that city fully armed with ecclesiastical authority. This intelligence which Ananias had of Saul, made him at first reluctant to attend to the divine message.

Thirdly, The *divine argument* with which the message was again urged : " The Lord said unto him, Go thy way : for he is a chosen vessel unto me." The argument is, that Saul had been divinely ordained for great work and great trial. Saul's subsequent history realised all that is here stated. He bore the name of Christ to the Gentiles ; he made the heathen world ring through all its temples with the doctrine of the Cross. Before kings and rulers he stood expounding its meaning and enforcing its claims, (chaps. xxv., xxvi., xxvii.) " Great things " he suffered, too, for His " name's sake." The whole of his apostolic life was a life of martyrdom, (2 Cor. xi. 23–28.)

Fourthly, The manner in which the message was *carried out.* " And Ananias went his way, and entered into the house." It was carried out (1.) *affectionately.* When he entered the house, he approached the soul-stricken penitent, and " putting his hand on him " —not as an ecclesiastical ceremony, but as an Oriental sign of friendship, (Matt. xix. 13)—he said, " Brother Saul ! " The greeting of a fraternal heart this. The man who was once shuddered at as a fiend, was now addressed as a brother. The lion has become a lamb. It was carried out (2.) *faithfully.* He does not go in his own name, but acknowledges at once that " Jesus, that appeared unto thee in the way as thou camest, hath sent me, that thou mightest receive thy sight, and be filled with the Holy Ghost." Jesus, who struck thee to the ground with the effulgence of His presence and the force of His words, hath sent me, not to pronounce anathemas on thy head, but " that thou mightest receive thy sight, and be filled with the Holy Ghost." It was carried out (3.) *effectively.* " And immediately there fell from his eyes as it had been scales." No natural remedies were applied. Ananias had been divinely commissioned to effect the cure, and in virtue of his commission he did it. The apostle himself (Acts xxii. 13) describes the incident with a touching simplicity. " The same hour I looked up upon him." Who can imagine the emotions that Saul's first glance at Ananias awakened in his heart ? He " arose." It was a resurrection from the dead ; he was a new man. The arch-bigot was gone for ever ; and the apostle was up to do a work that the ages would bless, and which eternity would celebrate. He was " baptized." He submitted to the ordinance which symbolised adoption of a new faith. He " received meat " (food) and " was strengthened." The new feelings that had flooded his soul, had taken away his appetite, and he had fasted three days ; now his spirit was calmed by a new faith, his appetite returned, he took food and was revived. " Then was Saul certain days with the disciples which were at Damascus." Here is his introduction into Christian fellowship. He becomes a member of a noble brotherhood of Christians.

Such are the aspects, then, in which these verses present Paul to us. First, as an *enemy to the cause of Christ;* then, as *conquered by the revelation of Christ ;* and then, as *enlisted in the service of Christ.* What a change ! How great ! how divine ! how influential ! It was the opening of a perennial fountain in the world's desert, the kindling of a bright and quenchless guiding star in the world's firmament.

I scarcely feel justified in quitting this subject without exhibiting the conversion of Paul in three aspects, namely, *as illustrating that great moral change which is essential to the salvation of every sinner; as supplying a cogent argument in favour of the divinity of the Christian faith ; and as affording hope of mercy to the greatest sinner.*

I. Look at Saul's conversion as illustrating that GREAT MORAL CHANGE WHICH IS ESSENTIAL TO THE SALVATION OF EVERY SINNER. In many respects, perhaps in most, Saul's conversion resembles all genuine conversions. This will appear, if we consider—

First, *The feelings developed in connexion with it.* In Saul's case, for example, there was—

(1.) *A vivid consciousness of Christ.* He felt that the Son of God was present in the brilliancy that flashed in his eyes, and the voice that fell on his ears. Those who were with him saw the light and heard the sound, but they had no consciousness of Christ. Saul had, and this was the commencement of the revolution in his soul. This smote him penitentially to the dust. The vision of Christ as the Saviour of the world is the first step to conversion. Hence the work of the ministry is to exhibit to sinners Jesus Christ as manifestly crucified amongst them. There was also in his case the feeling of—

(2.) *Anxious inquiry.* Two questions rose from his agonised soul—" Who art thou, Lord ? " and " Lord, what wilt thou have me to do ? " Deep was the anxiety which he felt. This is ever the case in true conversion. The mind is not passive in the change ; its moral course is not reversed irrespective of its own anxious efforts. God does not change it as He shifts the winds and turns the tides. There was, moreover, in Saul's case—

(3.) *Profound contrition.* He falls prostrate to the earth, and the moral anguish of his soul makes him dead to all surrounding objects, and for three days destroys all natural desire for food. What were the thoughts that convulsed his nature during the three days he lay down in blindness without food or drink ? How would the memories of his enormous crimes torment him ! how would the forbearing mercy of Christ melt him with the fires of shame and self-reproach ! In all conversions there must be something of this, this self-loathing, this deep contrition for sin. There was, furthermore, in his case—

(4.) *Earnest prayer.* " *Behold he prayeth,*" says Christ. What wonder is this ? Was he not a Pharisee, and did he not often pray ? Yes ! often used the words and assumed the attitude of prayer, but never *prayed.* But now he prays with all the earnestness of a penitent. " Behold he prayeth." *He* prayeth ; he, the arch-bigot, the fiendish persecutor, who was just before " breathing out threatenings and slaughter," now prayeth. This praying was the first breathing of a new life, and is ever associated with conversion. In every conversion there is the prayer, " God be merciful to me a sinner." Thus the feelings connected with Saul's conversion are such as are more or less identified with all genuine conversions. The resemblance of Saul's conversion with all true conversions will appear if we consider—

Secondly, *The display of the human and the divine in effecting it.* God's sovereign agency is most strikingly displayed. It was the flash of the Shekinah that arrested him in his fiendish career ; it was the voice of the Lord that struck him with conviction ; it was the Holy Ghost that inspired him with new life. Paul always traced the event to the sovereign agency of that God who called him by His grace. But whilst the *divine* is seen in it, there is also the *human.*

(1.) There is the human in Saul. The wonderful display of the divine is not sufficient to account for Saul's conversion. There are instances of those who have had as striking a display of the divine as Saul, and yet have not been converted. Pharaoh, Balaam, Caiaphas, men who witnessed the miracles of God, or the wonderful phenomena connected with Christ's crucifixion, had the divine brought upon them as powerfully as it came upon Saul, and yet they remained unconverted. The fact is, God does not save a man without his will. " God," says one of the fathers, " created us without our consent, but cannot save us without it." There was something in the nature and character of this Saul of Tarsus that made him susceptible of the divine influence. Pharisee though he was, he was a sincere man ; he served God after the manners of his fathers, with a pure conscience. His errand to Damascus he undertook conscientiously, believing that he should serve God thereby. Bad as he was, he was candid, sincere, having a reverence for the divine will.

(2.) There is the human in Ananias. Christ employed the agency of Ananias to consummate the work. So it is ever : God converts man by man. Let no man, therefore, expect that the Almighty will convert him irrespectively of himself. The resemblance of Saul's conversion, with all true conversions, will appear if we consider—

Thirdly, *The thoroughness of the change.* How vast the difference between the man described in the 1st verse of the chapter, and the man described in the 20th verse, between the man " breathing out threatenings and slaughter against the disciples of the Lord," and the man preaching " Christ in the synagogues, that He is the Son of God !" Paul is a new creation. Listen to his own description of the change : " But what things were gain to me, those I counted loss for Christ. Yea, doubtless, and I count all things but loss for the excellency of the knowledge of Christ Jesus my Lord ; for whom I have suffered the loss of all things, and do count them but dung, that I may win Christ."

Brothers, are you conscious of a change in any way resembling that conversion which took place in the history of Saul ? If not, that change remains the grand necessity of your being.

II. Look at Saul's conversion as supplying a COGENT ARGUMENT IN FAVOUR OF THE DIVINITY OF THE CHRISTIAN FAITH. Lord Lyttleton has truly said and ably demonstrated, " that the conversion and apostleship of Paul alone, duly considered, is of itself a demonstration sufficient to prove Christianity a divine revelation." The truth of Christianity does not depend on this argument. Were the conversion of Paul nothing but a mere myth, were his apostleship an imposture, Christianity would still be divine. The biography of Christ is Christianity, and the truth of that biography is supported by its own sublime nature, by the voice of all history, by its fitness to the spiritual constitution and exigencies of man, and by the supernatural flood of influence it has poured into the ages. Albeit, every argument that tends in any way to strengthen in any the conviction of its truth, should be sought out, preserved, studied, and used when occasion requires. There are many ways of stating the argument arising from the conversion of Paul. I may shape it thus :—

First, *If the testimony of Paul concerning Christ be true, Christianity is divine.* Jesus was the grand theme of Paul's ministry, oral and written. Everywhere he exhibits Him in his discourses and letters as the Messiah predicted in the Old Testament, as the Son of God, and the Saviour of the world. He desired " to know nothing among men but Christ, and Him crucified," he gloried in His cross, he counted all things loss for the excellency of Him. Paul's testimony sustains the truth of the evangelists and the predictions of the prophets concerning Christ. If you believe in Paul, you *must believe in Christ.

Secondly, *If the conversion of Paul is a reality, his testimony must be true.* (1.) His conversion shows that he had the *necessary intelligence* to bear a credible testimony. It is necessary, in order to give credibility to testimony, that the witness should be thoroughly acquainted with the circumstances he narrates. If Paul was ignorant of Christ, if the statements he made were the reckless utterances of a blind fanatic, his testimony is worth nothing. But the history of his conversion shows that he became *thoroughly* acquainted with Christ. He *saw* Him, he *heard* Him, he *felt* Him. Christ became more real to him than any being in the universe ; Christ was revealed in him, he said. (2.) His conversion shows that he had the *necessary candour* to bear a credible testimony. If a witness is strongly prejudiced in favour of the things he declares, his testimony is, to say the least, but questionable. The conversion of Saul shows that his prejudices were all *against* Jesus. No name was so odious to him as the name of Jesus ; no cause so abhorrent to his nature as His cause. Malignity to Him bore him now to Damascus, the scene of his conversion. When he, therefore, states that Jesus is the Son of God, the Saviour of the world, he states what runs directly opposed to his prejudices, and thus shows a candour which gives a credibility to his word. (3.) His conversion shows that he had the *necessary disinterestedness* to bear a credible testimony. When a witness has a deep interest in proving what he wishes to establish, his word is justly looked upon with suspicion. The history of Paul's conversion shows that self-interest had nothing to do in prompting him to adopt the new faith. In truth he made enormous sacrifices to do so. His position as a member, which he probably was, of the great Council of the nation, his high prospects in Church and State as a young man of genius, culture, and a Hebrew of the Hebrews ; his dearest friendships, his worldly wealth and comforts, all were sacrificed on his adhesion to the cause of Christ. And obloquy, insult, want, persecution, and martyrdom he knew would follow his decision. If disinterestedness, therefore, is an element of credibility in a witness, Paul's testimony concerning Christ must be taken.

Such is, anyhow, the form of an argument in favour of the divinity of Christianity from the testimony of Paul. If his testimony is true, Christianity must be divine; and if his conversion is a reality, his testimony must be true. For he had all the necessary qualifications of a truthful witness—intelligence, candour, and disinterestedness.

III. Look at Paul's conversion as affording HOPE OF MERCY TO THE GREATEST SINNER. The apostle himself regarded his conversion in this light. These are his own words, (1 Tim. i. 16,) "Howbeit for this cause I obtained mercy, that in me first Jesus Christ might show forth all long-suffering, for a pattern to them which should hereafter believe on him to life everlasting."

Acts 9:20-25

PAUL'S MINISTRY AT DAMASCUS

" *And straightway he preached Christ*[1] *in the synagogues, that He is the Son of God. But all that heard him were amazed, and said, Is not this he that destroyed them which called on this name in Jerusalem, and came hither for that intent, that he might bring them bound unto the chief priests? But Saul increased the more in strength, and confounded the Jews which dwelt at Damascus, proving that this is very Christ. And after that many days were fulfilled, the Jews took counsel to kill him: But their lying await was known of Saul: and they watched the gates day and night to kill him. Then the disciples took him by night, and let him down by the wall in a basket.*"

EMENDATIVE RENDERING.—(1.) Jesus.

EXEGETICAL REMARKS.—" *Straight-way.*" Immediately. The ardour of his temperament, and the force of his new convictions, prompted him to instant service in the new cause.

" *He preached Christ (Jesus) in the synagogues, that He is the Son of God.*" The synagogue afforded a fine field for introducing the doctrines of Christianity to the Jewish people. They were wherever the Jews existed, and they admitted a free discussion. The position which Paul set himself to demonstrate was that Christ was the true Messiah. It is to be observed, that the commencement of Paul's preaching was not the commencement of his apostolic work. His work now was like the work of Philip, the voluntary work of an evangelist, not the mission of an apostle. His own statement, (Gal. i. 21-23,) indicates that what he had done previous to his return to Tarsus was not properly apostolic work.

" *All that heard him were amazed.*" No wonder at their astonishment. A well-known man advocating with all his power a doctrine, which a few days before he had done all in his power to destroy.

" *After many days.*" " Between," says a modern expositor, " this and the 22d verse, there is supposed to be a chasm of three years, (Gal. i. 18,) in which Saul withdrew from his former associates and resorts, and retired into Arabia, where he received divine revelations ; and, in the exercise of prayer and meditation, and the duties of benevolence to the many Jews dwelling there, nursed the spirit of the gospel in his heart to strength and maturity, and came forth fully prepared to discharge his sublime mission of benevolence. How he passed his time he does not inform us, but we can easily see how beneficial was this retirement and repose to so fiery a nature as that of Paul ; and how truly such a repose fitted him to preach Christianity, not only with intelligence, but deep and matured fervour. Some, however, conjecture that the breach in the narrative occurs between the first and last clause of verse 19. The Arabian frontier approaches near Damascus, and Paul may have retired but a short distance from the city in order to escape the vigilance of his enemies. The omission of this journey by Luke shows that there was no concert between the writers, and instead of weakening, strengthens the probability of truth and genuineness."

" *But their lying await was known of Saul: and they watched the gates day and night to kill him.*" They had plotted to kill him, and watched earnestly day and night for an opportunity to execute their malignant design. Saul knew of the conspiracy, and was on his guard.

" *Then the disciples took him by night, and let him down by the wall in a basket.*" The description here of Saul's mode of escape agrees with the structure of ancient cities, which were protected by walls, and with the custom that now prevails in some parts of the East, of letting people down in baskets. The precise part of the wall from which Saul was let down is pointed out by Christians to travellers who now visit the city of Damascus.

HOMILETICS.—Saul's conversion was his birthday into the world's history. We have in these verses the opening of his apostolic ministry in Damascus, and his ministry here reveals three things :—

I. THE CHARACTER OF HIS SPIRITUAL CHANGE. We learn—
First, That it was *radical.* He preached " Christ in the synagogues, that He is the Son of God." That is, he set himself to prove that Jesus of Nazareth was the true Messiah. The very *opposite* this to what he was doing the hour before the light of heaven shone round about him. Then he gave his whole being to deny it ; now he gives his whole being to demonstrate it. How thorough the change ! Here are two men : the one is Saul the persecutor, the other is Paul the apostle. We learn—
Secondly, That it was *genuine.* He preached in the " synagogues ; " the very scenes where he was well known as one commissioned by the high priest to avenge the insult offered to the religion of their fathers by the new faith. Had not his conversion been sincere, he would not have acted thus. No impostor would have ventured such a step. He knew that the synagogues afforded a fine opportunity for proclaiming his new convictions, and for enabling him to make some atonement for his past life. Unto the synagogues therefore he resorts. We learn—
Thirdly, That it was *startling.* " All that heard him were *amazed,* and said," &c. The worshippers in the synagogues, as they listened to him, were struck with the deepest surprise ; and well they might ; the change was so *sudden,* so *thorough,* and so *extraordinary.* His ministry at Damascus reveals—

II. THE NATURE OF HIS NEW FAITH. " Saul increased the more in strength, and confounded the Jews which dwelt at Damascus, proving that this is very Christ." From this we infer—
First, That his new faith was *growable.* " He *increased* the more in strength." The more he examined the claims of Christ, the stronger grew his confidence. The more he reflected on His truths, the warmer and more energetic became his affections. Christianity

is not a class of dry notions. It is a living germ. Once planted in the soul, and every earnest thought bestowed upon it will only serve to strike its roots deeper into the centre of our being. From this we infer—

Secondly, That his new faith was *discussible.* It was a thing that Paul felt he could talk about, take it into the synagogues, and submit it to men, in many respects, most competent to search into its merits. Christianity is not a mystic sentiment that admits of no explanation, not a musty prejudice that totters before the glance of scrutiny. It is intelligible in its facts, and rational in its theories. From this we infer—

Thirdly, That his new faith was *demonstrable.* He " *confounded* the Jews which dwelt at Damascus, *proving* that this is very Christ." He confuted and convinced them. By manifestation of the truth he commended himself to every man's conscience in the sight of God. The truth of Christianity admits of the highest possible demonstration. His ministry at Damascus reveals—

III. THE SPIRIT OF HIS FIRST AUDITORS. " And after that many days were fulfilled, the Jews took counsel to kill him," &c. The expression, "after many days," gives an indefinite interval which Luke has not filled up. This interval is supposed by many to be the period of three years which was spent in Arabia, (Gal. i. 18.) What he did during these "many days," these three years in the solitudes of Arabia, we may conjecture, but cannot determine. We may be sure, however, that the period was spent in intellectual and moral qualification for the discharge of his wonderful mission. Malignity, we are told, inspired the men whom he first addressed, and amongst whom he first laboured. " They took counsel to kill him."

First, *Their malignity was deadly.* " They took counsel to *kill* him." Violence has always been the argument of bigotry. No one was more earnest in its use than Saul of Tarsus. He understood it. Error always seeks to destroy the truth by killing its advocate. On the other hand, truth ever seeks to kill the error by saving the advocate.

Secondly, *Their malignity was deliberate.* They " took counsel ;" " they watched the gates day and night." They plotted his destruction, and watched with diligence their opportunity. Evil as well as good has its plans.

Thirdly, *Their malignity was frustrated,* Then the disciples took him by night, and let him down by the wall in a basket." In this deliverance of Saul two things are suggested—

(1.) The way in which Providence delivers the good. Providence could have launched a thunderbolt, and crushed Paul's enemies at once, but it acted not thus, and thus it seldom acts. It saved him by his own *caution,* and the *assistance* of the disciples. It suggested—

(2.) The inevitable doom of evil. The plans of evil, however ably and sagely constructed, must be broken. They cannot stand long. "He taketh the wise in their own craftiness." The profoundest schemes of hell will, in the light of eternity, be only as the baseless fabric of a dream.

Acts 9:26-30

PAUL'S FIRST VISIT AFTER HIS CONVERSION TO JERUSALEM

"*And when Saul was come to Jerusalem, he assayed to join himself to the disciples : but they were all afraid of him, and believed not that he was a disciple. But Barnabas took him, and brought him to the apostles, and declared unto them how he had seen the Lord in the way, and that he had spoken to him, and how he had preached boldly at Damascus in the name of Jesus. And he was with them coming in and going out at Jerusalem. And he spake boldly in the name of the Lord Jesus, and disputed against the Grecians : but they went about to slay him. Which when the brethren knew, they brought him down to Cæsarea, and sent him forth to Tarsus.*"

EXEGETICAL REMARKS. — "*When Saul was come to Jerusalem.*" He had probably been three years away from Jerusalem, away in the solitudes of Arabia, (Gal. i. 17, 18.) He left Jerusalem a furiously malignant persecutor of Christ's disciples. He returns as one of their loving number. He left it with the heart of a tiger, he returns with that of a lamb. "*He assayed to join himself with the disciples ; but they were all afraid of him.*" No wonder. Why? (1.) Some had not heard of the change. The distance between Jerusalem and Damascus was great. (2.) The persecution which commenced with the stoning of Stephen still raged perhaps in the holy city. (3.) The quarrel which subsisted between Herod and Aretas, probably cut off all intercourse between the two cities. (4.) Those who remembered Saul would feel a horror at the mention of his name on account of the atrocities which he had perpetrated. (5.) The few that might have heard of his conversion would be likely to suspect that it was a mere feint, a bait to catch the more easily to destroy. Confidence is a plant of slow growth.

"*But Barnabas took him and brought him to the apostles,*" &c. Notwithstanding the general distrust, which placed Saul in this embarrassing and mortifying position, Barnabas, either on account of former acquaintance, or some other reason unknown, gave heed to his story, accepted him as a genuine disciple, and as such introduced him to the Church at Jerusalem. "*He brought him to the apostles.*" Saul himself tells us afterwards that on this occasion he only saw two of them, Peter and James, (Gal. i. 18, 19.) The others perhaps were absent, or shunned him, for the want of confidence. "*And he was with them coming in and going out at Jerusalem.*" He was fully admitted to their friendship, and recognised as a true Christian brother. He went in and out, had free intercourse with them. His stay here, however, on this occasion, was only fifteen days, (Gal. i. 18.)

"*And he spake boldly in the name of the Lord Jesus, and disputed against the Grecians.*" He "*preached boldly,*" and "*disputed,*" &c. The Grecians were the Hellenists, or foreign Jews, of whom Saul was one himself. With those Stephen contended, and perhaps some of them were present to hear Saul, who had heard the martyr.

"*But they went about to slay him.*" His preaching produced the same effect upon them as the sermon of Stephen—stimulated them only to anger.

"*Which when the brethren knew, they brought him down to Cæsarea, and sent him forth to Tarsus.*" In Acts xxii. 17-21, Paul himself relates before the Jews, that Jesus appeared to him in a trance in the temple, and commanded him to depart quickly from the city, for his testimony would find no willing acceptance among them. Both accounts strikingly agree ; for if the plan of assassination were formed against Saul, this was the most striking confirmation of it, that the Jews at Jerusalem would not receive his testimony. And how easily is it imaginable that Saul would not yet have resolved, in consequence of what the brethren said to him, to forsake the city, but departed directly in consequence of an intimation from the Lord in a vision—LANGE. The course of his journey, and the countries he visited, are mentioned in Gal. i. 21, by which it has been inferred that he travelled by land ; in which case Cæsarea Philippi would lie more directly in his way than the seaport Cæsarea. This is the opinion of Witsius, Doddrige, Kenrick, and Olshausen, though many other critics contend that it was Cæsarea on the sea-coast.—LIVERMORE.

HOMILETICS.—Paul had escaped from Damascus in a way that made such an impression on his mind that he referred to it fourteen years after, (2 Cor. xi. 30.) It was the commencement of that long catalogue of perils by his own countrymen, which occupy so large a portion of his apostolic history. Rescued from Damascus, he wends his way to Jerusalem. He would go over the same road as that by which he came, but with a mind whose views and feelings had been so thoroughly revolutionised that every external object would be changed. When he entered Jerusalem it would be a new city to him. The old streets would start strange memories. Familiar faces would have a new significance. His relations to Gamaliel, to the Pharisees, to the Sanhedrim, had thoroughly altered. The outward is ever to us according to the inward. Thus dungeons are sometimes palaces, and palaces sometimes cells. Thus, according to the state of our mind, the brightest day of summer is a day of darkness as of darkness itself. In this visit to Jerusalem, two things took place —*his admission to church membership, and the commencement of his evangelic ministry.*

I. HIS ADMISSION TO CHURCH MEMBERSHIP AT JERUSALEM. "He assayed to join himself to the disciples."

First, *His admission sought.* "He assayed,"—that is, he endeavoured—to join himself to the disciples. Amongst the disciples there was Peter. Peter to him was a special attraction ; and therefore of this visit he writes long afterwards : "After three years I went up to see *Peter*, and abode with him fifteen days." He had heard, undoubtedly, much about Peter. His wonderful sermon on the day of Pentecost had perhaps been often pressed upon his notice before his conversion, and the Christians at Damascus would tell him much about this marvellous Galilean fisherman. Whilst Peter was a special reason for joining the disciples, that would not be the only one. James was there, the Lord's brother, (Gal. i. 18.) His endeavour to get into that new fellowship indicated *a wonderful change in his social character.* Those men he now felt drawn towards, were, three years before, objects of his loathing and indignation. It indicated, too, the *law of social life.* There is a craving for intercourse with those of kindred thoughts, sympathies, and aims. His old social world was gone. He had rushed from it as from a hell. He now seeks another suited to the instincts and appetites of his new nature.

Secondly, *His admission obstructed.* "They were all afraid of him, and believed not that he was a disciple." It would seem that he had no letters of commendation from the Christians at Damascus. The hurried manner in which he escaped thence for his life would account perhaps for the omission. So that we do not wonder at the fear and hesitation of the Jerusalem disciples. Their obstruction must however have been—

(1.) *Painful to him.* He had been three years now connected with the Christian faith. He had held fellowship with the disciples at Damascus, and "preached boldly" there, and had for three years, somewhere in the solitudes of Arabia, studied the Christian faith, and cultivated the Christian life ; so that he must have felt it hard now not to be heartily welcomed by the Church at Jerusalem. Though hard, he must have have felt it just ; and this would make it all the more painful to him. Their obstruction, though thus painful to him—

(2.) *Was natural.* The purity of their fellowship, and the peace of their communion, required that they should always be cautious in the admission of any to their fellowship. And then the apostle's case was a very suspicious one. They must have remembered his history. The "haling men and women to prison," and the martyrdom of Stephen, would be fresh upon their memories. They required, therefore, the strongest evidence, before they would believe that he was a genuine convert to the new faith.

Thirdly, *His admission attained.* His admission to the Church was chiefly effected by the kind offices of Barnabas. He was a man well known to them and honoured by them, for he had demonstrated the sincerity of his faith, he "having land, sold it, and brought the money, and laid it at the apostles' feet." It has been suggested that probably Barnabas and Saul were acquainted with each other before. Cyprus, the home of Barnabas, is within a few hours' sail from Cilicia, the home of Saul. The schools of Tarsus may naturally have attracted one, who though a Levite, was a Hellenist, and there the friendship may have begun which lasted through many vicissitudes, till it was rudely interrupted in the dispute at Antioch. Barnabas in introducing him now to the Church, pleads on his behalf *the only sufficient qualification for church membership.* He "declared unto them how he had seen the Lord in the way, and that he had spoken to him, and how he had preached boldly at Damascus in the name of Jesus." Vital connection with Christ is the true condition of church membership.

Fourthly, *His admission enjoyed.* " He was with them, coming in and going out at Jerusalem." It became his spiritual home; he walked amongst them in all the confidence and liberty of Christian love. He would " come in" to them with some new thought conceived, new impression gained, new deeds wrought for Christ, the narration of which would stimulate and cheer the brethren. He would " go out" with the breath of their prayers, and the word of their counsel and their love fresh on his soul, bracing him for heroic work. Blessed is the man that has a spiritual home. Such homes are scenes where moral giants are trained.

II. HIS FIRST PREACHING OF THE GOSPEL AT JERUSALEM. " He spake boldly in the name of the Lord Jesus." Observe—

First, *The subject of his ministry :* " In the name of the Lord Jesus." As a man of genius and learning, he could have taken to them many subjects. He could have discussed the beauties of their classic literature, charmed them with sketches of their wonderful history, or dilated on the ethics of revelation, the spirituality of the soul, the immortality of man, and other such themes of grandeur. Such subjects would have been acceptable to them ; but he selects a subject which they hated, which he once hated, but which now possessed him,—" Jesus of Nazareth." This became his subject for ever now, He determined to know nothing amongst men but this. He viewed everything through it. He judged the world by it, &c.

Secondly, *The sphere of his ministry :* " The Grecians." Hellenistic Jews were his auditors. The same zeal which had caused his voice to be heard in the synagogues in the persecution against Stephen, now led Saul in these same synagogues to declare fearlessly his adherence to Stephen's cause. His boldness in this was not recklessness. He knew well the spirit of his audience—knew well the fierceness of the flame of anger that his argument would kindle in their hearts.

Thirdly, *The style of his ministry.* It was *brave* and *argumentative.* " He spake boldly." Nothing but an invincible courage could have enabled him to appear before such an audience, with such a subject. His boldness was that of the strongest conviction, founded on irresistible evidence, and backed by his own conscience. He " disputed." He did not, as a fanatic would, pour mere declamation on their ears, but submitted his theses for reasoning and discussion. Those old synagogues are to be honoured for the liberty of speech on sacred themes which they allowed.

Fourthly, *The results of his ministry.* One result was *persecution to himself :* " They went about to slay him." The same fury which had caused the murder of Stephen, now brought one of its accessories to the verge of assassination. Another result was *the increased sympathy of the Church :* "Which when the brethren knew," &c. Like the brethren in Damascus, they, who at first feared to admit him, now eagerly rescued him from the fury of his enemies.

Thus Paul departs from Jerusalem. "Fifteen days" is the measure of his visit and ministry in the metropolis of his country. Though the wrath of man drove him from it, it was according to the plan of heaven concerning him. Whilst praying in the temple one day, he fell into a trance, and Jesus appeared to him and said, "Depart: for I will send thee far hence unto the Gentiles," (Acts xxii. 17, 21.) The account leaves him at Tarsus, the home of his childhood. There he would preach to Gentiles, whom, when he lived there before as a Pharisee, he despised.*

Acts 9:31

PROSPEROUS CHURCHES

"*Then had the churches rest throughout all Judea and Galilee and Samaria, and were edified ; and walking in the fear of the Lord, and in the comfort of the Holy Ghost, were multiplied.*"

EMENDATIVE RENDERING.—" So then the Church had peace throughout all Judea and Galilee and Samaria, being built up and going onward in the fear of the Lord, and was multiplied by the exhortation of the Holy Spirit."—ALFORD.

EXEGETICAL REMARKS.—"*Then had the Churches rest.*" The storm of persecution which Stephen had evoked, and Saul had promoted, and which raged throughout Palestine, has for a while abated. Serenity for a time prevails throughout the Churches. Dr Lardner accounts for this cessation in the following manner :—"Soon after Caligula's accession, the Jews at Alexandria suffered very much from the Egyptians in that city, and at length their oratories there were all destroyed. In the third year of Caligula, A.D. 39, Petronius was sent into Syria, with orders to set up the emperor's statue in the temple at Jerusalem. This order from Caligula was to the Jews a thunder-stroke. The Jews must have been too much engaged after this to mind anything else, as may appear from the accounts which Philo and Josephus have given us of this affair. Josephus says, "That Caligula ordered Petronius to go with an army to Jerusalem, to set up his statue in the temple there ; enjoining him, if the Jews opposed it, to put to death all who made any resistance, and to make all the rest of the nation slaves. Petronius therefore marched from Antioch into Judea with three legions and a large body of auxiliaries raised in Syria. All were hereupon filled with consternation, the army being come as far as Ptolemais." Other reasons might perhaps be suggested : such as the conversion of Paul, the leader of the persecution, and the fact that the great mass of Christians had been driven by the storm into other lands."

* See Conybeare, *in loco.*

HOMILETICS.—The passage leads us to consider PROSPEROUS CHURCHES.

I. THE EXTERNAL CIRCUMSTANCES OF PROSPEROUS CHURCHES : " Rest." The Churches had been in a hurricane of persecution. The storm was now hushed ; and under the genial influences of peace they grew. Peace in the nation is the time for people to build houses and develop their resources. Peace in nature is the time to sow your seed and cultivate your garden. Persecution, like storms, may deepen the roots of piety where it exists, but is unfavourable to the dissemination of seed and the growth of fragile plants.

First, *This external condition Churches in modern England have.* We can sit under our own vine, &c. Once our Churches were very differently circumstanced. Their foundations trembled before the thunders of the Star Chamber and the Inquisition.

Secondly, *This external condition we in England are bound to improve.* Great is our responsibility. All the waste land should be cultivated. Every spot brown with barrenness should be made emerald with life.

II. THE MUTUAL RELATIONSHIP OF PROSPEROUS CHURCHES. There was—

First, *Organic independence.* These Churches are spoken of as distinct ; and they were doubtless distinct organisations, each having its own laws and managing its own affairs, knowing no head but Christ.

Secondly, *Spiritual unity.* They are all spoken of as belonging to *one* generic class, and subject to one general condition, and pursuing the same order of life. There is a vital unity between all true Churches—the unity of Spirit, Aim, Headship. The Churches scattered through all Judea, Galilee, and Samaria were, after all, but members of an invisible spiritual system, of which Christ is the Head. "We are," as Paul has it, "all members of one body," &c. That which really unites Churches is not "unions," "conferences," "synods," "convocations," "alliances," but Christ's Spirit of truth, love, and goodness.

III. THE INTERNAL CONDITION OF PROSPEROUS CHURCHES. "Walking in the fear of the Lord, and in the comfort of the Holy Ghost." This expression implies two things—

First, *Living in godly reverence.* Alford says, it is not "following after the fear," nor "walking according to the fear," nor "advancing in the fear." It is living in the fear of the Lord ; reverential regard for God reigning over the life ; God filling the soul.

Secondly, *Receiving sacred influences* : "By the exhortation of the Holy Spirit." These are the conditions of Church prosperity : reverence for God, and constant participation in divine influence.

IV. THE LEADING SIGNS OF PROSPEROUS CHURCHES. These signs are—

First, *The increase of strength:* "Were edified." The word in the Greek probably refers to both external and internal strength, and accession of grace. Paul commonly uses it of *spiritual* building-up.

Secondly, *The increase of numbers:* "Were multiplied." The multiplying of individuals, and the multiplying of Churches. Strong Churches, like strong nations, will colonise.

Are the Churches in England prosperous? Are they increasing in *strength*—strength of spiritual intelligence, benevolent sympathy, righteous character? Numerically, are they advancing? Not much, we fear. Compared with the growth of the world's wickedness and the increase of its population, the condition of Churches appears anything but prosperous. Why is this? Not for the lack of *Rest!* Why? Let each reader take the question up.

Acts 9:32-35

PETER AT LYDDA

" *And it came to pass, as Peter passed throughout all quarters,[1] he came down also to the saints which dwelt at Lydda. And there he found a certain man named Æneas, which had kept his bed eight years, and was sick of the palsy. And Peter said unto him, Æneas, Jesus Christ maketh thee whole : arise, and make thy bed. And he arose immediately. And all that dwelt at Lydda and Saron saw him, and turned to the Lord.*"

EMENDATIVE RENDERING.—(1.) Passed throughout all believers.

EXEGETICAL REMARKS.—" *Throughout all.*" " It is probable that as soon as the gospel spread in Samaria and Galilee, the apostles began to make circuits from Jerusalem, and visit the churches."—W. and W. Understand των αγιων " among all the saints." During this auspicious period of cessation from persecution Peter undertakes an apostolic journey of visitation and inspection. Some think that the occurrences here related took place during Saul's sojourn in Arabia.

" *He came down also to the saints which dwelt at Lydda.*" This Lydda is Lud in Hebrew, (Ezra ii. 33,) a city inhabited by Benjamites after the captivity—was a few miles east of Joppa, on the way to Jerusalem. It

was burned by the Romans in the war of Judea, but was rebuilt, and called by the Greeks Diospholis—the city of Jupiter. It is now in ruins, but bears the old name. Here Richard Cœur de Lion built a church to St George, the ruins of which are said to be still visible. It is now a considerable village of small houses.

" *And there he found a certain man named Æneas, which had kept his bed eight years, and was sick of the palsy.*" From the name of this paralytic, for such he was, it has been concluded that he was a Hellenist. But the distinguished Trojan hero, whose calamities and adventures are sung by Virgil, bore this name. This man was eight years bedridden.

" *And Peter said unto him, Æneas,*

Jesus Christ maketh thee whole : arise, and make thy bed. And he arose immediately." Here is a miracle of mercy wrought in the name of Christ. Peter was but the instrument, Christ was the agent.

"And all that dwelt at Lydda and Saron saw him, and turned to the Lord." The miracle seems to have been wrought publicly ; the man was well known. *"Saron,"* Hebrew, *Shareni*, was an extensive and fruitful plain, extending from Carmel to the vicinity of Joppa. It was proverbial for the fragrance of its flowers. The miracle which Peter wrought was the occasion of a general conversion to the new religion in that part of the country.

HOMILETICS.—Look at this miracle—

I. AS EXPRESSING THE GENIUS OF CHRISTIANITY. Æneas, a wretched sufferer for eight long years, Peter restored to health. In this he expressed the *benign* spirit of that new religion of which he was an apostle. Christianity is—

First, *The offspring* of mercy. It is a stream from the eternal fountain of love, &c.

Secondly, *The revealer* of mercy. "Herein is love," &c.

Thirdly, The *organ* of mercy. Through it humanity is to be redeemed from all evil, &c. Look at the miracle :—

II. AS SYMBOLISING THE MISSION OF CHRISTIANITY. This was a restorative miracle. The mission of Christianity is *Restorative.* Christ came to seek and to save, &c. The gospel is the *power* of God unto salvation. It does not create new faculties ; it only restores. It restores *souls*—

First, To *God's knowledge.*

Secondly, To *God's fellowship.*

Thirdly, To *God's image.* Look at the miracle—

III. AS INDICATING THE POWER OF CHRISTIANITY. "And Peter said unto him, Æneas, Jesus Christ maketh thee whole : arise, and make thy bed." It is suggested—

First, *That its restorative power is derived from Christ :* "Jesus Christ maketh thee whole." It is not the letter of Christianity that restores, it is the spirit ; and the spirit is Christ.

Secondly, That this restorative power is derived from Christ *by faith.* What brought this power from Christ to Peter ? His faith. Christ's power is with him who believes ; Christ's power is according to faith.

IV. AS REPRESENTING THE INFLUENCE OF CHRISTIANITY: Men "turned to the Lord." To turn to the Lord is to turn :—

First, *From the creature to the Creator.*

Secondly, *From the destroyer to the Restorer.*

Thirdly, *From the wrong and miserable to the holy and happy.*

Acts 9:36-43

DORCAS—THE MINISTRY OF DEATH AND THE MINISTRY OF LIFE

" *Now there was at Joppa a certain disciple named Tabitha, which by interpretation is called Dorcas: this woman was full of good works and almsdeeds which she did. And it came to pass in those days, that she was sick, and died : whom when they had washed, they laid her in an upper chamber. And forasmuch as Lydda was nigh to Joppa, and the disciples had heard that Peter was there, they sent unto him two men desiring him that he would not delay to come to them. Then Peter arose and went with them. When he was come, they brought him into the upper chamber : and all the widows stood by him weeping, and shewing the coats and garments which Dorcas made while she was with them. But Peter put them all forth, and kneeled down, and prayed; and turning him to the body said, Tabitha, arise. And she opened her eyes : and when she saw Peter she sat up. And he gave her his hand, and lifted her up, and when he had called the saints and widows, he presented her alive. And it was known throughout all Joppa; and many believed in the Lord. And it came to pass, that he tarried many days in Joppa with one Simon a tanner.*"

EXEGETICAL REMARKS. — " *There was at Joppa a certain disciple.*" — Joppa, or Jaffa, as it is now called, is one of the oldest towns of Asia, situated on a sandy promontory, jutting out from the eastern coast of the Mediterranean between Cæsarea and Gaza, and thirty-seven miles north-west of Jerusalem. Three of its sides are washed by the sea. It was, and still is, the principal seaport of the land of Judea, and of course of great commercial importance, (2 Chron. ii. 16 ; Ezra iii. 7 ; Jonah i. 3,) but its harbour is bad, and ships generally anchor a mile from the town. Several interesting incidents in Peter's life occurred here, as here and in chap. x. It was also a prominent place in the history of the Crusaders, and in the Egyptian campaign of Bonaparte. The modern city is surrounded by a wall twelve or fourteen feet high, and contains 4000 inhabitants, chiefly Turks and Arabs, and perhaps 600 nominal Christians, (Acts ix. 43.)— EADIE.

" *A certain disciple named Tabitha, which by interpretation is called Dorcas.*" The former is Hebrew, the latter is Greek, signifying gazelle or antelope, a graceful animal to which the Oriental poets frequently liken beautiful women.

" *Full of good works and almsdeeds.*" Her conduct justifies her name, and accounts for the deep interest which her friends and neighbours manifested in her death.

" *Whom they had washed.*" In ancient times it was customary to wash the body before burial. It is customary now amongst some civilised nations. The modern Jews use warm water, with roses and camomile.

" *When he was come, they brought him into the upper chamber.*" The "two men" that were despatched from Joppa to Lydda to invite Peter to visit the dead, succeeded in their mission—he came. He entered the "upper chamber" where the corpse was ready for interment.

" *All the widows stood by him weeping, and shewing the coats and garments which Dorcas made, while she was with them.*" The graphic minuteness of detail imparts to the narrative a charm of reality.

" *But Peter put them all forth,*" &c.

Peter had witnessed his Master do this in the house of Jairus, (Matt. ix. 25; Luke viii. 51.) When the room was cleared he kneeled down "and prayed, and then turning to the dead body he said, Tabitha, arise." "*And she opened her eyes, and when she saw Peter, she sat up. And he gave her his hand, and lifted her up, and when he had called the saints and widows, he presented her alive.*" The resurrection of Tabitha was as little as the cure of Æneas an independent act of Peter as an apostle; it was an act of Christ, for it was an answer to Peter's prayer.

"*Many believed in the Lord.*" This was the moral purpose of the miracle, and it was realised. The apostles were endowed with this power, not for the sake of bringing the dead back to natural life, but in order to win souls to faith and confidence in that Christ who alone can quicken the soul.

HOMILETICS.—In this miraculous incident we see the *ministry of death* and the *ministry of life*.

I. THE MINISTRY OF DEATH. Whilst death is one of the commonest events in human history, and is coeval with the race, it sometimes is associated with circumstances that give it a peculiar impressiveness and significance. It was so now in Joppa. Its victim here was *interesting in person, Christian in character*, and *useful in society*.

First, *Interesting in person.* Dorcas was probably invested with the charm of *beauty*. It is supposed by some that her parents gave her this name on account of the peculiar brightness of her eye and beauty of her form, as the animal from which her name is derived is one of the most graceful and lovely amongst the irrational tribes. She was also probably young. Age had not stolen the brightness from her eye, the bloom from her cheek, or the vigour from her limb. Beautiful and young, yet death assails her, and she falls a ghastly corpse.

Secondly, *Christian in character.* She was a "disciple," not of heathen philosophers nor of Jewish rabbis, but of Jesus Christ. Christ had been preached to her, and she believed in Him, and became His disciple. She is the first woman, after the names in the Gospels, whose name is mentioned in the history of the Church. How her Christian character must have heightened the charms of her personal beauty! What an unearthly dignity it would give to her bearing! what an angelic expression to her countenance! what a magic fascination to her spirit and her words!

Thirdly, *Useful in society.* She did not live to herself. She laid out her energies in the cause of humanity. "This woman was full of good works and almsdeeds which she did." (1.) We learn that her benevolence was *abounding*. "She was full of good works." There was nothing stinted in her charity, nothing narrow in her sympathies. Hers was not that miserable charity which requires constant importuning and impassioned appeals before you can get it to act; not that charity which is constantly calculating how little it can give, and yet be on good terms with conscience.

What she gave, she gave from the spontaneous impulses of her own generous nature; what she gave, she gave with all her heart and to the extent of her means. Her benevolence was an overflowing fountain within. "She was *full* of good works and almsdeeds;" her brain teeming with plans of usefulness that her generous impulses suggested. (2.) Her benevolence was *practical.* It did not expend itself in sentimental sighs or songs, nor in generous promises that ended in words. She worked—worked unostentatiously and perseveringly. She made "coats and garments" for poor widows. She did the work *herself,* she did not, as is customary with many in these days, employ others to do it for her, and feel that she had done her duty by giving a subscription for the purpose; she used her own hands, she plied the needle herself. There is no account that she had any companions in the work to excite and encourage her. Her own generous heart supplied her with all excitement necessary to do the noble service. Greatly was her kindness valued. Poor widows whom she relieved gathered around her lifeless frame "weeping, and shewing the coats and garments which Dorcas made while she was with them." There is a beautiful touch of nature in this. Our appreciation of blessings heightens as they depart. The good deeds of our friends to us come up to memory with a soul-subduing force when we see them in their coffins, or follow them to their graves. Those poor widows never felt the value of those garments as they felt them now. Every stitch became precious to them as they gazed at the fingers that plied the needle now stiff in death. "And all the widows stood by him weeping, and shewing the coats and garments which Dorcas made while she was with them."

Such is the ministry of death before us. Death in every case is terrible, but never does it appear so terrible to us as when it comes and strikes down the interesting in person, the Christian in character, and the useful in social life. The old, the corrupt, the worthless, when they depart, there is much to lament on their behalf, but the world can spare them and go on better without them. Not so the young, the Christian, and the useful. Their death is a loss to the race.

II. THE MINISTRY OF LIFE. Death has done its work on Dorcas. There she lies in an "upper chamber" in her house, washed and laid out, and ready for the grave. Is it all over with Dorcas? Is that fountain of goodness dried up for ever? Will that sweet countenance never beam with life again? Will that frame never be animated any more? Is there nothing stronger than death? "If a man die shall he live again?" "O God, wilt thou show wonders to the dead, shall the dead arise and praise thee?" Powerful as death is, a power has come into the world greater than it, the power of Him "who has abolished death, and brought life and immortality to light." He is the life of man, "the Resurrection and the Life." This life came now to Joppa, and entered the chamber where Dorcas lay dead. And here observe three things—

First, *The organ of this life.* It was not Peter that raised Dorcas; it was Christ in Peter. Peter was the mere instrument, nothing more. The life of Christ was manifest in him, and wrought through him. The Acts of the Apostles are in truth the acts of Christ. The book is as truly a biography of Christ as any of the four Gospels. In the Gospels you have Christ working wonders, speaking divine thoughts, and breathing holiest prayers in the form of *one* man whose nature was untainted by any sin. In the Acts of the Apostles you have the same Christ working miracles, preaching sermons, offering prayers through *many* men whose natures notwithstanding were tainted with moral impurity. Christ was in them; and they felt that it was not they who wrought, but He. It was Christ in Peter that now came to Joppa, entered the chamber where Dorcas lay, witnessed the tears of the weeping widows, and said, "Tabitha, arise," and struck life into her frame. Observe—

Secondly, *The power of this life.* It was stronger than death. It overcame it. Dorcas arose, she opened her eyes, and stood up before the "saints and widows." This display of Christ's power over death is *prophetic.* What He did for Dorcas now, one of His disciples, He will one day do for all His disciples, of every age and clime. He will enter the death chamber of each, and say to each, "Arise," and each will stand forth in a living frame, and die no more. "Behold, I show you a mystery; we shall not all sleep, but we shall all be changed," &c. This display of Christ's power over death is *encouraging.* Awful as death at times appears, I am not left to sink in despair before him as an all-mighty tyrant; he is not all-mighty. Christ, who is our life, He is the all-mighty power. He has the keys of death and hell at His girdle. Observe—

Thirdly, *The blessedness of this life.* The spiritual result of this miracle was that "many believed in the Lord." What does this mean? It means that many dead souls were quickened, that many polluted spirits were cleansed, that many condemned were pardoned. To believe on the Lord is to be translated from darkness to light, from the kingdom of Satan to the kingdom of God, to rise from the miseries of sin to the joys of immortality. A higher blessedness than this there is not for creature spirits. This is the result the miracle produced, and the result it was intended to effect. This subject teaches—

(1.) The immense importance of Christian beneficence. Why was this woman raised from death rather than other Christian disciples, many of whom had died undoubtedly since Christ's ascension to heaven, some of whom perhaps were lying dead at the time that Dorcas was? It would seem that she was selected as the object of this extraordinary blessing on account of her great beneficence, her kindness to the widows. There is no duty more explicitly, frequently, and urgently enforced in the Word of God than that of showing mercy to the poor. How often was this injunction enforced on the Israelites, " Thou shalt not harden thy heart nor shut thy house on thy poor brother ! " In the Old Testament, he to whom life was promised was he who gave bread to the hungry, and covering to the naked. One apostle tells us. " Pure religion and undefiled before God and the Father is this, to visit the fatherless and widows in their affliction." And another exhorts us to bear " one another's burdens, and so fulfil the law of Christ." Christ has told us that it is that *one* thing that will determine man's destiny in eternity. What is the reason that He will say to some " on that day," " Come ye blessed of my Father," &c.? Because they were orthodox in their opinions, bold professors of religion, regular in their attendance at church, punctual in all their religious observances. No ! Here it is, " I was an hungered, and ye gave me meat," &c. Learn—

(2.) The world's obligation to Christ. Had Christ not appeared, there would have been nothing here but the *ministry of death,* covering our heavens with sackcloth, and crushing our spirits into despair. But now we have the *ministry of life.* Those that the prophets and Christ and His apostles raised to life are the proofs of its existence, and the pledges of its universal manifestation.

Acts 10:1-32

PETER'S FIRST GOSPEL SERMON TO THE GENTILE WORLD

1.—*The Supernatural Preparation*

" *There was a certain man in Cæsarea, called Cornelius, a centurion of the band called the Italian band, a devout man, and one that feared God with all his house, which gave much alms to the people, and prayed to God alway. He saw in a vision evidently, about the ninth hour of the day, an angel of God coming in to him, and saying unto him, Cornelius. And when he looked on him, he was afraid, and said, What is it, Lord ? And he said unto him, Thy prayers and thine alms are come up for a memorial before God. And now send men to Joppa, and call for one Simon, whose surname is Peter : he lodgeth with one Simon a tanner, whose house is by the sea-side : he shall tell thee what thou oughtest to do.*[1] *And when the angel which spake unto Cornelius was departed, he called two of his household servants, and a devout soldier of them that waited on him continually ; and when he had declared all these things unto them, he sent them to Joppa. On the morrow, as they went on their journey, and drew nigh unto the city, Peter went up on the house-top to pray about the sixth hour. And he became very hungry, and would have eaten : but, while they made ready, he fell into a trance, and saw heaven opened, and a certain vessel descending unto him, as it had been a great sheet knit at the four corners,[2] and let down to the earth; wherein were all manner of four-footed beasts of the earth, and wild beasts and creeping things, and fowls of the air. And there came a voice to him, Rise, Peter; kill, and eat. But Peter said, Not so, Lord; for I have never eaten anything that is common or unclean. And the voice spake unto him again the second time, What God hath cleansed, that call not thou common. This was done thrice : and the vessel was received up again into heaven. Now, while Peter doubted in himself what this vision which he had seen should mean, behold, the men which were sent from Cornelius had made enquiry for Simon's house, and stood before the gate, and called, and asked whether Simon, which was surnamed Peter, were lodged there. While Peter thought on the vision, the Spirit said unto him, Behold, three men seek thee. Arise therefore, and get thee down, and go with them, doubting nothing : for I have sent them. Then Peter went down to the men which were sent unto him from Cornelius, and said, Behold, I am he whom ye seek : what is the cause wherefore ye are come ?[3] And they said, Cornelius the centurion, a just man, and one that feareth God, and of good report among all the nation of the Jews, was warned from God by an holy angel to send for thee into his house, and to hear words of thee. Then called he them in, and lodged them. And on the morrow Peter went away with them,[4] and certain brethren from Joppa accompanied him. And the morrow after they entered into Cæsarea. And Cornelius waited for them, and had called together his kinsmen and near friends. And as Peter was coming in,[5] Cornelius met him, and fell down at his feet, and worshipped him.[6] But Peter took him up, saying, Stand up; I myself also am a man. And as he talked with him, he went in, and found many that were come together. And he said unto them, Ye know how that it is an unlawful thing for a man that is a Jew to keep company, or come unto one of another nation; but God hath shewed me that I should not call any man common or unclean. Therefore came I unto you without gainsaying, as soon as I was sent for : I ask therefore for what intent ye have sent for me ? And Cornelius said, Four days ago I was fasting until this hour; and at the ninth hour I prayed in my house, and, behold, a man stood before me in bright clothing, and said, Cornelius, thy prayer is heard, and thine alms are had in remembrance in the sight of God. Send therefore to Joppa, and call hither Simon, whose surname is Peter : he is lodged in the house of one Simon a tanner, by the sea-side who, when he cometh, shall speak unto thee."*

EMENDATIVE RENDERINGS.—(1.) Omit these words. (2.) Tied by four rope ends. (3.) Omit these words.—ALF. (4.) And on the morrow he rose up and went away with them. (5.) When Peter had come in. (6.) Omit "him."

EXEGETICAL REMARKS.—"*There was a certain man in Cæsarea*"—a city on the coast of the Mediterranean between Joppa and Tyre, about seventy miles north-west of Jerusalem. It is sometimes called Cæsarea *Palestine*, to distinguish it from Cæsarea *Philippi.* Herod the Great enlarged the city, and gave it its name in honour of Augustus Cæsar, the Roman Emperor. Its inhabitants were chiefly Greeks : it contained a fine harbour, many splendid temples, palaces, and other buildings. It was the seat of the Roman governor, and became the capital of Palestine after the over-

158 / Acts of the Apostles

throw of the Holy City. It was one of the most magnificent cities of the Eastern world. After the destruction of Jerusalem, when Judea became a Roman province, Cæsarea was the chief city of Palestine, (Acts xxiv. 27, xxv. 1-13,) and was often visited by Paul, (Acts ix. 30, xviii. 22, xxi. 8.) It was here that he made his eloquent defence before Felix, Festus, and Agrippa, (Acts xxiii., xxv., xxvi.,) and here he suffered two years' imprisonment. Philip the Evangelist resided here, (Acts xxi. 8.)

"*Called Cornelius, a centurion of the band called the Italian band.*" Cornelius was a centurion of the Italian cohort, which had its name, no doubt, in distinction from these cohorts who were raised in Palestine and Syria, and embodied in the Roman army. It was composed of native Romans, at least Italians, and formed the nucleus of the garrison. Probably the procurator had already taken up his residence in Cæsarea, as the Roman garrison lay there. Cornelius was, without doubt, an Italian by descent.

"*A devout man, and one that feared God, with all his house, which gave alms to the people, and prayed to God alway.*" Though the Almighty Father made special revelations to the Jewish people, He did not neglect Gentile heathendom. Of old He spoke to Abimelech, to Pharaoh, to Nebuchadnezzar, to Job, to the Eastern Magi ; and here is a Pagan soldier, Cornelius, who had learnt from Him the true religion.

"*He saw in a vision evidently, about the ninth hour of the day,*" &c. "There prevails throughout this section a great circumstantiality of detail. The

narrative is limited to a small circle ; but the minutest traits and circumstances, both of time and place, are accurately and carefully given ; and although several times reference is made to earlier incidents, that which had once been told is not assumed to be known by a single reference, but it is repeated on each occasion ; so that the vision which appeared to Cornelius is thrice told, (see ver. 3, 6, 30, 32, xi. 13, 14 ;) as also the vision seen by Peter is likewise recounted three times, (see ver. 10, 16, 28, xi. 5-10.) This striking fulness of detail and circumstance is intended to give us a practical proof of the great importance which the narrator himself ascribed to the subject-matter of this paragraph. . . . First of all there appears to Cornelius, while in a state of trance, an angel, who commands him to send for Peter from Joppa. On the next day, while the centurion's messengers are on their way to Joppa, the equality of the Gentiles with the Jews, in regard to admission to the kingdom of God, is revealed to Peter by means of a symbolical vision. Lastly, a third revelation is made likewise to Peter, which, after the arrival of the messengers, announces their coming to the apostle, and, commands the Spirit, to go with them, nothing doubting. And in perfect correspondence with this miraculous introduction, we have, at the close of the interview between Cornelius and Peter, a divine communication vouchsafed by means of a miraculous speaking with tongues, which really brings about the result to which all these marvels have been pointing—the baptism of the Gentiles by the apostle."—BAUMGARTEN.

HOMILETICS.—This chapter is the record of a new epoch in the development of Christianity. The Gospel crosses the boundary of the Jewish race, enters the Gentile world, and sounds the trumpet of salvation there. Up to this point the apostles had confined their ministry to the seed of Abraham and the Jewish proselytes ; and nothing was more foreign to their views and repugnant to their prejudices than the extension of their mission to the unconverted heathens. But in this chapter we have Peter among the Gentiles, preaching, with all his wonted vigour, the new doctrine.

The general heading which we give to the whole of this chapter and the first eighteen verses of the succeeding one is,—PETER'S FIRST GOSPEL SERMON TO THE GENTILE WORLD. And the whole presents to our notice, five subjects for thought in relation to this first sermon :—First, *The supernatural preparation.* Secondly, *The interesting audience.* Thirdly, *The glorious doctrines.* Fourthly, *The direct results.* And Fifthly, *The ecclesiastical opposition.* The first, namely, THE SUPERNATURAL PREPARATION, is the subject which these thirty-two verses bring under our attention.

The preparation consisted in two things :—

I. IN A MIRACULOUS COMMUNICATION TO CORNELIUS. It required a special divine interposition to prepare in the Gentile world an audience for a gospel sermon, and such interposition occurred in the case of this heathen soldier.

First, He is *visited* by an angel : " He saw in a vision evidently (clearly), about the ninth hour of the day, an angel of God." This celestial messenger approached him in *human* form : " A man stood before me in bright clothing." Thus celestial intelligence appeared in patriarchal times. Painters and poets give us angels with wings, but in few of the records of angelic visits to our world do we find them thus endowed. The appearance of this messenger struck fear into the heart of Cornelius : " He was afraid, and said, What is it, Lord ? " The sentimental may talk about the beauty of angels, but to the heart of man as a sinner their appearance is always connected with terror and alarm.

Secondly, He is *encouraged* by an angel : " And he said unto him, Thy prayers and thine alms are come up for a memorial before God." *Genuine goodness includes piety and philanthropy.* The virtues of man on earth are recognised in heaven. Every breath of prayer, and every generous act, go " up as a memorial before God." The spirit of goodness in man, wherever it exists, moves heavenward, as a sweet curling incense from the altar of the heart. What more encouraging to Cornelius could there be than an assurance that heaven approved of his prayers and his alms ?

Thirdly, He is *directed* by an angel : " Send men to Joppa, and call for one Simon, whose surname is Peter : he lodgeth with one Simon a tanner, whose house is by the sea-side : he shall tell thee what thou oughtest to do." Why not tell it thyself, thou angelic spirit ? Thou knowest perhaps what Cornelius ought to do as well as Peter. *The Gospel is to be preached by men, not angels.* " We have this treasure in earthen vessels."

This supernatural communication answers the end. Cornelius is prompt to obey. No sooner had the angel departed, than " he called two of his household servants, and a devout soldier of them that waited on him continually ; and when he had declared all these things unto them, he sent them to Joppa." · What Abraham is to the Jewish saints, Cornelius is to the Gentile Christians—the first called out miraculously by God—the moral father of the great family. The Gentile is thus prepared to receive the Gospel, and an invitation is sent to its great apostle to come and preach it. The preparation of the heart for the reception of the Gospel is a work for the Lord. When He, the great Husbandman, prepares the soil, the sown seed will germinate and flourish. The preparation for this sermon consisted—

II. IN A MIRACULOUS COMMUNICATION TO PETER : " On the morrow, as they" (viz., the deputation sent from Cornelius) "went on their journey, and drew nigh unto the city, Peter went up upon the house-top to pray," &c., &c.

Observe three things concerning this supernatural communication to Peter—

First, *His spiritual exercise and physical state before it occurred, and his mental state at the time.* (1.) His *spiritual exercise.* He had just been employed in *prayer.* He had gone up to the house-top, the roof, as was usual, "to pray, about the sixth hour ; " that is, about twelve o'clock at noon. He who would see "heaven opened," must pray. Prayer parts the folds of material firmaments. (2.) His *physical state :* "He became very hungry, and would have eaten." , Both his soul and body, therefore, were in a craving state ; his soul craving for communications from God, and his body for sustaining food. (3.) His *mental state :* "He fell into a trance." This is a state of utter abstraction from all external objects ; a state in which the soul is so taken up with its own trains of thought that the senses are sealed to all surrounding objects. It was whilst he was in this state that the vision came. He "saw heaven opened, and a certain vessel descending unto him," &c. There was something of a natural connexion between his physical state of hunger and the creatures that he saw. In God's revelations to man, He allows the human oftentimes to play an important part. The vision was *symbolic.* The vessel may denote the human creation, containing the Jews and the Gentiles ; its descension from heaven indicating that the Gentiles—the "unclean"—had an origin as *divine* as the Jew ; and the command to "kill, and eat," expressing the advent of a dispensation to annul all that was narrow and ceremonial in the Judaic religion. Indeed, taking the human race generally, as they are let down from age to age from heaven to the four corners of the earth, they are like "all manner of four-footed beasts of the earth, and wild beasts, and creeping things, and fowls of the air." They are in some respects as dissimilar as the diverse tribes of the irrational kingdom : yet they are all from heaven. God " hath made of one blood," &c. The vision may teach—

(*a*) *The divine origin of the race.* "All let down" from heaven. Every human birth is a divine emanation. All souls come fresh from God. On this earth there is nothing *new* but souls.

(*b*) *The great diversities in the race.* All manner of "four-footed beasts." Great are the distinctions amongst men—physical, mental, and moral ; yet all from heaven.

(*c*) *The ceremonialisms that divide the race.* They are to be *killed* by the apostles of Christianity. The Gospel is to destroy all these " partition "-walls.

Secondly, *His strong antagonism to the grand purpose of this wonderful vision.* The purpose was to convince him that the Gentile world, which the Jew had esteemed as unclean and profane, was as admissible to the privileges of Christianity as the Hebrew people. Peter's opposition to the idea comes out in the fourteenth verse : " Not so, Lord ; for I have never eaten anything that is common or unclean." He was a Jew that attended rigorously, perhaps, to the Levitical law concerning food : so rigorously, that no hunger would tempt him to an infringement. This repugnance to prohibited food is intended to express the strong prejudice of his soul to the placing of the Gentile on the same ground as the Jew in relation to divine privilege. The fact that the vision occurred " *thrice*," plainly indicates how potent his religious antipathies were.

Thirdly, *The providential agency by which this antagonism was overcome.* While Peter was in *doubt* about the vision, and unable of himself to reach any satisfactory solution, just at *that point* the deputation from Cornelius reached him : " Behold, the men which were sent from Cornelius had made inquiry for Simon's house, and stood before the gate," &c. If our *doubt* is honest, as was Peter's, Providence will send us the interpreter. Providence will make a straight path for the feet of him who, on his way, has reached a point of embarrassment and is earnest for direction. The Spirit wrought with the means : " *While Peter thought on the vision, the Spirit said unto him, Behold, three men 'seek thee.*" Peter's interview with the deputation—their address to him—his entertainment of them for the night—his proceeding with them to Cæsarea on the morrow—his reception by Cornelius—the explanation of his reason for going to Cæsarea and visiting Cornelius, and also the account that Cornelius gave him of the vision he had had four days before, and the influence of it on his mind, are all fully recorded, (ver. 20–33.)

Thus these *two supernatural* communications removed the prejudice of the *Gentile* mind against the Jew, and that of the *Jewish* mind against the Gentile, which were the great barriers to the entrance of the Gospel to the heathen world. All now is ready ; Peter is in the house of Cornelius, who has gathered together a willing audience, and who says to him, " Now therefore are we all here present before God, to hear all things that are commanded thee of God."

Acts 10:33

PETER'S FIRST GOSPEL SERMON TO THE GENTILE WORLD

1.—*A Model Audience*

" *Immediately therefore I sent to thee; and thou hast well done that thou art come. Now therefore, are we all here present before God, to hear all things that are commanded thee of God.*"

EXEGETICAL REMARKS.—" *Thou hast well done.*" A formula of praise. He praises Peter, because he had not delayed to come.

" *Are we all here present.*" Cornelius, in his own house, speaks as if he and his friends were in that of Peter. They had received a religious preparation. The soil was good, and therefore the fruit grew rapidly.

" *Before thee,*" Beng., *God*—the most ancient reading. A transcriber easily mistook τοῦ Θεοῦ, for σοῦ, *thee*, either from the end of the verse, or from ver. 31. (But the common reading, *before God*, is right.—TISCH., ALF.)

" *That are commanded thee.*" It does not appear that Peter had been previously ordered what to say. (For Θεοῦ, *God*, read Κυρίου, the *Lord*.—TISCH., not ALF.)—C. E. T.

HOMILETICS.—The congregation assembled to hear Peter's sermon was composed of Cornelius and his family. Before we proceed to characterise this audience, we may say a word in passing concerning two improper views that have been taken of the piety of Cornelius. (1.) Some have regarded his recorded piety as a sanction for war. It has been said that Cornelius was a soldier, and that the Bible regarded him as a pious man, and, therefore, a soldier's life is divinely right. It is a sufficient answer to this to say that his piety, though genuine, was imperfect: he was only very partially enlightened on the question of duty and religion. Christianity and war are essentially and eternally antagonistic. A Christian soldier is an expression as incongruous and absurd as that of an intellectual fool. (2.) Some have regarded his recorded piety as sufficient to show that the Gospel is not indispensable to man. It has been said that if men can be made good without the Gospel, why, at an immense sacrifice of life and property, prosecute missionary enterprises ? To this we might reply—(*a*) That such a case is impressively exceptional. The appearing of such men as Socrates and Cornelius, in different ages among untold numbers of corrupt and benighted heathens, if rightly considered, tends to demonstrate the insufficiency of natural religion to meet the condition of fallen men. (*b*) That such men probably became what they were by the influence which the facts of revelation exerted on their minds. Cornelius, living in a city where there were so many Jews, and so near to Jerusalem, would not only know the leading facts of the Jewish religion, but would have heard a great deal about the history of Christ, the wonders of Pentecost, the martyrdom of Stephen, the conversion of Saul, and other facts connected with the new religion.

Concerning this MODEL CONGREGATION there are three remarks suggested :—

I. IT WAS EARNEST. Its earnestness is obvious from two circumstances—

First, *The religious character that is given to it.* It was composed of Cornelius and the members of his family. And in the second verse we are told that " he was a devout man, and feared God with all his house, which gave alms to the people, and prayed to God alway." His religion was *domestic*—" all his house ;" *generous*—" he gave alms to the people; " *habitual*—" he prayed to God alway." The religious spirit therefore pervaded this audience. There were no frivolous or volatile spirits amongst Peter's listeners.

Secondly, *The invitation they give the preacher :* " Immediately therefore I sent to thee." Messengers from Cæsarea were dispatched to Joppa requesting Peter to come. The centurion's messengers knocking at Peter's door have been represented as proud heathenism knocking at the gates of Christ's kingdom. " The embassy from Cæsarea to Joppa," says Lechler and Gerok, " is, first, a sad testimony of the poverty of heathenism ; secondly, an honourable testimony for the Gospel ; thirdly, a glorious testimony that God will have all men to be saved." Another remark suggested concerning this model congregation is—

II. IT WAS SOLEMN : " Now therefore are we all here present *before God.*" The expression " *before God,*" implies—

First, *Belief in the existence of the one God.* Cornelius and his house believed in the one absolute and eternal God, Creator of heaven and earth, &c. They were neither atheists, pantheists, nor polytheists.

Secondly, *Belief in the presence of the one God.* He is here : He, not merely His influence, but He himself, here in this room. We are " *before*" Him.

Thirdly, *Belief in the claim of the one God.* We are before Him ; He is our Maker, Proprietor, Sustainer, Judge ; demanding the homage of our souls ; and we must be sincere, serious, and devout.

They all had a *consciousness of God's presence.* They felt themselves in God's sight. Such a consciousness as this would not only sweep from their minds for the time all that was secular, sceptical, and frivolous in thought, but fill them with a profound *solemnity.* Would that all congregations had this consciousness ! Another remark suggested concerning this model congregation is—

III. IT WAS INQUIRING : " To hear all things that are commanded thee of God." They were assembled, not as a matter of *custom*, not to sit passive, to be acted upon by the speaker, not for a mere performance, but to *inquire*.

First, They were *profoundly religious* in their inquiry. They were in quest of the divine: " Commanded thee of God." They were not seekers after a knowledge of Peter's private speculations, or of aught that was human in thought. They desired information concerning the *divine* will. " Lord, what wilt Thou have me to do ? " This was their spirit.

Secondly, They were *thoroughly free* in their inquiry : " To hear *all* things." Their minds were untrammelled by prejudices, unbiassed by theological dogmas. They wanted to know " *all* "—the " whole counsel of God."

May not such a congregation as this be justly regarded as model ? Such a congregation as this methinks would not tolerate the pulpit crudities, the priestly assumptions and fooleries, of these modern times.

Acts 10:34-43

PETER'S FIRST GOSPEL SERMON TO THE GENTILE WORLD

3.—*The Glorious Doctrines*

" *Then Peter opened his mouth, and said, Of a truth I perceive that God is no respecter of persons : but in every nation he that feareth Him, and worketh righteousness, is accepted with Him. The word which God sent unto the children of Israel, preaching peace by Jesus Christ; (He is Lord of all ;)*[1] *that word, I say, ye know, which was published*[2] *throughout all Judea, and began from Galilee, after the baptism which John preached ; how God anointed Jesus of Nazareth*[3] *with the Holy Ghost, and with power ; and went about doing good, and healing all that were oppressed of the devil : for God was with Him. And we are witnesses of all things which He did, both in the land of the Jews, and in Jerusalem; whom they slew, and hanged on a tree :*[4] *Him God raised up the third day, and shewed Him openly ;*[5] *not to all the people, but unto witnesses chosen before of God, even to us, who did eat and drink with Him after He rose from the dead. And He commanded us to preach unto the people, and to testify that it is He which was ordained of God to be the Judge of quick and dead.*[6] *To Him give all the prophets witness, that, through His name, whosoever believeth in Him shall receive remission of sins.*"

EMENDATIVE RENDERINGS.—(1.) All men. (2.) Ye know the matter which was published.—ALF. (3.) Jesus of Nazareth, how that God anointed Him.—ALF. (4.) And we are witnesses of all things which He did, both in the land of the Jews and in Jerusalem ; whom they slew by hanging on a tree.—H. B. HALL. (5.) Permitted Him to become manifest.—ALF. (6.) Which is ordained by God, which is Judge of quick and dead.—ALF.

EXEGETICAL REMARKS.—" *Is no respecter of persons.*" " This is a single word in Greek, which, with the cognate forms, respect of persons, and to respect persons, is of Hebrew origin, and relates to judicial partiality, or the preference of one party to another, upon other grounds than those of right and justice. The same thing is repeatedly denied of God in Scripture, (Deut. x. 17 ; 2 Sam. xiv. 14 ; 2 Chron. xix. 7 ; 1 Peter i. 17,) and prohibited to man, (Lev. xix. 15 ; Deut. i. 17 ; xvi. 19 ; James ii. 1–9)." —ALEXANDER.

" *The word which God sent unto the children of Israel,*" *&c.* This word is the Gospel, (see Acts xiii. 26.) " The construction of verses 36–38, in which Peter recalls the chief facts of the life of Jesus as being to his hearers not entirely unknown, is somewhat loose. There are three successive sentences, to each of which ὑμεῖς οἴδα τε belong as the governing words. What the hearers already knew in a general way is indicated in a threefold manner :— 1. As the word of a message of God to the Israelites, τον λόγον, &c., (ver. 36 ;) 2. As an historical event, το γενόμενον ῥῆμα, &c., (ver. 37 ;) 3. As the person of Jesus of Nazareth, Ἰησοῦ, &c., (ver. 38.) This is undeniably a climax. Peter supposes that the history of Jesus was not altogether strange to His hearers, although Gentiles, partly by reason of their residence at Cæsarea in the Holy Land, and partly by reason of their religious disposition and susceptibility ; and that it had come within the sphere of their observation—(*a*) as a word addressed to the Israelites ; (*b*) as an occurrence in the land in which they dwelt ; and (*c*) as the appearance of the divine person of Jesus of Nazareth."

" *We are witnesses of all things,*" *&c.* Cornelius and the other members of Peter's auditory might have known the things of which Peter spoke by report ; but Peter and his fellow-labourers were " witnesses" of those things. The " things " were the great facts of Christ's history.

" *Whom they slew, and hanged on a tree, him God raised up on the third day.*" Striking contrast here between man's treatment of Christ and God's. Man crucified Him, hanged Him on a tree. God raised Him from the dead.

" *Shewed him openly, not to all the people.*" Referring undoubtedly to the many appearances of Christ after His resurrection from the dead,—appearances made, not to the people generally, but to His disciples exclusively.

" *And He commanded us to preach unto the people,*" *&c.* He—God, (chap. v. 29.) " *Unto the people.*" This corresponds to the commencement of ver. 41.

" *To testify*"—understand.

" *Even to the Gentiles,*" (chap. i. 8 ; Matt. xxviii. 19.)

" *Ordained*"—by an unchangeable decree.

" *Judge.*" This name by *synedoche* (a part of the whole) implies all the glory of Christ, and in reference to believers, signifies the consummation of Christ's benefits, (2 Tim. iv. 8. Comp. Heb. xii. 23.) He will judge the Jews who condemned Him ; the Romans who were in possession of Cæsarea, the seat of the Jewish government ; the dead, from among whom He arose, who will also rise again in due time, (1 Pet. iv. 5. Comp. chap. xvii. 31.) So the Lord Jesus also testified of Himself as the Judge, before He mentioned His own ascension, (John v. 22.)—C. E. T.

HOMILETICS.—" Then Peter opened his mouth." Here is an epoch in the annals of the race. Next to the incarnation of Christ, the day of Pentecost, and the conversion of Saul, in grand historic magnitude and influence, stands this sermon of Peter to the Gentile world. What are the doctrines of this sermon ?

First, *The absolute impartiality of God.*
Secondly, *The necessary elements of moral goodness.*
Thirdly, *The Mediatorship of Christ.*

I. The absolute impartiality of God : "God is no respecter of persons." These words do not teach either of the three following things :—(1.) That God pays no regard to men at all. The deist would have us to believe this. Reason, consciousness, analogy, and the Bible, however, refute this. The words do not teach, (2.) That God looks at men indiscriminately—regards them merely in the mass. No ; He looks at each individually. The words do not teach, (3.) That God bestows blessings on some which He imparts not to others. This is a manifest truth. He has given to each some distinguishing blessing of mind, body, or estate. But this is not what they mean. What, then, do they mean ?

First, *That God does not respect persons in the same sense that man does.* (1.) Man's respect for persons is very limited. How little man knows of his race. God knows the millions—knows all. (2.) Man's respect for persons is very superficial. He judgeth from appearance. God looks to the heart. (3.) Man's respect for man is selfish. Man respects another because of his disposition or capacity to help him. Not so with God. (4.) Man's respect for man is popular. Man respects the man whom the multitudes applaud. (5.) Man's respect for man is adventitious. It is because of what he *has*, rather than what he *is*.

Secondly, *That God does not respect persons in the sense of disturbing for any the settled conditions of happiness.* The conditions of health, intellectual development, and spiritual training are the same to all.

Thirdly, *That God does not respect persons in the sense of limiting His salvation to any particular class.* This is no doubt the sense in which the apostle now employed the words. God's provisions of mercy are for the world :—(1.) The merits of the atonement are sufficient for all. (2.) The force of moral motive is adapted to all. (3.) The agency of the Spirit is available to all.

What a change in the mind the announcement of this great truth indicates ! Peter's soul has broken through all the cerements of old prejudices, and, inspired with the free spirit of the Gospel, he looks upon *all* nations as *equal* in the eye of God. " God is no respecter of persons." Grand truth this !—a truth which, like the pillar that guided the Israelites in the wilderness, has a bright and a dark side ; —a dark side toward the ungodly among the worldly great, a bright side to the godly among the worldly poor.

II. The necessary element of moral goodness : "He that feareth God and worketh righteousness." "Feareth God." The fear here of course is not the servile, but the *filial ;* it is the fear of a love "that casteth out" all slavish feeling. The word stands here, as in numerous other places in the Bible, to represent that state of mind which God requires from every man. It means *godliness.* It exists nowhere where there is not a supreme love for the Supremely Good.

It is a fear that "worketh *righteousness.*" The "fear" must be of that character which inspires and secures obedience to the everlasting laws of right,—leads to a right conduct in relation to man, God, and the universe,—right both in relation to earth and in relation to heaven. There is a fear towards God that worketh *nothing.* It is inoperative. It just touches the soul occasionally, and goes off in a sigh. There is a fear that worketh *wrong.* It is a superstitious feeling that leads to an unnatural and an intolerant life. There is a fear that worketh *right.* This alone is the genuine thing. This is the essence of moral goodness.

Now Peter says that this is that in man which God accepts and respects wherever it is found. He does not accept a man because of his Judaism or his Gentilism ; not because of his birth, his country, or his particular form of worship; not because he lives in heathendom or Christendom ; but because of his moral rectitude. He that is right, whether he be a Socrates or a Paul, a Cornelius or a John, is accepted of Him. For no other reason will God accept man. The Bible is full of this truth : 2 Kings xxii. 19 ; Ps. xxxiv. 18, lii. 15-19 ; Deut. x. 12 ; 1 Sam. xv. 22 ; Hosea vi. 6 ; Micah vi. 8 ; Matt. v. 8.

III. THE MEDIATORSHIP OF CHRIST. Peter goes on to refer to that "Word," that Gospel which is God's instrument to generate in humanity this *rectitude* of soul. "The Word which God sent unto the children of Israel, preaching peace by Jesus Christ," &c. &c. What he says about the mission of Christ here is, in substance, the same as he proclaimed in his discourse on the day of Pentecost. He shows—(1.) that His mission was divine in its origin; (2.) redemptive in its purpose; (3.) universal in its aspect; (4.) involving His death upon the cross by the hands of wicked men, and His resurrection from the dead by the interposition of Almighty God. Every sentence of the apostle's discourse is fraught with significance, and would repay the minutest examination. When Peter now "opened his mouth" he poured forth a mighty stream of truth, which divides itself into numerous branches, that wind into districts of soul-stirring interest and sublimity.

Acts 10:44-48

PETER'S FIRST GOSPEL SERMON TO THE GENTILES

4.—The Direct Results

" *While Peter yet spake these words, the Holy Ghost fell on all them which heard the word. And they of the circumcision which believed were astonished, as many as came with Peter, because that on the Gentiles also was poured out the gift of the Holy Ghost. For they heard them speak with tongues, and magnify God. Then answered Peter, Can any man forbid water,¹ that these should not be baptized, which have received the Holy Ghost as well as we ? And he commanded them to be baptized in the name of the Lord. Then prayed they him to tarry certain days."*

EMENDATIVE RENDERING.—(1.) The water ·

EXEGETICAL REMARKS.—" *The Holy Ghost fell.*" The Jewish doctors taught that the Holy Spirit would neither dwell upon any heathen nor on any Jew in a heathen country. The Divine Spirit, it would seem, came upon the audience while Peter was preaching, in some audible and visible form —came in a similar way to His advent upon the day of Pentecost. His manifestation now was a testimony from Heaven that Gentiles as well as Jews might enter the divine kingdom.

" *They of the circumcision,*" &c. These were, no doubt, the companions of Peter from Joppa, who were Jews. They were astonished. Though they had believed, received Christianity, they were astonished, which shows how difficult it is to shake off an old prejudice.

" *They heard them speak with tongues, and magnify God.*" "There was no room for doubt," says a modern expositor, "as to the fact that the Spirit had been given, as there might have been in the case of mere internal spiritual changes. These were likewise wrought, as in every case of genuine conversion : but besides these, there were other gifts imparted, which were cognisable by the senses, and thus served as incontrovertible proofs of what had taken place. The one here mentioned is the gift of tongues, the same with that described in chap. ii. 4, notwithstanding the omission of the epithet there used, (other,) which, so far from implying a difference between the cases, is a mere abbreviation,

tacitly referring to the more complete description previously given. Here again it seems still more evident than in the other case, that the gift of tongues was not intended merely as a practical convenience, but as a miraculous token of God's presence, and a type of the reconciliation between Jew and Gentile, whose alienation had for ages been secured and symbolised by difference of language. They did not merely hear them say they had received the Holy Spirit : *they heard them* (actually) *speaking with tongues,* (*i.e.,* in foreign languages,) not unintelligibly or at random, but like the disciples on the day of Pentecost, in praise of God. This occasion has been well styled the Gentile Pentecost."

" *Can any forbid water ?*" ὕδωρ, the water. It means the water suitable for baptism. "Ordinarily baptism was administered before the advent of the Holy Ghost. But in this instance there was room for doubting whether they should be baptized without circumcision ; and so it fell immediately upon those who heard the Word, teaching us that the Holy Spirit can dispense with water-baptism at His pleasure, and warning the Church not to put baptism in the place once held by circumcision."—ALF. The expression, " *Can any forbid water ?*" conveys the idea that water was to be brought to them, and not they to the water.

" *Commanded them to be baptized.*" It will be seen from this that the apostle did not baptize himself, but left the work for others.

HOMILETICS.—These words bring under our notice the *immediate* results of this, Peter's first Gospel sermon to the Gentiles.

I. THE EFFUSION OF THE HOLY SPIRIT. There are two expressions used to represent the advent of the Spirit on this occasion. It is said the Holy Ghost "fell." The influence came from above. It is said that it was "poured out," conveying the same idea,—that it came from above. Two facts are stated—

First, *That it came to those who heard the Word.* The Divine Spirit, in its regenerating and redemptive influences, ever goes with the Word. The Gospel is the channel through which its holy influences flow to the soul. The Gospel is the chariot on which the Divine Conqueror goes forth to crush the enemies of the human soul, and to bring it forth to freedom, to light, and to glory. It is true that God's Spirit works through *all* nature for various purposes ; but for the grand purpose of *spiritual salvation* it works through the Gospel.

Secondly, *That it produced miraculous as well as moral effects.* Those who were the recipients spoke with "*tongues.*" In what particular language they expressed their feelings of gratitude and praise to God we are not told. Now, as on the day of Pentecost, souls had new thoughts and emotions, and they require a new dialect.* Change the thoughts and emotions of the world, and you will change the language of the world.

II. THE ADMINISTRATION OF BAPTISM. "Can any forbid water?" From what is here said about baptism we conclude—

First, *That baptism is a sign of a spiritual good.* They were to be baptized *after* they had received the Holy Ghost. The application of water to the person was a symbol of the action of the Divine Spirit on the soul ; not only, perhaps, in its cleansing influence, but also in its mode of communication, for the Spirit is here represented as being "poured out."

Secondly, *That baptism is a ceremony of easy observance.* "Can any forbid the water?" The language implies—(1.) That the water was in the house of Cornelius ; (2.) That the water could be brought to the parties. Christianity is a universal system, and any ordinance attached to it that cannot be attended to anywhere and at all times, has no vital connexion with it ; it is a mere fungus.

Thirdly, *That baptism is a service of subordinate importance.* "He commanded them to be baptized." Peter does not do it himself ; He has a *higher* work. It is said "that Christ baptized not," (John iv. 3,) and Paul said, "Christ sent me not to baptize, but to preach the Gospel." There is nothing vital about the ordinance.

* See p. 27.

Acts 11:1-18

PETER'S FIRST GOSPEL SERMON TO THE GENTILES

5.—*The Ecclesiastical Opposition*

"*And the apostles and brethren that were in Judœa heard that the Gentiles had also received the word of God. And when Peter was come up to Jerusalem, they that were of the circumcision contended with him, saying, Thou wentest in to men uncircumcised, and didst eat with them. But Peter rehearsed the matter from the beginning, and expounded it by order unto them,[1] saying, I was in the city of Joppa praying: and in a trance I saw a vision, A certain vessel descend, as it had been a great sheet, let down from heaven by four corners;[2] and it came even to me: Upon the which when I had fastened mine eyes, I considered, and saw four-footed beasts of the earth, and wild beasts, and creeping things, and fowls of the air.[3] And I heard a voice saying unto me, Arise, Peter; slay, and eat. But I said, Not so, Lord: for nothing common or unclean hath at any time entered into my mouth. But the voice answered me again from heaven, What God hath cleansed, that call not thou common.[4] And this was done three times: and all were drawn up again into heaven. And, behold, immediately there were three men already come unto the house where I was, sent from Cœsarea unto me. And the Spirit bade me go with them, nothing doubting. Moreover, these six brethren accompanied me, and we entered into the man's house: And he shewed us how he had seen an angel[5] in his house, which stood and said unto him, Send men to Joppa, and call for Simon, whose surname is Peter; who shall tell thee words, whereby thou and all thy house shall be saved. And as I began to speak, the Holy Ghost fell on me, as on us at the beginning. Then remembered I the word of the Lord, how that he said, John indeed baptized with water; but ye shall be baptized with the Holy Ghost. Forasmuch then as God gave them the like gift as he did unto us, who believed[6] on the Lord Jesus Christ, what was I, that I could withstand God? When they heard these things, they held their peace, and glorified God, saying, Then hath God also to the Gentiles granted repentance unto life.*

EMENDATIVE RENDERINGS.—(1.) But Peter began and rehearsed unto them in order.—ALF. (2.) Ropes.—ALF. (3.) Saw the four-footed beasts of the earth, and the wild beasts, and the creeping things, and the fowls of the air.—ALF. (4.) What things God hath cleansed, those call not thou common.—ALF. (5.) The angel.—(6.) When we believed.—ALF.

EXEGETICAL REMARKS. — These verses should not have been divided by the commencement of a new chapter from what goes before. They are the continuation of the same narrative, the sequel of the story of Cornelius.

"*And the apostles and brethren that were in Judœa, heard,*" &c. The de-scent of the Holy Spirit on the Gentiles at Cæsarea, and their reception into the Church, was an event so extraordinary that the tidings of it would soon reach the ears of the other "*apostles and brethren,*" who were still resident in Judœa.

"*They that were of the circumcision.*" These were not merely Jews, for all the Church at Jerusalem was circumcised, but those converted Jews who attached too much importance to the Jewish ceremonies. They were those who, notwithstanding their adhesion to the gospel, still regarded circumcision as a duty not to be dispensed with.

" *Contended with him.*" This shows that the apostles and early Christians did not regard Peter as having any particular supremacy over the Church. Had they regarded him as being in a particular sense the vicar of Christ upon earth, they would not have questioned the propriety of his conduct.

"*But Peter rehearsed the matter from the beginning.*" His defence is a bare historical recital of the facts, with a concluding question showing how they bore upon the point in question.

" *I was in the city of Joppa praying,*" &c. &c. The fact stated in these verses, 5-14, we have already noticed in chap. x. 9-43. " The variations in this form," says an able expositor of the narrative, "from those preceding, although unessential, are not unworthy of attention, as indicative of conscious accuracy in the writer, with a certain freedom from restraint as to the mere form of expression or minute details."

" *The Holy Ghost fell on them as on us at the beginning.*" " The figure of falling, as in chap. x. 10, denotes an influence or impulse from above, *i.e.* from a superior power. It is also worthy of remark, that in this baptism of the Spirit, the act described is that of pouring, not of plunging or immersing. *The Holy Spirit* is expressed in the original very emphatically and precisely, *the Spirit, the*

Holy (One). The words *as also* (ὥσπερ καί) mean *as really,* and *as evidently,* as on us, *i.e.* on the apostles and first converts on the day of Pentecost. This is here called *the beginning* of the Christian dispensation or the Christian Church, which dates from the effusion of the Holy Ghost at that time, corresponding to the organisation of the Mosaic Church by the Theophany and giving of the law at Sinai, which Pentecost, according to a highly probable tradition of the Jews, was partly instituted to commemorate."—ALEXANDER.

" *Forasmuch then as God gave them the like gift as he did unto us, who believed on the Lord Jesus Christ ; what was I that I could withstand God ?* " " The argument is, as the Lord has granted to them the same baptism of the Holy Ghost as to us, they are therefore to be reckoned among *us.* As they are included in the Βαπτισθήσεσθε, they were included in the *ὑμεῖς.*"—WEBSTER and WILKINSON.

" *When they heard these things they held their peace.*" His argument was conclusive and satisfactory ; and more than this, for it is said *they glorified God,* "they devoutly rejoiced in the new conviction that God had also *to the Gentiles granted repentance unto life.*" In consequence of Peter's statement, " the objectors not only expressed themselves satisfied, (ἡσύχασαν,) so that they in silence withdrew their reproaches, but they glorified God, because that God had also to the Gentiles given repentance unto life. The distinction of time between ἡσύχασαν and ἐδόξαζον gives us to understand, that the pacification of the opponents was instantaneous, whilst their thanks and praise to God were enduring."— LECHLER and GEROK.

HOMILETICS.—This first sermon of Peter to the Gentiles in the house of Cornelius at Cæsarea created, as we have already stated, a new epoch in the history of the world. It was the breaking of the Gospel-day over the gloomy hills of heathendom. It was the first battle in that bloodless campaign which will give to Christ " the heathen for *his* inheritance, and the uttermost parts of the earth for *his* possession." It shattered that huge partition-wall of ceremony which divided the Israelitish people from all other races of mankind. It gave the shock of an earthquake to the old prejudices of the Jews.

It awoke a controversy in the Church which raged for centuries, and has left a permanent impression in the records of Christendom. The Jews claimed the Messiah as all their own. They considered that if the Gentiles were blessed by Him, they could only be blessed by first becoming Jews—that they must bow to the yoke of Moses before they could reach the liberty of Christ. Even those of them who had been converted to Christianity felt this at first. Nor did the apostles easily free themselves from this national prejudice.

The paragraph before us is the sequel of the story of Cornelius given in the preceding chapter. It gives us an insight into the state of mind which Peter's sermon to the Gentiles produced in the Jewish Christians, and details the method by which he justified his conduct to them, and got them to acquiesce in what he had done. In it we discover four things worthy of attention—*a striking imperfection in the first church; a great man censured for a noble work; an inspired apostle conciliating his brethren; and a glorious victory over an old prejudice.*

We have here—

I. A STRIKING IMPERFECTION IN THE FIRST CHURCH. " And the apostles and brethren that were in Judæa heard that the Gentiles had also received the word of God. And when Peter was come up to Jerusalem, they that were of the circumcision contended with him, saying, Thou wentest in to men uncircumcised, and didst eat with them." The first Church was that at Jerusalem; there the disciples met before the day of Pentecost; there the first Gospel sermon was preached, when thousands were converted. Jerusalem was the mother Church of Christendom, and its members, up to this hour, were all converts from Judaism to the new faith. They were Christian Jews, who " were of the circumcision," and who not only had been circumcised themselves, but looked on circumcision as an obligation never to be abrogated. The members of this Church, made up of " apostles and brethren," very soon heard of what Peter had done in Cæsarea in eating with the Gentiles, preaching to the Gentiles, and baptizing the Gentiles. A fact so extraordinary and so opposed to all that was tender and strong in Jewish feeling, would, even in those distant days, without railroad or telegraph, rapidly spread from district to district, until it reached the metropolis of the country. They soon heard, therefore, " that the Gentiles had also received the word of God." The " word of God"—the Gospel—the sublimest utterance of the Divine mind.

The point here to be observed is, *the highly improper state of mind* which this information evoked in this *first* Church. They " contended with him, saying, Thou wentest in to men uncircumcised, and didst eat with them." Instead of *rejoicing* at the event, and congratulating him in the name of God, they called him to account and treated him as a criminal. Now, beyond all controversy, this state of mind was unworthy their profession, and utterly unchristian. The discovery of such imperfection in this mother Church is not without its lessons. It teaches—

First, *That antiquity in ecclesiastical matters is no infallible authority.* There are sections of the Church of Christ—the Romish and the Anglican, for example—that are constantly directing us to the ancient and patristic in order to attain a final settlement of all disputed questions in religion. Nay, more, there are men of such antiquarian proclivities in connexion with every section of the Church, who are everlastingly referring us to the past for the unerring and the perfect. Now, the fact that we discover imperfection in the very first Church, formed and taught by the inspired apostles, is sufficient to expose the folly of such conduct, and to shake faith in the infallibility of all ancient Churches. The fact is, that while infallibility dwells in no Church, it is far more reasonable to look to the most modern than to the most ancient for it ; for the more modern the Church, the greater its facilities for reaching certitude. Infallibility, however, dwells *only* in the Head, Jesus, the Son of God. It teaches—

Secondly, *That Christianity does not perfect its disciples at once.* These "apostles and brethren" were, of course, converted men. They were genuine disciples ; albeit, not perfect. They had many errors to correct, many old prejudices to uproot, many unvirtuous habits to overcome. Hence there were disputes even among the apostles, and fierce controversies raged among the first Churches. The fact is, Christian excellence is a growth, only the germ of which is given in conversion ; and unless the soil is well looked after, and the noxious weeded out, it will continue a frail and imperfect thing. Instead of the oak braving the tempest, it will be the sapling bending to the zephyr. Instead of the man, firm in limb and heroic in temper, it will remain the child, feeble in body, peevish and petulant in soul. Hence the work that is urged upon every disciple is to " grow in grace, and in the knowledge of our Lord and Saviour Jesus Christ."

We have here—

II. A GREAT MAN CENSURED FOR A NOBLE WORK. A nobler work than that which Peter wrought when, having come from Joppa to Cæsarea, he entered the house of Cornelius, and there preached the Gospel of Christ and baptized the converts, was never achieved by mortal. That work was full of God ; God inspired, guided, and strengthened him. That work was the opening of the fountain of life in the barren wilds of paganism ; the planting of the Sun of Righteousness in the black firmament of heathendom. Yet for this noble work there were men who censured him. " Thou wentest in to men uncircumcised, and didst eat with them." Instead of rapturous congratulation, here is the snarl of discontent. We are not to suppose that this is all they said to him, nor is it necessary to suppose that they uttered these very words ; but this was the pith of the censure. There is something *à fortiori* suggested, as if they had said—" To enter the house of Gentiles and to eat with them is an enormity, but how much more heinous the offence of placing them on a religious equality with the Jew, preaching the Gospel to them, and baptizing them in the Christian faith." We may rest assured there was a great deal of that miserable, narrow, and malign feeling peculiar to intolerant religionists expressed to Peter on this occasion. We may learn from the censure of these Christians at Jerusalem—

First, *That Peter was not regarded as an infallible dictator in spiritual matters.* The circumstance that he is here called to account by the whole body of Christians, goes certainly against the assumption that he was the vicar of Christ—a pope. " Call no man Rabbi : One is your Master, even Christ."

Secondly, *That men's works must not be determined by the judgment of contemporaries.* The sublimest works of the divinest workers on earth have generally met with censures from contemporaries. Men ahead of their time generally awaken envy and alarm. The greatest theological writers were heretics to the men of their age. The greatest religious heroes were martyred by their contemporaries. Preachers that woke the world to a new life were branded as fanatics. Do a great work, brother, and the great serpent of evil that winds around thy path will hiss at thee at every step.

We have here—

III. AN INSPIRED APOSTLE CONCILIATING HIS BRETHREN. How did Peter treat these fault-finders ? With the haughtiness of modern primacy ? There was nothing of the *primate* in this apostle. Peter might have utterly disregarded their remarks, heard them with silence, and withdrawn in contempt ; or he might have denounced them on account of their ingratitude and narrow sectarianism. Many, perhaps most, he had converted—given them, under God, the new life that they had—and their obligations to him should have made them cautious and respectful in pronouncing upon his conduct. But he listens to them attentively ; speaks, but when he speaks not a whisper of censure escapes his lips. He is calm, generous, dignified in what he says ; and he says that which was most adapted to justify himself and conciliate them. He does two things.

First, *He recites facts.* He gives a clear, brief, telling history of the circumstances that induced him to visit the Gentiles with the Gospel, the reception he met with, and the spiritual influences that attended his sermon. His account differs a little in form from the facts recorded in the preceding chapter ; but the difference being simply formal, serves to show his consciousness of accuracy, and the freedom he allowed himself in the communication of Divine realities. It is noteworthy that the apostle gives no account whatever of his sermon at Cæsarea. One might have expected that a discourse that was attended with such wonders would have been referred to on this occasion. Not so! He utters not a syllable about it. He bases his defence not upon what *he said*, but upon what *God did*. This retiçency of his concerning his sermon—(1.) *indicates his own modesty ;* and (2.) *rebukes vanity in preachers*.

Secondly, *He makes an appeal.* "Forasmuch then as God gave them the like gift as he did unto us, who believed on the Lord Jesus Christ ; what was I, that I could withstand God?" This is the logic of his address. He regarded the facts as showing unmistakably that it was God's will that the Gentiles should have the Gospel, and that therefore it would have been the utmost presumption on his part to have attempted to withstand that will. "What was I, that I could withstand God?" It was God who urged me to it; could *I* resist Him? Who was *I?* Was *I* powerful enough to hinder God?

Could anything be more adapted to win the hostile brethren over to his views on the question than this address, consisting of an unvarnished statement of Divine facts with their necessary moral inference? Facts are stubborn things, it has been said ; so they are. They will not move an inch for you. They stand unmoved as the mountains amidst the thunders of the Vatican. If when you are accused you have facts on your side, you need not fear ; you may rest on them as on a rock.

We have here—

III. A GLORIOUS VICTORY OVER AN OLD PREJUDICE. "When they heard these things, they held their peace, and glorified God, saying, Then hath God also to the Gentiles granted repentance unto life." From this we learn—

First, *They heartily acquiesced in the fact.* "They held their peace." They ceased to censure and to chide ; they felt that the apostle had done the right thing—that he had moved as God willed it. Every ground of opposition was gone—hushed were all contentious elements.

Secondly, *They devoutly rejoiced in the fact.* "They glorified God." They more than acquiesced ; they thrilled with a religious joy. That which had just before pained them, now filled them with delight. A spirit of universal brotherhood expelled, for a time, all the narrow feelings of nationality and sect.

Thirdly. *They joyfully declared the fact.* "Then hath God also to the Gentiles granted repentance unto life." "Repentance unto life" —stages in the way to a happy destiny; reformation, progress, and blessedness. Or the words may be regarded as implying three things, as—(1.) Salvation is the life of man ; (2.) Repentance is essential to salvation ; (3.) Repentance is the gift of God through the Gospel ministry.

Thus the old national prejudice was conquered, at least for a time. Peter's plain statement shattered their old notions, and gave them new and comprehensive thoughts concerning the Gospel. Now, for the first time, they felt that all men were brethren, that the Messiah was for humanity, and that the Gospel was for the wide world.

Acts 11:19-30

CHRISTIANITY IN ANTIOCH

"*Now they[1] which were scattered abroad, upon the persecution that arose about Stephen, travelled as far as Phenice, and Cyprus, and Antioch, preaching the word to none but unto the[2] Jews only. And some of them[3] were men of Cyprus and Cyrene, which, when they were come to Antioch, spake unto the Grecians,[4] preaching the Lord Jesus. And the hand of the Lord was with them: and a great number believed, and turned[5] unto the Lord. Then tidings of these things[6] came unto the ears of the Church which was in Jerusalem; and they sent forth Barnabas, that he should go as far as Antioch. Who, when he came, and had seen the grace of God, was glad, and exhorted them all, that with purpose of heart they would cleave unto the Lord. For he was a good man, and full of the Holy Ghost, and of faith: and much people was added unto the Lord. Then departed Barnabas to Tarsus, for to seek Saul: and when he had found him, he brought him unto Antioch. And it came to pass, that a whole year they assembled themselves with the Church, and taught much people. And the[7] disciples were called Christians first in Antioch. And in these days came prophets[8] from Jerusalem unto Antioch. And there stood up one of them, named Agabus, and signified by the Spirit that there should be great dearth throughout all the world: which came to pass in the days of Claudius Cæsar. Then the disciples, every man according to his ability, determined to send relief unto the brethren which dwelt in Judæa: which also they did, and sent it to the elders by the hands of Barnabas and Saul.*"

EMENDATIVE RENDERINGS.—(1.) So then they. (2.) Jews omit "*the.*" (3.) But some of them. (4.) Grecians also. (5.) Which believed, turned. (6.) Tidings of them. (7.) And that the. (8.) Came down.—ALF.

EXEGETICAL REMARKS.—There are several important places mentioned in these verses which must be described at the outset.

"PHENICE." This was a province of Syria, which in its largest sense comprehended a narrow strip of country lying on the eastern coast of the Mediterranean, and extending from Antioch to the borders of Egypt. But Phenice proper extended only from the cities of Laodicea to Tyre, and included only the territories of Tyre and Sidon. This country was called sometimes simply Canaan.

"CYPRUS." This is one of the largest islands in the Mediterranean Sea. It is of a triangular form, 140 miles long, and its breadth varies from about fifty almost to five. It is one of the earliest places out of Palestine into which the Gospel was carried. Some suppose it to be the same with Chittim (Num. xxiv. 24; Dan. xi. 30). The chief productions of Cyprus are, as formerly, wines, oil, honey, and wool. It is a famous place in mythological history, and was distinguished for the licentiousness of its inhabitants.

"ANTIOCH." The capital of Syria, situated on the river Orontes, near its mouth. It was founded by *Antigonus*, one of the generals of Alexander the Great, and from him called *Antigonia*, but afterwards received the name of *Antioch*, from *Antiochus*, another king of Syria, who completed it. During the predominance of the Christian religion it was called *Theopolis*, the divine city. It was rich, populous, and refined, and was at one period accounted the next city after Rome and Alexandria in the Roman empire. Cicero describes it as a noble and celebrated place, abounding with learned men and liberal studies. It was a great resort of the Jews, and afterwards of Christians, on account of the toleration here granted to different religionists. In all ages, it has been exposed to those terrific enemies of Oriental cities, wars and earthquakes. In A.D. 558, no less than 60,000 persons perished in an earthquake ; and in 1822 it was reduced to a heap of ruins by the same tremendous agent. Its present name is *Antakia*, and it numbers about 10,000 inhabitants.

"CYRENE." A province in the city of Lybia, lying about ten miles from the sea.

"*Now they which were scattered abroad upon the persecution that arose about Stephen,*" &c. These words connect this verse with chapter viii. 4. The scattered ones, it would appear, were not apostles, but the simple members of the Church. These are the men that we are told travelled as far as Phenice, Cyprus, and Antioch. Because Luke here takes up the thread of discourse left off at viii. 4, some suppose that the conversion of the Gentiles at Antioch was an event later in time than the conversion of Cornelius. The verse, however, distinctly states that these scattered evangelists preached "the word to none but the Jews only."

"*Spake unto the Grecians, preaching the Lord Jesus.*" "Ελθόντες is far better attested than εἰσελθόντες, in the

Textus Receptus, which has only one MS. for it. The reading, Ἕλληνας stands opposed to Ἑλληνιστάς. The number of testimonies are, indeed, in favour of Ἑλληνιστάς. Almost all cursive MS., and many fathers support it. Ἕλληνας has A.D. (in the writing of the original scribe), the Sinaitic MS., Eusebius, Chrysostom, Theophylact, and Œcumenius for it. Internal reasons decide for Ἕλληνας, for that only forms a contrast to Ἰουδαίοις, ver. 19 ; whilst the preaching the Gospel to the Hellenists was nothing new and remarkable. Therefore, already, Grotius, Usher, and Bengel preferred Ελληνας, and it is received by Griesbach, Lachmann, and Tischendorf."— L. & G.

It is evidently the intention of Luke, in this verse, to affirm that the men of Cyprus and Cyrene preached to those who were not Jews, and thus their conduct was distinguished from those mentioned in the preceding verse, who preached to the Jews only.— Grecians here, then, does not mean Hellenists, but Greeks ; all those who were not Jews—the Gentiles. Thus it seems that the " accession of Cornelius and his party was not the first admission of uncircumcised Gentiles into the Church. Nay, we read of no influence which the accession of Cornelius and his house had on the further progress of the Gospel among the Gentiles ; whereas there here open upon us operations upon the Gentiles from quite a different quarter, and attended with ever-growing success. The only great object served by the case of Cornelius was the *formal recognition of the principles which that case afterwards secured.*"

" *Then tidings of them,*" not of *these things.* It means news of the doings of the voluntary missionaries evangelising Hellenists, mentioned in verse 20.

" *Came unto the ears of the Church which was in Jerusalem, and they sent forth Barnabas, that he should go as far as Antioch.*" The mother Church sent forth this good man Barnabas on a mission of inquiry. And who could they have selected to inquire into the proceedings of those Cyrenians and Cypreans than a good man, who was himself a native of Cyprus ? Besides, Antioch was not far from Cyprus.

" *Then departed Barnabas to Tarsus for to seek Saul.*" Saul had fled from Jerusalem to Tarsus, his native place, for safety. Barnabas had ascertained the kind of spiritual work required at Antioch, and no one knew the spiritual aptitudes of Saul for such a work better than he. He introduced Saul first to the Church at Jerusalem.

" *And when he had found him, he brought him unto Antioch.*" Thus Saul stepped upon the theatre where his peculiar work was to be developed, both in extent and in depth, and for "*a whole year they assembled themselves with . the Church, and taught much people.*"

" *And the disciples were called Christians first in Antioch.*" This name originated not within but without the Church ; not with their *Jewish* enemies, by whom they were styled "Nazarenes " (chap. xxiv. 5), but with the *heathen* in Antioch ; and (as the form of the word shows) with the *Romans*, not the *Greeks* there. It was not at first used in a good sense, as chap. xxvi. 28 and 1 Peter iv. 16 show, though hardly framed out of contempt ; but as it was a noble testimony to the light in which the Church regarded Christ—honouring Him in their only Lord and Saviour, dwelling continually on His name and glorying in it—so it was felt to be too apposite and beautiful to be allowed to die.

" *And there stood up one of them, named Agabus, and signified by the Spirit that there should be great dearth throughout all the world.*" Nothing is known about this Agabus, except what is mentioned here and in chapter xxi. 10. He was in all probability a Christian disciple, and was now inspired by God to foretell the approach of a terrible calamity.

" *Which came to pass in the days of Claudius Cœsar.*" History tells us that four different famines occurred in this man's reign, and this one in Judæa and the adjacent country occurred in A.D. 41 (see Josephus' *Ant.* xx. 2, 5).

" *Then the disciples, every man according to his ability, determined to send relief unto the brethren which dwelt in Judæa.*" Wherever the Gospel is practically received there is ever a deep, tender, active philanthropy. Love to man is the effect and proof of love to God.

" *Which also they did, and sent it to the elders by the hands of Barnabas and Saul.*" πρεβυτέρους. " This is the first occurrence of the word in an ecclesiastical sense ; *presbyters*, literally *elders, aldermen*. Hence our word *priests*. The term implies *dignity* rather than *age*, as senator from *senex*, γερουσια from γέρων. The name and office were both derived from the Jewish Sanhedrim. In chap. xx. 28 they are called ἐπίσκοποι, overseers of the flock or Church at large. πρεσβύτερος is uniformly rendered *elder* in the E.V. ; never *priest*, which is ιερεύς. The πρεσβύτεροι in this passage must have included the apostles themselves. —WEBSTER and WILKINSON.

As Paul here appears for the first time in his apostolic character, we may present the following chronological table of the principal events of his life after his conversion, as recorded in this book :—

A.D.		
37.	Conversion,	Acts ix. 1
38, 39 (part).	Visit to Arabia,	ix. 22 (G. i. 17)
39.	To Jerusalem (first visit),	ix. 26–29
	And Tarsus,	30
40–42.	At Tarsus.	
42–44.	At Antioch (first residence),	xi. 25
43.	Prophecy of Agabus,	28
44.	To Jerusalem (second visit) with Barnabas,	xi. 30 to xii. 25
45–47.	First apostolical journey,	xiii. 2 to xiv. 26
47–51.	At Antioch (second residence),	xiv. 28
	Visit to Jerusalem (? third) with Barnabas and Titus,	xi. 30 n. (G. ii. 1)
50.	Visit (fourth) to Jerusalem—Council,	xv. 6
	Return, and third (short) residence in Antioch,	xv. 35
51–54.	Second apostolical journey,	xv. 41

HOMILETICS.—This paragraph records another magnificent stride taken by Christianity in its triumphant march. It indicates, to use the language of Baumgarten, the *rise of the first Gentile Churches.* Christianity enters Antioch, and there works its spiritual marvels. The narrative leads us to consider—

I. THE ENTRANCE OF CHRISTIANITY INTO ANTIOCH. " Now they which were scattered abroad upon the persecution that arose about Stephen, travelled as far as Phenice, and Cyprus, and Antioch, preaching the word to none but unto the Jews only. And some of them were men of Cyprus and Cyrene, which, when they were come to Antioch, spake unto the Grecians, preaching the Lord Jesus." In the entrance of the Gospel into this city several things are here suggested worthy of notice. We discover—

First, *Evil overruled for good.* The evil is referred to in the 19th verse : " The persecution that arose about Stephen." The 7th chapter of this book, on which we have already commented, gives a full account of that spirit of diabolical intolerance on the part of the Jewish Sanhedrim, that resulted in this martyrdom of Stephen. His death, instead of satiating the rage, stimulated it. The taste of blood whets the appetite of the wild beast. " There was a great persecution against the Church which was at Jerusalem." On this account the members of the Church at Jerusalem, which must have been very numerous at that time, were scattered abroad throughout the regions of Judæa and Samaria, and other parts of the world. Now through many populous and influential parts the disciples, driven from Jerusalem by fear, travelled to Antioch. No doubt they preached the Gospel wherever they went. The thing to be observed here is this, that the very efforts of enemies to crush Christianity gave it a new vigour and a wider sweep. The blood of the martyr became the seed of the Church. The blow struck by evil became the instrument of good. Thus it has ever been. He who is stronger than the devil baffles him in every attempt, and makes his wrath to praise Him. In the long run of destiny the universe will see that evil has been, from its birth to its death, only the servant of good. We discover—

Secondly, *The invincibility of Christian courage.* Though these disciples fled from Jerusalem to escape the wrath of their persecutors, they did not flee from the cause they had espoused, or relax in their efforts to advance it. They knew their cause was an unpopular one; they knew that everywhere it would excite the same ire that it awoke in Jerusalem; still they deserted it not. They were found "*every-where preaching the word.*" True courage does not consist in callous indifference to danger, nor does it always require the risking of life. But it demands evermore adherence to principle, eternal fealty to duty. They felt it their solemn obligation to speak the "things they had seen and heard" concerning Christ. This spirit reigned in them as an unconquerable power. We discover—

Thirdly, *The legitimacy of lay preaching.* Who were these men who travelled as far as Phenice and Antioch preaching the word? Were they apostles? Nay, were they in any sense official ministers of Christ? No. By the general consent of all acknowledged critics they were the *common* disciples of Christ, the common members of the Church at Jerusalem. Now it is remarkable, aye and significant too, that the planting of Christian Churches in various parts of the old world, and even in Antioch itself, was the work, *not of apostles, but of private men holding no ecclesiastical office whatever.* This shows (1.) that it is the duty of every man who knows the Gospel to proclaim it; and (2.) that those who would restrict the work of preaching to those who are professional and ordained, arrogate an authority the most injurious to the spiritual interests of man, and the most antagonistic to the genius of New Testament history. He who in heart understands the Gospel needs no licence from bishop, pope, or king. He has a divine right to do what these humble disciples did, "go everywhere preaching the Word." We discover—

Fourthly, *The universality of the Gospel.* Whilst at first it would seem from the 19th verse that some of them preached "unto the Jews only," those of them from Cyprus and Cyrene "spake unto the Grecians, preaching the Lord Jesus." The Greek language, it would seem, was spoken both in Cyprus and Cyrene; the Christians, there-fore, who came from that district were peculiarly qualified to preach the Gospel "unto the Greeks." By the "Grecians" Luke means Greeks or Gentiles. (1.) The circumstance that the historian mentions it as *a new fact* favours this view. In the preceding verse he had stated that these missionaries from Jerusalem had preached the Gospel to the "Jews only." To say in the next verse that they had preached merely to the Greek-speaking Jews would be no fresh information—would, in fact, be a repetition of a common occurrence unworthy the character of such a writer as Luke. (2.) The interest that the fact awakened favours this view. We are informed that when the tidings reached the mother Church at Jerusalem that these "Grecians," whoever they were, had been preached to at Antioch, they at once despatched Barnabas as a deputation to the scene. It is scarcely credible that, had they been Jews, such an excitement would have been produced at Jerusalem, for to preach to the Jews was an everyday occurrence. But nothing was more natural than that the Christians at Jerusalem should be stirred to the very heart that the Gospel had been preached to the Greeks at Antioch. (3.) The best critical authorities adopt this view. We regard, therefore, the inspired historian as saying, that these missionaries from Jerusalem preached the Gospel to the Gentiles in the great city of Antioch, and this was a wonderful fact. Whether they did this before Peter preached to Cornelius or after, is a question which alters not the wonderfulness of the fact. The fact shows the *universality* of the Gospel—shows that it is a system as suited to the Greek as to the Hebrew mind, and equally essential to the highest interests of both. It is the power of God unto salvation, " to the Jew first, and also to the Greek."

II. THE ACHIEVEMENTS OF CHRISTIANITY AT ANTIOCH. The narrative before us tells us not only of the *entrance* of the Gospel to this grand city of the ancient world, but of its triumphs there, and from it we learn the following things concerning its achievements there. The achievements—

First, *Involved a Divine change in the characters of many.* " And the hand of the Lord was with them : and a great number believed, and turned unto the Lord." Observe—(1.) The Divine power which attended their ministry. " The hand of the Lord was with them." The meaning is, that there was a manifest display of Divine energy in their preaching. Observe—(2.) The faith which their ministry generated. " A great number believed." They believed undoubtedly the great facts concerning the crucified and risen Messiah ; the facts which Peter proclaimed on the day of Pentecost. The Gospel ministry can only exert its beneficent power amongst the hearers as they *believe.* Force in the pulpit depends on faith in the pew : the preacher's voice is mere sound if the people's souls are not believing. Observe— (3.) The revolution which their faith effected. " Turned unto the Lord"—that is, to God, as manifested in His Son. They turned to Him in contrition, love, assimilation. Such was the Divine change effected amongst a great number in Antioch by the simple preaching of these missionaries from Jerusalem. The achievements—

Secondly, *Attracted the attention of the mother Church.* " Then tidings of these things came unto the ears of the Church which was in Jerusalem ; and they sent forth Barnabas, that he should go as far as Antioch." It was natural that the preaching of the Gospel to the Gentiles, and its wonderful success in that splendid city, should soon be heard of in Jerusalem, and there excite feelings of the deepest interest. Two things followed upon this excitement in Jerusalem.

(1.) *Barnabas was sent as a deputation to visit the scene.* " They sent forth Barnabas." Certain of the more thoughtful expositors have called special attention to two facts connected with the sending of Barnabas. (1.) That he was not an apostle, but merely an influential teacher at Jerusalem. No ecclesiastical dignitary was deputed on this occasion. (2.) That he was not deputed by the apostles, but by the Church which was in Jerusalem. The apostles who were present on this occasion gave their votes, and perhaps counsel, but no more. The feelings and conduct of Barnabas when he appeared amongst them, his own high religious character, and the great spiritual good resulting from his labours, which are contained in the 23d and 24th verses, suggest the following remarks in relation to personal Christianity :—

(i.) That personal Christianity *is essentially identified with Divine grace.* " The grace of God." He *saw* Divine grace in the conversion of the Gentiles, and the new life developed through the preaching of the Gospel.—(1.) Personal Christianity *originates* in Divine grace. " Of his own will begat he us," &c. (2.) Personal Christianity is *sustained* by Divine grace. (3.) Personal Christianity is a *reflection* of Divine grace. Wherever there is true personal Christianity, there is the highest display of the loving heart of God.

(ii.) That personal Christianity, *wherever it exists, is an observable fact.* " Barnabas *saw* it at Antioch." Personal Christianity is not an inoperative sentiment, not a candle that can be concealed under a bushel. It must reveal itself.—(1.) The ruling spirit of life is new. There is a new heart. Old things are passed away.—(2.) The master-purpose of life is new. The aim is not to serve sense, or self, or the world, but to glorify God in everything. —(3.) The prevailing conduct of life is new. It is the characteristic of converted men, that they are about their Father's business.

(iii.) That personal Christianity, *in its extension, delights the heart of the good.* " Barnabas was *glad.*" There is nothing so adapted to gladden the heart of a truly devout and philanthropic spirit as the extension of Christianity in the world. They know that, as that spreads—(1.) The world's happiness will be promoted. It is the only power that works off evils, social, political, and moral. —(2.) God's character will be revealed. It clears away from the mind the cloud that conceals the moral beauty of the great God of the universe.

(iv.) That personal Christianity *requires on behalf of its subjects the most persevering effort.* He " exhorted them all, that with purpose of heart they would cleave unto the Lord." (1.) There are many forces to separate us from the Lord ; evils within and social influence around us, &c. (2.) These forces can only be counteracted by the most strenuous efforts—" purpose of heart." There must be watching, praying, running, &c.

Brother, though thy Christianity is of " the grace of God," that grace has made its growth and continuance dependent on thine efforts. With an invincible purpose, adhere to the Lord, hold on with the tenacity of thy being to the truths of His Word and the promises of His love.

The other thing that followed this excitement was—

(2.) *Prophets from the Holy City were attracted to the spot.* "And in those days came prophets from Jerusalem unto Antioch" (ii. 27). The word "prophets" means inspired teachers, although some of them had the power of foretelling future events, such as Agabus, who signified by the Spirit that there should be a great dearth throughout all the world. The sending of Barnabas, and the voluntary visit of these prophets, are only indications of that *immense interest* which the work of the Gospel in Antioch awakened amongst first Christians, wherever the tidings reached. The achievements—

Thirdly, *Led to the settlement of Barnabas and Paul for twelve months in the city.* "Then departed Barnabas to Tarsus, for to seek Saul, and when he had found him, he brought him unto Antioch. And it came to pass, that a whole year they assembled themselves with the Church, and taught much people." How Paul spent his time at Tarsus until Barnabas met him, we know not. No doubt active in evangelic labour. We should like to have known the exact scene and circumstances in which this noble Barnabas found *him* who became the great apostle of the Gentiles. All we know is, he did find him, and that they both go lovingly together to the Syrian capital, and there continue "a whole year." Who would not like to have a history detailing all the labours and all the events in the history of these two great men during that "whole year?" The result of their labours, however, was the growth of a church in a city which became a missionary centre for diffusing the Gospel through the heathen world. The achievements—

Fourthly, *Gave a new name to the disciples of Christ.* "And the disciples were called *Christians* first in Antioch." It is only used twice elsewhere in the New Testament (Acts xxvi. 28; 1 Peter iv. 16). If given in derision, the appellation has become the most glorious symbol in the world. It towers above every other name on earth. The highest titles of earth pale before it. It represents the highest thinking, the divinest sympathies, the grandest enterprises, and the sublimest characters of all lands and times. Oh! come the day when all the appellations that designate little sects, parties, denominations, shall be lost in that one grand name—*Christian*—a name that shall live and brighten when the most brilliant titles that dazzle a foolish world are lost in forgetfulness. The achievements—

Fifthly, *Developed a new spirit of beneficence in the people.* "Then the disciples, every man according to his ability, determined to send relief unto the brethren which dwelt in Judæa: which also they did, and sent it to the elders by the hands of Barnabas and Saul." Their beneficence was—

(1.) *Individual.* "Every man." There was not one who did not contribute something. The new love glowed in every heart, and found its expression in the gift of every hand.

(2.) *Proportionate.* It was "according to his ability." Not according to what other people did, or what other people expected, but "according to his ability." Each did the utmost he could.

(3.) *Prompt.* It was done at once. They did not postpone it or adjourn it for future consideration. They "determined to send relief."

(4.) *Judicious.* They arranged for its distribution in a most effective and judicious way. They "sent it to the elders by the hands of Barnabas and Saul." The elders were those that were regarded as the most experienced members of the various Churches ; and Barnabas and Saul were deputed to take the contributions to them, and entrust them with the distribution as their discretion would dictate. Here, then, we have a beautiful display of that philanthropy which the ancient seers beheld as the light of coming ages, and which has been ever the inspiration of the godly. It is

> "That bright chain of love which God hath given,
> Reaching from heart to heart, and thence to heaven."

Acts 12:1-19

PETER IN PRISON—THE WEAKNESS OF SATAN

" *Now, about that time, Herod the king stretched forth his hands to vex certain of the church.*[1] *And he killed James, the brother of John, with the sword. And because he saw it pleased the Jews, he proceeded further to take Peter also.. (Then were the days of unleavened bread.) And when he had apprehended him, he put him in prison, and delivered him to four quaternions of soldiers to keep him ; intending after Easter*[2] *to bring him forth to the people. Peter therefore was kept in prison ; but prayer was made without ceasing of the church*[3] *unto God for him. And when Herod would have brought him forth,*[4] *the same night Peter was sleeping between two soldiers, bound with two chains: and the keepers before the door kept the prison. And, behold, the angel*[5] *of the Lord came upon him, and a light shined in the prison :*[6] *and he smote Peter on the side, and raised him up, saying, Arise up quickly. And his chains fell off from his hands. And the angel said unto him, Gird thyself, and bind on thy sandals: and so he did.*[7] *And he saith unto him, Cast thy garment about thee, and follow me. And he went out and followed him ; and wist not that it was true which was done by the angel ; but thought he saw a vision. When they were past the first and the second ward, they came unto the iron gate that leadeth unto the city ; which opened to them of his own accord: and they went out, and passed on through one street ; and forthwith the angel departed from him. And when Peter was come to himself, he said, Now I know of a surety, that the Lord hath sent his angel, and hath delivered me out of the hand of Herod, and from all the expectation of the people of the*

Jews. *And when he had considered* [8] *the thing, he came to the house of Mary the mother of John, whose surname was Mark ; where many were gathered together praying. And as Peter knocked* [9] *at the door of the gate, a damsel came to hearken, named Rhoda. And when she knew Peter's voice,* [10] *she opened not the gate for gladness, but ran in, and told how Peter stood before the gate. And they said unto her, Thou art mad. But she constantly affirmed that it was even so. Then said they, It is his angel. But Peter continued knocking : and when they had opened the door, and saw him, they were astonished. But he, beckoning unto them with the hand to hold their peace, declared unto them how the Lord had brought him out of the prison. And he said, Go show these things unto James, and to the brethren. And he departed, and went into another place. Now, as soon as it was day, there was no small stir among the soldiers, what was become of Peter. And when Herod had sought for him, and found him not, he examined the keepers, and commanded that they should be put to death. And he went down from Judæa to Cæsarea, and there abode.*"

EMENDATIVE RENDERINGS.—(1.) Laid his hands upon certain of the Church to vex them. (2.) The Passover. (3.) By the Church. (4.) Was about to bring. (5.) An angel. (6.) The chamber. (7.) He did so. (8.) Knew. (9.) And when he had knocked. (10.) And knowing Peter's voice.—ALF.

EXEGETICAL REMARKS. — "*Now about that time.*" That is about the time when Barnabas and Saul came from Antioch to Judæa, as mentioned in the preceding verses, and about fourteen years after the ascension of Christ. Whilst Barnabas and Saul were distributing the charities of the Church of Antioch amongst the needy disciples in Judæa, a new persecution of the Christians sprang up at Jerusalem, which is here recorded. "*Herod the king stretched forth his hands,*" &c. This was Herod Agrippa, the elder, or the great son of Aristobulus, the son of Herod the Great, by Mariamne. Aristobulus was put to death by his father through jealousy and court cabals. Herod Agrippa was educated at Rome, where he contracted dissipated and extravagant habits, in the luxurious reign of Tiberius. He was favoured by the succeeding emperors, Caius Caligula and Claudius Cæsar, and appointed king over the territories of Batanea, Trachonitis, Abilene, Galilee, Samaria, and Judæa,—a dominion about as extensive as that of Herod the Great, his grandfather. Archelaus (Matt. ii. 22) and Herod Antipas, who put John the Baptist to death, were his uncles (Matt. xiv. 1-12,) and Herodias was his sister. The Agrippa introduced in

chap. xxv. 13, and also Bernice, were his children. He ruled seven years, from A.D. 37 to A.D. 44. The manner of his death is related in ver. 23.

"*And he killed James the brother of John with the sword.*" This was James the son of Zebedee, one of the earliest followers and most confidential friends of Christ. He is never mentioned in the Gospels but with John his brother. His martyrdom may be regarded as the fulfilment of Christ's words, Mat. xx. 22. It is remarkable that, as far as we know, one of these inseparable brothers was the first, and the other the last, that died of the apostles. James, it would seem, was the first of the twelve who sealed his fidelity with his blood. It is related by Clement of Alexandria, though the story is probably legendary, that "as the apostle was led forth to the place of execution, the person who had accused him was so touched with the courage and constancy which he displayed, that he repented of what he had done, came and fell down at his feet, and earnestly begged pardon for what he had said against him. St James tenderly raised him up, kissed him, and said to him, ' Peace be to thee, my son, and the pardon of thy faults.' At this, his former accuser publicly professed himself a Christian, and so both were beheaded at the same time."

"*And because he saw 'it pleased the Jews, he proceeded further to take Peter also.*" He discovered, perhaps what he did not expect at first, that the persecution which he had set on foot against the Christians, and the martyrdom of James, was *popular*, and this prompted him to proceed to apprehend or arrest Peter.

"*He put him in prison, and delivered him to four quaternions of soldiers.*" That is, to four parties of soldiers of four each, corresponding to the four Roman watches ; two watching in prison, and two at the gates, and each party being on duty for the space of one watch.

"*Intending after Easter to bring him forth to the people.*" "*After Easter*, an absurd confusion of the Christian with the Jewish festival, transcribed into King James' version from the older ones of Tyndale, Cranmer, and Geneva, while Wiclif, and the Rhenish version go to the opposite extreme, of retaining the original without translation (*after pask* or *pasche*). There is no imaginable reason why it should not be translated here, as in every other place where it occurs, by its exact equivalent, *the Passover.* See Matt. xxvi. 2 ; Mark xiv. 1 ; Luke ii. 41 ; John ii. 13 ; 1 Cor. v. 7 ; Heb. xi. 28 ; and more than twenty other instances, to which the one before us is the sole exception."—ALEXANDER.

"*Bound with two chains.*" He was chained to the arms of two soldiers, a method of confinement spoken of by other ancient writers, especially by Seneca. Ordinarily, however, it would seem that a prisoner was bound only to one soldier : Peter was therefore doubly secured,—chained to two and guarded by fourteen others.

"*And behold the angel of the Lord came upon him.*" The angel could not have been a mere human messenger, or some providential event, such as an earthquake or lightning, but a superhuman intelligence commissioned by Peter's Lord and Master to effect his deliverance. What the angel is said to have done, is a work

of a personal and superhuman agent. He "smote Peter on the side." He raised him up. He spoke,—"Arise up quickly."

"*Chains fell from his hands.*" Literally *the* chains. What human hand could have snapped those manacles, and freed him without the knowledge of his guards ? Would the shock of an earthquake or the flash of lightning have done it without injuring him or the soldiers ?

"*Gird thyself, and bind on thy sandals*," &c. Here again is personal intelligence. The angel did for Peter what he could not do for himself,—break his fetters ; but does not do for him what he could do for himself —put on his tunic and mantle.

"*Which opened to them of his own accord.*" That is the iron gate which enclosed the prison from the city. "His" should be its,—its "own accord." The historian means to say that it opened without any human instrumentality. All the details indicate supernatural interposition.

"*And when Peter was come to himself,*" &c. Naturally enough his miraculous deliverance had stunned him with amazement. He was bewildered ; at first all seemed a dream to him. Now he returns to his normal state, and feels that it is the Lord's work. "I know of a surety that the Lord hath sent his angel," &c.

"*He came to the house of Mary, the mother of John, whose surname was Mark.*" "This John Mark is no doubt the same who is mentioned in verse 25, and reappears in xiii. 13 ; xv. 37-39. He is also supposed to be the same whom Peter calls his son (1 Peter v. 13), *i.e.*, his spiritual son, or convert : whom Paul names in three of his epistles as his fellow-labourer (see Col. iv. 10 ; 2 Tim. iv. 11. ; Philemon xxiv.), and to whom an old and uniform tradition ascribes the composition of the second Gospel."—ALEXANDER.

"Mary must have had a house with some pretensions to receive a large number: her pecuniary means agree with what we know of her brother Barnabas (iv. 37). She must also have been distinguished for faith and courage among the believers, to allow such a meeting in the face of persecution. These nocturnal assemblies became very frequent among Christians. She is spoken of as the mother of Mark, because he was so well known, *συνηθρ. κ. προσευχ.* Two things are intended to be set before us,—that there was a congregation assembled, and that they were engaged in prayer, in intercession for Peter."—WEBSTER and WILKINSON.

" *And as Peter knocked at the door of the gate, a damsel came to hearken, named Rhoda.*" Rhoda, or rather Rhode, as the name is Greek, denotes a rose-bud. Females were frequently called after the names of flowers and trees, as Susannah, a lily ; Hadana, a myrtle ; Tamah, a palm.

" *And when she knew Peter's voice, she opened not the gate for gladness, but ran in and told how Peter stood before the gate.*" "There is great naturalness in this stroke of the historian, such as a fictitious writer would have hardly imagined. Her joy, instead of leading her to admit Peter instantly, as would seem to be the spontaneous dictate, impelled her first to gladden the company with the joyful news of his escape."—LIVERMORE.

" *And they said unto her, Thou art mad.*" The strongest expression of their incredulity. Perhaps they felt not only that the news was too extraordinary, but too good to be believed.

" *Then they said, It is his angel.*" Some understand by this, messenger: it is his *messenger*. But though this is the original meaning of the Greek word, and occurs in a few places (Matthew xi. 10 ; Luke vii. 24 ; ix. 52 ; James ii. 5), it cannot be taken in that sense here. Eastern nations believed in tutelary angels, or guardian spirits. Christ's disciples shared this belief (Matthew xvii. 10). Whether they meant by this, it is his disembodied spirit, or his supernatural guardian, it is, perhaps, impossible to determine ; in either case, however, a belief in a world of spirits is undoubtedly expressed.

" *And when they had opened the door, and saw him, they were astonished.*" Their astonishment implies—(1.) That they had entered into no conspiracy to free the apostle. (2.) That though they had prayed for his deliverance, they did not dare to hope for it. His rescue to them seemed hopeless.

" *Go, shew these things unto James.*" This was James the Less. James the Elder had just been put to death (see verse 2). James is singled out, perhaps, because he had begun to take the oversight of the Church at Jerusalem, where we afterwards find him (chap. xv.) A strong argument for credibility of the Scriptures may be drawn from the fact, that in S. S. there is an exceedingly full and minute mention of *particular individuals* and *particular circumstances*, especially as connected with miraculous events. Now, a *false* witness is careful to avoid such mention : he introduces as few names as possible : he expresses himself in terms the most loose and general. Not so the inspired writers. The very name of the person who, wounded by Peter, was healed by Christ, is recorded, that all men might actually refer to him or his friends. Those who doubted the facts had the power of ascertaining the truth by the witnesses pointed out. Thus we have here Mary, James, Rhoda.

" *Now, as soon as it was day, there was no small stir among the soldiers what was become of Peter.*" His mysterious deliverance created great excitement and confusion. Fear and wonder filled them with mental tumult " as soon as it was day." Day would reveal the enormity of the night, and the revelation would produce " no small stir," &c.

" *And when Herod had sought for him, and found him not, he examined the keepers, and commanded them that they should be put to death.*" "This is not to be regarded as an act of extraordinary cruelty in Herod, but as a simple application of the Roman military law, with which he was familiar. It is not necessarily implied that the miraculous deliverance of Peter was known either to the king or to the guards ; but as the latter could give no account of his escape, there seemed to be no doubt that they must either have connived at it, or slept upon their post, a capital offence in Roman soldiers."—ALEXANDER.

HOMILETICS.—Every chapter in the voluminous history of the Church develops the old decree of heaven, that enmity should exist between "the seed of the serpent and the seed of the woman," between the votaries of Satan and the disciples of Christ. This is the battle of all the battles of the world, the under-lying spring of all the commotions, anarchies, persecutions, and wars of all the ages that have been, and of all the troubled ages that have yet to dawn. But how does the "old serpent" carry on his battle? What form does the infernal anarch assume in carrying out his malignant aims? Does he come in the form of a serpent? No! Nor in any supernatural appearance. It is in the form of man he comes, and by man he works. The strongest human forms he assumes, the forms by which he works the direst deeds, are the forms of tyrannic kings and wily priests. It is in the form of a *king* he appears to us in this chapter. Herod is his incarnation, his instrument. "Now about that time, Herod, the king, stretched forth his hands to vex certain of the Church." Here is (1.) *malignity:* "He vexed the Church, and killed James." Here is (2.) *servility:* "Because he saw it" (the murder of James) pleased the Jews, he proceeded to take Peter also." It was not because he had aught against Peter; it was because he courted the favour of the Jews. He crouched before public sentiment. The Spirit of Satan is a cringing, servile, crawling spirit: "On thy belly shalt thou go."

The subject I shall use this narrative to illustrate is this: *The weakness of Satan, even when invested with the regal authority of earth.* We learn from this narrative that there are four things he cannot do :—

I. SATAN CANNOT RENDER UNAVAILING THE INTERCESSIONS OF THE GOOD. "Peter therefore was kept in prison : but prayer was made without ceasing of the Church unto God for him." The Church, the small assembly of Christ's disciples, hearing of the imprisonment and imminent danger of Peter, their leading apostle, betake themselves to their knees. "It is evidently," says Baumgarten, "the wish of St Luke, that you should look on this incessant prayer of the Church as the cause why the fate of St Peter took so different a form from that of St James." The *united* and *incessant* intercessions of these disciples in this Church, were, under God, the means of the apostle's deliverance.

Against the force of the prayer of these men whom Herod despised Satan was *powerless*. It would have been easier work for him to have controlled the winds of heaven than to have neutralised the prayers of these poor, persecuted men. Mighty as is the power the devil has over the world, he cannot prevent our prayers penetrating the heavens and entering the heart of God. He was mighty in Pharoah of old, who trod with an iron despotism upon the liberty and lives of the Jewish people ; but a few of the oppressed ones prayed ;

their cries entered the ears of the Lord God of Sabbaoth, and their long-struggled-for deliverance came at last. He was mighty in Nebuchadnezzar, who set up his image in the plains of Dura, and commanded all his people to worship it, at the peril of their lives; but those amongst them who were true, prayed to the God of heaven, and they were rescued from his demon grasp to his own confusion and dismay.

II. SATAN CANNOT DESTROY THE MORAL PEACE OF A GOOD MAN.

"And when Herod would have brought him forth, the same night Peter was *sleeping* between two soldiers, bound with two chains: and the keepers before the door kept the prison." What an instance of sublime composure this! Think of the place. A prison—a dark, filthy cell. Think of his position. Chained to two soldiers—linked to two wretches from whom his nature must have recoiled with horror. Think of those who were watching him. He was delivered to "four quaternions of soldiers" (sixteen soldiers). Think of the time. It was the night when Herod intended to bring him forth and put him to death. Peter must have been aware of his danger. He knew that the wretch who was "vexing the Church," who had just killed James, and who had imprisoned him, intended to take away his life. Yet he sleeps; sleeps far sweeter and safer than his bloody persecutor could sleep that night. Herod, with his dungeon, his quaternions, and his iron chains, could not steal from Peter his sleep. His sleeping in these circumstances suggests three things :—

First, *A gracious Providence.* Here is an illustration of the promise, "He giveth His beloved sleep." Sleep is one of the choicest of the animal gifts of God. How it re-invigorates the frame! "Tired nature's sweet restorer, balmy sleep." How it drowns our sorrows and our cares for the time, as in a placid sea of forgetfulness! How it restrings the harp of life, and fits it for the new melodies of the coming day! How it binds up afresh our energies, and regales our senses as with the balmy airs of Elysium. What more did Peter want than sleep? It was the right and needful thing for the season, sleep for the night. Had he had one of the most comfortable chambers in Cæsar's palace, and rested his frame upon the softest bed of down, could he have had more than sleep? "He giveth His beloved sleep."

> "O earth, so full of dreary noises!
> O men, with wailing in your voices!
> O delvèd gold, the wailer's heap!
> O strife, O curse, that o'er it fall!
> God strikes a silence through you all,
> And giveth His beloved sleep."—*Mrs Browning.*

Secondly, *An approving conscience.* A condemning conscience would have kept sleep away. Peter knew that he was engaged in the right work.

Thirdly, *A sense of security.* He had no fear or alarm about the future. He had committed himself to the care of heaven! He felt himself safe in the hands of his Master. He knew that Christ had said, "I give unto my sheep eternal life." What need we fear when this is done? "God is our refuge and strength, a very present help in trouble."

III. SATAN CANNOT PREVENT THE VISITATION OF ANGELS TO THE GOOD. "And, behold, the angel of the Lord came upon him, and a light shined in the prison: and he smote Peter on the side, and raised him up, saying, Arise up quickly. And his chains fell off from his hands," &c. The Bible not only teaches the existence of angels, but their ministration. "Are they not all ministering spirits?" &c. This chapter, we are told, reveals more about angels than any other in this book. This case of the angel suggests two things :

First, *The ease with which an angel does his work.* With what ease he approaches Peter! The massive walls, the chains, the gates, the Roman guards, presented no obstruction to this angel. Silently he entered the prison, and with exquisite ease he liberated the apostle. "He touched him on the side, raised him gently, said, Arise up quickly," &c. The chains fell off. No effort; no struggle; there was a divine ease in all this. With what ease, too, he led him forth from the prison. "When they were passed the first and second ward," &c. God's greatest agents work *quietly.*

Secondly, *The extent to which an angel does his work.* The angel only does for a good man what a good man *cannot* do for himself : no more. "And the angel said unto him, Gird thyself, and bind on thy sandals," &c. Peter could bind up his tunic, tie on his sandals, and throw on his cloak himself, and the angel would not therefore condescend to do this. But Peter could not snap the chains that bound him, could not extricate himself from the grasp of his guards, could not get away from the iron prison ; and the angel did this for him. Angels will not do for us what we can do for ourselves.

IV. SATAN CANNOT PREVENT THE FRUSTRATIONS OF HIS OWN PURPOSES. "And when Peter was come to himself, he said," &c. That Herod's purpose was frustrated is seen—

First, *In the deliverance of Peter.* His deliverance was—(1.) Consciously divine : "I know of a surety," &c. (2.) Very wonderful : "He came to the house of Mary, the mother of John," &c. They were "*astonished.*" The inmates would not believe the messenger, and charged with madness, Rhoda, who told it.

Secondly, *In the progress of truth.* "And he said, Go shew these things unto James," &c. What an impulse this fact must have given to the new cause !

Thirdly, *In his confusion.* "Now, as soon as it was day, there was no small stir among the soldiers," &c. Satan's plans may be very subtle in their structure, vast in their sweep, imposing in their aspect, and promising in their progress; but their *failure* is *inevitable.* They must break down, and their author and abettors must be everlastingly confounded in their wreck. Take heart, ye children of the truth, God's world will one day be delivered from the devil and his plans. "As soon as day" comes, and come it will, "there will be *no small stir*" amongst God's enemies.

Acts 12:20-25

HEROD SMOTE BY THE ANGEL—AN OLD PICTURE OF HUMAN SOCIETY

" *And Herod was highly displeased with them of Tyre and Sidon: but they came with one accord to him, and, having made Blastus the king's chamberlain their friend, desired peace ; because their country was nourished by the king's country. And upon a set day, Herod, arrayed in royal apparel, sat upon his throne, and made an oration unto them. And the people gave a shout, saying, It is the voice of a god, and not of a man. And immediately the angel of the Lord smote him, because He gave not God the glory : and he was eaten of worms and gave up the ghost. But the word of God grew and multiplied. And Barnabas and Saul returned from Jerusalem, when they had fulfilled their ministry, and took with them John, whose surname was Mark.*

EXEGETICAL REMARKS. — " *Herod was highly displeased.*" " The word Θυμομαχῶν occurs only in the later classics, in Polybius, Plutarch, Diodorus, Siculus, and, as it appears, always in the sense of external, and even fierce war and fighting (Steph. Thes.) But as an actual campaign of Agrippa against the Phœnician cities, likewise in alliance with Rome, is in itself improbable and entirely unknown, we are obliged to take the word in the sense that Herod was embittered (Θυμα) against the Tyrians and Sidonians, and made war upon them (μαχῶν), as well as he could, perhaps closing up the frontiers against them, to which what follows points."—L. and G.

" *But they came with one accord to him.*" That is, ambassadors came conjointly from both cities, Tyre and Sidon. The men of these two cities came in the representatives that they appointed.

" *Having made Blastus the king's chamberlain their friend.*" This man they gained over, by arguments or bribes, to their cause.

" *Desired peace, because their country was nourished by the king's country.*" " They were dependent upon the territories of Herod for their grain : a species of trade which they had carried on from very early times with Palestine (1 Kings v. 9-11 ; Ezra iii. 7 ; Ezek. xxvii. 17). Nothing is related in Josephus, or any other historian of that period, of the animosity of Herod to the Phœnicians, as it was not perhaps of much moment compared with many occurrences of the times. But it is appropriately introduced by Luke, as explaining the occasion on which the adulation of the people was paid to the king as to a god."

" *And upon a set day, Herod, arrayed in royal apparel,*" &c. The account which Josephus gives of this is so accordant and corroborative that we cannot forbear presenting it in connection with the comments of a modern critic :—" On the second day of the shows, early in the morning, he came into the theatre dressed in a robe of silver, of most curious workmanship. The rays of the rising sun, reflected from so splendid a garb, gave him a majestic and awful appearance. In a short time they began, in several parts of the theatre, flattering acclamations, which proved pernicious to him. They called him a god, and entreated him to be propitious to them, saying, ' Hitherto we have respected you as a man : but now we acknowledge you to be more than mortal.' The king neither reproved these persons, nor rejected the impious flattery. Soon after this, casting his eye upwards, he saw an owl sitting upon a certain cord over his head. He perceived it to be a messenger of evil to him, as it had been before (according to a German soothsayer, when he was imprisoned by Tiberius) of his prosperity, and was struck with the greatest concern. Immediately after this he was seized with pain in his bowels, extremely violent at the very first. Then turning himself toward his friends, he spoke to them in this manner : ' I, your god, am required to leave this world—fate instantly confuting these false applauses just bestowed on me : I, who have been called immortal, am hurried away to death. But God's appointment must be submitted to. Nor has our condition in this world been despicable : we have lived in the state which is accounted happy.' While he was speaking these words, he was oppressed with the increase of his pains. He was carried, therefore, with all haste to his palace. These pains in his bowels continually tormenting him, he expired in five days' time, in the fifty-fourth year of his age, and

of his reign the seventh.' The correspondences between this account and the briefer narrative of Luke are numerous and striking, while the differences also bear witness to their independence and truth. (1.) Both assign Cæsarea as the place of Herod's death. (2.) Luke speaks of a set day : Josephus styles it the second day of the shows. (3.) They agree respecting the splendour of the king's dress, one giving a minute, and the other a general description of it. (4.) Luke says, he sat upon his throne and made an oration ; the Jewish historian represents him going to the theatre to preside over the shows, where, probably, a kind of throne was erected for the convenience of the monarch. (5.) Luke apparently attributes the impious flattery of the people to their satisfaction with his speech ; while Josephus introduces it directly after his account of the majesty and splendour of his apparel ; but both causes might have contributed to produce it. (6.) Both represent him as receiving without rebuke the blasphemous adulation of the people. (7.) Both harmonise essentially respecting his disease, both as to its cause as a judgment of Heaven against his impiety, and as to its nature, as loathsome and agonising ; though it has been observed, Luke, supposed to be a physician (Col. iv. 14), describes the symptoms, while Josephus states results."—LIVERMORE.

" *The word of God grew.*" This stands in sublime contrast with the end of the persecutor : the persecutor is gone, but the persecuted cause moves grandly on.

" *And took with them John.*" " Barnabas and Saul," we are told, " returned from Jerusalem," having discharged their commission (chap. xi. 30), and now they return, taking with them John whose surname was Mark.

HOMILETICS.—The first nineteen verses of this chapter, treating of Peter in prison, we have already discussed. The paragraph now before us gives us an insight into the state of human society in the age and land of Herod. It is indeed more or less a true picture of human society as it appears at all times. We discover in the social life then and there, what we see here and now—*national inter-*

dependence, class wickedness, retributive justice, and remedial ministries.

Here we have—

I. NATIONAL INTERDEPENDENCE. The great fact which the incident illustrates is that of national interdependence. The Phœnicians wanted in this case what the Palestinians had, and the Palestinians no doubt needed what the Phœnicians could give them in return. A glorious fact in God's government of man is this fact of national interdependence. Throughout the earth one zone produces something which other zones have not, and the peculiar products of each contribute towards the consummation of man's well-being. This interdependence of nations serves—

First, *To stimulate human activities.* It presses ever on the sense of need and the love of gain in man, and thus keeps his powers in constant action. His faculties are ever on the stretch in contriving and constructing methods to work to the greatest advantage the soil on which he is placed, and to increase the facilities of transit. He makes seas his high-road, electricity his messenger, winds and fire the carriers to bear away his commodities to other lands. It serves—

Secondly, *To check all monopolies.* There are narrow souls who would keep all that their land produces to themselves, and within its own limits. Ignorant alike of the laws of the universe, the genius of the world in which they live, and the insignificance of their own existence, they vainly and proudly talk about their " *national independency.*" Nature laughs them to scorn. Creature independence is a solecism. A universe of creatures cannot make an independency. It serves—

Thirdly, *To promote international concord.* A free commerce throughout the world is one of the best means by which men can become mutually acquainted. The free interchange of commodities involves to some extent the free interchange of thought. Buyers and sellers mutually show themselves in their transactions. Feuds and wars are generated in the darkness of ignorance. The evil passions of the human soul go forth like the beasts of prey to devour in the shadows of night. Foreigners are miserably suspected, if not hated, until they are known. Knowledge turns the figure which looked grim and ghastly in the dark, into a man with loving sympathies and radiant look. Whilst knowledge of man is promoted by such commerce, interest in him is also advanced by it. It is to the interest of traders to be on terms of amity and free intercourse. The commercial interests of the world are against war, and will one day lead the world to look at soldiering as a clog on the wheels of industry which should be thrown away. There is, however, a higher concord even than this, a concord of *true brotherhood of soul,* a concord which commerce can only effect as it becomes thoroughly inspired and ruled by those high principles and that self-sacrificing benevolence which were embodied in the life of Him who came to break down all the partition-walls which divide men from men, and nation from nation.

Here we have—

II. CLASS WICKEDNESS. The two grand classes of society are the *rulers* and the *ruled*. These are the poles of social life. In this narrative you have their two characteristic evils in relation to each other, unbounded arrogance and base servility. Here is—

First, *Unbounded arrogance:* " And upon a set day, Herod, arrayed in royal apparel, sat upon his throne, and made an oration unto them." This " set day," it would seem, was a grand day at Cæsarea. Some say it was the second day of Herod's games, or public shows, in honour of his patron, Claudius: whilst others think it was a day to celebrate his return from Britain, which about this time he had reduced to his subjection as a Roman province. The occasion, certainly, was a grand one. Cæsarea was crowded with pleasure-seekers, gathered from all the surrouuding districts. The king enters that theatre which had been erected by his grandfather, the notorious murderer of the innocents. " The stone seats," we are told, " rising in a great semicircle, tier above tier, were covered with an excited multitude." Every eye can see the royal seat, and there sits the king clothed in magnificent robes, brilliant and costly with silver. He now makes " an oration unto them." What he said we know not : we may be sure it was very *grand*, like most modern " *orations.*" Every sentence was inflated with vanity, and every tone had the ring of one who would be thought a god. It would be as gorgeous in its form as was his costume ; as arrogant in its spirit as were his pretensions. In this oration, we suppose, he pronounced himself on the message which he had received through his ambassador, Blastus. Whether it was favourable or not, we are not informed. Now to us, at the distance of eighteen centuries, the impious arrogance of this man is astounding ; and yet it is *common to his class.* The haughtiness of rulers is proverbial. Many of them treat their fellow-men as if they themselves were a race of gods. For the want of a royal heart they assume royal pageantry. They would dazzle the people by the gorgeousness of their show, and rule them by the absoluteness of their will. This arrogance in rulers has ever been the fruitful source of all national feuds and insurrections.

Here is—

Secondly, *Base servility:* "And the people gave a shout, saying, It is the voice of a god, and not of a man." The " people," we suppose, means here the vast assembly which crowded the amphitheatre. If the monarch in his *oration* gave out a favourable answer to the Phœnician envoys, they would heartily join, if they did not even lead, the thunders of acclamation. Now there could be no sincerity in this demonstration. It is scarcely supposable that the shrewd trader from Phœnicia, and the cultured Greeks and Jews too, who might have been there, could have believed that this man was a god. It was simply base flattery. It was the shout of that servility which has been the sin and curse of the ruled in all ages. It is not uncommon, even in these days of enlightenment, to see men, crushed to poverty by the injustice of rulers, shouting hosannas in their ears. There is no greater obstruction to a free government, wholesome law, and national advancement, than the servile spirit of the millions towards those who are above them. It is not until the people practically reverence the rights of their manhood, practise self-reliance and honest individualism, that any true reform can be obtained, or, if obtained, truly valued. No government can help the man who respects not the high prerogatives of his own humanity.

Here we have—
III. RETRIBUTIVE JUSTICE. "And immediately the angel of the Lord smote him, because he gave not God the glory : and he was eaten of worms, and gave up the ghost." This Herod was one of those empty men who took the flattery in. He lacked that royalty of nature necessary to chastise his flatterers on account of their impiety. He wished to pass for what he was not, to receive even the honours of a god when he could get them. Little did he or his minions think that the Nemesis of retribution was there, heard all, peered into his heart, and resolved on avengement. "The angel of the Lord smote him." Does the "angel" here mean a fatal disease which arrested him and sealed up at once the fountains of his life, or a messenger despatched from heaven as an officer of Eternal Justice? The latter, I think. Angels had often done such work before (Exod. xii. 21 ; 2 Kings xix. 35 ; 2 Sam. xxiv. 16 ; 2 Chron. xxxii. 21). Whether or not Herod saw an owl perched upon a cord above his head, as Josephus states, it is clear from the passage before us that the king's terrible fate came upon him as a judgment from God. This event took place, according to Josephus, in the fifty-fourth year of Herod's age and the fourth of his reign, A.D. 44.

The *justice* of this man's fate is as clear as sunshine. Surely he who had just killed by the sword James the brother of John, who had imprisoned Peter, who had commanded that the keepers of the prison whence Peter escaped should be put to death, and who now with impious arrogance received the worship of a god, deserved the terrible end which now befell him. All consciences looking at it must be constrained to say, "The Judge of all the earth does right." Such instances of retributive justice had occurred with Pharaoh and Belshazzar, and others before, and have occurred since, but they are confessedly rare, as compared with the number of enormous offenders belonging to every age. Yet though rare, they are sufficient to show that there is a moral government in the world, that there is justice which sees the wrong and will avenge it, quite sufficient to prophesy with unmistakable clearness the coming of a period when retribution shall be fairly dealt out to all. They are to the period of the world's assizes what the buddings of early spring are to the fruits of autumn, what the first rays of the sun playing upon the mountains are to the full tide of noon—patterns and precursors.

Here we have—

IV. REMEDIAL FORCES. Though there was so much that is bad and terrible in Cæsarean society at this time, there was something good and delightful at work, and it is thus expressed : " The word of God grew and multiplied. And Barnabas and Saul returned from Jerusalem, when they had fulfilled their ministry, and took with them John, whose surname was Mark." We have here two remedial forces which were now at work and prospering.

First, *The Word of God*. This, we are told, "grew and multiplied." A word is the revelation of mind, and is great and mighty in proportion to the mind it represents. The gospel is *the* Word of GOD, the revelation of an omnipotent mind. God has other words, other revelations, but this is the Word. Christ, the substance of the Gospel, is the *Logos*—the fullest expression of Himself. The heavenly germ had been planted in the minds of the apostles, and they were planting it now among their fellow-men. Their work was prospering. The seed was growing everywhere, not only amongst the Jews, but amongst the Gentiles too. The fruit rising out of this new life is the antidote to the world's evils, the provision for the cravings of the human soul. Herod had done his best to crush it, so had his predecessors, so had the Jewish Sanhedrim ; but it went on, and as it advanced it elevated and blessed. The other remedial force is—

Secondly, *The agency of the good*. Here are Barnabas, Saul, and John, all working to help on the world in the true and the right. Barnabas and Saul, as we have already seen, had been deputed by the Church at Antioch to carry "relief unto the brethren which dwelt in Judæa." They had fulfilled their mission, and were returning to Antioch to give an account of their visit and to prosecute their work. They brought " John, whose surname was Mark," back with them to act as a coadjutor.

Thus Christianity, the " Word of God," and good men—Barnabas, Saul, and John—are working for the world's salvation ; whilst men like Herod, and those who gathered in the amphitheatre, were outraging every principle of morality, and adding to the crimes and disgrace of the race.

Thank God, the remedial forces are here with us, and they are our hope. We have still the Word of God and the agency of good men.

Part 3. The Church Among the Gentiles
Acts 13-28

Acts 13:1-12

*The designation of Barnabas and Saul to their missionary work,
and the glorious effects of their ministry.*

" *Now there were in the church that was at Antioch certain prophets and
teachers ; as Barnabas, and Simeon that was called Niger, and Lucius of
Cyrene, and Manaen, which had been brought up with* ¹ *Herod the tetrarch,
and Saul. As they ministered to the Lord, and fasted, the Holy Ghost
said, Separate me Barnabas and Saul for the work whereunto I have called
them. And when they had fasted and prayed, and laid their hands on
them, they sent them away. So they, being sent forth by the Holy Ghost,
departed* ² *unto Seleucia ; and from thence they sailed to Cyprus. And
when they were at Salamis, they preached the word of God in the synagogues
of the Jews : and they had also John to their minister. And when they
had gone through the isle unto Paphos, they found a certain sorcerer, a false
prophet, a Jew, whose name was Bar-jesus : which was with the deputy of
the country, Sergius Paulus, a prudent man ; who called for Barnabas
and Saul, and desired to hear the word of God. But Elymas the sorcerer
(for so is his name by interpretation) withstood them, seeking to turn away
the deputy from the faith. Then Saul, (who also is called Paul,) filled with
the Holy Ghost, set his eyes on him, and said, O full of all subtilty and all
mischief, thou child of the devil, thou enemy of all righteousness, wilt thou
not cease to pervert the right ways of the Lord ? And now, behold, the hand
of the Lord is upon thee, and thou shalt be blind, not seeing the sun for a
season. And immediately there fell on him a mist and a darkness ; and
he went about seeking some to lead him by the hand. Then the deputy,
when he saw what was done, believed, being astonished at the doctrine of the
Lord.*

EMENDATIVE RENDERINGS.—(1.) Foster-brother of. (2.) Went down.—ALF.

EXEGETICAL REMARKS.—With this chapter begins the third great division in apostolic history. The first part, extending from the first to the eighth chapter, is a history of ⋅the Church among the Jews ; the second, from the eighth to the thirteenth, a history of the Church in its passage from the Jews to the Gentiles. The third, a history of the Church among the Gentiles, extending from the thirteenth to the end, and is a record of the progress of Christianity from Antioch, through various districts, till it reaches Rome, the empress of the world.

The first missionary tour we shall divide, for the sake of convenience, into four sections. From Antioch in Syria to Paphos; from Paphos to Iconium; from Iconium to Lystra and Derbe; and from Lystra and Derbe back to Antioch in Syria.

" *Now there were in the church that was at Antioch certain prophets and teachers,*" &c. The writer gives the names of a few of these " teachers and prophets " as specimens. " There is," to use the language of another, " a certain interest attached to each of them. SIMEON is one of those Jews who bore a Latin surname in addition to their Hebrew name; like John, whose surname is Mark, mentioned in the last verse of the preceding chapter; and like Saul himself. LUCIUS, probably the same as is mentioned in Rom. xvi. 21, is a native of Cyrene, that African city abounding with Jews, and which sent to Jerusalem our Saviour's cross-bearer. MANAEN is spoken of as the foster-brother of Herod the tetrarch. This was Herod Antipas, the tetrarch of Galilee; and since we learn from Josephus that this Herod and his brother Archelaus were children of the same mother, and afterwards educated at Rome, it is probable that this Christian prophet or teacher had spent his early childhood with these princes, who were now both banished from Palestine to the banks of the Rhine." " SAUL," he who was destined to be the greatest amongst the universal Church, is mentioned last. At present, perhaps, he had not distinguished himself, and remained in apparent obscurity.

" *As they ministered to the Lord, and fasted,*" &c. The word " ministered" here is the Greek from which our word "liturgy" is derived, and literally means any public service or official function.

" *So they being sent forth by the Holy Ghost, departed unto Seleucia,*" &c. Their route seemed as follows:

First, *They first go to Seleucia.* This was the port of Antioch, lying about fifteen miles west of that city, on the Mediterranean, at the mouth of the river Orontes, in Syria. It took its name from one of the successors of Alexander the Great, Sileucus Nicanor, by whom it was built. How they tra-

velled these fifteen miles we do not know—whether they walked or rode —nor are we told whether they went alone, or whether they were accompanied by members of the church. It would seem that John, otherwise called Mark, was with them as "their minister," or servant. They required such an attendant. Having to travel from place to place, they would need some one to attend to their secular concerns, and to provide for their wants. Their mission was spiritual, and the necessary temporalities were to be attended to by others.

Secondly, *From Seleucia they sailed to Cyprus.* Here they found some skiff bound to this island, and accordingly embarked. The island of Cyprus was sixty miles south-west of Seleucia; they had, therefore, sixty miles to go by sea. Travelling by sea was a very different thing in those days from what it is now; sixty miles then were more than six hundred now. The accommodation which modern vessels afford to their passengers, making even long voyages a pleasure, was of course unknown in those ancient times. Cyprus was a large island, renowned in former times for wealth, fertility, and luxury. It was now a Roman province, and ruled by a proconsul. Five reasons have been suggested for their making Cyprus their first destination: (1.) Its contiguity to the mainland of Syria. (2.) Its visibility from the sea by reason of its high mountains. (3.) The constant marine traffic, especially in summer seasons, which was carried on between it and Seleucia. No sooner, perhaps, did the apostles reach the latter, than they found a craft ready. (4.) It was the native place of Barnabas, and instinct as well as policy would suggest it to him as the most favourable scene for first labour. (5.) The Jews were numerous in that island. Although their mission was to the Gentiles, their surest course for reaching them was through the synagogues, for there they found the proselytes and the Hellenistic Jews.

Thirdly, *They direct their steps to the capital of Cyprus, Salamis.* Here, we are told, " they preached the word of God in the synagogues of the

Jews." The synagogues furnished excellent openings for the introduction of the gospel, and the apostles availed themselves everywhere of them.

Fourthly, *They proceeded from Salamis to Paphos.* This place was situated on the western extremity of Cyprus, and was famous for its luxury and licentiousness. It contained a splendid temple, dedicated to Venus, whose worship was of the most dissolute character. The extent of the island of Cyprus from east to west was about four hundred miles. The apostles probably traversed the whole, and visited everywhere where there was a population. Such were the scenes which the missionaries *first* visited. How long they were occupied in these first journeyings we know not. The fatigues, the inconveniences, and the perils of traversing these districts can hardly be appreciated by us in these days, when facilities for travelling are so numerous and complete.

HOMILETICS.—The paragraph now under notice may lead us to consider *the designation of Barnabas and Saul to missionary work, and the glorious effects of their ministry.*

I. THEIR DESIGNATION TO THE MISSIONARY WORK. Three things are observable here :—

First, *The persons by whom they were designated.* Simeon that was called Niger, Lucius of Cyrene, and Manaen, " which had been brought up with Herod the tetrarch." Observe—(1.) They were designated by the most *influential* of the members. It is not to be supposed that these were the only members of the church at Antioch. They are mentioned as the most prominent and representative men. (2.) They were designated by the direction of the Divine Spirit : " Separate me Barnabas and Saul," &c. (3.) The Divine Spirit directed them as they were devotionally engaged. It was " as they ministered to the Lord, and fasted." The whole Church, it is likely, was at this time taken up with special religious devotions, importuning Heaven, it may be, for some fresh revelation of duty. The communication from the Spirit must be regarded as an answer to their supplications.

Secondly, *The reason why they were designated.* Why were Barnabas and Saul to be sent forth as missionaries more than any other members of that church ? The answer we have in the words of the Spirit. It is, " the work whereunto I have called them." They were divinely selected and divinely qualified for this missionary undertaking. The call of the Spirit is that alone which gives validity to any ordination to spiritual office. If the Spirit call us to a work, we are divinely ordained : if He call us not, " the ordination services " of churches are a mockery, nothing more.

Thirdly, *The ceremonies by which they were designated.* " And when they had fasted and prayed, and laid their hands on them, they sent them away." They implored the benediction of Heaven upon the missionaries elect ; then they " laid their hands on them," as a sign of transfer from the ordinary services of the church into a special mission. The act was *moral*, not *official ;* designed not to confer the gifts of the Spirit, or authority from any ecclesiastical body, but to invoke a blessing upon those beloved and gifted ones who were about to plunge into the midnight of the Gentile world, and encounter all the terrible dangers and sufferings of persecution.

Paul repeatedly and earnestly asserts his apostolic authority from God, not from man (Rom. i. 1; 1 Cor. i. 1; 2 Cor. i. 1; Gal. i. 1; Eph. i. 1; Col. i. 1; 2 Tim. i. 1). "The nature and design of this proceeding have been variously understood in accordance with various conclusions or hypotheses as to church organisation. (1.) It could not have been an ordination to the ministry, for the very two men set apart were already eminent and successful ministers, far more illustrious in the Church than those who are supposed to have ordained them. (2.) It could not have been a consecration (so called) to the diocesan episcopate, for, even admitting its existence, why should all those prelates be attached to one church? or, if not prelates, how could they bestow a higher office than they held themselves? (3.) It could not have been, as some allege, an elevation of these two men to the apostleship, to fill the places of the two Jameses; for how could ordinary ministers, or even bishops, create apostles? or how could such an act be reconciled with Paul's asseveration that his apostleship was not from men, nor even through men? or with the fact that Barnabas is nowhere subsequently called an apostle, except on one occasion in conjunction with Paul, and even then in a dubious sense? The only remaining supposition is, that this was a designation, not to a new rank or office, but to a new work, namely, that of foreign missions; or, rather, to this single mission, which they are subsequently said to have 'fulfilled.' It is not necessarily implied that this was the first intimation made to Barnabas and Saul of their vocation to the work of missions. The divine communication mentioned may have been previously made, and they may have come to Antioch for the very purpose of obtaining a dismission from the Church there; and it may have been in reference to this request that the prophets and teachers were engaged in special prayer and fasting for divine direction."—ALEXANDER.

Such was the designation of these missionaries. The Church, obeying the voice of the Spirit, set them apart; laid their hands upon them, implored the divine benediction, and sent them away.

II.—THEIR SUCCESS IN THE MISSIONARY WORK

There are two striking facts recorded in connexion with the first missionary tour: both occurred at Paphos.

First, *The vanquishment of evil in the person of Elymas.* At Paphos " they found a certain sorcerer, a false prophet, a Jew," &c. Observe the *two very opposite* aspects in which this man stands before us; the one in which he stood before the eyes of his corrupt age, and the other in which he stood before a divinely-inspired apostle.

(1.) In the eye of his *depraved age* he is a very *great man*. He is a magician, a prophet, "Bar-jesus"—the son of some distinguished Joshua. He was regarded no doubt with a superstitious reverence by the men of his city and times. Even "Sergius Paulus, a prudent man," an enlightened Roman, the "deputy of the country," representing Cæsar himself, was greatly under the influence of this Elymas. He was a great man with his age. He assumed the prerogatives of Deity, and people then, as now, accepted assumptions.

(2.) In the eye of *true men* he is a *contemptible character*. Paul, "filled with the Holy Ghost, set his eyes on him, and said, O full of all subtilty and all mischief, thou child of the devil, thou enemy of all righteousness." The "son of Jesus" in the estimation of the world, is the "child of the devil" in the eye of Paul. The world's great sage and seer was to Paul a man "full of all subtilty and all mischief." The apostle peers into the man's heart, strips off all his assumptions, exposes and denounces his miserable dishonesties, impieties, and corruptions. There is a fire of holy indignation in the apostle's words. The spirit that enabled Paul to read this impostor's heart, enabled him also to chastise him on account of his sins. "Behold, the hand of the Lord is upon thee, and thou shalt be blind, not seeing the sun for a season." And it was so. "And immediately there fell on him a mist and a darkness." Here is the vanquishing of evil. This Elymas is the type of all the ungodly classes who pass in society for what they are not. Great they may be in the estimation of their contemporaries, but contemptible in the eye of Christianity. They have only to be exposed to be vanquished.

Secondly, *The creation of the good in the person of Sergius Paulus.* This proconsul was won to the gospel. "Then the deputy, when he saw what was done, believed." Here is the greatest man in the island converted to the new faith.

What Christianity did at Paphos it is ever doing—(1.) *vanquishing the evil;* and (2.) *creating the good.*

Acts 13:13, 14

THE FIRST MISSIONARY TOUR.—II. FROM PAPHOS TO ICONIUM

1.—*The new name given to Saul, and the withdrawal of John from Perga.*

" *Now when Paul and his company loosed from Paphos, they came to Perga in Pamphylia: and John departing from them returned to Jerusalem. But when they departed from Perga, they came to Antioch in Pisidia, and went into the synagogue on the sabbath day, and sat down.*"

EXEGETICAL REMARKS. — "*Now when Paul and his company loosed from Paphos.*" Paphos, a city at the western extremity of the land (Cyprus), where they had laboured for some time, where they had converted Sergius Paulus and smitten Elymas the sorcerer with blindness, is the port from which they start.

"*They came to Perga in Pamphylia, &c.* The first city they next come to is Perga in Pamphylia. Pamphylia was a province of Asia Minor, lying over against Cyprus; and Perga was the metropolis of the province, situated not on the sea-coast, but on the river Cestus, about twelve miles from its mouth. Cicero says that this city was distinguished by possessing the most ancient and sacred temple of the goddess Diana. Their stay at Perga on this occasion seems to have been short. Nothing is recorded of anything they said or did there. The only thing that occurred there of importance was, "John departing from them returned to Jerusalem."

"*They departed from Perga, they came to Antioch in Pisidia.*" They seem to have visited Pamphylia at this time only as the key or entrance to this Antioch in Pisidia, where they did a large amount of spiritual work and produced much excitement. This Antioch is called Antioch in Pisidia to distinguish it from Antioch in Syria. It was situated about ninety miles north of Perga. It was built by the founder of the Syrian Antioch, and in the age of the Greek kings of the line of Seleucius, and was a town at this time of considerable importance. Here Paul on this occasion preached his first *recorded* sermon, which effected the conversion of numbers, and raised at this time such a fierce spirit of persecution · as led to the expulsion of the apostles from the locality.

" *They went into the synagogue.*" Synagogues, which were places of public worship among the Jews, were coextensive with the Jewish people. Wherever there was a colony of Jews there was a synagogue. They varied, it would seem, in magnitude and decoration from the simple proseucha at Philippi, to the magnificent prayer-house at Alexandria.

HOMILETICS.—Now, in looking at this section of their missionary tour, we discover two things of such interest and significance as to require special attention,—viz. *the new name which is given to Saul, and the withdrawal of John.*

I. THE NEW NAME WHICH WAS GIVEN TO SAUL. " Now when Paul and his company loosed from Paphos." Paul !—a new name this in evangelical history. It is true that in the ninth verse it is said that he is "also called Paul;" but here the name is first written by the historian as the name by which the great apostle would henceforth be known. Up to this point he had uniformly been called Saul by the historian; hence on, he is uniformly designated Paul. Henceforth, too, the apostle himself, in all his epistles, without any exception, speaks of himself under this name. Peter also calls him "our beloved brother Paul." Why the name Saul is dropped and that of Paul assumed, is a question open to much speculation. Was it because he had just converted a distinguished Roman by that name —Sergius Paulus? Or was it to mark the change that had been effected in his life by his conversion to Christianity? Or was it because the resignation of a Jewish and the adoption of a Roman name would facilitate his introduction among the Gentiles? I can scarcely say yea to either. It seems to me probable that the apostle had this Roman name before, as well as the other Hebrew name Saul, and that, now he was going to live and labour amongst the Gentiles, he drops the Jewish cognomen for the Roman.* What a different life these two names, in the history of the same man, represent. Under the name Saul there stands before you a man of great intellect, great culture, great genius, great enthusiasm, consecrating for the most part his mighty powers to the cause of bigotry, religious intolerance, and the devil. Under the name Paul you have all the energies and resources of the same great man, most self-sacrificingly and enthusiastically employed to extend the divine gospel of love, to ameliorate the woes of the world, and to raise humanity to the blessedness of heaven. Around this name, Paul, the sympathies of the Church in all ages have gathered, nor will it lose the charm of that name whilst its memory endures.

II. THE WITHDRAWAL OF JOHN AT PERGA. "And John departing from them, returned to Jerusalem." This is an incident that should not be overlooked. There is to us a saddening interest about it. Who was this John? His surname was Mark. He was the son of that Mary into whose house Peter went after the angel had delivered him from prison out of the hand of Herod, where "many were gathered together praying" (Acts xii. 12). He was probably the Mark who wrote the Gospel bearing his name. He was the son of Mary, the sister of Barnabas. He had not been long with the apostles. He left Jerusalem with Barnabas and Saul when they were returning to Antioch, after they had dispensed relief for the distressed in Jerusalem, and had gone forth with them from Antioch to Cyprus, and had tended on them at Salamis and Paphos; but now at Perga he leaves them. Why did he leave them? Was *love of home* the cause? Had he one of those domestic natures that

---

* See Conybeare and Howson, who on this point in the apostle's history, as well as on every other, throw considerable light.

are happy nowhere but at the family hearth? Was he impelled from a desire to see his pious mother, and to mingle again with his old companions at Jerusalem? Or was it lack of the power of endurance? Did he find himself physically incapable of bearing up under such a life of privation, toil, and excitement as that to which the missionaries were committed? Or was it cowardice? Did the dangers that threatened them everywhere, by sea and land—dangers arising from their modes of travelling and the bloody persecution which their mission awoke—so intimidate his soul and upset his nerves that he could go on no longer? Or was it because he was discontented with the unexpected transfer of authority from Barnabas, his uncle, to Paul? Hitherto Barnabas was the active man, and took the lead in all; now Paul, from the superiority of energy, not against the consent of Barnabas, but with it, rose supreme in influence. His nephew might have felt this. He might have felt that it was not the thing that his uncle, who was the elder Christian and minister too, and who, moreover, had introduced Paul both to the mother Church at Jerusalem, and the Gentile Church at Antioch, should be thrown into a secondary position. This I think the most probable reason. Hence we find (chap. xv. 36–38), when Paul suggested to Barnabas that they should go again and visit every city where they had preached the word of the Lord, and Barnabas wished to take John his nephew with them, that Paul positively refused to have him. "But Paul thought not good to take him with them; who departed from them from Pamphylia, and went not with them to the work." This little incident is sufficient to teach three things:

First, *The imperfection of the best human fellowship.* Three better men than Paul, Barnabas, and John, were not to be found. When they went forth from Jerusalem together, the hearts of the trio throbbed in happy unison; but here is a jar, here is a disruption. We learn—

Secondly, *The insufficiency even of religion to make the society of all thoroughly congenial.* There are constitutionally in men social affinities and antipathies which grace regulates but does not overcome. There are natures with whom we cannot blend, nor can they blend with us. These three men were good, but they could not coalesce. We learn—

Thirdly, *The importance of relying on self and God in our labours, rather than on the support of coadjutors.* It is natural to seek for co-operation in labour; it would be unjust to refuse it when offered, if good; but to depend on it is irreligious, unmanly, and generally disappointing.

Acts 13:15-41

THE FIRST MISSIONARY TOUR.—FROM PAPHOS TO ICONIUM *(continued)*

2.—*The substance of Paul's first reported sermon.*

" And after the reading of the law and the prophets, the rulers of the synagogue sent unto them, saying, Ye men and brethren, if ye have any word of exhortation for the people, say on. Then Paul stood up, and beckoning with his hand, said, Men of Israel, and ye that fear God, give audience. The God of this people of Israel chose our fathers, and exalted the people when they dwelt as strangers in the land of Egypt, and with an high arm brought he them out of it. And about the time of forty years suffered he their manners in the wilderness. And when he had destroyed seven nations in the land of Chanaan, he divided[1] their land to them by lot. And after that he gave unto them judges, about the space of four hundred and fifty years, until Samuel the prophet. And afterward they desired a king : and God gave unto them Saul the son of Cis, a man of the tribe of Benjamin, by the space of forty years. And when he had removed him, he raised up[2] unto them David to be their king, to whom also he gave testimony, and said, I have found David the son of Jesse, a man after mine own heart, which shall fulfil all my will. Of this man's seed hath God, according to his promise, raised unto Israel[3] a Saviour, Jesus : When John had first preached before his coming the baptism of repentance to all the people of Israel. And as John fulfilled his course, he said, Whom think ye that I am ? I am not he : but, behold, there cometh one after me, whose shoes of his feet I am not worthy to loose. Men and[4] brethren, children of the stock of Abraham, and whosoever among you feareth God,[5] to you is the word of this salvation sent. For they that dwell at Jerusalem, and their rulers, because they knew him not, nor yet the voices of the prophets, which are read every sabbath-day, they have fulfilled them in condemning him. And though they found no cause of death in him, yet desired they Pilate[6] that he should be slain. And when they had fulfilled all that was written of him, they took him down from the tree, and laid him in a sepulchre. But God raised him from the dead : And he was seen many days of them which came up with him from Galilee to Jerusalem, who are his witnesses unto the people. And we declare unto you glad tidings, how that the promise which was made unto the fathers, God hath fulfilled the same unto us their children, in that he hath raised up Jesus again ;[7] as it is also written in the second psalm, Thou art my Son, this day have I begotten thee. And as concerning that he raised him up from the dead, now no more to return to corruption, he said on this wise, I will give you the sure mercies of David.[8] Wherefore he saith also in another psalm, Thou shalt not suffer thine Holy One to see corruption. For David, after he had served his own generation by the will of God, fell on sleep, and was laid unto his fathers and saw corruption : But he, whom God raised again, saw no corruption. Be it known unto you therefore, men and brethren, that through this man is preached[9] unto you the forgiveness of sins : And by *him all that believe are justified from all things, from which ye could not be justified by the law of Moses.*[10] *Beware, therefore, lest that come upon you which is spoken of in the prophets; Behold, ye despisers, and wonder, and perish : for I work a work in your days, a work which ye shall in no wise believe, though a man declare it unto you.*

EMENDATIVE RENDERINGS.—(1.) And he destroyed seven nations in the land of Canaan and divided. (2.) And he removed him and raised up. (3.) Of this man's seed hath God according to promise brought unto Israel. (4.) Omit *men and.* (5.) Those among you who fear God. (6.) And when they found no cause of death in him they desired Pilate. (7.) Omit this word. (8.) The mercies of David, holy and sure. (9.) Announced. (10.) And in Him every one that believeth is justified from all things, from which ye could not be justified in the law of Moses.—ALF.

EXEGETICAL REMARKS.—" *After the reading of the law and the prophets.*" The law of Moses was divided into various sections, one of which was read each Sabbath-day, and the whole in the course of the year. Bengel suggests " that as each portion was read in conjunction with a portion from the prophets, it is not likely that Deut. i. and Isa. i. were read together on this occasion."

" *The rulers of the synagogue sent unto them saying, Ye men and brethren.*" Each synagogue had three rulers who regulated all its concerns, and they granted an opportunity to whomsoever they pleased to preach and exhort.

" *And after that, he gave unto them judges about the space of four hundred and fifty years, until Samuel the prophet.*" " As this appears to contradict 1 Kings vi. 1, various solutions have been proposed. Taking the words as they stand in the Greek, thus, ' after that, by the space of 450 years, he gave judges,' the meaning may be, that about 450 years

elapsed from the time of the covenant with Abraham *until* the period of the judges, which is historically correct, the word ' about ' showing that chronological exactness was not aimed at. But taking the sense to be as in our version, that it was the period of the judges itself which lasted about 450 years, this statement also will appear historically correct, if we include in it the interval of subjection to foreign powers which occurred during the period of the judges, and understand it to describe the whole period from the settlement of the tribes in Canaan to the establishment of royalty. Thus, from the Exodus to the building of the temple were 592 years (Josephus, *Antiquities*, viii. 3. 1): deduct forty years in the wilderness ; twenty-five years of Joshua's rule (Josephus' *Antiquities*, v. 1. 29) ; forty years of Saul's reign (v. 21) ; forty of David's, and the first four years of Solomon's reign (1 Kings vi. 1) ; and there remain just 443 *years;* or, in round numbers, about 450 years."—P. C.

HOMILETICS.—This paragraph leads us to consider *the substance of Paul's first reported sermon.*

The *day* on which the sermon was delivered was the " Sabbath-day." It was on this day the Jews and the proselytes invariably met in the synagogues. It was the day when they would be found there in greater numbers, and which was set apart for special purposes of religious instruction and worship. Into one of these synagogues now at Antioch, Barnabas and Paul entered and sat down. After the prayers were recited, extracts from the law and the prophets read, the book returned to the minister, the rulers of the synagogue sent to the strangers, saying, " Ye men and brethren, if ye have any word of exhortation to the people, say on." Paul seized the opportunity, accepted the invitation, and, with the bearing of an orator, " beckoning with his hand," and the zeal of an apostle, commenced by saying, " Men of Israel, and ye that fear God, give audience."

Looking at the sermon, we discover in it three great facts which he seemed anxious to impress on their attention.

I. THAT THEIR SCRIPTURES, WHICH EXHIBITED GOD'S SPECIAL KINDNESS TO THEM AS A PEOPLE, CONTAINED THE PROMISE OF A MESSIAH. After reminding them of certain striking facts in their history, showing how wondrously kind God had been to them as a people, extending from verse 17 to 21, he directs them at once to the great prophetic truth that there was, according to their Scriptures, to come a Messiah. He states—

First, *That David was to be the progenitor of that Messiah.* " And when he had removed him, he raised up unto them David to be their king ; to whom also he gave testimony, and said, I have found David the son of Jesse, a man after mine own heart, which shall fulfil all my will. Of this man's seed hath God, according to his promise, raised unto Israel a Saviour, Jesus."

Secondly, *That John the Baptist, one of the greatest prophets of their age, was to be His forerunner.* " When John had first preached before his coming the baptism of repentance to all the people of Israel. And as John fulfilled his course, he said, Whom think ye that I am ? I am not he. But, behold, there cometh one after me, whose shoes of his feet I am not worthy to loose " (24, 25). This fact, namely, that their Scriptures pointed to a Messiah, they would be prepared, of course, readily to admit. Hence he proceeds to another fact arising out of this which would not be so easily admitted.

II. THAT THE MESSIAH PREDICTED BY THEIR SCRIPTURES HAD ACTUALLY APPEARED ON THE EARTH. " Men and brethren, children of the stock of Abraham, and whosoever among you feareth God, to you is the word of this salvation sent." He states facts that occurred in the history of the Messiah while here.

First, *That he was crucified and buried according to their Scriptures.* " For they that dwell at Jerusalem, and their rulers, because they knew him not, nor yet the voices of the prophets which are read every Sabbath-day, they have fulfilled them in condemning him. And though they found no cause of death in him, yet desired they Pilate that he should be slain. And when they had fulfilled all that was written of him, they took him down from the tree, and laid him in a sepulchre " (27–29). In their Scriptures they would find an account of just the treatment He actually met with on the earth.

Secondly, *That God actually raised Him from the dead, also, according to their Scriptures.* " But God raised him from the dead : and he was seen many days of them which came up with him

from Galilee to Jerusalem, who are his witnesses unto the people."
He states that Christ's resurrection was *well attested* by living witnesses. " And he was seen many days of them," &c. (31). He
states that His resurrection formed the *glad tidings* which they had
to declare unto them. " We declare unto you glad tidings " &c. (32).
He states that His resurrection was *a fulfilment of their Scriptures.*
" God hath fulfilled the same unto us their children, in that he hath
raised up Jesus again," &c., &c. (33-35).* In quoting these passages he seemed to anticipate that some of his audience would say
that they referred to David ; but this he declares is impossible, as
that David " was laid unto his fathers, and saw corruption." The
other great fact we discover in this sermon is,

III. THAT THIS MESSIAH IS THE MEDIATOR THROUGH WHOM
THE WORLD IS TO BE SAVED. He states—
First, *That faith in Him will secure the forgiveness of all sins.*
" Be it known unto you, therefore, men and brethren," &c.† He
states—
Secondly, *That the rejection of Him is of all crimes the most to
be deprecated.* " Beware, therefore, lest that come upon you which
is spoken of in the prophets ; Behold, ye despisers, and wonder, and
perish : for I work a work in your days, a work which ye shall in no
wise believe, though a man declare it unto you." (1.) *That sometimes the Divine judgments following the rejection of God's word
have been foretold.* It is the principle of the divine government
that punishment shall ever follow unbelief. Numerous instances in
the Bible might be cited. The apostle quotes a case here where such
punishment had been predicted. The passage is taken from Hab. i.
5. The original design of the prediction was to proclaim the ruin
that would come upon the Jewish nation by the Chaldeans. The
reason why that ruin came on them from God was their unbelief.
(2.) *That the judgments that have followed unbelief in past times
should be taken as types and warnings of those that will follow the rejection of God's word in Jesus Christ.* Thus the apostle uses Divine
judgment here. The passage which he quotes from the Septuagint,
not by any means with literal accuracy, he cites to show, not that this
particular prophecy will be fulfilled in the experience of the rejectors
of Christ, but that something as terrible. From the language
we may infer—(*a*) That the judgment, when it comes, will fill the
victim with *amazement*—" Behold, ye despisers, and wonder." What
wild amazement seized the antediluvians, the men of Sodom, &c.,
when the judgment came. (*b*) That the judgment, when it comes,
will effect *utter destruction*—" perish." (*c*) That the judgment that
is to come is *incredibly tremendous.* It is " a work which ye shall
in no wise believe, though a man declare it unto you."

* See a homily on this part of the passage, Homilist, 2d series, vol. iv. p. 359.
† See a homily on this text, Homilist, 1st series, vol. vi. p. 276.

Acts 13:42-52

THE FIRST MISSIONARY TOUR.—FROM PAPHOS TO ICONIUM
(continued)

3.—The effects of Paul's first reported sermon

And when the Jews were gone out of the synagogue, the Gentiles besought [1] *that these words might be preached to them the next sabbath. Now when the congregation was broken up, many of the Jews and religious proselytes followed Paul and Barnabas: who, speaking to them, persuaded them to continue in the grace of God. And the next sabbath day came almost the whole city together to hear the word of God. But when the Jews saw the multitudes, they were filled with envy, and spake against those things which were spoken by Paul, contradicting and blaspheming. Then Paul and Barnabas waxed bold, and said, It was necessary that the word of God should first have been spoken to you: but seeing ye put it from you, and judge yourselves unworthy of everlasting life, lo, we turn to the Gentiles. For so hath the Lord commanded us, saying, I have set thee to be a light of the Gentiles, that thou shouldest be for salvation unto the ends of the earth. And when the Gentiles heard this, they were glad, and glorified the word of the Lord: and as many as were ordained to* [2] *eternal life believed. And the word of the Lord was published throughout all the region. But the Jews stirred up the devout and honourable women, and the chief men of the city, and raised persecution against Paul and Barnabas, and expelled them out of their coasts. But they shook off the dust of their feet against them, and came unto Iconium. And the disciples were filled with joy and with the Holy Ghost.*

EMENDATIVE RENDERINGS.—(1.) And they having gone out, they besought.—ALEX. (2.) Disposed of.—BLOOMFIELD.

EXEGETICAL REMARKS. — " *Might be preached to them the next sabbath.*" Margin,—In the week between, or in the Sabbath between.

" *And the next Sabbath-day came almost the whole city together.*" The crowd was probably increased by the instructions and appeals of Paul and Barnabas during the interval between these Sabbaths.

" *And spake against those things which were spoken by Paul, contradicting and blaspheming.*" " *Spake against* and *contradicting* are in Greek but two forms of the same verb, which includes the meaning of both English ones, to wit, the idea of denial and that of vituperation or abuse."—ALEXANDER.

" *It was necessary that the word of*

God should first have been spoken unto you.*" The recipients and pupils of the earlier dispensation were to have the first offer of the blessings of the new. —Luke xxiv. 47.

" *But seeing ye put it from you, and judge yourselves unworthy of everlasting life.*" This is irony. They did not judge themselves unworthy, but they acted as if they did, and their conduct proved their unworthiness.

" *Lo, we turn to the Gentiles.*" This does not mean that Paul now for the first time was directed to the Gentiles, nor that henceforth he would no more address himself to the conversion of the Jews, but that he now turned from the Jewish portion of his audience to the Gentiles.

" *And as many as were ordained to*

eternal life believed." The word " ordained" here does not necessarily mean appointed or decreed, but rather prepared or disposed. The true version seems to be, " As many as were disposed, bent on, or inclined to eternal life, believed." The reference is of course to the Gentiles, in contradistinction to the Jews. The Jews were hostile to the gospel, and would not listen ; the Gentiles were disposed to listen, and believed.

HOMILETICS.—This paragraph brings under our notice the *results of Paul's first reported sermon.*

What were the effects produced by this first reported sermon of the great apostle ?

I. A GENERAL SPIRIT OF RELIGIOUS INQUIRY. "And when the Jews were gone out of the synagogue, the Gentiles besought that these words might be preached to them the next sabbath." According to the latest critics, the words " Jews," " synagogues," and " Gentiles," in this verse, have all been interpolated by the copyist. The reading now adopted would be, " And they—the apostles—having gone, they —the hearers—besought that these words might be preached to them the next Sabbath-day. The sermon had aroused such a spirit of inquiry in the audience that there was an earnest request that the same discourse should be delivered on the next Sabbath-day. A sermon has done much when it has broken the monotony of thought, and excited the spirit of religious inquiry.

II. THE CONVERSION OF MANY OF THE HEARERS. "Now when the congregation was broken up, many of the Jews and religious proselytes followed Paul and Barnabas : who, speaking to them, persuaded them to continue in the grace of God." In the last clause of this verse, as in the first of that before it, the subjects of the verbs are not expressed, so that it may either mean that these Jews and proselytes persuaded Paul and Barnabas to persevere in the good work they had begun, or that Paul and Barnabas persuaded them to persevere in their inquiries after saving truth, here called " the grace of God." The former construction is of course inadmissible. The meaning is, that Paul and Barnabas exhorted them to continue in " the grace of God ; " and this implies, of course—

First, *That they had received it.* Had been converted.

Secondly, *That there was a danger of losing it.*

III. A GREAT EXCITEMENT AMONGST ALL CLASSES. " And the next sabbath day came almost the whole city together to hear the word of God." The words of Paul had struck into the heart of the population, and set the minds of all alive. During the previous week, his sermon was the one thought in all minds, the one subject of talk in all circles. All felt anxious to hear more ; so that now, at the dawn of the Sabbath-day, they gather in crowds to hear the wondrous truths again. The gospel breaks the stagnant atmosphere of the mind, and unchains the strong winds of thought.

IV. The stirring up of a bitter persecution. "But when the Jews saw the multitudes, they were filled with envy, and spake against those things which were spoken by Paul, contradicting and blaspheming." When the Jews saw the crowds of Gentiles flocking to the apostles, admitting their judgment on the claims of the Messiah, and treated by them as on terms of equality with the chosen people, their envy was kindled, the fiendish flame raged in their bosoms, and they began to contradict and blaspheme. They spake against them, dealt in calumny, reviled them as heretics and false teachers. True and powerful sermons will excite antagonism as well as win converts.

V. The increased power of the apostles in their work. "Then Paul and Barnabas waxed bold and said, It was necessary that the word of God should first have been spoken to you: but seeing ye put it from you, and judge yourselves unworthy of everlasting life, lo, we turn to the Gentiles. For so hath the Lord commanded us, saying, I have set thee to be a light of the Gentiles, that thou shouldest be for salvation unto the ends of the earth." Like all true men, they grew greater in the presence of difficulties—they grew braver as perils thickened around them. Opposition never intimidates great natures in a good cause. On the contrary, it brings out their manhood in defiant attitudes. Hence we are told that Paul and Barnabas "waxed bold." In the text we have three things :

First, *The gospel offered by a divine plan.* "It was necessary," said the apostles to those unbelieving and persecuting Jews, "that the word of God should first have been spoken to you." Necessary? What made it necessary? The purpose of Christ. He commanded "that repentance and remission of sins should be preached in his name among all nations, beginning at Jerusalem." The Jews were to have the first offer. There were good and wise reasons for this. Their offer to the Jew "first" was—(1.) *The strongest proof of the sincerity of their own faith.* The Jew lived on the very scenes where the great facts of Christianity occurred. They were eye-witnesses of the whole. Their offer to the Jew "first" was—(2.) *The strongest proof of the mercifulness of their system.* The loving genius of their religion came out in this. The Jew was the greatest sinner ; the Jews crucified the Lord of life and glory. Christ's true ministers, in offering the provisions of the gospel, are directed by a divine plan. There is no caprice or accident in their movements. In the text we have—

Secondly, *The gospel rejected by an unbelieving people.* "Seeing ye put it from you, and judge yourselves unworthy of everlasting life." "Judge yourselves unworthy!" Is not this withering irony? The Jew think himself unworthy of eternal life! Proud spirits ; they considered nothing too good in heaven or earth for them ; they felt themselves worthy of heaven's choicest gifts. (1.) *Man's conduct is his true verdict upon himself.* A man is not what he may think he is, or say he is, or what others may judge he is, but *is what his conduct is.* His every-day life pronounces the true sentence upon himself—the only sentence that conscience will accept. (2.) *Man's sentence upon himself when he rejects the gospel, is terribly awful.* " Unworthy of everlasting life." The man who rejects the gospel declares by the very act his thorough unworthiness, unfitness for eternal life. He dooms himself to eternal death. In the text we have—

Thirdly, *The gospel promoted by earnest men.* " Lo, we turn to the Gentiles." We have no time to lose. Souls by millions around us want the salvation we are commissioned to offer. We have offered it to you. You have rejected it. Adieu, we hasten to other spheres. "We turn to the Gentiles." Two things are suggested here : (1.) *A lamentable condition for a people.* These unbelieving Jews are left—the apostles turn from them—the gospel is withdrawn. A greater calamity this to a people than if the sun went down and left their heavens in sackcloth. Mercy will not always continue with a people. " My spirit shall not always strive with man." (2.) *An obvious duty for a ministry.* It was right for these gospel labourers to leave a rocky, sterile and unproductive soil, and try elsewhere. Their field is the world. Ministers are not only justified, but often bound to leave their sphere of labour. That ministry which is unsuccessful in one sphere, is often gloriously prosperous in another. These apostles wrought wonders amongst the Gentiles. In the text we have—

Fourthly, *The gospel designed for the world by the mercy of God.* " For so hath the Lord commanded us, saying, I have set thee to be a light to the Gentiles," &c. They assured them first of *God's* SPECIAL *kindness to them.*

VI. A PRACTICAL ACCEPTATION OF THE GOSPEL BY A LARGE NUMBER OF THE GENTILES. "And when the Gentiles heard this, they were glad, and glorified the word of the Lord : and as many as were ordained to eternal life believed. And the word of the Lord was published throughout all the region." The idea is, that as many as were disposed unto eternal life—the gospel—believed in it. If the verse had been translated according to the proper meaning of the original, it would have run thus : "As many as were disposed for eternal life believed." And Bloomfield, in speaking of this passage, says, " So far from favouring the system of actual election, the words rather support the opposite direction, namely, that God, while

'Binding nature fast in fate,
Left free the human will.' "

The idea is, that those who are *disposed* for the gospel believe in it, and this is evermore the case.

VII. THE EXPULSION OF THE APOSTLES FROM THEIR COASTS, AND THEIR DEPARTURE TO ICONIUM. " But the Jews stirred up the devout and honourable women, and the chief men of the city, and raised persecution against Paul and Barnabas, and expelled them out of their coasts. The words " devout " and " honourable " are not to be taken in a spiritual, but in a conventional sense ; they were " devout " in the sense of being proselytes, " honourable " in the sense of social rank. The persecuting Jews used the influence of these women to banish the apostles. Women have often been used as tools in the hands of persecutors. The persecutors so far succeeded that the apostles withdrew. " But they shook off the dust of their feet against them." The act does not mean indignation. No fires of revenge or resentment glowed in their bosoms. Shaking the dust off their feet was a dramatic act expressing abhorrence of their conduct in desecrating the most sacred of missions. They " came unto Iconium," where we shall again have to observe their movements, and to study their utterances and works.

Acts 14:1-5

THE FIRST MISSIONARY TOUR.—FROM PAPHOS TO ICONIUM
(*continued*)

4.—*The ministry of the Apostles at Iconium*

" And it came to pass in Iconium, that they went both together into the synagogue of the Jews, and so spake, that a great multitude both of the Jews and also of the Greeks believed. But the unbelieving Jews stirred up the Gentiles, and made their minds evil affected against the brethren.[1] Long time therefore abode they speaking boldly in the Lord, which gave testimony unto the word of his grace, and granted signs and wonders to be done by their hands. But the multitude of the city was divided: and part held with the Jews, and part with the apostles. And when there was an assault[2] made both of the Gentiles, and also of the Jews, with their rulers, to use them despitefully, and to stone them."

EMENDATIVE RENDERINGS.—(1.) But the Jews which believed not, stirred up and embittered the minds of the Gentiles against the brethren. (2.) A stir or movement. —ALF.

EXEGETICAL REMARKS.—" *It came to pass in Iconium.* The apostles are now at Iconium. This city was the capital of Lycaonia, about one hundred and twenty miles from the Mediter- ranean Sea ; its present name is Koniah. The climate is delicious ; it is embosomed by lofty mountains, gardens, and meadows, spread out in great beauty around it ; it holds a distinguished place in history; it is famous as "the cradle of the rising power, the conquering Turks." The elements of its population at the time when the apostles visited it would be as follows:—"A large number of trifling and frivolous Greeks, whose principal places of resort would be the theatre and the market-place; some remains of a still older population coming in occasionally from the country, or residing in a separate quarter of the town; some few Roman officials, civil or military, holding themselves proudly aloof from the inhabitants of the subjugated province; and an old-established colony of Jews, who exercised their trade during the week, and met on the Sabbath to read the law in the synagogue."

"*They went both together into the synagogue.*" "*Together.*" Though Paul was the prominent speaker, yet Barnabas always accompanied him. They went into the synagogue together. The synagogue was the medium of intercourse not only with the Jews, but with the serious Gentiles.

"*And so spake that a great multitude, both of the Jews and also of the Greeks, believed.*" "Some," says Alexander, "deny that heathen Greeks would frequent the synagogue, but such a practice is not only natural and probable, but actually mentioned in the classics, which bear witness to the interest felt in Judaism, and the practice of attending on its worship, even in Rome. It is said, indeed, that these were proselytes; but how could they become such if entirely unacquainted with the Jewish worship?" "*And so spake.*" They spoke with such remarkable force, warmth, and unction, that many of their hearers believed.

"*Long time, therefore, abode they speaking boldly in the Lord.*" In spite of opposition they continued "speaking boldly in the Lord," *i.e.* in dependence on Him.

HOMILETICS.—This paragraph leads us to consider the *ministry of the Apostles at Iconium.* Here they "so spake, that a great multitude both of the Jews and also of the Greeks believed." There are four things noteworthy connected with their ministry here.

I. AN EXTENSIVE CONVERSION. It is said that "a great multitude both of the Jews and also of the Greeks believed." What they said concerning Christ was said in such a manner, and so sanctioned by the Holy Spirit, that an extensive faith in Christianity was produced both among the Jews and the Gentiles. "A great multitude believed." The preaching that ends in enlightened practical faith is the preaching that Christ ordained and that the world wants. There is a preaching—(1.) That produces mere *passing emotion;* (2.) That produces *superstition;* (3.) That produces *scepticism.*

II. A VIOLENT OPPOSITION. "The unbelieving Jews stirred up the Gentiles, and made their minds evil affected against the brethren." The spiritual victories they won in the synagogue over the mind of the Jew and the Gentile, roused the antagonism of the unbelieving Jew, who used his great social influence to their disadvantage and injury. They "stirred up the Gentiles," *i.e.*, excited and embittered their minds with hostile passions. It is ever true that those who reject the gospel themselves seek to deter others from accepting it. "Ye neither go in yourselves; ye prevent those that would," is a divine allegation, ever true of the rejectors of Christianity.

III. A DIVINE DEMONSTRATION. Opposition neither drove them at once from the sphere of their labour, nor lessened the displays of divine power. On the contrary, they *abode* there, " speaking boldly in the Lord ;" and as they spoke, divine power was manifested in " signs and wonders." Divinity appears in their subject, their spirit, and their miracles.

First, In their *subject.* The " word of His grace," that is, His gracious word, the gospel. This is indeed a gracious word to humanity. Whatever doctrines men draw from the gospel that are not gracious, are not logical, not true. The gospel is a *gracious* word of infinite love.

Secondly, In their *spirit.* " Speaking boldly." They show a heroism more than human in continuing in the very scene of persecution, and speaking with so much intrepidity. " Long time therefore *abode* they speaking *boldly* in the Lord." The Spirit of God is manifest in that indomitable courage of theirs.

Thirdly, In their *miracles.* The Lord " granted signs and wonders to be done by their hands." The works they wrought are not recorded, but they were such as transcended human power, and were evidently the products of God. Thus the stronger the evil one appeared in Iconium opposing the mission of the apostles, the higher rose the manifestations of God in their behalf. " As thy days, so shall thy strength be."

IV. A SOCIAL SEPARATION. " But the multitude of the city was divided : and part held with the Jews, and part with the apostles." " Divided"—the Greek word from which *schism* is derived. There was a rent, a schism created in the city through the ministry of the apostles. Such unity of sympathy as existed before in the population was divided, and part flowed towards the Jews and part towards the apostles. It was predicted of Christ that through Him the "thoughts of many hearts should be revealed." The searching ministry of the apostles at Iconium made bare the hearts of the people. Those who took part with the Jews made " an assault" upon the apostles, " to use them despitefully, and to stone them." They rushed on them with malignant insolence and outrage. The storm raised, however, was under the direction of God. It was a divine breeze, to bear the precious seeds of truth to regions farther on, to Lystra and Derbe. The apostles fled unto Lystra and Derbe, not from fear, but from the instinct of duty.

Acts 14:6-13

THE·FIRST MISSIONARY TOUR.—III. FROM ICONIUM TO LYSTRA AND
DERBE.

1.—*The Theology of Heathendom*

" *They were ware of it,*[1] *and fled unto Lystra and Derbe, cities of Lyca-*
onia, and unto the region that lieth round about : And there they preached
the gospel. And there sat a certain man at Lystra, impotent in his feet,
being a cripple from his mother's womb, who never had walked : The same
heard Paul speak : [2] *who steadfastly beholding him, and perceiving that he*
had faith to be healed, said with a loud voice, Stand upright on thy feet.
And he leaped and walked. And when the people saw what Paul had
done, they lifted up their voices, saying in the speech of Lycaonia, The gods
are come down to us in the likeness of men. And they called Barnabas, Jupi-
ter ; and Paul, Mercurius, because he was the chief speaker. Then the
priest of Jupiter, which was before their city, brought oxen and garlands unto
the gates,[3] *and would have done sacrifice with the people.*

EMENDATIVE RENDERINGS.—(1.) Having considered it.—HALL. (2.) Was listening to
Paul speaking. (3.) Brought bulls and garlands unto the doors.—ALF.

EXEGETICAL REMARKS.— "*Fled unto*
Lystra and Derbe, cities of Lycaonia."
The original order of the clause is,
"to the cities of Lycaonia, Lystra and
Derbe." The district of Lycaonia
extends from the ridge of Mount
Taurus, on the borders of Cilicia, on
the south, to the Cappadocian hills,
on the north. It is perhaps the largest
plain in Asia Minor.

The cities of Lystra and Derbe were
somewhere about the base of the
Black Mountain. Their exact sites,
however, are unknown. As there is
no reference to any synagogue or any
Jews at Lystra, it has been inferred
that few, if any, of the Hebrew race,
resided there. It was the home of
the Gentiles, the scene of heathenism.
In Lystra, Timothy was circumcised,
probably born. Derbe was the native place of Gaius, and Cicero mentions it as the residence of his friend
Antipato.

" *There sat a certain man at Lystra,*
impotent in his feet, being a cripple
from his mother's womb, who never had
walked," &c. There is a remarkable
similarity between the miracle here

and that recorded in Acts iii. The
strong resemblance between these,
the subjects of both being lame men,
and both being occasions of discourses
and persecutions, " so far from tending to discredit either narrative, seems
rather to confirm both as authentic,
on the principle that like causes produce like effects : so that these two
narratives, instead of being copied
one from the other, are only specimens of what was frequently experienced in that age on a larger or a
smaller scale. That one of these remarkable examples is recorded in
each great division of the history is
no proof of a disposition to assimilate
the life of Paul to that of Peter, but
a natural result of the plan on which
the whole book is constructed, and
agreeably to which one apostle is
especially conspicuous in one part,
and the other in the other. The resemblance in the miracles themselves
can be a difficulty only on the supposition that they were fortuitous, and
under no particular divine direction."
—ALEXANDER.

The miracle here was most striking, beneficent, and symbolic. It was conditional on personal faith, and thus indicated that the rectification of the soul guarantees the rectification of the body.

"*And they called Barnabas Jupiter, and Paul Mercurius.*" "Jupiter, the Roman name of the divinity whom the Greeks called Zeus, and in the early ages Dis, the accusative of which word (Dia) is the one here used." Jupiter, the most mighty of all the deities of the ancients, the father of gods and men, the Ammon of Africa, the Bel of Babylon, the Osiris of Egypt, was all but universally worshipped. Seated on a throne of ivory, holding in one hand a thunderbolt, and in the other a sceptre of cypress, his dominion was regarded as extending over gods and men. "*Mercurius,* more usually written with an English termination, Mercury, like Timotheus and Timothy (2 Cor. i. 1–19), the Roman name corresponding to the Greek Hermes, the interpreter or spokesman of the gods, and represented in the popular mythology as commonly attending Zeus or Jupiter in his visits to the earth." He was regarded as the god of eloquence, as

light, rapid, quick in his movements. Some suppose that these heathens considered Barnabas to be Jupiter because he was the man of the more grand and imposing appearance. Paul was thought to be Mercurius, because he spoke most on the occasion.

"*Then the priest of Jupiter, which was before the city.*" Jupiter, it would seem, had a temple or image in front of the city of Lystra, or near the gates. Ancient cities were regarded as under the protection of particular deities, and their figures were placed in conspicuous places in the city. His leading priest now brought oxen and garlands unto the gates, in order to sacrifice. Bulls and bullocks were regarded both by the Jews and Gentiles as the most costly of offerings, and such were offered to the chief or father of the gods. Oxen and garlands were now to be presented. The heathens adorned the statues of their gods about to be worshipped with garlands and wreaths of flowers. Thus Virgil :—

" The victim ox that was for altars pressed,
Trimmed with white ribbons, and with garlands dressed."

HOMILETICS.—This paragraph brings under our notice *the theology of heathendom.* "When the Lystrians saw what Paul had done, they lifted up their voices, saying, in the speech of Lycaonia, The gods are come down to us in the likeness of men," &c. In the words and acts of these heathen Lystrians, there comes out what I should call the native theology of human hearts everywhere and in all conditions.

There are three great theological beliefs involved in their conduct :

I. THAT THE DIVINITY IS ALWAYS MANIFEST IN THE MIRACULOUS "When the people saw what Paul had done, they said in the speech of Lycaonia, *The gods are come down to us.*" They regarded the miracle wrought by the apostles as a demonstration of the presence of their deities. Their *instinctive* faith was, that a miracle was the product of divine power. This seems to be an inbred belief. Though logically, perhaps, it could not be proved that divine power exclusively can perform a miracle, man everywhere believes it. Whenever anything extraordinary in nature occurs, the human spectators, as well in civilised as savage states, involuntarily *feel* that God is at work. This doctrine, thus held by the heart of depraved humanity, accords with the teachings of the Bible, which everywhere ascribe the miraculous to the direct agency of God.

Another belief involved in their conduct is—

II. THAT THE DIVINITY ASSUMES HUMAN FORMS. "The gods are come down to us in the *likeness of men.*" This was the general belief of heathendom. Through all its regions men held that their gods came from heaven to earth, assumed human forms, and travelled from place to place to inspect the affairs of men. Thus Homer sings concerning them :—

> " They curious oft of mortal actions, deign
> In forms like these to round the earth and main ;
> Just and unjust recording in their mind,
> And with sure eyes inspecting all mankind."

And Ovid speaks of Jupiter as descending from heaven to redress the wrongs of earth :—

> " The clamours of this vile, degenerate age,
> The cries of orphans, and th' oppressor's rage,
> Had reached the stars : I will descend, said I,
> In hope to prove this loud complaint a lie.
> Disguised in human shape I travelled round
> The world, and more than what I heard I found."

The universal belief in such theophanies may be regarded—

First, *As a dim memory in the soul of Paradise, where God held fellowship in human form with man.*

Secondly, *As a prophetic sentiment of that grand incarnation* " *when the* WORD *was made flesh and dwelt amongst us.*"

Another belief involved in their conduct is—

III. THAT THE DIVINITY IS TO BE WORSHIPPED WHEN APPEARING IN THE HUMAN FORM. These heathens believing that the gods had come down, that Barnabas was Jupiter, and Paul, Mercurius, began their worship : " Then the priest of Jupiter which was before their city, brought oxen and garlands unto the gates, and would have *done sacrifice with the people.*" The principle which they expressed in all this is, that the Divinity is to be worshipped, even when manifested in human nature.

Now, the theology which comes out from the hearts of these heathens, and which is written in the souls of all, serves several important purposes :

First, *As an eternal hindrance to the reign of atheism.* Atheism is a contradiction to the profoundest faith of the human heart. Whatever system of doctrine is contrary to the intuitions of humanity cannot stand.

Secondly, *As indicating the responsibility of heathens.* " There is

a light that lighteth every man that cometh into the world."* God
has left no man without some measure of inner light.
Thirdly, *As presumptive evidence in favour of the gospel.* The
gospel agrees with the primitive beliefs of human hearts.
Fourthly, *As a guarantee for the spread of Christianity.* The
congruity of Christian theism with the theism of the soul is a pledge
of its ultimate triumph : "Now, we believe, not because of thy saying," &c. The gospel brings God to man in miraculous works and
in a human form, and all this that he might worship.

Acts 14:14-19

THE FIRST MISSIONARY TOUR.—FROM ICONIUM TO LYSTRA AND DERBE
(continued)

2.—*The sublimity of Christianity and the worthlessness of human
popularity*

" *Which when the apostles, Barnabas and Paul, heard of, they rent their
clothes, and ran in* [1] *among the people, crying out, And saying, Sirs, why
do ye these things ? We also are men of like passions with you, and preach
unto you, that ye should turn from these vanities* [2] *unto the living God,
which made heaven, and earth, and the sea, and all things that are therein :
Who in times* [3] *past suffered all nations to walk in their own ways. Nevertheless he left not himself without witness, in that he did good, and gave us
rain from heaven, and fruitful seasons, filling our hearts with food and
gladness. And with these sayings scarce restrained they the people,* [4] *that
they had not done sacrifice unto them. And there came thither certain
Jews from Antioch and Iconium, who persuaded the people,* [5] *and, having
stoned Paul, drew him out of the city, supposing he had been dead.*

EMENDATIVE RENDERINGS.—(1.) Rushed forth. (2.) Vain gods. (3.) The generations. (4.) The multitude. (5.) The multitudes.— ALF.

EXEGETICAL REMARKS.—" *They rent
their clothes.*" This was a customary
Oriental method of expressing grief,
and also indignation and abhorrence
of impiety or blasphemy committed
in one's presence.—See Matt. xxvi.
65 ; Mark xiv. 63.
" *And saying, Sirs, why do ye these
things ?*" "*Sirs,*" literally men, nearly
equivalent to our gentlemen.—ALEX-
ANDER.
" *We also are men of like passions
with you.*" " This rendering gives an
improper turn to the passage. The
original stands,—We are men, not
gods, like affected with you."
" *In that he did good.*" It was a
remark of Sinisyus, a bishop of Cyrene, that to do good, so to speak,
was the very nature of the Deity, as
much as fire to burn or for light to
shine. It is even so. Who is God ?
It is He who does good, and good only,
and good for ever and everywhere.
" *And gave us rain from heaven.*"
" The mention of rain," says a modern
expositor, " in particular, as one of the
clearest manifestations of the divine

* See Homilist, series iv., vol. ii., page 48.

benignity, was in accordance with the old Jewish saying, that "there were three keys—of life, rain, and resurrection—always kept in God's hand," not given to any delegate or proxy; as indicating a more direct or special act of power on the part of the Supreme. The apparent irregularity with which it falls, the difficulty of foretelling it, and its absolute necessity to the prolonged existence of either animate or vegetable creatures, single the rain out as worthy of emphasis in this brief record of Heaven's gifts to man. "The circuit of the waters," in their wonderful passage from the sea into the atmosphere by evaporation, their condensation into clouds and rain, their fall upon the earth into streams and mighty rivers, and their return to the great reservoir of the ocean from which they issued in an invisible form, is to every devout mind a perpetual miracle of celestial power and goodness" (Jer. v. 24). "If we hearken to the voice of the world," says an ancient philosopher, "we shall hear it say nothing but God hath made me."

"*And having stoned Paul, drew him out of the city.*" Jews from Antioch and Iconium, we are told, instigated the people to this act of cruelty. Years afterwards, Paul refers to this : "Once was I stoned" (2 Cor. xi. 25).

HOMILETICS.—This passage gives an illustration of *the sublimity of Christianity and the worthlessness of human popularity.*

I. The SUBLIMITY of CHRISTIANITY. Its sublimity is seen in three things :—

First, *In the spirit it generates.* What a sublime spirit the apostles manifested on this occasion! They repudiated with horror the homage that was about to be rendered to them : "Which when the apostles Barnabas and Paul," &c. It is the characteristic of mean-natured men that they seek homage from their fellows. The meaner the spirit, the fonder of praise and adoration. Many of the heathen emperors put themselves up as gods and sought divine honours ; and there are those now in every circle of society who are craving to be the idols of their sphere. But here you have two men to whom the highest honours were offered—offered by a whole community, and offered enthusiastically, and offered under most tempting circumstances—repudiating them with a holy indignation. "They rent their clothes" as an indication of their intense dislike to such honours. "We also are men of like passions with you." What gave them this spirit which made them so superior to popularity and fame? Christianity! The man who has this spirit is too great, not only to seek, but to receive the honours which worldly men covet. Its sublimity is seen—

Secondly, *In the God it reveals.* What a view did the apostles here give the Lystrians of God! They speak of Him (1) *as the absolutely living One*—" the living God ;" not like their gods, dead idols. The God of Christianity *lives*—lives independently, everywhere, and for ever. His life is the life of the universe. They speak of Him (2) *as the universal Creator*, "which made heaven, and earth, and the sea, and all things that are therein." In the beginning this God created the heaven and the earth. Whatever is in the universe

He made : the only Creator. They speak of Him (3) *as the patient Governor of men :* "Who in times past suffered all nations to walk in their own ways." "Nations" here refers to all Gentile nations, and they walked in their own ways ; not in the ways of truth, and virtue, and God, but "in their own ways," and they did so because He *suffered* it. He permitted them thus to go on. Their conduct was offensive to Him, and opposed to His requirements ; but He suffered them to go on from generation to generation. He allowed them full scope for the play of their intellect, their genius, and their passions. They speak of Him (4) *as the constant Worker in the universe.* "Nevertheless he left not himself without witness, in that he did good, and gave us rain from heaven, and fruitful seasons, filling our hearts with food and gladness." The operations of nature were only His power in action. Rain came from heaven, fruitful seasons came round, and the hearts of His creatures were gladdened with food ; not as pseudo-philosophers tell us, as the result of laws, but as the operations of His hand. He works everywhere in nature, always doing good, and all His works are "witnesses" of Himself. The visible are the effects, expressions, and proofs of the invisible God. Such is the God whom Christianity gives to man—the living, creating, patient, constantly-working God. This discourse of the apostles shows how they adapted their subject to their hearers. When they address Jews, they deal with the Hebrew Scriptures ; when they address heathens, they open the Bible of nature and expound its chapters. Its sublimity is seen—

Thirdly, *In the revolutions it effects.* The apostles here describe the great change which Christianity accomplishes in a few striking words. We "preach unto you that ye should turn from these vanities unto the living God." This is the work of Christianity ; to turn souls from the *false* to the *true,* from the *shadowy* to the *real,* from the *creature* to the *Creator.* The gods of men are *vanities,* whether Jupiter or Mercurius, or worldliness, fashion, pleasure, or pride. What a grand thing, then, is Christianity ! What on earth is comparable to it ? All the systems of men to it are as tapers to the sun.

II. The Worthlessness of human popularity. How long did this public desire to worship the apostles continue at Lystra? How long did their popularity remain? It had a very brief existence, for in the nineteenth verse we read, "And there came thither certain Jews from Antioch and Iconium, who persuaded the people, and having stoned Paul, drew him out of the city, supposing he had been dead." What a rapid reaction ! The apotheosis is followed by a persecution ; the enthusiastic adorers are transformed to malignant foes ; the men who are honoured as gods one hour, are treated the next as wretched criminals deserving death. They stoned Paul until they thought him dead. This is popularity. "Hosanna" to-day, "Crucify" to-morrow. What a worthless thing ! How much beneath the man to value, still less to court. He who worships popularity worships—

First, A *corrupt* god. So long as the world is depraved, the popular thing must be wrong.

Secondly, A *capricious* god. It approves to-day what it denounces to-morrow. Little men go after popularity, and their little souls adore it ; great men are followed by popularity, and their great natures care nothing for it.

Paul was not, however, dead, as his enemies thought : " As the disciples stood around about him, he rose up, and came into the city; and the next day he departed with Barnabas to Derbe." All we hear of them in Derbe is that they "preached the gospel."

Acts 14:20-28

THE FIRST MISSIONARY TOUR.—IV. FROM LYSTRA BACK TO ANTIOCH IN SYRIA,

Their work on their way to Antioch and at Antioch

" *Howbeit, as the disciples stood round about him, he rose up, and came into the city : and the next day he departed with Barnabas to Derbe. And when they had preached the gospel to that city, and had taught many,*[1] *they returned again to Lystra, and to Iconium, and Antioch, confirming the souls of the disciples, and exhorting them to continue in the faith, and that we must through much tribulation*[2] *enter into the kingdom of God. And when they had ordained*[3] *them elders in every church, and had prayed with fasting, they commended them to the Lord, on whom they believed.*[4] *And after they had passed throughout Pisidia, they came to Pamphylia. And when they had preached the word in Perga, they went down into Attalia ; and thence sailed to Antioch from whence they had been recommended to the grace of God for the work which they fulfilled. And when they were come, and had gathered the church together, they rehearsed all that God had done with them, and how*[5] *he had opened the door of faith unto the Gentiles. And there*[6] *they abode long time with the disciples.*"

EMENDATIVE RENDERINGS.—(1.) Made many disciples. (2.) Many tribulations. (3.) Elected. (4.) They prayed with fasting and commended them to the Lord, on whom they believed. (5) That.—ALF.

EXEGETICAL REMARKS.—" *Howbeit as the disciples*," &c. At Lystra the persecution raised against the apostle Paul was so violent that it led almost to his death. He was carried out of the city *supposed to have been dead.* Fortunately for mankind, his death was only a supposition : " As the disciples stood round about him, he rose up, and came into the city : and the next day he departed with Barnabas to Derbe." Some think that he was actually dead, and raised by a miracle ; others, that he lay stunned by the blows he had received, or was in a swoon ; and others that he was all but dead, and that by miraculous agency he was restored. There is no way of determining the case with certainty. It may be that it was a mere delirium or swoon, occasioned by the violence of his persecutors, and that in that swoon he had that wondrous trance described by himself in 2 Cor. xii. 3, when he knew not "whether he was in the body or out of the body." It is thought that Timothy was a witness of St Paul's persecution at Lystra, and that he might have been among that group of disciples who surrounded his lifeless body outside the walls of Lystra. No sooner has the apostle recovered than he starts with Barnabas to Derbe, in which city both preached the gospel and taught many. From Derbe they determine on their return to Antioch in Syria, whence they started on their missionary tour.

"*And when they had preached the gospel to that city, and had taught many, they returned again to Lystra and to Iconium and Antioch.*" Derbe was the ultimate point of their tour. It is worthy of note, that they return not by the route geographically nearest, by the province of Cilicia, bounding Lycaonia on the south-east. They left this, the direct course, and journeyed back by the same cities they had visited on their way out.

"*Confirming the souls of the disciples.*" The word "*confirming*" (Ἐπιστηρίζοντες) means strengthening. It has no reference whatever to that rite of confirmation which is practised in some Churches. If the rite of confirmation is built upon this word, it is on a sandy foundation. Confirmation here does not refer to laying hands on people's heads to make them superstitious, but laying truth on people's souls to make them strong in heart and duty.

"*And when they had ordained them elders.*" Literally "chosen by vote." Compare chap. vi. 2-6. The Greek word does not express the idea of ordination as now understood. The spirit of ritualism, taking this word in an ecclesiastical sense, makes it to denote a setting apart to an office by the imposition of hands. It has no such signification. Only in one other place does the word occur, 2 Cor. viii. 19, where it is applied to Luke and translated "who was also the chosen of the churches." The word means simply an election. "*Elders.*" This word, in the Greek "presbyters," must be taken in such a generic sense as to include all church officers, pastors, and deacons.

"*And had prayed with fasting.*" Literally *fastings—fasts*, the plural form referring to ordinations in the several Churches.

"*And after they had passed throughout Pisidia, they came to Pamphylia. And when they had preached the word in Perga, they went down into Attalia.*" We have already indicated the sites and circumstances of Pisidia, Pamphylia, and Perga. All these places, with the exception of Attalia, they had visited before on their way out. At Perga, however, they had only time to land on that occasion (see chap. xiii. 13) ; now in returning they "preached the word" there. "*Attalia*" was a city of Pamphylia at the mouth of the river Catarrhactes, built by Attalus Philadelphus, king of Pergamus, and is still a seaport of considerable size and commerce, under a slightly altered name.

"*And thence sailed to Antioch.*" "Not, of course, the Antioch of verse 21, which was in Pisidia, but the city of this name in Syria (chap. xiii. 1). They had been absent, according to the computations of some, about three years on this first apostolical journey ; during which time they had visited Salamis and Paphos, on the island of Cyprus ; and Perga, Antioch, Iconium, Lystra, Derbe, Attalia, and other places,—in three of the provinces of Asia Minor, viz., Pamphylia, Pisidia, and Lycaonia."—LIVERMORE.

HOMILETICS.—The passage that we have read presents two things to us : their *work on their way back to Antioch; and their work when they reached Antioch.*

I. THEIR WORK ON THEIR WAY BACK TO ANTIOCH. "Confirming

the souls of the disciples, and exhorting them to continue in the faith. This shows—(1.) *That duty in them was superior to fear.* They go from Derbe to Lystra, Iconium, and Antioch ; pass through the very scenes where they had roused the bitterest hostility, endured persecution, and endangered their lives. " They counted not their lives dear unto them." It shows—(2.) *That duty in them was superior to convenience.* They could have reached their beloved Antioch much easier and sooner, but they felt it their duty to visit those whom they had converted to the faith. It will be seen by these verses that the work was *indoctrinating, organising, and dedicating.*

First, *Their work was indoctrinating.* " Confirming the souls of the disciples, and exhorting them," &c. The apostles confirmed them in the faith—(1.) *By urging duty.* The duty was to " *continue in the faith.*" They had embraced the faith ; there were strong influences tending to loosen their interest in it, and it was of the highest moment to them that they should hold it fast. There is no better way of strengthening our souls in the faith than by continuing our duty in relation to it. Obedience is the best interpreter of doctrine, the most successful school of theology. " He that doeth the will of God shall know of the doctrine." They confirmed them in the faith— (2.) *By inculcating principle.* " We must through much tribulation enter the kingdom of God." The principle is, that trial is the condition of true elevation. Ever since the introduction of sin, the cross has been the way to the crown. We must sow in tears to reap in joy. The vine must be pruned to make it fruitful. The cup must be bitter to make it remedial. Heavenly dignities are reached, not as some voyagers reach their haven while sleeping, but as heroes reach their laurels by agony of soul and torture of limb. " These are they that have come up out of great tribulation," &c. Thus, these apostles endeavoured to *strengthen* the souls of their new converts. What a divine work was theirs ! What is the work of the mere sage, hero, politician, artist, compared with the work of making souls *strong* in all that is true in thought, holy in sympathy, and righteous in purpose.

Secondly, *Their work was organising.* " And when they had ordained them elders in every church." Because the oldest men are supposed to have the greatest knowledge and experience, the most influential officers in the Church are spoken of as " *elders.*" The words do not mean that the elders were ordained for the apostles, but that the apostles ordained them for the Church. The churches which the apostles had planted were young and inexperienced. They were now leaving them, and they took from their number some of the most competent to take care of their temporal concerns, and to promote their spiritual interest—to take charge, in fact, of the churches in the absence of the apostles. They instructed, exhorted, managed.

Thirdly, *Their work was dedicating.* " And had prayed with

fasting, they commended them [the disciples] to the Lord, in whom they believed." They did not commend them to the officers they had appointed to take charge of them, but to "the Lord, the great shepherd, the bishop of souls." Probably these apostles had no prospect of ever seeing them again, and in the spirit of true affection to them and loyalty to their Master, they commended them to His keeping.

The passage presents—

II. THEIR WORK WHEN THEY REACHED ANTIOCH. "And after they had passed through Pisidia, they came to Pamphylia. And when they had preached the word in Perga, they went into Attalia." This is the first account we have of a Christian missionary meeting, and it is therefore of special interest. The words touch upon the scene, the deputation, the attendance, and the speeches of this first missionary meeting. (1.) *The scene was Antioch,* an ancient city, exceedingly important on account of its wealth, numbers, and influence. It was the capital of Syria, about three hundred miles north of Jerusalem, and second only to Rome and Alexandria in importance. It had a history, but no fact in its history was of more intrinsic importance than the fact of its being the scene of the *first* missionary meeting. There were many good reasons for holding the meeting here. It was a very populous place, and consequently the meeting was likely to obtain large publicity. The population was made up of Jews and Gentiles, and these two great sections of the ancient world would have an opportunity of knowing something about the triumphs of this new religion. It was a place abounding with wealth, and therefore was able to render a temporal support to the good cause. It was, moreover, the place whence the mission had proceeded (Acts xiii. 1). There was great propriety therefore in holding this missionary meeting at Antioch. (2.) *The deputation was Paul and Barnabas.* These two men were very different in certain attributes of being. Barnabas does not seem to have had that force and fire of nature which distinguished Paul; still, however constitutionally dissimilar, they were morally harmonious. A child may be morally one with an archangel; the feeblest infant may become the coadjutor of a seraph. They were the missionaries, and they spoke at this missionary meeting. Missionary meetings should be addressed by missionaries rather than by men who are invited to speak either because they have long purses or long tongues. (3.) *The audience was the Church.* "They gathered the Church together," that is the assembly of Christian believers that lived there. The mission was theirs, they had set it on foot; they had probably contributed to its support, and they were bound to sustain it. (4.) *The speeches were narrations.* They "rehearsed all that God had done." They did not deal in those prettyisms of rhetoric and tricks of oratory which are too often employed in modern missionary meetings, to get a cheer and wake the loud applause. They merely " *rehearsed,*"—related what they had done ; and they had wonderful things to tell. The following things are taught by this first missionary meeting :—

First, *That the missionary enterprise is unquestionably right.* It has apostolic precedent. In saying that the missionary enterprise is right, we are far enough from saying that every missionary *society* is right. A missionary society may be a mere commercial affair baptized with a Christian name. But however corrupt these modern societies may have become, the enterprise itself is undoubtedly right. It is based upon the authority of Christ, and supported by the conduct of the apostles. " Go into all the world," &c.

Secondly, *That the missionary enterprise demands our prayers.* Paul and Barnabas had been " recommended to the grace of God" (see also Acts xiii. 1–3). The true missionary should have the prayers of the Church. Whilst their mission is an arduous one, their exposure to dangers is of no common order.

Thirdly, *That the missionary enterprise is the cause of the Church.* " They gathered the Church together ;" that is, the Christian people together ; not any particular officers of the Church, but the whole Church. It was that which concerned every individual member, and that in which every member would be interested.

Fourthly, *The missionary enterprise has a history worth relating.* These missionaries " rehearsed all that God had done with them." We have a short account of their tour (Acts xiii. 4–51, xiv. 1–24). There is no history so interesting or so valuable as the history of the triumphs of the gospel over men of every creed and clime, character and circumstances. Those triumphs are the strongest arguments for the common origin of the race and the divinity of Christianity.

Fifthly, *The missionary enterprise is under the special direction of God.* This missionary deputation traced all their success to God ; they " rehearsed all that God had done with them, and how that he had opened the door of faith unto the Gentiles." They regarded Him as giving access to the Gentiles. " He had opened the door." In modern times there has been an immense amount of clap-trap about opening the door to the gospel. Ignorant men in the name of the gospel of peace have spoken of *war* as opening the door for the gospel. So long as mind is mind, violence must ever shut the door of the heart. The breaking down of the walls of China by military violence, instead of opening a door for the gospel, may only be the building up around that vast population a moral barrier against the entrance of Christian truth.

Acts 15:1-5

THE FIRST ECCLESIASTICAL COUNCIL

1.—*The nature of the dispute.*

" *And certain men which came down from Judea taught the brethren, and said, Except ye be circumcised after the manner of Moses, ye cannot be saved. When therefore Paul and Barnabas had no small dissension and disputation with them, they determined that Paul and Barnabas, and certain other of them, should go up to Jerusalem unto the apostles and elders about this question. And*[1] *being brought on their way by the church, they passed through Phenice and Samaria, declaring the conversion of the Gentiles : and they caused great joy unto all the brethren. And when they were come to Jerusalem, they were received of the church, and of the apostles and elders, and they declared all things that God had done with them. But there rose up certain of the sect of the Pharisees which believed, saying, That it was needful to circumcise them, and to command them to keep the law of Moses.*"

EMENDATIVE RENDERING.—(1.) So then.—ALF.

EXEGETICAL REMARKS.—This chapter records the transactions of the first synod of the Christian Church, or, as it has been called, the Apostolic Council. It was held in order to settle a dispute which certain Judaising teachers had introduced into the Church at Antioch in relation to circumcision.

" *And certain men came down from Judea.*" The appearance of certain men from Judea, and what they proposed at Antioch, reveals to us at once a deep fermentation in the Church, and an important question, which must be solved and debated. Luke describes those who cast the stone into the water, which caused ever-widening circles, as τινές ἀπὸ τῆς Ἰουδαίας, certain who were from Judea, who came from it. This is undoubtedly not to be understood merely geographically, but it likewise points to the engrained Jewish disposition and mode of thought."—L. & G.

" *Certain men.*" Names omitted either perhaps on account of their own personal insignificance or out of contempt for their conduct.

" *Except ye be circumcised after the manner of Moses.*" The term *circumcision*, though it refers to a particular

rite, stands here, perhaps, for the whole ceremonial law of Moses, just as the baptism of John stands for the whole ministry of John (Acts i. 22), the cross for the whole gospel (1 Cor. i. 18 ; Gal. vi. 12-14). Circumcision here stands for Mosaic ritualism.

" *When therefore Paul and Barnabas had no small dissension.*" Paul and Barnabas stood earnestly, no doubt, for the side of freedom and Catholicity (Eph. iii. 2-6).

" *They determined that Paul and Barnabas, and certain other of them, should go up to Jerusalem.*" All argument seemed lost on those " *certain men,*" and hence a deputation to the mother Church at Jerusalem was resolved on. " *Go up to Jerusalem.*" " Up" in a moral sense. There was the seat of religious authority to the Jewish mind ; there was the scene too of the Saviour's suffering, death, and resurrection ; there too the apostles resided ; and there the day of Pentecost had shone in its splendour.

" *And being brought on their way by the Church, they pass through Phenice and Samaria.*" They went with the full sympathy and concurrence of the

Church, represented by its leading officers. "*Phenice and Samaria*" lay directly on the route from Antioch to Judea.

"*Declaring the conversion of the Gentiles, and they caused great joy unto all the brethren.*" Great joy, because it was unexpected; it attested the universal love of the great Father and the adaptation of the gospel to all.

"*And when they were come to Jerusalem they were received of the Church and of the apostles and elders.*" Here was a meeting of the two Churches the Church at Antioch and the Church at Jerusalem. All the members of each Church, of course, were not there in person, but they were there by representation. Was this visit of Paul to Jerusalem the same as that which he mentions in Gal. ii., and placed fourteen years after his conversion? It is generally thought so. On the question, however, see Schaff, vol. i. p. 288.

HOMILETICS.—These words lead us to consider the *nature* of that dispute which now agitated the Church. Modern science informs us that the fiercest hurricanes revolve around a perfect centre of calm —that no tempests can break the serenity within the circle of that centre. It should have been ever thus with the Church. The chapter, however, informs us that there is disturbance in the centre of the moral world—the Church. Whilst Paul and Barnabas were employed in Antioch, for there "they abode long time with the disciples," "certain Judaising teachers came down from Judea," and introduced a serious controversy among the brethren.

A little examination of this Church dissension in Antioch will show that it has the leading features of most of the ecclesiastical controversies in all ages; that it is, in truth, more or less, a *type* of all Church disputes. It was a conflict between the *ritualistic* and the *spiritual*, the *traditional* and the *progressive*, the *fettering* and the *free*.

I. THE CONFLICT WAS BETWEEN THE RITUALISTIC AND THE SPIRITUAL. Except ye be circumcised after the manner of Moses, ye cannot be saved. The names of these breakers of Church peace are not given, nor do we require them. They are unworthy of mention. They were not persons of any distinction or authority. They came as the stern advocates of a rite which they held as *essential to salvation*. They were *ritualists ;* their religion had more to do with the senses than with the soul, with the form than with the spirit. I can conceive of them urging at least two arguments for the enforcement of this rite : (1.) That the law of Moses was the law of God, and therefore immutable ; (2.) That the religion of Messiah was to develop and not abrogate the Levitical economy. The new religion which the apostles had carried into the Gentile world was, on the other hand, pre-eminently spiritual ; it taught that "circumcision or uncircumcision availeth nothing, but a new creature in Christ Jesus."

II. THE CONFLICT WAS BETWEEN THE TRADITIONAL AND THE PROGRESSIVE. For many ages the Jewish people had been the repository of spiritual life, the Gentile who sought religious light could only obtain it through the Jew. These Judaising teachers had felt that what had been must continue, that if the Gentiles accepted Christianity they must accept it through the medium of Jewish institutions —they were institutional conservatives, they could not give up the past. Whatever new thing arose, it must not even clash with the old, still less supersede it; nay, it must recognise, honour, and support the old. On the other hand, Christianity was pre-eminently progressive; it made the old a mere starting-point. Its new life broke through the cerements of the past. It left Palestine for the world, the Jew for the race, the temple of Jerusalem for the temple of the universe, teaching men everywhere that "God is a Spirit: that they that worship Him must worship Him in spirit and in truth."

III. THE CONFLICT WAS BETWEEN THE FETTERING AND THE FREE. To bind the Gentile converts to this Jewish rite would be to enslave their souls; hence Peter, in his speech on the subject before the Church at Jerusalem, exclaimed, " Why tempt ye God to put a yoke on the necks of the disciples?" To tie the soul to a ceremony is to enslave it, and this those bigots now sought to do. They would fetter the limbs of a new faith with the trammels of old ceremonies. Christianity is freedom; it invests the soul with " the glorious liberty of the children of God."

Now, see ye not in this contest much of what has been going on in all the contests of the Church that are past? The men who have broken its peace have always been like these " certain men who went down from Judea to Antioch," men who would bind the spirit of Christianity to the ritual and the past. It is the *ritualistic* and *traditional* members of churches that are generally the exciters of ecclesiastical discord.

Acts 15:6-21

THE FIRST ECCLESIASTICAL COUNCIL

2.—*The settlement of the dispute—(a.) The first stage.*

" *And the apostles and elders came together for to consider of this matter. And when there had been much disputing, Peter rose up and said unto them, Men and brethren, ye know how that a good while ago God made choice among us*[1] *that the Gentiles by my mouth should hear the word of the gospel, and believe. And God, which knoweth the hearts, bare them witness, giving them the Holy Ghost, even as he did unto us ; and put no difference between us and them, purifying their hearts by faith.*[2] *Now therefore why tempt ye God to put a yoke upon the neck of the disciples, which neither our fathers nor we were able to bear ? But[3] we believe that through the grace of the Lord Jesus Christ[4] we shall be saved, even as they. Then all the multitude kept silence, and gave audience to Barnabas and Paul, declaring what miracles[5] and wonders God had wrought among the Gentiles by them. And after they had held their peace, James answered, saying, Men and brethren, hearken unto me : Simeon hath declared how God at the first did visit the Gentiles, to take out of them a people for his name. And to this agree the words of the prophets; as it is written, After this I will return, and will build again the tabernacle of David, which is fallen down; and I will build again the ruins thereof, and I will set it up : that the residue of men might seek after the Lord, and all the Gentiles, upon whom my name is called, saith the Lord, who doeth all these things. Known unto God are all his works from the beginning of the world. Wherefore my sentence is, that we trouble not them, which from among the Gentiles are turned[6] to God : but that we write unto them, that they abstain from pollutions of idols, and from fornication, and from things strangled, and from blood. For Moses of[7] old time hath in every city them that preach him, being read in the synagogue every sabbath day."*

EMENDATIVE RENDERINGS.—(1.) You. (2.) Their faith. (3.) Howbeit. (4.) Omit this word. (5.) Signs. (6.) Turning. (7.) From of.—ALF.

EXEGETICAL REMARKS.—"*And the apostles and elders came together for to consider of this matter.*" They assembled for the express purpose of settling the dispute, not by arbitrary authority, but by calm deliberation.

"*Peter rose up and said unto them.*" How long the "much disputing" continued, and what was said before Peter arose, we are not told. True to his nature, he came first to the front. Nor could any of them indeed have stronger claims to the first speech on this occasion. He was probably the most aged, had been the most accustomed to public speaking, and was perhaps the first to preach the gospel to the Gentiles.

"*Ye know how that a good while ago God made choice amongst us that the Gentiles by my mouth should hear the word of the gospel.*" Here he refers, it is thought by some, to the vision which he received at Joppa some ten years before. He means to say, "Ye know how that God appointed me some time ago to preach the gospel to the Gentiles."

"*Why tempt ye God to put a yoke upon the neck of the disciples.*" Some critics read this, "Why tempt ye God *by putting* a yoke," &c. Here is

a frank confession of the burdensome character of the Mosaic ritual. With the numerous traditions of the Rabbins it had become intolerable. Indeed, Christianity in some Churches now is so Judaised, has become so burdensome, as neither our fathers nor we are able to bear. "The great excess and multitude of ceremonies hath so increased in these latter days that the burden of them was intolerable. St Augustine complained that, in his time, the estate of Christian people was in worse case in that matter than were the Jews. Christ's gospel is not a ceremonial law as much of Moses' law was ; but it is a religion to serve God, not in bondage of the figure or shadow, but in the freedom of the Spirit."—WEBSTER and WILKINSON.

"*Then all the multitude kept silence, and gave audience to Barnabas and Paul.*" The speech of Peter had produced a hush, and disposed the audience to listen to further teaching on the subject. The speeches of Barnabas and Paul are not recorded ; they seem to have been mere narrations, historic sketches of the wonders God had wrought among the Gentiles by them.

"*And after they had held their peace, James answered, saying,*" &c. James responded to what Paul and Barnabas had just said. "James is supposed by many to be 'James thè brother of the Lord' (Gal. i. 19), not one of the twelve, but an unbeliever (John vii. 5), till convinced by Christ's appearing to him after His resurrection (1 Cor. xv. 7), surnamed the Just, and put to death by the Jews soon after the close of the New Testament history. There is, however, a strong presumption that the person holding so distinguished a position in the Church at Jerusalem, while the apostles still survived, was himself one of their number: and as James the son of Alpheus was probably a cousin of our Saviour, he might be called his brother (Gal. i. 19), in strict accordance with biblical and oriental usage (see Gen. xiv. 16; xxix. 12–15; Rom. i. 13, ix. 3; 1 Cor. i. 1). It is very possible that James resided in Jerusalem more constantly than any other of the twelve, and had special charge of the Church there, not, however, as an ordinary pastor, much less as a diocesan bishop, but as a resident apostle." —ALEXANDER.

"*And to this agree the words of the prophets.*" "The book of the minor prophets, of whom Amos, who flourished about 780 or 790 B.C., was one."

"*As it is written*" (see Amos ix. 11, 12). 'The particular aim of the prophet seems to have been, to describe the restoration of the Jewish prosperity, the rebuilding of the temple after the Babylonish captivity, and the spread of the true faith even beyond Judæa, all which was fulfilled about two hundred years afterwards. James employed this by way of accommodation, as illustrative of the admission of the Gentiles into the Messiah's kingdom. Peter had reasoned from the gifts of the spirit and the purification of faith, granted to the Gentiles (verses 8, 9); Paul and Barnabas, from miracles done, by the divine power and ap-

probation, among the heathen; and James adduces the voice of the elder dispensation itself, which embraced the Gentiles in its plan of mercy."— LIVERMORE.

"*Known unto God are all His works from the beginning of the world.*" Many modern critics reject the greater part of this verse; they only recognise the words, "known from the beginning," as of canonic worth.

"*That we write unto them, that they abstain.*" The conclusion that James came to was, that the Gentiles should not be troubled with the question of Jewish ritual, but that a letter should be addressed to them embodying the views of the council.

"*Pollutions of idols.*" After a sacrifice had been offered in a heathen temple, and a portion had been given to the priests, the remainder was either exposed for sale in the market, or served up by the worshipper for the entertainment of his friends (1 Cor. viii.; x. 14–53).

"*From things strangled, and from blood.*"—Suffocated or strangled flesh was regarded by the heathens as very delicious; such, however, was an abomination to the Jews. The precept of James is against cruelty, luxury, and intemperance.

"*For Moses of old time hath in every city them that preach him,*" &c. Three reasons have been suggested for James making this statement. One is, that he gives it because it was not necessary to enjoin abstinence on the Jewish converts; another, to indicate that he gives it in order to assure them that there was no danger that Moses would grow obsolete in consequence of this indulgence to the Gentiles; and the other to remind the Gentile Christians that they should not by any heathen usages fall behind their Jewish brethren, who were consequently preserved from such corruptions by the regular reading of the law.

HOMILETICS.—This paragraph leads us to consider the *first stage in the settlement of the dispute,* which comprises—

I. A DEPUTATION FROM THE CHURCH AT ANTIOCH, AND A FULL DISCUSSION OF THE SUBJECT AT A GENERAL ASSEMBLY OF THE

CHURCH. " And when they were come to Jerusalem, they were received of the Church, and of the apostles and elders, and they declared all things that God had done with them." Here is the Church of Antioch in the person of Paul, Barnabas, and certain others, meeting with the mother Church at Jerusalem. They are heartily welcomed. The brethren welcomed them, the apostles welcomed them ; so did the elders and all the men in office give them a hospitable reception. Both were mother Churches. Barnabas and Paul stated to them at once " all the things that God had done with them." After this " there rose up certain of the sect of the Pharisees which believed, saying, that it was needful to circumcise them, and to command them to keep the law of Moses." It is a *general* synod, not a mere meeting of the apostles and elders. It is not necessary to believe that every member of the Church at Jerusalem was present, but that all were represented in that council. It was a *popular* assembly. Lightfoot says—" It was not a convention premeditated and solemnly assembled, but only occasionally emergent." The case in dispute was to be submitted, not to a set of ecclesiastical functionaries, but to a general judgment of the believers. We have no account of this " much disputing " which preceded the formal speeches. Of neither the speakers nor their arguments are we informed. It was, perhaps, very general and desultory, preliminary to the *following discussion.* Whilst four men spoke on this occasion—Peter, Paul, Barnabas, and James—we have only the report of two, which we shall now notice.

First, *The speech of Peter.* " Peter rose up and said unto them." It is noteworthy that in speaking at this council there is no assumption of superiority on Peter's part. He does not appear as a primate, or even as a moderator ; he does not even seem to have been the chairman of the occasion. He does not take upon himself to sum up the arguments or to pronounce a judgment. He speaks only as one of their number, strongly as he would speak, but with deference to the common judgment. In his speech he shows that Jewish ritualism was unnecessary, inexpedient, and contrary to his faith.

(1.) He shows that it was *unnecessary.* He quotes his own experience in proof of this. " Men and brethren, ye know how that a good while ago God made choice among us," &c. His reference is to the conversion of Cornelius, which occurred perhaps ten years before. This fact was well known to them. It was a fact so sublimely strange in its nature, so significant in its character, so mighty in its influence, that every convert to Christianity must have known it.

He states that his ministry to the Gentiles was—(*a*) By the appointment of God. " God made choice among us." Was (*b*) Divinely sanctioned : "Giving them the Holy Ghost." The Spirit accompanied his ministry. Was (*c*) Productive of the same spiritual results : " Put no difference between us and them, purifying their hearts by faith." The gospel, when believed, produced the same effect upon the Gentile as the Jew, and that effect was the purifying of the heart. This work it effects as well without Jewish ritualism as with it; this work in all cases it achieves in connexion with faith and the agency of the Holy Ghost. In his speech he shows—

(2.) That it was *inexpedient.* "Now therefore why tempt ye God to put a yoke upon the neck of the disciples, which neither our fathers nor we were able to bear?" (*a*) Ritualism is a yoke to the soul which sometimes becomes intolerable. (*b*) Men by their bigoted conduct may tempt God to put this yoke upon people. Men may so oppose the will of God, and thus so try his patience, that He may allow the evils of the past to come upon the present. Were England to renounce her Protestantism, she would in this way tempt God to put the terrible yoke of Popery upon this country. In his speech he shows—

(3.) That it was *contrary to his faith.* "We believe that through the grace of the Lord Jesus Christ we shall be saved, even as they." The "we," of course, refers to the converted Jews : "we, converted Jews," in which Peter included himself. The "they," we think, refers, not, as some suppose, to the Jewish people, but to the Gentile converts. The doctrine, however, in which Peter expresses his faith is, *that salvation of the soul is through Jesus Christ, and not through any ritualism whatever.* Peter's meaning may be, that the Gentiles have been saved, their hearts have been purified without ritualism, simply through the grace of Jesus Christ; and we, though brought up in connexion with ritualism, may be saved in the same way without it. Jews and Gentiles are both saved in the the same way, that is, by grace; why, then, should we impose on them a ceremony which does us no good? Luther says—"We must not yield or give up this article, though heaven and earth, and whatever will not endure, perish." This is the last speech we have of Peter. Adieu, great apostle !

Secondly, *The speech of James.* It appears that Paul and Barnabas spoke next. "Then all the multitude kept silence, and gave audience to Barnabas and Paul, declaring what miracles and wonders God had wrought among the Gentiles by them." "All the multitude," implying a much larger number than the apostles and elders,—a *general* gathering. The speech of Peter had produced such a deep impression that there was a breathless "silence" when he sat down, and when Barnabas and Paul arose. Barnabas is mentioned first, for probably he spoke first, as being better known, or perhaps better loved in Jerusalem than Paul. Their speeches are not recorded; only so much is said about them as to show that they were historic—a recitation of the leading events connected with their missionary tour to the Gentiles. They related "what great signs and wonders God had done among the Gentiles through them." They did not parade these as their own achievements, but ascribed them all to God. What they said fell into the current of Peter's sentiment, and made the river of evidence roll with all but a resistless force through the assembly.

But the speech of James is given : " And after they had held their peace, James answered, saying, Men and brethren, hearken unto me," &c. James, who was probably *chairman* of the assembly, summed up the matter, and gave his judgment as to the course to pursue. Neander remarks, " that on account of his strict observance of the law, he was held in utmost reverence by the Jews, and that, therefore, in his words the greatest confidence would be placed." He accepts the position of Peter that " God at first did visit the Gentiles, to take out of them a people for his name," and he supports it by a prophetic quotation. " And to this agree the words of the prophets ; as it is written," &c. James employs this prediction in the way of accommodation, as illustrating the admission of the Gentiles into the Messiah's kingdom. The quotation from the prophet is made from the Septuagint version, because, no doubt, he spoke in Greek, and used the current version. The passage points to three things :

(1.) *A great restoration among the Jewish people.* The building up of that which was in ruins.

(2.) A restoration that would *lead the Gentiles* to seek after the Lord. " The residue of men " here evidently refers to all who were not Jews.

(3.) A restoration *effected by that God who sees the end from the beginning.* " I will return and will build again the tabernacle of David, which is fallen down," &c. Who is this ? It is He " who doeth all these things, . . known from the beginning." The words teach, therefore—(*a*) *That the world had a beginning ; (b) That the world is the theatre of divine operations ; (c) That the divine operations are the development of an intelligent plan stretching on through all ages.*

He pronounces, as the conclusion, his judgment, and gives his advice: " Wherefore my sentence is, that we trouble not them, which from among the Gentiles are turned to God " (*i.e.*, that we do not seek to impose on them any of the Jewish rites) ; " but that we *write* unto them that they abstain from pollutions of idols, and from fornication, and from things strangled, and from blood."

The decision contained four prohibitions. " *Pollutions of idols :* " The injunction is to abstain from the eating fleshly food which had been offered in sacrifices. Another prohibition was " *fornication :* " this is mentioned in connexion with idolatry, because horrible licentiousness mingled with the devotions of those heathens. Another prohibition was " *from things strangled :* " they were to refrain from eating the flesh of things strangled, which were held in abomination among the Jews, and in high esteem among the heathens. Another prohibition was from " *blood*." Abstinence from blood is enjoined in Gen. ix. 4; Lev. x. 14; Deut. xii. 23; 1 Sam. xiv. 34. Such were the prohibitions in James's counsel.

Milman remarks,—"That the influence of James effected a discreet and temperate compromise. Judaism, as it were, capitulated on honourable terms. The Christians were to be left to that freedom enjoyed by the proselytes of the gate, but they were enjoined to pay so much respect to those with whom they were associated in religious worship, as to abstain from those practices which were most offensive to their habits. The partaking of the sacrificial feast in the idolatrous temples was so plainly repugnant to the first principles either of the Jewish or the Christian theism, as to be altogether irreconcilable with the professed opinions of a proselyte to either. The using of things strangled, and blood, for food, appears to have been the most revolting to Jewish feeling; and perhaps among the dietetic regulations of the Mosaic law, none in a southern climate was more conducive to health. The other article in this celebrated decree was a moral prohibition, but not improbably directed more particularly against the dissolute rites of the Syrian and Asiatic religions, in which prostitution formed an essential part, and which prevailed to a great extent in the countries bordering upon Palestine." Although no burden of ritualistic law was to be imposed upon the Gentiles, it was the duty of the Gentiles to abstain from all those customs that were repugnant to the mind of a Jew.

James advised that all the Gentile Christians should be communicated with upon the subject. " *That we write unto them.*" They were already very numerous and widely scattered; therefore they should be written to. The twenty-first verse seems to be a general reason which the apostle assigns for enforcing these prohibitions upon the Gentiles. "For Moses of old time hath in every city them that preach him, being read in the synagogues every Sabbath-day." The sense of the verse appears to be, that as these things were prohibited by the Jewish law, and as the Jewish law was read every Sabbath in the synagogue, it was not necessary to impose these prohibitions on the Jewish converts; that since Jewish prejudice was general and inveterate, this yielding was necessary.

Acts 15:22-35

THE FIRST ECCLESIASTICAL COUNCIL

2.—*The settlement of the dispute (continued).—(b.) The second and third stages*

" *Then pleased it the apostles and elders, with the whole church, to send chosen men of their own company*[1] *to Antioch with Paul and Barnabas ; namely, Judas surnamed Barsabas, and Silas, chief men among the brethren. And they wrote letters by them after this manner : The apostles and elders and brethren*[2] *send greeting unto the brethren which are of the Gentiles in Antioch and Syria and Cilicia : Forasmuch as we have heard, that certain which went out from us have troubled you with words, subverting your souls, saying, Ye must be circumcised, and keep the law :*[3] *to whom we gave no such commandment : it seemed good unto us, being assembled with one accord, to send chosen men unto you with our beloved Barnabas and Paul, men that have hazarded*[4] *their lives for the name of our Lord Jesus Christ. We have sent therefore Judas and Silas, who shall also tell you the same things by mouth. For it seemed good to the Holy Ghost, and to us, to lay upon you no greater burden than these necessary things ; that ye abstain from meats offered to idols, and from blood, and from things strangled, and from fornication : from which if ye keep yourselves, ye shall do well. Fare ye well. So when they were dismissed, they came to Antioch ; and when they had gathered the multitude together, they delivered the epistle : which when they had read, they rejoiced for the consolation. And Judas and Silas, being prophets also themselves, exhorted the brethren with many words, and confirmed them. And after they had tarried there a space, they were let go in peace from the brethren unto the apostles.*[5] *Notwithstanding it pleased Silas to abide there still.*[6] *Paul also and Barnabas continued in Antioch, teaching and preaching the word of the Lord, with many others also.*"

EMENDATIVE RENDERINGS.—(1.) To choose out men of their own company, and send them. (2.) The apostles and the elder brethren. (3.) Omit these words, from *saying* to *law*. (4.) Delivered up. (5.) Them that sent them. (6.) Omit this verse. —ALF.

EXEGETICAL REMARKS.—" *Then pleased it the apostles and elders, with the whole church, to send chosen men,*" *&c.* The result of the deliberations of that council was a resolution to send a deputation of two influential men of their number, with a circular letter agreed upon, to Antioch. The men sent, we are told, were Barsabas and Silas, called elsewhere Silvanus. Nothing is known of the former, unless he is the person nominated to the vacant place in the apostleship (chap. i. 23) ; the latter is mentioned chap. xvi. 25, xvii. 4 ; 2 Cor. i. 19.

" *And they wrote letters by them*"— Greek : " having written." It does not mean that they wrote more than one epistle.

" *Send greeting unto the brethren which are of the Gentiles in Antioch and Syria and Cilicia.*" The controversy raged principally in those places, though the letter was for all lands and all times. The substance of the letter we have noticed already in the speech of James.

"*So when they were dismissed, they came to Antioch; and when they had gathered the multitude together, they delivered the epistle.*" The great body of the Church at Antioch met to receive the epistle that had been sent to them from the Church at Jerusalem. They rejoiced in the communication.

HOMILETICS.—The passage leads us to consider the *second* and *third* stages in the settlement of the dispute.

II. A DEPUTATION BACK FROM THE CHURCH AT JERUSALEM TO THAT AT ANTIOCH, WITH THE RESULTS OF THE DELIBERATION. "Then pleased it the apostles and elders, with the whole Church, to send chosen men," &c. The assembly is satisfied; discussion is over; the judgment and counsel of James are accepted and acted upon, and "chosen men of their own company"—leading members of the Church, among whom are Barsabas and Silas—are appointed to go down to Antioch with Paul and Barnabas. They take with them the letter, which runs as follows :—"The apostles and elder brethren send greeting," &c. This circular letter rehearsed the occasion of its promulgation, and directed its readers for further information as to its verbal statements to its bearers, enumerated four special prohibitions which had been enunciated by James in the assembly, and concluded by a solemn release from all ceremonial restrictions of every kind. This letter may be looked upon in three aspects :

First, As a homage to the right of private judgment. It is not an enactment enforced by penalties, nor is it a mere moral appeal addressed to a corporate body; it is directed to the judgment of every individual member of the Christian Church through all the districts of Antioch, Syria, and Cilicia. The questions at issue were vital to every individual man, and to every man appeal is made. In truth the whole Bible recognises the right of private judgment. This letter may be looked upon—

Secondly, As a condemnation of ecclesiastical decrees. The benign and tender spirit of this missive, the touching references it contains, its popular and advisory features, give it a character that stands in striking contrast to the deliverances of most ecclesiastical councils in later days. Little men who claim to be the successors of these apostles, have, from their assemblies, issued decrees whose arrogance and intolerance insult the Christian name. This letter may be looked upon—

Thirdly, As a charter of the Church's liberties. With this letter issuing from the great council of the mother Church at Jerusalem, the result of apostolic deliberation and heavenly guidance, we claim a liberty from the reign of ritualism.

The other stage in the settlement of the dispute is—

III. THE ASSEMBLING OF THE CHURCH AT ANTIOCH TO RECEIVE THE COMMUNICATION FROM THE MOTHER CHURCH AT JERUSALEM. " So when they were dismissed, they came to Antioch: and when they had gathered the multitude together, they delivered the epistle," &c. The whole Church is assembled at Antioch. Paul and Barnabas, Barsabas and Silas, having returned from Jerusalem, enter the assembly, and deliver the LETTER. This yields great "consolation." Barsabas and Silas, being the greater strangers, address the assembly. They exhort the brethren with many words, and confirm them. Those who had come down with Paul and Barnabas from Jerusalem after a little while return home.

Such was the method of settling this first discussion in the Christian Church. How simple, wise, and successful ! Had the example been imitated in after-times by contending members, how much persecution would have been avoided! how much disgrace would have been spared the Christian name! This ecclesiastical assembly at Jerusalem is a model for all times. It brought forth a spirit which frees from the yoke of the ritualist, the prejudices of the bigot, the arrogance of the self-righteous.

Acts 15:36-40

THE QUARREL OF BARNABAS AND PAUL

" *And some days after, Paul said unto Barnabas, Let us go again and visit our*[1] *brethren in every city where we have preached the word of the Lord, and see how they do. And Barnabas determined*[2] *to take with them John, whose surname was Mark. But Paul thought not good to take him with them, who departed from them from Pamphylia, and went not with them to the work. And the contention was so sharp between them, that they departed asunder one from the other : and so Barnabas took Mark, and sailed unto Cyprus ; and Paul chose Silas, and departed, being recommended by the brethren unto the grace of God.*" [3]

EMENDATIVE RENDERINGS.—(1.) The. (2.) Was minded. (3.) The Lord.—ALF.

EXEGETICAL REMARKS.—"*Some days after, Paul said unto Barnabas, Let us go again and visit our brethren.*" In this Paul manifests his wonted zeal as well as his watchfulness for souls. He knew the perils to which young converts were exposed, from heathenism on the one hand, and Judaism on the other ; and he was anxious " to establish them in the faith."

" *And Barnabas determined to take with him John, whose surname was Mark.*" This John was Mark the evangelist. He had been with them before as a travelling companion (chap. xii. 15, xiii. 35). He was the son of a sister of Barnabas (Col. iv. 10), and probably affection rather than judgment guided him in this wish.

" *But Paul thought not good to*

take him with them, who departed from them from Pamphylia." The wish of Barnabas, Paul could not respond to. We know not the reason ; perhaps incompetency. After this, however, we find Paul speaking of this John with interest (Col. iv. 10 ; 2 Tim. iv. 11 ; Philem. i. 24).

" *And the contention was so sharp between them.*" The word sharp ($\pi\alpha\rho o$-$\xi\upsilon\sigma\mu\delta s$) is that from which our word paroxysm is derived. The persistence perhaps of Barnabas in favour of his nephew excited the warm temperament of Paul into momentary rage. The difference, however, between them was not enduring. Though they had separated now, we find that they became travelling companions again (1 Cor. vii. 6 ; Gal. ii. 9).

HOMILETICS.—These words record a quarrel between two of the best of men and most eminent apostles of Jesus Christ. The contention seems to have been no trifling affair. The temper of both was more than slightly ruffled ; it was tempestuous. Two great souls came into collision, and the deeps of passion were broken up. The altercation between them was so fierce and fiery that the tie of old friendship gave way for a time, and they separated from each other. The fact that such a scene as this in apostolic life is *recorded*, proves to me the *genuineness* of these men. Had it been their object to impose upon mankind, such a scene as this, instead of being set forth in all its nakedness, would have been either not mentioned at all, or, if mentioned, it would have appeared in such a form as to conceal altogether what is morally offensive. Such moral infirmities would never have appeared in the history of these men if they had been impostors. As genuine men, they reveal themselves to us in the costume of real life, with all their imperfections about them.

This apostolic quarrel illustrates several truths that require to be pressed upon our attention.

I. THAT PROBABILITY IS NO CERTAIN GUIDE FOR US IN JUDGING THE FUTURE. To the members of the Church at Antioch, and, indeed, to all who were acquainted with these apostles, nothing could have appeared more improbable than that they should ever quarrel, and especially at such a crisis in their history. Who were these apostles ? They were both *good men.* Love to Christ and souls filled and fired their natures. More, they were *old friends.* They had, it would seem, been schoolfellows together at the feet of Gamaliel. Barnabas had conferred upon Paul some years before a favour sufficiently great to have bound them together in amity for ever. It was Barnabas that took Paul by the hand when he returned a convert from Damascus to Jerusalem, and introduced him into the fellowship of those disciples who otherwise would have recoiled from him with horror as their recent persecutor. They had been *fellow-labourers* for a long time. They had taken a long, trying, and perilous missionary tour from Antioch, and had returned. They had stood side by side in many fierce battles with the heathen, groaned together under many a wound, and won together many splendid victories for Christ. They had recently returned from the mother Church at Jerusalem, where they had been settling a great ecclesiastical dispute. They were *apostles* too, acting under the inspiration and direction of Christ. And now they were projecting another missionary tour together. " Paul said unto Barnabas, Let us go again and visit our brethren in every city where we have preached the word of the Lord, and see how they do." Under such circumstances, I ask, could anything appear more *improbable* than that such men should quarrel? Yet they did. We look to the future, and say, probably such an event will happen ; yet how often the future falsifies our calculations and disappoints our hopes. We do not know what convulsions may occur to-morrow in communities the most compact, what disruption in friendship the most consolidated by time and consecrated by love. Science may give correct prophecies concerning events in the natural universe. It may tell when the tide will overflow its boundaries, when an eclipse will take place, or when another comet will sweep the heavens ; but no *uninspired* intelligence can predict with certainty the future of the *spiritual* world. Souls are *free :* they have the power of self-motion. There are hidden forces and passions in the human heart which only await the advent of certain circumstances in order to produce revolutions which no finite mind can foretell.

This quarrel illustrates the truth—

II. THAT LITTLE THINGS ARE OFTEN MORE TRYING TO THE TEMPER THAN GREAT. These men for years had been in the most trying circumstances together, both on sea and land. They had contended together with the bigoted Jew and the idolatrous Gentile. They had just returned from Jerusalem, where they had engaged in a most exciting debate, involving interests the most precious and questions the most momentous, and yet we have no record of the slightest ebullition of temper on the part of either. They seem to have gone through the whole of these great things with the most unbroken equanimity of soul. But now the mere question as to whether John should accompany them in the projected mission or not, produces great irritation, a *paroxysm* in each. Barnabas, perhaps, wished John to go rather on the ground of *personal* feeling than of the general good. He was the son of his sister, and it was somewhat natural to desire to take him with them as a travelling companion. The affection of Barnabas would be likely to magnify unduly the merits of his nephew. Paul, on the other hand, viewed the question on *public* grounds, and estimated John by his aptitude for such a mission. He did not forget how John deserted them at an important stage in their journey before. " But Paul thought not good to take him with them, who departed from them from Pamphylia, and went not with them to the work." Now, as to whether they should take John with them or not seems to us a *small* matter,—very small, compared with other things that engaged their united attention; and yet it was this that broke the harmony of their friendship. It is often so. The small things of life have generally a greater power to try the temper than the great things. Call men together to discuss *small* questions, and they will quarrel; call them to work out a great object, and they will be cordial and unanimous. The best way to promote church union is to engage in great works. It is the little things that annoy. Flies irritate the noble steed more than the roll of the chariot wheel. This quarrel illustrates the truth—

III. THAT CHRISTIANITY ALLOWS SCOPE FOR DISCRETIONARY ACTION. These apostles took upon themselves to decide as to whether John should accompany them or not. No principle was involved in it—it was a mere question of expediency. We are allowed no discretionary action either as to *moral principles* or *cardinal truths*. We are bound to obey the moral laws of heaven: we disobey at our peril. We are also bound to believe in the cardinal truths of the gospel: woe be to us if we reject them. But there is much in connexion with the methods of extending and the policy of establishing Christianity that is left entirely with our judgment. Hence it is noteworthy that the discussion at Jerusalem, which involved vital truths, was, we are informed, under the direction of the Holy Spirit. "It seemed good to the Holy Ghost," said James. But in this discussion between Barnabas and Paul concerning John, there seems to have been no special direction at all. It was left with their own judgment to determine. Many such questions are left for such treatment. The questions of church government, &c.
This quarrel illustrates the truth—

IV. THAT THE BEST OF MEN ARE NOT ABSOLUTELY INFALLIBLE. When the apostles spoke and acted under the inspiration of the Eternal Spirit of Truth, they were infallible. But they did not always thus speak and act, as the event we are discussing shows. They were now left to their own judgment, and infirmity of temper is the result. There is but *One* perfect example, and thank God there is One; and He is to be followed through evil as well as good report.
This quarrel illustrates the truth—

V. THAT UNDER THE GRACIOUS RULE OF HEAVEN, EVIL IS MADE SUBSERVIENT TO THE PROGRESS OF GOOD. Their quarrel led them to abandon the proposed journey—nothing more. The quarrels of some Christians lead to the abandonment of their principles. "And so Barnabas took Mark, and sailed unto Cyprus; and Paul chose Silas, and departed, being recommended by the brethren unto the grace of God. And he went through Syria and Cilicia, confirming the churches." This disruption led to two things :

First, An increased *area* of usefulness. Instead of one district for both, which was contemplated, there were two, one for each. It led Paul into Europe.

Secondly, An increased *power* of usefulness. Instead of two men, Paul and Barnabas, there were four. Paul took Silas, and Barnabas, Mark ; and thus, we believe, greater good resulted than would have been accomplished had they remained united. Evil must ever be overruled for good.

> " All good proceedeth from Thee,
> As sunbeams from the sun ;
> All evils fall before Thee,
> Thy will through all is done."

This quarrel illustrates the truth—

VI. THAT EARNEST WORK WILL INEVITABLY RECTIFY OUR TEMPERS. They had not been parted long, I presume, before every particle of animosity went out. The first Christian effort extinguished every spark. We find Paul referring kindly to Mark (Col. iv. 10 ; 2 Tim. iv. 11 ; Philem. 24), and also to Barnabas (1 Cor. ix. 6).

Acts 15:41-16:8

PAUL'S SECOND MISSIONARY TOUR.—I. FROM ANTIOCH IN SYRIA TO TROAS

Paul a model for all Gospel ministers

"*And he went through Syria and Cilicia, confirming the churches. Then came he to Derbe and Lystra : and, behold, a certain disciple was there, named Timotheus, the son of a certain woman, which was a Jewess, and believed ; but his father was a Greek : Which was well reported of by the brethren that were at Lystra and Iconium. Him would Paul have to go forth with him ; and took and circumcised him, because of the Jews which were in those quarters : for they knew all that his father was a Greek. And as they went through the cities, they delivered them the decrees for to keep, that were ordained of the apostles and elders which were at Jerusalem. And so were the churches[1] established in the faith, and increased in number daily. Now, when they had gone throughout Phrygia and the region of Galatia, and were forbidden of[2] the Holy Ghost to preach the word in Asia, after they were come to Mysia, they assayed to go into Bithynia : but the Spirit[3] suffered them not. And they, passing by Mysia, came down to Troas.*"

EMENDATIVE RENDERINGS.—(1.) So then the churches were. (2.) Being hindered by. (3.) The Spirit of Jesus.—ALF.

EXEGETICAL REMARKS.—" *He went through Syria and Cilicia.*" These were regions of which Antioch and Tarsus were capitals : and to the Gentile Christians in these districts the ecclesiastical letter drawn up by the apostles at Jerusalem was specially directed. This was the natural and necessary route to take by land from Antioch into Asia Minor. Some suppose that Paul preached in Cilicia and the adjacent parts of Syria a few years after his conversion.

"*Confirming the Churches.*" Although the gospel had been preached in these regions before, there is no evidence that Churches were formed, and perhaps the work of the apostle now was to organise the converts into Churches, giving them permanent directions and counsels for their conduct, and thus "*confirming*" them.

"*Then came he to Derbe and Lystra.*" These two places are named together, as in chap. xiv. 6, but in the reverse order, as they were now approached from the opposite direction. Paul and Silas had probably come through the famous Cilician gates, a pass in the Tarsus range leading from north to south, and eighty miles in length. —ALEX.

"*Behold, a certain disciple.*" He was a disciple of Christ—a Christian. Probably he was one of Paul's converts, won by him on his first visit to that place. Hence Paul calls him his "son" (1 Cor. iv. 17; 1 Tim. i. 2). "He may have been in that group of disciples that surrounded the apparently lifeless body of the apostle outside of the walls of Lystra, on the occasion of his first visit" (2 Tim. iii. 10, 11).

"*The son of a certain woman, which was a Jewess, and believed: but his father was a Greek.*" We learn elsewhere (2 Tim. i. 5), that his mother's name was Eunice, and his grandmother's name Lois, both eminent for faith. His father was a Greek and a heathen, for the word "*believed*" is not added to his name as it is to his wife's. Though it was contrary to the Jewish institution to contract matrimonial alliances with heathen nations (Ezra ix. 12), it was sometimes done, and was regarded as less heinous for females to marry Gentile husbands than for males to marry Gentile wives.

"*Which was well reported of by the brethren which were at Lystra and Ico-*

nium." His reputation for Christian principle and for consistency was exalted and perhaps wide-spread. This testimony corresponds to his general character, as portrayed in both the epistles which Paul addressed to him (Philip. ii. 19–23; 1 Cor. iv. 17, xvi. 10, 11; 1 Thess. iii. 1–6).

"*Him would Paul have to go forth with him, and took and circumcised him, because of the Jews which were in those quarters: for they knew all that his father was a Greek.*" "It was customary, according to the Talmud, for the father to have control of his children's religious observances; and because his father was a Gentile, Timothy was not circumcised. "As Paul wished to employ him as a co-worker with himself among the Jews as well as Gentiles, the rite of circumcision was performed as a mere prudential regulation, in deference to Jewish prejudices, since for a half Jew not to be circumcised would be worse than for one Gentile born to neglect it. Paul was firm to withstand to the last point the requirement of circumcision as an essential to the Christian profession, as is evident from the case of Titus. The decree of the Christian assembly at Jerusalem had decided that matter in relation to the pure Gentiles; but Timothy was partially a debtor, so to speak, by his birth, to the Jewish law; and though the apostle was so unyielding where the rite was demanded as necessary, he would, in the exercise of a generous charity, yield much to the scruples of his weaker brethren, where no principle would be compromised."—LIV. Here is apostolic sanction of the principle of expediency.

"*And as they went through the cities.*" Where Paul had preached before—Derbe, Lystra, Iconium, and Antioch.

"*They delivered them the decrees.*" Literally dogmas. These dogmas or decrees were the substance of the letter which had been drawn up at Jerusalem, exempting the Gentile converts and all others from the burdensome ritual of Moses.

"*Now, when they had gone throughout Phrygia.*" "A large central province of Asia Minor, surrounded by

Cappadocia, Galatia, Mysia, Lydia, Caria, Lycaonia, Pisidia, Lysia, and Bithynia. Its inhabitants claimed to be the most ancient people in the world; and even the Egyptians yielded them the palm in that respect. The capital was Apamea. And, of "the seven churches" mentioned in the Apocalypse, two, Laodicea and Colosse, to which Paul wrote one of his epistles, were situated in this district."—LIV.

"*The region of Galatia.*" Galatia was occupied by the Gauls and Celts three hundred years before Christ. One of the epistles of St Paul is addressed to the Galatians.

"*And were forbidden of the Holy Ghost.*" How the Spirit restrained the apostles from going whither they intended, whether by a revelation, the presence of opposing circumstances, or a mysterious impression which they could not shake off, does not appear. The fact alone is stated—the apostles were prevented by God. They were hindered from carrying out their own volitions. The Divine Spirit is ever restraining men, and turning them from their own ways.

"*Asia.*" This is not the great Asiatic continent, nor the rich peninsula now called Asia Minor, but only so much of its western coast as constituted the Roman province of Asia.

"*After they were come to Mysia.*" This place was situated in the north part of Asia Minor, and had for its boundaries Bithynia, Phrygia, Lydia, the Mediterranean, Hellespont, and Propontis. Its principal town was Pergamos.

"*They assayed (endeavoured) to go into Bithynia.*" A province lying farther east than Mysia.

"*But the Spirit suffered them not.* Why did the Spirit prevent them? Some think that because Europe was ripe for labours, and that other men would be honoured to establish the gospel in those regions. Indeed, we are informed by Pliny, that by the end of the first centuries Bithynia was filled with Christians. "*Spirit.*" What spirit? The spirit of Jesus, τὸ πνεῦμα Ἰησοῦ, as the best ancient authorities read. "This is the first time that the Holy Ghost is expressly spoken of as determining the course they were to follow in their efforts to evangelise the nations; and it was evidently designed to show that whereas hitherto the diffusion of the gospel had been carried on in unbroken course, connected by natural points of junction, it was now to take a leap to which it could not be impelled but by an immediate and independent operation of the Spirit. And though primarily this intimation of the Spirit was only negative, and referred but to the immediate neighbourhood, we may certainly conclude that Paul took it for a sign that a new epoch was now to commence in his apostolic labours.—BAUMGARTEN.

"*And they passing by Mysia.*" Probably meaning passing through without stopping.

"*They came down to Troas.*" A seaport near the site of ancient Troy. It is immortalised as being the scene of the epic poem of Homer, the *Iliad*, and also part of the *Æneid*, by Virgil. Here they were opposite to Greece, and near to it, so as to be ready to enter on their new field of missionary labour.

HOMILETICS.—We have briefly followed Paul in his first missionary tour, when he started from Antioch with Barnabas and Mark. We have also noticed the many serious and significant things that took place at Antioch after his returning: the holding of the first missionary meeting : the discussion at the first ecclesiastical council, in order to settle a severe controversy that had broken out : and the quarrel between Barnabas and himself. A second missionary deputation now starts from this same Antioch, consisting not of the same parties, nor taking the same route. Paul and Barnabas no longer go together ; a certain alienation of soul has taken place between them which disqualifies for cordial and mutual co-operation. Barnabas takes Mark, his nephew, who had offended Paul, and occasioned the quarrel between the two old apostolic friends; and both of them, Barnabas and Mark, "sailed unto Cyprus," and we lose sight of them. The historian lets them drop from the page. Their subsequent doings were no doubt of a character worthy of historic record, but no such record has come down. Their record is on high. Whilst the historian leaves Barnabas and Mark, he follows Paul and Silas, and even joins them in their adventures.

We shall look at this fragment of history as presenting Paul as a *model for all gospel ministers.*

I. He recognises the importance of ESTABLISHING NEW CONVERTS IN THE FAITH. "He went through Syria and Cilicia confirming the Churches." His main object is not to convert, but to "confirm." In this visit he does not break new ground, but goes over the old scenes ; visits Derbe and Lystra, scenes where he had been shamefully and cruelly persecuted. Who that remembers the malignant treatment which he met with on his former visit to Lystra can fail to admire his magnanimity and dauntless heroism in entering this place again ? But the work he had commenced in those places was unfinished, and he returns. The passage presents two things in relation to his confirmatory work :

First, The method : "And as they went through the cities they delivered them the decrees for to keep." He carried with him wherever he went, and expounded, the apostolic letter from Jerusalem (xv. 23–29). He indoctrinated them with the spirit of that document.

Secondly, The success : "And so were the Churches established in the faith, and increased in number daily." The result was twofold :—(1.) Moral increase—"established in the faith." Their views became clearer ; their principles struck a deeper root ; their attachment to Christ attained a greater strength. Their religion passed from the region of theories and feelings into their heart and life. (2.) Numerical increase—"increased in number daily." Let Christians improve in character, and converts will multiply daily. A morally improved Church will swell the number of converts. This confirmatory work, this work of improving the character of Christians, is pre-eminently the work of Christians in this age and land of ours.

We have a deep impression that a re-converted Church is essential to the conversion of the world.

II. He recognised the importance of ENLISTING TRUE COADJUTORS IN THE WORK. "Paul chose Silas," and he would have Timotheus to "go forth with him." On the great page of human history stands there a man more brave in heart, more mighty in his own strength, more entirely self-dependent, than Paul, the "apostle of Jesus

Christ?" Not one! Yet he needs a companion. He lost Barnabas, and he " chose Silas," and took with him Timotheus. Christ knew our social needs, and hence, in sending out His disciples and apostles, He sent them in twos. One supplements the deficiencies of the other; in the breast of one there lies a spark to rekindle the waning fire of the other's zeal. He selected the best man as his social helper. He would not have Mark, and he declines taking Barnabas again; but he wants some one. The Church at Antioch at this time was numerous. There were many to 'choose from, but he selected one of the "chief men among the brethren" of the mother Church at Jerusalem, that numbered its thousands, and with him a noble young soul, Timotheus. In a great work, link not yourselves to spiritually common men when you may get moral peers and princes.

III. He recognised the importance of ACCOMMODATING HIMSELF TO PUBLIC SENTIMENT. The Jews believed in circumcision. It was with them a most sacred rite; a rite which they considered distinguished them from all other nations, and marked them as the children of God. Although the rite had been abrogated, was no longer binding, it had not been branded as a sin—it was not yet a moral wrong; and hence Paul, in accommodation to the popular sentiment, circumcises Timothy. "Had," says a modern expositor, "Timothy not been circumcised, a storm would have gathered round the apostle in his further progress. His fixed line of procedure was to act on the cities through the synagogues, and to preach the gospel to the Jew first, and then to the Gentile. But such a course would have been impossible had not Timothy been circumcised. He must necessarily have been repelled by that people who endeavoured once to murder St Peter because they imagined he had taken a Greek into the temple (chap. xxi. 29). The very intercourse of social life would have been almost impossible, for it was still "an abomination" for the circumcised to eat with the uncircumcised. In all this Paul was consistent with himself, with his own grand axiom, "I am all things to all men, that I might save some."

IV. He recognised the importance of YIELDING TO THE DICTATES OF THE DIVINE SPIRIT. "After they were come to Mysia, they assayed to go into Bithynia : but the Spirit suffered them not." There is a Divine Spirit, and that Spirit has access to the human spirit. The fact that He influences men is not only a doctrine of the Bible, but is also a matter of consciousness. The modes of His operation are various and often inexplicable. "The wind bloweth where it listeth," &c. If we are the true ministers of Christ, His Spirit, according to His promise, is with us—" Lo, I am with you always." (1.) The will of that Spirit *must be obeyed* : to oppose that is sin, weakness, ruin. (2.) The will of that Spirit is *knowable :* He gives indications by *impressions* within and by *events* without.

Acts 16:9-12

PAUL'S SECOND MISSIONARY TOUR.—II. FROM TROAS TO PHILIPPI

The cry of the Macedonian to Paul

" *And a vision appeared to Paul in the night : there stood a man of Macedonia, and prayed him, saying, Come over into Macedonia, and help us. And after he had seen the vision, immediately we endeavoured to go into Macedonia, assuredly gathering that the Lord*[1] *had called us for to preach the gospel unto them. Therefore, loosing from Troas, we came with a straight course to Samothracia, and the next day to Neapolis ; and from thence to Philippi, which is the chief city of that part of Macedonia,*[2] *and a colony : and we were in that city abiding certain days.*"

EMENDATIVE RENDERINGS.—(1.) God. (2.) The first Macedonian city of the district.—ALF.

EXEGETICAL REMARKS.—"*And a vision appeared to Paul in the night.*" "The divine will is now more fully made known by a vision or preternatural appearance. "*In*" (through, during, in the course of) "*the night.*" Perhaps the night of their arrival. "*Appeared to Paul,*" as in chap. ii. 3, vii. 2, xxvi. 30–35, ix. 17, xiii. 31. It is not said, in a dream,— which expression occurs only in the case of Joseph (Matt. ii. 13, xix. 22), and of Pilate's wife (Matt. xxvii. 29). Some believe the supposition of a dream to be excluded here, as the lowest form or stage of divine communication, never used with the apostles."—ALEX.

" *There stood a man of Macedonia,*" &c. "*A man ;*" not Lydia nor the Philippian gaoler, but some one that represented the Macedonians—a representative man, for he says, "*help* US." Paul knew him to be a Macedonian, perhaps by his language or his apparel.

" *Therefore, loosing from Troas :*" a nautical term—sailed away.

" *With a straight course :*" over the Ægean Sea, the Archipelago.

" *To Samothracia.*" "Or Samothrace. This was an island in the Ægean, about thirty miles in circumference. It was called Samothrace, or the Samos of Thrace, to distinguish it from other places of the same

name. It was an asylum for criminals and adventurers. Its modern name is Samandrachi."—LIV.

" *And the next day to Neapolis.*" "A city of Macedonia, on the Ægean coast, known in modern times as Napoli. It is represented by the modern Caralla. It is situated between one and two hundred miles from Troas."

" *And from thence to Philippi.*" "A city of Macedonia, formerly called Dathos, and Krenides, or the springs; but being rebuilt and greatly enlarged by Philip, father of Alexander the Great, it took from him the name of Philippi. It is at the head of the Ægean Sea, twelve miles north-west of Neapolis. Its modern name is Filiba. It lay on the great plain between Hamus and Pangæus, and was upon the great road from Rome to Asia—the *via Egnatia*. It was a place of great celebrity in profane history."—EADIE. It is famous in history as the scene of the great battle forty-two years before the Christian era, which decided the fate of the Roman republic, and in which Brutus and Cassius were defeated by Octavius and Anthony. Those who wish a more full and graphic description of Paul's tour from Antioch to Philippi, should read the magnificent description given by Conybeare and Howson.

HOMILETICS.—We may look at this cry of the Macedonians to Paul as expressing the cry of the heathen world to the Christian Church in all ages.

I. THE CRY WAS HUMAN. "There stood a *man* of Macedonia." A *man*, (1.) Not an angelic intelligence. A *man*, (2.) Not a member of a class, but of a race. It was not a philosopher, artist, priest, warrior, king; but a *man*. It is the *humanity* in heathendom that is in moral distress. The aid that is so deeply required is not secular, political, educational, military, but *moral.* Help to the conscience, soul; help to man as man in his spiritual and eternal relationships. That man which appeared in vision to Paul represents the suppliant attitude of heathens everywhere in relation to Christianity.

II. THE CRY WAS SIGNIFICANT. "Come over and help us." It implies—

First, *A sense of need.* Man everywhere feels that there is something wanting to make matters right between him and his God. "Wherewithal shall I come before the Lord?" It implies—

Secondly, *Conscious inability to supply the need.* The Macedonian man felt that the Macedonians, with all their wealth and intelligence, could not supply the necessity. Heathenism has no self-redemptive power. It implies—

Thirdly, *Faith in the power of Christians to help.* The Macedonian man took it for granted that Paul could help. How he knew we cannot tell. Perhaps that Spirit that works with heathens as well as with Christians gave him that impression. Macedonia may be taken to represent the western world as it then existed; and with all the brilliant civilisation of Greece and Rome, it wanted something which Christianity alone could supply. Once this call sounded for help from the heathen West to the Christian East; now it sounds from the heathen East to the Christian West.

III. THE CRY WAS OBEYED. Paul is not disobedient to the cry; he attends at once to the call. "And after he had seen the vision, immediately we endeavoured to go into Macedonia; assuredly gathering that the Lord had called us for to preach the gospel unto them." "Never," says Mr Binney, "in this world was there a ship equal to that in which these men sailed to Macedonia! One of our distinguished writers, Thomas Carlyle, refers to the little ship *Mayflower*, which sailed from Southampton in 1620, having on board the Pilgrim Fathers—men of strong hearts, with religious faith in them, having an intense love of liberty, and determined to go where they could have freedom to worship God. In that little ship were the seeds and elements of the intelligence, civilisation, literature, religion, which were one day to be developed in a new national life beyond the sea. But was there ever a *Mayflower* like this? When these men went down to the quay to look for a vessel, how little the world thought, how little those who saw them thought, how little they themselves knew, what history they were making! What effects were to flow from this movement of theirs! What an influence it was to have on the future character of dominant races! And yet, in appearance, it was one of the most ordinary things that could possibly take place. These four men go on board a vessel—Paul, with his fervent soul and his strong intellect; Silas, with his zeal and his prophetic gifts; Luke, with his scholarly culture and professional accomplishments; and Timothy, with his youthful earnestness, and as yet undeveloped powers for work. These four men, guided by the Divine Spirit, COME TO EUROPE; and that ship in which they sailed has in it the seeds of all that is to be developed in the religion and learning, the philosophy, legislation, art, science, and everything else that has made European nations the acknowledged regal masters of the world."

Acts 16:13-15

PAUL'S SECOND MISSIONARY TOUR.—III. THE GOSPEL IN EUROPE

" *And on the sabbath we went out of the city[1] by a river side, where prayer was wont to be made; and we sat down, and spake unto the women which resorted thither. And a certain woman named Lydia, a seller of purple, of the city of Thyatira, which worshipped God, heard us :[2] whose heart the Lord opened, that she attended unto the things which were spoken of Paul. And when she was baptized, and her household, she besought us, saying, If ye have judged me to be faithful to the Lord, come into my house, and abide there. And she constrained us.*"

EMENDATIVE RENDERINGS.—(1.) Out of the gate. (2.) Was listening.—ALF.

EXEGETICAL REMARKS.—" *On the Sabbath-day we went out of the city by a river side.*" Sacred rites were frequently performed and temples built near waters. Probably they reached Philippi in the early part of the week, and they remained for the Sabbath, being the time for public worship.

" *Where prayer was wont to be made.*" It would seem that the Jews were accustomed to assemble on the banks of this river on the Sabbath for worship. Because of this the apostles resorted thither.

" *A certain woman named Lydia, a*

seller of purple, of the city of Thyatira." Thyatira is situated on the confines of Lydia and Mysia, in Asia Minor, between Pergamos and Sardis, and was famous in the ancient world for its purple dye. Lydia's occupation was to dispose, by sale, of this dye.

" *Whose heart the Lord opened.*" Her mind was disposed by the Spirit of God to listen to the doctrines of Paul.

" *And when she was baptized and her household, she besought us,*" &c. We are not told whether baptism was administered by immersion, pouring, or sprinkling; nor are we told of whom the household was composed, males or females, children or adults, or both.

"*She besought us, saying, If ye have judged me to be faithful to the Lord, come into my house, and abide there.*" From this, it would appear that she was a woman of means and of mod-

esty. She had an establishment at Philippi, large enough to accommodate the missionary party, and to receive her wares from her native town. There is a beautiful modesty of spirit in the expression, "If ye have judged me to be faithful to the Lord."

HOMILETICS.—Paul, Silas, Timotheus, and I suppose Luke too, are now at Philippi. Thither they had gone, not by their own choice. The Eternal Spirit, who is in all, and over all, had by a vision to Paul brought them to this important city in Europe. Great cities are great fountains of social influence; their streams run through the world. These great fountains are greatly polluted, and require above all places the cleansing influence of gospel truth ; hence, thither God especially directs His ministers. It would seem that the apostles, when they entered the city, did not announce their approach at once. "We were in that city abiding certain days." One might have supposed that Europe would have rung out such a loud ALL HAIL ! to these messengers of mercy, that all Philippi would have crowded about them immediately on their entrance. But no ; as ever, "the kingdom of God cometh not with observation." The passage leads us to consider *three* things :

I. THE FIRST GOSPEL PREACHING IN EUROPE. "And on the Sabbath we (Luke included) went out of the city by a river side, where prayer was wont to be made, and we sat down, and spake unto the women which resorted thither." An exquisitely simple and unostentatious record of the opening of the mission in Europe. No long preamble, no parade. Observe—

First, The *season* of this first gospel preaching. It was on the "Sabbath," the seventh day, held as most sacred by the Jews. On this day the religious sentiment would be more active in the Jewish mind, generally, than on other days, and therefore would be more disposed to listen to the new revelation which the God of their forefathers had made. It is well for ministers to study the *mental moods* of men in their dispensation of truth. There are days and circumstances that throw souls into moods specially suited for religious impressions. There are tides in the affairs of spiritual as well as secular concerns. Observe—

Secondly, The *scene* of this first gospel preaching in Europe. " Out of the city by a river side, where prayer was wont to be made." They retired from the hum and bustle of the city into the solitudes and sublimities of nature. "By a river side." What river was this ?—the stream that flowed near Philippi into the Strymon ? We know not, nor does it matter. Few objects in nature are more beautiful and suggestive to a reflective devotion than a river. Emblem of life, ever changing ; emblem of the universe, flowing on for ever and for ever. But by this river prayer was wont to be made." The Jews were accustomed to have their *proseuchœ* (oratories), places of prayer, built near water, that they might attend to the various ablutions connected with their religious rites. Such was the scene where the first preaching in Europe took place. To Christianity all places are alike sacred. "God is a Spirit," &c. Observe—

Thirdly, The *style* of this first gospel preaching in Europe. "And we sat down and spake unto the women which resorted thither." How beautifully free and natural! They did not stand erect in the attitude of orators, they "sat down," mingled with the people. They did not deliver set discourses, but "spake," talked ; nothing more. Perhaps each said something, though Paul said most. What did they talk about? The beauties of nature? the immortality of the soul? the providence of the Eternal? If they referred to these, they were not their *grand* theme. *Christ* and *His cross* were, we may rest assured, their great subject.

II. THE FIRST GOSPEL HEARERS IN EUROPE. Who were they? Poets, statesmen, philosophers, heroes, kings? No! "*Women.*" They "spake unto the women." Why were women there and not men? Was it because the men came at one hour and the women at another? or because the women had a special service for themselves? Did wives meet there to pray for their husbands, and sisters for their fathers and their brothers? We know not the reason. All we know is, that women are always more religiously disposed than men.

The fact that the gospel was first preached to women in Europe, suggests to us three things :—

First, That the gospel is *universally appreciable*. Had the apostles felt that the truths they had to communicate required for their appreciation intellectual culture, logical force, philosophic acumen, they would have gone first, not only to men, but to men of the higher type of mind. But they felt that the gospel, being a revelation of facts, character, love, all that was required to understand it was the common intuitions and sympathies of a woman's affectionate nature. The fact suggests—

Secondly, That the gospel *honours the female character*. All religions but that of the Bible degrade woman. Throughout the glowing East, yes, and throughout the world where Christianity is not, woman is regarded as the mere instrument of man's greed and lusts. Everywhere she is a slave ; and though, as in the more civilised parts of the world, she may be petted and fondled, she is still a slave to man. The gospel honours woman. The Saviour of the world was born of a woman. He talked to the woman of Samaria. Women were amongst His followers. He showed Himself to women after His resurrection, and women were amongst the converts under the Pentecostal sermon, and the apostles now preached in Europe *first* to *women.* Woman is under special obligation to the gospel. The fact suggests—

Thirdly, That the gospel has a regard to *social influence.* It is no flattery to woman to say that she has a greater influence on her race than man has. When she acts worthily of her nature, her influence as sister, wife, mother, is regal. Woman, in influence, is not the weaker, but the stronger vessel.

III. THE FIRST GOSPEL CONVERT IN EUROPE. "A certain woman named Lydia," &c. Observe three things here concerning her :—

First, *Her secular calling.* "A seller of purple." Purple was a colour got from a shell-fish, and of great cost and richness. It was chiefly worn by the wealthy and great. This woman was in trade. She sold in Philippi and other places, perhaps, the costly colour which she obtained in Thyatira.

Secondly, *Her religious character.* "Which worshipped God." This does not mean that she was genuinely religious in heart, but that she was a proselyte. She was a formal worshipper of the God of Abraham.

Thirdly, *Her spiritual change.* "Whose heart the Lord opened," &c. (1.) The *subject* of the change. The "heart." This, notwithstanding her religious profession, had been closed. The Spirit of truth had not entered it. It was shut. Avarice, prejudice, habit, shut up the heart. (2.) The *cause* of the change. "The Lord opened" it. Not by a miracle, not irrespective of means, but by the influences that were brought to bear upon her on this occasion— Sabbath-day associations, natural scenery, the presence and speeches of the apostles, &c., disposed her to listen to what Paul had to say. (3.) The *proof* of the change. (*a*) *Teachableness.* "She attended unto the things which were spoken of Paul." As a thirsty soul she drank in the new truths. (*b*) *Profession.* What did she avow? The necessity of a *cleansing* influence for herself and household. She does this symbolically—"She was baptized." This case of baptism does not prove that faith is a necessary condition of the ordinance, for it is not said that her household believed. (*c*) *Gratitude.* "If ye have judged me to be faithful to the Lord, come into my house," &c.

What a wonderful history! The gospel is preached to many women, and only one seems to have been converted. Lydia becomes the *first Christian in Europe,* and the mother of the Philippian church. A hundred years before this, by a battle of carnage and blood, in this Philippi, the foundation of the empire of Augustus was laid ; now a bloodless battle was fought here by the apostles, that laid the foundation of Christ's ever-growing kingdom in Europe.

Acts 16:16-22

PAUL'S SECOND MISSIONARY TOUR.—III. THE GOSPEL IN EUROPE
(*continued*)

"*And it came to pass, as we went to prayer,*[1] *a certain damsel possessed with a spirit of divination met us, which brought her masters much gain by soothsaying : The same followed Paul and us, and cried, saying, These men are the servants of the most high God, which show*[2] *unto us the way of salvation. And this did she many days. But Paul, being grieved, turned, and said to the spirit, I command thee, in the name of Jesus Christ, to come out of her. And he came out the same hour. And when her masters saw that the hope of their gains was gone, they caught Paul and Silas, and drew them into the market-place unto the rulers, and brought them to the magistrates, saying, These men, being Jews, do exceedingly trouble our city, and teach customs which are not lawful for us to receive, neither to observe, being Romans. And the multitude rose up together against them ; and the magistrates rent off their clothes, and commanded to beat them.*"

EMENDATIVE RENDERINGS.— (1.) The place of prayer.   (2.) Tell.—ALF.

EXEGETICAL REMARKS.—"*A certain damsel possessed with a spirit of divination,*" or, as the margin reads, *of Python.* In the Greek mythology that was the name of a serpent which guarded an oracle on Mount Parnassus, and was slain by Apollo, thence called *Pythius,* as being himself the god of divination. That she was not, as some suppose, a mere ventriloquist, or sheer impostor, nor a mere somnambulist or lunatic, but a demoniac, is clear from Paul's address to her.—ALEX. This woman met the apostles as they went to prayer ; that is, to the place of prayer.

"*Which brought her masters much gain by soothsaying.*" This woman had keen masters, and they, availing themselves of the credulity and superstition of their neighbours, turned her remarkable power to their own account.

"*The same followed Paul and us, and cried, saying, These men are the servants of the most high God, which show unto us the way of salvation.*" What she said concerning these apostles—Paul, Silas, Timothy, and Luke—was an undoubted truth. But how did she come to know this ? Pro-

bably she had heard it from the lips of the apostles themselves.

"*And this did she many days.*" She persevered in this, pursuing them wherever they went, and uttering these words.

"*But Paul, being grieved.*" The word "grieved," would be more exactly rendered "wearied." Losing his patience with the constant annoyance, turned and said to the spirit, "I command thee in the name of Jesus to come out of her." The spirit that was in her, and acting through her, was some evil personality.

"*In the name of Jesus Christ.*" By His authority, and as His representative.

"*And he came out the same hour.*" Her deliverance from the evil spirit was miraculous and instantaneous.

"*And when her masters saw that the hope of their gains was gone, they caught Paul and Silas, and drew them into the market-place unto the rulers.*" They were grieved—were enraged at the loss, and under its influence they proceed to lay violent hands on the apostles.

HOMILETICS.—This remarkable incident leads us to consider the DEVIL OF AVARICE in two aspects.

I. IN THE PURSUANCE OF ITS PURPOSE. This maid was the mere organ and agent of mercenariness. This in truth was the demon which inspired her. In pursuing its sordid aim we discover three things which have ever marked its history :—

First, *The prostitution of mind.* This young woman's nature was *sold* to mammon. Her sympathies, talent, intuitions, genius, all were consecrated to the greed of her masters. Does not greed ever thus prostitute mind ? It hires the genius of the world for its service. A more terrible sight can scarcely be witnessed than the prostitution of souls to the mere purpose of gain. We discover—

Secondly, *The practice of falsehood.* This woman was a soothsayer. She pretended to withdraw the dark veil of the future, penetrate to its mysterious arena, and foretell coming events. She did all this for money. " She brought her masters much gain by soothsaying." This is only a specimen, alas ! of that falsehood which characterises the history of avarice. Men build up their fortunes by falsehoods. Lies are considered the life of trade. We discover—

Thirdly, *Religious profession.* To impose upon the spectators, she professed her acquaintance with the apostles and almost a reverence for them. " These men," said she, " are the servants of the most high God, which show unto us the way of salvation." This declaration was truth, truth well spoken, though truth spoken undoubtedly for mercenary ends. Perhaps she had sufficient prescience to see that the mission of the apostles would be successful, and that her declaration of their success would heighten her reputation and increase her authority. Alas ! avarice uses religion for its own ends, puts on its garb, uses its vocabulary, and kneels to its heroes.

This remarkable incident leads us to consider the devil of avarice—

II. IN THE FRUSTRATION OF ITS PURPOSE. Paul thwarts avarice in the person of this girl. " Paul, being grieved, turned, and said to the spirit, I command thee in the name of Jesus Christ to come out of her. And he came out the same hour." Does this mean the exorcising of a *personal* spirit of evil who had taken possession of her ? or does it mean the expulsion of the *spirit of evil* from her ? I incline to the latter opinion, and regard Paul as effecting her conversion. This he did, and this he did as all conversions are accomplished, " in the name of Jesus Christ," and at once—" in the same hour." The change which Paul effected in her now, whatever it was, interfered with the gains of her masters. The " masters saw that the hope of their gains was gone." Critics observe that there is a paronomasia or play upon the words in the original which is lost in our version, for the same verb is here used as that in the preceding verse which describes the departure of the spirit from her.* Observe—

First, *The vindictiveness of this frustrated avarice.* "They caught Paul and Silas, and drew them unto the market-place unto the rulers." Nothing enrages a selfish man so much as interference with his gains. Snatch a little of his gold from his grasp, and he will rage like a demon. Selfish men will oppose any enterprise, however divine, that interferes with their gains. Vested interests are the great antagonists of truth everywhere.

Secondly, *The hypocrisy of this frustrated avarice.* When they brought the apostles before the magistrates, what charge did they allege against them? Did they say these men have interfered with our traffic or our gain? This would have been truth. No; they prefer a false accusation. "These men, being Jews, do exceedingly trouble our city, and teach customs which are not lawful for us to receive, neither to observe, being Romans." The false charge they make is such that covers their sordid natures with the garb of loyalty and patriotism. These wounded grubs would be thought patriotic heroes.

Thirdly, *The power of this frustrated avarice.* These rich men had sufficient power to move the multitude in their favour, and to command the magistrates to do their work. "And the multitude rose up together against them : and the magistrates rent off their clothes, and commanded to beat them. And when they had laid many stripes upon them, they cast them into prison, charging the jailor to keep them safely." Such was the power which *avarice* had in Philippi eighteen centuries ago, and such is the power, alas ! which it has ever wielded, and still wields. It can move magistrates and monarchs. "Money answereth all things," " and the love of it is the root of all evil."

Acts 16:23-40

PAUL'S SECOND MISSIONARY TOUR.—III. THE GOSPEL IN EUROPE
(*continued*)

"*And when they had laid many stripes upon them, they cast them into prison, charging the jailor to keep them safely : who, having received such a charge, thrust them into the inner prison, and made their feet fast in the stocks. And at midnight Paul and Silas prayed, and sang praises unto God : and the prisoners heard them.*[1] *And suddenly there was a great earthquake, so that the foundations of the prison were shaken : and immediately all the doors were opened, and every one's bands were loosed. And the keeper of the prison awaking out of his sleep, and seeing the prison doors*

* ἐξῆλθεν, and he went out ; ἐξῆλθεν, was gone out.

open, he drew out his sword, and would have killed himself,[2] *supposing that the prisoners had been fled. But Paul cried with a loud voice, saying, Do thyself no harm; for we are all here. Then he called for a light,*[3] *and sprang in, and came trembling, and fell down before Paul and Silas, and brought them out, and said, Sirs, what must I do to be saved? And they said, Believe on the Lord Jesus Christ,*[4] *and thou shalt be saved, and thy house. And they spake unto him the word of the Lord, and to all that were in his house. And he took them the same hour of the night, and washed their stripes; and was baptized, he and all his, straightway. And when he had brought them*[5] *into his house, he set meat before them, and rejoiced, believing in God with all his house. And when it was day, the magistrates sent the serjeants, saying, Let those men go. And the keeper of the prison told this saying to Paul, The magistrates have sent to let you go: now therefore depart, and go in peace. But Paul said unto them, They have beaten us openly uncondemned, being Romans, and have cast us into prison: and now they thrust us out privily? Nay verily; but let them come themselves and fetch us out. And the serjeants told these words unto the magistrates: and they feared, when they heard that they were Romans. And they came and besought them, and brought them out, and desired them to depart out of the city. And they went out of the prison, and entered into the house of Lydia: and when they had seen the brethren, they comforted*[6] *them, and departed."*

EMENDATIVE RENDERINGS.—(1.) Paul and Silas, in their prayers, were singing praises unto God, and the prisoners were listening to them. (2.) Was about to kill himself. (3) Lights. (4.) Omit this word. (5). Them up. (6.) Exhorted.—ALF.

EXEGETICAL REMARKS.—*"And when they had laid many stripes upon them, they cast them into prison, charging the jailor to keep them safely."* Stripped of "their clothes, afflicted with many 'stripes,' bruised, and bleeding, the apostles were thrust into prison, and their feet were, in the inner prison, made fast in the stocks."

"And suddenly there was a great earthquake," &c. Here is the miraculous interposition of their great Master. He causes the prison to shake to its foundation, the doors to fly open, and the chains to fall from their bleeding limbs.

"He drew out his sword, and would have killed himself, supposing that the prisoners had been fled." Roused from his slumbers by the crash of the earthquake, and seeing the prison doors thrown wide open, overwhelmed with terror, the keeper of the prison attempts to destroy himself. The sword was at hand. Probably he wore it at his side. Self-destruction was considered by the Romans as not only lawful, but a duty or a virtue under certain circumstances. Cato's

suicide was celebrated as a heroic act; and by a singular historical coincidence, that very city of Philippi, or its neighbourhood, had been signalised within a hundred years, not only by the great defeat of Brutus and Cassius, but by the suicide of both, and by a sort of wholesale self-destruction on the part of their adherents, who had been proscribed by Octavius and Anthony.

"But Paul cried with a loud voice, saying, Do thyself no harm; for we are all here." But how, it has been asked by recent sceptical critics, could Paul, in his inner prison, know what the jailor was about to do? In many conceivable ways, without supposing any supernatural communication. Thus, if the jailor slept at the door of the "inner prison," which suddenly flew open when the earthquake shook the foundations of the building; if, too, as may easily be conceived, he uttered some cry of despair on seeing the doors open; and if the clash of the steel, as the affrighted man drew it hastily from the scabbard, was audible but a

few yards off in the dead midnight stillness, increased by the awe inspired in the prisoners by the miracle—what difficulty is there in supposing that Paul, perceiving in a moment how matters stood, after crying out, stepped hastily to him, uttering the noble entreaty here recorded?"— P. C.

"*He came trembling, and fell down before Paul and Silas.*" His conscience is roused into terror; he sees Paul and Silas standing before him with the chains struck off, and notwithstanding the marks of suffering that were on their person, standing with the calm dignity of gods, and he falls to their feet and exclaims, "Sirs, or lords, masters, what shall I do to be saved?" What new light has broke into the man? At once he discovers a grand dignity in the men who appeared to him but just before as miserable criminals. He calls them lords.

"*Believe on the Lord Jesus Christ, and thou shalt be saved, and thy house.*" Of course, it is quite possible, says

Stier, that the ἵνα σωθῶ might mean nothing more than this : If I am to "do myself no harm"—and, now I am come to myself, I no longer desire it —what am I to do, so that no further harm may arise to me out of this earthquake, and the bursting open of my prison, and that I may be able to come out safe from the whole matter? But if the jailor meant temporal salvation, Paul meant spiritual.

"*And he took them the same hour of the night, and washed their stripes and was baptized, he and all his, straightway.*" His hard heart is touched into mercy, and he begins at once to alleviate their sufferings, and to show them hospitality.

"*Nay verily; let them come themselves and fetch us out.*" The magistrates, alarmed, sent early in the morning to release their prisoners, saying, "Let these men go." But Paul, being a Roman, would not accept such a release. He stood upon his rights as a Roman citizen, and demanded a satisfactory acknowledgment, which he finally obtained.

HOMILETICS.—This fragment of apostolic history sets forth in the most striking and inspiring aspects the *surpassing power of personal Christianity.*

I. WE SEE HERE CHRISTIAN PIETY ELEVATING THE SPIRIT ABOVE THE GREATEST TRIALS. "At midnight Paul and Silas prayed, and sang praises unto God." Where were they in these midnight hours, and what was their physical condition? The preceding verses inform us that they were in *the inner prison*, the darkest part of the dungeon; their bodies lacerated with the stripes of the *lictors*, and their feet made fast in the stocks. At "midnight," kind nature's season for sleep, they were sleepless. They could not sleep;—their bleeding wounds drove sleep away. Yet, instead of spending those midnight hours of physical torture in bitter imprecations on their enemies, or rebellious murmurings against heaven, they "prayed" and "sang." Those old prison walls, which were accustomed to echo groans and sighs, resounded now with unearthly strains of joy and praise. There was midnight without, but sunshine within; their bodies were in chains, but their souls were free. Their religion bore them aloft to regions of unrestricted liberty and unclouded light.

What gives religion this power to raise the soul above such torturing and terrible trials?

First, *Faith in the Divine superintendence.* The apostles knew that they were not in their present wretched condition by accident or chance, but that the whole was under the wise and kind control of the Eternal Father. This is consoling. Job felt this. "He knoweth the way that I take," &c.

Secondly, *Consciousness of God's approval.* Had their consciences accused them of having acted contrary to the will of Heaven, there would have been darker midnight and a severer suffering within than without. But the reverse was their consciousness. The "well done" of Heaven echoed within, and set all to music. "If God be for us, who can be against us?" "Being justified by faith, we have peace with God," &c.

Thirdly, *Memories of Christ's trials.* The religion of man is vitally connected with Christ. His intellect is filled with memories, and his heart with the spirit, of his Master. He compares his trials with those which He endured, and he experiences a support by the comparison.

Fourthly, *Assurance of a glorious deliverance.* "Our light afflictions, which are but for a moment," &c. "I reckon that the sufferings of this present time are not worthy to be compared with the glory which shall hereafter be revealed in us."

These things explain, to some extent at least, the soul-elevating force of religion. He who has this religion has a well-spring of joy within himself. He can glory in tribulation, and find a paradise in a dungeon.

II. WE SEE HERE CHRISTIAN PIETY ENSURING THE INTERPOSITION OF THE GREAT GOD.—" And suddenly there was a great earthquake, so that the foundations of the prison were shaken, and immediately all the doors were opened, and every man's bands were loosed." This was an undoubted miracle, and demonstrated in the most impressive manner the fact *that God takes special care of the good.* The GREAT ONE observes all, sustains all, directs all, owns all; but has a special regard for pious souls.

First, *Reason would suggest this.* Would not reason suggest that the Eternal *Spirit* would feel a greater interest in *mind* than in matter?—That the Eternal *Father* would feel a greater interest in His offspring than in His mere workmanship?—That the Source of all love and holiness would feel a greater interest in those who participate in His own moral attributes than in those who do not?

Secondly, *The Bible teaches this.* (1.) In explicit declarations. "To that man," says the Almighty, "will I look, even to him that is poor and of a contrite spirit, and trembleth at my word." "As a father pitieth his children, so the Lord pitieth them that fear Him." "Wherefore if God so clothe the grass of the field," &c. (2.) In the biography of the good. Did He not specially interpose on behalf of the patriarchs, prophets, and apostles? God will ever interpose for the good. If necessary He will make the heavens rain bread, and the rock out-pour refreshing streams. He will divide the sea, and stop the mouth of lions.

III. WE SEE HERE CHRISTIAN PIETY CAPACITATING THE SOUL FOR THE HIGHEST USEFULNESS.

First, *The Philippian jailor was prevented from self-destruction.* "The keeper of the prison, awaking out of his sleep, and seeing the prison doors open, he drew out his sword, and would have killed himself, supposing that the prisoners had fled." Imagining the wondrous escape of the prisoners, and being held by the Roman government responsible for the safe custody of the prisoners, he was overwhelmed at the fearful penalties to which he was exposed. He determined to kill himself. Instead of regarding such an act as a crime, he would, perhaps, attach a virtue and nobleness to it. But Paul prevented this. "Do thyself no harm ; we are all here." The voice of Christianity to man is, "Do thyself no harm ;"—no harm of any kind. The good are ever useful in preventing evil.

Secondly, *The Philippian jailor was directed to true safety.* "Sirs, What shall I do to be saved ?" This question indicates, we think, a complex state of mind. He had regard not only to material and civil deliverance, but to spiritual and eternal. The question implies a *sense of peril*, and a sense of the *necessity of individual effort.* What shall I do ? Something must be done. Paul, without circumlocution and delay, in the fewest possible words, and at once, answers, "Believe on the Lord Jesus Christ and thou shalt be saved." Some paraphrase it, "Heartily embrace the Christian religion and thou shalt be saved." Believe on Him as the Representative of God's love for the sinner, as the Atoner to God's character, as the Guide to God's heaven.

Thirdly, *The Philippian jailor experienced a delightful change of mind.* "And he took them the same hour of the night, and washed their stripes, and was baptized, he and all his, straightway. And when he had brought them into his house, he set meat before them, and rejoiced, believing in God with all his house." What a change ! The ruffian who "thrust them into the inner prison, and made their feet fast in the stocks," and who felt perhaps not one single pang of sympathy for their intense suffering, now tenderly washes their "stripes," and entertains them with pious hospitality. The terror-struck soul who "called for a light, and sprang in, and came trembling, and fell down" in utmost horror, before Paul and Silas, is now full of joy and faith. "He rejoiced, believing in God."

In this question and answer you have three things requiring a separate discourse—

(a.) THE INITIATIVE STAGES TO CONVERSION. First, *A terrible sense of danger.* The earthquake, and the strange and sublime conduct of the prisoners, roused his guilty conscience. Secondly, *An earnest spirit of inquiry.* "What shall I do to be saved?" Thirdly, *A readiness to do whatever is required.* This is implied in the question. Something must be done by me; I'll do it, whatever it is. Here you have—

(*b.*) THE EXCLUSIVE MEANS OF CONVERSION. "Believe on the Lord Jesus Christ." Faith in Christ is indispensable to produce this moral change. First, *A change of character requires a change in beliefs.* We are controlled and moulded by motives: motives are beliefs. Secondly, *The new beliefs necessary to produce the true change must be directed to Christ.* Christ alone gives us *the true ideal of character,—the true way of reaching it,—and the true aids to enable us to do so.* Here you have—

(*c.*) THE GLORIOUS ISSUE OF CONVERSION. "Thou shalt be saved." What is salvation? It is not in any sense a *physical* change, not merely an *intellectual* change, not necessarily a *local* change. It is a *moral* revolution. It is the soul rising from sensualism to spirituality, from selfishness to benevolence, from the world to God. First, *This conversion will ensure the salvation of our own souls.* "Thou shalt be saved." Secondly, *Will lead to the conversion of others.* "And thy house." It does not mean, of course, that his belief would save his family independently of their own belief; but that it would prompt him to use such efforts that would, under God, lead his family to a faith unto salvation.

IV. WE SEE HERE CHRISTIAN PIETY INVESTING THE SOUL WITH THE TRUEST INDEPENDENCY. "And when it was day the magistrates sent the sergeants, saying, Let those men go."

First, *Here you see their independency of soul in their superiority to the fear of man.* As soon as they were miraculously delivered from prison, they might have hurried away from such a scene of enemies; but they remained, although the magistrates gave them liberty to depart. They were not afraid. They could chant the 46th psalm, "God is our refuge and strength," &c.

Secondly, *Here you see their independency in refusing great benefits, because offered on improper grounds.* "Paul said unto them," the messengers of the magistrates, "They have beaten us openly uncondemned, being Romans, and have cast us into prison, and now do they thrust us out privily? Nay, let them come themselves, and fetch us out." Glorious independency! As if Paul had said, These Roman magistrates, as they are called, in beating us openly uncondemned, and thrusting us secretly into prison, have violated the laws of Rome, and trampled on our rights as citizens; politically we have not deserved this treatment, and we will not accept as a favour that which we demand as a right. Let these magistrates come themselves and fetch us out; and this will be a practical confession that they were wrong, and a practical vindication of our conduct as citizens. A great soul will repudiate favours offered on mean, unjust, or unworthy grounds. A good man will refuse liberty, social influence, wealth, unless they can be honourably and righteously obtained.

Thirdly, *Here you see their independency triumphing over their enemies.* The magistrates, feeling they had done wrong, "came and besought them, and brought them out, and desired them to depart out of the city." These tyrants became fawning suppliants at the feet of their prisoners.

Such is Christian piety as *first* displayed in *Europe*, and displayed in Europe in a *prison.* Piety is not that weak simpering thing which has often passed for it, and still too often passes for it. It is the mightiest force on earth. It lifts the soul into rapture, light, and grandeur, amidst the most terrible physical suffering, darkness, and thraldom. It ensures Divine interposition on its behalf, and moves the arm of Omnipotence in its favour. It qualifies for the highest usefulness, checks the progress of evil, directs souls to the true means of salvation, and works out a glorious transformation in the character of man. It invests the soul with the loftiest independency ;—an independency which defies antagonism, repudiates benefits unless righteously and honourably presented, and makes governments do it homage. True Christians have not received "the spirit of fear, but of love, power, and of a sound mind."

Acts 17:1-9

PAUL'S SECOND MISSIONARY TOUR.—IV. FROM PHILIPPI TO
THESSALONICA

Paul's preaching at Thessalonica

" *Now when they had passed through Amphipolis and Appollonia, they came to Thessalonica, where was a synagogue of the Jews : And Paul, as his manner was, went in unto them, and three Sabbath days reasoned with them out of the Scriptures ; opening and alleging, that Christ must needs have suffered, and risen again from the dead ; and that this Jesus, whom I preach unto you, is Christ. And some of them believed, and consorted with Paul and Silas ; and of the devout Greeks a great multitude, and of the chief women not a few. But the Jews which believed not,*[1] *moved with envy, took unto them certain lewd fellows of the baser sort, and gathered a company,*[2] *and set all the city in an uproar, and assaulted the house of Jason, and sought to bring them out to the people. And when they found them not, they drew Jason and certain brethren unto the rulers of the city, crying, These that have turned the world upside down are come hither also;*

whom Jason hath received: and these all do contrary to the decrees of Cæsar, saying that there is another king, one Jesus. And they troubled the people and the rulers of the city, when they heard these things. And when they had taken security of Jason, and of the other,[3] they let them go."

EMENDATIVE RENDERINGS.—(1.) Omit *"which believed not."* (2.) Made a riot. (3.) The rest.—ALF.

" EXEGETICAL REMARKS. — *" Now when they had passed through Amphipolis."* This was the chief town in the southern region of Macedonia, and it was situated on the river Strymon, at no great distance from its entrance into the Ægean Sea. It derived its name, which signified *around the city,* from the circumstance of the river flowing around it, and forming a peninsula, or, as others say, an island. It was originally a colony of the Athenians, and occasioned many difficulties between that nation and the Spartans. In the middle ages it was styled *Chrysopolis,* or the Golden City. A town still exists upon the ancient site, under the name of *Empoli,* or *Yamboli.*—LIV.

"And Appollonia." This city was on the route from Philippi to Thessalonica. It was a colony formed by the Corinthians, and a place of considerable trade.

" They came to Thessalonica." This place, unlike some other places of which we read in Scripture history, has retained its importance, and almost its name, to this very day. It is an imposing city, rising, tier above tier, on a steep ascent fronting the sea ; and contains still some seventy thousand inhabitants, of whom many now, as in St Paul's days, are Jews by race.

" Where was a synagogue of the Jews." At Philippi there seems to have been no synagogue, only a customary place of prayer by the river side. But in this city there is not merely a synagogue, but *the* synagogue, a place for all who dwelt in the city and neighbourhood.

" And Paul, as his manner was, went in unto them, and three Sabbath days reasoned with them out of the Scriptures." The apostles, like Christ, preached the gospel in synagogues. Paul's preaching, it seems, was chiefly expository, and designed to prove from the Old Testament that Christ was the true Messiah.

" And some of them believed, and consorted with Paul and Silas." That is, adhered to Paul and Silas. Paul and Silas.—Where are Luke and Timothy ? They were with them in the vessel from Troas to Philippi, and abode together in the latter place for certain days. Perhaps both for the present are still at Philippi. From the first Epistle to the Thessalonians it appears that the converts were nearly all Gentiles (1 Thess. i. 9, 10).

" But the Jews which believed not, moved with envy." This passion has ever been an obstruction to the progress of truth. It inspired men to the crucifixion of Christ. It hunted the apostles to prison and to death. Inspired with envy now, we are told the Jews gathered " them certain lewd fellows of the baser sort, and gathered a company, and set all the city on an uproar, and assaulted the house of Jason, and sought to bring them out to the people." They used the "lewd fellows of the baser sort," the idle loungers, the low rabble of the market, to gather a mob, and to create a riot. And they succeeded, for they set all the city in an uproar, and " assaulted the house of Jason," where Paul was lodged and entertained. He seems to have been of the same trade as Paul, and probably the apostle wrought with him for his livelihood.

" And when they found them not, they drew Jason and certain brethren unto the rulers of the city." *" Rulers of the city,*—in Greek one compound word, *Politarchs*—the proper designation of the elective magistrates of this free city, as distinguished from the prætors or duumviri (στρὰτηγοι) of a Roman colony. Luke's unstudied but exact precision in the use of these official titles has been justly urged as a strong incidental proof of authen-

ticity. A further confirmation of his accuracy is afforded by an ancient arch still standing in Thessalonica, inscribed with the names of the seven *Politarchs,* three of which, by a curious coincidence, are also the names of three Macedonians elsewhere mentioned as Paul's travelling companions, viz., Soapter, Gaius, and Secundus.—ALEX.

" *Crying, These that have turned the world upside down are come hither also.*" The charge which they brought was twofold—that they were turning the world upside down, and that they were acting in opposition to Cæsar, " saying that there is another king, one Jesus."

" *And when they had taken security of Jason, and of the other, they let them go.*" The security could not have been for the appearance of the apostles, but rather for their departure, that the public peace might not be disturbed by them any more. Here is strong friendship—Jason putting himself in the place of Paul.

HOMILETICS.—This paragraph leads us to notice Paul's preaching at Thessalonica.

I. His preaching was EVANGELIC.

First, *His grand theme was Christ.* (1.) He showed the necessity of His suffering and His resurrection. He " must needs have suffered, and risen again from the dead." The cross of Christ was his great subject. He exhibited that in all its high aspects. (2.) He showed that He was the *true* Messiah. " This Jesus, whom I preach unto you, is Christ"—is the Messiah of your Scriptures.

Secondly, *His grand authority was the Scriptures.* He " reasoned with them out of the Scriptures." He did not attempt to derive his arguments and illustrations from general literature or philosophy, but from the Scriptures. He would, perhaps, quote the old prophecies (Gen. xlix. 10 ; Isa. xl. 1–10 ; liii. ; Dan. ix. 24–27 ; Micah v. 6, &c.), and show that in the life of Jesus of Nazareth, who suffered and rose from the dead, those wonderful prophecies were fulfilled. Reasoning with the Jews, his authority was *Scripture,* and with the Gentiles, *Nature,* as at Athens.

Thirdly, *His grand method was reasoning.* " He " reasoned with them." " Opening and alleging." " Opening" (διανοίγων), means to *explain,* to *unfold.* " Alleging" (παρατιθέμενος), means *laying down the proposition.* He laid down his propositions, and he argued their truth from the Scriptures. This is model preaching. Let ministers give to men now the Christ of the *Scriptures,* not the Christ of their *theology.*

II. His preaching WON CONVERTS. " And some of them believed, and consorted with Paul and Silas ; and of the devout Greeks a great multitude, and of the chief women not a few." The " devout Greeks" were those who renounced heathenism, had become proselytes to the Jewish religion, and worshipped at the synagogue. They were called by the Jews, " proselytes of the gate." The " chief women," were females of influence, members of families of high rank. The converts were—

First, *Numerous.* " A great multitude."

Secondly, *Influential.* " Chief women." Some of the leading women of the city.

Thirdly, *Thoroughly united.* They "consorted with Paul and Silas." Common beliefs awaken common sympathies. Christ gathers men of different types of character and grades of life together.

III. His preaching AWOKE OPPOSITION. " But the Jews which believed not, moved with envy," &c. In this opposition we see four things :—

First, *The force of envy.* " The Jews which believed not, were moved with envy." This malignant passion of evil natures had been excited in the Jews by the moral conquest which the apostles had won in their synagogue. This passion has always been the inspiration of all persecutions. It shows itself now in a thousand forms.

Secondly, *The servility of mobs.* These Jews took unto them certain lewd fellows of the baser sort, and gathered a company, and set all the city on an uproar," &c. The persons referred to were those unprincipled idlers that are found lounging about places of public resort, the lazy rabble that fill workhouses with paupers, and jails with prisoners. *Certain evil fellows of the market-place.* These are always ready instruments to the hands of evil men in power. The demagogue can cajole them, and the rich can purchase their services with cash. *Vox populi, vox diaboli.*

Thirdly, *The revolutionising power of the gospel.* " These that have turned the world upside down are come hither also." These men spoke a truth, though unintentionally. The gospel does turn the world upside down, for the moral world is in the wrong position.

Fourthly, *The falsehood of wickedness.* " These all do contrary to the decrees of Cæsar." The charge they brought against them was that of sedition and rebellion against the Roman emperor, high treason against the crown. These men covered their envy under the garb of patriotism.

Such was Paul's preaching at Thessalonica, and what the gospel did at Thessalonica, when preached as Paul preached it, it will ever do—win numerous converts, and awaken strong opposition.

Acts 17:10-14

PAUL'S SECOND MISSIONARY TOUR.—V. FROM THESSALONICA TO BEREA

Spiritual nobility

" *And the brethren immediately sent away Paul and Silas by night unto Berea : who, coming thither, went into the synagogue of the Jews. These were more noble than those in Thessalonica, in that they received the word with all readiness of mind, and searched¹ the scriptures daily, whether those things were so. Therefore many of them believed ; also of honourable women which were Greeks, and of men, not a few. But when the Jews of Thessalonica had knowledge that the word of God was preached of Paul at Berea, they came thither also, and stirred up the people.² And then immediately the brethren sent away Paul to go as it were to the sea : but Silas and Timotheus abode there still."*

EMENDATIVE RENDERINGS.—(1.) Searching. (2.) At Berea also they came, stirring up and troubling the multitude there likewise.—ALF.

EXEGETICAL REMARKS.—"*And the brethren immediately sent away Paul and Silas by night unto Berea.*" The brethren were those who had received the gospel at Thessalonica, and who had "consorted" with Paul and Silas. They acted now as one man, and were zealous in their efforts to rescue the lives of the apostles from the perils that threatened them. They lost no time—"*immediately.*" They did it secretly, "by night," when their enemies were off their guard. He was sent to Berea. Berea, now *Verria*, is a city of Macedonia, about twenty miles west of Thessalonica, near Mount Pindus.

"*Who, coming thither, went into the synagogue of the Jews.*" Persecution had not cooled their zeal nor weakened their determination. No sooner do they reach Berea, than they begin their evangelic work.

"*These were more noble than those in Thessalonica.*" The primary sense of the words "more noble," is better

born. Their nobility consisted in this case, in frankly receiving the Word, and daily searching into its meaning.

"*But when the Jews of Thessalonica had knowledge that the word of God was preached of Paul at Berea, they came thither also, and stirred up the people.*" "Stirred up the people"— excited a popular commotion. The verb contains a figure as it is derived from the word *tous*, the surge from the sea. The persecutors from Thessalonica agitated the Berean mind as the tempest agitates the sea.

"*And then immediately the brethren sent away Paul, to go as it were to the sea.*" The words do not mean that they pretended to go to the sea, but that they went actually in the direction of the sea. Pydna was the nearest seaport running up from the Ægean Sea. It is not known, however, whether he took his journey to Athens by land or by water.

HOMILETICS.—These words suggest certain thoughts in relation to spiritual nobility. *Nobility* is a grand word, but does not always represent a noble thing. It is often applied to physical prowess and ancestral lineage ; but the word in such applications is more or less degraded. He only is *noble* who has a noble soul. There is a mental and moral nobility. The latter is the greatest of all ; it is God-like. It is, however, *mental nobility* for which the Bereans seem to be commended. There are three things recorded here that indicate their mental nobility:—

I. They rendered a CANDID ATTENTION TO NEW DOCTRINES : "They received the word with all readiness of mind," &c. They did not allow prejudice to seal their ears, and close their souls ; they were prepared to listen.

First, This conduct is *ever befitting finite minds*. As there must always be to the highest finite intelligences universes of truth of which they know nothing, it becomes even a seraph to be *docile*, and ever ready to hear. Angels, we presume, are so; they have no prejudices against what is new; they crave for it. How much more becoming in man is this state of mind—man, who knows so little, and that little often so imperfectly.

Secondly, This conduct is *very rare amongst mankind.* Somehow or other men for the most part grow up with preconceptions that close the soul to all that does not blend with them. Their pre-formed ideas they treat as absolute truths, and recoil with a jealousy from all that is new. Nothing is more repugnant to these men than a *teaching pulpit.* It is *noble*, therefore, to have the mind so free from these prejudices as to listen *candidly to new doctrines.*

II. They gave a PROPER EXAMINATION TO NEW DOCTRINES: "And searched the Scriptures daily, whether those things were so." They were not mere passive listeners, receiving impressions which led to no effort, and which passed away in the hour. They set to work; they examined.

First, They examined *independently.* They searched the Scriptures for *themselves.* They were not swayed by the authority of others, nor did they accept the statement of the apostles on their own credit. They took the old Scriptures in their own hands, unrolled the parchment, deciphered the characters, and sought the meaning. This is what all should do. There is much talk about the *right* of private judgment; we want more about the *duty.* Men are block-heads in theology, and priest-ridden in religion, because they search not the Scriptures for themselves.

Secondly, They examined *perseveringly:* "And searched the Scriptures *daily."* So vast the area and so deep the mines of Scripture, that you can know but little of it by a glance or two. Desultory, occasional and unsystematic efforts will be useless. You must be at it *daily,*—walk some new field, scale some new mountain, penetrate some new depth *daily.* If thou wouldst get wisdom, thou must search for it as for hid treasure.

III. They yielded to the EVIDENCE OF NEW DOCTRINES: "Therefore many of them *believed."* They bowed to the force of evidence. It is childish—alas! it is common—to believe without evidence. It is wicked to resist evidence. It is *noble* to surrender to its force.

First, Their faith *was intelligent.* It came as the result of investigation. It was not a blind prejudice, a traditional idea; it was a living conviction. This is the faith that is wanted, the only faith of any worth.

Secondly, Their faith *was general:* "Many believed." Influential women and men not a few.

Oh! for more of this *mental nobility* in pews—aye, in pulpits too!

Oh ! haste the day when men shall so honour their minds, truth, and the God of both, as to use their own faculties in an independent and persevering quest of what is divine !

Acts 17:15, 16

PAUL'S SECOND MISSIONARY TOUR.—VIII. FROM BEREA TO ATHENS

Paul's moral survey of the city

" *And they that conducted Paul brought him unto* [1] *Athens : and receiving a commandment unto Silas and Timotheus for to come to him with all speed, they departed. Now, while Paul waited for them at Athens, his spirit was stirred in him, when he saw the city wholly given to idolatry.*"

EMENDATIVE RENDERING.—(1.) As far as.—ALF.

EXEGETICAL REMARKS.—"*And they that conducted Paul brought him unto Athens.*"—" Athens, a city of Minerva, the capital of Attica in Greece, situated on the Saronic Gulf, forty-six miles east of Corinth, and five miles from the coast. Its three harbours, the Pyraeus, Munychia, and Phalerus, and the broad long walls by which they were joined to the city, are often alluded to in Grecian history. The architectural beauty of the city, especially of its temples, has commanded the admiration of all succeeding ages. Athens, by her commercial enterprise, collected the richest productions of surrounding countries. Her citizens were proud of their metropolis, and often bled for its defence. Yet the great proportion of the inhabitants were slaves, doomed to hopeless drudgery. The limestone rock on which Athens stands supplied the ordinary material for its buildings, and also from many of its quarries the marble for its nobler structures. The plain is bounded by ranges of hills— on the north-west, by Mount Parnes ; on the south-east, by Mount Hymettus ; and on the north-east, by Mount

Pentelicus ; out of which rises the higher pinnacles of Lycabettus. West of it was a smaller rock, the Areopagus ; to the south-west, about a quarter of a mile distant, was the Pnyx, the place of the great popular assemblies. Here, on a *bema* or stone block, the orators stood, and addressed often a crowd of 12,000, gathered together in a semicircular area."—EADIE.*

" *Receiving a commandment unto Silas and Timotheus for to come to him with all speed, they departed.*"— Paul had left his companions, Silas and Timotheus, at Berea, and had been escorted by some new friends to this celebrated city. He was left here, it would seem, for some time alone ; the Bereans who had accompanied him had departed, and Silas and Timotheus had not come. He wished, however, for them "to come to him with all speed." When they came to him we are not told. According to 1 Thess. ii. 17, iii. 2, we may, however, suppose that Timotheus soon came to him, but was sent back with instructions to Thessalonica. The reason why the visit of Timotheus to him is passed over in silence may be ac-

---

* See a magnificent description of Athens, and Paul's entrance into it, in Conybeare and Howson, *in loco*.

counted for by the fact that Luke the historian was still in Philippi.

"*His spirit was stirred in him.*" "Or, more exactly, sharpened, set on edge,—the verb from which comes paroxysm, violent excitement, as a medical term signifying the access or fit of an acute disease, as an ethical term commonly applied to anger, but admitting of a wider application here, where we may readily suppose Paul to have felt, not only indignation in the proper sense, but grief, shame, wonder, and compassion likewise." ---ALEX.

"*He saw the city wholly given to idolatry.*"—The margin has it "full of idols," κα τείδωλον. All history agrees with this representation. Pausanias says that it had more images than all the rest of Greece, and other ancient writers speak of it as the one great altar and the one great sacrifice of Attica.

HOMILETICS.—Our subject is, Paul's *moral survey of Athens.* What did he discover in Athens thus so intensely to distress his heart?

I. GREAT GENIUS PERVERTED.

First, *He saw developments of great genius.* He was *alone* in a city which was the distinguished seat of philosophy, learning, and the arts; where the most famous poets, statesmen, sages, and heroes of the heathen world were either born or flourished. Although at this time deprived of all political importance, it was still revered throughout the world for what it had achieved in the cause of freedom, literature, and art. It was called the eye of Greece, the inventor of letters, the light of the civilised world. Her schools still attracted the flower of the Roman youth, and the names of her great men were held in sacred veneration.

Everywhere he saw manifestations of wondrous genius. The city on all hands presented proofs of what man's intellect could achieve. There stood the Parthenon, the Temple of Athene—a pile which even now, after the lapse of centuries, remains the wonder of the world. There stood the Erechtheium, the most venerated of all Athenian sanctuaries; there, too, was the Lyceum, where Aristotle lectured; the Cynosarges, where Antisthenes the Cynic expounded his harsh and crabbed doctrines; and the Academy, where Plato gave his lessons, was there. It was, in fact, a city of architectural magnificence and monumental splendour. Deities were numerous there, and almost every deity had its temple. The triumphs of mind in its architectural skill, æsthetic creations, and philosophical theories were visible on all hands. What Jerusalem has been in the true religious culture of humanity, Athens has been in the culture of the æsthetical and reasoning powers of mankind.

Secondly, *He saw perversions of great genius.* Though possessing a mind qualified by nature and cultivation to appreciate in a high degree the splendid works of architecture and sculpture which lay about him, in an atmosphere peculiarly transparent, and under a sky beautifully genial, we have no record of any expression of delight which escaped him as he beheld the city. But the contrary : his spirit was *"stirred in him."* He was thrown into an agony of grief at what he beheld. He had a standard of character unknown to any Athenian sage. He looked upon humanity with a new eye—an eye that peered through all its surroundings into its moral heart. Paul was not dead to the *æsthetic,* but he was intensely alive to the *moral,* and he felt that the æsthetic glory of Greece was but a gorgeous covering which genius had woven and spread over a vast cemetery of moral corruption. Whilst he could admire the skill that chiseled the marble into such exquisite forms, and piled it into magnificent superstructures, and the ingenuity of intellect, and the adroitness of logic, that propounded and discussed philosophical hypotheses, he felt that all this power was *perverted,* since it was all on the side of idolatry; and this *"stirred"* his spirit. Genius and intellect *wasted*—nay, worse than that, employed for immoral and impious ends. As a cultured and devout son of temperance gazes without one thrill of admiration on the æsthetic magnificence of some gin-palace, and feels only the most poignant distress at the thought to what the building is devoted—aye, and the greater the display of genius in the architecture, the greater his agony of soul on account of the immoral purposes for which it is employed ; so Paul looked at Athens now. There is nothing in mere material civilisation, even in its highest forms, to delight a truly enlightened soul.

II. THE GREAT GOD DISHONOURED. With all the display in the city of æsthetic genius and intellectual power, there was a miserable lack, if not an utter absence, of all the higher elements of soul.

First, *They had no grand moral purpose in life.* They spent their time in nothing else but *"* either to tell or hear some new thing." Empty theories and idle gossip occupied their chief attention; since they knew not the only true God, they had no grand purpose in life. The deeper and diviner parts of their souls were undeveloped.

Secondly, *They had no love for the true God.* Supreme love for the supremely good, and those aspirations of philanthropy which have regard to the moral interest of souls, they knew not. Athens, by wisdom, knew not God. " It was easier," says an old writer, " to find a god than a man." Far enough are we from disparaging what is called the light of nature, or from underrating the capabilities of the human mind for searching out God in the works of His hand ; but all history shows that where the Gospel has not gone, man has never reached the true religion, and never felt the higher inspiration of his being. (See Romans i.) The best of the Athenian gods were but men—men that had been, or were supposed to have been—whose attributes were exaggerated by superstitious fancy, and whose very lusts and passions in some cases were of the most revolting kind. Paul knew that the destiny of the soul depended upon its worship ; that if it worshipped any object but the ONE true and living God, it must inevitably sink lower and lower for ever. There is but one being in the universe that has a claim to the worship of man—the Creator. He claims the supreme homage and service of all souls. His claim is just: no conscience can dispute it. Because the apostle loved supremely this supreme object of worship, he felt intense pain at seeing His righteous claims contemned. "I beheld the way of transgressors, and was grieved."

Acts 17:17-21

PAUL'S SECOND MISSIONARY TOUR.—IX. AT ATHENS

1. *Paul's discussions in the synagogue and the market-place*

" *Therefore disputed he in the synagogue with the Jews, and with the devout persons, and in the market daily with them that met with him. Then certain philosophers of the Epicureans, and of the Stoics, encountered him. And some said, What will this babbler say ?* [1] *other some, He seemeth to be a setter forth of strange gods : because he preached unto them Jesus and the resurrection. And they took him and brought him unto Areopagus,* [2] *saying, May we know what this new doctrine, whereof thou speakest, is ? For thou bringest certain strange things to our ears : we would know therefore what these things mean. (For* [3] *all the Athenians and strangers which were there spent their time in nothing else, but either to tell or to hear some new thing.)* "

EMENDATIVE RENDERINGS.—(1.) What meaneth this babbler to say ? (2.) The hill of Mars. (3.) Now.—ALF.

EXEGETICAL REMARKS.—" *Therefore disputed he in the synagogue with the Jews and the devout persons.*" There is nothing strange about his entry into the synagogue. This he did in every place where there was a synagogue. " In the synagogue he reasoned with the Jews and the devout persons," that is, the Gentile proselytes.

" *And in the market daily with them that met with him.*" The market-place —the Agora. This was a place near to the centre of the city, an open space, which was full of monuments commemorative of persons and events of that imperishable interest to the Athenian mind. Here people at all times met in concourse, some for business, some for speculative discussion, some for idle gossip. It was a place for whetting the intellect of the city, launching a new theory on the tide of discussion, as well as for gratifying the curiosity of the idle. It was a bold thing for this humble tent-maker of Tarsus, unable, perhaps, to speak their grand language with classic accuracy, to venture into the arena. He had, however, unbounded faith in the sublimity of the gospel, and was not afraid to submit it to the keenest genius and the loftiest intellects.

" *Epicureans.*" " The Epicureans, or Philosophers of the Garden, owed their name to Epicurus, who died at Athens in the year 270 before the birth of Christ, leaving his house and garden to be the constant seat of his philosophy, which was accordingly maintained there till the time of which we are now reading."

"*Stoics.*" "The Stoics, or Philosophers of the Porch, were so called from the Stoa Pœcile, or Painted Porch, adjoining one of the Athenian squares or markets, where their founder, Zeno, taught at the same time with Epicurus."—ALEX.

"*What will this babbler say?*" The Greek word in the margin, σπερμο-λόγος, is "base fellow." Literally, this means grain-picker, an epithet at first applied to birds, and then to beggars who collect and live on scraps, and hence became a term of contempt. The language is most contemptuous: it represents the apostle as the reporter of idle tales picked up from others.

"*He seemeth to be a setter forth of strange gods.*" It would seem, according to some critics, that they understood Paul as meaning, by Jesus and Anastasis (resurrection), a new god and goddess. Their misconception arose, not from want of simplicity on his part, but from want of unprejudiced minds on their part.

"*And they took him and brought him unto Areopagus.*" "The name Areopagus is derived from the Hill of Mars, which signifies either the court itself or the hill or spot on which it was held. It was a rocky elevation, almost in the centre of the city, and commanded a wide range of prospect. The eye looked around and below on works and wonders of art—statues, altars, and temples, and on the glorious scenery of nature—mountains, islands, and seas. The tribunal that assembled here was most ancient in origin and venerable in character: and among other objects of trust and jurisdiction, civil, social, and political, had particular cognisance of all blasphemies against the heathen gods."—EADIE. Four hundred and fifty years before this, Socrates was arraigned in this court for introducing strange and foreign gods, the charge which was now hinted against Paul. It was not, however, as a criminal that Paul was conveyed to this spot. The expression, "they took him," conveys no idea of coercion, but of gentle handling.

HOMILETICS.—Three things are here to be observed—*The parties with whom Paul reasoned; The subjects on which he discoursed;* and *The effects of the discussion.*

I. THE PARTIES WITH WHOM PAUL REASONED. With whom did the apostle argue—carry on a dialogue after the Socratic method? With the effeminate and uncultured in mind, the mental rabble, those without power to stand against the force of his influence? No—"*Jews,*" "*Epicureans,*" "*Stoics.*" These may be looked on in two aspects:—

First, *Theologically.* The "Jews" were *monotheists.* They believed in the one true and living God, and in Moses as His great minister to man. The "Epicureans" were *atheists.* They ascribed the creation of the world to chance; they had no faith in the one infinite Creator of heaven and earth. The Stoics were *pantheists.* They confounded the universe with God, or regarded it rather as God. Paul had to deal, therefore, with these three great intellectual systems. Each would require a very different line of argument.

Secondly, *Ethically.* Ethically, these three represented three great cardinal moral evils, *self-righteousness in the Jew, carnality in the Epicurean, indifferentism in the Stoics.*

II. THE SUBJECTS ON WHICH HE DISCOURSED. What is the grand

subject that Paul brought under their notice? Some newly-dis-covered fact in nature, or some philosophic truth that had engaged the attention of the greatest thinkers? No. *"He preached unto them Jesus and the resurrection;"* he proclaimed Jesus as the true Messiah, and His resurrection from the dead. His subject was—

First, The greatest *person* in the history of the race. Christ was the grand theme in the apostle's discussion with these philoso-phers. He spread out His wonderful history before them, and endeavoured to show its significance and grand aim. He was not "ashamed to speak of Him who was rejected and despised of men— a man of sorrows and acquainted with grief."

Secondly, The greatest *fact* in the history of this the greatest per-son, is His *resurrection*.

III. The effects of the discussion. What were the *immediate* effects which this discussion produced in the Agora amongst the Stoics and Epicureans? The immediate effects seemed very un-satisfactory. There was—

First, *Contempt:* *"What will this babbler say?"* Paul was probably no orator in their sense, nor could he speak their language in perfect measure and cadence, nor was he of commanding presence. They would regard him, therefore, as a mere "babbler."

Secondly, *Misconception.* They thoroughly misunderstood him. *"He seemeth to be a setter forth of strange gods."*

Thirdly, *Curiosity.* Though they did not understand him, yet what they heard so heightened their curiosity that they wished to hear more. "And they took him and brought him unto Areopagus, saying, May we know what this new doctrine, whereof thou speakest, is? For thou bringest certain strange things to our ears: we would know, therefore, what these things mean." This was so far the most favourable result. The apostle's teaching succeeded up to this point in generating in them the desire to know something more about the new doctrine.

Acts 17:22-31

Paul's second missionary tour.—IX. at athens *(continued)*

2. *Paul's discussion on Mars-Hill*

"Then Paul stood in the midst of Mars-Hill, and said, Ye men of Athens, I perceive that in all things ye are too superstitious.[1] *For as I passed by, and beheld your devotions, I found an altar with this inscrip-tion, TO THE UNKNOWN GOD. Whom therefore ye ignorantly*

worship, him declare I unto you.[2] *God,*[3] *that made the world, and all things therein, seeing that he is the Lord of heaven and earth, dwelleth not in temples made with hands; neither is worshipped*[4] *with men's hands, as though he needed any thing, seeing he giveth to all life, and breath, and all things; and hath made of one blood all nations of men for to dwell on all the face of the earth, and hath determined the times before appointed,*[5] *and the bounds of their habitation; that they should seek the Lord,*[6] *if haply they might feel after him, and find him, though he be not far from every one of us: For in him we live, and move, and have our being; as certain also of your own poets have said, For we are also his offspring. Forasmuch then as we are the offspring of God, we ought not to think that the Godhead is like unto gold, or silver, or stone, graven by art and man's device. And the times of this ignorance God winked at;*[7] *but now commandeth all men every where to repent: Because he hath appointed a day, in the which he will judge the world in righteousness by that man whom he hath ordained; whereof he hath given assurance unto all men, in that he hath raised him from the dead.*"

EMENDATIVE RENDERINGS.—(1.) Very religious. (2.) For as I passed by and beheld your devotions, I found also an altar with this inscription, TO AN UNKNOWN GOD. What, therefore, ye ignorantly worship, that declare I unto you. (3.) The God. (4.) Served by. (5.) And caused every nation ·of man, sprung of one blood, to dwell on all the face of the earth, and determined the times appointed. (6.) God. (7.) Overlooked.—ALF.

EXEGETICAL REMARKS. — "*Then Paul stood in the midst of Mars-Hill.*" The Areopagus has been already described. He is now on the heights, behind him is a crowd of citizens who have followed him from the Agora; in that crowd there are philosophers and artists, poets, warriors, and judges. Before him lies Athens in all her beauty, natural and artistic; the Acropolis lies on the east of where he stands, abrupt ·and vast, covered with the noblest monuments of Grecian art: temples, and theatres, and statues, and sculptured groups, rising up in majestic beauty to the sublime Parthenon, the masterpiece in the glory of ancient architecture. "On the other side, hard by the Agora, rises the Pnyx, the place of the assemblies of the people, where stands the famous stone on which the orators addressed the assembled multitudes, and from which Demosthenes had often rolled his thunders." What a position for a poor foreigner —an obscure Jew like Paul—to take! Yet he takes it, and thus begins his sermon. "*Ye men of Athens.*" His exordium shows that he had all the attributes of a consummate orator: a calm, dignified self-possession, a remarkable facility of so distributing his thoughts and constructing his arguments as not to offend the taste or irritate the prejudices of his auditory, and withal a power of reaching and bringing down to the capacity of his hearers those lofty themes of thought in which all are interested, and which all can appreciate, and before whose majesty those little opinions that divide men melt away into nothingness. He is *direct*— "*Ye men of Athens*"—a style in which Demosthenes and their great orators used to address them. "*Men* of Athens," not to mere human beings, but *to men.* I speak not to men indiscriminately, but to "*you men of Athens,*" men of the most exalted city in the world. He is *appreciative.* He does not parade their evils; he recognises their excellencies, and gives them full credit for the good he had seen.

"*I perceive that in all things ye are too superstitious.*" This is not a felicitous translation of δεισιδαιμονεστερ- ους. *God-fearing* would be better than *superstitious.* He means, I presume, to give them credit for great *religiousness;* he does not mean" that their religiousness was rightly directed. Far otherwise ; but he meant that they had it to a remarkable extent. *They had an excessive awe of invisible beings* All their buildings and sculpture appear to him the product and expression of religious sentiment.

" *For as I passed by, and beheld your devotions, I found an altar with this inscription,* TO THE UNKNOWN GOD." Not only were they so religious as to worship known deities, but the *unknown* one ; for in his walks through the city Paul saw an altar with the inscription 'Αγνωστῳ Θεῷ. What the Athenians meant by such an altar it is difficult to surmise, unless it was to express the feeling that, with all their gods, there were some gods wanted—that the known gods did not gratify the cravings, and fill up the capacity of their religious nature. What they wanted, Paul now stood up to give them.

" HIM *declare I unto you.*" *Him* —the *One* you are unconsciously seeking after, the One you want, *declare I unto you.* Mark the word *declare.* He does not say, Him *define* I unto you, nor, Him *describe* I unto you; for who can define the Unsearchable, who can describe the Infinite ? But, *Him declare I.*

" *God that made the world and all things therein.*" The profoundest philosophers of Greece were unable to see any distinction between God and His universe. Paul here states it clearly. " *He dwelleth not in temples made with hands.*" This thought was familiar to the Jews (1 Kings viii. 27 ; Isa. lxvi. 1 ; vii. 48).

" *As though he needed any thing.*" This is also familiar to the Jews. (Job xxxv. 6–8 ; Psalm xvi. 2, 3 ; Isa. xl. 14, 18).

" *And giveth life and breath, and all things.*" This is the culminating point of a pure theism.

" *And hath made of one blood all nations of men to dwell on all the face of the earth.*" Holding, with the Old Testament teaching, that in the blood is the life (Gen. ix. 4 ; Lev. xvii. 11 ; Deut. xii. 23), the apostle sees this life-stream of the whole human race to be one, flowing from one source.—BAUMGARTEN.

" *The times of this ignorance God winked at.*" This is an inaccurate translation — *overlooked* is the best word. It means that those past times were times of Divine forbearance ; those times being passed, God demanded repentance now.

HOMILETICS.—Homiletically, we have to notice the *substance* and *effects* of this sermon.

THE SUBSTANCE OF THE SERMON

The great subject is God. " Him declare I unto you." He declares to them God in two aspects :—

I. IN RELATION TO THE UNIVERSE IN GENERAL.

First, *He declares God as the Creator of the universe :* " God that made the world," &c. The declaration that God created the universe would strike at once against the error of Epicurean philosophy, which regarded the universe as springing from a fortuitous concourse of atoms—the work of chance : and against the Stoical philosophy, which regarded the universe as existing from eternity. The universe is the evolution of the eternal existence : creation is the possibility of the infinite mind springing into actualities by its own sovereign volition.

Secondly, *He declares God as the Ruler of the universe :* " He is

Lord of heaven and earth." He holds an undisputed sovereignty over all matter and mind—all worlds and all systems. The universe is not like a great machine built to manage itself, and which the builder has left to its own operations; on the contrary, it is an order of things kept in being and harmony every moment by the unremitting agency of the Creator.

Thirdly, *He declares God as the Life of the universe:* "*He giveth to all life, and breath, and all things.*" And then in the 28th verse he says, "*In Him we live, and move, and have our being.*" In His hand is the life of every living thing and the breath of all mankind. What the root is to the branch, what the blood is to the body, God is to the universe—the life. The deductions which the apostle draws from this representation of God are two, and they are irresistible. (*a.*) *That God is unlocalised.* "*He dwelleth not in temples made with hands.*" He has no special place of residence. Your city, as if the apostle had said, abounds with temples for your deities, but the "unknown" God whom I declare unto you requires no temple; "the heaven, yea, the heaven of heavens cannot contain Him." (*b.*) *That God is independent.* "*Neither is worshipped with men's hands as though He needed anything.*" The heathens thought their gods needed their services. They built temples with a great expenditure of skill and wealth, not for the accommodation of worshippers, but to gratify their deity. The sculpture and the æsthetic beauties connected with the place were provided not to inspire the devotee, but to gratify and propitiate the gods. The God whom Paul declared did not require that. "He *needed not* anything." The God of the universe is without needs. He is independent alike of our loyalties or rebellions. "*If thou art righteous, what does it profit Him?*" &c. *All He needs from His creatures is for His creatures to feel their need of Him.* He declares to them God—

II. In Relation to Mankind in Particular.—He refers to what the God of the universe is to *man*. "*And hath made all nations to dwell,*" &c. He states several things concerning this God in relation to man.

First, *That He gave to all mankind a unity of nature.* "*Made of one blood all nations of men.*" There are immense diversities subsisting between men occupying different regions of the earth. The European, the Mongolian, the Hottentot, how striking the differences between these races! These differences have led many a scientific man to conclude that they have descended from various stocks. Without touching on arguments of a scientific kind, such as those drawn from anatomy, physiology, philology, in favour of the unity of the race, we merely say that we ground our belief chiefly—First, *On mental resemblances.* The faculties of thinking, loving, hating, fearing, hoping, worshipping, self-commending, self-condemning, are common to the race. Secondly, *On Scriptural statements.* There is not a single passage in the Bible to suggest a doubt as to the homogeneity of the race, and the descent from one pair. The Bible gives the genealogy of the race up to the days of Christ. The most brilliant names in science have maintained the unity of the race: Buffon, Linnæus, Soemmering, and Cuvier, in natural history; Blumenbach, Müller, and Wagner, in anatomy; Prichard, Latham, Pickering, among ethnologists; Adeling, W. von Humboldt, and Bunsen, among philologists; and Alexander von Humboldt, "at whose feet all science had laid down its treasures."

Secondly, *That He appointed to all mankind their boundary in life.*

"*And hath determined the times before appointed, and the bounds of their habitation.*" The word *bounds* is generally used to represent the boundary of a field. Two thoughts may illustrate the apostle's meaning. (*a.*) There is a boundary for every man in relation to the *place* of his existence. The sphere which individuals occupy is a sphere which God has appointed. He has drawn a line around it, detached it from the spheres of others. Every man has an orbit of his own, and that orbit is appointed by Him. The same with nations. Nations have their geographic boundary, and these have been drawn by heaven. Though they may proximately grow out of the diversity in men's organisations, customs, laws, habits, still God hath made them. (*b.*) There is a boundary for every man in relation to *time*. There is an "appointed time for man on the earth," for the individual man and the nation. Men and nations have their day, and the length of that day even to the minute is determined. There is no room for chance in human history.

Thirdly, *That He requires from all mankind the recognition of His existence.*

"*That they should seek the Lord, if haply they might feel after Him, and find Him, though He be not far from any one of us.*" There are two things here:

(1.) *Man's distance from God.* This distance is *moral*, and is to be overcome by effort on man's part. That they should seek the Lord.

(1.) *God's nearness to man.* This utterance is so pregnant as to require a separate discourse.

" NOT FAR FROM ANY ONE OF US."

Let us dwell a little on this expression, "NOT *far* from any one of us." He is in a direct, constant, and vital contact with all existence, however vast or minute, however remote or near. This is a doctrine recognised by universal consciousness, established by all true philosophy, explicitly affirmed, cogently enforced, and variously illustrated in the glorious old Bible. In relation to this truth, our race may be divided into five classes:

First, *Those who enjoy His presence.* The Psalmist, who said, " When I awake I am still with thee," may be taken as a representative of this class.

Second, *Those who are stolidly insensible of His presence.* The unconverted men of Ephesus, referred to by Paul (Eph. ii. 12) as being

" without God and without hope in the world," are representatives of this class,—the dominant class of all ages and climes.

Third, *Those who are in horrific dread of His presence.* The ungodly spoken of by the patriarch of Uz (Job xxi. 14) are types of this miserable class. They say unto God, " Depart from us, for we desire not a knowledge of Thy ways." " Depart ! "—this is the unceasing cry of hell.

Fourth, *Those who are in earnest search of His presence.* Job, in one period of his history, represented this class. Their cry is, " Oh that I knew where I might find him ! that I might come even to his seat !" (Job xxiii. 3). This class comprehends all earnest inquirers.

Fifth, *Those who theoretically deny His presence.* This class is represented by those words in which Eliphaz (Job xxii. 12, 13) very unjustly included Job. Their language is—

> " Is not God in the height of heaven ?
> And behold the height of the stars, how high they are.
> And thou sayest, How doth God know ?
> Can He judge through the dark cloud ?
> Thick clouds are a covering to Him and He seeth not ;
> And He walketh in the circuit of heaven."

The deist, who denies that God takes any interest in the individual affairs of individual life, belongs to this class.

It is needless to say, that the different opinions and feelings of all these classes do not alter, even to the shadow of a shade, the fact, that GOD IS NEAR. The earth sweeps her majestic course around the sun, though all the priests of Catholic Europe deny the fact of her motion. What if some do not believe, their unbelief does not make the truth of God of none effect. Let us then for a moment illustrate this, the grandest and most solemn of all truths. God is *near* in several respects :

I. HE IS LOCALLY NEAR. " Do not I fill heaven and earth ?" saith Jehovah" (Jer. xxiii. 24). Reason replies that if thou art *absolute* in thine existence it must be so—an absolute existent has no relation to time or place. He, not some portion of Him—if such language is admissible—not merely His influence, but He, Himself, in all the glorious completeness of His personality, fills all. No metaphysics can explain, no finite thought can comprehend, how He can be equally present in all places at the same time ; but the denial of it involves philosophical contradictions, undeifies God, and contravenes the plainest and the sublimest teachings of inspiration. Labouring reason, exhausted and confounded in thy futile endeavours to compass this transcendent truth, come to the Bible—live and revel in the sublimity of the thought. Man, take up the grand psalm of Unconditioned Existence, and chant it with the truthful, joyous heart of godly love—

> " Thou hast beset me behind and before,
> And laid Thine hand upon me.

> Whither shall I go from Thy Spirit ?
> Or whither shall I flee from Thy presence ?
> If I ascend up into heaven, Thou art there—
> If I make my bed in hell, Thou art there," &c.

Among the many practical truths which grow out of the nearness of God, we merely mention three : (1.) That all men should live under a constant impression of His presence ; (2.) That all attempts at secrecy in sin are to the last degree futile and absurd ; and (3.) That death can effect no local separation of the soul from God.

II. HE IS RELATIONALLY NEAR. He is the nearest *relation* we have. He is our *Sovereign*, overruling all things pertaining to us and our history ; but He is infinitely *nearer* than that—He is our Father ; but He is *nearer* than that—He is our Creator, has made every particle and faculty of our being ; but He is *nearer* than that—He is our Proprietor, the owner of all we are and have ; but He is *nearer* than that—He is our LIFE. We cannot move a muscle, we cannot breathe a breath, we cannot think a thought, we cannot feel an emotion, without Him. He is the energy of our force, the impulse of our activities, the life of our life. " In Him we live, and move, and have our being." Two truths are inferable from His relational nearness.

First, *That the necessity of the atonement cannot be satisfactorily argued, to thinking minds, on the remote relationship of God as the Governor of man.* The necessity of the atoning work of Christ I hold with an earnest and growing tenacity ; but to argue it on such a basis, is only to awaken doubt in the minds of the thoughtful.

Secondly, *That the preservation of man's perfect freedom of moral action is very wonderful.* Whilst He moves us, we are morally free in moving. The *how* of this, is the problem with which all thoughtful ages have wrestled hard, and to this hour it remains unsolved. *Logic*, proceeding from the vital connexion of God with me, demonstrates that I am a mere machine ; but *consciousness*, which is more powerful than logic, demonstrates to me that I am free. I *feel* that I am free, and no argument can destroy this feeling.

III. HE IS SYMPATHETICALLY NEAR. We are nearer to His heart, than we are to the heart of any other. How close is the heart of a mother to her sweet babe ! All the sympathies of her existence twine around it, and she clasps it to her heart with an energy stronger than death. But we are nearer to the heart of God than the babe to the heart of that mother.

> " Can a woman forget her sucking child,
> That she should have no compassion on the son of her womb ?
> Yea, she may forget,
> Yet will I never forget thee.
> Behold, I have graven thee upon the palms of my hands ;
> Thy walls are continually before me."

There are three things that show the nearness of His heart to us. First, *His distinguishing goodness in the creation of our existence.*

He has given us greater capacities for happiness than He has to any
other creatures of which we have any knowledge. There are some
beings who have only capacities for sensuous enjoyment, and there
are others who have perhaps only capacities for mental enjoyment—
we have both. We can derive happiness both from the material and
spiritual universe. *Sensuous, intellectual, social, and religious* enjoy-
ments are ours.

Secondly, *His wonderful forbearance in the preservation of our
existence.* We are rebels against His government as fallen creatures,
yet how He forbears. Listen to the language of His heart, "How
shall I give thee up, Ephraim?" &c. (Hosea ii. 8.)

Thirdly, *His infinite mercy in the redemption of our existence.* Here
is the climax of love. "God so loved the world," &c. "God commendeth
His love towards us, in that while we were yet sinners Christ died for
us." Brothers! in the light of this wonderful theme, *indifferentism,
hypocrisy, and ceremonialism,* to the last degree are absurd and vile.
Is it true that the heart-searching God is thus near us? Then our
indifference is more anomalous than the conduct of him who lies
down to sleep upon the bosom of that volcano which is up-flinging
its floods of fire. Is it true that He is thus near us? Then how pre-
posterous and how wicked are all the attempts at dissembling our
conduct before Almighty God. Hypocrites try to see without light,
or breathe without air : the effort will be wiser than any attempt you
can make to impose upon the all-present and all-seeing God. Is it
true that He is thus near us? Then ceremonialists, why be so particular about the rituals, the places, and the times of worship? "God
is a Spirit."

> "Oh! tell me, Mighty Mind, where art Thou?
> Shall I dive into the deep? Call to the sun
> Or ask the roaring sea for their Creator?
> Shall I question loud the thunder,
> If in that the Almighty dwells,
> Or holds He furious storms in straiten'd reins
> And bids fierce whirlwinds wheel His rapid car?
> What mean these questions? trembling, I retract—
> My prostrate soul adores the present God."

Another thing he states in this sermon concerning this God in
relation to man is

Fourthly, That He is the *Father of all mankind.*

"WE ARE ALL HIS OFFSPRING."

This is such a grand expression that we must not pass away from
it too hastily.

"It appears," says a modern writer, "that Paul was conversant with
Greek literature, as well as with the peculiar learning of the Jews.
The sentiment of his quotation is found in several ancient poets, with
a heathen application. In a hymn to Jupiter, by Cleanthes, a Stoic
philosopher and poet of Troas, successor to Zeno as the master of that
system of philosophy, occurs the following passage—

> " Majestic Jove, all hail ! to thee belong
> The suppliant prayer, the tributary song ;
> To thee, from all thy mortal offspring due,
> From thee we came, from thee our being drew :
> Whatever lives and moves, great Sire ! is thine,
> Embodied portions of the soul divine !''

But more particularly, in a poem upon descriptive Astronomy, entitled " Phenomena," and written by Aratus, B.C. 250, a native of Cilicia, the country of Paul, we have the exact words of the text—

> " From Jove we sprung, whom we mortals should never
> Leave unsung. Of Jove the public walks are
> Full : and councils of all men : both the sea
> And shore are full of him. From Jove comes all
> That we enjoy ; for we are of his offspring."

The original forms half of an hexameter verse. Hesiod, Pindar, and Lucretius, expressed the same idea, with slight verbal variations.

I. THIS GLORIOUS FACT IN OUR NATURE INDICATES CONSTITUTIONAL RESEMBLANCE TO GOD. To be the " offspring" of God means something more than to be the creatures of God. The earth, the sea, the skies, are His creatures ; but it would be as improper to call them His offspring, as it would be to call the building the offspring of the architect, or the machine the offspring of the machinist. It implies a resemblance in the *essential* attributes of being. The child, in the fundamental properties of his nature, is like his parent. Man is as much more like his Maker than the material and immaterial universe is, as the son of the artist is more like his father than any of the productions of his father's genius. Man resembles God—he is like Him *in spiritual personality, intellectual perception, moral sensibility, loving sympathy, spontaneous activity.*

First, *This resemblance constitutes man the highest natural revelation of God.* Though a mere atom in space as compared with the stupendous systems that roll about him, he is the brightest reflector of the Infinite. As I see the ocean in a dewdrop, and the sun in a particle of light, I see God in man.

Secondly, *This resemblance accounts for our power of forming ideas of God.* Had we no resembling attributes, His existence would be to us a blank for ever ; had we no conscious personality, we could form no conception of His absolute individuality ; had we no intellectual perception, we could form no idea of the wisdom of His plans, or the truth and propriety of His revelations ; had we no moral sensibility, we could never reach a conception of the holiness of His character, or the rectitude of His procedure ; had we no loving sympathies, divine love, mercy, compassion, would be words that could convey no meaning whatever to us ; and had we no spontaneous activity, an idea of His freedom and almightiness could never enter our minds. These properties of nature which resemble His, are the mirror which reflect His infinite being and attributes upon the soul. The eagle aloft in its sunny realm, with eyes keener than ours, takes a vaster view of material nature than we can; yet it sees no God in all. The view of a thousand landscapes, and the light of a thousand suns, can give no idea of the Infinite to this imperial tenant of the air. Why? Because it is not made, like us, in the image of the Creator.

II. This glorious fact in our nature suggests the rationale of divine laws. Why has God given us laws for the regulation of our conduct,—laws which prohibit one course of action and enforce another,—laws associated with sanctions of eternal moment and duration? Is it for the sake of restricting our freedom of action or curtailing our pleasures? No. Do His laws, like those of human monarchs, arise from the policy of selfishness or fear? The thought is blasphemy. Is He obliged, like little mortal rulers amongst men, to guard His throne by legislation? Such an idea, though current in some theologies, we hold to be essentially incompatible with His almightiness, and derogatory to His character. Parental love is the principle, the ultimate *reason*, of all His laws. His laws are the considerate directions of a loving Father, profoundly desirous that His offspring shall escape all evils, and realise the highest good. The Decalogue is the voice of a Father's love:—a few rough hints of duty which He has mercifully given, and which the loving heart of a dutiful child will in the course of ages elaborate into volumes which the world could not contain. You cannot legislate for love, it is a law unto itself. It is only the unfilial heart that regards His laws as the rigorous severities of a mighty monarch. He who has the true spirit of a child will always say with the Psalmist, "O how I love thy law!" If any question this interpretation of the Divine code, let him do two things : *First*, Carefully examine the character of those laws, and see if he can find one that does not tend to happiness ; and, *Secondly*, Let him consult the experience of the obedient, and see if he can find one who will not say, "In the keeping of thy commandments there is a great reward."

III. This glorious fact in our nature explains the interposition of Christ. Why did the Infinite Creator send His Son into our world to do and endure what He did? What was there in insignificant and sinful man to enlist this marvellous interposition of Divine mercy? Was it the *intrinsic value* of the human soul? The soul, it is true, is a superior existence as compared with the inanimate and irrational universe ; but it is inferior, perhaps, when compared with other intelligence in the universe ; and as compared with the Infinite mind, What is it? Not as much as a dim spark compared with the central fires of immensity. By one volition He could create innumerable worlds, and people them with spirits far transcending in intrinsic worth the souls of men. Sometimes the value of the soul is dilated upon as if it were the *reason* of the Divine interposition for our recovery. But such a notion, wherever entertained, is but the flattering dream of a proud imagination. I find the reason, not in the soul's *worth*, but in the soul's *relationship*, as the "offspring of God." Parental love amongst men, instead of being weakened and cooled by the infirmities of the child, is heightened and fired by them. It seems a law in the government of parental hearts, that the weaker the child, the stronger the parent's love. This principle, which is a divine implantation, enables me to understand, in some humble measure, *why* the Infinite Father should show all this wonderful compassion to men. We are the weak infirm children in His great family. "We are His offspring," weak, wayward, infirm ; and this explains His merciful interposition.

IV. THIS GLORIOUS FACT IN OUR NATURE EXPOSES THE ENORMITY OF SIN. What laws are so binding,—what authority so sacred as a true Father's ? First, How heinous does sin, *in relation to God*, appear when you think of Him as a Father ! The greatest ingratitude is that which overlooks a father's kindness ; the greatest criminality is that which violates a father's precepts ; the greatest rebellion is that which contemns a father's authority. Secondly, How heinous does sin, *in relation to society*, appear when you think of Him as a Father. We are all brothers and sisters. How enormously iniquitous then are *slavery, war, cruelty,* and *oppression* of every kind !

V. THIS GLORIOUS FACT IN OUR NATURE AIDS US TO ESTIMATE THE TRANSCENDENT BLESSEDNESS OF THE DUTIFUL. The office of a father is to provide for his children. He provides *guardianship, education,* and *nourishment* for his children. As a guardian, He protects the mind as well as the body, guards our existence with all its rights and interests,—is our everlasting SHIELD. As an educator, He develops all the wonderful powers of our nature, trains us not only for some office in time, but for the high services of eternity. As a nourisher, He has supplies for all wants now and for ever.

Man, reverence thy nature ! act worthy of thy high relationship ; thou art a child of the Infinite. The great universe is thy Father's house. Seek through Christ the pardon of thy sins, and the true spirit of adoption, and thou shalt find at last in the great eternity, a "mansion" prepared for thee.

Another thing he states in this sermon concerning God's relation to man is (5.) *He demands repentance from all.* " And the times of this ignorance God winked at ; but now commandeth all men everywhere to repent, because He hath appointed a day in the which He will judge the world in righteousness by that man whom He hath ordained ; whereof He hath given assurance unto all men, in that He hath raised Him from the dead."

So far Paul, in this celebrated sermon on Mars Hill, propounds the doctrines of natural religion,—doctrines written on the pages of nature. In the verses before us he directs to subjects not found in the volume of nature, and revealed only in the Word of Inspiration. We must make this passage also the subject of a separate discourse.

THE GOSPEL AGE

First, *God's relation to the world before the gospel age.* "The times of this ignorance God winked at." The ages before the gospel were "times of ignorance." The ignorance here, of course, refers not to ignorance of things in *general,* for the ancients knew many things, but to the grand subjects of religion—to God and His relations. The heathens were ignorant of the One True and Living God —"the world by wisdom knew not God." Their ignorance, it must be remembered, was a *guilty* ignorance, for had they not the means of knowing? Outward nature, and the intuitions of their own souls, were sufficient to teach them the knowledge of God ; but the means they neglected, and their ignorance was *guilty.* This ignorance, we are told, "God winked at." What does this mean? Certainly not that He connived at it. The original word here used means, "overlook ;" and this is the idea we are to attach to it here. It means not that God did not *observe* the wickedness of these times, but that He exercised great forbearance. He dealt leniently with those dark ages. He suffered the ignorance to begin, and to grow, and to develop itself. He did not interpose *specially,* either in vengeance or in grace. Why did the Almighty permit these ages of ignorance to continue? This is a question which, if proper to ask, is impossible to solve. We may discover certain useful ends answered by it ; and these ends will be sufficient to satisfy us that His forbearance with this ignorance was worthy of Himself. It serves to show, for example—(1.) The insufficiency of human reason in matters of religion. God gave human reason plenty of time to exhaust all its resources in endeavours to find Him out. It serves to show—(2.) The necessity of a special revelation. Since God gave mankind so many ages to endeavour to find Him out, and they failed, grew darker and darker over the questions of religion up to the time of Christ, men are left without the shadow of a foundation for supposing that they can do without the gospel of Jesus Christ.

These verses present to us—

Secondly, *God's relation to the world in the gospel age.* God's conduct NOW towards the world is changed. He who *overlooked* in forbearing mercy the wickedness of past times, *now* commands "every man everywhere to repent." The text presents us three things in connexion with the gospel age—

I. THE ONE GREAT DUTY OF MAN IN THE GOSPEL AGE. What is the duty ? It is to *repent.* It means something more than contrition for sin—more than a change of opinion, or renunciation of a habit ; it means a change of soul. What is a change of soul ? A change in the *ruling disposition* of life. Every man is under some *ruling* disposition ; a disposition into which you can resolve all the actions of his every-day life. This is the *heart* of the man. Repentance is a change in this. It means, in general, the same thing as " conversion," " regeneration," " renewal," &c. This reformation of soul is the *one* urgent duty of every man in this gospel age. What said John the Baptist ? " Repent ye, for the kingdom of God is at hand." What said Jesus ? " I am come to call sinners to repentance." What said Peter on the day of Pentecost ? " Repent, and be baptized every one of you in the name of Jesus Christ, for the remission of sins." And this is the duty—the *one* duty—which God presses upon the world now : " He commandeth all men, everywhere, to repent." All men—whatever their age, their country, their colour, their circumstances, their intellectual and moral condition—*everywhere*, on whatever zone of the globe. Why repent ? (1.) Because it is *right*. All men, everywhere, are in the *wrong*, and eternal rectitude demands a change. (2.) Because it is *indispensable*. There is no possibility of being happy without it. Nothing will do without it ; all may be blessed with it. " Marvel not that I said unto thee, Ye must be born again ; " " Except a man be born again, he cannot see the kingdom of God."

The text presents us with—

II. THE ONE GRAND PROSPECT OF MAN IN THE GOSPEL AGE What is the grand thing looming before men in this age ? The *day of judgment*. " He hath appointed a day in which He will judge the world."

First, *The period* is appointed. That day who shall describe ? No mortal can. The Judge himself can alone describe it. He has done so. " When the Son of man shall come in His glory " (Matt. xxv.) Who knows when the day will dawn ? No one. It will come, perhaps, as the flood came—whilst men are eating and drinking, &c. ; or as Christ came—in the deep hush of darkness, when men were all asleep. We know not *when*, but we know it is *fixed*. It is registered in His unfulfilled plans. His Providence is getting nearer to it every hour. " God hath appointed a day." It *must* come.

Secondly, *The Judge* is appointed. " By that *man* whom He hath ordained." " The Father judgeth no man." When He stood as a criminal at the bar of Caiaphas, He said, " Hereafter shall ye see the Son of man sitting on the right hand of power." This *man* is to be the Judge. And He will judge " in righteousness." This *man* has heretofore ever dealt in mercy. Now eternal *rectitude* is the rule of His conduct. Such is the wonderful prospect held out to mankind in this the gospel age. The grand thing that loomed in the future of the men who lived *before* the gospel was the gospel age itself. The gospel age has come, and the grand thing that looms in the future of humanity now is *the day of judgment*.

What an argument for repentance is this *righteous* judgment before us. We must be *made right* to be enabled to stand in that day.

The text presents us with :—

III. THE ONE DEMONSTRATING FACT FOR MAN IN THE GOSPEL AGE. "Whereof he hath given *assurance* unto all men in that He hath raised Him from the dead." The apostle means one of two things by this expression. Either that *the resurrection of Christ* is an assurance that there will come a day of judgment, or that the resurrection of Christ is an assurance that He is the Divine Judge of all. The latter, perhaps, is the most likely idea. Although, in truth, the fact answers both purposes. The resurrection of Christ is the fact that demonstrates the divinity of Christ's teaching. Paul always regarded it as such. By His resurrection from the dead, "Christ was declared to be the Son of God with power." But how does the resurrection of Christ demonstrate the divinity of His teaching ; or, in other words, the truth of Christianity ? For the sake of brevity and point, the question may be answered syllogistically—

First, *Any teacher, living a holy life, rising from the dead, according to his own announcement, must be divine.* Suppose in this age a man of spotless character were to appear as a teacher, proclaiming truths congruous with men's common sense, common conscience, and common experience, who announced that he should die in a certain way, and rise from the dead so many days after his burial: and suppose that he did die, and did rise, according to the very letter of his own word, would not the fact be regarded by all as the most *conclusive* proof that could be possibly furnished of the divinity of his teaching ? For who but God could raise the dead ?

Secondly, *Christ, as a teacher, did live a holy life, and did rise from the dead according to His own announcement.* Was He not holy ? Did He not foretell His resurrection, and did He not rise in exact conformity with His own words ? What is the conclusion ? He is a divine teacher. Who can escape this inference ? Thank God He has given us the *assurance.*

Such is the gospel age—*the age* in which we are living.

Having examined the substance of Paul's sermon at Athens, we have now to attend to

THE EFFECTS OF THE SERMON

"And when they heard of the resurrection of the dead, some mocked, and others said, We will hear thee again of this matter. So Paul departed from among them. Howbeit certain men clave unto him and believed," &c., &c.

First, *That whatever might be the diversity in the positions, talents, and sentiments of men, the doctrines of the true religion are important to all.* To the " Jews," " Epicureans," and " Stoics," the apostle proclaimed the same doctrines.

Secondly, *That whatever might be the power with which the great verities of the true religion are urged, a necessary and uniform result is not to be expected.* " Some mocked," &c. The same tool, wielded by the same hand, and with the same force and skill, could produce the same effect upon the same species of stone, metal, or timber ; but the same doctrines urged by the same man, at the same time produce widely different results in the same place upon the same congregation. As you look upon Paul standing there, on Mars' Hill, and declaring with all the skill of a dialectician, the grace of an orator, and the zeal of a seraph, the great verities of religion, you might suppose that he would carry the whole of his audience with him on the majestic flow of his own great thoughts. But no !

Here are three moral classes :—

I. SOME AMONGST HIS AUDIENCE HEARD HIM WITH DERISIVE IN-CREDULITY. " And when they heard of the resurrection of the dead, some mocked." The Epicureans would especially do this. They denied a future state, and regarded death as an eternal sleep. Three things would probably induce them to ridicule this doctrine. First, It stood opposed to their preconceived notions. For three hundred years their school had been teaching the non-existence of any after life. Many a sceptic rejects Christianity on this same ground. It contains things contrary to his preconceived notions, therefore he treat it with derision. How foolish, how arrogant is this! Are their little notions the measure, the sum of all truth ? Secondly, It was apparently improbable to them. They would be likely to say, Resurrection of the dead ! How can that be ? Are not the genera-tions of men reduced to dust? Have not the particles of which their bodies were composed been wrought into the texture of every species and form of plant and of animal life ? Where are the symptoms of a resurrection? Does not an eternal silence reign over cemeteries? Thus their notions of improbability would be likely to induce them to ridicule this idea. But how foolish this ! The men who saw the priests endeavouring to level the walls of Jericho, by blowing in the rams' horn, would probably " mock " them on this account, but the walls fell notwithstanding. Lot seemed as one that " mocked unto his sons-in-law," when he warned them of the approaching judgment; but the tempest of fire came albeit, &c. Thirdly, He who proclaimed the doctrine to them, was not a recognised teacher. He did not be-long to their school. He was not even an Athenian ; he was a poor Jew. What did he, therefore, know about these things ? These were probably some of the reasons that induced these men to deride the doctrine, and these reasons, alas ! act now.

II. SOME AMONGST HIS AUDIENCE HEARD HIM WITH A PROCRAS-TINATING RESOLVE. " Others said, We will hear thee again of this matter." Probably these were some of the Stoics, who believed in a future state, and who were disposed to give the subject a little attention at some future time. However, whoever they might be, they were evidently interested in the "matter." This procrastinating of the subject of religion is exceedingly foolish for the following reasons—First, Because it is, of all subjects, the most important. Secondly, Because an important step towards its reception has been taken when an interest has been created. Men generally are thoroughly indifferent; but here there was some interest. Thirdly, Because any portion of future time is very uncertain, and even should it be vouchsafed, the existing interest may never be renewed. There is no reason to believe that those men did ever hear Paul again. He immediately departed, and probably never returned. A "more convenient season" may never come.

III. SOME AMONGST HIS AUDIENCE HEARD HIM WITH PRACTICAL FAITH. "Howbeit certain men clave unto him," &c. Dionysius and Damaris are mentioned because, probably, they were persons of some note in the world. These two names suggest—That Christianity is alike suited to both sexes. Both the man and the woman will find in it whatever their peculiar organisations, talents, dispositions, and circumstances may require. Let the woman stand as the representative of the *intuitional* power, and the man as the *logical;* Christianity meets both. Or let the woman stand as the representative of those who have to attend to the more *private* and *domestic* duties, and the man as the representative of those who have to be out in the *open world*—in the field, the market, the shop, the senate-house—battling with difficulties. Christianity is suited to all spheres. It is great enough for the greatest, and simple enough for the simplest. From the whole we may learn—(1.) That the gospel is moral in its influence upon the world. It does not bear man down by violence and force. (2.) That the gospel is not to be restricted to any class. (3.) That ministers should not despair for want of success. Though some deride, and some procrastinate, some will believe.

Acts 17:33

PAUL'S SECOND MISSIONARY TOUR.—X. HIS ADIEU TO ATHENS

" *So* [1] *Paul departed from among them.*"

EMENDATIVE RENDERING.—(1.) And thus.—ALF.

HOMILETICS.—We have looked at Paul in connexion with Athens ; we have marked the feelings with which he surveyed the city, his conduct with the philosophers of the Agora, and his wonderful sermon on Mars' Hill. The sentence before us presents him leaving the famous city, never more, perhaps, to visit it.

I. He leaves Athens, having considerably ALTERED its SPIRITUAL CONDITION.

First, *He left it a new stimulus to thought.* He that heightens my impulses to thought influences my condition and destiny. Our thoughts make us. What a stimulus to thought did Paul give to the Athenian mind! He gave to their understandings a new theory of the universe, a new method to happiness, a new manifestation of God —" God in Christ," &c. There was, perhaps, more thinking in Athens on the night after the discourse on Mars' Hill than there had ever been before. The springs of intellect were touched, and the wheels of thought were in rapid motion.

Secondly, *He increased its responsibility.* Responsibility is measured by privileges. Athens had been highly favoured for ages. Great men had lived and laboured there—men with many a divine thought within them—Plato, Socrates, and Aristotle ; but Paul was greater than all. He gave more of the divine in thought to them than was found in the combined wisdom of all their philosophers. O Athens, better a thousand times that Paul had never entered thee, than that thou shouldst fail in the new-imposed responsibility ! Paul changed the position of Athens in the moral world. Geographically and materially it remained the same, but in the moral empire of God it was a changed place. The men there would never feel again exactly as they had felt, would never think again exactly as they had thought.

II. He leaves Athens with a HEIGHTENED ESTIMATE of CHRISTIANITY. The apostle made a *great experiment* in taking the gospel to Athens. Perhaps he felt it so the day he walked the city, surveying it, previous to the opening of his mission. He had undoubtedly heard about their great sages, and was perhaps in some measure acquainted with their vast systems of thought. He had no doubt received a deep impression of the inventiveness, energy, and æsthetics of their intellect in the gorgeous architecture and brilliant statuary of their city. How will such men, he may have asked, regard the tale I have to tell them of Jesus of Nazareth ? How will my story stand before the keen intellect of these men, especially when presented by mê, a man without dignity of presence, without oratorical power, without a name amongst them, and without such a knowledge of the niceties of their noble language, as will qualify me to address them with any great acceptance ? Somewhat thus, perhaps, he questioned. After his discussion, however, in the Agora, and his sermon on Mars' Hill, all these misgivings would give place to an unbounded confidence in the glory of his message. He soon found that the gospel enabled him to measure souls with Athenian sages, and to make their grandest systems of thought appear paltry in the light of his teaching. He felt that the gospel "was mighty through God in pulling down the strongholds," &c. Christianity has been tested by every school of philosophy, every grade of intellect, and by every system of religion, for long centuries since Paul left Athens, and it has always come forth the triumphant power. How unbounded, therefore, should be our confidence!

III. He leaves Athens, NEVER PERHAPS TO VISIT IT ANY MORE. There is something very affecting in a parting of this kind. It was affecting to see Moses leaving Pharaoh to meet him no more until the judgment; the young lawyer leaving Christ, going away sorrowful; and now Paul leaving Athens. Though he would not return to them again—

First, *He had discharged his conscience.* He had declared unto them the whole counsel of God; he was clear of their blood. Though he would not return to them again—

Secondly, *He would be engaged in the diffusion of the gospel.* He was off to Corinth, and thence on, for his gospel was a gospel for humanity.

Thirdly, *Though he would not return to them again, he would anticipate meeting them at the retribution.* He had told them of a day of judgment, and on that day he would meet them.

Acts 18:1-11

PAUL'S SECOND MISSIONARY TOUR.—XI. FROM ATHENS TO CORINTH.

1. *Paul's ministry at Corinth*

" *After these things Paul departed*[1] *from Athens, and came to Corinth; and found a certain Jew, named Aquila, born in Pontus, lately come from Italy, with his wife Priscilla (because that. Claudius had commanded all Jews to depart from Rome), and came unto them. And because he was of the same craft, he abode with them, and wrought: for by their occupation they were tent-makers. And he reasoned in the synagogue every Sabbath,*[2] *and persuaded the Jews and the Greeks. And*[3] *when Silas and Timotheus were come from Macedonia, Paul was pressed in the spirit, and testified to the Jews that Jesus was Christ.*[4] *And when they opposed themselves, and blasphemed, he shook*[5] *his raiment, and said unto them, Your blood be upon your own heads; I am clean: from henceforth I will go unto the Gentiles.*[6] *And he departed thence, and entered into a certain man's house, named Justus, one that worshipped God, whose house joined hard to the synagogue. And Crispus, the chief ruler of the synagogue, believed on the Lord with all his house; and many of the Corinthians hearing believed, and were baptized. Then spake the Lord to Paul in the night by a vision, Be not afraid, but speak, and hold not thy peace: for I am with thee, and no man shall set on thee to hurt thee, for I have much people in this city. And he continued there a year and six months, teaching the word of God among them."*

EMENDATIVE RENDERINGS.—(1.) He departed. (2.) Was earnestly occupied in discoursing. (3.) But. (4.) The Christ. (5.) Shook out. (6.) I shall henceforth with a clear conscience go unto the Gentiles.

EXEGETICAL REMARKS. — " *After these things.*" That is, after what had occurred at Athens, the record of which is in the preceding chapter.

" *Paul departed from Athens, and came to Corinth.*" Corinth was a famous Grecian city. It stood on the isthmus between Northern Greece and the Peloponnesus. It had two ports; the one fronting Asia, the other Europe. Though destroyed by the Romans about the same time that Carthage was destroyed (B.C. 146), it was rebuilt by Julius Cæsar, and was, when Paul entered it, in a most flourishing condition. It was the capital of Achaia, one of the two great provinces into which Greece was divided by the Romans, the other being Macedonia. It was the great emporium of the world, the meeting-place of nations for traffic. It held the keys of commerce, and swarmed with a trading population. It was far famed in its day, not only for trade, but for wealth, luxury, and vice. On account of its licentiousness and debauchery it has been called by some the Venice, and by others the Paris of the Old World. " To play the Corinthian" was a proverbial expression for being a man addicted to dissipation and debauchery. Mental culture was not, however, wholly neglected in this scene of voluptuous revelry and money-making traffic. Literature and the arts advanced to considerable perfection. One of our best styles of architecture sprang from Corinth, and carries its name through all times. Paul, having left Athens, now enters this city, not many miles distant. They were, however, cities very different in character. Athens was the seat of learning. Corinth was the centre of business and political power. Athens was "a city of loungers, a place of indolent curiosity, and of leisurely speculation." Corinth was a city of business; there men of different countries resorted in order to buy, and sell, and get gain. Two reasons might have influenced Paul in visiting this city for apostolic labour. First, Its connexion with the world in general. Corinth stood " in immediate connexion with Rome and the west of the Mediterranean; with Thessalonica and Ephesus in the Ægean, and with Antioch and Alexandria in the East." Secondly, Its connexion with the Jews in particular. Being one of the world's great centres of merchandise, Jews were there in great numbers. What Jerusalem was to them religiously, such a place was Corinth to them commercially. The gospel proclaimed in the markets and squares of Corinth would rapidly spread throughout the world. No place could have been better selected fer radiating the influence of the gospel through the world than Corinth.

" *And found a certain Jew named Aquila, born in Pontus, lately come from Italy, with his wife Priscilla.*" From these Latin names one would conclude that they had resided so long in Rome as to sink their Jewish family names. " *Pontus,*" the most easterly province of Asia Minor, stretching along the southern shore of the Black Sea. From this province there were Jews at Jerusalem on the great Pentecost (chap. ii. 9), and the Christians of it were included among "the strangers of the dispersion," to whom Paul addressed his first epistle (1 Peter i. 1). Whether this couple were converted before Paul made their acquaintance commentators are much divided. They may have brought their Christianity

with them from Rome (Olshausen),
or Paul may have been drawn to them
merely by like occupation, and, lodging with them, have been the instrument of their conversion (Meyer).—
P. C.

"*Because that Claudius had commanded all Jews to depart from Rome.*"
The Roman emperor had by an edict
expelled all the Jews from the imperial city. Of this Claudius, Suetonius
the biographer narrates the fact, and
thus furnishes a strong incidental
proof of the veracity and fidelity of
Luke as the chronicler of the events
of apostolic history.*

"*And because he was of the same
craft he abode with them, and wrought:
for by their occupation they were tent-
makers.*" "What is commanded of
a father towards his son ?" (asks a
Talmudic writer). "To circumcise
him, to redeem him, to teach him the
law, to teach him a trade, &c. R.
Judah saith, He that teacheth not
his son a trade, does as if he taught
him to be a thief. Rabban Gamaliel
saith, He that hath a trade in his
hand, to what is he like ? He is like
to a vineyard that is fenced. So some
of the great wise men of Israel had
been cutters of wood. Rabban Jo-
chanan Ben Zaccai, that was vice-
president of the Sanhedrim, was a
merchant four years, and then he fell
to the study of the law." "Rabbi
Judah, the great cabalist, bore the
name and trade of Hhajat, a shoe-
maker or tailor."—Lightfoot, vol. iii.,
pp. 227, 228 ; viii., p. 131. According to (this) old Jewish custom, which
was well-nigh as binding as law, Paul
learned a trade, that of a maker of tent-
cloth. Michaelis (Int., vol. ii., p. 1338,
edit. 4) represents Paul as a machine-
maker. A passage in Julius Pollux
led him into this singular mistake.
(See Hug's introduction, part ii., p.
86.) The Fathers suppose Paul to be
a worker on leather, or a tent-maker.
Chrysostom says, "By his trade he
was employed upon skins." The fact
that war tents were made of leather,
induced the old writers to suppose
that Paul worked on this material.
The probability is, that as a kind of

shagged, rough-haired goat was very
common in Cilicia, and as the hair
of this animal was manufactured into
a thick, coarse cloth, and as this
manufacture may have been very
common in Paul's native province,
he therefore selected it as his employment. The cloth thus manufactured was called *Cilicia*. It was
used for the covering of tents in war,
and upon ships : also for shepherds'
tents, especially in Syria and on the
Euphrates. It is not to be supposed,
however, that Paul never made tent-
cloth except from materials procured
in his native region." (See Dr Tho-
luck's Life and Writings of Paul.)

"*And he reasoned in the synagogue
every Sabbath.*" How he reasoned
we may learn in a passage from one
of his letters afterwards. "When I
came to you, I came not with excellency of speech or of wisdom, declaring unto you the testimony of God.
For I determined not to know anything among you save Jesus Christ
and Him crucified. And I was with
you in weakness, and in fear, and
in much trembling."

"*And when Silas and Timotheus
were come from Macedonia.*" Paul had
been alone at Athens, now he is joined
by Silas and Timotheus, — the one
from Berea, the other from Thessalonica.

"*Paul was pressed in the spirit,*"
or as some read it, "*was pressed with
the word.*" Preaching the gospel was
felt by him as of great urgency.
We learn this from his own letters
(1 Cor. ii. 1–5, 1 Thess. iii. 1–10). He
now wrote under this feeling his first
epistle to Thessalonians.

"*And when they opposed themselves
and blasphemed, he shook his raiment.*"
He "shook his raiment," as an expressive act of shaking off the guilt of their
condemnation, and indicating that he
would have nothing more to do with
them.

"*Your blood,*" &c. The guilt of your
destruction is your own, an allusion
perhaps to Ezek. iii. 4–9.

"*And he departed thence, and entered into a certain man's house named
Justus,*" &c. Not changing his lodg-

* See Conybeare and Howson

ing, as if Aquila and Priscilla up to this time were with the opponents of the apostle (Alford), but merely ceasing any more to testify in the synagogue; and henceforth carrying on his labours in this house of Justus, which, "joining hard to the synagogue," would be easily accessible to such of its worshippers as were still open to light. Justus, too, being probably a proselyte, would more easily draw a mixed audience than the synagogue. From this time forth conversions rapidly increased.—P. C.

"*And Crispus, the chief ruler of the synagogue, believed on the Lord and all his house.*" This Crispus is mentioned in 1 Cor. i. 14, as being one of the few whom Paul baptized with his own hands.

"*Then spake the Lord to Paul in the night by a vision, Be not afraid, but speak, and hold not thy peace.*" The increasing success of the apostle so increased the rage of his opponents as probably to suggest to him the necessity of leaving Corinth as he had left the other places. The Spirit, however, came to him to reassure him. "*For 1 am with thee, and no man shall set on thee to hurt thee; for I have much people in this city.*" Two reasons are here given to encourage him to persevere in his labours. First, Divine protection; "I am with thee," &c. Second, The assurance of future success; "I have much people in this city." There are souls here concealed from you who will practically respond to your message and be saved. Dissolute though it was, Corinth afforded a finer field for religious influence than Athens. "*In this city*"—the most dissolute city in the world—there was "much people."

"*And he continued there a year and six months, teaching the word of God among them.*" During this eighteen months he wrote the two epistles to the Thessalonians.

HOMILETICS.—In this brief sketch of Paul's *eighteen months'* ministry, there are several things worthy of our attention.

I. A PROPITIOUS CONCURRENCE OF CIRCUMSTANCES in connexion with the preaching of the gospel. He enters the city of Corinth a poor, penniless stranger, but see what arrangement has been made for his accommodation. He "found a certain Jew named Aquila, born in Pontus, lately come from Italy," &c., &c.

Observe all the incidents concur here to favour Paul's ministry at Corinth—(1.) The Roman emperor had by an edict expelled all the Jews from the Imperial city. "Claudius had commanded all Jews to depart from Rome." (2.) These Jews, Aquila and his wife Priscilla, thus expelled from Rome, came to Corinth. Many, no doubt, of the banished ones went elsewhere, but these, for some reason or other, came to the very city where Paul was about entering on his apostolic mission. (3.) Aquila "was of the same craft as Paul." This was another event of interest. (4.) Paul found them out. And that he, a perfect stranger, should find out these strangers in such a large city is also noteworthy. Is there not something remarkable in the concurrence of these circumstances?

They were *Jews*, this would give them some interest in the apostle; they were *strangers* banished from their own homes, this would also dispose them to sympathise with Paul, who was a stranger amongst strangers; and, moreover, they were of the *same trade and social grade* in life; and this would, undoubtedly, tend still further to heighten their sympathies; and these strangers in a large city, found each other out *at once*, as if there was some mystic affinity between them, blindly bringing them together. Is not Divine superintendence to be seen in this propitious concurrence of circumstances? Truly the angel of Providence went before Paul into Corinth, and prepared for him a house, employment, fellowship, and an open door for the gospel. " In Rome," says Lange, " the emperor must expel the Jews, in order that Aquila may come to Corinth, and offer house and board to the apostle." Thus the all-ruling God uses the designs of princes, and the changes of the world, to provide for His children, and to advance His kingdom.

II. THE VALUE OF HANDICRAFT IN CONNEXION WITH THE PREACHING OF THE GOSPEL. " And because he was of the same craft, he abode with them, and wrought: for by their occupation they were tent-makers." The Jews, as we have seen, were accustomed to teach all boys some trade, even those who received a liberal education, both as a means of subsistence, and a moral safeguard. The old Jews were undoubtedly right in this. Industry is a Divine ordinance; idleness not only often tempts to dishonest acts, but is *essentially* dishonest. He who consumes without producing is a social thief. " He abode with them and wrought." This statement agrees with many passages in the apostle's letters (1 Cor. iv. 12; 2 Cor. xi. 9; 1 Thess. ii. 9; 2 Thess. iii. 8). The fact that the great apostle wrought at his trade to support himself in Corinth, shows—

First, That there is no *disgrace in manual labour*. A greater man than Paul never lived, and here we see him working at his trade in the house of a poor exiled Jew. The fact shows—

Secondly, *The necessity of independency in a minister*. No man held with a deeper conviction, and urged with greater force, the duty of the Church to support him who ministers to it the Word of life. He taught that the " Lord hath ordained that they which preach the gospel should live by the gospel" (1 Cor. ix. 14). Notwithstanding this, he felt the necessity of being independent of the means that might come, and *ought* to come, from those to whom he ministered. He was determined by the labour of his own hands to maintain an honourable independency. " In all things I have kept myself from being burdensome unto you, *and so will I keep myself*" (2 Cor. xi. 9). Those hands of his enabled him to move as an independent man amongst the men of Corinth. The Sabbath-day he reasoned in the synagogue; but on all the other days he toiled hard for his bread at his trade during his eighteen months' ministry. He wanted nothing in worldly riches of them. He sought not theirs, but them. Most desirable is it for all ministers to be thus *independent* of the people. The pulpit which is felt to be the means of bread to the minister is often terribly degraded, and no wonder.

III. The stimulating influence of co-operation, in connexion with the preaching the gospel. "And when Silas and Timotheus were come from Macedonia, Paul was pressed in the spirit, and testified that Jesus was Christ." He had encountered all the difficulties of his mission in Athens single-handedly and alone. Their advent to Corinth would be now rapturously hailed by him, and the effect of their arrival upon his mind was only to intensify his zeal in the cause of his Master. "*Paul was pressed in spirit.*" The word translated "pressed" is the same which our Lord employs, "I have a baptism to be baptized with, and how am I *straightened* till 'it be accomplished." The sight of his companions and fellow-labourers fanned his earnestness into a stronger flame. No doubt they imparted to him most refreshing and stimulating information concerning the triumphs of the gospel, which they had witnessed during their separation from him. Timotheus had just visited the Church of Thessalonica, and the news he brought concerning that Church, most probably, prompted Paul to address a letter forthwith to the Thessalonian converts.* The effect of this renewed earnestness, this pressure of soul, was the testifying to the Jews that Jesus was Christ. He laboured more strenuously in the cause. It sometimes happens that an increase in our coadjutors lessens our own diligence; it was not so with Paul. The arrival of his fellow-labourers struck new fire into his soul, and urged him to yet greater activity.

IV. The law of responsibility, in connexion with the preaching of the gospel. "And when they opposed themselves and blasphemed, he shook his raiment, and said unto them, Your blood be upon your own heads; I am clean." The renewed zeal and efforts of the apostles stirred up yet fiercer opposition. They not only "*opposed,*" but "*blasphemed*"—used impious revilings and contumely. Paul felt two things, now, in relation to the law of responsibility.

First, *That having been faithful to his conscience, his duty was discharged.* He had declared honestly and fully the truth to them, and had nothing of which to accuse himself. "He shook his raiment" before them, and thus dramatically declared that he was free, and with emphatic words he exclaimed, "*Your blood be upon your own heads; I am clean.*" There is no implication or threat, but an emphatic assertion that if they perished they would perish by their own folly.

Secondly, *He felt that, having rejected the gospel, they had increased their own responsibility.* They rejected the spiritual life offered to them, and were guilty of self-murder; they had no one to blame. "*Your blood be upon your own heads.*" Probably the

---

* Those letters derive a higher interest and deeper significance when read with a knowledge of Paul's circumstances when he wrote them at Corinth.

apostle felt at this time the force of those wonderful words which the Almighty addressed to Ezekiel (chap. xxxiii. 8, 9).

V. A CHANGE OF SPHERE IN CONNEXION WITH THE PREACHING OF THE GOSPEL. Up to this time it would seem he had confined his ministry entirely to the Jew. " He reasoned with the Jews in the synagogue." But now he turns to the Gentiles. *" From henceforth I will go unto the Gentiles,* and he departed hence and entered into a certain man's house, named Justus, one that worshipped God, whose house joined hard to the synagogue." Instead of preaching in the synagogue, he now preached in a private house, the house of Justus. He was not particular where he preached. At Rome it was in his "own hired lodging" (Acts xxviii. 30). At Ephesus, it was the school of Tyrannus (Acts xvi.) At Philippi, by the river-side (Acts xvi.) Here, at Corinth, it was a house close to the synagogue. Was there any special reason for Luke stating that the house joined hard to the synagogue ? Did he wish to make known the fact that Paul was not afraid of the Jews, notwithstanding their intolerance and persecution, inasmuch as he goes next door to their synagogue to preach ? The fact that Paul thus changed his field of labour shows—

First, *His belief that the gospel is equally adapted for all, the Gentile as well as the Jew.*

Secondly, *A conviction that his ministry was too precious to be wasted upon incorrigible souls."* He knew that the discourses which he preached in the synagogues to the Jews, and which were rejected, would, if preached elsewhere, turn many from darkness to light. When a minister finds that he is amongst a people he cannot benefit, casting pearls before swine, it is his duty to select another sphere.

VI. MORAL TRIUMPHS IN CONNEXION WITH THE PREACHING OF THE GOSPEL. " And Crispus, the chief ruler of the synagogue, believed on the Lord, and all his house; and many of the Corinthians hearing, believed and were baptized." His conversion, being a man of distinction (the chief ruler of the synagogue), would be a signal demonstration of the power of the gospel, and afford a mighty impulse to its advancement in the city. His family believed also as well as many of the Corinthians. We have elsewhere the names of several of those who became Christians in Corinth. Apenetus, Caius, Aquila, and Priscilla, as well as Crispus. The class of converts here, it would seem from Paul's own pen, were not generally of the philosophers or nobles, but the most profligate and degraded (1 Cor. vi. 11). The fact that the gospel won converts in Corinth, the most depraved and dissolute city in the whole world, is a demonstration that it is equal to the conquest of the world.

VII. DIVINE ENCOURAGEMENT IN CONNEXION WITH THE PREACH-

ING OF THE GOSPEL. " Then spake the Lord to Paul in the night by a vision, Be not afraid, but speak, and hold not thy peace: for I am with thee, and no man shall set on thee to hurt thee ; for I have much people in this city." Probably Paul at this time had reached the period he refers to, when he said, "I was with thee in fear and much trembling" (1 Cor. ii. 3). And he needed this interposition from Heaven—this assurance of the Divine presence and protection. Observe—

First, *The kind of service Christ requires of His ministers.* It is the service of bold speech, " Be not *afraid,* but speak."

Secondly, *The encouragement He vouchsafes to His ministers*—(1.) Protection ; " I am with thee, and no man shall set on thee to hurt thee." (2.) Success ; " I have much people in this city."

Acts 18:12-17

PAUL'S SECOND MISSIONARY TOUR.—XI. FROM ATHENS TO CORINTH (*continued*)

2.—*His ministry at Corinth.*—*Gallio*

" *And when Gallio was the deputy of Achaia, the Jews made insurrection with one accord against Paul, and brought him to the judgment-seat, saying, This fellow*[1] *persuadeth men to worship God contrary to the law. And when Paul was now about to open his mouth, Gallio said unto the Jews, If it were a matter of wrong or wicked lewdness, O ye Jews, reason would that I should bear with you : but if it be a question*[2] *of words and names, and of your law, look ye to it ; for I will be no judge of such matters. And he drave them from the judgment-seat. Then all the Greeks took*[3] *Sosthenes, the chief ruler of the synagogue, and beat him before the judgment-seat : And Gallio cared for none of those things.*"

EMENDATIVE RENDERINGS.—(1.) Man. (2.) If there be questions. (3.) Then they all took.—ALF.

EXEGETICAL REMARKS.—"*And when Gallio was the deputy of Achaia.*" He was the brother of Seneca, the famous philosopher, who describes him as a man of uncommon mildness and simplicity. He was appointed proconsul of Achaia by the Roman emperor Claudius, A.D. 53.

" *The Jews made insurrection.*" Or rose up against.

" *With one accord.*" Unanimously.

" *And brought him to the judgment-seat.*" The tribunal of the governor, to which the Romans attached great importance and sanctity.

" *Saying, This fellow.*" " Fellow " is not expressed in Greek, it is supplied by our translators.

" *Persuadeth men to worship God contrary to the law.*" The law, not the Jewish, but the Roman law ; for Gallio, as a Roman magistrate, would not concern himself with the latter.

" *Gallio said unto the Jews, If it were*

a matter of wrong." Literally, an injustice.

"Or wicked lewdness." That is, reckless immorality, as distinguished from a legal act.

"O ye Jews, reason would that I should bear with you." A Roman magistrate could take cognisance of injustice and gross immorality, but not of religious ceremonies.

"But if it be a question of words and names." A mere verbal controversy on religious questions.

"Look ye to it." That is your concern, not mine.

"For I will be no judge of such matters. And he drave them from the judgment-seat." That is, he peremptorily dismissed them.

"Then all the Greeks took Sosthenes, the chief ruler of the synagogue." This Sosthenes, who had succeeded Crispus, was probably the leader and instigator of the insurrection, and he now became the victim of popular vengeance.

HOMILETICS.—In this fragment of apostolic history we have four things worthy of notice :—

I. RELIGIOUS INTOLERANCE. " The Jews made insurrection." The religious intolerance of these Jews is seen in three things—

First, In the *reason* of their opposition to Paul. What was the reason? Was it because he had violated any law, invaded any of the rights of men, broken the public peace, or insulted the public morals? No, but simply because he had " persuaded" men to *worship* God, in a way not exactly agreeable to their own views. This was all. And what right had they to interfere with him on this account? The very essence of religious intolerance is interference with others on account of diversity of religious views. Their religious intolerance is seen—

Secondly, In the *spirit* of their opposition to Paul. " They made insurrection with one accord." They were exasperated themselves, and they also woke the passions of the people against the apostle. They were indignant with him because his religious opinions did not agree with theirs. What madness! But how common this! How the bigot through all ages has hated and denounced the man who would not adopt his views! Their religious intolerance is seen—

Thirdly, In the *means* of their opposition to Paul. What means did they adopt in opposing Paul? Arguments, suasion, or any such moral means? No, bigotry cannot reason. It substitutes rage for reason, abuse for argument. These bigots sought to crush the apostle by invoking the arm of civil authority. They applied to Gallio. Such is bigotry. It is the blackest of all the black crimes in the world's long roll of wickedness. It was bigotry that put to death the Son of God himself. We have here—

II. MAGISTERIAL PROPRIETY. How did Gallio treat this case Did he, like Pilate, bow to public wish? No, he would not even *entertain* the case. " And when Paul was now about to open his mouth, Gallio said unto the Jews, If it were a matter of wrong or wicked lewdness, O ye Jews, reason would that I should bear with you: but if it be a question of words and names, and of your law, look ye to it; for I will be no judge of such matters. And he drave them from the judgment-seat." He meant, I presume, that the question of religious differences came not within the authority of a civil magistrate. On this principle the Roman government always acted; to its praise be it said, it allowed the greatest freedom in matters of religious opinions.

First, Gallio, in *acting* thus as a magistrate, *acted* justly towards *himself.* The magistrate who dares to interfere with the religious opinions of the people, incurs an amount of responsibility too great for any man to bear. He who dares to legislate for conscience, not only insults his Maker, but perpetrates an injury upon himself.

Secondly, Gallio, in *acting* thus, *acted* justly to his *fellow-subjects.* "Look ye to it." As if he had said, Religion is not to be settled in courts of law, but in courts of conscience. Magnificent type of magistracy is this magistracy of Gallio !

> "Let Cæsar's due be ever paid,
> To Cæsar and his throne ;
> But consciences and souls were made
> To be the Lord's alone."

Here we have—

III. SOCIAL RETRIBUTION. "Then all the Greeks took Sosthenes, and beat him before the judgment-seat." "With what measure ye mete, it shall be measured to you again." Society often gives back to a man what he has given it. The persecutor is often persecuted. This case of social retribution develops—

First, *The natural sense of justice in humanity.* These Greeks had witnessed this Sosthenes in his wicked endeavours to crush Paul, a righteous man, and their sense of justice was outraged; and now their opportunity occurred for vengeance. This sense of justice is a spark from divinity, a ray from the eternal throne, and a pledge that one day justice will be done to all. This case of social retribution develops—

Secondly, *The reproductiveness of evil in man.* Sosthenes had dealt out vengeance to Paul, and now it came back to him in a rich harvest. Violence begets violence ; anger, anger, &c. The propagating power of evil is immense. Evil cannot overcome evil. "Satan cannot cast out Satan." Christ has taught the true theory of this moral expulsion. This case of social retribution develops—

Thirdly, *The power of the gospel.* It is far more than probable that the Sosthenes referred to in 1 Cor. i. 2 is the same person as that referred to in the text. He was a convert to Christianity, a member of the church at Corinth, and esteemed by Paul himself as a "brother." "Paul and Sosthenes our brother unto the church of God." So that over this fierce persecutor Paul's gospel so triumphed, that he became a brother in the holy cause. "The gospel is truly mighty to the pulling down," &c.

Here we have—

IV. LAMENTABLE INDIFFERENCE. "He cared for none of these things." We can scarcely think with some expositors that this means nothing more than a mere *magisterial* unconcernedness to the religious disputes which the Jews now brought under his notice. This he undoubtedly developed on the occasion, according to his own language in the preceding verse ; and this was right and proper, as we have seen. But here I think the reference is to his *personal* indifference concerning religious questions themselves. As an educated, moral, and high-minded Roman, he regarded the religion of Paul as *beneath his notice.* Gibbon tells us that the various modes of worship which prevailed in the Roman world, " were all considered by the people as equally true, by the philosopher as equally false, and by the magistrate as equally useful." Gallio, therefore, we take as a type of this prevailing *religious indifferentism.* This is one of the greatest and most prevalent evils of this age too, and it is *infidelity in its worst form.* Mere theoretical infidelity you can put down by argument. But this is beyond the reach of all logic. It generally assents to every article in your creed, and often repeats its beliefs, and sings its psalms.

First, Religious indifference is *unreasonable.* No question is of such transcendent moment to man as religion, and therefore it is madness on his part to neglect it.

Secondly, Religious indifference is *criminal.* It is contrary to the wishes and the labours of the holiest men ; it involves the abuse of all the means of spiritual improvement ; and it is a practical disregard to all the commands of God.

Thirdly, Religious indifference is *perilous.* The danger is great, increasing, but still, thank God, at present avoidable.

Acts 18:18-22

PAUL'S SECOND MISSIONARY TOUR.—XII. FROM CORINTH TO ANTIOCH

" And Paul after this tarried there yet a good while, and then took his leave of the brethren, and sailed thence into Syria, and with him Priscilla and Aquila ; having shorn his head in Cenchrea, for he had a vow. And he came to Ephesus, and left them there : [1] *but he himself entered into the synagogue, and reasoned with the Jews. When they desired him to tarry longer time with them,* [2] *he consented not ; but bade them farewell, saying, I must by all means keep this feast that cometh in Jerusalem : but I*

will return again unto you, if God will. And he sailed from Ephesus.[3] And when he had landed at Cæsarea, and gone up, and saluted the church, he went down to Antioch."

EMENDATIVE RENDERINGS.—(1.) They came to Ephesus, and he left them there. —ALF. (2.) Omit these words, *with them.* (3.) But bidding them farewell, and saying, I will return again unto you, if God will, he sailed from Ephesus.—ALF.

EXEGETICAL REMARKS.—*" Paul after this tarried there yet a good while."* He had already been eighteen months, and notwithstanding this insurrection, he continued longer.

" And sailed thence into Syria, and with him Priscilla and Aquila." "Into Syria," that is, on his way to Antioch. In passing from Corinth to Ephesus by sea, you sail amongst the islands of the Greek Archipelago. In ancient times no voyage across the Ægean Sea was more frequently made than that between Corinth and Ephesus. They were the capitals of the two flourishing and peaceful provinces of Achaia and Asia, and the two great mercantile towns on opposite sides of the sea. It required some thirteen or fifteen days with a fair wind to accomplish the voyage. The vessel in which the apostle embarked was bound for Syria, and only put in at Ephesus on her way. How he spent those days on the waters, whether the voyage was rough or smooth, what were the leading incidents on board during the period—of all this we are uninformed.

" Having shorn his head in Cenchrea, for he had a vow." The expression, "having shorn his head in Cenchrea," has occasioned not a little controversy. To whom does the personal pronoun "*his*" refer, Paul or Aquila? This is the question on which there are divided opinions, and contending argument. Chrysostom, Hammond, Grotius, and many others, including Conybeare and Howson, regard Paul as the person who had made the vow. We cannot better express our view of the subject than by quoting the words of Dr C. J. Vaughan:—" It is impossible to decide the question absolutely: and persons will be guided in their opinion chiefly by their idea of the probability of the case. Was it likely—and the question answers itself differently in different minds—that St Paul, on any occasion of danger, by land or sea, should have made a vow to God in case of deliverance? a vow indicated, like the Nazarite's, by suffering the hair to grow uncut during its continuance, and now terminated by the sign here described. We know from chapter xxi. that St Paul did not consider such a vow wrong: he was still a Jew, and observance of the law, in any of its ceremonies, was not wrong for him; we can only say that the form of the sentence is ambiguous in the original, and that the word, "*having shorn,*" might be connected either with the nearer name (Aquila), or with the more remote."

" And he came to Ephesus." The capital of Ionia and Asia. It lay about forty miles south of Smyrna, and five from the sea, and contained the splendid temple of Diana, one of the seven wonders of the world. This splendid edifice was about 400 feet long, 200 high, and supported by 127 marble columns, 60 feet high, which had been the offerings of as many kings, each one contributing a pillar. It was not finished until 220 years after its commencement. It was burnt by the torch of an incendiary, who sought thus to immortalise his name, on the night of the birth of Alexander the Great; but it was rebuilt in more than its former glory. Yet the ruins of the city are now with difficulty identified.—LIV.

" I must by all means keep this feast that cometh in Jerusalem." "This feast is," says a modern accomplished expositor, " commonly supposed to have been Pentecost, as navigation was not commonly resumed before the Passover, and no other annual solemnity was absolutely called "the feast." In this grand festival, Jerusalem would be full of people, gathered from all parts of the Jewish world, and thus a splendid oppor-

tunity would be afforded to the apostle to make known the gospel of Jesus Christ."

"*Landed at Cæsarea.*" "This city was formerly called Strato's Tower. It is situated on the coast of the Mediterranean, at the mouth of a small river, and has a fine harbour. It is 36 miles south of Acre, about 62 north-west of Jerusalem, and about the same distance north-east of Azotus. This city is supposed by some to be the Hazor mentioned in Joshua xi. 1. It was rebuilt by Herod the Great, and named Cæsarea in honour of Augustus Cæsar. The city was dedicated to him. The seaport was called Sebaste, the Greek word for Augustus. It was adorned with most splendid houses, and the temple of Cæsar was erected by Herod over against the mouth of the haven, in which was placed the statue of the Roman emperor. It became the seat of the Roman governor

while Judea was a Roman province." —BARNES.

"*Gone up.*" This refers undoubtedly to Jerusalem. It was very common for the sacred writers, in speaking of going to Jerusalem, as going up. See Matt. xx. 17 ; Mark x. 32 ; Luke ii. 42 ; John v. 1, vii. 8, xi. 58, xii. 20 ; Acts xi. 2 ; xv. 2 ; Gal. 1. 17, 18 ; ii. 1, 2.

"*He went down to Antioch.*" Down from Jerusalem to Antioch. Thus from one mother church he passes to another—from the mother church at Jerusalem he comes down to the other mother church at Antioch. This is the second missionary tour that he completes at Antioch.

How sketchy is inspired history. It only indicates by a specimen event or two spiritual operation and circumstances which would take folios to record. The whole of Paul's history at Corinth we must await eternity to disclose.

HOMILETICS.—These verses may be taken as an illustration of *apostolic earnestness.* Paul constitutionally was an earnest man. His temperament was pre-eminently sanguine, his heart was in all he did, and with all his might he wrought. He was fervent in business ; every chapter in his life before, and after, his conversion, shows him to be a man whose purposes were made red hot with the passion of an ever-glowing nature. His earnestness in apostolic work comes out in the short paragraph before us. It is here seen—

I. IN HIS NOBLE DEFIANCE OF DANGER. The Jews had " made insurrection with one accord " against him, and he must have felt, even after Gallio the Roman magistrate had refused to forward, or even entertain their malignant purposes, their ire was still unsubdued, and all aflame. Yet he quits not the scene of duty. "*Paul tarried there yet a good while.*" Though at every turn he would undoubtedly meet with men with condemnation on their lips, and curses on their tongues, yet he paused not in the prosecution of his work. His glowing sympathies with Christ and the divine purpose raised him above the fear of all danger. " He counted not his life dear unto him." His apostolic earnestness is here seen :—

II. IN HIS SURRENDER OF FRIENDSHIP. There are several things in this narrative which show the trials which his social heart must have felt.

First, *His adieu to his brethren at Corinth.* " He took his leave of the brethren." He entered this Paris of the old world to fight the battles alone, and the antagonism was immense, and he left it with numerous converts and a prosperous church. The members of that church were " *his brethren :* " he loved them. The two letters which he afterwards wrote to them show the depth of his affection. Yet he leaves them at the call of duty.

Secondly, *His separation from his dearest companions at Ephesus.* Priscilla and Aquila, we are told, he left at Ephesus. It must have been not a little painful to a man of Paul's tender sensibilities, to separate from those with whom he had been so closely and so lovingly connected. They had been his fellow-workers and friends ; and inspired with the spirit and purposes that animated him, they had embarked in the same mission, and accompanied him to Ephesus. " He came to Ephesus, and left them there."

Thirdly, *His departure from Ephesus in opposition to the earnest request of his friends.*" " When they desired him to tarry longer time with them, he consented not." " Whosoever loveth father and mother more than me, is not worthy of me." Paul proved himself worthy of Christ. His apostolic earnestness is here seen :—

III. IN HIS CONSECRATION TO DUTY. " I must by all means keep this feast that cometh in Jerusalem : but I will return again unto you, if God will."

First, *He felt that God's will called him to Jerusalem now.* " I must by all means keep this feast." He had no doubt about the Divine will upon this point, and hence he was prepared to make any sacrifices to carry it out.

Secondly, *He was willing to return to Ephesus, if it were God's will.* " I will return again unto you, if God will." Consecration to the Divine will, which was the very spirit of his life, was the philosophy of his greatness,—his heroism and his marvellous achievements. *Deo volente.* This should always be the devout proviso in all our plans.

The following homiletical remarks of Lechler and Gerok are worth quoting :—" 1. No hostile hatred restrains him, where the Lord sends him (ver. 19). 2. No brotherly love retains him, when the Lord calls him away (ver. 20). 3. No place is too distant to him ; he hastens when the Spirit draws him thither (ver. 21). 4. No place is too pleasant to him ; he takes his leave when the Lord cannot use him there (ver. 22). I must go to Jerusalem, the watchward of a pilgrim of God, by which he breaks through all the temptations of the world, in love and suffering, from friend and foe."

Acts 18:23-28

PAUL'S THIRD MISSIONARY TOUR.—XIII. FROM ANTIOCH TO EPHESUS

1. *Apollos*

" *And after he had spent some time there, he departed, and went over all the country of Galatia and Phrygia in order, strengthening all the disciples. And a certain Jew, named Apollos, born at Alexandria, an eloquent man, and mighty in the scriptures, came to Ephesus. This man was instructed in the way of the Lord; and, being fervent in the spirit, he spake and taught diligently the things of the Lord,*[1] *knowing only the baptism of John. And he began to speak boldly in the synagogue: whom when Aquila and Priscilla*[2] *had heard, they took him unto them, and expounded unto him the way of God*[3] *more perfectly. And when he was disposed to pass into Achaia, the brethren wrote, exhorting the disciples to receive him: who, when he was come, helped them much which had believed through grace: for he mightily convinced the Jews, and that publicly, shewing by the scriptures that Jesus was Christ.*"

EMENDATIVE RENDERINGS.—(1.) The things concerning Jesus. (2.) Priscilla and Aquila (see Rom. xvi. 3; 2 Tim. iv. 19). (3.) Omit these two words.—ALF.

EXEGETICAL REMARKS.—" *He departed.*" "This third missionary journey, occurring in the year 54 or 55 after Christ, was at first—exactly as the second missionary journey—directed to the churches already established. However, Phrygia and Galatia only are here named. Pisidia, Pamphylia, and Lycaonia, are not mentioned. Whether these provinces, on account of the extreme brevity of the narrative, are unintentionally passed over in silence, or whether Paul only visited the churches in Galatia and Phrygia, founded on his second missionary journey, cannot be determined. Neither are we informed who were his companions ; but from chap. xix. 22, it is evident that Erastus and Timotheus must have journeyed with him."—L. & G.

" *Went over all the country.*" " He not only planted, but watered what he had planted. Like his Master, he went about doing good. His spirit rises with the vastness of his work, and his zeal kindles to a higher, purer flame at every encounter of opposition. He grasps the most distant cities in his plans of benevolence, flies from country to country to preach the gospel, and from youth to age strains every energy and faculty of his powerful genius, and uses every gift of the heaven-descended Spirit, to push forward the work of human salvation. Glorious being ! upon what a grand scale was every virtue of the gospel lived out, and every truth of heaven enforced and adorned."—LIV.

" *And a certain Jew named Apollos.*" Luke, the historian, here breaks away for a moment from the narrative of the *third* missionary tour of the apostle to introduce the name, character, and doings of a certain celebrated Jew named " Apollos." This episode is so interesting and instructive, that we have reason to be thankful for the momentary interruption of the narrative concerning Paul. From what is here recorded of this Apollos, as well as from Paul's reference to him in his letters to the Corinthians, we may regard him as a type of all great preachers.

" *Born at Alexandria.*" A celebrated city in Egypt, named after its founder, Alexander the Great. At this time it was not only a great commercial emporium, but an illustrious seat of Greek and Hebrew learning. It was here that the Septuagint version, and also the school of Platonising Jews, represented by Philo, had their origin. It had the greatest library in the old world.

"*An eloquent man.*" Although the word *eloquent* literally means *learned*, yet as Scripture learning is specially mentioned afterwards, the word must be taken in the common and current acceptation.

"*Being fervent in spirit.*" Literally means boiling, and is a phrase used by the apostle in another place (Rom. xii. 11).

"*Diligently.*" This is not the meaning of the Greek word, but accurately, exactly, or correctly.

"*Baptism of John.*" The ministry of John.

"*When he was disposed.*" Literally, he desiring.

HOMILETICS.—Looking at Apollos as a type of all great preachers, we have presented to us a man of superior biblical intelligence, great power of expression, fine attributes of spirit, and varied capacity for usefulness.

I. SUPERIOR BIBLICAL KNOWLEDGE. It is here said he was "mighty in the Scriptures," and that he was "instructed in the way of the Lord." The Scriptures which he possessed were, of course, the writings of Moses, the prophets, and the Psalms. "In these he was mighty." What is it to be *mighty* in the Scriptures? It is not to have a mere knowledge of the *letter*. A man's verbal knowledge of the Scriptures may be very extensive and correct, and yet he may be very *ignorant* of the spiritual import and purpose of the Bible. True mightiness in the Scriptures may include three things.

First, *A knowledge of the leading historical facts of the Scriptures.* The Bible is a wonderful history of divine *events* and *actions.* These embody and represent principles that have to do both with the procedure of God and the duty and destiny of man. No man can be *mighty* in the Scriptures who is not well versed in these facts.

Secondly, *A knowledge of the leading principles of the Scriptures.* Principles constitute the heart and worth of the Bible. All its facts are valuable only as they are the casket and mirror of principles. These principles are of two kinds, *doctrinal* and *ethical*— theoretic and regulative. The man who knows the mere facts and not the principles, cannot be said to be *mighty* in the Scriptures.

Thirdly, *A knowledge of the leading aims of the Scriptures.* What is their *grand* aim? To build up creeds, to establish sects, to make man the creature of dogmas, rituals, and pietistic moods? No. Such a use, which, alas! has been common, is an impious and an accursed perversion. Its grand aim is to make men *morally good;* to regenerate, ennoble, and beautify the soul. In other words, "to redeem men from all iniquity." He who does not understand this to be its grand purpose, however conversant he may be with its leading facts and principles, cannot be *mighty* in the Scriptures or "understand the way of the Lord." No man can be a great preacher who is not thus "*mighty* in the Scriptures." He may be mighty in linguistical attainments, in classic lore, in general literature, in the arts and sciences, but unless he is "mighty in the Scriptures," he will never be a *great* preacher.

II. EFFECTIVE POWER OF EXPRESSION.

He is said to be an "*eloquent man*." What is eloquence? From the earliest Greek writers on the subject, down to the treatises of Cicero and Quintilian, and even to Blair, Campbell, and Whately, of the present age, we have numerous and oftentimes conflicting definitions of eloquence. *Influential expression* is our definition of it. It is such an expression of a man's own soul as makes his audience feel *one* in heart with him in the question discussed. The power of eloquence will depend mainly on two things:

First, *The power of the subject on the speaker's own mind.* If he has so compassed it with his intellect that he can hold it before his heart until it melts, thrills, and permeates him, he has in him the first condition of eloquence.

Secondly, *Adequate communicative organs on the speaker's part.* A man may have the subject so in him as to inflame his own soul, and yet be unable, through the lack of communicative organs, to make his audience pulsate with his own emotions. He may lack in *voice.* Its modulations may be incapable of conveying what is in him. He may lack in *language.* His vocabulary may be too poor, and his tongue too hesitant. He may lack in *gesture.* It may be stiff, awkward, repulsive. He may lack in *countenance.* The eye may be too dead to flash the fire; the muscles of the face too rigid to quiver; the whole face too fleshy to radiate the divine. He in whom all these unite in the greatest perfection has the most effective organs of expression.

Although true eloquence is a *gift* rather than an attainment, it may be reached to some extent by cultivation. Men who have it not by nature, and who strive to be eloquent in their discourses by oratorical contrivances, often disgust the common-sense portion of their auditory. Daniel Webster, the celebrated American, expressed views on this subject more consonant with our own than any other writer of modern times. When public bodies are to be addressed on momentous occasions, when great interests are at stake, and strong passions excited, nothing is valuable in speech further than it is connected with high intellectual and moral endowments. *Clearness, force,* and *earnestness,* are the qualities which produce conviction True eloquence, indeed, does not consist merely in *speech.* It cannot be brought from far. Labour and learning may toil for it, but they will toil in vain. Words and phrases may be marshalled in every way, but they cannot compass it. It must exist in the *man,* in the *subject,* in the *occasion.* Affected passion, intense expression, the

pomp of declamation, all may aspire to it : they cannot reach it.
It comes, if it come at all, like the outbreaking of a fountain from
the earth, or the bursting forth of volcanic fires, with spontaneous,
original, native force. The graces taught in the schools, the costly
ornaments and studied contrivances of speech, shock and disgust men
when their own lives, and the fate of their wives, their children, and
their country, hang on the decision of an hour. Then words have
lost their power, rhetoric is vain, and all elaborate oratory contemptible. Even genius itself then feels rebuked and subdued, as in the
presence of higher qualities. Then patriotism is eloquent—then self-
devotion is eloquent. The clear conception outrunning the deductions of logic, the high purpose, the firm resolve, the dauntless spirit
speaking on the tongue, beaming from the eye, informing every feature, and urging the whole man onward to his object. This, then, is
eloquence ; or, rather, it is something greater and higher than all
eloquence. It is action—noble, sublime, godlike action.

III. FINE ATTRIBUTES OF SPIRIT. This man's spirit is indicated
here. We learn—
First, *That it was earnest.* "Being fervent in spirit." Earnestness is the necessary result of genuine faith in the gospel, and is
essential to all eloquence in its advocacy. Earnestness is the soul
of eloquence, and the condition of success both in spiritual culture
and Christian propagandism. We learn—
Secondly, *That it was faithful.* The meaning is, that he taught
faithfully so far as he knew. He did not say more than he knew,
did not pretend to a knowledge which he had not ; but spoke out
firmly his convictions concerning the things of the Lord, namely, the
gospel. There was much that he did not know, for as yet he only
knew the "*baptism of John.*" He had not come up to a full knowledge of Jesus Christ as the true Messiah. We learn—
Thirdly, *That it was courageous.* "He began to speak boldly in
the synagogue." He was not satisfied with talking in a more *private*
way concerning the things of the Lord, but he entered the synagogue,
stood up before the congregation, and, with an undaunted courage,
spoke to the bigoted Jews. We learn—
Fourthly, *That it was docile.* This great man, who was " mighty
in the Scriptures"—this man of genius and eloquence—feels his
ignorance, and modestly submits to the teaching of Aquila and
Priscilla—" whom when Aquila and Priscilla had heard, they took
him unto them, and expounded unto him the way of God more
perfectly."
This beautiful little incident furnishes an example both to hearers
and preachers. (1.) *Here is an example to hearers.* Aquila and
Priscilla, though they knew, through the teaching of the great apostle
Paul (who had been their guest at Corinth for some time), much more
of the things of the Lord than Apollos, yet they attended his ministry

at the synagogue. If they could not derive much profit from his ministry, they were there to encourage him by their presence, and to assure him of their sympathies and prayers. They did not scoff at his ignorance, or parade his defects, but they took him unto them, "*and expounded unto him the way of God more perfectly.*" They endeavoured to give him a more accurate idea of the gospel than he had. They did not do this publicly or ostentatiously, but privately and with becoming modesty. Enlightened and experienced Christian hearers may do great service to young ministers in this way.

This incident furnishes—(2.) *An example to preachers.* This eloquent young man, who had just come from the university of Alexandria, the greatest school in the world, was not above learning of this humble tent-maker and his wife. Great souls are always docile. The unlearning preacher—a no uncommon character, alas !—dishonours his office and imposes on his hearers.

IV. VARIED CAPACITY FOR USEFULNESS. "And when he was disposed to pass into Achaia," &c. What disposed him to pass into Achaia does not appear. He had heard, perhaps, of the triumphs of Paul at Corinth, and desired to help forward the good cause. It would seem from 1 Cor. i. 12, iii. 4, 5, that his eloquence had so wonderfully charmed certain members of the Church at Corinth, that division sprang up. The description of his work here in these two verses shows that he had a twofold capacity for usefulness :—

First, *A capacity for confirming those who believed.* It is said, "he helped them much which had believed." He helped them, no doubt, by dissipating their doubts, enlarging their conceptions, strengthening their faith, argumentatively vanquishing their assailants.

Secondly, *A capacity for convincing those who did not believe.* It is said that he "mightily convinced the Jews, and that publicly." It appears, therefore, from these verses, that he was a man capable of performing the *two* grand functions of the true preacher—*edifying* the Church, and *converting* the sinner.

Here, then, are the leading features of a *great preacher :*—Superior biblical knowedge, effective power of expression, fine attributes of spirit, and varied capacity for usefulness.

Acts 19:1-12

PAUL'S THIRD MISSIONARY TOUR.—XIII. FROM ANTIOCH TO EPHESUS
—(continued)

2. The best method of evangelising a city

" And it came to pass, that, while Apollos was at Corinth, Paul, having passed through the upper coasts,[1] came to Ephesus: and finding certain disciples, he said unto them, Have ye received the Holy Ghost since ye believed? And they said unto him, We have not so much as heard whether there be any Holy Ghost. And he said unto them, Unto what then were ye baptized? And they said, Unto John's baptism. Then said Paul, John verily baptized with the baptism of repentance, saying unto the people, that they should believe on him which should come after him, that is, on Christ[2] Jesus. When they heard this, they were baptized in the name of the Lord Jesus. And when Paul had laid his hands upon them, the Holy Ghost came on them ; and they spake with tongues, and prophesied. And all the men were about twelve. And he went into the synagogue, and spake boldly for the space of three months, disputing and persuading the things concerning the kingdom of God. But when divers were hardened, and believed not, but spake evil of that way[3] before the multitude, he departed from them, and separated the disciples, disputing daily in the school of one[4] Tyrannus. And this continued by the space of two years ; so that all they which dwelt in Asia heard the word of the Lord Jesus,[5] both Jews and Greeks. And God wrought special miracles by the hands of Paul : so that from his body were brought unto the sick handkerchiefs or aprons, and the diseases departed from them, and the evil spirits went out of them."

EMENDATIVE RENDERINGS.—(1.) Parts. (2.) Omit this word. (3.) The way. (4.) Omit this word. (5.) Omit this word.—ALF. ; TISCH.

EXEGETICAL REMARKS. — " Paul, having passed through the upper coast, came to Ephesus." This chapter gives an account of Paul's second visit to Ephesus. His first visit seems to have been incidental and very brief (Acts xviii. 19–21). When he departed from it on the first occasion, he left behind his old friends, Priscilla and Aquila, and faithfully promised, to return " if God willed." According to that promise, he is now, after extensive journeyings, great perils, and labours, once more in that famous city of the ancient world. " Upper coast" here may refer to Phrygia and Galatia, or the country between them and Ephesus. Ephesus was a very ancient city of Ionia, near the mouth of the Cayster, famous for its wealth and commerce, and for the temple of Diana, just without its walls, built in the sixth century before Christ, burnt down in the fourth, on the night that Alexander the Great was born, and rebuilt in such a style as to be reckoned by the ancients one of the seven wonders of the world. Ancient Ephesus was always flourishing, and under the Roman domination the greatest city of Asia Minor, whereas now it exists only in ruins, near the Turkish village of Asayluk ; while Smyrna, by a singular but not uncommon contrast, is now more flourishing and populous than ever."—ALEX.

"*And finding certain disciples.*" These "certain disciples" included some, if not all, of those referred to in chap. xviii. 21. Some little progress in the evangelisation of Ephesus had no doubt been made since Paul's former visit. Aquila and Priscilla had not neglected the holy work, and Apollos had made his mighty eloquence tell in the right direction. It is probable that Paul at Ephesus was the guest of Aquila and Priscilla, as he had been at Corinth, and that in their humble home he wrought at his own trade for a livelihood ; indeed, in his farewell address to the Ephesian elders at Miletus, he declares that "his own hands had ministered to his necessities" during his sojourn in their city.

"*He said unto them, Have ye received the Holy Ghost since ye believed ?*" The meaning is, Did ye receive the Holy Ghost when ye believed ? The answer which they give to this question explains what is meant here by receiving the Holy Ghost :

"*And they said unto him, We have not so much as heard whether there be any Holy Ghost.*" Literally, the words are, "We did not even hear whether the Holy Ghost was given,"—meaning at the time of their baptism under John. On that occasion, they had not heard of the great day of Pentecost.

"*And he said unto them, Unto what then were ye baptized ?*" "This implies, what is otherwise most probable, that Christian baptism was administered from the beginning in the form prescribed by Christ himself (Matt. xxviii. 19), and that no one therefore could receive it without hearing of the Holy Ghost, in whose name, as well as in the Father's and the Son's, every convert was baptized. Since they could not be baptized into Christ without so much as hearing of the Holy Spirit, Paul infers that they had not been so baptized at all, and asks them into what they were baptized, *i.e.*, into what profession or communion, into what creed or system, into what faith or religion, they had been initiated by the rite to which they had submitted."—ALEX.

"*And they said, Unto John's baptism.*" The baptism of John means here, as elsewhere, the ministry of John. To be baptized into John's baptism means here to be baptized into his ministry, to be initiated by that rite into the doctrine of repentance which he taught. John's baptism or ministry was one of repentance and preparation. This the apostle expresses in the 4th verse.

"*And when they heard this, they were baptized in the name of the Lord Jesus.*" When they heard this,—not the mere words reported in verse 4, but the *subject expounded.* According to the tenor of these words, they were baptized—not, however, by Paul himself (1 Cor. i. 14)—in the name of the Lord Jesus, into the whole fulness of the new economy, as now opened up to their believing minds.—P. C.

"*And when Paul had laid his hands upon them, the Holy Ghost came on them.*" "Paul having laid (his) hands upon them, they prophesied,—not foretold, but spoke by inspiration. The effect is similar to that described in viii. 17, x. 44, except that in the latter cases baptism had not yet been administered, and there was no imposition of hands."—ALEX.

"*And all the men were about twelve.*" There were only twelve disciples in this state of infantile intelligence and experience.

"*He departed from them, and separated the disciples, disputing daily in the school of one Tyrannus.*" His three months' disputation in the synagogue, mentioned in verse 8, did not realise the results he desired ; hence he changed the scene of his ministry, withdrawing from the synagogue, and occupies the school of one Tyrannus. Nothing is known with certainty of this Tyrannus.

"*And this continued by the space of two years,*"—that is, this school of Tyrannus, daily preaching the gospel, making in all two years and three months of evangelising work in that city on this visit.

"*So that all they which dwelt in Asia heard the word of the Lord Jesus, both Jews and Greeks.*" *All*—a natural hyperbole. It means that the gospel spread far and wide through Asia

Minor. It is probable that at this time the seven Churches addressed in the Book of Revelations were planted. During these two years and three months likewise it is supposed Paul wrote his Epistle to the Galatians and the first to the Corinthians.

"*And God wrought special miracles* (literally powers) *by the hands of Paul: so that from his body were brought unto the sick handkerchiefs or aprons, and the diseases departed from them, and the evil spirits went out of them.*" "*From his body,*" χρὼς, is the *skin, the surface of the body.* It is evident that here his power of working miracles attained its height. "*Aprons,*" with which they were girded. "*From them.*" We read of evil spirits having frequently caused apparently natural diseases.—C. E. T.

HOMILETICS.—These verses may be regarded as indicating the best method of *evangelising* a city. When Paul enters Ephesus, does he stand up at once to harangue indiscriminate multitudes on the great subjects of the gospel? Not he. He goes philosophically to work; he proceeds on a plan that is admirably wise. When he reaches a new scene of labour, before he opens his mission, he thoughtfully surveys it, inquires into its condition, endeavours to ascertain whether there are any persons in any degree prepared to accept his doctrines. Three things are to be observed in his method here at Ephesus.

I. HE BEGINS WITH THOSE WHO ARE MOST ACQUAINTED WITH HIS DOCTRINES. At the outset we read of him "finding certain disciples," amounting in all to about twelve. These men, though not in possession of the whole truth, had been baptized unto John's ministry. They knew the doctrine of repentance, and were partially acquainted with the "Lamb of God, who taketh away the sins of the world."

They had made some progress in Christian knowledge. And they were genuine in their desires and efforts to live up to the point of their intelligence. It was a wise policy in Paul to go to these men *first.* Such men would be better qualified and more disposed to listen to the gospel, and such men, when cordially won to his cause, would become his most effective coadjutors. To establish in the faith "twelve" such men would prove more conducive to the advancement of truth than to elicit the thunderous cheers of a crowded and promiscuous auditory. It is interesting to observe how he deals with these.

First, *He promptly convicts them of the deficiency of their Christianity.* He does this by two questions:—(1.) "Have ye received the Holy Ghost since ye believed?" They said unto him, "We have not so much as heard whether there be any Holy Ghost." As disciples of John, they must have known something of the old Scriptures, and the old Scriptures teemed with references to the Holy Spirit. What they meant was, that they had not heard of the Spirit in such forms as it came down on the day of Pentecost, in the rushing mighty wind and cloven tongues of fire. The apostle puts another searching question to them. (2.) "Unto what then were ye baptized?" As if he had said, Baptism in Christianity is baptism in the name of the Father, Son, and Holy Ghost. You cannot have entered fully into the Christian system if you have not heard of the Holy Spirit. Their answer explains their ignorance. " They said, Unto John's baptism." They were the disciples of John, and had not yet come fully into the school of Christ, and therefore their ignorance. It is clear from the sequel that those questions of the apostle struck deep into their souls, and made them profoundly conscious of their deficiency.

Secondly, *He effectively ministers to their advancement in divine knowledge.* " Then said Paul, John verily baptized with the baptism of repentance, saying unto the people, that they should believe on Him which should come after him, that is, on Christ Jesus." By this he teaches them—(1.) That John's ministry was *reformative.* John, disgusted with the moral rottenness of conventional Judaism, and with the hollowness of the age, retires into the wilderness to search out truth, and to commune with God. The wild scenery around him, and the calm heavens above him, deepened his impressions of the real and everlasting. With the spirit of eternal reality fresh upon his heart, he issues from the solitudes where he had thought and prayed, and met with God, and appears before the masses of his countrymen thundering the urgency of reformation down into their souls. He teaches also—(2.) That John's ministry was *introductory.* John told his vast audiences to believe on Him thatw ould come after him, that is, Christ Jesus. John did not hold himself forth as an object of faith. He founded no Church; he established no religion of his own. Those whom he baptized, he baptized into something that was to come. He pointed men to Christ, " the Lamb of God who was to take away the sins of the world."

Now this teaching of the apostle was *effective,* for we are told that when they heard this " they were baptized in the name of the Lord Jesus." This act was an expression of that higher stage of experience to which Paul's ministry had raised them. It is not said that Paul baptized them ; nor is it even said that he required them to be baptized, nor are we told that they were baptized with water at all. The true baptism is the baptism of the Spirit.

Thirdly, *He conveys the miraculous gifts of the Spirit.* " And when Paul had laid his hands upon them, the Holy Ghost came on them; and they spake with tongues, and prophesied." The patriarchs were accustomed to lay their hands on those for whom they invoked the favour of heaven. The imposition of hands in the apostle's case now signified perhaps, not merely invocation, but *impartation* also. He acted thus as the agent through which the eternal Father communicated to these converted souls miraculous endowments. Hence it would seem that no sooner were His hands laid on them than the supernatural gifts came down, and they " *spake with tongues, and prophesied.*" The gift of tongues I am disposed to regard, not as the gift of new languages, but as the gift of speaking spiritual truths with supernatural fervour and force. The Spirit did not make them linguists, but spiritual orators; made their old words burn with new meaning. New ideas will make an old language new. Let souls burn with celestial thoughts, and they will speak with "tongues of fire." This gift of speech enabled them to prophesy,—" *they pro-phesied,*"—taught. " *He that prophesieth speaketh unto men to edi-fication and exhortation and comfort.*"

Such, then, was the conduct of Paul towards these "twelve dis-ciples," who constituted the nucleus of that Ephesian Church to which he afterwards addressed one of his most magnificent epistles. He has now taken a hold upon the city.

II. HE PROCEEDS TO THOSE WHO WERE NEXT TO THE " TWELVE " IN THEIR ACQUAINTANCE WITH HIS DOCTRINES. He resorts to the synagogue, according to his custom. The Hebrew Scriptures were recognised as authorities in the synagogue, and he there could reason with the Jews on common ground.

His ministry with the Jews was—

First, *Argumentative.* "Disputing." He gave reasons to sustain his propositions. He answered objections and presented convincing proofs. He was no empty declaimer, no whining sentimentalist. He spoke to men's judgment. It was—

Secondly, *Persuasive.* "Persuading." He plied them with motives rightly to excite their affections and determine their will. It was—

Thirdly, *Indefatigable.* He was " *daily*" at the work. He was instant in season and out of season.

III. HE ULTIMATELY GOES FORTH INTO THE WIDE WORLD OF GENERAL SOCIETY. He leaves the synagogue, and goes into the school of Tyrannus. And here "for the space of two years" he continues to preach. The result, we are told, was—

First, *A wide diffusion of the gospel.* "All they that dwelt in Asia heard the word," &c. It is very probable that the whole of that province of Asia heard of the new doctrine, if not directly from the lips of Paul, from his coadjutors, and from those whom he then ad-dressed. Ephesus was the metropolis of that region, and into it the population of the provinces were constantly flowing for purposes both of commerce and of worship. Hence the doctrines of Paul would rapidly and extensively spread.

Secondly, *The ejection of evil spirits.* "And the diseases departed from them, and the evil spirits went out of them." There were in Ephesus at this time what are found in all places at all times—chil-dren of suffering. There were men there, not only afflicted with corporeal diseases, but also afflicted by demoniacal possessions. There were there men so fallen that they became the residences and the organs of infernal spirits. Paul's supernatural ministry met the case of these afflicted ones. He cured them by a miraculous agency.

His supernatural ministry was (1.) *derived.* Unlike Christ, he had not the power of working miracles natural in himself. God wrought special miracles by the hand of Paul. His supernatural ministry was (2.) *beneficent.* It was put forth, not to wound or to injure men, but to heal and bless them. His supernatural ministry was (3.) *strikingly manifest.* The mere " *handkerchiefs or aprons* " which touched his body carried with them virtue to heal the diseased and to expel the devil from the possessed.

Acts 19:13-20

PAUL'S THIRD MISSIONARY TOUR.—XIV. AT EPHESUS

1. *The seven sons of Sceva—A spurious Christianity*

" *Then certain of the vagabond Jews, exorcists, took upon them to call over them which had evil spirits the name of the Lord Jesus, saying, We adjure you by Jesus, whom Paul preacheth. And there were seven sons of one Sceva, a Jew, and chief of the priests, which did so. And the evil spirit answered and said, Jesus I know, and Paul I know ; but who are ye? And the man in whom the evil spirit was leaped on them, and overcame them,[1] and prevailed against them, so that they fled out of that house naked and wounded. And this was known to all the Jews and Greeks also dwelling at Ephesus ; and fear fell on them all, and the name of the Lord Jesus was magnified. And many of them that believed came, and confessed, and showed their deeds. Many of them also which used curious arts brought their books together, and burned them before all men : and they counted the price of them, and found it fifty thousand pieces of silver. So mightily grew the word of God and prevailed.*

EMENDATIVE RENDERING.—(1.) Overcame both of them.—ALF.

EXEGETICAL REMARKS.—" *Then certain of the vagabond Jews, exorcists.*" Περιερχομένων, *going about,* like jugglers. These were men who undertook to dispel demons by the use of spells or charms, some of which, according to Josephus, are said to have been handed down from Solomon. In the days of Christ these itinerant exorcists seem to have been very numerous.

" *They took upon them to call over them which had evil spirits the name of the Lord Jesus.*" They used the name of Jesus no doubt because they had heard Paul use it, and desired to try its efficacy for themselves.

" *And there were seven sons of one*

Sceva, a Jew, and chief of the priests, which did so." Nothing is known of this Sceva but what is mentioned here. He was a Jew, and a chief priest. His seven sons were professional wonder-workers.

" *And the evil spirit answered and said, Jesus I know, and Paul I know ; but who are ye ?*" The language strongly expresses the doctrine of demoniacal possession. The evil spirit speaks through a man.

" *And the man in whom the evil spirit was leaped on them, and overcame them.*" The demon in the man attacked the presumptuous exorcists, " overcame them," treated them with violence.

" *And fear fell on them all, and the*

name of the Lord Jesus was magnified." The discomfiture of these impostors, and the violence which the demon inflicted on them, struck a general feeling of awe and solemnity, "and the name of Jesus was magnified."

"*Many of them also which used curious arts brought their books together,*" &c. " Ephesus was a city with one dominant superstition—the worship of the goddess Diana—and with a host of smaller superstitions growing out of it. In particular, it was the head-quarters of magical art. All sorts of charms and incantations were devised and sold there. Am-ulets, which were to preserve men from bodily danger, and formulas, which were to ward off demoniacal fascination, constituted no unimportant part of the very trade of Ephesus. Mysterious symbols, called *Ephesian letters*, copied (I believe) from inscriptions on various parts of the great tutelary idol, were purchased and carried about as a safeguard to the possessor from perils ghostly and bodily. " The study of these symbols was an elaborate science, and books both numerous and costly were compiled by its professors."—Dr J. C. Vaughan.

HOMILETICS.—This fragment of apostolic history strikes us at the outset with two remarkable subjects—

First, *Man's craving for the supernatural.* The men of Ephesus seemed to feel themselves ever in a supernatural atmosphere. Under the shadow of Diana, which overhung their city, superstitions were rife, and ghostly priests and miracle-workers abounded. Man feels that he has a relation to something deeper than the hard earth beneath him, and higher than the blue vault above him. He is, in fact, a spiritual being, and has spiritual affinities and wants. He craves for that which lies beyond the realm of sense.

The other thought with which this incident strikes us at the outset is—

Secondly, *Accommodation in the work of Christian propagandism.* The apostle, on entering Ephesus, meets the *tendency* of the inhabitants for the supernatural by performing miracles himself. " And God wrought special miracles by the hands of Paul : so that from his body were brought unto the sick handkerchiefs or aprons, and the diseases departed from them, and the evil spirits went out of them." Though we are not to suppose that the apostles were always able to perform miracles, yet inasmuch as such an influx of supernatural power was now given to Paul to heal diseases and expel evil spirits, we are authorised to regard his miracles *here* as indicating the will of God that His messengers should accommodate themselves in some degree to the minds of the people to whom they are sent. Had the Ephesians possessed no faith in the miraculous, and been pure naturalists, it is not likely that Paul would have had either the capacity or the will to have achieved the marvellous. As Moses met and fought the magicians of Egypt on their own ground, confounding them by the supernatural, so Paul now confronts and confounds the deluded supernaturalists of Ephesus. He accommodates himself to their state of mind, and thus acts upon the principle which he elsewhere lays down as a guiding rule in his apostolic work : " I am made all things to all *men,* that I might by all means save some." There is a policy to be observed in Christian evangelisation. We are recommended to be "wise as serpents and harmless as doves." The policy, however, is foreign to truculency ; it is wedded to truth, and guided by rectitude.

We shall take this extraordinary narrative as an illustration of a *spurious* Christianity. It presents to us a spurious Christianity in three aspects—

I. As an impious mimicry of the divine. "Then certain of the vagabond Jews, exorcists, took upon them to call over them which had evil spirits the name of the Lord Jesus, saying, We adjure you by Jesus, whom Paul preacheth. And there were seven sons of one Sceva, a Jew, and chief of the priests, which did so."

These "*exorcists*" were to all intents and purposes spurious religionists. They were "vagabond impostors," who itinerated amongst men, professing to expel evil spirits, and to correct the moral ills of the world. The "seven sons of one Sceva, a Jew," are especially mentioned in the passage as engaged in the work. They now *imitated* Paul. They had witnessed the marvels that the apostle had wrought, and they impiously tried their hands at the same. The work they imitated was divine in two respects—

First, *In its object*. Paul had expelled *evil spirits ;* and this was the grand work of Christianity. Christ came to "destroy the works of the devil"—to free men from the ideas, desires, impulses, habitudes of evil spirits—and to fill the soul with the spirit of God. These *exorcists* attempted this work.

The work was also divine—

Secondly, *In its method*. Paul accomplished his work in the "name of Jesus Christ." He never attempted it in his own power. The name of Christ was the argument he employed, the talisman he wielded. These exorcists imitated him in this. They used the same name : "*We adjure you by Jesus, whom Paul preacheth*."

As in the case of these exorcists, a *spurious* Christianity is ever a mimicry of the divine. It has two distinctive forms in Christendom —the *naturalistic* and the *ritualistic*. The former strips the gospel of all its supernatural attributes, reduces its narrative to a common history, its hero to the dimensions of a common man. It is regarded as a system of human ideas, running above the average of human conceptions it may be, but still human. The latter makes Christianity consist mainly in sacraments, observances, priestly interventions, vestments, and such like puerilities. Even the two rites which the gospel sanctions, baptism and the Lord's Supper, are employed, not as commemorative, symbolic, and educational, but as mystic media through which saving grace flows into the soul.

Now, a spurious Christianity, in these and all other forms, does, as the "seven sons of Sceva " did, imitate the divine both in the object and the method. The object they aim at is to cast out devils, and the method they employ is, " the name of Jesus."

This narrative presents to us a spurious Christianity —

II. As the indignant scorn of hell. " And the evil spirit answered and said, Jesus I know, and Paul I know ; but who are ye ?" The evil spirit is here spoken of as a *person* distinct from the man. He belonged to another race of beings, to another world. He was one of the Satanic tribe and realm. He speaks through the organs of the man whom he possessed. His words must be taken as representing the thought and spirit of hell, to which he belonged, and from them therefore we may infer —

First, *That hell knows and respects Christ and His true followers.* " Jesus I know." Once, in the synagogue (Mark i. 23), one of the infernal host cried out to Christ, " I know thee, who Thou art, the Holy One of God." And now another, perhaps the same, exclaims, " Jesus I know." I heard of Him millenniums ago in the promise made in Eden. I know Him. He encountered and conquered our leader in the wilderness, and bruised his head upon the cross. The key of our world is at His girdle. The chain He forged by His ministry is round our spirits. He has triumphed over us. " Jesus I know." Our hell grows hotter as His trophies multiply. And "Paul I know." Once he was on our side, consenting to the death of Stephen, and zealously persecuting the followers of Christ. I know him — he is an earnest and successful preacher of the faith he once endeavoured to destroy. The devils know Christ and his followers ; and, more, they *respect* them. Not a word does this evil spirit say either against Jesus or Paul. Devils have consciences, and their consciences bind them to reverence the holy and the true. We infer —

Secondly, *That hell despises and avenges religious pretenders.* "Who are ye?" The question expresses both indignation and contempt. " Who are ye? What right have you to use that wonderful *name* at which we tremble?" Hell has no respect for its own emissaries. Those who serve it best it most loathes ; it cannot love. Not only does the evil spirit express its indignation and contempt by the question, " Who are ye?" but wreaks vengeance on the head of the pretenders. " And the man in whom the evil spirit was leaped on them, and overcame them, and prevailed against them, so that they fled out of that house naked and wounded." This strange incident suggests — (1.) *That the efforts of a spurious Christianity only increase the force of evil.* The evil spirit in the man seemed to get new strength from the efforts of the exorcists. He "*leaped*" and "*overcame.*" That which is not Christian *in spirit* can never be Christian in effect. The work in which there is not the Christian heart is an evil work, and goes to swell the tide of evil in the world. That which is not the genuine gospel gives strength to the devil.

" He that is not with me is against me." Grapes spring not from thorns. This strange incident suggests—(2.) *That Heaven employs evil to punish evil.* The evil spirit, by the divine permission, acts the officer of justice and wreaks vengeance on the heads of these religious pretenders. As a rule, God punishes wickedness by wickedness. The sinner is the tormentor of the sinner here and everywhere, now and for ever.

This narrative presents to us a spurious Christianity—

III. As DIVINELY OVERRULED FOR GOOD. We are told in verse 20, " *so mightily grew the word of God and prevailed.*" Its influence gained force, its adherents number. The narrative shows that three useful results grew out of the efforts of these exorcists.

First, *A popular excitement in favour of the true.* " And fear fell on them all." The undoubted reality and striking wonderfulness of the miracles wrought by Paul, as contrasted with the futile attempts and confounding discomfiture of his hypocritical imitators, became known, we are told, to " all the Jews and Greeks at Ephesus," and struck deep religious awe into their hearts. The marvellous intelligence spread with electric swiftness through the whole city, broke the monotony of thought, and set the Ephesian mind thinking upon the new faith. The " name of Jesus " became the dominant subject of general thought, the leading theme of general talk. Much is done for truth when the general mind of the community is excited towards it. Mental monotony is one of the most potent and prevalent obstructions to truth. There is a sad tendency in human souls to run in old ruts, or sleep on the stagnant thoughts of their ancestors. This is especially the case in religious matters. Men will tread the beaten path of thought, though vast fields of glorious truths lie around inviting them to new directions. Providence, the divine handmaid of truth, often permits, and often creates, events in a community that startle them like the blast of a thousand trumpets, and force them into new trains of thought. Sometimes, as is the case before us, the abominations of a spurious Christianity have so broken forth upon the public mind as to startle it from its slumbers, and to excite it into earnest inquiry after the truth. Witness Popery in the days of Luther. And is not modern Ritualism in the Anglican Church now beginning to act in this way ?

Another result that grew out of the efforts of these exorcists was—
Secondly, *An open profession of Christian faith.* " And many that believed came and confessed, and showed their deeds." It would seem from this that there were those in Ephesus who believed in Christ prior to this occurrence. Like Nicodemus and Joseph of Arimathea they were secret disciples. They had not sufficient moral courage to declare convictions so repugnant to popular belief, to acknowledge a religion so antagonistic to the dominant superstition.

This event, however, brought them to a crisis, so deepened their faith, and roused their conscience, as to force them to a public acknowledgment. They came out from their own companions. They renounced their old practices, they confessed their old crimes, and stood forth valiantly as adherents to the new faith.

Another result that grew out of the efforts of these exorcists was— Thirdly, *A conscientious renunciation of evil practices.* " Many of them also which used curious arts brought their books together, and burned them before all men ; and they counted the price of them, and found it fifty thousand pieces of silver." Here is a remarkable illustration of the force of conscience. The event struck the moral chords of the soul into thunder. Conscience rose from serfdom to sovereignty. The force of conscience is seen—

(1.) In the sacrifice of secular interest. The books they burnt were worth " fifty thousand pieces of silver," a price equal to two thousand pounds of our money. These books were famous in the ancient world. Books in those days were costly things, and books of this class had a special worth. They were supposed to be invested with a mystic virtue. By them, moreover, these people obtained their livelihood. Yet a sin-convicted conscience strips them of their value, and compels their destruction. The silver which Judas clutched so fondly in his hand became red hot at the glare of conscience. Conscience makes light work of trades, crafts, professions, fortunes. Let England's conscience be divinely touched, and many of her trades, crafts, and callings will go off in flame.

The force of conscience is seen—

(2.) In the outrage on historic feeling. These books were not only valuable on account of their supposed mystic virtue and their power to get gain, but there were associations connected with them that made them priceless. They had been handed down from sire to son. Many a loved one had possessed them. Many a venerated hand had touched them. They were associated with many a tender name and with many a thrilling event in life. Notwithstanding that, conscience would have them go. Prudence might have pleaded " Keep them, but do not use them any more ; or, if you do not keep them, sell them, and give the produce to the poor." No ; conscience is deaf to such pleadings, and her stern voice fulminates, " Burn them, burn them ! "

This subject urges several important facts upon our attention—

First, *That evil spirits are amongst men.* The sons of Sceva as well as Paul, Ephesus as well as Jerusalem, Paganism as well as Christianity, recognise this fact. There is something in fallen man inspiring him to actions which his conscience deprecates, and subjugating his higher nature to that which he feels to be foreign to his being, antagonistic to his interest, and not of God. The impurities, unkindnesses, carnalities, and impieties which work within him, so clash with his moral ideas, that he knows them to be importations from the evil sphere. Their presence in him implies the presence of the devil. Are not men possessed when they live the irrational, immoral, and ungodly?

Secondly, *That evil spirits must be expelled.* This is a fact also felt as truly by the "vagabond exorcists" as by Paul. Men of every school, and sect, and age, and clime, who have desired the good of their kind, have felt this, and wrought according to their respective light to rid the world of fiends. Who shall cast out the devils? Whoever does it is the philanthropist, the saviour.

Thirdly, *That evil spirits can only be expelled by genuine faith in the name of Christ.* Paul did so now because he had a real and genuine faith in *that name.* The exorcists failed because they pronounced that name, and had no faith in it. Thousands of men in Christendom this day are trying to cast out fiends from souls by pronouncing the transcendent name of Christ without any faith.

What are the "High Ritualists," as they are called, doing in our Protestant England? Trying to cast out devils. But how? By histrionic exhibition, sacerdotal badges, and curling incense. What are all these better than the "*Ephesian letters?*" This ritualistic work in the name of Christianity is an imposture—an attempt to charm away the devil by a species of clumsy magic.

Acts 19:21, 22

PAUL'S THIRD MISSIONARY TOUR.—XIV. AT EPHESUS (*continued*)

2. Christianity: the beneficence of its spirit, the aggressiveness of its disciples, and the authority among its ministers

"*After these things were ended, Paul purposed in the spirit, when he had passed through Macedonia and Achaia, to go to Jerusalem, saying, After I have been there, I must also see Rome. So he sent into Macedonia two of them that ministered unto him, Timotheus and Erastus; but he himself stayed in Asia for a season.*"

EXEGETICAL REMARKS. — "*After these things were ended.*" What things? The things respecting the exorcists, in the preceding passage.

"*Purposed in the spirit.*" This is said of a holy purpose; of a wicked purpose, "*hath conceived in thy heart,*" chap. v. 4. Paul's purpose was pleasing to the Lord; for He himself adds the promise, chap. xxiii. 11.

"*When he had passed through Macedonia and Achaia.*" The two great provinces into which Greece was divided at the Roman conquest.

"*To go to Jerusalem.*" His object in going there was to carry the collections which he had been making, or about to make, for the poor saints there. This appears from first of Corinthians, written from this place at this time (1 Cor. xvi. 1-9; Rom. xv. 25, 26, 31).

"*Saying, after I have been there, I must also see Rome.*" Jerusalem and

Rome, the two metropolitan cities, the one ecclesiastically, the other politically. " I *must* also see Rome." Why must ? It was a part of the divine plan which he was engaged in executing. The same purpose is expressed in his Epistle to the Romans, xv. 28, 29. The perfect and unstudied agreement of these passages with that before us, is one of the incidental evidences in favour of the genuiness of the inspired record. —See PALEY'S HORÆ-PAULINÆ.

" *So he sent into Macedonia two of them that ministered unto him, Timo-*

theus and Erastus." These both were his personal attendants and fellow-labourers in the gospel (1 Thess. iii. 2 ; 2 Cor. viii. 23 ; Rom. xvi. 21 ; Phil. ii. 25 ; Col. iv. 11). These were now despatched, in all probability, in order to set on foot the collection mentioned above (1 Cor. xvi. 1–10). Erastus is in all likelihood the same person mentioned in Rom. xvi. 23, and 2 Tim. iv. 20.

" *But he himself stayed in Asia for a season.*" That is, he remained in Ephesus, the capital of Asia, for some time.

HOMILETICS.—The strange things connected with the imposture of the itinerant exorcists are over. Events, like men, have their day. The loudest hurricane sinks into silence. The divine spirit of evangelism in Paul, instead of passing away with these events, wakes to new energy and effort. Paul at once projects new labour. " He purposed in the spirit," &c.

These two verses present to us several things relative to Christianity.

I. A PRACTICAL BENEFICENCE IN ITS SPIRIT. The Christians at Jerusalem, it would seem, were at this time in great temporal distress. Their distress awoke that compassion in the mind of the apostle which led to practical effort for their relief. He appeals to the churches of Macedonia, composed, no doubt, largely of Gentile converts, for their charitable contributions. The beneficence here operates with all the calm force of a natural law. There is distress in Jerusalem. Paul feels that something must be done for its relief. He communicates it to Timotheus and Erastus, and they feel the same ;—they go to the churches of Macedonia and Achaia ; they feel also, and relief comes as a matter of course. It was not a subject in those days requiring to be enforced by argument and declamation. The fact of distress evoked it. In the letter which Paul wrote from this place and at this time to the Corinthians, he indicates the order in which the collection should be made, but uses no argument to enforce the duty (1 Cor. xvi. 1-9). This is as it should be. True Christians are all members of *one* spiritual body ; and the feeling of one member should be participated in by the whole.

These two verses present—

II. AN HEROIC AGGRESSIVENESS IN ITS DISCIPLES. Paul " purposes in the spirit," not only to go to Jerusalem to relieve the temporal distresses of the saints, but to go to Rome also. " *After I have been there, I must also see Rome.*" See Rome ! What for ? Merely to see it, in order to gratify curiosity, to study the institutions and habits of a wonderful people, to enrich his experience of life, to increase his acquaintance with men and things? Not mainly, if at all so, but to carry the gospel into the heart of the imperial city. His purpose to visit Rome indicates his *belief* in three things :—

First, *That Christianity could stand the scrutiny of the most enlightened people.* He had such intellectual confidence in the system he had espoused as to invite to it the most penetrating eyes of the world. Christianity is simple enough for the mind of a child, and sublime enough for the genius of a seraph.

Secondly, *That no intellectual or social advancement can supersede the necessity of the gospel.* The apostle knew that the greatest statesmen, artists, poets, heroes, sages, lived at Rome. Yet none of them could do the work of the gospel. Nay, all of them were in urgent need of its provisions.

Thirdly, *That the work of evangelisation should have a special regard to the most influential centres of the human population.* It is evidently God's plan, in diffusing the gospel through the world, to establish it in the most influential towns, cities, peoples, great radiating centres. The apostles observed this plan. Hence Paul determines now to visit Rome. If modern missions had observed this order, they would not show to-day such miserable results for the long years of labour, the millions of money, and the sacrifice of life and talent expended. These two verses present—

III. AN OFFICIAL AUTHORITY AMONGST ITS MINISTERS. The gospel employs various men as officers to extend its influence. " When Christ ascended up on high He gave some to be apostles," &c. In these verses there are three officers, Paul, Timotheus, and Erastus, and there is a manifest subordination. Paul is the superior. He " *sent* into Macedonia two of them that ministered unto him." We have no account that he even consulted them on the subject. The authority here, which seems to have been mightily potent, was not legal or prescriptive, but simply *moral.* Paul had greater genius, scholarship, and a richer and diviner experience than Timotheus and Erastus, and hence his mere wish to them would be law. In a society where all minds are spiritually pure, the simple wish of the greatest soul is the greatest law. He only is the true ruler in the Church of God whose words and thoughts and spirit and bearing are felt to have a heavenly royalty. These two verses present—

IV. AN INCIDENTAL ARGUMENT FOR ITS GENUINENESS. In the account which is here given by Luke of Paul's purpose to visit Rome, and that which he gives himself many years afterwards, there is one of those undesigned coincidences so frequent in the New Testament, and which, properly regarded, constitute an incontrovertible argument for the truth of Christianity.

Acts 19:23-28

PAUL'S THIRD MISSIONARY TOUR.—XIV. AT EPHESUS (*continued*)

3. *The speech of Demetrius an argument for the divine power of the gospel*

"*And the same time there arose no small stir about that way. For a certain man named Demetrius, a silversmith, which made silver shrines for Diana, brought no small gain unto the craftsmen; whom he called together with the workmen of like occupation,*[1] *and said, Sirs, ye know that by this craft*[2] *we have our wealth. Moreover ye see and hear, that not alone at Ephesus, but almost throughout all Asia, this Paul hath persuaded and turned away much people, saying that they be no gods which are made with hands: so that not only this our craft is in danger to be set at nought, but also that the temple of the great goddess Diana should be despised, and her magnificence should be destroyed, whom all Asia and the world worshippeth. And when they heard these sayings, they were full of wrath, and cried out, saying, Great is Diana of the Ephesians.*"

EMENDATIVE RENDERINGS.—(1.) Employment. (2.) Employment.

EXEGETICAL REMARKS.—"*And the same time there arose no small stir about that way.*" "That way" is Christianity. Christianity is a way to a certain kind of thinking, loving, and living. The cause of the "stir" about that way is revealed below.

"*For a certain man, named Demetrius, a silversmith, which made silver shrines for Diana, brought no small gain to the craftsmen.*" Diana was one of the twelve superior divinities, of which the Roman poet Ennius gave a list in the following couplet :—

"Juno, Vesta, Minerva, Ceres, Diana, Venus, Mars,
Mercurius, Jovis, Neptunus, Vulcanus, Apollo."

She was adored as Luna, or the moon in heaven, Diana on the earth, and Hecate or Proserpine in Hades. She was the goddess of hunting, of travelling, of chastity, of childbirth, of enchantment, &c., and was worshipped in different countries under different names, and different qualities were ascribed to her. But, at Ephesus, she was represented with a great number of breasts, and regarded as Nature, the mother of mankind. Thus, one of the inscriptions on an image of Diana was "Nature, full of varied creatures, and mother of all things." —LIV. Now, the temple of this goddess was so vast and beautiful as to be ranked among the seven wonders of the world. "Pliny tells us that it was 425 feet long and 220 in breadth, and that it was adorned with 100 columns each 60 feet high, 27 of which were curiously carved, and the rest polished. It occupied 220 years in building. All Asia contributed to its erection, and 127 magnificent columns were bestowed on it by as many kings. Its altar was furnished by the famous Praxitetes, and Apelles contributed a portrait of Alexander the Great. Little silver models of the temple, with a goddess enshrined in them, were made for sale, and sold in such quantity as to afford profitable work for many hands." — EADIE. This Demetrius, the silversmith, carried on a prosperous trade in these silver shrines, and engaged a large number of the men of Ephesus in his employment.

" Whom he called together, with the workmen of like occupation." Work-men—lit., *craftsmen.* There were both τεχνῖται, *artificers* of a higher class, and ἐργαται, *workmen.*—C. E. T.

"So that not only this our craft is in danger to be set at nought, but also that the temple of the great goddess Diana should be despised." Eventually even the temple itself and the great goddess Artemis would be counted for nothing.—ALF. This crafty Demetrius appeals to just the two elements in his audience which would tend to excite in them their self-ishness and superstition. Hence when they heard these sayings they were wroth, "and cried out, saying Great is Diana of the Ephesians."

HOMILETICS.—The *meeting* which Demetrius now addressed was a very remarkable one. It gives us an insight into three things—

First, *Into the perversion of human handicraft.* Here is an assembly of men whose inventive genius and skilful labour were employed in the manufacturing of things offensive to Heaven and debasing to souls; things to foster in man the superstition which has ever been at once his disgrace and his curse. Alas! this perversion of human handicraft has ever been lamentably common. Much of the industry of the world is employed in fabricating that which is bad in itself—beverages which brutalise the reason, arts which inflame the lusts, and horrid implements of torture and death. So corrupt is the *commerce* of the world, that men traffic in the bad, and build up fortunes by selling the productions of wickedness.

This meeting gives us an insight—

Secondly, *Into the force of the mercantile spirit.* What was it that brought these men together, and inspired Demetrius, the speaker, to exert himself to the utmost to arrest the progress of the truth in Ephesus? Cupidity. "Our craft is in danger to be set at nought." This it was which roused him and his artisans to oppose the gospel. This fired them with enthusiasm. This mercenary spirit is ever the unceasing antagonist to the truth. Preach the divine doctrine of human liberty to the slaveholders who traffic in their species; preach the divine doctrine of peace to those who get their living in providing deadly weapons for the field of battle; preach the doctrine of spiritual independency to men who derive their revenue and influence by arrogating dominion over men's faith; and in all these cases you will have the mercenary spirit rising and thundering in full tide against you.

This meeting gives us an insight—

Thirdly, *Into the revolutionary power of the gospel.* It was the revolution which the gospel was effecting in Ephesus that roused their fears. "So mightily grew the Word of God and prevailed," that many of the magicians who drove a lucrative trade in their imposture, "brought their books together, and burned them before all men." Demetrius felt now that the very foundations of idolatry were being sapped by the doctrines of the apostle. "Moreover ye see and hear," &c. Here is a public declaration of the wonderful success of the gospel at Ephesus. We shall take this declaration as *an argument for its divine power.* There were four things connected with its triumph in this city, which, taken together, will amount to an argument of considerable force in favour of the position that it is " *the power of God.*"

I. The triumphs of the gospel at Ephesus, according to Demetrius, involved a RELIGIOUS REVOLUTION. The mercenary orator alleges that Paul had succeeded in turning " away much people, saying, that they be no gods which were made with hands." The revolution effected in the minds of the people was that which involved the abandonment of those objects which had gathered about them the strongest and the profoundest affection of their nature ;—their *gods.*

First, Such a change as this *religious* change is always the most *radical.* *The god of the soul,* whatever it is, is in all cases the object of the soul's supreme affection. It is that which gathers about it and centres in itself more of the sympathies of human nature than any other object in existence. This paramount affection is, in sooth, the very fount and root of man's life. What man loves most, moves and controls him in all the activities of his being ; it is at once the engine that propels, and the rudder that guides his bark on the sea of active life. Out of this supreme love—which is, without figure, the moral heart of a man—are the " issues of life." Change this in a man, and you change the whole current of the river of his existence; you reverse the action of all the wheels in the machinery of his being. The man in fact becomes, to use Scripture phraseology, a "new birth," a "new creation," a "new man." Such is the *radical* change which the gospel is designed and fitted to effect. This is its grand mission; where it has not wrought this revolution, whatever else it has accomplished, it has failed of its purpose.

Secondly, Such a change as this *religious* change, is always the most *difficult.* The strongest attachments in human nature, whenever they are developed, are the *religious.* Men who *feel* that they have gods, will hold to them with all the tenacity of their being. Where this religious attachment exists, men have ever been ready to give thei ɔproperty, their wives, their children, their very lives for their goᴀs. Religiousness is the soil in which the soul strikes its deepest roots. This grand tree in God's spiritual forest will part sooner far with every leaf and branch, and even bark itself, than with its rootings ; it will hold on to these till every fibre quivers in the chilly blast of death. Even the bigoted proselytiser in this age, who seeks to turn men from other sects to his own, be it from synagogue to church, from Popery to Protestantism, or from Conformity to Dissent, knows, to the vexation of his narrow soul, the *difficulty* of effecting the slightest change in men religiously. But the change he aims at is not a thousandth part as difficult as the change the gospel aims to achieve ; the change, not of a man's creed or sect, but the change of his deepest inward life.

There were circumstances, it should be remembered, connected with the age and sphere in which the gospel was first introduced which contributed not a little to augment the natural difficulty. The old religions to which the Jew and the heathen were attached, had a grand history, a gorgeous aspect, and a world-wide popularity, which gave them an immense influence over their devotees. The Sanhedrim of Jerusalem, and the legions of Rome, stood in terrible antagonism to the man who would dare abandon the old religion, and threatened death to him who would venture to promote such a new and hostile system as the gospel.

Having thus noticed the radicalness and difficulty of the work involved in the revolution which the gospel set itself to accomplish, we observe :—

II. The triumphs of the gospel at Ephesus, according to Demetrius, were UNDENIABLE FACTS. Demetrius says, " Ye see and hear, that not alone at Ephesus, but almost throughout all Asia, this Paul hath persuaded and turned away much people, saying that they be no gods which are made with hands." He suggests three kinds of evidence :—

First, The evidence of *personal observation :* " Ye see," &c. The men he addressed had ocular demonstration of the fact. They had seen with their own eyes the change which the gospel had wrought among the men of Ephesus. They had seen the change which had come over not a few of the men and women in the city to whom Paul had preached. They had renounced their old associations, their old habits, their old ideas, their old religion, and adopted a new course of life,—a course which was attractive at once by its strangeness and injurious bearing upon their own craft. They *saw* these changes ; there was no denying them. Such ocular evidence of the revolutionary power of the gospel most men in Christendom are privileged to possess. Who has not known the drunkard, the blasphemer, the licentious, and the selfish, become, by the power of the gospel, temperate, reverent, chaste, and generous ? Thank God, such instances occur now—would they were multiplied a millionfold !

Another kind of evidence suggested by Demetrius is—

Secondly, The evidence of *general testimony :* " Ye *hear.*" Some of their own townsmen, perhaps, whom they were bound to believe, had told of changes effected upon persons within their particular sphere of observation. Such evidence, if the witnesses are intellectually and morally competent, is nearly as conclusive as the former, and is often available in cases where the former is not. Most of our knowledge is derived from this source. What we have *seen* is but a fraction compared with what we have *heard.* Our personal vision has only given us the area of a few acres, and the range of a few years; general testimony gives us the universe and the ages. From such a source we learn much of the brilliant achievements of the gospel in the days that are gone. "We have heard with our ears, O God; our fathers have told us what work Thou didst in their days, in the times of old." From the testimony of Paul we are assured that in Colosse, Ephesus, Rome, and Corinth, wonderful religious revolutions had been effected by the gospel he had preached. His success in Corinth, the most corrupt and dissolute city of the old East, may fairly be taken as a specimen of his achievements elsewhere. After enumerating some of the classes of sinners that dwelt in that metropolis of iniquity, such as "fornicators, idolators, adulterers, thieves, covetous, drunkards, revilers, extortioners," he says, "such were some of you; but ye were washed, but ye were sanctified, but ye were justified in the name of the Lord Jesus, and in the Spirit of our God." Clement, one of the Church fathers, who died in Rome in the year 102, confirms, in a letter which he wrote thirty years after the Church was established at Corinth by Paul, this testimony of the apostle as to the great and radical change effected by his preaching in that city. Others of the Christian fathers furnish abundant testimony of the wonderful changes which the gospel effected through the whole Roman empire during the first three centuries of the Christian era.

Another kind of evidence suggested by Demetrius is—

Thirdly, The evidence of *avowed enemies*. Demetrius was an *avowed enemy*, and yet here he publicly affirms the triumphs of the gospel. Could he have denied, or even have ignored its effects, rest assured he would have done so. But so patent and influential were the changes wrought in the city, that he was bound thus publicly to avow them. The wonderful revolutions which Christianity has effected in the character and lives of thousands, in every age, are so manifest and influential, that hostile historians, such as Gibbon, are bound to chronicle them as the fountains of striking epochs.

From such evidence, then, as is suggested by Demetrius, and which abounds in this age and land of ours, all are forced to admit the radical changes which Christianity has effected in the conduct and spirit of multitudes of mankind. These triumphs of the gospel stand forth amidst the flowing events of human history in the eighteen centuries that are gone, with an existence as undeniable, and a brilliancy as marked, as the fixed stars of night amidst the floating clouds and the passing meteors of our sky.

III. The triumphs of the gospel at Ephesus, according to Demetrius, were CONFINED TO NO PARTICULAR TYPE OF MEN. Demetrius affirms that the religious revolutions effected by Paul's preaching were widely spread. "Not alone at Ephesus, but almost throughout all Asia." Though there might be in this broad statement something of that exaggeration which often marks the utterances of an impassioned speaker, or something of that civic egotism which often deludes a man with the notion that his own little country is the world—we are warranted in accepting it as conveying the idea that the influence was not confined to any particular type of men, natural or social. The Jew and the Gentile, the refined Greek and the brave Roman, the tradesman, the artist, the poet, the sage, the statesman, the warrior—some of all types became the subjects of its renovating power. On the day of Pentecost the representatives, perhaps, of all races became the subjects of the change. By the end of the second century, Tertullian, addressing the Roman magistrates, speaking in the name of the Christians, said, "We are but of yesterday, and we have filled up every place—towns, islands, castles, boroughs, councils, camps, tribes, wards, palace, senate, forum; we have left you nothing but your temples." And, in modern times, not a type of men has yet been discovered on whom the gospel has not effected its religious change. The dreamy Hindoo, the degraded Hottentot, the stalwart sons of Polynesia, the African, the Asiatic, and European races, all have furnished examples of its regenerating power. This fact lends not a little force, we think, to the argument. Had the religious changes which the gospel effected been confined to any particular type of men, they might have been ascribed rather to the natural peculiarities of the subjects than to the divine energy of the system. It might have been said that these men experienced its influence because of the deficiency of this faculty, or the predominance of that; the keenness of this sensibility, or the bluntness of that. But since men of all types are undeniably susceptible of its renovating power, its energy is more manifestly divine. The Maker of man is the Author of the system, since it can work out in him the change which is the grand aim of its mission. The fact is, that man, the world over, and the ages through, needs that which the gospel alone can supply. He needs an object of supreme love that can satisfy his conscience, and become the happy centre of his soul ; he needs a reconciliation to that Deity from whom he feels himself estranged by the wickedness of his life ; he needs the hope of a happy future beyond the grave ; he needs some plan of social unity that shall bind all the opposing sections of the race in the bonds of a loving brotherhood. To all these deep needs of humanity the gospel appeals by ministering to them that which meets them in every point, and up to their fullest demand. It satisfies the *desire of nations ;* it responds to the cry of the race ; it has "good tidings of great joy" for "all people."

IV. The triumphs of the gospel at Ephesus, according to Demetrius were ACHIEVED BY THE AGENCY OF MAN AS MAN. How does Demetrius say that the gospel worked this revolution at Ephesus, and throughout all Asia ? Here are his words :—"This *Paul* hath persuaded and turned away much people, saying that they be no gods which are made with hands." "This Paul;" not these angels; not these magistrates backed by victorious legions; but this *Paul,* a poor Jew, a tent-maker. How did he do it? By wielding civil authority? No. All political power was against him. By miraculous instrumentality? He was, it is true, endowed with this power, but the great moral results of his ministry are not ascribed to miraculous agency. Here is the agency he employs:—He "*hath persuaded.*" He used arguments to convince their understandings, and plied them with motives to influence their wills. He brought the light of his own ideas upon their intellect, and the warmth of his own sympathies upon their hearts. His words, as they fell upon their ears, bore with them not only a truth to bring their judgments to his conclusion, but a love to bring their hearts into unison with his own. This is the noblest of works. He who wins one soul to the true and the right, achieves a conquest that throws the most brilliant victories of the Cæsars, Alexanders, and Napoleons into contempt. The suasive energy is truth spoken in love; it is a sword forged in heaven; its victories bless humanity, gladden the universe, and encircle the conqueror with an imperishable renown.

There is much in connexion with the agency of Paul at Ephesus which impresses us with divine power.

First, *We discover divine power in his daring to enter such a place as Ephesus.* Ephesus was one of the greatest cities of the ancient world. In the days of Paul it was the capital of Asia. The temple of Diana was the great thing in this great city; it was the great attraction; it was to the population the means of livelihood as well as the scene of their devotions. Foreigners from a distance were constantly pouring into the city in order to worship the far-famed goddess in her majestic fane. Thus the *mercenary* united with the *superstitious* to bind men's hearts to Diana. What valour, more than human, must have enabled Paul to have entered such a city as this to proclaim a doctrine that would strike at once against the worldly interests and the religious predilections of the population! I know of no courage in the history of worldly men approaching that which this Paul displays in carrying his unpopular message into such places as Antioch, Corinth, Athens, Ephesus, Rome, the head-quarters of idolatry, sensualism, and wickedness in all its forms. This heroism of his can only be explained by the fact that the power was of God and not of him.

Secondly, *We discover divine power in what, by his simple agency, he accomplished there.* Just in proportion to the simplicity of the agency which this man employs is the manifestness of the divine power in the wonders that he achieved. "We have this treasure in earthen vessels, that the excellency of the power may be of God, and not of man." Such agency as that which Paul employed at Ephesus, an agency of suasion, is that by which the gospel, in every age, has accomplished its grand results. It spreads, not by the sword of the warrior, the enactments of statesmen, or the edicts of monarchs, but by the simple persuasion of its disciples and its messengers. By their words and spirit, and conduct, and life, they persuade the ungodly world to turn from its idols ; and thus the work goes on. Does not this simple agency by which the gospel succeeds attest its divinity? Had it worked out its revolutions by some grandly imposing instrumentality, it might have been concluded that the instrumentality did the work.

Brothers, duly weigh all the circumstances which the words of Demetrius at Ephesus suggest in relation to the triumphs of the gospel, in order to deepen and strengthen your faith in the almighti-ness of its power. Mark well the nature of the change it effects. It is *religious*, it is a revolution in the supreme forces of the soul. Other changes, more external and less vital, it has effected on a grand scale in the world's history, and for these we may indeed claim for it a power nothing less than divine. Great intellectual, domestic, social, ecclesiastical, and political revolutions it has wrought in human his-tory. It has sapped the foundations of pagan systems, and they are tottering to the fall. In its brightness the Crescent has become dim; it has stripped priestcraft of its mask, and thrown light into the spectral realms of superstition. Systems that once held the world in awe it has exploded. It has stabbed autocracy to the heart, and the death-throes of despotism are everywhere seen. The seeds of liberty it has scattered over the two hemispheres. It has given laws to the ruling empires of the world. The first geniuses of the race have been kindled into splendour with its themes. It has coloured the literature of the world, and tempered the spirit of the age. Its symbol is the chief ornament of Christendom ; it is hung in the halls of science and the palaces of sovereigns ; it is interwoven into the thoughts and hearts, into the hopes and fears, into the designs and doings, and general experience of that race of men who are inevitably destined to become the civil, intellectual, and moral mas-ters of the world.

But these revolutions are but shadows of that *religious* revolution in men's souls of which we have been speaking, and which it is its great aim and glory to accomplish. It is in this deep and inner revolution of spirit-life and destiny that I see not only the ful-filment of its mission, but the demonstration of its divinity. In this its divine power beams out in a soul-inspiring radiance upon our spirits. Deeply do we need a strong faith in the divine power of this old gospel. Its genuine *religious* revolutions are now, alas ! so rare that we are in danger of regarding it as something feeble, if not effete. Oh, for an agency to wield it like Paul— an agency which, by its intelligence, prayerfulness, and self-sacri-ficing benevolence, shall bring out its latent renovating force ! He supplies the world with the strongest argument for the divinity of the gospel, who is most successful in bringing out the soul-renovat-ing force which sleeps within it as the electric fire of God.

Acts 19:29-41

PAUL'S THIRD MISSIONARY TOUR.—XIV. AT EPHESUS (*continued*)

4. *The statesman-like address of the town-clerk*

" *And the whole*[1] *city was filled with confusion : and having caught Gaius and Aristarchus, men of Macedonia, Paul's companions in travel, they rushed with one accord into the theatre. And when Paul would have entered in unto the people, the disciples suffered him not. And certain of the chief of Asia, which were his friends, sent unto him, desiring him that he would not adventure himself into the theatre. Some, therefore cried one thing, and some another : for the assembly was confused ; and the more part knew not wherefore they were come together. And they drew Alexander out of the multitude,[2] the Jews putting him forward. And Alexander beckoned with the hand, and would have made his defence unto the people. But when they knew that he was a Jew, all with one voice, about the space of two hours, cried out, Great is Diana of the Ephesians. And when the town-clerk had appeased the people,[3] he said, Ye men of Ephesus, what man is there that knoweth not how that the city of the Ephesians is a worshipper[4] of the great goddess[5] Diana and of the image which fell down from Jupiter ? Seeing then that these things cannot be spoken against, ye ought to be quiet, and to do nothing rashly. For ye have brought hither these men, which are neither robbers of churches,[6] nor yet blasphemers of your[7] goddess. Wherefore if Demetrius, and the craftsmen which are with him, have a matter against any man, the law is open,[8] and there are deputies ; let them implead one another. But if ye inquire anything concerning other matters, it shall be determined in a[9] lawful assembly. For we are in danger to be called in question for this day's uproar, there being no cause whereby we may give an account of this concourse. And when he had thus spoken, he dismissed the assembly.*"

EMENDATIVE RENDERINGS.—(1.) Omit this word. (2.) Some of the multitude drew forth Alexander. (3.) Multitude. (4.) Temple-keeper. (5.) Omit this word. (6.) Temples. (7.) Our. (8.) Court days are held. (9.) The.—ALF.; TISCH.

EXEGETICAL REMARKS.—" *Having caught Gaius and Aristarchus, men of Macedonia, Paul's companions in travel, they rushed with one accord into the theatre.*" The original order of the sentence is " they rushed with one accord into the theatre, seeing Gaius," &c. The name Gaius was common among the Romans. It is not therefore certain whether here it designates the same person as mentioned elsewhere. The probability, however, is that he is the same person as mentioned in Rom. xvi. 23 ; 1 Cor. iv. 13. Aristarchus is in all

probability the same who afterwards attended Paul to Palestine, and shared in his imprisonment (Col. iv. 10, Phil. xxiv.) The " *theatre* " was not only the amphitheatre for dramatic spectacles and games, but was also the gathering place of the people to hold assemblies, hear harangues, and judge cases. These edifices were of immense size, and would hold many thousands. They were without roofs, and the seats gradually sloped up from the centre, on every side, so that those on the back were raised very high.—LIV.

"*And when Paul would have entered in unto the people, the disciples suffered him not.*" Paul's desire was to go into the theatre, where the mob had gathered, in order to make his defence, to rescue his beloved companions. "Paul fought with beasts at Ephesus" (1 Cor. xv. 32). Brave man! No military valour was equal to his. He was now anxious to rush into this theatre of wild beasts to defend Gaius and Aristarchus, and to denounce the worship of Diana.

"*And certain of the chief of Asia, which were his friends,*" &c. These Asiarchs were not civil magistrates nor priests in the ordinary sense, although their office was connected with religion. They were annually chosen in the cities of the province to conduct the sacrificial services and public games in honour of Diana. They derived their title from the name of the province, as the corresponding officers in Cyprus, Syria, and Lydia were called Cypriarchs, Syriarchs, Lydiarchs, &c. —ALEX. These Asiarchs seem to have been Paul's friends, for they desired "*that he would not adventure himself into the theatre.*"

"*Some, therefore, cried one thing and some another : for the assembly was confused ; and the more part knew not wherefore they were come together.*" This verse contains a graphic description of a mob : some shouting one thing, and some another ; confusion presiding, and most not even knowing why they were assembled, but having been borne away by a popular sympathy.—LIV.

"*And they drew Alexander out of the multitude, the Jews putting him forward.*" This man seems to have been the very coppersmith of whom Paul speaks 2 Tim. iv. 14. He was of the same trade as Demetrius. The Jews put him forward to speak, no doubt in their defence.

"*But when they knew that he was a Jew, all with one voice, about the space of two hours, cried out, Great is Diana of the Ephesians.*" Having known him as a Jew, they would not hear him. It would seem that he persisted in his attempt to address the tumultuous mob, for they continued their shouting for "*about the space of two hours.*"

"*And when the town-clerk had appeased the people,*" &c. The "*town-clerk*" does not represent here the same humble office as that which it represents amongst us. It represents a magistrate of high dignity and authority. The words would have been better rendered, "the town-clerk having stilled the crowd," &c.

"*Ye men of Ephesus, what man is there that knoweth not how that the city of the Ephesians is a worshipper of the great goddess Diana, and of the image which fell down from Jupiter ?*" "*What man is there.*"—Paul would have spoken otherwise. (But the raving multitude was unworthy of his preaching.) Nevertheless, the town-clerk's language is ambiguous. He may have thus spoken either from persuasion or from expediency, for in ver. 37 he says, not *our*, but *your* goddess. "*Of the Ephesians.*"—By the repetition of the proper name their renown is signified. "*Is.*"—At that very time the Ephesians were proud of this distinction. On this account there was a great gathering of men to these sacred games. "*Worshipper.*"—The Pernethians adored Hercules ; other nations, other gods ; the Ephesians, Artemis (Diana). "*Which fell down from Jupiter.*" —They supposed that their image fell from heaven, *from Jupiter.*— C. E. T.

"*Seeing that these things cannot be spoken against, ye ought to be quiet, and to do nothing rashly.*" Like a truly legal man, he urges that such was notoriously the constitution and fixed character of the city, with which its very existence was all but bound up. Did they suppose that all this was going to be overturned by a set of itinerant orators ? Ridiculous. What did they mean, then, by raising such a stir ?"—P. C.

"*For ye have brought hither these men, which are neither robbers of churches, nor yet blasphemers of your goddess.*" Noble testimony this to the character of the apostle. They were neither temple-plunderers, sacrilegious persons, nor the blasphemers of Diana. The apostle, in preaching about idolatry, ever studiously avoided insulting those whom he addressed.

Wherefore, if Demetrius and the craftsmen which are with him, have a matter against any man, the law is open.' The meaning is, if they have done anything illegal, the assizes or court-days are being held ; take the matter into court before the constituted authorities.

" *And there are deputies ;* " literally pro-consuls. " *Let them implead one another ;*" that is, plead against each other, have the thing legally discussed.

HOMILETICS.—The address of the town-clerk is so wise in its statesmanship, and so successful in its issue, that it is worth our while to look a little carefully into it. The speech of Demetrius had roused the city into wild confusion. What made his speech so powerful and so popular ? Simply the congruity of its spirit with the selfish feelings and the idolatrous prejudices of an audience deeply sunk in moral corruption. The philosophy of an eloquent speech is to be found in the sympathy of the audience with its animating spirit and leading opinions. So long as the majority of the world are depraved, the most popular speakers will be ever those most in sympathy with the current thought and feeling of the masses. Demetrius was intensely mercenary ; so were the craftsmen he addressed ; and hence his words kindled them into flame. The excitement ran like an electric spark through the city. From every house and shop and street people rush forth. They gather into groups, and then into a dense crowd. The dense, lawless mass throbs with one pulse, and heaves with one passion. But few in the mass could tell *why* they are there. A mystic feeling has drawn them together, and they are prepared for anything. "The majority knew not why they had come together :" a most truthful description this of all mobs. What is to be done ? The peace of the city is broken ; precious lives are in danger ; Gaius and Aristarchus are already in their hands ; St Paul is in imminent peril ; property is jeopardised. What is to be done ? Who shall disperse that senseless, lawless, infuriated multitude, and restore the city once more to peace and security ? This is the question which now pressed upon the peaceable citizens. Happily there is one man equal to the task. He makes the effort, and succeeds. Let us examine his speech.

In analysing it we discover four telling elements—*conciliation, conscience, counsel,* and *caution.*

I. THERE IS CONCILIATION. He allays their passions at the outset by the intimation that the goddess of whose honour they were so anxious was of such unquestionable and universally admitted dignity as rendered all their solicitude perfectly unnecessary. " Ye men of Ephesus " (the usual Greek formula of popular address), " what man is there that knoweth not how that the city of the Ephesians is a worshipper (and a temple-keeper) of the great goddess Diana, and of the image which fell down from Jupiter." As if he had said, These poor Jews cannot in any way weaken the authority, limit the influence, or dim the glory of Diana. You may as well be anxious about the radiance of the quenchless stars as to be anxious about Diana. "Seeing then that these things cannot be spoken against, ye ought to be quiet, and to do nothing rashly." As there is not the slightest occasion for all this tumult, *be quiet ; act as men, not as children.*

II. THERE IS CONSCIENCE. He speaks out the *just* as well as the politic. He reminds them that Paul and his companions had not been guilty either of profaning the temple or calumniating the goddess. "For ye have brought hither these men, which are neither robbers of churches, nor yet blasphemers of your goddess." They were neither sacrilegious nor insolent in relation to their religion. They took nothing from the temple with their hands, nor did they with their lips outrage the feelings of Diana's worshippers. This is a high testimony from a learned and dignified pagan to the conduct of the apostles as the promoters of a new faith. It shows—

First, *That they exhibited a respectful deference to the feelings of the errorists.*

Secondly, *That they set forth God's truth rather than battled with men's opinions.*

Thirdly, *That their language was kind and not reproachful.*

Would that all promoters of truth had imitated the example of the apostles in this respect. We thank this grand old chancellor of Ephesus for such a testimony to apostolic conduct as this.

III. THERE IS COUNSEL. He administers wise advice. He tells them that should there be one of their number who had committed any wrong against them, the court of justice was open, and they could make an appeal to the proconsul. "Wherefore, if Demetrius and the craftsmen which are with him have a matter against any man, the law is open, and there are deputies : let them implead one another." As if he had said, If any of you have a charge of wrong against any of these men, go into the court of justice with them, and have the case fairly and impartially tried. And if these men have not committed any wrong against Demetrius and the craftsmen, but have offended in some other matter of which the court of justice will not take cognisance,—matters in relation to opinions or tastes, or social usage—let such matters be settled "*in a lawful assembly.*" This assembly is an unlawful one. It is disorderly, tumultuous, the creature of unreasoning passion ; let there be an assembly of men lawfully called together to settle the matter in dispute.

IV. THERE IS CAUTION. In conclusion, he gives them a word of warning. He tells them that such an uproar exposed the city of Ephesus to the displeasure of the Romans. "We are in danger to be called in question for this day's uproar, there being no cause whereby we may give an account of this concourse." His speech was successful. Right reason can calm the tide of tumultuous passion, Reason! thou canst conquer the world, if thou wouldst only rise from thy lethargy, shake off thy trammels of prejudice, come into the "true light," and speak out honestly the rational things.

Acts 20:1-6

PAUL'S RETURN FROM HIS THIRD MISSIONARY TOUR.—I. HIS DEPART-
URE FROM EPHESUS, AND HIS ARRIVAL AT TROAS

" And after the uproar was ceased, Paul called unto him the disciples, and embraced them, and departed for to go into Macedonia. And when he had gone over those parts, and had given them much exhortation, he came into Greece, and there abode three months. And when the Jews laid wait for him, as he was about to sail into Syria, he purposed to return through Macedonia. And there accompanied him into Asia, Sopater of Berea;[1] and of the Thessalonians, Aristarchus and Secundus; and Gaius of Derbe, and Timotheus; and of Asia, Tychicus and Trophimus. These, going before, tarried for us at Troas. And we[2] sailed away from Philippi after the days of unleavened bread, and came unto them to Troas in five days; where we abode seven days."

EMENDATIVE RENDERINGS.—(1.) Sopater, the son of Pyrrhus, a Beræan. (2.) We ourselves.—ALF.

EXEGETICAL REMARKS.—" Departed for to go into Macedonia," &c. &c. Paul now fulfils his purpose of proceeding to Macedonia and Greece (chap. xix. 21). He seems, however, to have been hurried away earlier than he intended by the uproar created by Demetrius and his partisans. Before departing, he calls together the " disciples, and embraced them." He saluted them with parting expressions of kindness (Rom. xvi. 6 ; 1 Cor. xvi. 20 ; 2 Cor. xiii. 12 ; 1 Thes. v. 26). " And when he had gone over those parts." The parts of the country in and near Macedonia. Probably he went to Macedonia through Troas, expecting to find Titus (2 Cor. ii. 12). But not finding him there, by himself to Philippi, Thessalonica, &c., and then returned to Greece proper. " And had given them much exhort-

ation, he came into Greece." " Into Greece," of which Athens was the capital. While in Macedonia, it would seem from 2 Cor. vii. 5–7, he was in great anxiety and trouble, but was at length comforted by the coming of Titus, who brought him intelligence of the liberal collections of the churches of Greece for the poor saints at Jerusalem. It is supposed that the Second Epistle to the Corinthians, was written during this time in Macedonia, and sent to them by Titus. " And there abode three months." The greater part of these three months was probably spent at Corinth, where he is supposed at this time to have written the Epistle to the Romans, which he sent by Phœbe, a member of the church at Cenchrea (Rom. xvi. 1). Some rough work he anticipated on his arrival at Corinth (2 Cor. x. 1-8 ; xiii. 1-10). In his first visit he had spent two years in Corinth ; he now spends three months here, making it his head-quarters, visiting the surrounding churches, and promoting the collection for the poor Christians in Palestine.

"*And when the Jews laid wait for him, as he was about to sail into Syria, he purposed to return to Macedonia.*" His first intention was to go by sea to Syria, reach Antioch, which would complete his third missionary tour, and thence proceed to Jerusalem with the sums of charity he had collected in Macedonia and Achaia; but intelligence of contemplated murder reached him, so he changes his plan. "*The Jews laid wait for him.*" Though we are not informed of the exact nature of the plot, it was no doubt a conspiracy against his life. Several conspiracies had been thus formed against him (Acts ix. 23 ; 2 Cor. xi. 32 ; Acts xxiii. 2). Though a man of invincible courage, yet knowing his life was in danger, and that he could avoid the danger without sacrifice of principle, detriment to his reputation, or injury to his usefulness, he does so. He changes his route, retraces his steps by land northwards, and finds himself once more among his beloved friends at Philippi.

"*And there accompanied him into Asia, Sopater of Berea,*" &c. These names are elsewhere mentioned. Sopater is called (Rom. xvi. 21) Sosipater, who was a kinsman of Paul. Tychicus held a high place in Paul's esteem and love (Eph. i. 21, 22) ; Timotheus is well known. These men did not attend him, it would seem, from Achaia to Macedonia, but went with him to Asia, having gone before him and joined him at Troas. The presence of these seven men, on this occasion, has been variously explained and understood. It was evidently not fortuitous, but according to previous arrangement. That they simply attended Paul to aid him in his missionary work at this point is peculiarly improbable, for he is about to leave this field of labour, and to have less need of such assistance than before. That they accompanied him as a body-guard, to protect him from the violence or machinations of the Jews, seems inconsistent with the fact recorded in the next verse, that at the very outset of his journey, and before he left the country where his life had been in danger, they were sent before him, and were separated from him at least five days, and possibly much longer. Perhaps the most felicitous conjecture which has been proposed is that these men went as representatives of the Gentile churches lately founded in the presence of the mother church ; and the apostles—three representing Europe and four Asia, two of the latter the interior, and two the western coast of Asia Minor. If they were also bearers of a general contribution from the Gentile churches for the poor saints at Jerusalem, as some infer from certain passages in Paul's epistles written about this time or not long before (1 Cor. xvi. 1-4 ; 2 Cor. vii. 1-5 ; Rom. xv. 25-28), the whole number (seven) may have had some reference to that of the almoners, or deacons in the mother church itself.

"*These, going before, tarried for us at Troas.*" "For us." This is an incidental mention of Luke, the historian, whose name has not appeared since chap. xvi. 17.

"*And we sailed away from Philippi after the days of unleavened bread.*" "The impression is, not that either the whole or part of them had gone from Corinth or Cenchrea to Troas, but that all had sailed from Philippi, and that Paul and the writer of the Acts were soon to follow. The writer, by the way, could not have been Timothy, as he was among those who had gone on before ; nor Silas, as, from all that we know of him, he was now at Jerusalem."—BINNEY. "*After the days of unleavened bread,*" means, after the seven days of the passover. The journey was accomplished in "*five days.*" Paul, when he crossed it on a former occasion, did it in two days (chap. xvi. 11, 12). The navigation, however, of the Ægean Sea being uncertain, they were hindered, probably, by contrary winds.

HOMILETICS.—These verses bring under our notice some points worthy of attention.

I. THE FRAGMENTARY CHARACTER OF GOSPEL HISTORY. The few sentences before us extend over a period of nearly twelve months. During those twelvemonths, what wonderful things had occurred in the history of Paul! What privations endured, what perils braved, what discourses preached, what discussions conducted, what souls converted, what labours accomplished ! Why, the events of his life during his journey from Ephesus to Troas would no doubt have filled volumes. " In our day," says a modern writer, " we have biographies of two, four, six, and even eight volumes. The late Mr Simeon of Cambridge left directions in his will, that if any life was written of him, it was not to extend beyond one volume. The direction was obeyed, and obeyed to the letter, but in that only, for though his friends got his biography into one volume, that one volume was thick enough to have made two or three!" We almost wish there had been journalists in those days to have chronicled all the items in Paul's wonderful life.

II. THE MYSTERY OF DIFFICULTIES IN CONNECTION WITH DUTY. Antecendently one might have thought that the great Father of man would have made clear and sunny the path of those of His children who endeavoured with all their souls to carry out His will ; that a man like Paul would have had no thorns in his path, no clouds in his sky. But the fact is otherwise. Though no man was ever engaged in a higher mission than Paul, nor threw into it diviner impulses, few ever had a rougher or a darker path. Read his own sketch of his own difficulties and dangers : " In labours more abundant, in stripes above measure, in prisons more frequent, in deaths oft. Of the Jews five times received I forty *stripes* save one. Thrice was I beaten with rods, once was I stoned, thrice I suffered shipwreck, a night and a day I have been in the deep," &c., &c. Herein is mystery : impenetrable, confounding, sometimes soul-crushing mystery. We must patiently await the great explaining day.

III. THE UNCONQUERABLENESS OF A CHRIST-LIKE LOVE. Mark it in Paul's remaining at Ephesus until the *"uproar '* was ceased. He did not abandon the vessel in the storm, but, like a brave captain, remained with it until it was secure in the haven. Mark it in the affectionate spirit with which he withdrew from Ephesus. Instead of quitting the scene with the fire of indignation flaming within him, on account of the insults and injuries he had received, he calls the disciples together and *"embraced them."* No amount of trial, danger, opposition, or disappointment could cause Paul to relinquish his blessed mission. His Christ-like love bore his soul triumphantly above all. " The love of Christ constraineth me," he says. His love dared the prisoner's chains and the martyr's tortures.

Acts 20:7-12

PAUL'S RETURN FROM HIS THIRD MISSIONARY TOUR.—II. HIS MINISTRY
AT TROAS.

Religious institutions

" And upon the first day of the week, when the disciples[1] came together to
break bread, Paul preached unto them, ready to depart on the morrow ; and
continued his speech until midnight. And there were many lights in the
upper chamber where they[2] were gathered together. And there sat in a window[3] a certain young man named Eutychus, being fallen into a deep sleep :
and as Paul was long preaching, he sank down with sleep, and fell down
from the third loft, and was taken up dead. And Paul went down, and
fell on him, and, embracing him, said, Trouble not yourselves ; for his life is
in him. When he therefore was come up again, and had broken bread,[4]
and eaten, and talked a long while, even till break of day, so he departed.
And they brought the young man alive, and were not a little comforted."

EMENDATIVE RENDERINGS.—(1.) We. (2.) We. (3.) On the window-seat. (4.)
The bread.—ALF.

EXEGETICAL REMARKS.—"*And upon
the first day of the week.*" This day
appears to have been used by the
apostles instead of the Jews' Sabbath,
being the day of the resurrection of
Jesus, for the purpose of worship and
communion (1 Cor. xvi. ; Rev. i. 10).
This is the first trace of observance of
Sunday in the history of the Church,
and the allusion here to it shows that
its observance had become customary.
   "*To break bread.*" This means to
celebrate the Lord's supper.
   "*Paul preached unto them.*"
" Preached " — the word elsewhere
translated reasoned and disputed. It
primarily signifies colloquial discourse
or conversation.
   "*And there were many lights in the
upper chamber where they were gathered
together.*" Jowet, a modern missionary in that region, remarks, "that the
very great plenty of oil in that neighbourhood would enable them to afford
many lights." And again, " On entering my host's door, we found the
ground-floor entirely used as a store ;
it is filled with large barrels of oil,—
the produce of the rich country for

many miles round." He further observes, in relation to the " upper
chamber," that " the rooms on the
second floor are very ordinary, and
occupied by the family for their daily
use ; but on the next story all their
expenses is lavished, and in such an
apartment Paul was invited to preach
his parting discourse,—a secluded,
spacious, and commodious room."
   "*And there sat in a window a certain young man named Eutychus, being
fallen into a deep sleep ; and as Paul
was long preaching, he sunk down with
sleep, and fell down from the third loft,
and was taken up dead.*" Young man
— Παῖς, boy, ver. 12. *Being fallen* . . .
he fell down, Gr. καταφερομενος . . . κα-
τενεχθείς. Participles of the same verb,
but of different tenses : ἤνεγκον expresses more than φέρω. Sleep surprised him as he sat : being *borne*
down by sleep, he fell. (*On the window-seat*). In the East the apertures
for windows were without glass, and
sometimes without shutters.—C. E. T.
   "*And Paul went down, and fell on
him, and, embracing him, said, Trouble
not yourselves ; for his life is in him.*"

"*Fell on.*" Christ did not use this action ; but Elijah, Elisha, and Paul did. "*Trouble not yourselves.*" In the gravest affairs, undue agitation was forbidden : Exod. xiv. 13 ; 1 Kings vi. 7 ; Isa. viii. 6. The temple was built without noise. In war, tranquillity was required of the people. "*Is in him.*" Paul speaks with a view of removing sudden terror ; we must not therefore take his words in too literal a sense. He does not say *as yet* or *again* ; but simply states that the youth is alive, as if he had not fallen. The miracle was patent.—C. E. T.

"*When he therefore was come up again, and had broken bread.*" "*Had broken bread.*" This was Paul's special act on departing. It was distinct from that which had occurred the day previous (ver. 7).—"*Talked.*" More familiarly after the solemn address spoken of in ver. 9. "*So.*" Without the intervention of any repose. "*They brought the young man alive.*" They brought, not *carried ;* he was not at all enfeebled. "*Alive.*" Not even through this accident did they receive any damage from Paul (2 Cor. vii. 9).—C. E. T.

HOMILETICS.—Paul, sailing from Philippi across the Ægean Sea, reaches Troas, a city of Phrygia, on the Hellespont, between Troy north and Asia south. In this region the events recorded in the "Iliad" of Homer are supposed to have occurred. The verses now before us, briefly sketching as they do his work at Troas, and recording the striking event connected with Eutychus, present to us some remarks connected with religious institutions.

We have here—

I. RELIGIOUS INSTITUTIONS SANCTIONED BY CHRISTIANITY. "And upon the first day of the week, when the disciples came together to break bread, Paul preached unto them," &c. Here are three *religious institutions* sanctioned by Paul—

First, "*The first day of the week.*" This is the first account we have of the Christian Church observing this day. From this time down to the present, "the first day of the week" has been observed for religious purposes (1 Cor. xvi. 2 ; Rev. i. 10). It is a wise ordination that the day on which the resurrection of Christ took place —the grand fact of redemption—should be thus employed.

Secondly, *The Lord's Supper.* The disciples came together to "break bread." This evidently refers to the Eucharistic bread (Acts ii. 46). This is an ordinance which Christ himself instituted "the night on which He was betrayed." It has been observed by the Church through all ages to the present hour.

Thirdly, *The preaching of the gospel.* "Paul *preached* unto them." Preaching is a *divine* institution. Christ gave the commission after His resurrection, and after His ascension He sent down His Spirit to qualify men for the work. In meeting together, therefore, on "the first day of the week, and in breaking bread" to commemorate the sufferings of Christ, and in preaching the gospel, we are doing what the apostles sanctioned by their example, and what the good have attended to during eighteen centuries.

We have here—

II. RELIGIOUS INSTITUTIONS INTRUDING ON THE CLAIMS OF NATURE. " Paul continued his speech until midnight." Night is the time for rest, not for labour. The body, exhausted with the activities of the day, requires the reinvigorating repose of night. Hence, as Paul was pushing the religious services beyond their proper limits, one of his hearers (Eutychus) fell asleep, "and fell down, and was taken up dead." Many reasons would perhaps justify Paul in thus protracting his discourse. The people were very ignorant on the most vital of all questions. He had much to communicate. His heart was full of sympathy, and he had to depart on the morrow. Still, as he thus intruded on the claims of nature, a result occurred which marked such *long services* as an evil. It is remarkable that no fault is found with Eutychus. He could not help it. Perhaps his nature was overtasked ; his spirit might have been willing, but his flesh was weak, and he gave way.

Religious institutions intrude on the claims of nature—

First, *When they are employed for the purposes of inordinate excitement.* The history of what was called " the revival" in Ireland and elsewhere a few years ago furnishes many sad examples.

They intrude on the claims of nature—

Secondly, *When they are protracted beyond a certain period.* Long sermons are a sin against nature. More than half the sermons preached are somnific. Were there many in every congregation who, like Eutychus, " sat in a window" during the service, instead of in seats well secured, what accidental deaths would be reported in our journals ! Many modern preachers, under such circumstances, would make the sexton busy.

We have here—

III. RELIGIOUS INSTITUTIONS ASSOCIATED WITH SUPERNATURAL POWER. "And Paul went down, and fell on him, and, embracing him, said, Trouble not. yourselves, for his life is in him." This was an undoubted miracle, performed in somewhat the same manner as that which Elisha wrought on the Shunammite's son (2 Kings iv. 33-35). This miracle may be regarded as emblematic of that divine power of restoration which is associated with the preaching of the gospel.

First, Man is the *organ* of it. God could have raised Eutychus directly without the intervention of Paul or of any secondary instrument. But He worked through Paul ; so in quickening dead sinners now, He employs the ministry of the word.

Secondly, Man is the *subject* of it. Eutychus was raised. God brings the supernatural power of restoration to bear upon man through man.

Acts 20:13-21

PAUL'S RETURN FROM HIS THIRD MISSIONARY TOUR.—III. HIS FAREWELL ADDRESS AT MILETUS

1. *His conscious fidelity in the discharge of his ministry*

"And we went before to ship, and sailed unto Assos, there intending to take in Paul : for so had he appointed, minding himself to go afoot. And when he met with us at Assos, we took him in, and came to Mitylene. And we sailed thence, and came the next day over against Chios; and the next day we arrived at[1] Samos, and tarried at Trogyllium ; and the next day we came to Miletus. For Paul had determined to sail by Ephesus, because he would not[2] spend the time in Asia ; for he hasted, if it were posble for him, to be at Jerusalem the day of Pentecost. And from Miletus he sent to Ephesus, and called the elders of the church. And when they were come to him, he said unto them, Ye know, from the first day that I came into Asia, after what manner I have been[3] with you at all seasons, serving the Lord with all humility of mind, and with many[4] tears, and temptations, which befell me by the lying in wait of the Jews; and how I kept back nothing that was profitable unto you, but have showed you, and have taught you publicly, and from house to house, testifying both to the Jews, and also to the Greeks, repentance towards God, and faith towards our Lord Jesus Christ." [5]

EMENDATIVE RENDERINGS.—(1.) Put into. (2.) That he might not have to. (3.) Was. (4.) Omit this word. (5.) Omit this word.—ALF.

EXEGETICAL REMARKS.—"He leaves Troas, where, as we have already seen, he had met the disciples on " *the first day of the week,*" " *broke bread,*" and preached to them until midnight. Under his discourse there, Eutychus, sinking to a sleep, falls down, and is taken up dead, and Paul raises him to life again by a miracle. The apostle does not start with his companions in the ship, for the historian says, " *And we went before in a ship to Assos, there intending to take in Paul.*" The " *we*" here includes Luke, and the persons mentioned in vers. 4 and 5. Paul prefers walking from Troas to Assos, which was a small seaport upon the Ægean, about twenty miles. Why Paul preferred going alone and walking this distance does not appear ; perhaps he preferred solitude, or desired to visit some of the inhabitants on the way and talk to them about salvation. The ship reaches Assos, Paul enters it, and they first reach Mitylene, an island between thirty and forty miles distant from Assos. The next day they reach Chios, about forty miles still farther on, and the next day Samos, an island about fifty miles south-west of Chios, the birthplace of Pythagoras. They tarried a few hours at Trogyllium, a town opposite Samos, a few miles distant, and the next day sailed to Miletus, a seaport upon the coast of Ionia, where Thales, one of the seven wise men of Greece, was born, and where there is a famous temple to Apollo, about thirty miles east of Ephesus. Paul was anxious to reach Jerusalem to attend the feast of Pentecost, and he had no desire to visit Ephesus again.

" *Paul had determined to sail by Ephesus.*" " *By*" does not mean that he intended to take it on his route, but to pass it by and take a nearer direction. Yet the ship, either by the arrangementsof the captain, or by an unexpected accident, or by the wish of Paul and his companions, remains for some time at Miletus. While there, Paul sends to Ephesus, about thirty miles distant, requesting the elders of the Church to visit him. They come and he delivers to them one of the most touching, fruitful, and solemn farewell discourses that was ever delivered. We are not told who the elders were who visited him on this occasion, nor are we told their number. They were, however, the guardians and representatives of the Church at Ephesus, and Paul's sermon to them must be regarded as addressed to all the disciples at Ephesus and the regions round about.

HOMILETICS.—Let us mark the way in which he takes his leave of them in this farewell discourse. *He leaves them with a consciousness of having rightly discharged his mission.* " *Ye know from the first day that I came into Asia, after what manner I have been with you at all seasons,*" &c., &c. " *Ye know,*" as if he said, You have had opportunities during the three years I have been at Ephesus of knowing me thoroughly, and you know how I have lived and laboured amongst you. " *Ye know,*" notwithstanding the malignant calumnies that have been put in circulation by those " *beasts*" with whom " *I fought at Ephesus.*" How does he say that he discharged his mission amongst them ?

I. HUMBLY : "With all humility of mind." Though endowed with miraculous power, and specially called to his high mission, he carried himself amongst them with great humility. Paul was a humble man. His humility was not the lowliness of a mean spirit. It was that moral sobriety of a soul that felt the solemnity of life, the greatness of God, and the responsibility of its mission. " Unto me, who am the least of all saints," &c.

II. TENDERLY : " With many tears." Paul was a man of tender spirit. He often wept. Not, however, on account of his own personal sufferings or trials. These he bore with a magnanimous spirit. These he gloried in. His tears were tears of compassion for perishing souls, and tears of love for Christ ; tears of regret at the inconsistency of those who were the professed disciples of his Lord and Master, " Of whom I tell you weeping, they are the enemies of the cross of Christ."

III. FULLY—" How I kept back nothing that was profitable unto you." He did not temporise. He did not present to them so much truth as would be agreeable to their prejudices, and reserve whatever was unpopular ; but whatever truth was right for them to know, or necessary to their salvation, whether they liked it or disliked it, he pressed upon their attention ; he " kept nothing back."

IV. INDEFATIGABLY—" Have taught you publicly from house to

house." He was not content with delivering discourses in the public assembly, but went from house to house amongst them : he was "instant in season and out of season."

V. UNRESTRICTEDLY—"From house to house." He did not confine his ministry to any class. He preached to man as man everywhere. "Jews, also to the Greeks."

VI. EVANGELICALLY—What was the grand theme of his discourses ? "Repentance towards God and faith in our Lord Jesus Christ." Repentance means change of mind in relation to God. Faith in the Lord Jesus Christ means practical confidence in Him as the true Messiah, the Saviour of the world, the Mediator between God and man. Paul urged a change of mind in relation to God as the great thing needed, and enforced the only means of attaining it.

Acts 20:22-24

PAUL'S RETURN FROM HIS THIRD MISSIONARY TOUR.—III. HIS
FAREWELL ADDRESS AT MILETUS (*continued*)

2. *The spirit of duty*

" *And now, behold, I go bound in the spirit unto Jerusalem, not knowing the things that shall befall me there: save that the Holy Ghost witnesseth in every city, saying that bonds and afflictions abide me. But none of these things move me, neither count I my life dear unto myself, so that I might finish my course with joy,[1] and the ministry which I have received of the Lord Jesus, to testify the gospel of the grace of God.*"

EMENDATIVE RENDERING.—(1.) But I hold my life of no account, nor precious to me, in comparison of finishing my course, and the ministry which I received from the Lord Jesus, to complete my testimony of the gospel of the grace of God.—ALF.

EXEGETICAL REMARKS.—" *Now, behold, I go bound in the spirit.*" Paul knew that he would be bound in body at Jerusalem. He already felt himself bound in mind, bound by a sense of obligation, impelled by a feeling of duty.

" *Not knowing the things that shall befall me there.*" He knew that trials severe and terrible awaited him in Jerusalem. But of their particular character he was ignorant.

" *Save that the Holy Ghost witnesseth in every city, saying that bonds and afflictions abide me.*" (Chap. ix. 16.) As he passed from city to city, he was constantly admonished by divine warnings that he would be persecuted and imprisoned at his arrival at Jerusalem. Chap. xxiv. 4–11 illustrates this. The faith which sustained him and his associates is vividly portrayed, 2 Cor. iv. 8–18.

" *But none of these things move me,*"

neither count I my life dear unto myself, so that I might finish my course with joy, and the ministry which I have received of the Lord Jesus, to testify the gospel of the grace of God." There is much difference of reading here. The best text is, ἀλλ' οὐδένος λόγου ποιοῦμαι τὴν ψυχὴν τιμίαν ἐμαυτῷ ὡς τελειῶσαι, &c. —Tisch., Alf., Mey., *i.e.*, literally, *of no word* (account) *esteem I my life worthy for myself; that I may finish,*

&c.—Mey. "*None*"—No misfortune. "*Unto myself*"—As far as I am concerned (chap. xxi. 13; Phil. i. 21, 22). The denial of self. "*So that*"—Lit. *so*, that is, do I think it so precious? "*Finish*"—He did finish his course after a long space (2 Tim. iv. 7, 8). "*Course*" —A speedy one. "*Of the grace*"—Of the New Testament. "*Of God*"—God's name is very forcibly repeated in ver. 25-27.—C. E. T.

HOMILETICS.—We take the subject of these words to be—*the spirit of duty*, and the words suggest three things in relation to this spirit :—

I. IT IS A BINDING SPIRIT : "I go bound in the spirit unto Jerusalem." What does this mean? Simply impelled in mind, urged by the force of his convictions of obligation to Christ. He was not urged to visit Jerusalem merely to renew old associations; the imperious sense of duty impelled him. The binding does not imply reluctance; it does not mean that he would not go if he could help it. To be bound by the spirit of duty is to be self-bound, is to be free. "I go bound in spirit." I *must* go. The necessities of souls, the claims of Christ, demand my presence in Jerusalem. The experience he expresses here is the same that Peter and John had when they said, "We cannot but speak," &c., the same that he had at other times when he said, "Necessity is laid upon me." The divine spirit of duty, when it possesses a man, is all-commanding. Everything must yield to it. It will listen to no excuses based upon inconveniences, or apparent inexpediences. It makes me feel that I must be *faithful*, I must be *honest*, I must be *spiritual*, I must *teach*, I must *do good*. Spiritual Christianity is a sublime despotism —a despotism, however, in which the soul finds its highest freedom.

II. IT IS A HEROIC SPIRIT. This spirit raised the apostle above all fear. It inspired him with an undaunted courage.

First, *He was not afraid of threatened persecutions*. Although he seems to have been ignorant of the exact kind and measure of persecution and suffering, he was certain by a divine *presentiment* that terrible afflictions awaited him there : "Not knowing the things that shall befall me there : save that the Holy Ghost witnesseth in every city, saying that bonds and afflictions abide me."

Though he was in darkness as to the particulars of the suffering, he was in certainty as to the fact. The afflictions he did meet with there are narrated in the next chapter. But all those afflictions as they loomed before him now in the future depressed him not. He looked at them with a fearless heart : "None of these things move me."

Secondly, *He was not afraid of death itself:* "Neither count I

my life dear unto myself." Duty was dearer to him than life.
Life is a *precious* thing, felt to be more precious to most than worlds.
" Skin for skin, yea, all that a man hath, will he give for his life."
Yet duty is far more precious to a Christ-inspired soul. Like Christ,
the Chief of all noble souls, the truly good have ever been ready to
sacrifice life for duty. The sacrifice of our mortal life for duty conduces in every way to our well-being. The sacrifice of duty for the
preservation of life conduces to our degradation and our ruin.

III. IT IS AN ABIDING SPIRIT : " So that I might finish my course
with joy, and the ministry which I have received of the Lord Jesus,
to testify the gospel of the grace of God." Here we have the grand
object to which he made everything subservient—namely, the faithful prosecution of his mission. These words give us a view—
First, *Of the life of man.* (1.) Paul regarded life as a *course.* " My
course." The allusion is to the Grecian race. (2 Tim. iv. 7, 1 Cor.
ix. 24.) It is in truth, a race, measured, so long and no longer—
withal very short. (2.) He regarded it as a course which *would have
an end*—"finished." There is an end to this course. (3.) He regarded
life as a course that *should* be finished with " *joy*"—not with terror,
amazement and anguish, but "joy." It is Heaven's wish that we
should all meet with a happy end. The words give us a view—
Secondly, *Of the life of a minister.* (1.) The life of a minister is
that of a most responsible *trustee.* He has "received from the Lord
Jesus the gospel of the grace of God." It is committed to his
charge. (2.) The life of a minister is that of a solemn *witness* " to
testify the gospel." He is to bear witness to the world of the sovereign and unbounded love of God to sinners as manifested in the
gospel ; he is to testify the gospel by life as well as death, spirit as
well as speech.
The spirit of duty constrains a man to make all things in life subservient to the prosecution of his mission during his course on earth.
It is an *abiding* spirit. Paul did not feel it binding him at one
period of life, or in one class of circumstances, but in all ; through the
whole course, and through the whole ministry. The divine spirit of
duty does not enter a man as a passing visitant ; it takes up its abode
in the soul as the sole and permanent monarch.

Acts 20:25-27

PAUL'S RETURN FROM HIS THIRD MISSIONARY TOUR.—III. HIS
FAREWELL ADDRESS AT MILETUS (*continued*)

3. *Ministerial responsibility*

" *And now, behold, I know that ye all, among whom I have gone preaching the kingdom of God,*[1] *shall see my face no more. Wherefore I take you to record*[2] *this day, that I am pure from the blood of all men. For I have not shunned to declare unto you all the counsel of God.*"

EMENDATIVE RENDERINGS.—(1.) Omit these two words. (2.) Witness.

EXEGETICAL REMARKS.—" *I know that ye all among whom I have gone preaching the kingdom of God, shall see my face no more.*" " *I know*"—This expresses not absolute certainty, but assured persuasion. " *Shall see my face no more*"—He was bound on a dangerous journey, and it was probable that he would never see them again. Whether he afterwards visited Ephesus or not is a matter of doubtful inference, though critics have conjectured that he re-visited this region. See Phil. i. 25–27 ; ii. 24 ; Philemon 22.

" *Wherefore I take you to record this day that I am pure from the blood of all men.*" " *Wherefore*"—A deduction from ver. 20. " *I take you to record*"—

Your conscience will bear me witness. This is the meaning of the middle voice. " *This day*"—This phrase has explanatory force. " *Pure*"— This should be the chief anxiety on the part of those who are bidding farewell.—C. E. T.

" *For I have not shunned to declare unto you all the counsel of God.*" " *Have not shunned to declare*"—This indicated how he had fulfilled his high duty, viz., by a full and fearless proclamation of the truth, and the whole truth of the gospel, even that unpalatable doctrine, that Gentiles, without submitting to the yoke of Moses, were entitled to all the privileges and promises of the Christian faith.

HOMILETICS.—Great is the responsibility of a minister of the gospel. His charge is the weightiest that Heaven imposes on mortals. He touches the primal springs of human action, and influences the destinies of souls. The verses before us present ministerial responsibility in three aspects :—

I. As DEEPLY FELT. Paul always felt it, but never more so than now, in addressing his audience with the certainty that it was the last time. " And now, behold, I know that ye all among whom I have gone preaching the kingdom of God, shall see my face no more." Every Sunday there are ministers who preach their *last* sermons to the people, who ascend their pulpits, announce their text for the last time, *but they do not know it.* If they knew it, how overwhelmed they would be with the sense of their responsibility.

They would feel—

First, It is the last time, and we must correct any wrong impressions that we may have made upon these people.

Secondly, It is the last time, and we must bring forward every vital truth that may have been too much overlooked.

Thirdly, It is the last time, and we must use every argument in our power to effect the conversion of souls. Whatever correction is to be made, must be made now, or never. Whatever deficiency is to be supplied, must be done now, or never. Whatever argument is yet to be employed, must be employed now, or never. "They shall see my face no more." This is just what Paul felt now. As he spoke, he felt that the men he addressed would never see him any more in the flesh. Ought we not ever to preach as dying men to dying men?

II. As TERRIBLY SOLEMN. "Wherefore I take you to record this day, that I am pure from the blood of all men." Two solemn facts will throw light on this wonderful utterance :—

First, *That preaching may involve the contraction of enormous guilt, either on the part of the preacher, the hearer, or both.* The preacher who makes an unfaithful representation of the gospel, contracts guilt in every discourse ; and the hearer who rejects the overtures of redemptive mercy, increases his condemnation. "Son of man, I have made thee a watchman unto the house of Israel : therefore hear the word at my mouth, and give them warning from me. When I say unto the wicked, Thou shalt surely die ; and thou givest him not warning, nor speakest to warn the wicked from his wicked way, to save his life ; the same wicked man shall die in his iniquity ; but his blood will I require at thine hand. Yet if thou warn the wicked, and he turn not from his wickedness, nor from his wicked way, he shall die in his iniquity ; but thou hast delivered thy soul."

Secondly, *That the preacher who rightly discharges his mission clears himself of any participation in the guilt that may have been contracted.* "I am pure" (clear), says Paul, "from the blood of all." Why? Here is the reason. "For I have not shunned to declare unto you all the counsel of God." He kept nothing back that was profitable. In ministering the truth he did not study what was agreeable to their prejudice, whether it was palatable or popular, but fearlessly proclaimed what was essential to their salvation. If there was blood therefore, anywhere, it was not on him. He was clean.

III. As CONSCIOUSLY DISCHARGED. The apostle had the sublime consciousness that he had faithfully discharged his duty amongst them. He looks them in the eye, and he appeals to them. "Wherefore I take you to record"—I summon you as witnesses this day—"that I am pure from the blood of all men." "This day." An expression very strong in the original, meaning *this very day.*

This very day, when I stand before you for the last time, when I preach to you this final discourse, when I feel myself in the presence of the Eternal Judge—this very day.

What a blessed ministerial consciousness this is! Blessed is the preacher that can always retire from public services with this exalted feeling.

Acts 20:28-31

PAUL'S RETURN FROM HIS THIRD MISSIONARY TOUR.—III. HIS FAREWELL ADDRESS AT MILETUS (*continued*)

4. *The Church of God*

" *Take heed therefore unto yourselves, and to all the flock over which the Holy Ghost hath made you overseers,*[1] *to feed the church of God, which he hath purchased with his own blood. For*[2] *I know this,*[3] *that after my departing shall grievous wolves enter in among you, not sparing the flock. Also of your own selves shall men arise, speaking perverse things, to draw away disciples*[4] *after them. Therefore watch, and remember, that, by the space of three years, I ceased not to warn every one night and day with tears.*"

EMENDATIVE RENDERINGS.—(1.) Bishops. (2.) Omit this word. (3.) Omit this word. (4.) The disciples.—ALF.

EXEGETICAL REMARKS.—"*Take heed therefore unto yourselves.*" First, to yourselves, and then to the flock. Personal goodness is a primary qualification for spiritual usefulness.

"*Over which the Holy Ghost hath made you overseers.*" The original is *bishops*, as translated,· Phil. i. 1 ; 1 Tim. iii. 2 ; Titus i. 7 ; 1 Pet. ii. 25. These officers were identical in the first church with presbyters or elders. All the orders of modern episcopacy and papacy were not found in the first Churches, and they are without scriptural sanction.

"*The church of God, which he hath purchased with his own blood.*" The true reading is, τὴν ἐκκλησίαν τοῦ κυρίου, *the Church of the Lord.*— TISCH., MEY., DE W., &c. ALF. defends the *common* text, *of God*, but on insufficient grounds. Many, with the Sclavonic version, τὴν

ἐκκλησίαν κυρίου καὶ Θεοῦ, *the Church of the Lord and of God.* Paul often uses the phrase, *the Church of God*, and in the Epistles to the Thessalonians, Corinthians, Galatians, Timothy ; never *the Church of the Lord.* He never uses the expression *Lord and God*, interposing the particle *and.* We must *therefore* read *the Church of God* ; although if in this passage Paul said *Church of the Lord*, according to the parallelism of the Old Testament, it would be *the Church of Jehovah, which he hath purchased.* It, therefore, is a most precious flock. "*His own*"—For it is the blood of the Son of God (1 John i. 7). —C. E. T.

"*For I know this, that after my departing shall grievous wolves enter in among you, not sparing the flock.*" Two classes of coming enemies are here announced, the one more external to themselves, the other bred in the bosom of their own community. Both were to be teachers, but the one "grievous wolves, not sparing," *i.e.*, making a prey of "the flock;" the other simply sectarian, "perverters" of the truth, with the view of drawing a party after them. Perhaps the one pointed to that subtle poison of Oriental Gnosticism, which we know to have very early infected the Asiatic Churches; the other to such Judaising tendencies as we know to have troubled nearly all the early Churches. See the Epistles to the Ephesians, Colossians, and Timothy; also those to the seven Churches of Asia (chaps. ii., iii.)— P. C.

HOMILETICS.—These verses lead us to look upon the *Church of God* in three or four striking lights—

I. AS A SOCIETY OF PRICELESS VALUE. *"It is a flock,"* a name given to the Church of the Old Testament (Isa. xl. 11, lxiii. 11 ; Jer. xiii. 17, xxiii. 2, xxxi. 10 ; Ezek. xxxiv. 3 ; Micah vii. 14, &c. &c.) A name, too, which Christ also applied to His disciples (Luke xii. 32.) It was a favourite figure with the apostle Peter (1 Pet. v. 2, 3.) This flock, or assemblage of human souls, is incalculably precious. Why? It is said to have been purchased with *" the blood of God."* Instead of the words *" of God,"* it should have been *of the Lord,* referring to the Lord Jesus Christ. No idea can be more repugnant, either to our intelligence or intuitions, than the idea that the absolute Spirit who fills immensity could shed blood. The true reading is, as maintained by most of the best critics, *the Church of the Lord, which He hath purchased with His own blood.* The idea is, the Church is the product of Christ's vicarious sacrifice. Other societies exist amongst men, to some extent irrespective of Christ's mediation—such as scientific societies, political societies, commercial societies, &c. But the society called the Church is acquired by the sacrifice of Jesus Christ. Had He not died, it never would have been. Of all, therefore, the societies on earth, none so precious as this—the Church. The anthem of this Church in heaven is, " Unto Him that washed us in His own blood," &c.

Another light in which these verses lead us to look upon the the Church of God is—

II. AS A SOCIETY WELL GUARDED. This flock, this society, is by the Holy Ghost put in charge of holy men.

First, *It is put in charge of earthly shepherds.* " Take heed therefore unto yourselves, and to all the flock." There is here (1.) Self-vigilance : " Take heed, therefore, unto yourselves." The spiritual overseer or the shepherd must take care of himself first. He must enlighten his own judgment, discipline his own heart, and train his own soul into Christian virtues first. He must save himself before he can save others (1 Tim. iv. 14). (2.) Church vigilance. " And to all the flock." They are to take heed of the Church, to instruct, guide, guard it, and in every way promote its spiritual welfare.

Secondly, *The earthly shepherds are appointed by the Holy*

Ghost. He hath made the overseers; He calls and qualifies men for this high office, makes them true bishops. All ministers are bishops in the New Testament sense. There were now several bishops in the Church at Ephesus. The Church, then, is a society divinely guarded. It has human shepherds, and also the Divine Shepherd, who is the Bishop of souls. Another light in which these verses lead us to look upon the Church of God is—

III. AS A SOCIETY ASSAILED BY ENEMIES : " For I know this, that after my departing shall grievous wolves enter in among you, not sparing the flock." The apostle refers to two classes of enemies—
First, *Those who would come to them from without.* Those who would "enter in among" them—worldly men, malignant persecutors, "grievous wolves."
Secondly, *Those who would spring up from within.* "Also of your own selves shall men arise speaking perverse things," &c. From some of the professed members such will arise. The greatest enemies of the Church perhaps have sprung from its own bosom.

IV. AS A SOCIETY DEMANDING THE UTMOST ATTENTION. "Therefore watch, and remember that, by the space of three years, I ceased not to warn every one night and day with tears." Paul holds out his own conduct as an example and motive. His labour for three years amongst them, was—
First, *Incessant :* "Night and day." He was instant in season and out of season.
Secondly, *Earnest :* "With tears." It does not mean, of course, that he was always weeping, but that he was always animated by the tenderest affection.

Acts 20:32

PAUL'S RETURN FROM HIS THIRD MISSIONARY TOUR.—III. HIS
FAREWELL ADDRESS AT MILETUS (*continued*)

5. *The well-being of man*

" *And now, brethren,*[1] *I commend you to God, and to the word of his grace, which is able to build you up, and to give you an inheritance among all them which are sanctified.*"

EMENDATIVE RENDERING.—(1.) Omit this word.

EXEGETICAL REMARKS. "*I commend you to God.*" "*To God,*" the almighty conservator of His people. And to "*the word of His grace,*" that message of His pure grace (ver. 24), by the faith of which He keeps us (1 Pet. i. 5). Which, *i.e.*, God, is able to build you up, and to give you an inheritance, &c. Observe how salvation—not only in its *initial stages* of pardon and regeneration, but in all its *subsequent stages* of "up-building," even to its *consummation* in the final inheritance—is here ascribed to the "ability" of God to bestow it, as in Rom. xvi. 25 ; Eph. iii. 20 ; particularly Jude 24 ; and of 2 Tim. i. 12, where *the same thing is ascribed to Christ.* "*Among all them which are sanctified*" — Sanctification is here viewed as the final character and condition of the heirs of glory, regarded as one saved company.— P. C.

HOMILETICS.—These words lead us to consider two things :—

I. THE CONDITIONS ON WHICH MAN'S WELL-BEING DEPENDS. What are the great conditions of a soul's well-being? The text leads us to answer—

First, *Moral edification.* The apostle desired his hearers now to be built up—"build you up." The word "*build*" is architectural. A house is built by *plan, and by slow degrees.* Paul often speaks of the moral culture of the soul under the figure of building (1 Cor. iii. 10, xii. 14 ; Eph. ii. 20 ; Col. ii. 7). The soul in depravity is a temple in ruins. It requires to be built up upon the true foundation, and according to the true plan.

The other condition is—

Secondly, *Holy fellowship.* "Give you an inheritance among all them which are sanctified." The language implies—(1.) That there are *sanctified ones.* Who are they? All who have truly believed in Christ, and experienced a moral renewal of the Holy Ghost are *partially* sanctified. There are millions who are *perfectly* sanctified in heaven. John saw them—"a multitude which no man could number." Yonder in those bright heavens there are millions of "just men made perfect." (2.) That an inheritance with those sanctified ones is the grand *desideratum.* The sanctified ones dwell in social harmony, in unclouded intelligence, in spiritual purity, in divine fellowship. What higher good is there than to have an inheritance with them, to be with them, to dwell with them ? not as a matter of sufferance, but as a matter of right ; not temporarily, but for ever ; to "sit down with Abraham, Isaac, and Jacob," and with the great and good of all ages ?

These words lead us to consider—

II. THE AGENCY BY WHICH THESE CONDITIONS ARE ATTAINED. By what power can man attain this moral edification, this holy fellowship ? The text answers the question : "I commend you to God and to the word of His grace, which is able to build you up."

Two remarks are suggested—

First, *It works by the gospel:* "The Word of His grace." This is a beautiful designation of the gospel. The gospel is God's *Word* —God's Word of *grace*. It originates in grace, it reveals grace, it produces grace. This gospel is equal to the work ; it "is able to build you up." The gospel is no weak instrument. It is the power of God unto salvation. It is by this gospel that the great God is building up souls, and preparing them "for an inheritance among all them that are sanctified ! "

Secondly, *It is secured by prayer :* "And now, brethren, I commend you to God." How did he commend them to God ? In earnest prayer, invoking His interposition. Prayer is the appointed means for securing God's aid in the spiritual edification and salvation of men. "For all these things will I be inquired of," &c.

Acts 20:33, 34

PAUL'S RETURN FROM HIS THIRD MISSIONARY TOUR.—III. HIS FAREWELL ADDRESS AT MILETUS (*continued*)

6. *Honest labour*

"*I have coveted no man's silver, or gold, or apparel. Yea,*[1] *ye yourselves know, that these hands have ministered unto my necessities, and to them that were with me.*"

EMENDATIVE RENDERING.—(1.) Omit this word.

EXEGETICAL REMARKS. — "*I have coveted no man's silver, or gold, or apparel,*" *&c.* His labours had been not only faithful and earnest, but thoroughly disinterested. He did not covet their possessions. Good old Samuel, in relinquishing his office, made a profession of disinterestedness similar to this (1 Sam. xii. 3).

"*These hands have ministered to my necessities.*" Some suppose that he held his hands forth so as to show that they were hardened with toil.

HOMILETICS.—"Two men," says Carlyle, "I honour, and no third. First, the toil-worn craftsman, that with earth-made implement laboriously conquers the earth and makes her man's. Venerable to me is the hard hand, crooked, coarse, wherein notwithstanding lies a cunning virtue indefeasibly royal, as of the sceptre of this planet. The second man I honour, and still more highly, is he who is toiling for the spiritually indispensable—not to say daily bread— but the bread of life. These two in all their degrees I honour ; all else is chaff and dust, which let the wind blow whither it listeth. Sublimer in this world know I nothing than a peasant saint. Could such now anywhere be met with, such a one will take thee back to Nazareth itself. Thou wilt see the splendour of heaven spring from the humblest depths of earth like a light shining in great darkness."

In Paul, you have these two labourers which the sage of Chelsea so greatly honours. Paul was a noble toiler for the two breads—the material and the spiritual. The text leads us to consider labour in four aspects—

I. AS A GUARD AGAINST DISHONESTY. " I have coveted no man's silver, or gold, or apparel." Covetousness is dishonesty—the soul of theft. Why did the apostle not covet? The reason is in the next verse. He *wrought with his own hands* for his livelihood. Paul had a trade; he was a tent-maker. The old Hebrews were wise in this; they made a rule of training their children to some craft by which they could obtain their livelihood.

After, perhaps, Paul had been educated as a lawyer at the feet of Gamaliel, he was put to the trade of a tent-maker. At this he wrought diligently for his livelihood. During his arduous ministry at Corinth, he lived in the house of tent-makers, Aquila and Priscilla, and toiled with them at their craft. Such labour acts as a security against dishonesty in two ways—

First, *It raises a man above the need of another's property.* The great Creator has given to every man, as a rule, that natural• skill and strength, which, when industriously used, will secure all the temporal good he needs.

Secondly, *It trains a man to respect another's property.* The man who toils for what he has, alone knows the *value* of property. Laziness breeds covetousness, and is evermore the patron of dishonesty. The industrious habits of a people are the safeguards of a nation's property. The text presents labour—

II. AS A CONDITION OF INDEPENDENCY. There is a sublime spirit of independency in these words: "Ye yourselves know that these hands have ministered unto my necessities and to them that were with me." This feeling of independence in Paul must have been heightened by the fact that he knew that he had a divine claim to their temporal things (1 Cor. ix. 13, 14). Heightened also by the fact that on account of his influence over them, he might have extracted from them large portions of their property. There seems to be a tendency in men to present property to their pastor and spiritual adviser. The more ignorant and superstitious the people, the more they pamper their priests. Two thoughts are suggested here—

First, *That it is a desirable thing for a minister to be secularly independent of his people.* Why else does the apostle rejoice at it? The people who feel that their ministers are dependent upon them are likely to take advantage of his *poverty*, and to misinterpret his acts of purest generosity; and the minister who feels his dependency may come under a strong temptation to humour their prejudices, and under a painful sense of his own humiliation.

Secondly, *That a secular independence, therefore, every minister should endeavour to obtain.* Any man with two healthy hands can do it and ought to do it. " These hands "—thank God for them ! They are able to minister to our necessities. Agriculture, mechanics, trade, literature, medicine, law—the minister who wishes to be secularly independent of his people may get his livelihood from some of these.

The text presents labour—

III. As a source of beneficence. Paul says that his hands not only ministered to his necessities, but to *them that were with him,* so that they enabled him " to support the weak." Industrious labour is socially beneficent.

First, The industrious man *necessarily* enriches society. He produces what would *not* have been without him, and thus adds to the common stock of wealth on which society lives. The lazy man, on the contrary, consumes without producing, and thus impoverishes society. Every honest worker, whether he will or no, helps to support the weak.

Secondly, The industrious man *generally becomes both able and willing to help society.* Industry has the power, not only of supplying the means to alleviate the distress, but often generates the disposition to do so. Where Christianity is, as in the case of Paul, the disposition is. Thus, then, labour is a source of beneficence. The text presents labour—

IV. As a practice to be followed. " I have showed you all things, how that so labouring ye ought to support the weak." He who, like Paul, supports himself by his own industry, and distributes what he can spare by the proceeds of his own labour to ameliorate the distresses of others, is an *example for universal imitation.*

This is, in truth, the religious life : this is to fulfil the law of Christ. Were all men to follow the example of Paul, social and political evils would be unknown, and the world would be a paradise.

" Labour, then, brothers ; nature lives by labour—beast, bird, air, fire. The heavens and rolling world all live by action. Nothing lives at rest, but death, ruin."

But, whilst you labour, labour *generously,* not for your own greed and aggrandisement, but for the social weal. " A man," says Whately, " who gives his children habits of industry, provides for them better than by giving them a fortune." There is nothing too great for honest labour to achieve. It can gain the gift of tongues, make man understood in all countries, and influential among all peoples. " It is the philosopher's stone that can turn all metals into gold ; the wand of divinity that can make the wilderness blossom as the rose."

Acts 20:35

PAUL'S RETURN FROM HIS THIRD MISSIONARY TOUR.—III. HIS
FAREWELL ADDRESS AT MILETUS (*continued*)

7. *Receiving and giving*

" *I have showed you all things, how that so labouring ye ought to support
the weak, and to remember the words of the Lord Jesus, how he said, It is
more blessed to give than to receive.*"

EXEGETICAL REMARKS.—" *I have
showed you all things.*" The words of
our Lord Jesus. As neither all the
words nor deeds of Christ are recorded (John xxi. 25), it is not to be
wondered at that we do not find this
sentence in any of His addresses or
conversations. Their spirit, however,
is everywhere in His life and teaching.

HOMILETICS.—These words bring at the outset to our minds three
things in relation to Christ.

First, *The unrecorded portions of His words.* Nowhere in the
Gospels do we find the words which Paul here quotes as from Christ.
We find much that He said containing their import, but we do not
find the form of the sentence which is here ascribed to Him. We
have but little of Christ's biography. We are thankful for the little.
The great bulk of His words found no record, and are in oblivion.
We thank Paul for rescuing this fragment from forgetfulness.

Secondly, *The unworldly character of His teaching.* The maxim
here quoted stands in contrast with the practical opinions of the
world. The world says, " It is more blessed to *receive* than give."
It says, by its conduct, " Blessed is the man that accumulates the
most."

Thirdly, *The unselfish character of His life.* The words are not
a sentence borrowed from some ethical authority, nor are they the conclusion of His speculative reasoning ; they are the expressions of His
life. He received much from the Eternal ; He gave much to the
world—gave all His powers, His life ; and His testimony is, that
He was more happy in giving than in receiving.

The text brings three facts before us—

I. THAT RECEIVING AND COMMUNICATING ARE THE TWO GRAND
FUNCTIONS OF LIFE. All the actions men perform are either receptive or impartive.

First, *Man has acquisitive tendencies and powers.* His desire
for getting is ever active and ineradicable. Wealth, power, influence,
knowledge ; these are some of the objects he craves for.

Secondly, *Man has the impartive tendencies and powers.* His social and religious instincts urge him to give what he has attained ; to distribute property, to impart knowledge, diffuse happiness. All men, by the necessity of their nature, are engaged either in a right way or a wrong way in these two great functions—receiving and giving.

II. THAT THE RIGHT DISCHARGE OF BOTH THESE FUNCTIONS IS BLESSEDNESS. This is implied by the word *"more."* To receive in a *right* spirit, and for right ends, health, pleasure, property, knowledge, friendship, fame ; to receive the pleasant with gratitude, the painful with submission, and the whole with a loving acquiescence, is a truly blessed thing. God made us receptive beings, and a right reception of His gifts is blessedness.

First, *Receiving as the reward of effort is blessedness.* It is natural to feel happiness when the result laboured for has been reached.

Secondly, *Receiving as a consciousness of fresh power is blessedness.* A conscious augmentation of our powers and resources is joy.

Thirdly, *Receiving with religious gratitude is blessedness.* Gratitude is joy ; it is the inspiration of heaven's eternal anthems.

III. THAT THE BLESSEDNESS OF THE RIGHT DISCHARGE OF THE COMMUNICATING FUNCTION IS THE GREATER. " It is *more* blessed to give than to receive." He who gives what justly belongs to himself, what he esteems as valuable, cordially, disinterestedly, and religiously, is of all men most blessed. Why is it " more" blessed ?

First, *Because it is more spiritualising.* Every generous, disinterested act, in giving, tends to detach the soul from the material and temporary, and to ally it with the spiritual and eternal. The man who is constantly gaining and not giving, becomes more and more the slave of selfishness, materialism, and time. The giving man is unfettering himself as he gives.

Secondly, *Because it is more socialising.* In giving, you awaken in the social sphere sympathy, gratitude, and admiration. The loving man awakens love, and happiness has been defined as loving and being loved.

Thirdly, *Because it is more God-assimilating.* God gives, but cannot receive. He can gain nothing in intelligence, power, riches, glory. He gives all, and only gives. The grand function of His being is giving. He opens His hand evermore. The nearer we approach to God, the more blessed we are. Cicero says, that " men resemble the gods in nothing so much as in doing good to their fellow-creatures."

Acts 20:36-38

PAUL'S RETURN FROM HIS THIRD MISSIONARY TOUR.—III. HIS
FAREWELL ADDRESS AT MILETUS (*continued*)

8. *A parting prayer*

" *And when he had thus spoken, he kneeled down, and prayed with them all. And they all wept sore, and fell on Paul's neck, and kissed him: sorrowing most of all for the words which he spake,*[1] *that they should see his face no more. And they accompanied him unto the ship.*"

EMENDATIVE RENDERING.—(1.) Had spoken.

EXEGETICAL REMARKS.—"*And when he had thus spoken, he kneeled down, and prayed with them all.*" *These things having said* (or *saying*), *placing his knees* (upon the ground), *with them all he prayed.* The mention of his kneeling seems to imply that it was not a customary posture in public prayer, but one occasioned by the strength of his emotions. Long after, as we learn from Justin Martyr and others, it was the practice of the Church to stand in public, or on special occasions like the one before us. —"*Prayed with them.*" No doubt in the sense attached to the words now; to wit, that of leading the devotions, or praying in the name of all.—ALEX.

" *And they all wept sore, and fell on Paul's neck, and kissed him.*" There *was* (or *arose*) a *great* (or *sufficient*) weeping of *all, and falling on his neck* (*i.e.*, embracing him), *they kissed him* (an emphatic compound form, denoting frequency or tenderness). The childlike expression both of love and sorrow is to be explained, not merely from ancient or oriental usage, but as a proof of the intense regard which Paul appears to have commanded on the part of all who were in the bonds of spiritual friendship with him. As in many other cases, this attachment seems to have borne due proportion to the malice of his enemies.

HOMILETICS.—*He leaves them in the exercise of prayer and amidst deep emotion.* "And when he had thus spoken, he kneeled down and prayed."

I. IT WAS A JOINT PRAYER. He kneeled down on the shore of Miletus. No bodily attitude is more beseeming in prayer than this. It seems to be the natural gesture into which the soul, filled with intense emotion of worship, throws the human body. This prayer was a *joint* prayer. They all kneeled down, and they all prayed, the apostle uttering the words in which they all joined ; their souls going with every expressed petition. They would never pray together again. A more suitable way of parting there cannot be than that of blending the souls together in devotion. Christ parted with His disciples in prayer.

II. IT WAS A TENDER PRAYER. "They all wept sore," &c. What

emotions streamed out in those tears! There was *love*—love for Paul—love of gratitude, high esteem, and admiration. There might have been *regret.* It is not unlikely that they accused themselves with not having sympathised and co-operated with him as they ought, and with not having improved under his ministry as they ought. There was no doubt *apprehension.* They apprehended evils to him in Jerusalem; and probably they apprehended evils to themselves after his departure from their midst. We do not wonder that they wept at the loss for ever of such a man, such a friend, such a master; it was enough to break their hearts into floods of emotion.

They would see him no more. That struck a tender chord in each heart, and "tears unbidden flow." "We cannot," says a modern writer, "but observe how holy is that tie of spiritual interest, that clasping of soul with soul, and heartfelt recognition of human brotherhood. But a few years before, and what was Paul to the elders of Ephesus, or the elders of Ephesus to Paul? They knew not, cared not, for one another. But they imbibe the spirit of Jesus; they catch a glimpse of the hallowed ties that unite man to man, and man to God, and lo, they are new creatures; they are born, spiritually born, into a new universe. They look upon each other with different eyes, and feel that their connexion is no coarse or common one; but that it has been formed in heaven; that it is knit by the fingers of God, and will last evermore. How changed their interest in one another and in the mass of men! What a different spectacle does the world present to their sanctified vision! It is no longer a mere stage for the warrior to play his bloody part,—an amphitheatre with wild beasts,—an arena for the selfish strivings of men; but in very deed the world of God lighted up by Him, pervaded by His presence, alive with His wisdom and active love, and swarming with beings near and dear to the mighty Parent. Thus they taste a new delight, and enjoy a newly-created sense. They are now men, brethren, and feel for one another. They may be sundered by the events of this life, and see one another no more; but they now know—sublime assurance!—that man's true life is beyond this little span of being, and they have 'a hope built in heaven.' "

Acts 21:1-16

" *And it came to pass, that after we were gotten from them,[1] and had launched, we came with a straight course unto Coos, and the day following unto Rhodes, and from thence unto Patara : and finding a ship sailing over unto Phenicia, we went aboard, and set forth. Now, when we had discovered Cyprus, we left it on the left hand, and sailed into[2] Syria, and landed at Tyre : for there the ship was to unlade her burden. And finding disciples,[3] we tarried there seven days : who said to Paul through the Spirit, that he should not go up to Jerusalem. And when we had accomplished those days, we departed[4] and went our way ; and they all brought us on our way, with wives and children, till we were out of the city :. and we kneeled down on the shore, and prayed. And when we had taken our leave one of another, we took ship, and they returned home again. And when we had finished our course from Tyre, we came to Ptolemais,[5] and saluted the brethren, and abode with them one day. And the next day we that were of Paul's company[6] departed, and came unto Cæsarea : and we entered into the house of Philip the evangelist, which was[7] one of the seven, and abode with him. And the same man had four daughters, virgins, which did prophesy. And as we tarried there many days, there came down from Judea a certain prophet, named Agabus. And when he was come unto us, he took Paul's girdle, and bound his own hands and feet, and said, Thus saith the Holy Ghost, So shall the Jews at Jerusalem bind the man that owneth this girdle, and shall deliver him into the hands of the Gentiles. And when we heard these things, both we, and they of that place, besought him not to go up to Jerusalem. Then Paul answered, What mean ye to weep and to break[8] mine heart ? for I am ready not to be bound only, but also to die at Jerusalem for the name of the Lord Jesus. And when he would not be persuaded, we ceased, saying, The will of the Lord be done. And after those days, we took up our carriages,[9] and went up to Jerusalem. There went with us also certain of the disciples of[10] Cæsarea, and brought with them one Mnason of Cyprus, an old disciple, with whom we should lodge.*"

EMENDATIVE RENDERINGS.—(1.) Had torn ourselves away from them. (2.) Towards. (3.) Having sought out the disciples. (4.) We embarked in the ship. (5.) And finishing our voyage we came from Tyre to Ptolemais. (6.) Omit, *That were of Paul's company.* (7.) Being. (8.) What do ye, weeping and breaking ? (9.) Baggage. (10.) From.—ALF.

EXEGETICAL REMARKS.—Paul has taken his final farewell of the elders of Ephesus on the shore of Miletus, and the parting scene was most touching. His friends with sorrowing hearts and tearful eyes, having accompanied him into the ship, he pursues his voyage. And as this narrative is a continuation of the preceding history, we shall rapidly glance at HIS DEPARTURE FROM MILETUS, AND HIS ARRIVAL IN JERUSALEM.

"*And it came to pass, that after we were gotten from them, and had launched."* The expression, *"*gotten from them," means, *having torn ourselves from them :* so strong were the ties of loving sympathy that bound their hearts together on the shores of Miletus, that the disruption was an effort of agony.

" *We came with a straight course to Coos."* This is an island in the Ægæan Sea, about twenty-three miles in length, near the coast of Cairia, about forty nautical miles south of Miletus. It was a fertile spot, famous for its vineyards, its wine, silk, cotton, and for its worship of Esculapius, and the residence of Hippocrates. It is probable that they reached this island on the evening of the day on which they started from Miletus, for it would seem the vessel had an auspicious wind—" we came with a straight course unto Coos."

" *Unto Rhodes."* This was another island. It was south-east of Coos. It was celebrated for its gigantic ʼstatue of Apollo, a colossus regarded as one of the seven wonders of the world. The image was most stupendous ; it was made of brass, and strided the entrance of the harbour. Between its legs, ships in full sail entered and departed. The vessel reached this beautiful and far-famed island "the day following."

" *Thence unto Patara."* A town on the coast of Lycia, near the mouth of Xanthos, where Apollo was believed to utter oracles at certain seasons. Here Paul and his companions had to disembark. Paul was on his way to Jerusalem, bearing contributions from Macedonia and Greece to the destitute Christians in Judea, and he was anxious to be there in all haste, in order to attend the Pentecost. The vessel that had conveyed him to Patara had perhaps either finished her voyage there, or was proceeding in some other direction than to the ports of Phenicia.

"A ship sailing over unto Phenicia." Providence favours the good, and the apostle finds at Patara *" a ship."* He and his companions embarked without a moment's delay. And now the voyage was more propitious. Free from shoals and rocks, they sail no longer ʼhrough narrow channels, and under

the shadow of great mountains, but out in the open sea. The distance between Patara and Tyre, the capital of Phenicia, is three hundred and forty geographical miles, and if they had a favourable voyage, as the narrative seems to imply they had, they accomplished it in about forty-eight hours.

" *We had discovered Cyprus."* A famous island we have elsewhere described.

" *We landed at Tyre."* Perhaps in the course of a few hours after a glimpse of Cyprus, they landed at TYRE, one of the most famous cities of the ancient world—a city described by the old prophets in a state of splendour, where its *" merchants were princes, and its traffickers the honourable of the earth."*

" *There the ship was to unlade."* Perhaps she had brought grain from the Black Sea, or wine from the Archipelago. Here Paul and his companions discovered what to them was more precious than all the wealth of the city—followers of Christ.

" *And finding disciples, we tarried there seven days, who said to Paul through the Spirit, that he should not go up to Jerusalem."* Who these disciples were, in what way they were brought to Christ, and by what means the apostle now found them out in the city, are points on which we have no information. The *"* SPIRIT" in some way had informed them of the sufferings which Paul would endure at Jerusalem, and their love prompted them to dissuade him from his purpose to visit it. Their words were not a divine command to Paul, but their own inference, from the fact divinely revealed to them, that Paul was to suffer there. It was not the Spirit that said, he "should not go up," *but their mistaken love.* Having spent the seven days, the vessel having unloaded and taken in another cargo, she is ready for sea again.

"And when we had accomplished those days, we departed, and went our way ; and they all brought us on our way, with wives and children, till we were out of the city, and we kneeled down on the shore and prayed." Here is another parting scene presented,

with inimitable simplicity ; full of nature and of touching interest. The Christian families of Tyre, husbands and wives, parents and children, followed Paul and his companions with loving sympathies down to the beach, and there on the hard shore, under the open heavens, and amidst the howl of the sea, kneeled down in prayer. A modern traveller has sketched the very spot on which this touching scene occurred.

" *And when we had taken our leave one of another, we took ship,"* &c. The vessel is now ready, she is floating on the crested wave, the sails are hoisted, and the moment for separation has come. The last embrace is given.

" *We came to Ptolemais, and saluted the brethren, and abode with them one day."* This place, it was said, was named after Ptolemy, the first king of Egypt. Its modern European name is Acre. It was a Palestinian city of the Mediterranean, about thirty miles south of Tyre. It has been the perpetual theatre of war, constituting, as it does, the key of Syria, and has stood, perhaps, longer on the field of history than most of the other places mentioned in the Holy Book. The present population is about 20,000. They discovered " brethren " here : they saluted those brethren, and remained with them one day.

" *Cæsarea."* A city on the coast of the Mediterranean, about thirty-six miles to the south of Ptolemais, and about sixty north-west of Jerusalem. It was rebuilt by Herod the Great, and named Cæsarea, in honour of Augustus Cæsar. It has long since been blotted out of existence. Its Christian associations, however, possess an imperishable interest. It was the abode of the centurion Cornelius, the first Gentile believer in the new faith—the Abraham of Gentile believers. Here the angel smote Herod because he gave not God the glory. Here Peter unlocked the gates of the kingdom, and flung them open for the Gentile world. Here, as we shall see, Paul made Felix tremble, and Agrippa almost a Christian ; and here, for two long years, he was held a prisoner, and

from thence sent in bonds through storms and shipwreck to Rome. Here they remained some days, and were the guests of Philip the evangelist.

" *And we entered into the house of Philip the evangelist, which was one of the seven ; and abode with him."* He was one of the seven elected deacons of the Church at Jerusalem (Acts vi. 5), but since then had become an evangelist, a preacher of the gospel. After his conversation with the eunuch, he had " gone down to Cæsarea " (Acts viii. 40), and had continued ever since preaching the new faith. How many converts he had won we are not told, but we are told something of his family.

" *He had four daughters, virgins, which did prophesy."* In their case the prophecy was fulfilled (Joel ii. 8). While the apostle and his companions abode in the house of this distinguished family, a prophet came down to him from Jerusalem, dramatically warning him of the danger which awaited him there.

" *And as we tarried there many days, there came down from Judea a certain prophet named Agabus. And when he was come unto us, he took Paul's girdle, and bound his own hands and feet and said, Thus saith the Holy Ghost, So shall the Jews at Jerusalem bind the man that owneth this girdle, and shall deliver him into the hands of the Gentiles."* It is probable that this Agabus was the same man as he who foretold the famine, and gave occasion to Paul's first official mission at Jerusalem (Acts xi. 27–30). It was not an uncommon thing for the prophets to perform actions emblematic of the events they predicted. Thus Jeremiah, in order to denote the approaching captivity of the Jews, was directed to bury his girdle by the Euphrates (Jer. xiii. 4). And thus Isaiah, in order to indicate the captivity of Egypt, walked naked and with bare feet (Isa. xx. 3, 4). Many other instances of similar emblematic actions occur (see Jer. xxvii. 2, 3, xviii. 4 ; Ezek. iv., also xii.) Christ himself acted in the same way when He took a towel and girded Himself, and washed the disciples' feet (John xiii. 4, 5). Such symbolic actions added to the impressiveness of the declaration. The action of Agabus was felt to be impressive now.

"*And when we heard these things, both we and they of that place besought him not to go up to Jerusalem.*" Their hearts were smitten with sadness at the terrible dangers awaiting Paul which were thus so dramatically announced, and with tears they besought him not to go up to Jerusalem. Paul, however, had made up his mind ; he was not to be turned from his purpose, although he deeply felt the tenderness of their appeals.

"*Then Paul answered, What mean ye to weep and to break mine heart ? for I am ready not to be bound only, but also to die at Jerusalem for the name of the Lord Jesus.*" Seeing the invincibility of his purpose, they ceased to persuade him, saying, "The will of the Lord be done."

Having thus spent some days with Philip and his family, listened to the prophecies of his virgin daughters, received the terrible warning of Agabus, and overcome the powerful persuasions of his friends not to go to Jerusalem, he and his companions depart.

"*And after those days we took up our carriages, and went up to Jerusalem.*" The word carriages does not mean conveyances, but baggages. "*We took up our carriages,*" is in the Greek all in one participle, and means, taking up our luggage.

"*Brought with them one Mnason, of Cyprus, an old disciple, with whom we should lodge.*" Four things are indicated of this Mnason—that he was a native of Cyprus ; that he had been a convert to Christianity for some time ; he was called an "old disciple ;" and that he had a house at Jerusalem, to which the apostle was taken.

Thus we have followed Paul into Jerusalem, and here for the present we leave him.

HOMILETICS.—There are several subjects of a spiritual and useful character discoverable in this fragment of apostolic history, which we would endeavour, with great brevity, to bring into prominent impressiveness.

I. THE SOCIAL LOVE GENERATED BY THE GOSPEL. There is an affection which man has for man altogether apart from Christianity. It is an affection of animal sympathy, personal interests, mental reciprocities. But the social love generated by Christianity is of a purer and higher character. Several of its features are here displayed.

First, *Strong.* So strongly did it bind Paul and the Ephesians together on the shores of Miletus that they had to *tear* themselves asunder :—for such is the meaning of the expression translated "after we had gotten from them." Their souls had so deeply struck the roots of their love into each other's being, that a violent energy of will was required for the separation. The parting scene, too, on the Tyrian shore, and the tears wept on leaving Cæsarea, also indicated the strength of Christian love. The love which genuine Christians have for each other is not the thread of a passing sentiment, but the golden chain of an immutable law. It is that which binds all the hosts of heaven in an indissoluble unity of thought, aspiration, interest, and pursuit.

Secondly, *Hospitable.* It is probable that Paul and his companions were entertained in the homes of Christians wherever they stayed. It is distinctly stated that they abode with Philip. Paul a guest in Philip's house! This is one of the divine marvels which sometimes occur in the history of men. The name of Saul of Tarsus at one time was a terror to the heart of Philip. Elsewhere we have these remarkable words: " As for Saul, he made havoc of the church, entering into every house, and haling men and women, committed them to prison. Therefore they that were scattered abroad went everywhere preaching the word. Then Philip went down to the city of Samaria, and preached Christ unto them " (Acts viii. 3–5). We perceive from this, that terror of Saul drove Philip from his home at Jerusalem. Had they ever met since ? Probably never. What a change the gospel has accomplished. The lion has become a lamb. He from whose presence he rushed as from a fiend, he now entertains as a loving brother and a distinguished apostle of the Lord. Christian love is hospitable ; its doors are ever open to the faithful. Its motto is, " Share and share alike." It holds its possessions as the common property of the brotherhood. Use hospitality, &c.

Thirdly, *Tender.* Christianity quickens the sensibilities, and intensifies the feelings of the human heart. The more Christianity a man has in him the more tender he is. Lived there ever a man with more gospel in him than Paul, and was there ever a man more tender in soul ? In nearly all the partings recorded in these verses there were *tears.*

Fourthly, *Religious.* In parting with the Ephesians we are told that he kneeled down and prayed with them all, and in parting with the men of Tyre he did the same. " We kneeled down on the shore and prayed." Christian love turns to God as the opening flower to the sun. It presents its dear objects to the loving guardianship of the Eternal Father. The best way of serving one's friends is to commend them " to God," as Paul did, and to "the word of his grace." Apart from Him we can render them no help. Our best thoughts, our wisest counsels, our tenderest sympathies, our most costly gifts will be of little service apart from His benediction and superintending care.

Such, then, are some of the features here developed of that love which Christianity generates in the hearts of His disciples. Another subject discoverable in the piece of apostolic history before us is—

II. THE FALLIBILITY OF HUMAN AFFECTION. The good men of Tyre loved Paul, yet they sought to dissuade him from *duty ;* so also did the good men of Cæsarea : " *They besought him not to go up to Jerusalem.*" So urgent and powerful were they in their persuasions, that Paul exclaims, " *What mean ye to weep and to break mine heart ?*" We do not know the arguments they employed ; but we know that in both cases they quoted the Holy Spirit's influence. At Tyre we are told that the disciples said to Paul, "through the Spirit," that he "*should not go up to Jerusalem.*" And at Cæsarea, the prophet Agabus said, "*Thus saith the Holy Ghost.*" This reference to the Spirit would add power to the urgency of their loving appeals. He was deeply moved by it, but not mastered. All their arguments were the arguments of *mistaken* love—arguments which, if they had succeeded, might have injured the character and usefulness of Paul. Human affection often recommends that which is not good. The mistaken kindness of parents has ever proved the greatest curse to children. Never does the devil act so mightily upon the human heart as when his errors are urged on us by the arguments of those who love us most. Let us learn to act in relation to this mistaken kindness of our friends as Christ acted in relation to Peter, who from love attempted to dissuade Him from prosecuting the painful part of His mission, "*Get thee behind me, Satan.*" The counsels of the purest human love are not always wise. Another subject discoverable in this narrative is—

III. THE UNCONQUERABLENESS OF A CHRIST-INSPIRED PURPOSE. Mighty as was the influence which love brought to bear upon Paul both at Tyre and Cæsarea, to prevent him from going to Jerusalem, it could not break his purpose ; he was invincible in his determination. "*I am ready not to be bound only, but also to die at Jerusalem for the name of the Lord Jesus.*" His determination was not a caprice, not a mere wish, not an intention formed in haste, not a resolution based on mere natural desires or reasons of expediency. It was a determination based on the strongest convictions of his judgment, backed by the whole current of his sympathies, and deeply rooted in him by the spirit of Christ. Such a purpose cannot be broken ; it defies opposition, it removes mountains. Luther felt it to be so as well as Paul. When Spalatin, the beloved friend of the illustrious reformer, joined, with many others, in entreating him not to enter Worms, on account of the terrible dangers that there awaited him, his reply was, "Though there were as many devils in Worms as there are tiles on the house-tops, yet will I go thither." Such a purpose as this is the heart of true moral courage. Physical courage is a mere gift of nature, and often that which is called moral courage is nothing but mere insensibility and obstinacy of temperament. Paul seems to me to have been physically a weak man, and mentally a timid, nervous, sensitive soul. In writing to the Corinthians, he says, "*I was with you in fear and much trembling.*" And yet this man had an indomitable heroism, and that heroism is to be ascribed to his Christ-inspired purpose. Another subject discoverable in this narrative, is—

IV. THE SUBLIMEST VICTORY OVER SOUL. "*And when he would not be persuaded, we ceased, saying, The will of the Lord be done.*"

They did not conquer him with their combined power, but he conquered them single-handedly ; he did so by his invincible purpose. And what a conquest ! " *The will of the Lord be done.*" This does not mean, " We must bow to the *necessity.*" Many men are brought to do this who have no Christianity. The ungodly father, when life has fled from his child ; the reckless speculator, when he has played the game that has wrecked the whole of his fortune ; the criminal, when he is in the hand of justice : these and many others say, when all hope is gone, " *The Lord's will be done.*" In their case it means a soul whose energies are crushed, whose hopes are blighted, upon whom the night of despair has set in. But here it would be understood to mean a cordial acquiescence. And it implies a belief—

(1.) *That there is a God.* (2.) *That that God has a will in relation to individuals.* (3.) *That the working out of that will is the best thing.*

We say this is the sublimest conquest over souls :—

First, *It is a conquest over the folly of souls.* The greatest folly in the universe is to oppose the will of God. It is the folly that leads to all the perplexity, confusion, and misery of the world. The wisest thing is to acquiesce in that Will which is all-wise, all-good, all-mighty.

Secondly, *It is a conquest over the wickedness of souls.* Opposition to the divine will is the very essence of all sin ; the world's guilt, the world's crime, is rebellious hostility to the divine will.

Thirdly, *It is a conquest over the misery of souls.* Opposition to the divine will is hell. Obedience is heaven. The sublimest victory in the universe is this victory over soul ; the victory, this, for which Christ and His followers are fighting.

Acts 21:17-26

PAUL'S FINAL VISIT TO JERUSALEM

1. *His appearance in the Mother Church*

" *And when we were come to Jerusalem, the brethren received us gladly. And the day following, Paul went in with us unto James; and all the elders were present. And when he had saluted them, he declared particularly what things God had wrought among the Gentiles by his ministry. And when they heard it, they glorified the Lord,*[1] *and said unto him, Thou seest, brother, how many thousands of Jews there are which believe;*[2] *and they are all zealous of the law: and they are informed of thee, that thou teachest all the Jews which are among the Gentiles to forsake Moses, saying that they ought not to circumcise their children, neither to walk after the customs. What is it therefore ? the multitude must needs come together :*[3] *for they will hear that thou art come. Do therefore this that we say to thee: We have four men which have a vow on them. Them take, and purify thyself with them, and be at charges with[4] them, that they may shave their heads: and all may[5] know that those things, whereof they were informed concerning thee, are nothing ; but that thou thyself also walkest orderly, and keepest the law. As touching the Gentiles which believe, we have written and concluded[6] that they observe no such thing, save only that they keep themselves from things offered to idols, and from blood, and from strangled, and from fornication. Then Paul took the men, and the next day purifying himself with them entered into the temple, to signify the accomplishment of the days of purification, until that an[7] offering should be offered for every one of them."*

EMENDATIVE RENDERINGS.—(1.) God. the Jews which have become believers. (2.) How many thousand there are among (3.) A multitude will certainly come together. (4.) For. (5.) Shall. (6.) Which have become believers, we have written decreeing. (7.) The.—ALF. ; TISCH.

EXEGETICAL REMARKS.—Here we have an account of Paul's fifth and final visit to Jerusalem, the metropolis of Judæa, and the mother Church of Christendom. His previous four visits have occupied our attention, and are elsewhere recorded (chaps. ix. 26, xi. 30, xv. 4, xviii. 21, 22). The verses now under consideration reveal to us the treatment he met with in the holy city by the evangelical Christians.

First, They welcomed him.

"*And when we were come to Jerusalem, the brethren received us gladly.*" The word "*we*" includes Paul, Luke the historian, and those seven mentioned in the fourth verse of the preceding chapter. The "*brethren*" includes those Christian believers whom they met immediately on their arrival ; these, we are told, received Paul and his companions "*gladly.*" They rejoiced in their advent, as fellow-believers in the Messiahship of Christ, and as the representatives of Gentile Christianity, and as the bearers of charitable contributions from distant churches to relieve those of their brethren who were suffering from want in the Church at Jerusalem. We may be sure the apostle and his companions were welcomed heartily, both on the first night of their arrival in the city, and on the next day, in a more formal and more general way, but not the less cordial and warm.

Secondly, They listened in assembly to his apostolic reports.

"*And the day following Paul went in with us unto James, and all the elders were present. And when he had saluted them, he declared particularly what things God had wrought among the Gentiles by his ministry.*" James, the brother of the Lord, was at this time the head of the mother Church at Jerusalem. "*The elders*" were those official members of the Church who assisted in the conduct of its affairs, and the promotion of its spiritual interest. To the house of James and his companions now resort, and an official session of the Church is held to receive them. The most leading men of the Christian community are there. After Paul had "*saluted*" (greeted) in words of kindness and respect, he commences his address, and the subject of his address was God's work by him among the Gentiles.

"*He declared particularly what things God had wrought among the Gentiles by his ministry.*" The word "*particularly*" indicates the minuteness with which he entered into details ; he declared each one of the things "*which God did in the nations.*" No doubt he captivated their attention, and filled them with transports of delight.

Thirdly, They glorified God on his account.

"*And when they heard it, they glorified the Lord.*" At the intelligence of his triumph, they praised not Paul, but the Lord. Paul represented the work as so manifestly not his own achievements, but the Lord's, that to Him they at once ascribed the praise.

Fourthly, They inform Paul of a disastrous prejudice.

"*Thou seest, brother, how many thousands of Jews there are which believe; and they are all zealous of the law.*" "Thou seest, brother"—though probably James had uttered these words, they are the expression of the assembly, for he spoke in their name. "*Brother*"—an expression both of personal affection and official recognition ; the highest title given in the primitive Church, even to apostles. The fact brought under the attention of the apostle is, that there were thousands, literally myriads, meaning an indefinite multitude of Jews, who believed in Christianity, but were still *zealots* concerning the law of Moses. Whitby quotes various authors to show how intense was the zeal of the Jews generally for their law, and that they would rather die than forfeit their character as its faithful observers.

Fifthly, They reported a current slander against himself.

"*And they are informed of thee that thou teachest all the Jews which are among the Gentiles to forsake Moses, saying that they ought not to circumcise their children, neither to walk after the customs.*" This was a baseless calumny, for had not Paul circumcised Timothy, observed a religious vow, and come now to Jerusalem in order to attend one of the great national feasts ? It is true that the apostle had denied the necessity of Mosaic observances for personal salvation ; but he had never represented them as worthless or unlawful while the Temple was still standing : indeed, in consideration of Jewish attachments to Jewish form, he had carried expediency to the furthest point in order to conciliate their prejudices.

Sixthly, They propounded to him a method of conciliation.

"*What is it therefore ? the multitude must needs come together : for they will hear that thou art come. Do therefore this that we say to thee : We have four men which have a vow*

on them ; them take, and purify thyself with them, and be at charges with them, that they may shave their heads : and all may know that those things whereof they were informed concerning thee, are nothing ; but that thou thyself also walkest orderly, and keepest the law.*" "The assembled elders," says an accomplished scholar and able biblical expositor, "knew what St Paul was and was not, and aware, too, of this general misconception of his teaching, recommended to him the following expedient :—Let him show, by a practical proof, that he did not object to a Jew being a Jew still. There were four men, Jewish Christians, at that moment in Jerusalem, bound by a Nazarite's vow. That vow, made commonly at a time of personal danger by land or sea, by disease or accident, bound the person undertaking it to abstain from wine, and to let his hair grow uncut for a certain period, at the end of which particular sacrifices were to be offered, which were not always within the command of a poor man's purse. It was no means unusual for richer men to bear the expense of those sacrifices in behalf of the poor. The Christian elders recommend St Paul to do this : to include himself for a few days in the Nazarite's vow of these four Jewish Christians, and then to pay the cost of the prescribed offerings for all. '*Be at charges with them,*' the 24th verse says, '*that they may shave their heads,*'—that is, bear the charge, pay the expense, of those sacrifices, which must be offered before they can rid themselves of their vow, and cut the hair off their heads in sign of its termination. The advice was friendly, and St Paul followed it. He who had said in one of his letters, '*To the Jew I became as a Jew, that I might gain the Jews,*' acted now upon the principle. He had never made it a principle of doctrine that Jews should abandon their ceremonial law. *He* was a Jew : therefore he might perform one of those ceremonies with a safe conscience, if by so doing he might conciliate his countrymen, and thus, by God's grace, *save some.*" *

Concerning the expedient thus re-

* See " Church of the First Days," vol. iii. p. 194, by Dr C. J. Vaughan.

commended, two things are worthy of notice : (1.) Paul adopted it.

" *Then Paul took the men, and the next day purifying himself with them entered into the temple, to signify the accomplishment of the days of purification, until that an offering should be offered for every one of them.*" Whether Paul, with his deep insight into the spirituality of the gospel, and his love of spiritual liberty, was thoroughly satisfied with this advice or not, he followed it, and thus with the " weak became weak." His conciliation compromised no principle, and was for the good of others, not for the interest of himself. The expedient (2.) Was unsuccessful. It was well projected, well carried out, but, like most other expedients, answered not fully the end intended. Seven days had not ended before " *the Jews which were of Asia, when they saw him in the temple, stirred up all the people, and laid hands on him.*"

HOMILETICS.—From the whole of this we learn the following things :—

I. THE EARLY CONQUEST OF THE GOSPEL. During the quarter of a century which had elapsed since Paul's first introduction to the mother Church at Jerusalem, what wonders Christianity had wrought ! The historic sketch which Paul presented now before James and the elders, the marvels which he had accomplished by his ministry, seemed to fill his hearers with devout amazement : " *When they heard it they glorified the Lord.*" And there, too, on that occasion, they tell him that " *many thousands of Jews believed.*" The sermon of Peter on the day of Pentecost, and the ministry of Paul and the other apostles in various parts of Judea, brought thousands of Jews to believe the Messiahship of Christ. These triumphs of the gospel at the very outset of its career serve several important purposes.

First, *They serve to demonstrate the genuineness of gospel facts.* Those who believed at this period and in Judæa had ample opportunities of testing the truth of the facts which were presented to their attention.

Secondly, *They serve to show the amazing force of Christian truth.* What other systems of truth could have effected such revolutions? could have won such numbers of Jews, who were so strongly prejudiced against its founder and hero to believe in Him, to the salvation of their souls ?

Thirdly, *They serve to show the zeal with which the apostles prosecuted their ministry.* It was through the preaching of the truth that those conquests were won.

From this we learn—

II. THE TENACITY OF EARLY PREJUDICE. Those Jews who believed in Christ could not give up the ritualism of Moses, in which they had been brought up. " *They were still zealous of the law.*" Though those whose ministry won them to Christ taught them that the old ritualism was typical and temporary, that Christ was the end of the law, and that faith in Him was all that was necessary for salvation, they held with tenacity to the old rites. Early prejudices, especially in religion, often attain a potent and pernicious hold upon the human mind; they warp the judgment, they exclude the entrance of new light, they impede the progress of the soul in intelligence, liberty, and growth, in manly independency and power. Prejudices give a colour to the glass, through which the soul looks at truth, and thus prevent her from appearing in her own native hue.

From this we learn—

III. THE SLANDEROUSNESS OF RELIGIOUS BIGOTRY. We learn that those Jewish Christians, who were thus attached to the ritual of Moses, had been informed that Paul had taught " *all the Jews which are among the Gentiles to forsake Moses, saying that they ought not to circumcise their children, neither to walk after the customs.*" This was a foul slander, for Paul not only acted indulgently towards the scrupulous (Acts xvi. 3; Rom. i. 4; 1 Cor. viii. 7, x. 27), but in general he disapproved of native Jews relinquishing the observance of the law, and he himself observed it too (1 Cor. vii. 18, ix. 20). All he rigorously insisted upon was, that no prerogative, or claim to salvation should be built on the observance of the law; and that it should not be imposed as a burden upon Gentile believers. Who fabricated this slander? The bigoted Jews. Religious bigotry has always been libellous; it has an instinct for calumny. Now, as ever, it misrepresents and maligns the men who propound doctrines transcending its narrow notions. Against such its pulpits, its platforms, and its press are organs of the vilest slander.

From this we learn—

IV. THE CONCILIATORY GENIUS OF CHRISTIANITY. How anxious James, the president of that official meeting, and the elders, were to preserve peace on that occasion! They perceive that a schismatic spirit is rife, and they are anxious to destroy it, and promote concord. Hence their question, " *What is it therefore?*" Meaning, What is to be done? How shall this false impression be removed? And they proposed the expedient that Paul should join the four men amongst them that were Nazarites. All this shows their strong desire for brotherly harmony and concord. Peace is the instinct and mission of love. He who does not strive to harmonise social discords, crush social feuds, and heal social divisions, has not the true love within him. Love is ever on the wing, bearing the olive branch over the social tumults of the world.

This conciliatory spirit of Christianity is further developed in the conduct of Paul on this occasion. He joins the Nazarites, and observes their rites. " Paul is among the Nazarites," says Lange : " (1.) Not as a slave of human ordinances, but in the light of evangelical liberty, which had power over all things that promote the kingdom of God (1 Cor. vi. 12). (2.) Not as a dissembler before the people, but in the ministry of brotherly love, which bears the infirmities of the weak (Rom. xv. 1). (3.) Not as a fugitive from the cross, but in the power of apostolic obedience, which knows to deny itself from love to the Lord (Luke ix. 23)." Bold and invincible as was the apostle, his spirit of conciliation was very remarkable. In 1 Cor. ix. 1, he sketches his own conciliatory line of conduct. *" Unto the Jews I became as a Jew, that I might gain the Jews; to them that are under the law, as under the law, that I might gain them that are under the law; to the weak became I as weak, that I might gain the weak: I am made all things to all men, that I might by all means save some."* In his letters to the Romans he expresses the same spirit in language equally if not more strong. *" If meat maketh my brother to offend, I will eat no meat while the world standeth."* Fidelity to principle is not inconsistent with a studious endeavour to avoid giving offence to our fellow-men.

Acts 21:27-38

PAUL'S RETURN FROM HIS THIRD MISSIONARY TOUR.—HIS FINAL
VISIT TO JERUSALEM (*continued*)

" And when the seven days were almost ended, the Jews which were of [1] *Asia, when they saw him in the temple, stirred up all the people, and laid hands on him, crying out, Men of Israel, help : This is the man, that teacheth all men everywhere against the people, and the law, and this place : and further brought Greeks also into the temple, and hath polluted this holy place. (For they had seen before with him in the city Trophimus, an Ephesian, whom they supposed that Paul had brought into the temple.) And all the city was moved, and the people ran together : and they took Paul, and drew him out of the temple ; and forthwith the doors were shut. And as they went about* [2] *to kill him, tidings came unto the chief captain of the band, that all Jerusalem was in an uproar. Who immediately took soldiers and centurions, and ran down unto them : and when they saw the chief captain and the soldiers, they left beating of Paul. Then the chief captain came near, and took him, and commanded him to be bound with two chains ; and demanded who he was, and what he had done. And some cried one thing, some another, among the multitude : and when he could not know the certainty for the tumult, he commanded him to be carried into the castle. And when he came upon the stairs, so it was, that he was borne of the soldiers for the violence of the people.* [3] *For the multitude of the people followed after, crying, Away with him. And as Paul was to be led into the castle, he said unto the chief captain, May I speak unto thee ? Who said,*

Canst thou speak Greek ?   Art not thou[4] *that Egyptian which before these days madest an uproar, and leddest out into the wilderness four thousand*[5] *men that were murderers ?*

EMENDATIVE RENDERINGS.—(1.) From.   (2.) As they were seeking.   (3.) Crowd. (4.) Thou art not then.   (5.) Those four thousand.

EXEGETICAL REMARKS.—Having noticed the treatment which Paul met with at Jerusalem, the passage now before us narrates the treatment he met with from the intolerant Jew and the Roman authority.

ᴛ. First, His treatment by the intolerant Jew. "*And when seven days were ended.*" As the seven days were about to be fulfilled. The seven days which were to complete the observance of the vow (ver. 26). Perhaps the whole observance in this case was intended to be but seven days, as the time of such a vow was voluntary. The translation, " were almost ended," is not quite correct. The Greek implies no more than that the period of the seven days was about to be accomplished, without implying it was near the close of them when he was seized. By comparing the following places— chap. xxi. 18, 26 ; xxii. 30 ; xxiii. 12, 32; xxiv. 1, 11—it appears that the time of his seizure must have been near the beginning of those days.— DODDRIDGE.

" *Men of Israel, help.*" A short watchword to rouse the populace.

" *This is the man that teacheth all men everywhere against the people, and the law, and this place ; and further brought Greeks also into the temple, and hath polluted this holy place.*" " *This is the man.*" He is well known in Jerusalem ; his name was a household word, in all Israel. The charges of the infuriated mob, that this man spoke everywhere " against the people," were all false ; he had never spoken against the people, never against the law, never against the temple, and never polluted the holy place. This last would have been, according to Jewish law, a most criminal act, punishable by death. There was a court of the Gentiles, so called, within the precincts of the temple, into which they were allowed free admittance ; but beyond that,

into the holy place, or court of the Israelites, they were not suffered to penetrate ; and inscriptions were written upon the pillars, in the current languages, forbidding any but a Jew to cross the fatal threshold, as being unclean, and tending to desecrate the sanctuary of the Most High. " *This holy place.*" This was an interior court, in which some of the sacred things of the temple—as the altar of incense, golden table and candlesticks — were deposited and used. The Gentiles were not allowed to enter that, nor the *chel* or enclosure before it. Philo says that it was certain death for any one who was not a Jew to set his foot within the inner courts of the temple.—LIV.

" *For they had seen before with him in the city Trophimus, an Ephesian, whom they supposed that Paul had brought into the temple.*" The charge contained in the preceding verse was founded on a natural though inexcusable mistake of those who made it. " *Seen before*"—*i.e.,* before they saw Paul in the temple on the occasion just referred to. *Trophimus,* one of those who sailed from Greece before Paul, and awaited him in Troas. He and Tychicus were there described as Asians (or of Asia), which is here made more specific. " *Trophimus the Ephesian*" (not *an*)—*i.e.,* the one previously mentioned in more general terms, and also the one well known, both by name and person, to these Jewish countrymen. " *In the city*"— No doubt in the streets, beyond the temple area. " *They supposed*"—Were of opinion, or believed : a false impression, which might easily have been corrected, which they consequently had no right to propagate, but which exonerates them from the charge of sheer invention or malignant falsehood.—ALEX.

" *And all the city was moved, and the people ran together.*" The heart of

Jerusalem was stirred to its centre, and the mob, with characteristic haste and recklessness, ran together in pursuit of Paul.

"*And they took Paul, and drew him out of the temple.*" He had entered the temple in the fulfilment of a religious duty. The mob pursued him, and by violence drew him out, in order that they may not desecrate the holy place by shedding his blood in it. "*And forthwith the doors were shut.*" The shutting of the doors has been variously understood. According to some, it was intended to prevent Paul's taking refuge at the altar, as Adonijah and Joab did (1 Kings i. 50–53; ii. 28, 29), although the law of Moses recognised no right of asylum, except in the case of unpremeditated homicide (Exod. xxi. 12–14). Others suppose that it was meant to save the sacred precincts from the defilement of Paul's blood, whom they were now about to put to death. A third opinion is, that the shutting of the doors during the time of ceremonial service was a formal suspension of that service. Equally satisfactory with any of these explanations, and perhaps more natural than either, is the simple supposition, that the priests or Levites upon duty in the temple, when they saw Paul violently dragged out, shut the doors, in order to exclude both him and his assailants, with a view not only to their own security, but also to preserve the sanctuary from being made the scene of a tumultuous brawl.— ALEX.

Secondly, His treatment by the Roman authority. "*The chief captain of the band having heard that all Jerusalem was in an uproar, came in and took him, and commanded, and demanded who he was and what he had done.*" It appears from chapter xxiii. 26, that the name of this chief captain was Claudius Lysias. He was in charge of the garrison of the citadel of Antonio, near the temple. In the conduct of this Roman officer here, the following facts are observable:—

First, His presence checked the violence of the people. Having heard that all Jerusalem was in an uproar, he "*immediately took soldiers and centurions, and ran down with them.*"

Having probably a thousand men under his command, he hurried forth with a good body of soldiers to quell the disturbance. The sight of him put a stop to the cruelty that was being inflicted upon Paul. Mobs are great cowards. A few soldiers, as in this case, can overawe a mighty multitude.

Secondly, By his command Paul was bound in chains. He "*commanded him to be bound with two chains.*" The peace was broken. He supposed Paul to be the cause of it. His duty was to maintain order, and hence, perhaps, he thus captures Paul for future investigation. The Roman method of safe keeping was to chain the hands and feet of the prisoner, fastening him to a soldier on either side.

Thirdly, By his inquiries he fruitlessly sought to know the cause of the tumult. He "*demanded who he was, and what he had done.*" This was proper as a government officer. But in vain he sought the information : "*Some cried out one thing and some another among the multitude.*" The mass had no reason at all, and the few who had, felt perhaps that the reason was too bad to mention.

Fourthly, He directed Paul to be taken to the castle. This castle of Antonio, situated north of the temple, originally erected by the Maccabees, and called Baris, was rebuilt by Herod the Great, with much splendour and many conveniences, for the soldiers stationed in it, and named after Mark Antony. Its strength as a fortress was great, and it was so situated as to command the temple. Paul was conducted thither, probably in order to disperse the multitude, and to allow a further investigation. The soldiers bore him up the stairs on account of the violence of the people.

Fifthly, He misunderstood his history. "*And as Paul was to be led into the castle, he said unto the chief captain, May I speak with thee ? Who said, Canst thou speak Greek ? Art not thou that Egyptian* (xx., see note) *which before these days madest an uproar, and leddest out into the wilderness four thousand men that were murderers?*"

But Paul said, I am a man which am a Jew of Tarsus, a city in Cilicia, a citizen of no mean city." The fact that he made this mistake plainly indicates that he did not much concern himself with the religious history of the Jews, and felt no interest whatever in the progress of the Christian religion. Sixthly, He granted him permission to address the people. Paul's reply to his question threw new light upon his mind, and no doubt convinced him that his prisoner was no ordinary man. The apostle did not here exaggerate the importance of his birth-place, for Tarsus was the capital of Cilicia, and was famous for its schools of philosophy, and the high refinement and wealth of its people. Xenophon in his " Anabasis " calls Tarsus "a great and flourishing city;" and Josephus says that " it was the metropolis and most renowned city among the Cilicians." The bearing and the spirit of Paul in his answer induced the Roman to grant his request, and *" he gave him licence."* The wonderful advantage of this licence to Paul then and there to speak, will appear in the sequel.

HOMILETICS.—The narrative leads us to consider—

I. THE GENIUS OF RELIGIOUS INTOLERANCE. Three things come out in the conduct of these Jews which always characterise the spirit of religious intolerance :—

First, *Cunning.* This is indicated in the watchword they employed to rouse the populace—*" Men of Israel, help!"* hereby naïvely intimating that Paul was an enemy to all Israel ; that he was the opponent of every Jew, and that all should make a common cause in crushing him. Artifice has ever been the instrument of religious bigotry. Its miserable genius works by inuendo and insinuation. Another characteristic of religious intolerance is—

Secondly, *Falsehood.* It fabricates false allegations. " This is the man that teacheth all men everywhere against the people, and the law, and this place ; and further brought Greeks also into the temple, and hath polluted this holy place." Now this was all a spiteful fiction. Did Paul "teach all men everywhere against the people?" It is true he often denounced their bigotry, and their exclusiveness; but never a word of his was spoken against their race, and their high distinctions. Did he ever disparage "the law?" Never. It is true he often taught that its ceremonies were not binding upon Gentile disciples, nor of eternal obligation even upon the Jew ; but he never defamed it, never spoke of it with contempt. In truth, he always displayed a profound regard for it as a grand, old, and divine institution, the glory of the ancient world. Did he ever speak " against this place "—the temple itself? It is true that he taught that God dwelt not " in temples made with hands," but was to be worshipped everywhere ; but never a word did he utter in dishonour of the temple. Did he ever bring " Greeks into the temple, and pollute the holy place ? " This would have been a most criminal offence, and one punishable with death. For, although there was a court of the Gentiles within the precincts of the temple, into which Gentiles were allowed admission, their entrance into " the holy place," or court of the Israelites, was strongly prohibited. Inscriptions were written upon the pillars, prohibiting any but a Jew to cross the fatal threshold. Philo says it was certain death for any one who was not a Jew to set his foot within the inner courts of the temple According to a speech which Josephus puts into the mouth of Titus the Jews were suffered by the Romans themselves to kill even a Roman who guiltily entered this sacred place. But there was no evidence that the apostle ever took a Gentile within the sacred enclosure. The reason they had for the charge was a baseless supposition—" Trophimus," whom they " *supposed* " that Paul had brought into the temple. They " supposed "—they did not know it —they perhaps saw Paul walking in the streets with him, and they rushed to the conjecture.

But whilst those charges are so utterly groundless, they bear testimony to three things concerning Paul—

1. *His notoriety.* " This is the man," implying that he is well known, and that none in the city require any further particulars concerning him. This Paul has in a few short years rung his name into the ear of all Israel, and painted his image on the imagination of the Jewish people. These charges bear witness to—

2. *His industry.* They state that " he taught *all men, everywhere.*" Thus, they unwittingly confirmed the apostle's own description of his labours, and also his biographer's account of his marvellous activity. These charges bear witness to—

3. *His power.* Their charges imply more than their sense of his notoriety and indefatigability. They testify to his amazing influence over the age and land in which he lived. Had he been an obscure man, and of feeble influence, they would not have spoken or acted as they did. They felt he was not one of the common horde, whom they could easily crush, but a man of such colossal influence as required the force of a whole nation to arrest and confine.

There is yet another characteristic here of religious intolerance.

Thirdly, *Violence.* We are told, they " laid hands on him ; " " they drew him out of the temple;" " they went about to kill him; " and, more than this, they scourged him, for, we are told, "they left beating of Paul." Violence has ever marked the history of religious intolerance. It does not argue, for it lacks an intelligent faith in its own cause. It has, therefore, ever had recourse to fraud and force. The tongue of slander, the arm of law, and the implements of persecution, it substitutes for reason and suasion. The narrative of the hostility reveals—

II. THE GENIUS OF A MOB ASSEMBLY. Men are pretty well the same in all ages. The same classes, under similar circumstances, come out in similar phases. Mobs are the same everywhere, and in all time. The mob gathered in the streets of Jerusalem evinced just those things which mobs show now in Paris, New York, or London. Here is—

First, *Credulousness.* The false cry raised by the Asiatic Jews, and the false charges made, were taken up at once, were accepted without any inquiry. " All the city was moved." Man is naturally a credulous animal. He has a propensity for believing. And this propensity gets intensity in association with numbers. Hence it often turns out that what even a credulous man will not believe when alone, he readily accepts when issuing from the lip of a dema-gogue in a vast assembly. Men accept creeds in Churches which they repudiate in private discussion. Mobs are awfully credulous. They will swallow whatever is offered, without testing it by taste, or masticating it by inquiry.

Secondly, *Senselessness.* Why did the people rush forth from their houses, from along the streets, and crowd about the temple, in one vast and tumultuous mass? What did they know about the charges made against Paul? Nothing. Hence, when the chief captain " came near and demanded to know who Paul was, and what he had done," *some cried one thing, and some another.* They had no intel-ligent account to give. Reason had abdicated the throne ; they were the mere creatures of impulse. The mob in the streets of Ephesus on a previous occasion (Acts xix. 32) acted in the same way. Then, also, " some cried one thing and some another, and the more part knew not wherefore they were come together." A sad sight this. A vast multitude of human beings moved not by intelligent motives, but by blind impulse. It is this senselessness that makes the opinions of mobs so worthless, their movements so reckless, and their existence so dangerous.

Thirdly, *Contagiousness.* So liable were the multitudes to be affected by the iniquitous opinions of those Asiatic Jews, that no sooner were they uttered than this contagion was felt through the city. " *The people ran together,*" and when they came together their hearts surged with the same common passions. Their blood was heated with the same thought, their minds inspired with the same purpose. Their leaders, the bigots, said, " Men of ISRAEL, help," and the " *people ran together,*" and the " *multitude of the people followed after, crying, Away with him.*" With all our metaphysical science, how little we know of the many subtle elements by which man influences his fellow. How amazing it is, that one man's thought, whether good or bad, may influence a nation, making millions burn with the fire of a common sentiment !

CONCLUSION.—From the whole, many important subjects rise into prominence. We shall only mention three :—

First, *The great mixture of characters in social life.* Here, in Jerusalem, now what a diversity of character figures on the stage! Here are the evangelical Christians, under the presidency of James the apostle ; here are the Asiatic Jews, animated by all the malice of religious exclusiveness and intolerance ; and here are the Romans, despising, it may be, alike the religion of the Jew and Christian, but inflexible in their loyalty to legal order; and here is Paul exhibiting a type of spiritual nobility unapproached by the greatest of his age. Such is a picture of human society as it has ever been, and as it still appears. Though all, in every human community are of the same origin, made of the same materials, organised upon the same natural type, related to the same grand moral system, and doomed to the same eternity, yet in thought, and feeling, and character, there is a marvellous diversity. Human souls differ in their character and spheres as the stars of heaven in their nature and in their orbits.

Secondly, *The great advantage of civil government.* What enormities would not that infuriated and tumultuous mob, surging there about the glorious old temple in Jerusalem, have committed, had not the Roman officer and his soldiers showed their face and interposed. Paul was being beaten to death until the representative of civil law appeared. Civil governments are a necessity so long as society remains depraved; and God in His mercy has ordained, not, of course, their wrongs, nor, perhaps, their forms, but certainly their existence and their spheres.

Thirdly, *The antagonism of the depraved heart to Christianity.* Why was Paul that one central figure in Jerusalem now against which all that was corrupt in the city pelted its fury and hurled its anathemas? Simply because he embodied and radiated the pure morality, the spiritual worship, and the universal love of the gospel. Christianity clashes with the corrupt in human nature, stirs it into malice, and makes it rage with fury. Hence it is that its progress is ever a history of battles—battles fought on the arena of the sinner's heart.

Acts 21:39-22:21

PAUL'S FINAL VISIT TO JERUSALEM.—HIS ADDRESS ON THE STAIRS.

1. *His autobiographic defence*

" *But Paul said, I am a man which am a Jew of Tarsus, a city in Cilicia, a citizen of no mean city:*[1] *and, I beseech thee, suffer me to speak unto the people. And when he had given him licence, Paul stood on the stairs, and beckoned with the hand unto the people. And when there was made a great silence, he spake unto them in the Hebrew tongue, saying, Men,*[2] *brethren, and fathers, hear ye my defence which I make now unto you. (And when they heard that he spake in the Hebrew tongue to them, they kept the more silence: and he saith), I am verily[3] a man which am a Jew, born in Tarsus, a city in Cilicia,[4] yet brought up in this city at the feet of Gamaliel, and taught according to the perfect manner of the law of the fathers, and was zealous toward God, as ye all are this day. And I persecuted this way unto the death, binding and delivering into prisons both men and women. As also the high priest doth bear me witness, and all the estate of the elders: from whom also I received letters unto the brethren, and went to Damascus, to bring them which were there bound unto Jerusalem, for to be punished. And it came to pass, that, as I made my journey, and was come nigh unto Damascus[5] about noon, suddenly there shone from heaven a great light round about me. And I fell unto the ground, and heard a voice saying unto me, Saul, Saul, why persecutest thou me? And I answered, Who art thou, Lord? And he said unto me, I am Jesus of Nazareth, whom thou persecutest. And they that were with me saw indeed the light, and were afraid;[6] but they heard not the voice of him that spake to me. And I said, What shall I do, Lord? And the Lord said unto me, Arise, and go into Damascus; and there it shall be told thee of all things which are appointed for thee to do. And when I could not see for the glory of that light, being led by the hand of them that were with me, I came into Damascus. And one Ananias, a devout man according to the law, having a good report of all the Jews which dwelt there, came unto me, and stood, and said unto me, Brother Saul, receive thy sight. And the same hour I looked up upon him. And he said, The God of our fathers hath chosen thee, that thou shouldest know his will, and see that Just One, and shouldest hear the voice of his mouth. For thou shalt be his witness unto all men of what thou hast seen and heard. And now, why tarriest thou? arise, and be baptized, and wash away thy sins, calling on the name of the Lord.[7] And it came to pass, that, when I was come again to Jerusalem, even while I prayed in the temple, I was in a trance; and saw him saying unto me, Make haste, and get thee quickly out of Jerusalem: for they will not receive thy testimony concerning me. And I said, Lord, they know that I imprisoned and beat in every synagogue them that believed on thee: and when the blood of thy martyr Stephen was shed, I also was standing by, and consenting unto his death,[8] and kept the raiment of them that slew him. And he said unto me, Depart: for I will send thee far hence unto the Gentiles."*

EMENDATIVE RENDERINGS.—(1.) A citizen of no mean city in Cilicia. (2.) Omit this word. (3.) Omit this word. (4.) In Tarsus of Cilicia. (5.) Coming nigh unto Damascus. (6.) Omit *and were afraid.* (7.) His name. (8.) Omit *unto his death.* —ALF.

EXEGETICAL REMARKS. — Paul appears before us now in a new condition; he is a prisoner; he was "bound with two chains" (Acts xxi. 33). In this condition we shall find him now in every chapter to the close of his memorable life. He closes his connexion with this city by two defences of himself—the one addressed to the people, and the other to the great council of the nation. We have now to notice HIS DEFENCE BEFORE THE PEOPLE.

This subject will take us from the last verse of the 21st chapter to the 30th of the next. Indeed, the last verse of the 21st ought to have been put as the first of the 22d chapter; the division is unfortunate, unjustifiable, and unwise. The position from which the apostle delivered his defence before the people is noteworthy.

He "*stood on the stairs.*" The stairs were the steps leading from the area of the temple into the castle of Antonio, and up which he had been forcibly borne by the soldiers (Acts xxi. 35). His position was a commanding one, standing on an elevation commanding a view of the temple, with crowds assembled at the base of the building, protected from their fury by the soldiers, having the "licence" of the "chief captain" to speak, he addressed them with all the freedom of his noble and Christ-inspired nature.

"*And when he had given him licence, Paul stood on the stairs, and beckoned with the hand unto the people; and when there was made a great silence, he spake unto them in the Hebrew tongue, saying,*" &c. He "beckoned" with his hand to still the noise of the people, and he spoke in "the Hebrew tongue," not because they would not have understood Greek, but because he wished to command their sympathies by demonstrating that he was an Israelite. With great rhetorical adroitness, he further conciliates the good-will of his audience by the courteous and even affectionate terms with which he addresses them as "men, brethren, and fathers." So far he succeeds.

"*And when they heard that he spake in the Hebrew tongue to them, they kept the more silence, and he saith,*" &c. The multitude, which just before had raged like ocean in the storm, were reduced to a breathless stillness, with eager ear to listen to what the prisoner had to say. In Paul's defence on this occasion there is nothing like special pleading — no attempt to invalidate opposing evidence. As an honest man, who felt that his life would bear scrutiny, he gives a brief sketch of himself, that is all.

First, He avows himself a Jew by birth and education.

"*I am verily a man which am a*

Jew." This he avers in order to refute the charge on which he was arrested, namely, that of traitorous hostility to the religion of his fathers.

"*I am a Jew, born in Tarsus, a city in Cilicia*—(2 Cor. xi. 22; Phil. iii. 5) —*brought up in this city at the feet of Gamaliel.*" This Gamaliel, by general consent, was an eminent Pharisee, a member of the Sanhedrim, and appeared before in this history, (chap. v. 40). "*At the feet*"—In Bible language, the teacher is said to be at the head of his disciples (2 Kings ii. 3). The pupil sits at the feet,—an intimation of the intimate nearness and subjection to the teacher's authority.

"*And taught according to the perfect manner of the law of the fathers, zealous towards God, as ye all are this day.*" He was not only a Jew, a Jew, though born in Tarsus, yet brought up in Jerusalem, and taught by one of the most distinguished Rabbis, but he was taught perfectly — strictly in their law, and he was moreover "*zealous towards God*"—a zealot of God.

Secondly, He describes his persecuting zeal against the Christians.

"*And I persecuted this way unto the death, binding and delivering into prisons both men and women.*" "*This way*"—that new sect or religion. "*Unto death*"—not merely in desired intention, but in fact. He was implicated in the martyrdom of Stephen (chap. vi. 9). "He was exceedingly mad against them," &c.

"*As also the high priest doth bear me witness, and all the estate of the elders: from whom also I received letters unto the brethren, and went to Damascus, to bring them which were there bound to Jerusalem, for to be punished.*" Here he refers them to proof of the opposition, which he once felt, in common with them, "*this way*"—this Christianity. As if he had said, Do you doubt me? Ask the high priest before you, who commissioned me to persecute the Christians; ask the "*elders,*" your presbyters, who gave me letters of introduction when I went to Damascus on the mission of persecution.

Thirdly, He narrates his miraculous conversion.

"*And it came to pass that as I made my journey, and was come nigh unto Damascus.*" He begins his own account of his conversion, which must be compared with chap. ix. 13. The explanatory remarks which we have offered on that chapter preclude the necessity of going minutely into the account here. In comparing the account here with that given in chap. ix., we discover certain formal differences. (1.) There are points stated here which are not found there,—such, for example, as the "*trance*" (ver. 17). (2.) There are points stated here in a form somewhat different to what they are stated there. For example, it is stated in chap. ix., that they heard a voice, and here they heard not a voice. It is stated here that they "*that were with me saw indeed the light, and were afraid; but they heard not the voice of him that spake to me.*" And the words there are, "the men that journeyed with me heard a voice, and were speechless." There are, says Alexander, several possible solutions of this seeming inconsistency. One consists in referring the two statements to successive points of time, so that they are said to have heard the voice at last, but not at first, or *vice versâ.* Another makes a difference between the accusative and genitive construction of the verb *to hear*, the one denoting mere sensation, the other intellectual perception. Substantially identical with this, but simpler and more natural, is the distinction between hearing a voice speak and hearing what it says; as nothing is more common in our public bodies than the complaint that a speaker is not heard, *i.e.,* his words are not distinguished, though his voice may be audible and even loud. In these two obvious and familiar senses, it might be said, with equal truth, that Paul's companions heard the voice, *i.e.,* knew that it was speaking, and that they did not hear it, *i.e.,* did not know what it said. Whether this distinction was designed to be suggested by the difference of construction, or the change of case already mentioned, is a doubtful point, but one which does not affect the validity or truth of the solution. It is positively favoured, on the other hand, by the only remaining variation, namely, that instead of the *voice* (ix. 7), we have here the more explicit phrase, *the voice of the* (one) *speaking to me,* which, though it does not necessarily suggest, admits and justifies, the supposition that the voice which they did not hear was speaking, *i.e.,* an articulate, a distinguishable voice, and not mere vocal sound or utterance, without regard to words or language. A remarkable analogy is furnished by the case recorded in John xii. 28–30, where some said that it thundered, and others, that an angel spoke, implying that it was a voice (and not a mere sound) that they heard, while the Evangelist records the very words that it pronounced. In this case, as in that before us, it might well be said of the first class mentioned, that they did, and that they did not, hear the "voice from heaven." Their mistaking it for thunder proves at the same time that they heard it in the one sense, and that they did not hear it in the other.

Fourthly, He shows that his reception into the new body was by Jewish agency.

"*And one Ananias, a devout man according to the law*" (12–16). Here Paul omits the narrative of some things that Luke had stated in chap. ix., and adds other things which the historian had not recorded. The differences, such as they are, are incidental proofs of the genuineness of the history.

Fifthly, He gives an account of his apostleship amongst the Gentiles (17–21).

"*And it came to pass that when I was come again to Jerusalem, even while I prayed in the temple, I was in a trance.*" "*When I was come again*"—Paul's first return is mentioned in chap. ix. 26. The genitive προσευχομένου μου, *while I prayed,* follows this (Gr.) dative: *me orante* is the Latin equivalent of προσευχομένου μου: these words have a closer connexion with the *trance.*—C. E. T.

HOMILETICS.—In a very general glance at the whole of this autobiographic defence we mark several things as noteworthy.

I. IN IT SELF IS CRIMINATED. *He virtually denounces himself.* " I persecuted this way unto the death," &c. There is not a word here uttered by the apostle in vindication of his conduct prior to his conversion. He paints the whole in the dark colours of fact. He virtually denounces himself; he confesses guilt in connexion with the martyrdom of Stephen. What can any man discover in his history previous to his conversion on which he can look with complacency ?

II. IN IT CHRIST IS HONOURED. He honours Christ in several ways :—

First, *His conversion he ascribed to Him.* Christ's advent to him on the road to Damascus effected the great change. The apostle always ascribes his conversion to Christ: " *When it pleased God,*" &c.

Secondly, *His commission he ascribed to Him.* " He said unto me, Depart, for I will send thee far hence unto the Gentiles." Christ became everything to the apostle after his conversion : " For me to live is Christ, and to die is gain."

III. IN IT CONVERSION IS MEMORABLE. About twenty-five years had passed away since Paul's conversion, yet the incidents were so fresh in memory that he details them with all the minuteness with which they were detailed at first, as found in the ninth chapter. Conversion is the most *memorable* epoch in the biography of souls.

But looking with a little more minuteness, we find utterances in this autobiographic defence of the apostle on which many *sermons* could be preached.

We subjoin the following—

NO. I.—HIS FALLING TO THE GROUND.

" *And I fell unto the ground, and heard a voice saying unto me, Saul, Saul, why persecutest thou me ?* "

This remarkable verse presents to us four great general truths.

I. THAT MAN IS THE OBJECT OF DIVINE INSPECTION. Though Christ was now in heaven, yet His eye followed Saul on his way to Damascus. Little did Saul know that He whom he hated, whose disciples he sought to destroy, and whose name he endeavoured to blot from the earth, knew all about him—not only marked his every footstep, but saw his every passing thought and feeling. That the great God knows all about the life and conduct of the *individual* man, is obvious. First, *From the omniscience of His nature.* He who sees all things, sees each thing—the minute as well as the vast. Secondly, *From the history of mankind.* Hagar in the wilderness, Jacob at Bethel, Elijah in the cave, and now Saul on his way to Damascus. Thirdly, *From the teachings of the Bible.* (See Psalm cxxxix.; Prov. xv. 3; Heb. iv. 13.) This solemn fact should make us serious, circumspect, devout.

II. THAT CHRIST IS THE ORIGINATOR OF MORAL REFORMATION. What now gave the turning-point to Paul's life? The manifestation of Christ in the "light," the "voice," the address. "Saul, Saul," &c. Conversion does not originate with self; nor with the agency of man outside, but always with Christ. It is a resurrection. Who can raise the dead but He? It is a creation. Who can create but He? This fact agrees: First, *With the consciousness of the good.* The good everywhere involuntarily ascribe their goodness to Him. This is the burden of heaven's anthem. Secondly, *This agrees with the teachings of Scripture.* "Of His own will begat He us," &c. "When it pleased God to reveal His Son in me," &c.

III. THAT HUMILITY IS THE CONDITION OF HEAVENLY COMMUNION. When did Saul hear the voice of Jesus? When was his soul put *en rapport* with the divine mind? When he had fallen to the ground. Humility implies a deep sense of need, and without that sense the soul will never open its eye or its ear to the divine. We must take off the shoes from our feet, like Moses—fall to the dust, like Isaiah —smite our breast, like the publican, if we would hear what God has to say. "Unto that man will I look who is of a broken spirit," &c.

IV. THAT UNION WITH CHRIST IS THE PRIVILEGE OF THE GOOD. "Why persecutest thou ME?" What does this mean? Personally, Christ was in the heavens, beyond the reach of mortals. It means that so dear are His disciples to His heart, that their sufferings are His. He bears their infirmities, and carries their sorrows, even in heaven. They are "members of His body," and no part can be wounded without quivering to the sensorium. (See Matt. xxv. 40, 45.) "Inasmuch as ye have done it to the least of these," &c.

In this autobiographic defence there is another fertile subject for a sermon—

NO. II.—THE SOUNDS AND SIGHTS OF LIFE

"*And they that were with me saw indeed the light, and were afraid; but they heard not the voice of Him that spake to me*" (xxii. 9). "*And the men which journeyed with him stood speechless, hearing a voice, but seeing no man*" (ix. 7).

Here is a record of the *supernatural* in the life of Paul and his travelling companions when approaching Damascus. The fact that these supernatural phenomena were at "mid-day," and that the apostle's fellow-travellers were deeply sensible of them as well as the apostle himself, demonstrate that "the voice" that thundered in the ear, and "the light" that flashed around them were *objective* realities. The little discrepancy between the occurrence as given by Luke in the ninth chapter, and as stated by the apostle himself in the twenty-second, instead of invalidating, confirms the authenticity of the accounts. Identity of statement concerning the same occurrence, by two different individuals, after an interval of about twenty-five years, might justly awaken serious suspicions of collusion. You have here two things :—

First, *A voice heard by all, but understood only by Paul.* The voice produced, indeed, an impression on his companions. It vibrated on their ear, and so shocked their nervous system that they fell "speechless;" but it conveyed no idea. Whereas, it conveyed a wonderful message deep into Paul's soul. "I heard a voice saying to me in the Hebrew tongue," &c.

Secondly, *A light seen by all, but revealing nothing except to Paul.* The mystic light radiated about all with a brightness excelling that of "midday," and flooding them with feelings of alarm. But it revealed nothing. It was mere dazzling brightness; nothing more. But in that radiance what did Paul see? "The Lord, even Jesus, appeared unto" him.

Now, this *extraordinary* circumstance indicates what is *common* in human life. Everywhere there are men, hearing the same voice, but receiving different impressions; seeing the same lights, but observing different objects. A "voice" fraught with deep meaning to some, is mere empty sound to others. A "light" revealing the grandest realities to some, discloses nothing to others. There is everywhere through human society, diverse subjectivity under identical eternalism; or different mental phenomena under identical circumstances.

I. MEN'S LIVES IN RELATION TO MATERIAL NATURE SHOW THIS. The "*lights*" of nature, to the thoughtless multitude, reveal nothing but mere sensuous forms—just what they reveal to the brute, and nothing more. To the superstitious they reveal hosts of unearthly existences, presiding over the various operations of the world, dreaded as demons or worshipped as gods. To the sceptical philosopher they reveal nothing but a grand system of well-organised forces, moving and working by its own inherent impulse with all the resistlessness of an absolute fate. To the enlightened and devout Christian, they reveal a wise and loving Father, "WHO is God over all, blessed for evermore." The "*voices*" of nature, too, which are boundlessly varied, and set in every key, convey different impressions to different minds. To some nothing but mere sensation, to others superstitious awe, to others scientific intelligence, to others thoughts from God himself.

Thus it is that the same world is a different thing to different minds.

II. MEN'S LIVES IN RELATION TO HUMAN HISTORY SHOW THIS. The history of the world, from antediluvian days to this hour, is very differently regarded by different men. Its *lights* and *voices* reveal varied and almost opposite things. To some, history is *without any governing law at all.* Its social, mercantile, political movements are ascribable only to blind impulse and capricious passions. All is chaos. There is no law seen shaping or systematising the whole. To others, history *has only the governing law of human might.* These explain all on the principle that the strong preys upon the weak. The progress and decline of commerce, the rise and fall of empires, the fate of mighty battles, are all ascribable to superior might. To others, history *is governed exclusively by evil.* The devil is absolutely the god of the human world. The whole lives and acts under the shadow of his dark wings. He is in the schemes of the trader, the thunders of the orator, the edicts of the despot, the craft of the priest, the rage of the warrior. He inspires the activities of men, and shapes the destinies of the race. To others, history *is governed by the mediatorial plan of God.* The restorative purpose of Heaven, as revealed in the Bible, is seen running through the ages, stimulating, shaping, and subordinating all things. Even the bitterest sufferings of humanity are regarded as parturition throes giving birth to a higher order of things. Thus, then, through all human history it holds true that, as with Paul and his companions, the same sounds and sights differently affect different men.

III. MEN'S LIVES IN RELATION TO THE INSPIRED ORACLE SHOW THIS. The Bible has wonderful " *lights,*" and wonderful " *sounds,*" but nothing is more true than that they differently affect different men. Ecclesiastical history, theological polemics, as well as the religious life of our own age, are fraught with illustrations of this. The sceptic and the believer, the Papist and the Protestant, the Calvinist and the Pelagian, the Socinian and the Trinitarian, the Churchman and the Nonconformist, are examples as to how the same "light" and "voice" of the one Book affect different men. What is the articulate voice of God to one is mere hollow sound to another. And what is " *a light,*" revealing even the Eternal Himself, to one is either darkness or stupefying brightness to another.

IV. MEN'S LIVES IN RELATION TO THE GOSPEL MINISTRY SHOW THIS. How differently the same sermon is regarded by various members of the congregation! The sermon which, as a divine " *voice,*" speaks to the conscience of some, has no meaning to others; or which, as divine " *light,*" flashes moral conviction and reveals Christ to some, is either not seen at all, or regarded as a mere glare of human genius, or a blaze of human enthusiasm, revealing nothing divine.

CONCLUSION—

First, *This subject reveals a distinguishing attribute of human nature.* Men have the power of hearing and of seeing *with the soul.* Brutes have "the hearing ear and seeing eye," as we have, but all they see and hear terminate in the region of sensation. Souls have inner eyes and ears. Ezekiel, Isaiah, John on Patmos, our own Milton, &c., show what men can see and hear with those organs of the soul. Christ has told us that the pure in heart shall see God Himself. Man, in one word, has the power of *receiving, modifying,* and *interpreting* the impression the outward makes upon him.

Secondly, *This subject explains the great difference between spiritually and carnally minded men.* Society may be divided into two classes—the carnal and the spiritual : the one living to the flesh and for the flesh ; the other to the spirit and for the spirit. Why this difference? The one hears in the sounds, and sees in the sights of life what the other does not. The spiritual realises the spiritual even here. He looks away from " the things that are seen and temporal."

Thirdly, *The subject presents an object of life after which all should strive.* Each man should strive to get the eyes and the ears of his soul so quickened as to see and hear the divine everywhere in life. When the servant of Elisha had his eye and ear open, he saw and heard the supernatural. So it will be with us. We are now in the spiritual world. Spirits innumerable crowd around us. God is present. The voices of eternity are here, and yet we are deaf to them.

Here is another passage in his autobiographic defence, and the subject is—

NO. III.—THE DIVINE ORDINATION OF HUMAN LIFE

"*And he said, The God of our fathers hath chosen thee, that thou shouldst know his will, and see that Just One, and shouldst hear the voice of his mouth. For thou shalt be his witness unto all men of what thou hast seen and heard.*"

The verb, προεχειρίσατο, which is here translated, " chosen," only occurs in this form in one other place in the New Testament (xxvi. 16), where it has the sense of " making," or " appointing." The idea here is ordination, or setting apart. Ananias tells Paul that the God of their fathers had ordained him to the life specified in these verses. And truly the life is one of the highest that man can live on earth. What is the *ordination?* It is—

I. TO AN UNDERSTANDING OF THE HIGHEST SUBJECT. " *That thou shouldst know His will.*" God has a will—a will in relation to all existences—a will in relation to every individual man. His will is at once the spring of all existence, the rule of all motion, the standard of all character. To understand it is to understand the philosophy of all being, the cause of all phenomena, and the science of all duty. All true subjects of thought are related to it, and lead into it as radia to their centre. It is, therefore, the sublimest subject of thought. It expresses the divine nature, it reveals the universe. It is, therefore, the great theme for the study of eternity. To the study of this Paul was thus ordained. He began it then, he is at it now, he will continue at it for ever. He was ordained—

II. To a vision of the highest existence. " And see that Just One." Not only to understand the will which is the law of the universe, but to see the Lawgiver himself. " *That* Just One." Who? Evidently the Messiah—the God-man. (See Acts iii. 14.) He is called " that Just One," not merely because, as God, He is absolutely just, the fountain of eternal rectitude, nor merely because, as man, He " did no sin, neither was guile found in His mouth ;" but as Mediator who has engaged to make *unjust men just*. His work as Mediator is to make a world of unjust men just to themselves, just to their fellows, just to the universe, just to God. This is His work, and His work exclusively. Hence He is designated " *that* Just One." Paul was ordained to see Him.

First, *In order to renovate him as a sinner*. The vision of Christ is the soul-transforming force. " Beholding, as in a glass, the glory of the Lord, we are changed," &c.

Secondly, *In order to qualify him as an apostle*. It would seem that one of the necessary qualifications of an apostle was that he should have a personal view of Christ. Hence he says, " Am I not an apostle ? have I not seen Christ our Lord ?"

Thirdly, *In order to consummate his blessedness as a man*. What is the heaven of souls? The beatific vision of Christ. The sight of Him thrills all, brightens all, elevates all, enraptures all (Rev. v. 6, 12).

He was ordained—

III. To a reception of the highest communications. " And shouldst hear the voice of His mouth." To have a *direct* communication with Christ seemed necessary in order to put Paul on a level with the twelve apostles (Acts xiii. 3 ; Gal. i. 1). But whilst this was specially required for Paul as an apostle, it is a high privilege to which God " hath chosen," or appointed all good men. And what a privilege ! Who teaches like Christ? " Never man spake like this man." So they said who heard Him when on earth, when He spoke only the few things that they could bear. His words on earth were original, suggestive, soul-inspiring. But to listen to that voice in heaven, what an ecstasy of joy ! Every utterance of that voice will then dispel some cloud of mystery from the sky of spirits, and open up some new realm of thought to the intellect, some new domain of beauty to the imagination. What is the voice of your Platos, or even of your Pauls, compared to the voice of Christ? The glimmerings of rushlight to the light of day. He was ordained—

IV. TO A DISCHARGE OF THE HIGHEST MISSION. What work was he chosen to? "Thou shalt be His witness unto all men, of what thou hast seen and heard."

First, *To bear witness of the highest facts about the greatest Being.* Paul was appointed as a witness for Christ. He was to declare all that he knew from observation and experience concerning the Son of God. This he nobly did.

Secondly, To bear witness of the highest facts about the greatest Being *to all mankind.* "Unto all men." To the Jew as well as to the Gentile.

Oh, brothers! How earnestly should we aspire to such an ordination!

Here is another passage in his autobiographic defence requiring a separate discourse, and the subject is—

GETTING RID OF SIN

" *And now, why tarriest thou? arise, and be baptized, and wash away thy sins, calling on the name of the Lord.*"

The narrative in the ninth chapter records the execution of this proposition, but not the proposition itself. Here Ananias calls upon Saul to be baptized; there, we are told, that after he had received his sight "he arose and was baptized." The discrepancy here is not contradictory, but supplementary. The words suggest three remarks concerning the work of getting rid of sin. It is a *possible,* a *praying*, and an *urgent* work.

I. IT IS A POSSIBLE WORK. "Be baptized and wash away thy sins." The Holy Word represents the sinful state of the soul under different figures. *Sleep, slavery, disease, death, pollution.* Here *pollution*— the words imply, First, *That it is a cleansable* pollution. It is not ingrained. It is a something separable from the soul. It can be washed away. Baptism to Saul would not only be, what it ever was, the ordinance by which men passed from one religion to another, but would symbolise that moral cleansing of the soul which he so deeply needed. No water, of course, can wash the soul; all the waters of the Atlantic could not cleanse one moral stain. There is, however, a spiritual water, "the truth as it is in Jesus," by which the Eternal Spirit does cleanse (Ezek. xxxvi. 25, 27; 1 Cor. vi. 11; Titus iii. 7; Eph. v. 25, 26; Rev. i. 5, 6, vii. 14). Thank God, it is possible on this earth to separate the sin from the sinner. Secondly, That it is a pollution of which man must cleanse *himself:* "Wash away thy sins." No one can do it for us.

II. IT IS A PRAYING WORK. "Calling upon the name of the Lord." The correcter reading seems to be "calling on *His* name"—αὐτοῦ rather than κυρίου. Christ's name, however, is Himself; to call upon His name is to call upon Him.

First, *Christ is the efficient cleanser of human souls.* His work is to wash away the sins of the world, to purify the moral garments of humanity, to make them white, "without spot or wrinkle," &c.

Secondly, *Prayer is the ordained means of attaining His cleansing influence.* "Whosoever shall call upon the name of the Lord shall be saved" (Rom. x. 13). The prayer addressed to Him in the upper room at Jerusalem, brought down His cleansing influences on the day of Pentecost. You may get wealth by industry; intelligence by study; wisdom by experience; but moral purity only by prayer. Prayer takes the soul up to the Fountain opened for the washing away of all uncleanness.

III. IT IS AN URGENT WORK. "Why tarriest thou?" Or, more literally, why art thou about acting, instead of acting really? Do not hesitate a moment. Be prompt. What thou doest, do quickly. The importance of promptitude may be argued—

First, *From the greatness of the work.* Eternity depends upon it.

Secondly, *From the time already lost.* The whole life should have been given to it, but much has run to waste.

Thirdly, *From the increase of difficulties.* Disinclination, insensibility, force of habit—all increase by delay.

Fourthly, *From the character of the future.* It is (1.) *brief;* (2.) *uncertain.*

Here is another passage in his autobiographic defence requiring a separate discourse, and the subject is—

A COMMON THING REACHING THE WONDERFUL

"While I prayed in the temple, I was in a trance."

I. HERE IS A COMMON THING. A man *praying.* Prayer is an instinct of the soul. Danger seldom fails to rouse this instinct into a passionate supplication even in the most depraved. (See Psalm cvii. 13.) Volney, in a storm at sea, a striking example of this. Alas! more than half the prayers of the world are worthless. All worthless prayer may be divided into two classes—

First, *Prayer addressed to the wrong god.*

Secondly, *Prayer addressed to the right God in a wrong way.* The universal tendency of man to pray implies the soul's innate belief in some of the leading facts of theology, such as (1) the being, (2) the personality, (3) the presence, and (3) the entreatability of God.

II. Here is a common thing REACHING THE WONDERFUL. The trance, ἔκστασις, is the state in which a man has passed out of the usual order of his life, beyond the usual limits of consciousness and volition. To an " ecstasy " in the apostle Paul we owe the mission which was the starting-point of the history of the universal Church, the command which bade him " depart far hence unto the Gentiles." It is supposed by some, and with much probability, that it is to this trance Paul refers (2 Cor. xii. 1–5) when he speaks of being caught up to the third heaven, Now, it was *prayer*, a common thing, that conducted Paul into this *wonderful* state of ecstasy. It is prayer that lifts the soul into the transcendental.

CONCLUSION—
First, *Learn the sublime possibilities of the human soul.* By a mysterious power of abstraction it can close up all the physical senses, shut out the external universe, and transport itself on the wings of an angel into a world where there are scenes too grand for description, and communications surpassing utterance. Isaiah, Ezekiel, Daniel, John, as well as Paul, were often transported to these supernal states.

Secondly, *Learn the incomparable worth of true prayer.* It was while Paul was praying that he got into this trance. Prayer is the road into the celestial. While Daniel was praying, the man Gabriel touched him about the time of evening oblation, and said, " O Daniel," &c. (Dan. ix. 21–23). While Peter was praying on the housetop, he fell into ecstasy, and a man stood, &c. (Acts x. 9, &c.)

Acts 22:22, 23

PAUL'S FINAL VISIT TO JERUSALEM.—II. HIS ADDRESS ON THE STAIRS
BEFORE THE POPULACE

2. *An audience too prejudiced to be convinced*

" And they gave him audience unto this word,[1] and then lifted up their voices, and said, Away with such a fellow from the earth ; for it is[2] not fit that he should live. And as they cried out, and cast off[3] their clothes, and threw dust into the air."

EMENDATIVE RENDERINGS.—(1.) Saying. (2.) Was. (3.) Shook.

EXEGETICAL REMARKS. — Here we have the result of Paul's splendid defence. His auditory was too prejudiced to be convinced by any amount of argument. Though his address was so respectful, so frank, so sufficient in every respect for the occasion, no sooner did he refer to his mission to the Gentiles in the 21st verse, than they broke out into a violent interruption.

" *And he said unto me, Depart, for I will send thee far hence unto the Gentiles. And they gave him audience unto this word, and then lifted up their voices, and said, Away with such a fellow from the earth ; for it is not fit that he should live.* The word "*Gentiles*" fell from his lips like a spark upon the tinder of their bigotry. The *odium theologicum* raged so furiously within them that they could not listen to another word, or tolerate him for another moment. "Away with such a fellow from the earth ; it is not fit that he should live." They would not allow him to utter another word in justification. To them all the charges brought against him were more than true. He was a monster to be swept from the face of the earth —"away with such a fellow from the earth." The old voice that filled Jerusalem on the day of Christ's crucifixion comes out again in thunder. Their rage was ungovernable.

"*They cast off their clothes and threw dust into the air.*" The act described here may be either that of tossing up their loose cloaks or outer garments, or that of violently shaking them without removal ; not as a gesture of concurrence or applause, in which sense agitation of the dress is sometimes mentioned in the classics, but as a spontaneous expression of intense and irrepressible excitement. *Throwing dust into the air*—not as it has sometimes been explained, that it might descend upon their own heads as a sign of mourning—an idea probably connected with the false assumption that they rent their garments, whereas they only shook or tossed them. The act described is to be understood precisely like the one before it, as an outward symptom of internal rage resembling its expression in the lower animals, and said to be common in the East upon the part of whole crowds, when impatient or exasperated.—ALEX.

HOMILETICS.—These two verses are a sad revelation of prejudice.

I. ONE " WORD " DESTROYED THE EFFECT OF A WHOLE DISCOURSE. " They gave him audience unto this *word.*" What " word ? " " I will send thee far hence unto the Gentiles." Their prejudice was, that the Jews alone, of all the human race, were the objects of divine favour ; that Heaven recognised them, no other ; that the Gentiles were reprobate, outcast. Hence when Paul spoke of the Gentiles having a message of mercy sent to them, they were roused to the greatest excitement. Up to this time they had listened, if not with attention, yet with silence and external propriety. But with this word " *Gentiles* " all the glorious things and the cogent reasonings in the apostle's defence went for nothing.

How often is this the case ! Let the preacher in the course of a sermon filled with lofty truths utter a word that strikes against the prepossessions of some prejudiced hearer, and the whole sermon goes for nothing. " And they gave him audience unto this *word.*" Let not the preacher who studiously avoids striking at the prejudices of his hearers conclude, from the attention of his audience, that his sermon has been effectively accepted. Had Paul concluded his address before he uttered that " word," he might have inferred that his audience was brought into sympathy with his views.

II. ONE " WORD " ROUSED THE MALIGNANT PASSIONS INTO FURY. " They lifted up their voices, they cried out, they cast off their clothes, they threw dust into the air." This one word had hurled reason from the throne, opened the floodgates of passion, and made them the sport of a lawless rage. They roared like lions, they howled like wolves. In such a state of mind all argument fell powerless upon them.

III. ONE "WORD" TRANSFORMED THE BEST TEACHER INTO A WRETCH. "Away with such a fellow from the earth : for it is not fit that he should live." A better man, a nobler teacher than Paul, was not to be found on the earth, yet, because he now offended their prejudices, he became to them a monster whose existence was not to be tolerated for a moment longer. Thus offended prejudice has always acted. Thus towards Christ, thus towards the martyrs, thus towards the true teachers of all times.

> " The difference is as great between
> The optics seeing as the objects seen.
> All manners take a tincture from our own,
> Or some discolour'd through our passions shown,
> Or fancy's beam enlarges, multiplies,
> Contracts, inverts, and gives ten thousand dyes."—POPE.

Acts 22:24-29

PAUL'S FINAL VISIT TO JERUSALEM.—III. HIS ADDRESS ON THE STAIRS BEFORE THE POPULACE

3.—*The moral cowardice of warriors*

" *The chief captain commanded him to be brought into the castle, and bade that he should be examined by scourging ; that he might know wherefore they cried so against him. And as they bound him with thongs,*[1] *Paul said unto the centurion that stood by, Is it lawful for you to scourge a man that is a Roman, and uncondemned ? When the centurion heard that, he went and told the chief captain, saying, Take heed what thou doest :*[2] *for this man is a Roman. Then the chief captain came, and said unto him, Tell me, art thou a Roman ? He said, Yea. And the chief captain answered, With a great sum obtained I this freedom. And Paul said, But I was free born. Then straightway they departed from him which should have examined him : and the chief captain also was afraid, after he knew that he was a Roman, and because he had bound him.*" [3]

EMENDATIVE RENDERINGS.—(1.) With the thongs. (2.) What art thou about to do. (3.) When he bethought him that he was a Roman, and that he had bound him.

EXEGETICAL REMARKS.—" *The chief captain commanded him to be brought into the castle.*" To be brought from the stairs on which he was standing, and bade that he should be examined by scourging. Literally scourges. This was a species of judicial torture, somewhat like the Inquisition em-ployed in order to extort a confession, or compel a prisoner to accuse himself.

" *That he might know wherefore they cried so against him.*" Gr. ἐπεφώνουν. —C. E. T.

" *And as they bound him with thongs, Paul said unto the centurion that stood by, Is it law fulfor you to scourge a man that is a Roman, and uncondemned?" " They bound,"*—lit., *stretched him out.* — Gr. προέτειναν— That the apostle's back might be fully exposed to the stripes. This act is not ascribed to the centurion, who stood by, nor to the chief captain, who was not present even ; it refers to those of whom the commencement of ver. 22 speaks. *" With thongs"*— with which they bound him before inflicting the strokes. *Scourging* was threatened ; *thongs* differ from scourging, for they were employed to bind any one who was to be tortured by *scourging. "For you"*—Emphatic. It was nowhere lawful. *"A man that is a Roman"*—It was an evil deed, as Cicero tells us, to *bind* a Roman citizen : it was a heinous crime to *scourge* one. Paul did not assert his right of citizenship against the bonds (ver. 29), for bonds had been foretold: he did assert it against the scourge, that he might defend his body and life, with the object of hereafter preaching the gospel. *"And"*—that too.—C. E. T.

" And the chief captain answered,

With a great sum obtained I this freedom. And Paul said, But I was free born." "With a great sum," &c.— The right of Roman citizenship was at first granted only to such foreigners as had conferred distinguished services on the country, or as a mark of honour upon great and good individuals. But, in process of time, it could be purchased for money ; and under the corrupt emperors it was prostituted so low, to fill their treasuries, that it lost its value, and never again recovered its primitive distinction. The tribune, in the present instance, had purchased the privilege with a large sum of money. *" But I was free born."*—This is generally supposed to have been on account of Tarsus being made a free city by Augustus, and its inhabitants thus being admitted to the right of citizenship. Pliny, in his " Natural History," says, that " Tarsus was a free city ;" Appian, that " the people of Tarsus were free, and discharged from paying tribute ;" and other expressions are quoted from Dion Cassius and Philo, bearing upon the same point.—Liv.

HOMILETICS.—Here we have officers of law too weak to be generous or brave. " The chief captain commanded him to be brought into the ‑ castle, and bade that he should be examined by scourging, that he might know wherefore they cried so against him."

I. FEAR OF THE PEOPLE MADE THE CHIEF CAPTAIN CRUEL TOWARDS PAUL. Why did the chief captain—the Roman tribune—command Paul to be brought into the castle, scourged, and bound ? Not because he could have been in any way convinced of his guilt, but because he wished to conciliate the raging mob, who cried out, " Away with such a fellow from the earth !" For fear of the Jewish mob, this commander of the garrison examined him by scourging.

Here is base cowardice. The love of right should make the ruler superior to the fear of man.

II. FEAR OF THE ROMAN POWER FORCED HIM TO DESIST FROM HIS CRUELTIES. While the indignities and cruelties were being inflicted upon him, Paul, with the heroism of a great man, said, " Is it lawful for you to scourge a man that is a Roman, and uncondemned ?" From the conversation that took place from ver. 26–29, three things are observable :—

First, *Paul's self-command.* Tortured and bleeding under the lash, he speaks without rage or even excitement—speaks to the bold Roman himself : " Is it lawful for you to scourge a man who is a Roman ? "

Secondly, *The apostle's civic superiority.* He was superior to the Roman tribune himself. One was a "free-born" citizen of Rome, the other was a citizen only by purchase. " *With a great sum obtained I this freedom,*" said the captain.

Thirdly, *The force of the Roman name.* As soon as they heard that Paul was a Roman, the officer shrank with dread from the outrage he was committing, and the soldiers recoiled. "Then straightway they departed from him which should have examined him : and the chief captain also was afraid, after he knew that he was a Roman, and because he had bound him."

This incident accords with Roman history. Cicero, against Verres, says, " Whoever he might be whom you were hurrying to the cross, were he even unknown to you, if he but said that he was a Roman citizen, he would necessarily obtain from you, the prætor, by the simplest mention of Rome, if not an escape, yet at least a delay of his punishment." And again, "It is a heinous sin to bind a Roman citizen ; it is wickedness to beat him ; it is next to parricide to kill him ; and what shall I say to crucify him ? "

Acts 22:30-23:5

PAUL'S FINAL VISIT TO JERUSALEM.—I. HIS DEFENCE AS A PRISONER BEFORE THE SANHEDRIM

1. *The outrage of justice by a judge*

" *On the morrow, because he would have known the certainty*[1] *wherefore he was accused of the Jews, he loosed him from his bands, and commanded the chief priests and all their*[2] *council to appear,*[3] *and brought Paul down, and set him before them. And Paul, earnestly beholding the council, said, Men and brethren, I have lived in all good conscience before God until this day. And the high priest Ananias commanded them that stood by him to smite him on the mouth. Then said Paul unto him, God shall smite thee, thou whited wall : for sittest thou to judge me after the law, and command-est me to be smitten contrary to the law ? And they that stood by said, Revilest thou God's high priest ? Then said Paul, I wist not, brethren, that he was the high priest : for it is written, Thou shalt not speak evil of the ruler of thy people.*"

EMENDATIVE RENDERINGS.—(1.) Wishing to know the certainty. (2.) The. (3.) To assemble.

EXEGETICAL REMARKS.—We have noticed Paul's defence before the *people;* these verses present to us his defence before the Sanhedrim. His appearance as a *prisoner* before the great council of the nation takes place on the day following his defence before the people.

"*On the morrow, because he would have known the certainty whereof he was accused of the Jews, he loosed him from his bands, and commanded the chief priests and all their council to appear, and brought Paul down, and set him before them.*" It is here stated that Paul, by the commands of the chief captain, "was loosed from his bands." This does not mean that he was loosed of the bands mentioned in ver. 25, but the chains by which he was bound by two soldiers mentioned in ver. 33 of chap. xxi. Thus unchained, he stands before the assembled members of the Sanhedrim. The fact that the Sanhedrim was convened by the command of the Roman officer proves how completely the Jews were, even in the internal concerns of religion, subjects of the Roman sway.

"*And Paul, earnestly beholding the council, said, Men and brethren, I have lived in all good conscience before God until this day.*" He is now before the Sanhedrim, the great council of the nation. He has been brought down from the castle of Antonia into an apartment of the temple where the Sanhedrim held their meetings. "*Earnestly beholding*"—with a countenance displaying a good conscience; watching also to see whether any of the chief priests would question him. By this assertion he challenged them to accuse any of his former actions; and he showed that what he was about to state, (ver. 6), might fairly be alleged as the real ground of his imprisonment (chap. xxiv. 21). "*Conscience*"—(chap. xxiv. 16; 2 Cor. i. 12)—Paul speaks in particular of his state after conversion, for as to his previous condition

no one raised any question. Although in error, he had obeyed his conscience, and had done nothing to render him outwardly guilty. Now, inasmuch as he had not cast away the good he formerly had, but has received better things, the light of his present state enlightened his previous condition. "*Before God*"—although men did not approve of it.—C. E. T. Paul means, so far from neglecting the law, I have served God as a covenant Jew faithfully to this day.—ALF.

"*And the high priest Ananias commanded them that stood by him to smite him on the mouth.*" Who this Ananias is it is not certain. He presided, however, as the high priest on this occasion. The marvellous indignity which he ordered now to be inflicted on Paul, was in accordance with ancient and modern usages. Striking on the mouth was perhaps intended to express on this occasion that the tongue had been unlawfully employed, and that it should cease its utterances.

"*Then said Paul unto him, God shall smite thee, thou whited wall.*" White lime without and clay within; the lime is the colour and semblance of justice, within is injustice. The expression, translated into modern English, may mean "thou hypocrite."

"*And they that stood by said, Revilest thou the high priest? Then said Paul, I wist not, brethren, that he was the high priest,*" οὐκ ᾔδειν. A translation, suggested by Dr Burton, is worthy of attention : *I was not aware that there is now a high priest.* St Paul, too, had long been absent from Jerusalem; and it is quite consistent with the circumstances of the pontifical office at this time to suppose that Ananias wore no symbols of dignity, and did not occupy the president's chair on this occasion—γέγραπται (Exod. xxii. 28). Josephus says of the authority of the high priest, ὁτούτῳ μὴ πειθόμενος ιφέξει δίκην, ὡς εἰς τὸν θεὸν ἀσεβῶν.—W. and W. GREEK TESTAMENT.

HOMILETICS.—*The outrage of justice by a judge.* Ananias was the leading functionary in this judicial assembly; he was the president, the high priest. It appears from Josephus that there was a high priest by the name of Ananias at this time, and that he was an avaricious and intolerant man, and who, on account of his conduct with the Samaritans, had been sent by the Roman governor Quadratus to answer for himself before the emperor. Whether he was there detained or sent back to Judea, and if sent back to Judea, whether he continued or was reappointed high priest, are disputed points of no great moment. Luke's statement is quite sufficient, that a man bearing the name of Ananias now acted as high priest, and presided over this court of Jewish justice. This man, in the sacred name and temple of justice, now outraged the cause he professed to represent and administer. " He commanded them that stood by him to smite Paul in the mouth." Though this indignity accorded with the barbarism of both ancient and modern Oriental usages, it was not the less an outrage of all justice. The narrative suggests two remarks concerning it—

I. IT WAS MOST UNPROVOKED. Was there anything either in what Paul said or did to justify such gross insolence and injustice ? Let us see. Was there anything in that *look* of his ? He seems to have given them a wonderful look. And " Paul *earnestly* beholding the council." That look was the look *of conscious innocence and of searching observation.* We may rest assured there was nothing insolent or hard in that look, but everything that was reverent and tender. That *earnest* look of Paul at the council would scarcely fail deeply to affect his own heart. Some TWENTY-FIVE years had elapsed since he had been present perhaps as a member when Stephen the martyr stood as a criminal. To his death he then consented, and, as an intolerant Jew, received commission of the high priests to go and persecute the disciples of Christ. As he looked round he would be struck with the great changes that had been effected in that body. Many a familiar face was missing. Some had gone the way of all the earth. Others, very young, had become infirm with years and gray with time. His earnest look about that Sanhedrim must have filled him with melting memories. Certainly there could have been nothing in the look to have provoked the indignity which the high priest commanded to be dealt to him. Was there anything in his *address ?* What did he say ? " Men and brethren, I have lived in all good conscience before God unto this day." It has been remarked that the word *fathers,* which he employed in addressing the people (chap. xxi. ver. 21), is omitted in this address before the Sanhedrim. He only says here, " *Men and brethren.*" This omission might only be in the summary report ; or, if it were omitted from his actual address, it might have been a matter of accident, not intention. In any case, there is no ground for entertaining the neologic idea that Paul intended a rudeness. His declaration that he " had lived in all good conscience before God until that day" was far more adapted to conciliate than to offend. An opportunity will occur in the sequel of our exposition to offer remarks on a "*good conscience.*" All that Paul means by the expression here is a consciousness of rectitude. Conscientiousness, however, as will appear again, does not always imply a good conscience. Saul, even as a persecutor, was conscientious. Saul making havoc of the Church; Dominic founding the Inquisition; Calvin instituting the death of Servetus; the Puritans imprisoning and banishing Baptists and Quakers, were all conscientious. We can find nothing therefore, either in the attitudes, looks, or words of the apostle, in any way to justify the grossly insolent conduct of the high priest. The narrative of this outrage of justice by Ananias, shows—

II. IT WAS NOBLY MET.

First, *It was met with manly courage.* Did the spirit of Paul cower and cringe before this insult? No. It rose into noble defiance: " Then said Paul unto him, God shall smite thee thou whited wall: for sittest thou to judge me after the law, and commandest me to be smitten contrary to the law?" The Heavenly Teacher himself denounced the Pharisees as "*whited sepulchres.*" The words of the apostle may be either an *imprecation* or *prediction.* If the former, it was an outburst, not, we think, unjustified, of that warm temper of his which formed the foundation of his noble nature. Indignation in itself is not wrong. On the contrary, it is a virtuous passion when roused, as in this case, by the vision of a moral enormity. If the latter, a *prediction,* the apostle spoke under the inspiration of truth. Paul knew that the man who so outraged justice and law as Ananias did now, would inevitably meet with the retribution of Heaven. History shows that soon after he did become the victim of eternal justice. Josephus informs us that he, with his brother Hezekiah, were slain during the terrible excitement that occurred in Jerusalem when the insurgent ruffians, under their leader Manahem, had got possession of the Holy City. At first he attempted to conceal himself in an aqueduct, but afterwards was drawn forth and killed. But whether the apostle's language was that of imprecation or prediction, his courage in either case was strikingly manifest. It was not in the power of a mortal to crush into servility that Christ-inspired soul of his. This insult was also met—

Secondly, *By commendable candour :* " Then said Paul, I wist not, brethren, that he was the high priest: for it is written, Thou shalt not speak evil of the ruler of thy people." It appears that there were some in the Sanhedrim on this occasion who regarded Paul's words as profane and rebellious. " Revilest thou God's high priest?" The reply of the apostle is variously interpreted. " I wist not, brethren, that he was the high priest." Some suppose that the apostle speaks ironically; that he meant to say, I never could suppose that such an unjust man was a high priest, that a man who so outraged justice should sit in her seat and administer her affairs. Others suppose that he really meant what he said; that he really did not know that the man who commanded him to be smitten on the mouth was a high priest. Those who take the latter view—the view I incline to—must regard the apostle as in some measure apologising for the hastiness of his utterance, as virtually saying, I acknowledge my error and my haste; I have spoken unadvisedly with my lips; the insult and cruelty I have received have betrayed me into an undue warmth of temper; I know that the office of high priest is divine, however corrupt the man is who fills it, and respect for the office should have made me more cautious, for it is written, "Thou shalt not speak evil of the ruler of thy people" (Exod. xxii. 28). The best men on earth are liable to be overtaken by temper, and the candour which like Paul's hastens to acknowledge the defect is a rare attribute of excellence.

Acts 23:6-10

PAUL'S FINAL VISIT TO JERUSALEM.—I. HIS DEFENCE AS A PRISONER BEFORE THE SANHEDRIM (*continued*)

2. *The employment of policy by an apostle*

" *But when Paul perceived*[1] *that the one part were Sadducees, and the other Pharisees, he cried out in the council, Men and brethren, I am a Pharisee, the son of a Pharisee :* [2] *of the hope and resurrection of the dead I am called in question. And when he had so said, there arose a dissension between the Pharisees and the Sadducees ; and the multitude was divided. For the Sadducees say that there is no resurrection, neither angel, nor spirit ; but the Pharisees confess both. And there arose a great cry ; and the scribes*[3] *that were of the Pharisees' part arose, and strove, saying, We find no evil in this man ; but if a spirit or an angel hath spoken to him,*[4] *let us not fight against God.*[5] *And when there arose a great dissension, the chief captain, fearing lest Paul should have been pulled in pieces of them, commanded the soldiers to go down, and to take him by force from among them, and to bring him into the castle.*"

EMENDATIVE RENDERINGS.—(1.) But Paul being aware. (2.) The son of Pharisees. (3.) Some of the scribes. (4.) But peradventure a spirit or an angel hath spoken to him. (5.) Omit *let us not fight against God.*—ALF.

EXEGETICAL REMARKS.—" *But when Paul perceived that the one part were Sadducees, and the other Pharisees, he cried out in the council, Men and brethren, I am a Pharisee, the son of a Pharisee : of the hope and resurrection of the dead I am called in question.*" " *He cried out*"—he made an open acknowledgment that all in the crowd might hear (chap. xxiv. 21). Here, in a good cause, the maxim *divide et empera* (*divide and govern*), held good. Paul did not use subtle argument or logical quirks. He simply calls upon those of his hearers who were least distant from the truth to support him. *"I am a Pharisee"* — according to my former training, and am still, as far as concerns faith in the resurrection. *"The son of a Pharisee"* — Some read *the son of Pharisees.* They are confirmed by Tertullian. Paul calls himself a *"son of the Pharisees,"* not, of course, meaning his teachers, for this would be tautological to *"Pharisee, a son of the Pharisees."* He does not mention in chap. xxii. 3, a multitude of teachers, but only Gamaliel. He means that his parents, or father and grandfather, or that his ancestors, were Pharisees. (Comp. 1 Tim. i. 3.) Thus there is a climax: *" a Pharisee, the son of Pharisees: of the hope of the resurrection"* —A hendiadys (use of two nouns to express one idea, *the hope of the resurrection*). It was the resurrection they *hoped for. "I am called in question"* — In the present trial, in which Ananias acts as judge. Such is Paul's argument: it has come to this, that the hope of the resurrection of the dead is attacked. The predecessors of Ananias had been Sadducees (chap. v. 17). He himself was a Sadducee. And now, more than twenty years after the resurrection of Christ, they did not so persistently assail the preaching of Jesus Christ and His resurrection as the general doctrine of the resurrection from the dead, which was previously hateful to them, as indeed they had attacked it (chap. iv. 2) ; while the Pharisees in this matter were nearer the Christian faith. Paul, therefore, draws them over to his own side ; and therefore the Sadducees became the more furious. This was at that time the state of the controversy, which Paul subsequently mentions with much earnestness and fixity of purpose (chap. xxiv. 15, 21, xxvi. 6, 7, xxviii. 20."— C. E. T.

"And when he had so said, there arose a dissension between the Pharisees and the Sadducees, and the multitude was divided." The resurrection of the dead was the main point which divided the Pharisees and Sadducees into distinct sects. This doctrine the apostle threw as an apple of discord among them, and it produced what perhaps he intended, drew their attention from him, and gave the Pharisees, the most influential sect, for the time an interest in himself.

" We find no evil in this man ; but if a spirit or an angel hath spoken to him, let us not fight against God." Such was the verdict of the Pharisees, and such their recommendation.

" The chief captain, fearing lest Paul should be pulled in pieces of them, commanded the soldiers to go down, and to take him by force from among them, and to bring him into the castle." "The chief captain, fearing that Paul should be torn in pieces by the contending parties" (διασπασθῇ, whilst the one tried to lay hold on him in order to protect him, and the other did so in rage, so that he was pulled to and fro), therefore he ordered the soldiers to come from the castle, and to take him by force from the assembly, and to bring him again into the camp. The commander, doubtless in order not to affront the hierarchy, had not taken with him into the assembly a military detachment, but only an escort."—L. & G.

HOMILETICS.—Here we have *the employment of policy by an apostle.*

I. THE NATURE OF THE POLICY WHICH THE APOSTLE EMPLOYED. What was the expedient he employed? Seeing that there was no chance of having justice done him by that judicial assembly, he endeavoured at once to divert their attention from himself, by raising a question that would set them into a furious disputation among themselves. The members of the Sanhedrim were composed of Sadducees and Pharisees. One of the grand and chief questions that *divided* these parties was the doctrine of the *resurrection,* and the existence of a spirit-world. This question Paul now raised in their midst. "But when Paul perceived that the one part were Sadducees, and the other Pharisees, he cried out in the council, Men and brethren, I am a Pharisee, the son of a Pharisee: of the hope and resurrection of the dead I am called in question."

Some, indeed, have censured Paul for having had recourse to such an expedient. Those persons should remember that Paul stated nothing but the truth. (1.) It was true that he was a Pharisee, held all the theological tenets of that sect, and had been brought up from a child in that school. (2.) It was also true that the grand doctrine of the body's resurrection was one of the leading themes of his discourses everywhere (Acts xiii. 34, xvii. 31, 32, xxvi. 23–25 ; 1 Cor. xv.) And (3.) It was, moreover, true that the proclamation of this doctrine was the cause of much of his persecution. All, therefore, that he did was, with a master-stroke of policy, to declare a truth which would put him in sympathy with the Pharisees, who formed perhaps the most influential part of that judicial assembly before which he now stood as a criminal.

II. The effect of the policy which the apostle now employed. It answered the end he sought. It divided the Sanhedrim, and got the Pharisees on his side. "And when he had so said, there arose a great dissension between the Pharisees and the Sadducees, and the multitude was divided," &c.

Three results came out of the policy of the apostle on this occasion—

First, *A great excitement through a sectionising dogma.* "The resurrection of the dead," which was a grand truth to the apostle, was a mere dogma both to the Sadducees and Pharisees, accepted by the one and rejected by the other. But it was just that dogma that divided them into two sects, that marshalled them into opposing forces. As a rule, whatever idea divides one religious sect from another is the idea to raise in order to awaken sectarian bitterness and battle. Immersion, Episcopacy, Presbyterianism, Independency —these things make sects and raise them into discussion, and you will awaken irritation in the parties they divide. Paul knew human nature, and he just raised the question that divided the Sanhedrim, and thus diverted attention from himself by awakening a conflict between them. Another result is—

Secondly, *A demonstration of the apostle's innocence.* So little impressed was the Sanhedrim with the idea of the apostle's criminality, that they forgot all about it in the disputation amongst themselves ; and, more than this, the Pharisees actually said, "We find no evil in this man," and gave the advice which Gamaliel gave the same council some years before, "But if a spirit or an angel hath spoken to him, let us not fight against God." Another result that comes out from the policy employed by the apostle is—

Thirdly, *His deliverance from Jewish persecution.* " And when there arose a great dissension, the chief captain, fearing lest Paul should have been pulled in pieces by them, commanded the soldiers to go down, and to take him by force from among them, and bring him into the castle."

CONCLUSION. Do not get a wrong impression of Paul's *policy.* Though we have seen him on various occasions displaying great accommodativeness, now taking part in a Nazarite's vow in order to disarm the unreasoning hostility of his countrymen; now putting forward all the considerations which truth would authorise, in order to conciliate the mind of his Jewish audiences; now availing himself of his Roman citizenship, in order to avoid the infliction of a cruel and unjust torture; and now, in the case before us, taking advantage of the doctrine that divided his judges, in order to avoid their verdict of condemnation. In *none* of these strokes of policy is there the slightest approach to the disingenuous, the evasive, the shifting. In all there is an unbending honesty and an invincible courage.

Acts 23:11-35

PAUL'S FINAL DEPARTURE FROM JERUSALEM, AND HIS ARRIVAL
AT CÆSAREA

A visit from Christ, conspiracy of enemies, and an interposition of Providence.

" *And the night following, the Lord stood by him, and said, Be of good cheer, Paul ;*[1] *for as thou hast testified of me in Jerusalem, so must thou bear witness also at Rome. And when it was day, certain of the Jews*[2] *banded together, and bound themselves under a curse, saying that they would neither eat nor drink till they had killed Paul. And there were more than forty which had made this conspiracy. And they came to the chief priests and elders, and said, We have bound ourselves under a great curse, that we will eat nothing until we have slain Paul. Now therefore ye with the council signify to the chief captain that he bring him down unto you to-morrow, as though ye would enquire something more perfectly concerning him :*[3] *and we, or ever he come near, are ready to kill him. And when Paul's sister's son heard of their lying in wait, he went and entered into the castle, and told Paul. Then Paul called one of the centurions unto him, and said, Bring this young man unto the chief captain; for he hath a certain thing to tell him. So he took him, and brought him to the chief captain, and said, Paul the prisoner called me unto him, and prayed me to bring this young man unto thee, who hath something to say unto thee. Then the chief captain took him by the hand, and went with him aside privately, and asked him, What is that thou hast to tell me ? And he said, The Jews have agreed to desire thee that thou wouldst bring down Paul to-morrow into the council, as though they would enquire somewhat of him more perfectly.⁴ But do not thou yield unto them : for there lie in wait for him of them more than forty men, which have bound themselves with an oath, that they will neither eat nor drink till they have killed him; and now are they ready, looking for a promise from thee. So the chief captain then let the young man depart, and charged him, See thou tell no man that thou hast shewed these things to me. And he called unto him two centurions, saying, make ready two hundred soldiers to go to Cæsarea, and horsemen three score and ten, and spearmen two hundred, at the third hour of the night ; and provide them beasts that they may set Paul on, and bring him safe unto Felix the governor. And he wrote a letter after this manner : Claudius Lysias unto the most excellent governor Felix sendeth greeting. This man was taken of the Jews, and should have been killed of them: then came I with an army,⁵ and rescued him, having understood that he was a Roman. And when I would have known the cause wherefore they accused him, I brought him forth into their council ; whom I perceived to be accused of questions of their law, but to have nothing laid to his charge worthy of death or of bonds. And when it was told me how that the Jews laid wait for the man,⁶ I sent straightway to thee, and gave commandment to his accusers also to say before thee what they had against him. Farewell.⁷ Then the soldiers, as it was commanded them, took Paul, and brought him by night to Anti-patris. On the morrow they left the horsemen to go with him, and returned to the castle : who when they came to Cæsarea, and delivered the epistle to the governor, presented Paul also before him. And when the governor had read the letter, he asked of what province he was. And when he under-stood that he was of Cilicia; I will hear thee, said he, when thine accusers are also come. And he commanded him to be kept in Herod's judgment-hall."⁸*

EMENDATIVE RENDERINGS.—(1.) Omit this word. (2.) The Jews. (3.) As though ye would determine with greater accuracy. (4.) As though thou wouldst inquire. (5.) The troop. (6.) But when it was told me that a plot was prepared against the man. (7.) Omit this word. (8.) Herod's palace.—ALF. and TISCH.

EXEGETICAL REMARKS.—"*And the night following, the Lord stood by him, and said, Be of good cheer, Paul : for as thou hast testified of me in Jeru-salem, so must thou bear witness also at Rome.*" After all these labours, dangers, and rescues, the apostle needed some special communication from Heaven ; hence in " the night following" the exciting scenes re-corded in ver. 1–10, our Lord ap-peared to him, bade him " be of good cheer," recognised his faithful labours at Jerusalem, and assured him that he must do the same at Rome. Jeru-

salem and Rome, the two metro-politan cities of the world. Christ says he must go to Rome ; hence no enemies, no tumults, no shipwrecks can prevent it.

"*And when it was day, certain of the Jews banded together, and bound themselves under a curse, saying, that they would neither eat nor drink till they had killed Paul.*" " Bound themselves under a curse," *i.e.*, they made a vow, and invoked the malediction of Heaven if they did not fulfil it. It has been conjec-tured by Michaelis and others that this band of desperate men belonged to a class called *sicarii* (see chap. xxi. 38), who were also *zealots* for the law, and ready to engage in the grossest wickedness to gratify personal or religious animosities. *"Neither eat nor drink"* (1 Sam. xiv. 24.)—A common form or vow according to Jewish scholars. It might signify that they would abstain from their ordinary food until they had effected their purpose, rather than that they would literally take no nourishment whatever. But, if strictly bound to observe their oath to the letter, they could yet obtain an easy absolution from the Rabbins, or by some other expedient. Josephus relates that ten men had made a similar vow to take the life of Herod the Great, because he had departed from the customs of their nation.

" And when Paul's sister's son heard of their lying in wait, he went and entered into the castle and told Paul," &c. *" Paul's sister's son"*—This is all we know of the family of Paul. We are not told whether his nephew was young or old ; but here he shows his affection. Hearing of the conspiracy against his uncle, he enters the castle and gives information. Paul, on hearing this, calls one of the centurions, and requests him to bring his nephew to the chief captain in order to give him this intelligence. This was promptly attended to. The chief captain, being informed of the malignant purpose of the Jews, took measures to secure his protection.

"And he" (that is, the chief captain) *" called unto him two centurions, saying, Make ready two hundred soldiers to go to Cæsarea, and horsemen three score and ten, and spearmen two hundred, at the third hour of the night."* *" Spearmen two hundred"*—δεξιολάβους. Whether we read thus, or from one very ancient manuscript, δεξιοβόλους, the word refers to a class of soldiers of which nothing is known. (The former is doubtless the true reading— TISCH., &c. ; but the word has not been clearly explained.—ALF. Most probably a kind of light-armed troops. The word means simply *grasping with the right hand,* and seems to re-

fer to the kind of arms they bore.— MEY.) We may, therefore, wonder the more that *two hundred* of them were put under orders. An Arabic rendering has *eighty*. If, in addition to this Arabian evidence, we have any other, it might appear that two hundred had crept in from what precedes. At all events, far too many *soldiers* were set in motion against forty odd zealots.—C. E. T.

" And provide them beasts that they may set Paul on, and bring him safe." *" We should read διασώσητε, that ye may bring him safe,* not *διασώσωσι, that they may bring him safe."*

" Felix the governor," or procurator, whose residence was at Cæsarea. Antonius Felix was a freedman of Claudius Cæsar, the Roman emperor, and brother of Pallas, the favourite of Nero. According to the testimony of Tacitus, he governed his people with a servile mind, and indulged in every species of cruelty and lust ; and he says that he expected to escape with impunity in the commission of his wicked deeds on account of his great power. He had, at this time, been procurator about five years, and remained in office two years longer (chap. xxiv. 27), when he was succeeded by Porcius Festus.

" And he wrote a letter," &c. The letter addressed by Claudius Lysias to Felix here sets forth the simple facts which had just occurred in connexion with Paul's history. The letter extends from the 27th to the 30th verse.

" Antipatris." *"* A city built by Herod, and called in honour of his father, Antipater. It lay upon the route from Jerusalem to Cæsarea, about twenty miles from the latter, in a large fertile plain. Its location was identified by Robinson, in his late researches in Palestine and Arabia. The distance was great for one night's travel ; but the Roman soldiers were distinguished for their hardihood ; the march was a forced one, and the " night " might be used to include a considerable part of the following day."—LIV.

HOMILETICS.—Paul had made several visits to Jerusalem since his conversion. To the last visit he looked with great interest, as he was the bearer of the charitable contributions of the churches of Achaia and Macedonia to the poor saints at Jerusalem. For a long time his heart was on this visit; he struggled to perform it. The fear of death would not deter him from it; he made all circumstances bow to its accomplishment. But now he leaves that city never to return again; he leaves it as a prisoner in chains. He had just delivered an able defence, first before the people, and afterwards before the Sanhedrim, and in each case, instead of conciliating them, he only intensified their unreasoning, unrighteous, and savage hostility; so much so, that the " chief captain, fearing lest Paul should have been pulled in pieces of them, commanded the soldiers to go down and take him by force from among them, and to bring him to the castle." In glancing at the record here given of the circumstances connected with the termination of his connexion with Jerusalem, and his journey to Cæsarea, there are, at least, three things worthy of our special attention :—*A visit from Christ ; A conspiracy of enemies; An interposition of Providence.*

I. A VISIT FROM CHRIST. "And the night following, the Lord stood by him, and said, Be of good cheer, Paul; for as thou hast testified of me in Jerusalem, so must thou bear witness also at Rome." In what form "*the Lord stood by him,*" whether as He appeared on earth, or as He appears in heaven, is not said; but he saw Him not with his bodily eye, but with the eye of soul, for soul is endowed with faculties for perceiving the invisible. His advent to the apostle was—

First, *Opportune.* We may well suppose that Paul's sensitive nature would be subject to many painful memories, gloomy thoughts, and boding anxieties, on that "*night,*" as he lay, with a lacerated body, a prisoner in the castle. Mayhap he was permitted even to question the divinity of his cause and the rectitude of his mission. The best men have often had sceptical thoughts, and such thoughts to such men are as the bleak winds of winter midnight to the unsheltered and unclad. The advent of Christ on this night was, therefore, most opportune ;—a verification this of the promise that never fails, "*As thy day, so shall thy strength be.*" His advent now to the apostle was—

Secondly, *Cheering :* "Be of good cheer !" What a contrast to the words of falsehood, cursing, blasphemy, which during the previous days had been addressed to him ! Who shall tell the cadence in which they were spoken? The soothing music, inspiring energy, the winning tenderness of Christ's voice, who shall tell? None know but those whose hearts have caught its accents. There are two things in Christ's words suited to cheer the heart of the apostle—

(1.) Commendation: "*Thou hast testified of me in Jerusalem.*"

Had Paul been allowed the mental agony of questioning whether he had done the right thing in Jerusalem? If so, here is a scattering of the dark thought; here is a divine recognition and an approving testimony of his services. "Thou hast testified of me;" thou hast acquitted thyself nobly and faithfully—well done. Another thing in Christ's words suited to cheer Paul's heart was—

(2.) Information : "*So thou must bear witness also at Rome.*" Paul had long been intensely anxious to visit Rome. "After I have been there" (Jerusalem), says he, "I must also see Rome" (Acts xix. 21). In his epistles, too, his longings to visit Rome are strongly expressed (Rom. i. 10 ; xv. 23, 24). Rome, the mistress of the world, the home of poets, heroes, sages, artists, &c., how strongly he desired to be there, to preach Jesus and the resurrection. Perhaps he had just been thinking that there was no probability of his ever visiting Rome. Perhaps he had given up this long-cherished purpose, and had wept bitter tears of disappointment on the wreck of the loved hope. Christ's words assured him, however, that he should yet visit Rome. "For as thou hast testified of me in Jerusalem, so must thou bear witness also at Rome." This advent of Christ to Paul on this night suggests three general truths :—

First, *That great trials in duty are no evidence of unfaithfulness.* Paul was faithful, yet he was in a dungeon.

Secondly, *That great trials in duty are all known to Christ.* The trials of His people are not unforeseen casualties or misfortunes ; they are according to His arrangement. He knows where the sufferer is, He approaches him, He speaks to him.

Thirdly, *That great trials in duty do not release us from the obligation to persevere.* Paul was now told that he "must bear witness also at Rome."

Another thing worthy our special attention in this record of Paul's departure from Jerusalem for Cæsarea is—

II. A CONSPIRACY OF ENEMIES. "And when it was day, certain of the Jews banded together, and bound themselves under a curse, saying, that they would neither eat nor drink till they had killed Paul. And they were more than forty which had made this conspiracy," &c. The conspiracy formed against Paul was—

First, *Malignant.* Their avowed object was to "kill" him. The sufferings to which he was already subject did not satisfy them. Like wild beasts they thirsted for his blood. The conspiracy was—

Secondly, *Determined.* "They bound themselves under a curse." Let God curse us if we eat or drink before we murder this man. Nothing could express a more invincible resolve. The conspiracy was—

Thirdly, *Strong.* "More than forty" of these sanguinary despera-does banded themselves together for this purpose. The escape of Paul from the murderous hands of such a combination seemed all but impossible. The conspiracy was—

Fourthly, *Cunning.* Paul was in the custody of the chief captain, the Roman officer, well guarded. How could they get him into their hands? Only through the Sanhedrim. Hence they applied to the chief priests and elders for the purpose. They inform these Jewish officers of their bloody intent, and they request them that they should " signify to the chief captain, that he bring him down to them to-morrow, as though he would have heard something more concerning him." What they meant in their application to these Jewish authorities was this : " We are determined to kill Paul, but being in the charge of the Roman officer, we can get at him only through your aid." Whether the chief priests and elders agreed to this or not, one thing is certain, that the very fact that these wretches were emboldened to make such a request to them, demonstrates the horrible injustice and immorality that prevailed amongst the rulers of the Jews.

Another thing worthy of our special attention in this record of Paul's departure from Jerusalem for Cæsarea is—

III. AN INTERPOSITION OF PROVIDENCE. In the verses that follow (16–35), narrating the rescue of Paul, and his safe arrival in Cæsarea, we find Divine Providence doing the two great things which it is ever doing in this world—thwarting the evil and delivering the good.

First, *We find Providence thwarting the evil.* The discovery and defeat of this malignant plot is told with remarkable minuteness and inartistic simplicity in the following verses : " And when Paul's sister's son heard of their lying in wait, he went and entered into the castle, and told Paul. Then Paul called one of the centurions unto him, and said, Bring this young man unto the chief captain, for he hath a certain thing to tell him," &c.

In the method here recorded by which the purposes of evil men were thwarted, we find three things which generally characterise the procedure of Providence—

1. *Simplicity.* What was the agency employed ? " Paul's sister's son." This is all we know of the family of Paul. Here is a young man, probably uninfluential and obscure, who does the work. It has ever been Heaven's plan to employ apparently insignificant means for the accomplishment of great ends.

2. *Unexpectedness.* Little did the conspirators expect that their plan would be defeated by an obscure youth ; little did Paul expect that deliverance would come for him from such a quarter. Yet so it is : means often most unlikely are employed to accomplish important results. The waters of heavenly mercy often come to men from rocky Horebs.

3. *Naturalness.* The whole is beautifully natural. It was natural for Paul's nephew, having heard of the malignant plot, to seek access to his uncle, and to warn him of it. It was natural for his

uncle to despatch him to the chief captain to impart the intelligence
to him. It was natural for the chief captain, as a man of justice
and honour, to feel and act as he did. Thus God acts as a rule, in
all his procedure with men. Here—

Secondly, *We find Providence delivering the good.* Here is a
history of Paul's deliverance :—"And he called unto him two centurions, saying, Make ready two hundred soldiers," &c. These
verses show—

First, *That he secured a safe journey to Cæsarea.* It was *night*
when they started ; the road was intricate and perilous—a distance
of upwards of sixty miles,—but he was well guarded. A detachment
of four hundred and seventy brave and well-armed soldiers were appointed as an escort, to protect him against murderous plots and
all manner of violence. God's resources are greater than the devil's.
There were forty murderers in quest of Paul's life, but God raised
nearly five hundred brave soldiers to protect him. More are
they that are for us than they that are against us. Truly, the
angel of the Lord encamps round about them that fear Him, and
delivers them. These verses show—

Secondly, *That he secured a good introduction to the Roman
judge.* The letter that was written by Claudius Lysias to Felix,
whilst complimenting the governor, expressed the unrighteous persecutions to which Paul had been subject, and the dangers to
which he had been exposed, and by implication indicated his own
belief as to the apostle's innocence of the charges that were
brought against him. The result of the letter on the mind
of the governor was this:—"*I will hear thee,*" said he, " *when thine
accusers are also come. And he commanded him to be kept in
Herod's judgment-hall.*" So far Paul is safe, and on his way to
Rome, the imperial city he long desired to visit. Truly, "many are
the afflictions of the righteous, but the Lord delivereth him out of
them all."

Acts 24:1-9

PAUL AT CÆSAREA BEFORE FELIX.—(I.) HIS ACCUSERS

A picture of barristerial depravity

" *And after five days Ananias the high priest descended with the elders,*[1]
*and with a certain orator named Tertullus, who informed the governor
against Paul. And when he was called forth Tertullus began to accuse
him, saying, Seeing that by thee we enjoy great quietness, and that very*

worthy deeds are done unto this nation by thy providence, we accept it always, and in all places, most noble Felix, with all thankfulness. Notwithstanding, that I be not further tedious unto thee, I pray thee that thou wouldest hear us of thy clemency a few words. For we have found this man a pestilent fellow, and a mover of sedition among all the Jews throughout the world, and a ringleader of the sect of the Nazarenes :² who also hath gone about to profane the temple : whom we took, and would have judged according to our law : but the chief captain Lysias came upon us, and with great violence took him away out of our hands, commanding his accusers to come unto thee : by examining of whom thyself mayest take knowledge of all these things whereof we accuse him. And the Jews also assented, saying that these things were so."

EMENDATIVE RENDERINGS.—(1.) Some of the elders. (2.) The heresy of the Nazarenes.

EXEGETICAL REMARKS.—Paul is now at Cæsarea, a city situated on the coast of Palestine, on the great line from Tyre to Egypt. It is about half-way between Joppa and Dora, about thirty-five miles distant from Joppa, and fifty-five from Jerusalem by the nearest route. Its distance, however, to the metropolis by the common road would be from sixty-five to seventy miles ; hence it had taken the company of soldiers who had just conveyed Paul into the city nearly two days to do so. In Strabo's time there stood on its site a town called Strabo's Tower. In the time of Tacitus, Cæsarea is spoken of as being the head of Judea. Herod the Great made the change. Twelve long years he was engaged, at an immense cost of labour and wealth, in building this city, in honour of the Emperor Augustus. Josephus describes it as a city of " great magnificence." Like all human productions, however, it has had its day, and has long since passed away. The few ruins that remain as monuments of its existence are tenanted by snakes, scorpions, lizards, and wild boars. It is associated with many interesting events in New Testament history. Here Philip, one of the seven deacons of the young Church, lived for several years ; here Cornelius, the Italian centurion, was converted ; here the angel of the Lord smote Herod Agrippa the First, on account of his impious hardihood ; here Peter, when persecuted by Herod, found a tem-

porary refuge ; from hence St Paul sailed to Tarsus, when forced to leave Jerusalem on his return from Damascus ; here, too, he landed after his second missionary tour, and spent some time on his return from his third missionary journey ; and here now he is brought as a prisoner, and remains two long' years before his voyage to Italy. It was the home of Eusebius, the father of ecclesiastical history ; was the scene of some of Origen's labours, and the birthplace of Procopius, the eminent Byzantine historian. In this chapter we have an account of Paul as he appears before Felix, and it leads us to consider his accusers, his defence, and his judge. We take his judge last, because his character comes out more fully at the end of the chapter.

" *And after five days Ananias the high priest descended with the elders.*" Ananias was the man who a few days before, in Jerusalem, as Paul stood before the Sanhedrim (Acts xxiii. 2), commanded Paul to be smitten on the mouth, thus outraging justice and humanity. The " *elders*" were members of that ruling body who sanctioned such an outrage. These had " *descended*" locally, and, proud bigots, as they considered, morally, to Jerusalem, in order, if possible, to carry into execution the mortal hostility of the Sanhedrim against Paul.

" *With a certain orator named Tertullus, who informed the governor against Paul.*" As the name of this man is Roman, he was no doubt a Roman barrister of signal abilities, and perhaps of great reputation. The Jews, probably, for the most part being ignorant of Roman customs and laws, employed Roman lawyers to represent them in the courts of justice. Whatever the ability, the culture, the fame of this Tertullus, one thing is clear from the adulation which he addressed to Felix, that he was an *unscrupulous flatterer*, and therefore destitute of that sense of truthfulness which is essential to all moral worth. Mark how he opens the case : "*Seeing that by thee we enjoy great quietness, and that very worthy deeds are done unto this nation by thy providence, we accept it always, and in all places, most noble Felix, with all thankfulness.*" The character of this Felix, which will appear hereafter, will show this Tertullus to have been one of those unprincipled barristers who will outrage every noble sentiment of truth and justice in order to carry their point.

The charge is threefold :—

(1.) Sedition.

"*We have found this man a pestilent fellow, and a mover of sedition among all the Jews.*" A *pestilence*, or a pest, would be a more forcible translation, as well as a more literal one. The two great orators, Demosthenes and Cicero, speak of different persons as the pest of the Republic, the State, the Empire (*pestis republicæ, civitatis, imperii*). All the disturbances and commotions which Paul's enemies created were laid to his charge. To the Romans no crime was more heinous than that of sedition, for they seemed nervously afraid that their vast empire might in some part give way. Another charge was—

(2.) Heresy.

"*A ringleader of the sect of the Nazarenes.*" The disciples of Christ were contemptuously called Nazarenes, because they were the followers of Jesus of Nazareth, a place of notorious contempt. Paul is charged here with being the leader of that sect of heresy. This charge has the merit of truth. He was a standard-bearer in this little but rapidly growing army. The other charge was—

(3.) Sacrilege.

"*Who also hath gone about to profane the temple ; whom we took, and would have judged according to our law.*" The profanation of the temple was a serious but groundless charge. His enemies had asserted (c. xxii. 28) that he had introduced Greeks to the sacred place. This was a foul calumny. After these charges, this clever but unprincipled advocate does two things : (1.) Implies that the Sanhedrim at Jerusalem would have judged Paul righteously, if Lysias had not interposed : "*But the chief captain Lysias came upon us, and with great violence took him away out of our hands, commanding his accusers to come unto thee: by examining of whom thyself mayest take knowledge of all these things, whereof we accuse him.*" (2.) He gets the Jews, including Ananias and the elders whom he brought down, to assent to all he had stated. "*And the Jews also assented, saying that these things were so.*" I suppose it would scarcely matter what the barrister said, what falsehoods he stated, what fallacies he propounded ; if they went to ruin Paul, he would have the hearty corroboration of these Jews. Tertullus has now done ; he has stated his charge, and done his best to make the "worse the better reason."

Note—The passage beginning καὶ κατὰ τὸν, and would have judged, and ending with ἔρχεσθαι ἐπὶ σε, is omitted by Tisch. and Mey., and strongly suspected by Alf. It seems to be no part of the original text.—C. E. T. Alexander says, in relation to these sentences, "This clause, however, with the whole of the preceding verse, is rejected by the latest critics, because not found in the oldest extant manuscripts ; but this omission makes the speech, already brief, so strangely meagre, and the introduction of the passage is so hard to be accounted for, that its genuineness is, on the whole, more probable than its interpolation, as it may have existed in still older copies, now no longer extant. Upon this question of criticism depends the meaning of the other clause, which is admitted to be genuine."

HOMILETICS.—This piece of history presents to us, in the person of Tertullus, a picture of a corrupt barrister. The office of an advocate in judicial proceedings is one created by the wisdom and kindness of our ancestors. Many circumstances may occur to render the man unjustly accused of crime utterly incompetent to defend himself, and to clear his character. It is well, therefore, that there should be men who have the learning, the ability, and the legal right to take up their cause. But this office, like all other human things, has been sadly corrupted. Tertullus is an example. We see him doing two things which disgraced his profession :—

I. VENALLY ADOPTING A BAD CAUSE. What brought him down to Cæsarea from Jerusalem with Ananias the high priest, and the elders? Love of right—chivalry? No, *money.* He sold his services, and that to a bad cause.

First, *It was the cause of the strong against the weak.* Who are his clients? The whole Jewish Sanhedrim. Who was the man against whom he was to bring all the power of his learning and his eloquence? One poor man, a tent-maker. Chivalry ought to be the inspiration of an advocate, but, alas! how often is it cash.

Secondly, *It was the cause of the wrong against the right.* Were the weak in the wrong, men of the higher type would hesitate to go with the strong against them. But here is a man who was unquestionably right, and the mighty prosecutor manifestly wrong. The English courts of judicature exhibit something analogous to this sometimes. There are eminent members of the bar, some of whom are wonderfully pious in public meetings and in their place in Parliament on ecclesiastical questions, whose services in a *bad* cause can be easily secured by a handsome fee. We see this man—

II. WICKEDLY ADVOCATING A BAD CAUSE. In his advocacy we discover three things :—

First, *Base flattery :* "Seeing that by thee we enjoy great quietness, and that very worthy deeds are done unto this nation by thy providence, we accept it always, and in all places," &c. This Felix, a man steeped in depravity, and hated by the people, this venal advocate deifies with his flattery, ascribes to him deeds which were due to God alone.

Secondly, *Flagrant falsehood.* He lays, as we have seen, three charges against him—*sedition, heresy,* and *sacrilege,* not one of which had the shadow of foundation in fact.

Thirdly, *Suppressed truth.* The man who suppresses a truth when its declaration is demanded by the nature of the case, is guilty of falsehood, is a deceiver. This Tertullus did now. In stating his case he said nothing concerning the "forty" which had conspired in Jerusalem, and bound themselves by a solemn oath to kill Paul (xxiii. 14, 15).

CONCLUSION. This Tertullus was no doubt a great man in his own esteem, was perhaps affluent in legal lore, and endowed with high powers of oratory. Probably no professional advocate stood higher with the council at Jerusalem and the law courts of his times than he. Albeit in the case before us he has clothed himself with eternal infamy, and that because he became the venal advocate of the wrong against the right, the strong against the weak.

Acts 24:10-21

PAUL AT CÆSAREA BEFORE FELIX.—(II.) HIS DEFENCE

The Christianity of Judaism, and the characteristics of a great man.

" *Then, Paul after that the governor had beckoned unto him to speak, answered, Forasmuch as I know that thou hast been of many years a judge unto this nation, I do the more* [1] *cheerfully answer for myself : because that thou mayest understand, that there are yet but twelve days since I went up to Jerusalem for to worship. And they neither found me in the temple disputing with any man, neither raising up the people, neither in the synagogues, nor in the city : neither can they prove* [2] *the things whereof they now accuse me. But this I confess unto thee, that after the way which they call heresy, so worship I the God of my fathers, believing all things which are written in the law and in the prophets : and have hope toward God, which they themselves also allow, that there shall be a resurrection of the dead,* [3] *both of the just and unjust. And herein do I* [4] *exercise myself, to have always a conscience void of offence toward God, and toward men. Now, after many years, I came to bring alms to my nation, and offerings. Whereupon* [5] *certain Jews from Asia found me purified in the temple, neither with multitude nor with tumult : who ought to have been here before thee, and object, if they had ought against me. Or else, let these same here say, if they have found any evil-doing in me, while I stood before the council, except it be for this one voice, that I cried standing amongst them, Touching the resurrection of the dead, I am called in question by you this day.*"

EMENDATIVE RENDERINGS.—(1.) Omit *the more.* (2.) Prove unto thee. (3.) Omit *of the dead.* (4.) Do I also. (5.) Amidst which.

EXEGETICAL REMARKS.—" *Then Paul, after that the governor had beckoned unto him to speak, answered, Forasmuch as I know that thou hast been of many years a judge unto this nation, I do the more cheerfully answer for* myself.*" There is, says a modern expositor, a striking contrast here between the order and fairness of this Roman process, though conducted by a wicked man, and the passionate confusion of the Sanhedrim, although composed of priests, scribes, and elders of the people. It seems as if the Jews and Gentiles were beginning to change places as the guardians of the Church, a transposition afterward brought out in terrible relief at the destruction of Jerusalem, where Titus was as temperate and humane as the zealots were ferocious to themselves and others. This circumstance imparts new interest to the crisis which we have now reached, and in which Paul begins his third apology or apostolical defence of Christianity and of himself, not uttered, like the first, to a vast crowd of Jews from all parts of the world assembled to observe the feast of Pentecost; nor like the second, in the presence of the Sanhedrim or eldership of Israel; but before a Roman magistrate, and under the protection and restraint of the Roman arms, yet in the presence of the high priest and a deputation of the elders; so that he was still appealing to the chosen people, and before these Gentile witnesses attempting, for the last time, to convince them of the true religion between law and gospel, Christ and Moses. He begins, like Tertullus, with a regular *captatio benevolentiæ*, by ascribing to Felix at least one most important qualification for his present duty—that of long experience, and thorough knowledge of the men with whom he had to deal. He gives the judge credit, not for great intelligence, commanding ability, great usefulness, or high virtue, but merely for a knowledge of Jewish affairs and modern Jewish events. Here he expresses his pleasure in standing before one who knew the facts of the case. The apostle ventured to suppose that the judge knew that it was only " *twelve days* " since he went up to Jerusalem for to worship. The twelve days, says Lange, which the apostle mentions, may be reckoned as follows:—

I. Day after his arrival, visit to James (chap. xix. 18).

II. Levitical purification, and the first visit to the temple (chap. xxi. 26).

III.-VII. Days of the Nazarite offering; onset against Paul, and his capture (chap. xxi. 27).

VIII. The apostle before the chief councils (chap. xxii. 30; xxiii. 1).

IX. The conspiracy and its discovery; in the evening Paul is removed from Jerusalem (chap. xxiii. 12-31).

X. Arrival at Antipatris (chap. xxiii. 31).

XI. Arrival at Cæsarea (chap. xxiii. 32, 33).

XII. At Cæsarea.

XIII. Trial before Felix (chap. xxiv. 1). The trial before Felix accordingly took place on the fifth day (μετὰ πέντε ἡμέρας (chap. xxiv. 1) after Paul's departure from Jerusalem, if the day of departure be included. On the other hand, the fifth day had not yet elapsed, and, therefore, is to be excluded from the twelve days, as also is the day of the apostle's arrival at Jerusalem (ORIGEN). In his opening remarks he indicates two facts that bear powerfully on his own defence —(1.) His recent arrival in the country (twelve days), leaving him no time for such proceedings as were charged against him; and (2.) his purpose in visiting Jerusalem, which was to attend to the duties of that religion ("to worship") which they accused him of renouncing.

" *And they neither found me in the temple disputing with any man, neither raising up the people, neither in the synagogues, nor in the city: neither can they prove the things whereof they now accuse me.*" He disclaims, in the most unqualified way, any attempt on his part, whether in the city, temple, synagogues, or anywhere else among the people, to break the public peace, and boldly asserts the impossibility of sustaining any such charge by evidence.

" *This I confess unto thee, that after the way which they call heresy, so worship I the God of my fathers, believing all things which are written in the law and in the prophets: and have hope toward God, which they themselves also allow, that there shall be a resurrection of the dead, both of the just and unjust.*" The same Greek word as that translated " sect " in the fifth verse, is in this passage translated " *heresy;* " the word simply means division, schism, without any reference to the present popular notion of heresy as being an error of doctrine. A new sect in theology is always heretical in the eyes of the old. The apostle is not ashamed of being a Nazarene, but he denies that Christianity is a newly-formed heresy. On the contrary, he affirms that, as an apostle in the new .faith, he held the old. He worshipped the God of the Hebrews : "*So worship 1 the God of my fathers;*" as if he had said, "I propound no new divinity; the ancestral Deity I alone adore." He believed in the Old Scriptures, "believing " *all things that are written in the law and in the prophets;*" all things commanded by the law of Moses, and foretold by the old prophets, especially the things relating to the Messiah. His apostolic history was a proof of this, for wherever he went his arguments in defence of Christianity were drawn from the Hebrew Scriptures. He held to the *old hope : " And have hope toward God, which they themselves also allow."* The Old Scripture undoubtedly points to the resurrection of the dead (Job xix. 25-27 ; Isa. xxix. 19 ; Dan. xii. 2), and the Pharisees, the leading party of the nation, believed in it. Thus he affirms that his religion was not an apostacy from the old, but the faithful following out of the old in the new light.

HOMILETICS.—This passage presents to us two subjects—*the Christianity of old Judaism*, and *the characteristics of a great man*.

I. THE CHRISTIANITY OF OLD JUDAISM. The apostle's teaching, though he had become a believer in Christ, still had a vital connexion with the Jewish religion.

First, *He worshipped the Jews' God.* "So worship I the God of my fathers." The God of Judaism and the God of Christianity are identical. The apostle propounded no new divinity; the ancestral deity he alone adored.

Secondly, *He believed in the Jews' Scriptures.* "Believing in all things which are written in the law and in the prophets." Though he accepted Christ, he did not reject Moses and the prophets. Indeed, through Christ he saw them in a new and higher light.

Thirdly, *He believed in the Jews' resurrection.* "And have hope toward the God of my fathers." "They themselves also allow that there shall be a resurrection of the dead." The resurrection, which was dimly seen by the Hebrews, he saw in clear reality through the resurrection of Christ. Christianity is Judaism ripened into fruit, and brightened into noon. This passage presents to us—

II. THE CHARACTERISTICS OF A GREAT MAN.

First, *He is not ashamed of an unpopular cause.* "After the way which they call heresy, so worship I the God of my fathers." The thing that is universally denounced as a heresy he was not ashamed to hold and advocate. All new sects of Christians have been heretics, seceders, schismatics, and holding, in the judgment of opponents, an erroneous faith. Thus, Luther and Calvin were rank heretics in the eyes of Rome ; the Puritans and Methodists in the eyes of the Episcopal Church. Thus every new offshoot is a sect, a heresy from the old stock. Providence permits all this refinement from age to age in order that the Church at last might be without spot or blemish.

Secondly, *His highest aim is moral rectitude.* "Herein do I exercise, to have always a conscience void of offence toward God and toward men." In this declaration we have an illustration of *man and his mission.*

1. The greatest power in man—"*Conscience.*" What is conscience? I regard it not so much a faculty, a law, or a function of the soul, as its very essence, the moral self. That which connects us with moral government, constitutes our responsibility, and originates our weal or our woe. As is a man's conscience, so is he in the spiritual universe and before God. The New Testament attaches immense importance to conscience; no less than thirty times is it mentioned in its sacred pages. It was that in man to which the apostle appealed wherever he went. He sought to commend himself to "every man's conscience in the sight of God." The text reveals—

2. The divinest condition of man. What is the divinest condition? To have a conscience "*void of offence towards God and man.*" "The exact word," says Dr C. J. Vaughan, "is *unstumbling, not striking against stumbling-stones.* It is formed from that verb which we find in Ps. xci. (as quoted in our Lord's temptation), '*In their hands they shall bear thee up, lest at any time thou dash thy foot against a stone.*'" St Paul desires to have a conscience, or self-privity, free from such impact; free from collision with stones or rocks impeding its course. The figure is most expressive. He does not speak here of preserving his life from stumbling, but his conscience; not, therefore, of the act, or the word, or the idea of evil, but rather of the effect of such things upon his self-cognisance, upon his inward view and review, upon his feeling and his consciousness as he looks within. He is determined, God helping him by the grace of His Holy Spirit, that his introspection, his perpetual judgment upon himself, shall not find itself impeded and embarrassed in its course by stones and stumbling-blocks of evil done and good left undone; shall not trip here over a hasty or uncharitable word, and there over a neglected duty, and there over an injured soul, and there over a corrupt and polluting imagination; its course shall be clear as its judges; the straight and smooth and unstained surface of the life and soul shall present nothing for the self-cognisance to dash against as an upbraiding, accusing, or condemning object. This is the figure. The conscience, not the life only, must be kept void of offence. He would be able to say, "*I know nothing by (against) myself.*" The two chief departments of this *unstumbling* conscience correspond to the two great divisions of human duty—the one relating to God, and the other to man. "Void of offence toward God and *toward* man." The apostle does not say he has gained this blessed condition, but it was his *grand aim.* When a man's con-

science gets into this state, he has reached the true blessedness of his being. A good conscience is heaven. The text reveals—

3. The chief work of man. What is it? It is to get into this state. "Herein do I exercise myself." "Exercise, any kind of hard work, and specially applied to athletic strife or training, and then to moral discipline. . . . It here denotes not only constant and habitual practice, but methodical and systematic effort." The greatest work that a man has to do is with his moral self. Paul felt this ; his outward battles were as nothing compared to those that he fought on the arena of his own soul. "So fight I as not beating the air."

Another mark of Paul's greatness is—

Thirdly, *He is frank in explanation of himself.* The apostle now reverts to the purpose of his journey to Jerusalem, and to the charge as having come as a mover of sedition, and he goes into explanation. It was nearly *twenty-five* years since his conversion, and though he had paid occasional visits to Jerusalem, he had never resided there for any length of time. He informs the judge now, that his recent visit to the metropolis, after many years, was a benevolent one. "Now, after many years I came to bring alms to my nation, and offerings." The apostle had been the bearer of gifts from the churches of Macedonia and Achaia to. the poor saints in the city. This was his mission, a mission of mercy and worship, not of rebellion and impiety. He assures the judge that he was found in the temple by certain Jews from Asia "*purified*," not gathering a multitude and creating a tumult, and that those Jews who found him there ought to have been present. "Whereupon certain Jews from Asia found me purified in the temple, neither with multitude, nor with tumult, who ought to have been here before thee, and object, if they had aught against me. Or else, let these same here say, if they have found any evil-doing in me, while I stood before the council, except it be for this one voice, that I cried standing among them, Touching the resurrection of the dead I am called in question by you this day." He is open as the day in giving account of himself.

Acts 24:22-27

PAUL AT CÆSAREA BEFORE FELIX.—(III.) HIS JUDGE

The danger of religious delay

" *And when Felix heard these things,[1] having more perfect knowledge of that way, he[2] deferred them, and said, When Lysias the chief captain shall come down, I will know the uttermost of your matter. And he commanded a centurion to keep Paul,[3] and to let him have liberty, and that he should forbid none of his acquaintance to minister or come[4] unto him. And after certain days, when Felix came with his wife Drusilla, which was a Jewess, he sent for Paul, and heard him concerning the faith in Christ. And as he reasoned of righteousness, temperance, and judgment to come, Felix trembled, and answered, Go thy way for this time; when I have a convenient season, I will call for thee. He hoped also that money should have been given him of Paul, that he might loose him:[5] wherefore he sent for him the oftener, and communed with him. But after two years Porcius Festus came into Felix's room : and Felix, willing to show the Jews a pleasure,[6] left Paul bound.*"

EMENDATIVE RENDERINGS.—(1.) And Felix. (2.) Omit this word. (3.) Him. (4.) Omit *or come.* (5.) Omit *that he might loose him.* (6.) Willing to win favour with the Jews.

HOMILETICS.—Who was this Felix ? We need not go to Josephus or Tacitus, the latter of whom says, that in "the practice of all kinds of lust, crime, and cruelty, he exercised the power of a king with the temper of a slave," for proofs of the wickedness of this man's life sufficient for that comes out in the narrative. The narrative affords us a glance at him officially and morally.

First, *Officially.* How, as a judge, does he treat Paul ? He has heard the case, seen his accusers, listened to Tertullus, the advocate, looked at Paul, heard his noble defence, and if he possessed the most ordinary ability, penetration, and culture, he must have seen that the charges against the apostle were utterly groundless, and that the animus of his accusers was that of malignant and unscrupulous persecution. Hence, as a judge, he should have acquitted him at once. Instead of which, how does he act ? Though convinced, as he must have been, of the innocence and nobility of Paul, yet, in order to conciliate the Jews, he resorts to the cowardly expedient of delay. " And when Felix heard these things, having more perfect knowledge of that way, he deferred them, and said, When Lysias, the chief captain shall come down, I will know the uttermost of your matter." Legally, he could not condemn him ; morally, he was too cowardly to acquit. He was, therefore, shut up to an adjournment of the case, and the pretext was, that Lysias, when he came down to Jerusalem, would give further information of the matter. It is only fair, however, to this corrupt judge, to say, that he granted to Paul during his imprisonment some privileges. " And he commanded a centurion to keep Paul, and to let him have liberty, and that he should forbid none of his acquaintance to minister or come unto him." To be allowed to see his friends, though chained to a soldier, would, no doubt, be esteemed a great privilege by Paul. We may suppose that Philip and his family visited him—also Aristarchus, and Luke, the beloved physician, his companion, and biographer. The narrative leads us to look at him—

Secondly, *Morally.* " And after certain days, when Felix came with his wife Drusilla, which was a Jewess, he sent for Paul, and heard him concerning the faith in Christ. And as he reasoned of righteousness, temperance, and judgment to come, Felix trembled, and answered, Go thy way for this time ; when I have a convenient season I will call for thee. He hoped also that money should have been given him of Paul, that he might loose him ; wherefore he sent for him the oftener, and communed with him. But after two years, Porcius Festus came into Felix's room, and Felix, willing to show the Jews a pleasure, left Paul bound." In this we observe three facts touching this man's depravity, and illustrating the danger of religious delay. Observe—

I. HE IS CONVICTED BY PAUL'S PREACHING OF THE ENORMITY OF HIS WICKEDNESS. " *Felix trembled.*" What made him tremble ? It was Paul's discourse on the Christian religion—"faith in Christ," branching out into " *righteousness, temperance, and judgment to come.*" No doubt Paul knew the man's history well—knew his connexion with Drusilla, who sat by his side—knew well the most salient attributes as they came out in his conduct, and showed themselves in his looks and words, and, with all the force of his inspired genius, he brings the divine truth to bear upon his *conscience,* and the man trembles. The magistrate, the judge, the oppressor, the profligate, cowers with mysterious horror before the divine majesty of the prisoner's form and words.

II. HE TRIFLES WITH HIS CONSCIENCE BY ADJOURNING THE QUESTION OF REFORMATION. What does he do ? Does he at once yield to truth—renounce the old, and adopt the new light which the awakened conscience dictates ? No, but he stifles the feeling by promising to himself a more convenient season. " Go thy way for this time, when I have a convenient season I will call for thee." This trifling with an awakened conscience added enormously to his wickedness. Better conscience never awake, than it should awake with its reproofs, and be disobeyed.*

* See " Philosophy of Happiness," p. 35.

III. HE ADVANCES IN DEPRAVITY BY NOT BEGINNING AT ONCE THE WORK OF REFORMATION. He does send for Paul again, but what for ? *Not to help him out of his sins, but to gratify his greed.* " He hoped also that *money* should have been given him of Paul, that he might loose him, wherefore he sent for him the oftener, and communed with him." He had learnt from Paul's defence that he had been entrusted with funds for the poor at Jerusalem. He knew, too, that Paul had thousands who believed in him, many of whom were wealthy men, and he expected that money would be forthcoming to purchase by a bribe his liberty. Of all the base passions in the human heart, avarice is the basest, and this man had sunk deeply into that, after the convictions that he had received. Felix, to gratify his greed, and to please the Jews, let Paul remain for two years in his prison. Such, in Felix, was Paul's judge at Cæsarea.

The conscience of Felix was roused, under the ministry of Paul, and then was the " convenient " season-hour for his conversion. It was the favourable moral mood. He promised himself a " more convenient season," but it never came. Opportunities for seeing Paul came, and he availed himself of those opportunities again and again, but with none of those opportunities ever came the *moral mood.*

Acts 25:1-12

PAUL AT CÆSAREA BEFORE FESTUS

" *Now, when Festus was come into the province, after three days he ascended from Cæsarea to Jerusalem. Then the high priest,*[1] *and the chief of the Jews informed him against Paul, and besought him, and desired favour against him, that he would send for him to Jerusalem, laying wait in the way to kill him. But Festus answered, that Paul should be kept at Cæsarea, and that he himself would depart shortly thither. Let them therefore, said he, which among you are able,*[2] *go down with me, and accuse this man, if there be any wickedness in him. And when he had tarried among them more than ten days,*[3] *he went down unto Cæsarea ; and the next day sitting on the judgment-seat, commanded Paul to be brought. And when he was come, the Jews which came down from Jerusalem stood round about,*[4] *and laid many and grievous complaints against Paul,*[5] *which they could not prove : while he*[6] *answered for himself, Neither against the law of the Jews, neither against the temple, nor yet against Cæsar, have I offended anything at all. But Festus, willing to do the Jews a pleasure, answered Paul, and said, Wilt thou go up to Jerusalem, and there be judged of these things before me ? Then said Paul, I stand at Cæsar's judgment-seat, where I ought to be judged : to the Jews have I done no wrong, as thou very well knowest. For if I be[7] an offender, or[8] have committed anything worthy of death, I refuse not to die : but if there be none of these things whereof these accuse me, no man may deliver me unto them. I appeal unto Cæsar. Then Festus, when he had conferred with the council, answered, Hast thou appealed unto Cæsar ? unto Cæsar shalt thou go."*

EMENDATIVE RENDERINGS.—(1.) The chief priests. (2.) Which are powerful among you. (3.) Not more than eight or ten days. (4.) About him. (5.) Omit *against Paul.* (6.) Paul. (7.) If indeed I be. (8.) And.—ALF. and TISCH.

EXEGETICAL REMARKS. — These verses narrate Paul's *fourth* public appearance as a prisoner in defence of himself and his religion.

"*Now when Festus was come into the province.*" Festus comes into the place of Felix. From the scriptural narrative, as well as from Josephus, we infer that he was a better man and a more upright judge. His official life at Cæsarea seems to have been very short. He commenced office in the autumn of A.D. 60, and died in the summer of A.D. 62.

"*After three days he ascended from Cæsarea to Jerusalem.*" "*Ascended*" —The governors of Judea at this time generally resided at Cæsarea, but Jerusalem was regarded, for many reasons, as the seat of influence. Hence they spoke in those days of ascending or going up to Jerusalem, as we speak of going up to London.

"*Then the high priest and the chief of the Jews informed him against Paul.*" The word "informed" occurs in the first verse of the preceding chapter, and has the same meaning as here ; it has a forensic signification, and means laying criminal information. Although two years had passed away since they had charged him before Festus, their spirit of enmity was unchanged, and they urged the charge again.

"*And desired favour against him.*" The original language conveys the idea that they made this request as a *special* favour.

"*That he would send for him to Jerusalem, laying wait to kill him.*" Their object in endeavouring to get Paul's trial transferred to Jerusalem was that the nefarious plan of murdering him, mentioned in chap. xxiii. 15, might be accomplished.

"*Let them therefore, said he, which among you are able, go down with me, and accuse this man, if there be any wickedness in him.*" The word "wickedness," although not printed in italics, is supplied by the translators, and is to be found neither in the common texts nor the critical editions.

"*And when he had tarried among them more than ten days.*" The marginal reading, not more than eight or ten days, is regarded by the best authorities as the true text.

"*And when he was come, the Jews which came down from Jerusalem stood round about, and laid many and grievous complaints against Paul, which they could not prove.*" The expression "stood round about" indicates the eagerness with which they crowded around their long-lost victim. They felt a fiendish pleasure in having him, as they thought, once more within their reach. "*Grievous complaints*" — A repetition, most likely, of the charge before Felix (chap. xxiv. 5, 6).

"*Then, said Paul, I stand at Cæsar's judgment-seat, where I ought to be judged.*" The tribunal of Festus was, in authority and name, the bar of the Roman emperor, who went under the general designation of Cæsar, from Julius Cæsar, the first of the dynasty.

"*If there be none of these things whereof these accuse me, no man may deliver me unto them. I appeal unto Cæsar.*" As if he had said to Festus, "You dare deliver me to the Jews !" The right to appeal to Cæsar belonged to him as a Roman citizen, and it was strictly forbidden by the Lex Julien to put any obstruction in the way of a Roman citizen when he had appealed. Paul knew this, and he dared his judge by appealing to Cæsar—" Cæsar I invoke."

" *Hast thou appealed unto Cæsar ?* " " The right of appeal," says Alexander, " to the people in a body, or as represented by the tribunes, was one of the most valued rights of Roman citizens, and still continued to be so regarded even after the supreme judicial power of the people had been transferred to the emperors. Particular importance was attached to the right of appeal from the judgments of provincial magistrates. According to ancient writers, no delay or written form was requisite, the only act necessary to arrest the judg-

ment being the utterance of the word *Appello !* The magic power of this one word is described as similar to the talismanic phrase, *Civis Romanus sum !* Indeed, the two things coincided, as it was the Roman citizen, and not the mere provincial subject of the empire, who could thus transfer his cause from any inferior tribunal to that of the emperor himself. The possession of this citizenship, therefore, was the providential means of saving Paul at this critical juncture, not only from the power of his Jewish foes, but also from the weaknesses of his Roman friends."

HOMILETICS.—Felix, through *greed* and *love of popularity*, had kept Paul a bound prisoner in Cæsarea for " two " long years. Hoping to receive money for his liberation, and at the same time to restore his waning popularity among the Jews, this corrupt judge kept an innocent man all this time in bondage. Time, which works decay in all mortal things, wears out the power of despots, and rots the rods of tyrants and the hand that holds them, at last struck this despot down. When Porcius Festus was sent as a successor to Felix by Nero, the principal inhabitants of Cæsarea went up to Rome to accuse Felix, and condign punishment would have befallen him had it not been for the intercession which his brother Pallas made on his behalf. Wretched man ! He obtained neither gain nor popularity, the two things he sought, in keeping Paul in chains. He sought to conciliate the Jews by injustice, but their enmity towards him grew to a strength that struggled for his ruin. The plans of wickedness are doomed to frustration. Sooner or later all of them will float as miserable wrecks on the stream of destiny. The verses before us bring to our view the *antecedent,* the *attendant,* and the *resultant* circumstances connected with Paul's appearance before this Festus.

I. THE ANTECEDENT CIRCUMSTANCES CONNECTED WITH PAUL'S APPEARANCE BEFORE FESTUS. Here we have to notice—

First, *The arrival of Festus and his visit to Jerusalem.* " Now, when Festus was come into the province, after three days he ascended from Cæsarea to Jerusalem." After arriving, about the year A.D. 60, in Cæsarea, the seat of the civil government, and continuing there " three days," he goes up to Jerusalem, the metropolis of the Jewish people. This prompt departure to the Holy City arose, perhaps, not only from a curiosity to see a place so famous in the history of empires, but to study the spirit, institutions, and manners of a people with whose civil and political interests he would have, henceforth, much to do. Another circumstance connected with his appearance before Festus is—

Secondly, *The appeal of the Jews concerning Paul to Festus during his stay in Jerusalem.* " Then the high priest and the chief of the Jews informed him against Paul, and besought him, and desired favour against him that he would send for him to Jerusalem, laying wait in the way to kill him." Two things are manifest in these verses :—

(1.) *The national importance which the Sanhedrim attached to Paul.* More than two years had passed away since they raised the mob of Jerusalem against him, and since they followed him down to Cæsarea, and, with Tertullus, appeared against him before Felix. One might have thought that the changes which two years make in thought and feeling, and all human things, had destroyed their interest in Paul, and almost effaced his very name from their memory. Had it been merely *personal* enmity it would undoubtedly have been so. But it was the *religious* influence of this man, working wherever he had been, and working mightily in Jerusalem, before their eyes every day, that kept him before them as a terrible religious antagonist—who was sapping the very foundation of their religious system, prestige, and power. Their opposition is a tribute to Paul's mighty influence. Another thing manifest in these verses is—

(2.) *The servility and hypocrisy of religious bigotry.* " And desired favour against him, that he would send for him to Jerusalem." The arguments they employed are not given. No doubt they bowed before Festus as cringing, fawning sycophants, urging every consideration that the genius of bigotry could suggest and that was likely to tell effectively upon the mind of the Roman. They did not say, of course, what is stated in the last clause of the verse, that they were " laying wait in the way to kill him." Oh, no ! They pleaded no doubt, for justice, not murder. The nefarious plan recorded in chap. xxiii. 15, appears now to have been under the direct patronage of the " high priest and the chief of the Jews." Another circumstance connected with his appearance before Festus is—

Thirdly, *The reply of Festus to the request which the Jews made to him at Jerusalem.* " But Festus answered that Paul should be kept at Cæsarea, and that he himself would depart shortly thither "Let them, therefore," said he, "which among you are able to go down with me, and accuse this man, if there be any wickedness in him." Festus refuses. He does not say why he refuses. Perhaps he had one of those *presentiments* which is always strong, often indefinable, the offspring and the organ of God in the human soul. Anyhow, had he not refused, in all human probability Paul would have been murdered, and the Divine promise that had been made to him, that he should visit Rome, would have been frustrated (chap. xxiii. 11). But though he does not give the reason of his refusal, he promises an early trial, for " he would depart shortly thither." And he requests all who had the power to go down with him to Cæsarea, and to bring their accusation against Paul, "if there be any wickedness in him."

II. The attendant circumstances connected with Paul's appearance before Festus. "And when he had tarried among them more than ten days, he went down unto Cæsarea, and the next day, sitting on the judgment-seat, commanded Paul to be brought." Festus in this shows himself to be a man of his word, and a man prompt and punctual in action. He had promised to be there shortly ; there he is. The very day after his arrival at Cæsarea he is "on the judgment-seat," and commands "Paul to be brought." Two circumstances are to be noticed here as Paul stands before the judgment-seat.

First, *The charges of Paul's enemies, and his denial of them.*

(1.) Their charges. "And when he was come, the Jews which came down from Jerusalem stood round about, and laid many and grievous complaints against Paul, which they could not prove." What were they ? Judging from the answer which Paul made, they were the old ones—heresy, sacrilege, and treason ; crimes against the law of Moses, against the temple, and against the emperor. But whatever they were, the historian says that they were such that they could "not prove."

(2.) His denial of these charges. "While he answered for himself, Neither against the law of the Jews, neither against the temple, nor yet against Cæsar, have I offended anything at all." The way which he met those same charges before Felix is recorded in chap. xxiv. 10–21. His manner of treating them now was perhaps substantially the same ; hence the historian does not record his defence. The other circumstance to be noticed here as Paul stands before the judgment-seat is—

Secondly, *The request of Festus to Paul, and his refusal.*

(1.) The request of Festus. "But Festus, willing to do the Jews a pleasure, answered Paul, and said, Wilt thou go up to Jerusalem, and there be judged of these things before me ?" So far, we have discovered nothing censurable in the conduct of this Festus, but here evil shows itself. Popularity appears here dearer to him than justice. He had seen enough to feel in his conscience that Paul was an innocent man, and that he ought in all justice to be acquitted forthwith, but, for the sake of getting a good name with the Jews, he proposes to Paul another trial, and another trial at Jerusalem. Accursed love of popularity ! Pilate condemned Christ "to do the Jews a pleasure." Felix kept Paul bound two years "to do the Jews a pleasure," and Festus, "to do the Jews a pleasure," was willing to deliver an innocent man up to the murderous hands of his malignant enemies. All that can be said in palliation of the request of Festus is, that he did not enforce it, he merely submitted it to the choice of Paul.

(2.) The refusal of Paul. In his refusal there are three things worthy of notice :—(a) *His demand for political justice.* "Then said Paul, I stand at Cæsar's judgment-seat, where I ought to be judged." The apostle had committed no crime cognisable by the Jews, could hope for no justice from them, and was unwilling to hazard his life by returning into the midst of his bitter enemies. As a Roman citizen, he demanded Roman justice. In his refusal, we notice—(b) *His consciousness of moral rectitude.* "To the Jews I have done no wrong, as thou very well knowest." Festus, no doubt, knew that Paul had been tried by Felix, and that no fault was found then ; as a shrewd man, he must have seen that the spirit of his accusers was a spirit capable of fabricating the most groundless and malignant charges, and he must have learnt from the language, the spirit, and the learning of the apostle, that he was an innocent man. Paul had very good reason for saying, " *Thou very well knowest.*" His keen eye penetrated into the heart of the judge, and read there the sentence—" This man is not guilty." In his refusal, we notice —(c) *His sublime heroism of soul.* He dared death. Was he afraid ? Not he. "For if I be an offender, or have committed anything worthy of death, I refuse not to die." To a truly great man, truth, virtue, justice, honour, are far more precious than mortal life. Men's dread of death is always in proportion to their disregard of moral principles. He dared his judge too. "If there be none of these things whereof these accuse me, no man may deliver me unto them." As if he had said to Festus, "You dare deliver me to the Jews!" The right to appeal to Cæsar belonged to him as a Roman citizen, and it was strictly forbidden by the Lex Julien to put any obstruction in the way of a Roman citizen when he had appealed. Paul knew this, and he dared his judge, by appealing to Cæsar— " Cæsar I invoke."

III. THE RESULTANT CIRCUMSTANCES CONNECTED WITH PAUL'S APPEARANCE BEFORE FESTUS. "Then Festus, when he had conferred with the council, answered, Hast thou appealed unto Cæsar? unto Cæsar shalt thou go." The immediate result is, Paul is delivered from the power of the Jews, remanded into custody until an opportunity occurred of sending him into the imperial city. He was now destined for Rome.

In this, "Unto Cæsar shalt thou go," we may see the triumph of three things—

First, *The triumph of justice over policy.* Festus, in desiring him to go to Jerusalem to be tried, thought it a stroke of policy, but Paul's appeal to Cæsar forced him to abandon the purpose. In this, " Unto Cæsar shalt thou go," we see—

Secondly, *The triumph of generosity over selfishness.* A divine generosity—a generosity inspired by the gospel of Christ—had awakened in the heart of Paul a strong desire to go to Rome, in order to unfurl the banner of universal philanthropy in the metropolis of the world. " Paul purposed in the spirit, when he had passed through Macedonia and Achaia, to go to Jerusalem, saying, After I have been there I *must* also see Rome " (Acts xix. 21). And in his letter to the Romans he says, " I *long* to see you, that I may impart unto you some spiritual gift " (Rom. i. 11). And again, " Having no more place in these parts, and having a *great desire* these many years to come unto you, whensoever I take my journey into Spain I will come unto you ; for I trust to see you in my journey " (Rom. xv. 23, 24). This he wrote many years before, when he was at Corinth ; so that this generous desire to preach in Rome was one strengthened by years. But how had *selfishness,* working in the Jews especially, wrought earnestly in a thousand ways to thwart these heaven-born purposes of generosity ! Here, however, in the fiat " Unto Cæsar shalt thou go," is a triumph of his purpose. The door of Rome is thrown open to him : his way is made safe and sure. This incident I take as a cheering prophecy that the generous one day shall achieve the mastery of the world. In this, " Unto Cæsar shalt thou go," we see—

Thirdly, *The triumph of the divine over the human.* God had purposed that Paul should go to Rome. " And the night following the Lord stood by him, and said, Be of good cheer, Paul ; for as thou hast testified of me in Jerusalem, so must thou bear witness also at Rome " (Acts xxiii. 11). The purpose of the Jews was to kill him at Jerusalem, and had Festus acceded to their demands, Paul would never have seen the imperial city. But the Lord reigns, and so controls the opposing and conflicting passions of the world as ultimately to realise His own decree. God's revealed purposes may often seem to us most unlikely of fulfilment ; sometimes, indeed, all but frustrated ; yet they march forward to a grand consummation. As we believe, amid the darkness and desolations of the severest winter, that summer is on its march, and will cover the world with life and beauty, so let us believe, amongst all the workings of human depravity, that God's great purpose to redeem the world to holiness and bliss is marching on in stately certainty.

Acts 25:13-27

PAUL AT CÆSAREA BEFORE AGRIPPA.—I. HIS INTRODUCTION

" *And after certain days king Agrippa and Bernice came unto Cæsarea to salute Festus. And when they had been there many days, Festus declared Paul's cause unto the king, saying, There is a certain man left in bonds by Felix ; about whom, when I was at Jerusalem, the chief priests and the elders of the Jews informed me, desiring to have judgment against him. To whom I answered, It is not the manner of the Romans to deliver any man to die,*[1] *before that he which is accused have the accusers face to face, and have licence to answer for himself concerning the crime laid against him. Therefore, when they were come hither, without any delay, on the morrow I sat on the judgment-seat, and commanded the man to be brought forth. Against*[2] *whom, when the accusers stood up, they brought none accusation*[3] *of such things as I supposed : but had certain questions against him of their own superstition,*[4] *and of one Jesus, which was dead, whom Paul affirmed to be alive. And because I doubted of such manner of questions, I asked him whether he would go to Jerusalem, and there be judged of these matters. But when Paul had appealed to be reserved unto the hearing of Augustus, I commanded him to be kept till I might send him to Cæsar. Then Agrippa said unto Festus, I would also hear the man myself. To-morrow, said he, thou shalt hear him. And on the morrow, when Agrippa was come, and Bernice, with great pomp, and was entered into the place of hearing, with the chief captains and principal men of the city, at Festus' commandment Paul was brought forth. And Festus said, King Agrippa, and all men which are here present with us, ye see this man, about whom all the multitude of the Jews have dealt with me, both at Jerusalem, and also here, crying that he ought not to live any longer. But when I found that he had committed nothing worthy of death, and that he himself hath appealed to Augustus, I have determined to send him.*[5] *Of whom I have no certain thing to write unto my lord. Wherefore I have brought him forth before you, and specially before thee, O king Agrippa, that, after examination had, I might have somewhat to write. For it seemeth to me unreasonable to send a prisoner, and not withal to*[6] *signify the crimes laid against him.*"

EMENDATIVE RENDERINGS.—(1.) Omit these two words. (2.) Round about. (3.) No wicked accusation. (4.) Religion. (5.) But I found that he had committed nothing worthy of death : and seeing that he himself appealed to Augustus, I determined to send him. (6.) When sending a prisoner, not withal to.—ALF.

EXEGETICAL REMARKS. — These verses narrate Paul's *fifth* public appearance as a prisoner, in defence of himself and his religion.

" *And after certain days king Agrippa and Bernice came unto Cæ-* *sarea to salute Festus.*" " This man, Herod Agrippa the younger, was son of Herod the elder, and great-grandson of the so-called Herod the Great, and also brother to Drusilla. He was, on the whole, a much better man than his odious father. He had received his education at Rome as a special favourite of the Emperor Claudius; but when his father died (chap. xii. 23), who had retained the entire kingdom of Herod the Great, he was too young (being only seventeen years old) to succeed him. Claudius therefore sent Cuspius Fadius into the land as procurator, who was followed by Tiberius Alexander, Ventidius Cumanus, and Felix. Subsequently, two years later, when King Herod of Chalcis, uncle of the youthful Agrippa, died, the latter obtained, first, Herod's small kingdom or principality, then, after four or six years, he received instead the former tetrarchy of Philip (Luke iii. 1), which had hitherto been administered by a procurator, together with that of Lysanias, including, therefore, Batacæa, Auranitis, Trachonitis, and Abilene. Like all former tetrarchs, he caused himself to be styled 'king,' and, as Herod of Chalcis before him, possessed the right of control over the treasures of the temple, and also the power of nominating the high priest, although Judea, Galilee, and Samaria were ruled by a governor (now Festus). Agrippa was the last Jewish 'king,' and long survived the destruction of Jerusalem. The Bernice (or Berenice, Φερενίκη) who here appears with him was his and Drusilla's sister, and had been married to the above-named uncle, Herod of Chalcis. Having become a widow at his death, she came to stay with her brother Agrippa, and a very general public report accused the pair of living together in incest. To invert this suspicion, she again sought for matrimony with Polemon, king of Cilicia, whom, however, she abandoned in a short time, although for her sake he had adopted circumcision. She then returned to her former connexion with her brother. She must have been a person of the greatest beauty, and, as regards this point, no slight jealousy must have existed between the sisters Bernice and Drusilla. According to Tacitus, Bernice subsequently much endeared herself to Vespasian (as '*florens ætate formaque*'), and who, according to Suetonius, would have made her his empress, if the dissatis-

faction of the people had not deterred him, and compelled him to send her away."—STIER.

Here we have Paul's introduction to Agrippa, and in this introduction we have two things :—

First, Festus' statement of the case to the king in the absence of Paul. "*And when they had been there many days, Festus declared Paul's cause unto the king, saying, There is a certain man left in bonds by Felix.*" The statement of Festus before the king, extending from this verse to the 22d, is as near to that of Luke as would be natural in such a case. Much of this is but a recapitulation of facts, recorded by Luke in preceding verses, and which we have already noticed. The fresh elements, however, are noteworthy. They are—

(1.) The reason he gives for not delivering Paul up at first to the Jews. "*To whom I answered, It is not the manner of the Romans to deliver any man to die, before that he which is accused have the accusers face to face, and have license to answer for himself concerning the crime laid against him.*" There is a discrepancy between the reason here given and that contained in the fourth verse. The reason Festus assigned why Paul should be kept at Cæsarea, was his own convenience. This discrepancy admits of two explanations. One is, that Luke omitted to record the answer of Festus to the Jews on that occasion, and that he recorded only the personal inconvenience and not the political difficulty which is here mentioned. The other explanation is, that Festus now perpetrated a falsehood in his statement to Agrippa; that he reports to Agrippa not what he *did* say on that occasion, but what he *might* have said, or what, perhaps, he *ought* to have said. However, whether he made this reply or not, the reply itself bears an honourable testimony to that love of justice which distinguished the Roman rule. "It is not the manner of the Romans to deliver any man to die, before that he which is accused have the accusers face to face, and have licence to answer for himself concerning the crime laid against him." The statement of the text is substantiated by other authors : thus Appian says, "It is not their custom to condemn men before they are heard." Philo says of the Roman prefects, "They yielded themselves to the common judges, hearing equally the accusers and defendants, condemning no man unheard, prejudging no man, but judging without favour or enmity, according to the nature of the case." Tacitus also remarks, that "a defendant is not to be prohibited from adducing all things by which his innocence may be established." The justice of such laws is happily exemplified in our own judicature. Another fresh element here is—

(2.) The disregard for the religious questions in dispute. The question which brought the Jews into such a violent and deadly antagonism to Paul was what Festus calls their

"*Own superstition, and of one Jesus which was dead, whom Paul affirmed to be alive.*" The word "*religion*" would be better than "*superstition*" here, for it cannot be supposed that in speaking to Agrippa, who was a Jew, Festus would be so discourteous as to call his religion a "superstition" in our sense of the word. Still, of this religion, and this "one Jesus," Festus speaks with an air of manifest indifference. The whole seems to him to be unworthy of his notice. Of course, as a Roman judge, such religious questions were outside of his jurisdiction, but as a man they should have been regarded with a most vital concern. Another fresh element here is—

(3.) His motive for his desiring him to go to Jerusalem for trial.

"*And because I doubted of such manner of questions, I asked him whether he would go to Jerusalem, and there be judged of these matters.*" In the ninth verse we hear him ask Paul the question, "Wilt thou go up to Jerusalem, and there be judged of these things before me ?" Here he gives the reason for putting such a question. It was his own difficulty on the point. "I doubted of such manner of questions," or, as the margin has it, "I was doubtful how to inquire hereof."

Secondly, The statement of the case to the king in the presence of Paul. The result of the first statement of Festus was the desire on the king's part to hear Paul for himself. Consequently, the apostle is brought into his presence, and the circumstances of the interview were grand and imposing.

"*Then Agrippa said unto Festus, I would also hear the man myself. To-morrow, said he, thou shalt hear him. And on the morrow, when Agrippa was come, and Bernice, with great pomp, and was entered into the place of hearing, with the chief captains and principal men of the city, at Festus' commandment Paul was brought forth.*" The cold-hearted voluptuary, for such was Agrippa, had his curiosity awakened, and was anxious to see a famous man, and to hear a strange story. Accordingly, Paul is brought into his presence. Bernice comes with Agrippa into court "*with great pomp.*" The chief captains—chiliarchs, commanders of a thousand men—are there, and also the principal men of the city. The pomp, or, as the Greek is, the *phantasy*, was great to the eye of the sensuous and the thoughtless. It is worthy of notice that this parade of splendour was made almost on the very spot where Agrippa's father was a few years ago smitten by the angel, and devoured by worms, for the indulgence of a pride similar to that which Agrippa now exhibits. In the statement which Festus, in introducing Paul, now makes, he indicates two things—

(1.) His *personal* conviction in the matter. "And Festus said, King Agrippa, and all men which are here present with us, ye see this man, about whom all the multitude of the Jews have dealt with me, both at Jerusalem, and also here, crying that he ought not to live any longer. But when I found that he had committed nothing worthy of death, and that he himself hath appealed to Augustus, I have determined to send him." Here is a strong testimony to Paul's innocence. Festus had heard all that the Jews had to say against him, both at Jerusalem and at Cæsarea ; he had seen and spoken to Paul himself ; he had undoubtedly given much attention to the case, and here, in the open court of

Cæsarea, he declares that he had found "nothing worthy of death," and that he had no "*certain thing*" of which to accuse him. This indicates—
(2.) His *official* embarrassment. Festus was bound to send Paul to Rome, to the emperor, to be tried. Paul had demanded this, and the request he could not disregard ; but in sending him to the chief authority, whom he calls "*my lord*," it was his duty to specify the crimes that he had committed. But crimes he could not find. "Of whom I have no certain thing to write unto my lord. Wherefore, I have brought him forth before you, and specially before thee, O king Agrippa, that, after examination, I might have somewhat to write. For it seemeth to me unreasonable to send a prisoner, and not withal to signify the crimes *laid* against him." If Festus had done his duty, and acquitted Paul, he need not have sent him to Rome ; but now he was bound to send him to Rome, and here was his embarrassment. What was he to do ? He was unable to report the case to Nero without criminating himself. His hope, therefore, was, that something would come out before Agrippa that would solve the difficulty.

HOMILETICS.—In the fragment of apostolic history thus noticed, we have *four* states of mind which have ever prevailed in relation to the gospel—

I. BITTER ANTAGONISM. This is revealed in the Jews. This fired them against Paul. They hated "the *one Jesus* whom Paul preached as having died and risen again." They could not bear the mention of His name. There are men now who hate Christianity,—hate its principles, author, advocates, and disciples. The opposition, however, is as *futile* as it is malignant and wicked. The glorious cause of Paul has gone on and flourished, notwithstanding the fierce opposition of his contemporaries ; and so it will continue to do. The stone must smite the image.

II. IDLE CURIOSITY. This is revealed in Agrippa. "*I will also hear the man myself.*" Being a Jew, he could not have been ignorant of Paul's name, his history, or his cause, and now an opportunity occurred for him to see the man and hear his tale. His wish to hear Paul was not a wish for spiritual instruction. He had no heart-interest in the matter ; it was mere idle curiosity. It would afford him and his profligate companion an hour's gratification. That is all. Multitudes now go to hear preachers from the same motive.

III. PROUD INDIFFERENCE. This is revealed in Festus. He felt no interest in this superstition. He cared nothing about "*this one Jesus who was dead, and whom Paul affirmed to be alive.*" Not he. Religious indifferentism is the prevalent sin of Christendom. This is worse, for many reasons, than theoretic infidelity.

IV. VITAL FAITH. This is revealed in Paul. (1.) Paul had a *faith ;* (2.) His faith was *in Christ ;* (3.) His faith was his *very life.* To it he lived, and for it he was prepared to suffer and to die. "For me to live," he said, "is Christ, and to die is gain."

Acts 26:1-23

PAUL AT CÆSAREA BEFORE AGRIPPA.—II. HIS DEFENCE

1. *Its substance*

" *Then Agrippa said unto Paul, Thou art permitted to speak for thyself. Then Paul stretched forth the hand, and answered for himself: I think myself happy, king Agrippa, because I shall answer for myself this day before thee touching all the things whereof I am accused of the Jews; especially because I know thee to be expert*[1] *in all customs and questions which are among the Jews: wherefore I beseech thee to hear me patiently. My manner of life from my youth, which was at the first among mine own nation at Jerusalem, know all the Jews; which knew me from the beginning (if they would testify), that after the most straitest sect of our religion I lived a Pharisee. And now I stand and am judged for the hope of the promise made of God unto our fathers: unto which promise our twelve tribes, instantly serving God day and night, hope to come: for which hope's sake, king Agrippa, I am accused of the Jews. Why should it be thought a thing incredible with you, that God should raise the dead?*[2] *I verily thought with myself, that I ought to do many things contrary to the name of Jesus of Nazareth. Which thing I also did in Jerusalem: and many of the saints did I shut up in prison, having received authority from the chief priests; and when they were put to death, I gave my voice against them.*[3] *And I punished them oft in every synagogue, and compelled them to blaspheme; and being exceedingly mad against them, I persecuted them even unto strange cities. Whereupon, as I went to Damascus with authority and commission from the chief priests, at midday, O king, I saw in the way a light from heaven, above the brightness of the sun, shining round about me and them which journeyed with me. And when we were all fallen to the earth, I heard a voice speaking unto me, and saying in the Hebrew tongue, Saul, Saul, why persecutest thou me? it is hard for thee to kick against the pricks. And I said, Who art thou, Lord? And he*[4] *said, I am Jesus, whom thou persecutest. But rise, and stand upon thy feet: for I have appeared unto thee for this purpose, to make thee a minister and a witness both of these things which thou hast seen, and of those things in the which I will appear unto thee; delivering thee from the people, and from the Gentiles, unto whom now*[5] *I send thee, to open their eyes, and to turn them*[6] *from darkness to light, and from the power of Satan unto God, that they may receive forgiveness of sins, and inheritance among them which are sanctified by faith that is in me. Whereupon, O king Agrippa, I was not disobedient unto the heavenly vision: but shewed first unto them of Damascus, and at Jerusalem, and throughout all the coasts of Judea, and then to the Gentiles,*[7] *that they should repent and turn to God, and do works meet for*[8] *repentance. For these causes the Jews caught me in the temple, and went about to kill me.*[9] *Having therefore obtained help of God, I continue unto this day, witnessing both to small and great, saying none other things than those*

*which the prophets and Moses did say should come; that Christ should
suffer, and that he should be the first that should rise from the dead, and
should* [10] *shew light unto the people, and to the Gentiles."*

EMENDATIVE RENDERINGS.—(1.) Especially because thou art expert. (2.) If God
raiseth the dead. (3.) I gave my vote against them. (4.) The Lord. (5.) Omit
this word. (6.) That they may turn. (7.) Them of Damascus and Jerusalem,
and throughout all the country of Judea, and to the Gentiles. (8.) Worthy of
them. (9.) Endeavoured to kill me. (10.) If at least Christ was to suffer, and,
first rising from the dead, was to.—ALF., TISCH.

EXEGETICAL REMARKS.—This is a
continuation of Paul's fifth public
appearance as a prisoner in defence of
himself and his religion, and it neither requires nor admits of any division beyond that afforded by the
progress of the argument or drift of
the discourse.

" *Then Agrippa said unto Paul, thou
art permitted to speak for thyself.*"
As King Agrippa occupied the highest rank in the assembly, as the
guest of the procurator, he enjoyed
the honour of being president on this
occasion. Hence he opens the proceedings, and at last breaks up the
meeting. Alas! that the reign of evil
in our world should be so mighty as
to give tyrants a power over a good
man's tongue. "*Permitted to speak!*"—
Why, Paul had a divine right to speak,
and the world stands in urgent need
of his utterances.

" *Then Paul stretched forth the
hand, and answered for himself.*" He
stretched forth his hand, either because it was the usual attitude of
ancient orators, or to indicate that he
intended addressing himself exclusively to Agrippa; or in order, by the
chain that was on his hand fastening
him to the guard, to remind all in
the court of his unjust and cruel confinement.

"*I think myself happy, king Agrippa,
because I shall answer for myself this
day before thee touching all the things
whereof I am accused of the Jews.*" It
was gratifying to the apostle to be
permitted to speak at all on this occasion, for he had much that lay on his
conscience to say; much that would
throw light upon his history and his
religion. But it was especially gratifying to him to be able to speak on
this occasion before Agrippa.

" *Especially because I know thee to*

*be expert in all customs and questions
which are among the Jews: wherefore I
beseech thee to hear me patiently.*" This
was not the language of cringing flattery, but of truthful courtesy. King
Agrippa " *was expert,*" literally a
knower of Jewish customs and questions, and this to Paul was a great
advantage. The Roman magistrates,
Felix and Festus, before whom he
had defended himself, knew little or
nothing about Jewish customs and
questions; they were, therefore, incompetent to form an accurate judgment. Agrippa, on the other hand,
was "expert" in all these matters.
He was a Jew, who had lived a considerable time amongst his own people,
and who understood the doctrines and
rites of their fathers.

" *My manner of life from my youth,
which was at the first among mine own
nation at Jerusalem, know all the Jews;
which knew me from the beginning (if
they would testify), that after the most
straitest sect of our religion I lived a
Pharisee.*" He here asserts that he
was *well known* amongst the Jews.
Though born at Tarsus, he had been
sent early in life to Jerusalem to study
in the school of Gamaliel (chap. xxii.
3). He lived from youth up to his
conversion, not in an obscure province of the country, but in the heart
of the metropolis. He asserts that he
is well known among the Jews as one
of the strictest of Pharisees after the
most " straitest sect "—an *anomalous
pleonasm* not found in the original.
" *Of our religion* "—No sect was so
scrupulous in the observance, not only
of the Mosaic rituals, but also of all
traditional customs; and Paul was of
the strictest of these Pharisees. He
asserts that his Pharisaism was a *vital
thing*—" *I lived a Pharisee.*" Judaism,
to him, was not a mere letter, pro-

fession, or ceremonial, it was his life; he lived it, embodied it in his everyday actions. It would seem from his language that he was one of the most fanatical of the Pharisees.

"*And now I stand, and am judged for the hope of the promise made of God unto our fathers.*" For believing that the promised Messiah, the hope of the Church (chap. xiii. 22, xxviii. 30) has been fulfilled in Jesus of Nazareth risen from the dead.

"*For which hope's sake, king Agrippa, I am accused of the Jews.*" I am accused of the Jews, O king—of all quarters the most surprising for such a charge to come from. The charge of sedition is not alluded to in this speech.

"*Why should it be thought a thing incredible that God should raise the dead?*" The resurrection of Christ from the dead, and not the general resurrection, is what is referred to here. This, to Paul, was the crowning proof of Christ's Messiahship.

"*I verily thought with myself that I ought to do many things contrary to the name of Jesus of Nazareth.*" This verse should be read as connected with the fifth, and the words "so then" substituted for "*verily.*" The idea is, that because he was an inveterate Pharisee, he thought himself bound to oppose Jesus of Nazareth."

"*Which thing I also did in Jerusalem,*" &c. In this and the next verse he gives a brief sketch of the malignant and terrible persecutions which he inflicted upon Christians.

"*Whereupon, as I went to Damascus,*" &c. Here follows a history of his marvellous conversion, up to the sixteenth verse. As we have met with this before (chap. ix. 1-9, xxii. 6-11), we may merely point to the apparent discrepancies between this and the two previous accounts. Here, for example, is an addition to the two previous accounts as to the brightness of the sun, and it shining not only on Paul himself, but also upon those who were with him; here, too, is the addition of Paul's companions falling to the earth along with him : "*And when we were all fallen to the earth.*" In the other accounts it is said they "stood speechless." But the verb "stood" there used

may be rendered had stood still, or stopped, at the first appearance of the light, and is opposed not so much to lying prostrate as to going on. They may therefore have fallen after Paul did, whose prostration Luke records exclusively as that of the chief actor and great subject of the history.— ALEXANDER.

"*Saying in the Hebrew tongue.*" The Hebrew tongue was the language of Christ, and came from heaven. "It is hard for thee," &c. "Lightfoot says this is a Syrian proverb; but it is a Greek proverb, and is explained by a scholiast on Pindar as a metaphor from unruly oxen at work, who, when pricked with the goad, kick against it, and are but pricked the deeper."—C. E. T.

"*Rise, stand upon thy feet,*" &c. Here the apostle appears to condense into one statement various sayings of his Lord to him in visions at different times, in order to present at one view the grandeur of the commission with which his Master had clothed him." —ALFORD.

"*Delivering thee from the people, and from the Gentiles.*" The word "delivering" is understood by some not in the sense of rescuing, but in the sense of *selecting.* Both ideas are true concerning Paul : Christ rescued him from dangers to which he was exposed, both from the Jews and the Gentiles, and Christ also selected him from the great multitude of both as His minister.

"*I was not disobedient unto the heavenly vision.*" The expression seems to imply, that if he had yielded to selfish motives, he would have recoiled from a mission of such terrible responsibilities and hardships.

"*Saying none other things than those which the prophets and Moses did say should come: that Christ should suffer,*" &c. "Paul," says Lange, "puts the object of the biblical promise in an interrogative form, because it was disputed by the Jews. There were these three questions : — 1. Whether the Messiah is παθητός—*i.e.*, not only capable of suffering, but subjected to suffering, *necessitati patiendi obnoxius*, so throughout in the classical *usus loquendi.* 2. Whether the Messiah will rise again, and be the first in the domain of the resurrection. 3. Whether the Messiah will announce light (salvation) not only to the people of Israel, but also to the Gentiles. The two last thoughts are grammatically fused into one question, but, according to the nature of the subject, are to be regarded as separate."

HOMILETICS.—In this passage we have—

THE SUBSTANCE OF HIS DEFENCE

In looking at the various parts of Paul's defence here, there are five facts which he propounds :—

I. THAT THE THING FOR WHICH THEY ACCUSED HIM WAS THE GREAT BELIEF OF THE JEWISH NATION. Paul believed in a Messiah; so did the whole Jewish people. "And now I stand and am judged for the hope of the promise made of God unto our fathers : unto which promise our twelve tribes, instantly serving God day and night, hope to come : for which hope's sake, king Agrippa, I am accused of the Jews. Why should it be thought a thing incredible with you, that God should raise the dead ? "

These verses contain two great truths :—

First, *That the Messiah in whom he believed was the grand "* HOPE *" of the Jewish people.* It was a hope—(1.) Founded on a divine promise : "The promise made of God." The Old Testament abounds with divine promises of the Messiah.* It was a hope—(2.) Mightily influential. It was mighty in its *extent :* all had it—"Unto which promise our *twelve* tribes "—the whole Jewish people. It was mighty in its *intensity :* "instantly serving God day and night." "Day and night" with unwearied zeal they attended to all the ceremonies of the Jewish religion, *hoping* for the Messiah. Even to this day the hope of the Messiah burns in the heart of the Jewish people throughout the world. The disappointments of ages have not quenched it ; it flames on. Another truth implied here is—

Secondly, *That the resurrection of Jesus of Nazareth from the dead demonstrated that his Messiah was the true one.* This seems to be implied in the 8th verse ; "Why should it be thought a thing incredible with you, that God should raise the dead ? " They would not accept the fact of Christ's resurrection, though they could not deny it. The proofs, instead of winning them to the new faith, exasperated them. The language of the apostle implies that it was to the last degree absurd for them to consider the thing "incredible." "Why should it be thought a thing incredible with you, that God should raise the dead ? " Or, using the first word as an exclamation, "What ! should it be thought a thing incredible with

---

* Gen. iii. 15; xxii. 18 ; xlix. 10 : Deut. xviii. 15 : 2 Sam. vii. 12 : Ps. cxxxiii. 11 : Isa. iv. 11 ; vii. 14; ix. 6, 7 : Jer. xxiii. 15 ; xxxiii. 14–16 : Ezek. xxxiv. 23 . Dan. ix. 24 : Micah vii. 14 : Zech. xiii. 1–7 : Mal. iii. 1.

you that God should raise the dead?" Can it be possible that any rational being can question God's power to do so? Another fact that comes out in Paul's defence is—

II. THAT THE CAUSE HE NOW ESPOUSED HE ONCE HATED AS MUCH AS THEY DID.

He understood their prejudices, for they were once his own. "I verily thought with myself, that I ought to do many things contrary to the name of Jesus of Nazareth. Which things I also did in Jerusalem : and many of the saints did I shut up in prison, having received authority from the chief priests," &c.

Two facts he here states concerning himself—

First, *As a well-known Pharisee, he conscientiously set himself in opposition to Jesus of Nazareth.* As if he had said, " While I lived a Pharisee, I thought that I owed it to my country, to my religion, to my God, to oppose to the utmost of my power the claims of Jesus as the Messiah." Paul as a Pharisee was conscientious. Conscientiousness is not virtue.

Secondly, *He manifested his opposition by the most violent persecution of Christ's disciples.* He describes himself as feeling " exceedingly mad against them." So furious was his indignation, that he raged like a madman ; his ferocity overcame his reason. He gives a few specimens of his heartless cruelty towards them. He " shut them up in prison." He voted for their death. " When they were put to death, I gave my voice against them." Perhaps he was a member of the Sanhedrim, and always voted for their ruin. " He punished them oft in every synagogue, and compelled them to blaspheme," forced them to curse the name of Christ, and "persecuted them even unto strange cities."

Another fact that comes out in Paul's defence is—

III. THAT THE CHANGE EFFECTED IN HIM, AND THE COMMISSION HE RECEIVED, WERE MANIFESTLY DIVINE.

First, *The change effected in him was manifestly divine.* It is thus described : " Whereupon, as I went to Damascus with authority and commission from the chief priests, at mid-day, O king, I saw in the way a light from heaven, above the brightness of the sun, shining round about me and them that journeyed with me. And when we were all fallen to the earth, I heard a voice speaking unto me, and saying in the Hebrew tongue, Saul, Saul, why persecutest thou me? It is hard for thee to kick against the pricks. And I said, Who art thou, Lord? And he said, I am Jesus, whom thou persecutest." This is the third account of his conversion, and as it agrees substantially with the other accounts, which we have before noticed, we need offer no further observations.

Secondly, *The commission that he received at the time of his conversion was undoubtedly divine.* We have this in the

16th, 17th, and 18th verses. And these verses are so full of truth that they must be made the subject of a separate discourse.

APOSTOLIC MINISTRY

" *But rise, and stand upon thy feet: for I have appeared unto thee for this purpose, to make thee a minister and a witness both of these things which thou hast seen, and of those things in the which I will appear unto thee ; delivering thee from the people, and from the Gentiles, unto whom now I send thee, to open their eyes, and to turn them from darkness to light, and from the power of Satan unto God, that they may receive forgiveness of sins, and inheritance among them which are sanctified by faith that is in me.*"

These verses present to us three things concerning the ministry the apostle now received—

I. The THEME of his ministry. What had he to witness or testify?

First, All that he *had* seen of Christ: "That which thou hast seen." He had seen and heard great things amidst the bright light which struck him to the ground.

Secondly, All that he *should* see of Christ: "And of those things in the which I will appear unto thee." He would receive many more communications, and these were to become the theme of his ministry. A true minister will be *always* receiving fresh communications of truth, and he must proclaim the new as well as the old. "The Lord hath yet more light and truth to break forth from His Word."

II. The BENEFICENCE of his ministry: "To open their eyes," &c. He had to effect—

First, *The highest good.* There are four of the elements of highest good here :—

(1.) *Spiritual illumination:* "Open their eyes." An expression this implying three things—(*a*) The moral blindness of man as a sinner; (*b*) The restorative character of Christianity,—it does not give new eyes, but opens the old ones ; (*c*) The genuineness of Christ as a reformer,—the design of impostors is to close eyes.

(2.) *Soul emancipation:* "From the power of Satan unto God." Satan enslaves men by lust, worldliness, prejudice, superstition, &c. The minister's work is to manumit the slave.

(3.) *Divine forgiveness:* "That they may receive forgiveness of sins." The divine act of forgiveness is represented in the Bible as cancelling, forgetting, drowning sin ; separating the sinner from his sin, "as far as the east is from the west."

(4.) *Eternal blessedness:* "Inheritance amongst them which are sanctified," &c. The expression implies—(*a*) *Legitimate possession,* having a kind of right to it ; (*b*) *Social intercourse* "among them" not a scene of isolation; and (*c*) *Moral purity*—" sanctified." The Christian circle is holy. He had to effect—

Secondly, *The highest good by a simple method.* How is this highest good to be obtained? By no onerous labour or costly sacrifices, but by "faith that is in Me;" "*In Me,*" not in priests; "*In Me,*" not in human creeds; "*In Me,*" not in the opinions of men about Me. Faith in Christ is not a mere thing of the intellect, it involves the deepest sympathies of the heart. Nor is it even a thing of thought and feeling combined; it takes the form of *living acts;* it *moulds the life.*

(1.) Faith is in itself one of the *easiest* acts a man can perform. A child can believe; the propensity to believe is one of the strongest in human nature. Credulity has ruined the world.

(2.) Faith in itself is one of the most *influential* acts. What a man really believes sways his thoughts, controls his passions, and regulates his life.

Another fact in Paul's defence is—

IV. THAT THE DISCHARGE OF HIS MISSION WAS THE CAUSE OF HIS PRESENT PERSECUTION. "Whereupon, O King Agrippa, I was not disobedient unto the heavenly vision." Observe how he discharged this commission.

First, *Self-denyingly.* "I was not disobedient unto the heavenly vision," &c. "When it pleased God to reveal His Son in me, I conferred not with flesh and blood."

Secondly, *Contiguously.* He began where he was converted, and went on, "first to Damascus, to Jerusalem, throughout all the coasts of Judea, and then to the Gentiles." This is the true order. Begin with those nearest at hand, then gradually on.

Thirdly, *Reformatively.* His grand aim was spiritually to reform men, that "they should repent and return to God, and do works meet for repentance." A reform including two things—

(1.) A *renewed mind,* "That they should repent and turn to God:"—"Repent"—a thorough change—repenting and turning.

(2.) A *renewed life.* "Works meet for repentance:" the conduct answering the new state of the soul. This was his work, and because he did this, he says to Agrippa, "The Jews caught me in the temple, and went about to kill me." This was his only crime. Another fact in Paul's defence is—

V. THAT HIS MISSION WAS DIVINE, IMPARTIAL, AND IN STRICT ACCORDANCE WITH THE OLD TESTAMENT. "Having, therefore, obtained help of God, I continue unto this day, witnessing both to small and great, saying none other things than those which the prophets and Moses did say should come. That Christ should suffer, and that He should be the first that should rise from the dead, and should show light unto the people, and to the Gentiles."

First, *It was by divine help that he carried on his mission.* "Having obtained help of God." He had been in many dangers, and he could only trace his deliverance to God. His escapes were often miraculous. See 2 Cor. xi. 23-28.

Secondly, *It was with impartiality that he carried on his mission.* " Small and great." Small and great in stature, in mind, in social standing. His religion knew no distinction of persons, nor did he. All men were lost, and he sought their salvation. He was not too proud to speak to the meanest, nor too cowardly to address the greatest.

Thirdly, *It was in strict accordance with the Old Testament that he carried on his mission.* He said, "none other things than those which the prophets and Moses did say should come." He delivered no *new* doctrine. He simply says the prophecies concerning Christ have been fulfilled. The prophets declared that Christ should suffer (Dan. ix. 7 ; Isa. liii.) The words have been thus paraphrased : " Through the help of God I have maintained my ground to this day, bearing witness of the truth to men of all conditions, and discussing the great question, whether the Messiah of the prophecies was to die and rise again before He could be set forth as a Saviour both to Jews and Gentiles."

Acts 26:24-26

PAUL AT CÆSAREA BEFORE AGRIPPA.—III. HIS DEFENCE

2. *Its effects upon Festus*

" *And as he thus spake for himself, Festus said with a loud voice, Paul, thou art beside thyself; much learning*[1] *doth make thee mad. But he said, I am not mad, most noble Festus ; but speak forth the words of truth and soberness. For the king knoweth of these things, before whom also I speak freely : for I am persuaded that none of these things are hidden from him ; for this thing was not done in a corner.*

EMENDATIVE RENDERING.—(1.) Thy much learning.

EXEGETICAL REMARKS.—"*Festus said with a loud voice.*" It is not necessary to believe that his loud voice meant insolence or contempt ; it may only mean earnestness.

" *Thou art beside thyself.*" Thou art mad.

" *Much learning doth make thee mad.*" Literally many letters, which, according to its Greek etymology, may either refer to books or letters,

as in John v. 17, or the knowledge obtained from them, as in John vii. 15. It is an ancient opinion that great studies produce mental aberration.

" *I am not mad, most noble Festus.*" " Most noble," Paul intended not to apply, of course, to the man's *personal* character, but to his *official* position.

"*For the king knoweth of these things.*

" With admirable skill he parried the slighting charge of the cold-hearted Roman, who would naturally look on these subjects with an unsympathising mind, by appealing directly to the Jewish king, whose education had better prepared him to appreciate Paul's reasoning. He challenged the experience and observation of one who had enjoyed the opportunity of an enlarged acquaintance with Jewish affairs to bear witness to its truth." —LIV.

" *This thing was not done in a corner.*" The conversion of Paul was a matter of public notoriety. He was a well-known man before his conversion. His conversion was so extraordinary, and his subsequent conduct so wonderful in every respect, that his change became the subject of universal talk.

HOMILETICS.—These verses lead us to consider *the effects of his defence upon Festus.*

I. THE CHARGE OF FESTUS. The charge against Paul was mental derangement. He did not denounce him as a hypocrite or a knave, but rather as a brainless fanatic. This impression, though false, might have been sincere. The charge of madness against the earnest advocates of Christianity is *very easy, very common, and very foolish.*

First, *Easy.*—It requires no thought, no reflection. Nothing is less difficult than to dispose of great questions in this way.

Secondly, *Common.*—It is what the careless and the profligate are constantly alleging against earnest teachers.

Thirdly, *Foolish.*—Because no class of men are influenced by higher reason than the genuine advocates of religion. Posterity has long since decided who was the madman, Paul or Festus.

II. THE REPLY OF PAUL.

First, *He respectfully denies the charge.* " I am not mad, most noble Festus."

Secondly, *He describes the true character of his teaching :* " Words of truth and soberness." The " truth"here stands opposed to falsehood, and " soberness" to mental derangement. " I speak," as if Paul had said, " the words of *reality* and the words of *reason.*"

Thirdly, *He obliquely rebukes Festus.* He turns from him as if he would ignore his existence, and addresses himself to the king, saying, " For the king knoweth of these things, before whom also I speak freely : for I am persuaded that none of these things are hidden from him ; for this thing was not done in a corner." As if Paul had said to Festus, " It is not surprising that you cannot understand me ; you are not a Jew. You have already misunderstood me. I am not speaking to you, but to the king ; for the king knoweth of these things," &c. In thus acknowledging the king's acquaintance with the subject, Paul's aim was not to flatter the monarch, but to humble Festus.

Acts 26:27-30

PAUL AT CÆSAREA BEFORE AGRIPPA.—IV. HIS DEFENCE

3. *Its effects upon Agrippa*

" *King Agrippa, believest thou the prophets ? I know that thou believest. Then Agrippa said unto Paul, Almost thou persuadest me to be a Christian.*[1] *And Paul said, I would to God, that not only thou, but also all that hear me this day, were both almost and altogether such as I am, except these bonds.*[2] *And when he had thus spoken,*[3] *the king rose up, and the governor, and Bernice, and they that sat with them.*"

EMENDATIVE RENDERINGS.—(1.) With small persuasion thinkest thou that thou canst make me a Christian? (2.) I would to God, that, whether with little persuasion or too much, not only thou, but also all who hear me this day, might become as I am, except these bonds. (3.) Omit *when he had thus spoken.*—ALF., TISCH.

EXEGETICAL REMARKS. — " *Then Agrippa said unto Paul, Almost thou persuadest me to be a Christian.*" The expression has been very variously rendered, "but the simplest and most satisfactory interpretation," says Alexander, "although not even mentioned by some modern writers, is the one found in the oldest English versions—in a little, *i.e.*, in a small degree (Tyndale and Cranmer, *somewhat*). The idea then is, 'Thou persuadest me a little (or in some degree) to become a Christian,' *i.e.*, 'I begin to feel the force of your persuasive arguments, and if I hear you longer, do not know what the effect may be.' We cannot agree with Olshausen in regarding the words of Agrippa as something of a 'jocular character;' nor even with Baumgarten, as considering his words not devoid of a 'dash of irony.' We are inclined to adopt Stier's view, as regarding the king as saying, ' Much is not required for me to believe what thou sayest. If thou continuest to speak a little longer so clearly and so persuasively, I shall be forced to be a Christian.' If Stier's view is correct, which agrees with Tyndale, Cranmer, Alexander, and others, we want no change in our version: ' Almost thou persuadest me to be a Christian.'"*

HOMILETICS.—Paul appeals now directly to the king. " King Agrippa, believest thou the prophets ? I know that thou believest." He makes this appeal perhaps for two reasons :—to meet the charge of derangement that Festus had made, and to bring in the testimony of Agrippa, who understood the subject, to support his position, and also to strike on the conscience of Festus the great question of religion, " Believest thou the prophets? He does not wait for an answer, but with great oratoric skill he gives the answer himself, "I know that thou believest." But what was the effect upon the mind of Agrippa? "Almost." The king's confession and Paul's reply illustrate some features of gospel truth.

* See some excellent remarks upon this subject by Dr Stier in " Words of the Apostles."

I. THE MIGHTY POWER OF GOSPEL TRUTH. This is here seen—
First, *In shaking the religion of the monarch.* (1.) There is
no task more difficult than that of destroying a man's faith in
his own religion. Man has a religious nature—a nature made for
God, and every opinion that he has entertained on religion he
holds with more than an iron grasp. It is easier to argue a
man out of anything than out of his religious creed—he has
often given up his *home, friends,* and *life* for this. (2.) But
while it is thus difficult for men in general to exchange their creeds,
it was so especially with a Jew. The attachment of a Jew to
his religion is proverbial. No religion, Christianity excepted, ever
took such a hold upon the human mind as Judaism. Agrippa was a
Jew. (3.) But of all classes of men, no class would feel it more difficult to change their religion than *kings.* There are greater obstacles
in the way of a sovereign changing his religion than to any one else.
He is often a religious slave—the religion of the people must be his.
Pride, policy, or fear would bind him to his old creed. (4.) And yet
more, add to all this the circumstances of the new religion that was
presented to him. It was neither popular nor respectable. The
mass was opposed to it, and the high ranks frowned upon it with
contempt. Agrippa had just heard his noble friend Festus charge
the man with madness who was recommending to him this new religion. Notwithstanding all these obstacles, such was the power of
gospel truth, that in a few minutes the creed of the king was shaken
to its foundation. He seemed to feel that he was a deluded man,
and he felt an inclination to embrace the religion of the apostle.
" Almost thou persuadest," &c. Almost! Why, Agrippa, is it possible that thou art dissatisfied with the religion of thy fathers?
What strange thing has come over thee? Shall Agrippa stoop so
low, run such social and political risks, as to change his religion?
Why, the philosophy of Rome will laugh at thee, and every breeze
that sweeps over the Seven Hills shall be charged with ridicule for
thy folly, shouldst thou assume the degraded name of Christian.
Here is a glorious evidence of the power of our religion ! Blessed
be God, it is to triumph over all systems—it is to be the conqueror
of all religions. We care not what may be their antiquity, their
plausibility, their congeniality with depraved tastes. We care not
though their principles be inwrought into the moral heart of man.
Bring the religion of the cross in fair contact with them, and they,
like the mists of the morning in the summer's sun, shall vanish away.
Like Aaron's rod, the cross shall swallow up their enchantments.
It shall dispel every error that darkens the human judgment, snap
every fetter that enthrals the human soul—it shall give to every
spirit its right and freedom—the long-lost inheritance of man.
The mighty power of gospel truth is here seen—
Secondly, *In strengthening the heart of the apostle.* While Agrippa
trembles, Paul is calm ; there is a moral majesty on his brow. The

king must have felt himself a babe in the grasp of this giant—a serf in the presence of this iron-bound freeman. What was it that braced up the soul of the apostle with so much unconquerable energy? The same force that made Agrippa tremble—*gospel truth.* The cloudy pillar of old which shone brightly upon the Israelites in the Red Sea, frowned in midnight upon the Egyptians—the former it cheered and guided through the waters, the latter it terrified and overcame with dismay. So here, gospel truth had a very different effect upon these two men. And does it not always act thus? While it overcomes the sinner with the terrors of conviction, does it not fill the Christian with joy and peace in believing? It makes sinners feel their weakness, and believers their strength. It shakes the world, but establishes the Church. It is a system to pull down and build up—to uproot and to plant.

II. THE GRAND AIM OF GOSPEL TRUTH. What is its aim? To elevate man from the barbarous to the enjoyment of social life—to stir the human mind to action—to awaken it to a consciousness of its own precious being, and high relation and solemn condition—to dispel its ignorance, correct its errors, remove its opposition? It does all this, but its grand object is to make men *Christians.*

But what is it to be a Christian? This is the important question. Is it to be orthodox in creed? No; there are many wicked spirits profound theologians. Is it to be regular in our attendance on religious ordinances? No; the Scribes and Pharisees were so; and our Saviour said, " Except your righteousness exceed the righteousness of the Scribes and Pharisees ye shall in no case enter the kingdom of heaven." Is it to be attached to the person, character, and ministry of God's servants? No; Herod heard John gladly, but the vengeance of God overtook him even in this world. Is it conviction of sin? No; Judas repented, Felix trembled, and Agrippa was *almost* a Christian. What, then, is it to be a Christian? Paul answers the question—to be as *I am.* But what constituted Paul a Christian? Three things:—

First, *He accepted the atonement of Christ as the only hope of salvation.* How numerous and cogent were the arguments he employed to show that by the deeds of the law no flesh could be justified. " For if," said he " when we were enemies we were reconciled to God by the *death* of His Son; much more, being reconciled, we shall be saved by His life." On the sacrificial love of Christ, shed abroad in his own heart, he grounded his hope of heaven and acceptance with God. He disclaimed confidence in everything else. His talents, learning, and morality he thought nothing of—the cross of Christ was his all. " God forbid that I should glory, save in the cross of Christ my Lord."

Secondly, *He made the will of Christ the rule of his conduct.* " What wilt thou have me do?" was the first question he asked.

He regarded Christ as his Ruler, his King, as well as his Priest. He followed His directions—he obeyed His precepts—he cherished His spirit—he copied His example. Christ's example was the revelation of law. To imitate that example was to obey His will.

Thirdly, *He cherished the love of Christ as the inspiration of his life.* How earnest was Paul! He traversed continents, crossed seas, braved perils, and endured privations, to preach the gospel. But what was the motive? *Love!* "The love of Christ constraineth us," &c. He was so deeply impressed with the power of this love that at one time he said, "Though I give my body to be burned," &c.

These three things made the apostle what he was; these, too, are the essential elements of a Christian. Do you ask me what is the worth of this name, what is the value of the object which it is the design of gospel truth to confer? *I cannot tell.* It is a "name above every human name." A name that suggests matter for everlasting thought—that comprehends within its ample range all the pure, generous, free spirits of men of every age and clime; spirits that shall shine like stars in the kingdom of heaven for ever. A name that shall live in memory when the greatest names of earth shall be forgotten; when every title that emblazons the page of heraldry shall be blotted out by the hand of time. A name with which is connected the sublimest privileges. Are you a Christian? Then there is a close, and everlasting, though invisible, oneness between you, Christ, and every holy spirit—you live in the sympathies of the good, and in the arms of redemptive mercy. Are you a Christian? Then the great God is your Father, Jesus is your Brother, angels are your servants, and heaven at last will be your home. Are you a Christian? Then you can look and claim an interest in all. "All things are yours." How ardent, benevolent, and pious was that wish of the apostle's, "I would to God," &c. A nobler wish than this never entered a human heart. From it we learn that a Christian in *chains* is *freer, happier,* and *nobler* than a king upon his throne.

III. THE PRACTICAL METHOD OF GOSPEL TRUTH.

How does this powerful truth attain this sublime object? By sentimental rhapsody, priestly interpositions, theatrical ritualism, noisy declamations? No. These may rouse the passions, but cannot convince the judgment; may beget superstition, but never produce enlightened piety; are more adapted to make infidels than Christians. How then?—by baptismal water? This is an outrage on reason. By legislative enactment? There is no way by which coercion can travel to a man's soul, and touch the moral springs of action. Neither of these things separately, nor all conjointly, can effect the object. They who employ them for this purpose betray great ignorance of the laws of mind and the doctrines of the Bible. What then are the means? *Moral suasion.* "Almost thou persuadest me," &c. This implies two things—

First, *The existence of evidence to convince the judgment.* Persuasion, you are aware, is grounded on previous conviction. For example, before I could persuade an infidel to love and obey God, I must endeavour to convince him by evidence of the being, excellency, and claims of the GREAT ONE. Before I can persuade a sinner to seek salvation in Christ, he must be convinced of his own immortality, sin, and danger, and of the existence, suitability, and willingness of Christ as a Saviour. Where these things are not believed—and in every congregation there is an immense amount of scepticism in relation to them—the minister has to *argue*, he has to present evidence to the judgment! and until he can fasten convictions in them as to the reality of these things, he cannot *persuade*. He has no ground upon which to stand—no place on which to rest the great lever of the gospel. That the gospel has evidence to convince us of its truth, is a fact as clear as noon-day. If it can only make Christians by persuasion, and if there can be no persuasion without a conviction of its truth, then it follows that every Christian, whether a saint in heaven or a pilgrim on earth, is a living witness of its truth.

Secondly, *The existence of motives to change the will.* Persuasion consists in the presentation of motives in order to change the will, heart, and conduct. And how tremendous are the motives which the gospel contains for this purpose! Motives gathered from life and death, time and eternity, the resurrection morning and the judgment-day, the heights of heaven and the depths of hell, the scenes of Sinai and the mighty wonders of the cross. Oh, the cross contains a universe of motives in itself! Every page of gospel truth is charged with infinite motives to bow down the sinner's conscience and to change his will. The presenting of these motives to the mind is *persuasion*—is the means by which men are to be made Christians. This persuasion is a peculiarity of our religion. The religion of heaven needs no persuasion—the spirits there have only to know their duty in order to perform it. Other religions on earth are too false to depend upon it. If the religion of the " false prophet" is to be propagated, it must be by the sword; if Popery, by mystification; if Deism, by the construction of fallacies; but our religion can only spread by a fair exhibition to the mind : it has a self-propelling power. All it wants is to be presented fairly to the mind, in humble dependence upon that Spirit that has pledged to crown it with success. Was it not in this way that it spread in the first ages of the Church ?

IV. THE SOLEMN FAILURE OF GOSPEL TRUTH. "Almost" a Christian —only " almost." What was the reason he did not yield entirely to the divine influence now brought to bear upon him, and become a thorough Christian ? Not because the gospel had not sufficient motive to induce him to advance, but because he did not *think sufficiently and rightly upon it.* You are conscious that the power of argument upon your mind depends upon the consideration you give it. An individual may ply me with arguments ever so powerful, yet unless I think upon them, they will fall powerless upon my soul. Suppose you had an undutiful son who had left your home ; his conduct had often grieved your spirit ; his absence had nearly broken your heart ; it clothed your days with darkness, it made you sad and restless through the night. Tidings reach you concerning the place whither he has gone ; and the gay, foolish, sinful, and ruinous conduct he is still pursuing. Your paternal sympathies are stirred to their very depths ; you enter your private room, you resolve to address a letter to your undutiful, though much beloved boy. Into that epistle you throw all the pathos of a parent's heart, and all the arguments that paternal love could suggest to induce him to return to your bosom and home. After you have written your letter, you show it to the dear partner of your life, and the mother of your son. She returns it with a full heart, and says, If anything will move him this letter will. Now on what does the success of that letter depend? Not on its being sent; not on its being put into the hands of your son ; nor even on his reading it; but on his *thinking* properly upon it—thinking upon it as the expression of a father's heart—a heart which his conduct has well-nigh broken.

Just so it is with the gospel ; it is a letter sent down from the Everlasting Father to His undutiful children, containing the most powerful arguments to persuade them to return ; and the great reason why it succeeds not is, because they do not think. Hence He complains of their thoughtlessness. " O that my people were wise ! " Let men but think of these subjects—think of them, &c.

But was this a safe state of mind for Agrippa to be in? Did the gospel, to this extent of influence, do him any real good ? No ; if he lived and died in this state, better he had never seen Paul or heard of Christ.

Are you only almost Christians, brethren ? Then you are resisting the ministry of the gospel by striving against the light of your judgment and the conviction of your own conscience. *Almost a Christian!* Has the kingdom of God come so near to you, and will you not enter ? Have you heard the thunder, and seen the flashes of justice, and will you not flee from the wrath to come ? *Almost a Christian!* Why, the load of responsibility on your shoulders is tremendous ; as yet the many privileges you have enjoyed have done you no real good. *Almost a Christian!* you had better die a heathen. The nearer you are elevated to heaven, the deeper will be your fall. Methinks, if on the judgment-day there be one visage more impressed with agony and despair than another, it will be that of the " almost Christian ;" if there be one shriek more piercing, one wail of anguish more distressing amid the miseries of the lost, it will arise from the bosom of the " almost Christian." There are many sad failures. The failure of your health is sad, the failure of your business is sad, the failure of your country in some terrible campaign is sad—but all is nothing to this failure. If the gospel fail to save man, there is nothing else.

V. The philosophic genius of gospel truth. His reply to the king has a moral grandeur beyond description : " And Paul said, I would to God, that not only thou, but also all that hear me this day, were both almost and altogether such as I am, except these bonds." This forms a sublime peroration to this great defence, and a magnificent close to all his apologies. " Altogether such as *I am,*" implying that he felt that, though a bondsman, he was greater, nobler, happier, than the king and all before him. He was " heir of God, and a joint-heir with Christ." Here is *a spirit of the highest philanthropy.*

First, It was a *praying* philanthropy : " I would to God."

Secondly, It was a *forgiving* philanthropy. He desired the good of all his enemies, and nothing but their good ; he would have all of them enjoy his privileges, but none to share his bonds.

Thirdly, It was a *universal* philanthropy : " Not only thou, but *all* that hear me this day." Alas, they did not become what he wished them to be ! How did they separate from Paul ? Here is the result.

" And when he had thus spoken, the king rose up, and the governor, and Bernice, and they that sat with them." This seemed to be the impression of all.

"The king rose up," &c. " King Agrippa, like Felix and Festus, like his ancestors in the sacred story, flits now from the scene. Nothing came, we believe, of this strange interview between light and darkness, between sin and the gospel. Agrippa kept his useless idle faith in Jewish scriptures; kept, too, his heart's lusts, his obscene idol, his earth-bound life. Times of trial drew on. In the last Jewish wars he sided with the Romans, and then retired to drag out an inglorious age through thirty uneventful years, with a titular royalty and in real servitude, under the imperial shadow of Rome. In the year of our Lord 100, being the third year of the Emperor Trajan, he died there, the last prince of the blood-stained race of Herod. Yet, like all whose names, for good or for evil, are once stamped upon the holy page, Agrippa remains to all time for the edification and instruction of the Church which he despised " (Dr Vaughan). The court leaves Paul. The king, and all who heard him in the court, withdrew from him, never perhaps to see him again in this world. But he has not done with them. His thoughts will tell for ever on their destiny ; he will live in their memory ; he will meet them in another court.

Paul was emphatically a great man. He had an intellect that grasped the sublimest truths—a heart that loved his God, and bled with compassion for his race. He lived as well as preached Christianity. His conduct confirmed the doctrine that his lips declared.

He was a portraiture and a proof of the religion of Jesus. The peculiar estimation which he formed of the world was at once a result and an evidence of his singular greatness. His judgment was not carried away by show. The splendour of the world did not conceal from him its moral deformity. Standing upon an eminence unreached by the mass, he took a view of the world, and with the law of God as his standard, he formed a calm and deliberate judgment of mankind. He deprecated the religion of the religious, pitied the ignorance of the philosophical, and wept over the degradation of the great. He estimated no man according to his birth, office, attire, or wealth, but according to the real amount of Christian truth that lived in his heart and was embodied in his life. These remarks are suggested by the scene in which he appears before us in this chapter. Here the poet, the painter, and the sculptor may find a subject worthy of the highest effort of their genius. He stands before royalty as a criminal undaunted and brave. Neither the anathemas of his own countrymen, nor the scowl of the world, could crush that spirit of his which rose in triumph over all. He was in chains, and yet on the face of this globe there was no man more free than he; his spirit exulted in a liberty which no despot could injure, no time destroy. An outcast in the world was *he*, and yet its rulers trembled at the majesty of his looks and the power of his words. Here, with his great mind filled with love to God and man, his cogent rousing and eloquent appeals made Felix tremble and Agrippa exclaim, " Almost thou persuadest me to be a Christian."

Acts 27:1-20

PAUL'S VOYAGE FROM CÆSAREA TO ROME

1. *Man's counsellors in passing through life*

" *And when it was determined that we should sail into Italy, they delivered Paul, and certain other prisoners, unto one named Julius, a centurion of Augustus' band. And entering into a ship of Adramyttium, we launched, meaning to sail by the coasts of Asia;*[1] *one Aristarchus, a Macedonian of Thessalonica, being with us. And the next day we touched at Sidon. And Julius courteously entreated Paul, and gave him liberty to go unto his friends to refresh himself. And when we had launched from thence, we sailed under Cyprus, because the winds were contrary. And when we had sailed over the sea of Cilicia and Pamphylia, we came to Myra, a city of Lycia. And there the centurion found a ship of Alexandria sailing into Italy; and he put us therein. And when we had sailed slowly many days, and scarce*[2] *were come over against Cnidus, the wind not suffer-*

ing us, we sailed under Crete, over against Salmone; and, hardly passing it, came unto a place which is called The fair havens; nigh whereunto was the city of Lasea. Now, when much time was spent, and when sailing³ was now dangerous, because the fast was now already past, Paul admonished them, and said unto them, Sirs, I perceive that this voyage will be with hurt and much damage, not only of the lading and ship, but also of our lives. Nevertheless the centurion believed the master and the owner of the ship, more than those things which were spoken by Paul. And because the haven was not commodious to winter in, the more part advised to depart thence also,⁴ if by any means they might attain to Phenice, and there to winter; which is an haven of Crete, and lieth toward the south-west and north-west.⁵ And when the south wind blew softly, supposing that they had obtained their purpose, loosing thence, they sailed close by Crete. But not long after there arose against it⁶ a tempestuous wind, called Euroclydon.⁷ And when the ship was caught, and could not bear up into the wind, we let her drive. And running under a certain island which is called Clauda,⁸ we had much work to come by the boat: which when they had taken up, they used helps, undergirding the ship; and, fearing lest they should fall into the quicksands,⁹ strake sail,¹⁰ and so were driven. And we being exceedingly tossed with a tempest, the next day they lightened the ship; and the third day we¹¹ cast out with our own hands the tackling¹² of the ship. And when neither sun nor stars in many days appeared, and no small tempest lay on us, all hope that we should be saved was then taken away."

EMENDATIVE RENDERINGS.—(1.) A ship of Adramyttium, which was about to sail by the coasts of Asia, we put to sea. (2.) With difficulty. (3.) The voyage (4.) Omit this word. (5.) Looketh toward the north-east and the south-east. (6.) There blew down from it. (7.) Euraquilon. (8.) Cauda. (9.) The Syrtis. (10.) Lowered the gear. (11.) They. (12.) Furniture.—ALF. and TISCH.

EXEGETICAL REMARKS.—Paul has done with Cæsarea; he leaves it to return no more. Before Felix, Festus, and Agrippa, he had so triumphantly refuted the charges of his enemies, and established his own innocence, that Agrippa said, " This man might have been set at liberty if he had not appealed to Cæsar." The whole of this chapter is a history of his voyage so far as Malta, and the history is one of thrilling incident, and great moral significance. Its nautical details, which are very full, have borne the test of the most searching investigations.

" *And when it was determined that we should sail into Italy.*" The determination mentioned here does not refer to the purpose to visit Rome, which is expressed in ver. 12 of chap. xxv., but to the manner and time of going there. It was by sea, and immediately. The " *we* " includes Luke the historian, and Aristarchus a Macedonian Christian.

" *They delivered Paul and certain other prisoners.*" Who the other prisoners were, or what were their crimes, we are not told. With these criminals, Paul, the incorrupt and incorruptible, was delivered by Festus and others into the custody of " *Julius, a centurion of Augustus' band.*" And he is now in one of those merchant vessels on which, in those days, even generals and princes had to depend for transit from one part to another of the great empire. The ship was lying in the harbour of Cæsarea, and was bound for Adramyttium, a seaport of Lycia, on the western coast of Asia Minor.*

" *One Aristarchus.*" Aristarchus is

---

* See Conybeare and Howson for an excellent description of the ships and navigation of the ancients.

mentioned elsewhere as Paul's companion in travels (Acts xix. 29, xx. 4 ; Col. iv. 10.)

"*And the next day we touched at Sidon, and Julius courteously entreated Paul, and gave him liberty to go unto his friends to refresh himself.*" One day's sail brought them to Sidon. The gospel had been preached in Phœnicia long before (chap. xii. 19), and no doubt there was a Christian community at Sidon, some of the members of which, through the courtesy of Julius, Paul was now permitted to visit. The centurion "*gave him liberty to go unto his friends to refresh himself.*" His friends there would probably furnish him with supplies that would minister to his comfort during his long and perilous voyage. Why did the Roman soldier treat Paul with this consideration? Was it because of the good opinions which Festus and Agrippa had expressed, or was it because of the majesty and goodness his presence and his bearing exhibited? Probably he felt the influence of both.

"*And when we had launched from thence, we sailed under Cyprus, because the winds were contrary. And when we had sailed over the sea of Cilicia and Pamphylia, we came to Myra, a city of Lycia.*" The expression "*we sailed under Cyprus*," means they kept near to it for shelter and safety. The ancient navigators, ignorant of the mariner's compass, and other means and resources now enjoyed, were accustomed to creep along the shores as much as possible in sight of land. With the nautical advantages of modern times, the open sea is considered the least perilous. Thus sailing on over the sea of Cilicia and Pamphylia, they came to "Myra, a city of Lycia." Lycia was a maritime district of Asia Minor, bounded on the north by Pamphylia, and on the east, west, and south by the sea. Myra was the capital of the district, and situated on the coast. Here they landed.

"*And there the centurion found a ship of Alexandria, sailing into Italy; and he put us therein.*" The first part of the voyage is ended, the second part is commenced. The population of Rome, at this time numerous, were supplied with grain in a great measure from Egypt, whose Nile made it the granary of nations. The "*ship of Alexandria,*" now found at Myra, was laden with wheat. It must have been a large vessel, for, besides its cargo, it had *two hundred and sixty souls* on board, after the centurion, Paul, and his companions, and the prisoners, had embarked. Adverse winds had probably driven the ship on the coast of Asia Minor.

"*And when we had sailed slowly many days, and scarce were come over against Cnidus.*" This was a city, situated on a rocky and mountainous peninsula of the same name, in the province of Caria, between the island of Rhodos and Coos or Cos. It was distinguished for the worship of Venus, and contained the celebrated statue of that goddess by Praxiteles.

"*We sailed under Crete,*" now called Candia, an island fronting the Ægean Sea, one hundred and seventy miles long, and about thirty or forty broad, distinguished for its salubrity, fertility, and beauty.

"*Over against Salmone.*" A promontory at the east end of the island, which they doubled, and sailed under Crete, or south of it, to escape the contrary winds.

"*Hardly passing it.*" Having passed Salmone with great difficulty, being almost driven on it, they steered round the coast end of the island, and came to a roadstead, a species of harbour, "*called the Fair Havens,*" near the city of Lasea.

"*Now when much time was spent, and when sailing was now dangerous, because the fast was now already past, Paul admonished them,*" &c. "The fast was now already past." The fast of the great day of atonement, which occurred at the time of the autumnal equinox was, no doubt, meant. The fast, of course, is not mentioned here as influencing the weather, but as a period of time. Paul felt the crisis. Though not professionally a sailor, he was not ignorant of the navigation of that sea. He knew something of its dangers. Two years before this, in his letter to the Corinthians, he says, "Thrice have I suffered shipwreck, a night and a day have I been in the deep." He sounds the warning.

"*Sirs, I perceive that this voyage will be with hurt and much damage,*" *&c.* Whether he speaks from mere human forecast, or from supernatural inspiration, is a question answered by the distinct assurance he afterwards gave, as recorded in the 24th verse. His warning, however, goes for nothing.

"*The centurion believed the master and the owner of the ship more than those things which were spoken by Paul.*" It would seem that the "more part," the greater part of the crew, and the passengers agreed with the advice of the master and the owner. They considered that the haven was not sufficiently commodious to winter in, and hence they determined to leave "the Fair Havens."

"*The south wind blew softly. . . . Supposing that they had obtained their purpose, loosing thence, they sailed close by Crete.*" At first, when they moved off, things proved propitious, and appeared to indicate that they had taken the right course. The wind had probably before been a head wind, blowing from the west; it now veered to the south, and was favourable. A change, however, soon takes place.

"*But not long after there arose against it a tempestuous wind, called Euroclydon.*" "Euroclydon," derived from two words, meaning east wind and wave—may be rendered the wave-stirring east wind. This was a wind which veered to different points of the compass, from north-east to south-east, and is probably the one known at the present day under the name of *Levanter*—the country at the eastern extremity of the Mediterranean Sea being called the *Levant.*

"*And when the ship was caught, and could not bear up into the wind, we let her drive.*" They were soon plunged into distress. The wind seized her, and carried her along by its resistless force. Being unable to face the tempest, or poetically, as the original implies, to look it in the eye, they gave up all command, and let her drive along at the mercy of the tempest.

"*And running under a certain island which is called Clauda, we had much work to come by the boat.*" Clauda was a small island lying south-west of Crete. With the utmost difficulty, in consequence of the fury of wind and wave, they managed to reach the little boat which followed them, and lifted it on board the vessel.

"*Which when they had taken up, they used helps, undergirding the ship; and, fearing lest they should fall into the quicksands, strake sail, and so were driven.*" Having secured the boat, they commenced to undergird the ship, and to "strake sail." With cables or chains they girded the body of the vessel to prevent her timber from starting by the concussions of the sea; and to lessen the force of the wind upon the vessel, they "strake sail," lowered the mast, and "so were driven" on by the force of the elements.

"*We being exceedingly tossed with a tempest, the next day they lightened the ship,*" *&c.* This was a desperate effort. The sacrifice of the freight, the baggage, the rigging and the furniture of the vessel. "Skin for skin, all that a man hath, he will give in exchange for his life."

"*And when neither sun nor stars in many days appeared, and no small tempest lay on us, all hope that we should be saved was then taken away.*" What a terrific position! Mariners then having no compass, they could only tell their direction by the heavenly bodies, but the heavenly bodies had not shown themselves to these sailors for "many days," and the minds of all on board sunk in the depths of despair. "All hope that we should be saved was then taken away."

HOMILETICS.—This portion of the narrative serves to suggest certain lessons in relation to *man's counsellors in passing through life.*

I. That men in passing through this life have TRUE AND FALSE COUNSELLORS. Paul here stands for the true counsellor. He admonishes the mariners of their danger should they take a certain course (ver. 10). "The master and the owner of the ship" stand for the false counsellors. Their advice was contrary to that of Paul's (ver. 11). Thus it ever is, men have counsellors *true* and *false ;* some pointing them to the right path, and some to the wrong; some the apostles of God, and some the emissaries of hell. This fact urges on each—

First, *The necessity of an independent inquiry into the question of duty.* Let each use his own judgment. "Try the spirit," &c.

Secondly, *The necessity of Divine guidance in the question of duty.* "Guide me by thy counsel," &c.

II. That men are EVER DISPOSED TO FOLLOW THE FALSE RATHER THAN THE TRUE. The centurion and the "more part," the *greater portion* on board, rejected the counsels of Paul, and followed those of the master and the owner. It may be that some of them considered it a piece of impertinence on Paul's part, himself a landsman, to give nautical advice. Men ever follow the false in preference to the true. The false is, First, more *congenial ;* Secondly, more *popular ;* Thirdly, more *attractive.*

III. That following the false often APPEARS AT FIRST TO BE THE BETTER COURSE. When the vessel, contrary to the advice of Paul moved off from the "Fair Havens," things looked propitiously. " *The south wind blew softly.*" Perhaps under the bright sky, and before favourable winds, many on board laughed at Paul on the first day. So it is ; a false course frequently appears at first desirable. There are periods in our sinful life when the south winds blow softly— (1.) youth ; (2.) health ; (3.) prosperity.

IV. That the false ultimately CONDUCTS TO THE MOST TERRIBLE DISASTERS. The soft south wind gives way to the Euroclydon, which hurls the bark into the utmost distress. And then comes the period when all hope that they should be saved was taken away.

" No one," says Dr Howson, " who has never been in a leaking ship, in a long-continued gale, can know what is suffered under such circumstances. The strain both of mind and body, the incessant demand for the labour of all the crew, the terror of the passengers, the hopeless working at the pumps, the labouring of the ship's frame and cordage, the driving of the storm, the benumbing effects of the cold and wet, make up a scene of no ordinary confusion, anxiety, and fatigue." But two circumstances greatly aggravated the case of this ship's distress. There was the *darkness.* No sun or stars for many days appeared, not an unusual circumstance during a Levanter. There was *hunger,* "long abstinence." The want of food led to the pain of exhaustion and the bitter gnawing of hunger. This is what following the false leads to. " Sin, when it is finished, bringeth forth death."

Acts 27:21-26

PAUL'S VOYAGE FROM CÆSAREA TO ROME

2. *God's mode of dealing with man in his extremity*

" *But, after long abstinence, Paul stood forth in the midst of them, and said, Sirs, ye should have hearkened unto me, and not have loosed from Crete, and to have gained[1] this harm and loss. And now I exhort you to be of good cheer : for there shall be no loss of any man's life among you, but of the ship. For there stood by me this night the angel of God, whose I am, and whom I serve, saying, Fear not, Paul ; thou must be brought before Cæsar ; and, lo, God hath given thee all them that sail with thee. Wherefore, sirs, be of good cheer : for I believe God, that it shall be even as it was[2] told me. Howbeit we must be cast upon a certain island.*"

EMENDATIVE RENDERINGS.—(1.) Should have been spared. (2.) Hath been.—ALF.

EXEGETICAL REMARKS.—" *But after long abstinence, Paul stood forth in the midst of them, and said, Sirs, ye should have hearkened unto me,*" &c. When their distress had reached its extremity, when the last ray of hope had burnt out within them, and the cold shivering midnight of despair was settling on their spirits, at this point a light from heaven breaks on them, and that light leads to their salvation. That light comes through Paul.

" *Now I exhort you to be of good cheer, for there shall be no loss of any man's life among you, but of the ship.*" Though the apostle felt that they had done wrong in rejecting his advice, he cheers them by an assurance that there will be " no loss of any man's life," that the ship only would be destroyed.

" *For there stood by me this night the angel of God, whose I am, and whom I serve.*" This night. That is the previous night, for Paul made this speech in the day-time. This divine vision was the ground of his encouragement.

HOMILETICS.—These few verses suggest certain thoughts concerning *God's dealing with man in his extremity.*

I. HE BEGINS BY AGGRAVATING THE DISTRESS. " Sirs, ye should have hearkened unto me, and not have sailed from Crete, and to have gained this harm and loss." These words mean, You have brought all this distress upon yourselves ; you are virtually the authors of all this ; had you accepted instead of rejecting the counsel of wisdom, you would have been spared all this harm and loss. How would this reproof aggravate for the moment the agony of that dark hour ! It would call a new faculty up, *conscience,* and make it sting the sufferer. When a man is made to feel that his suffering is not merely a *calamity,* but a *crime,* it comes on him with new intensity and weight. Thus God ever deals with men. The first thing that He does to help a world in misery is to convince it that its misery is self-produced. His first words to it are, "O Israel, thou hast destroyed thyself." And He goes on to convince it of sin, righteousness, and judgment.

II. HE PROCEEDS TO MITIGATE THE DISTRESS. "Now I exhort you to be of good cheer; for there shall be no loss of any man's life among you, but of the ship." After the wound comes the salve. After sinners have passed through the agony of remorse, and experienced the workings of genuine repentance, there comes to them the message of divine comfort, "Let not your hearts be troubled, ye believe in God, believe also in me." After the tempest the still small voice. This is the divine order.

III. HE DOES BOTH THROUGH HIS SERVANTS. Through Paul God appealed to the distressed men on board the storm-tossed and sinking vessel. "There stood by me this night an angel of God, whose I am, and whom I serve, saying, Fear not, Paul; thou must be brought before Cæsar: and lo, God hath given thee all them that sail with thee."

Three things are here to be noticed—

First, *The essential character of God's servants.* What is *indispensable* in the character of a true servant? Paul's language here answers the question. (*a*) A practical consciousness of God's absolute claim to our being. "Whose I am." I am not the proprietor, but the trustee of myself. I am the property of another. (*b*) A constant working out of God's will in our being. "Whom I serve." The first question of Paul was, "Lord, what wilt thou have me to do?" Thou hast a will concerning me; that will I am bound and willing to follow out. This is the essence of a true servant.

Secondly, *The high privilege of God's servants.* What is that? Communication from the Heavenly Father : "There stood by me this night the angel of God." Why did God's angel come to Paul rather than to the rest on board that labouring barque? Because Paul was His true servant. "The secrets of the Lord are with them that fear Him, and He will show them His covenants."

Thirdly, *The social value of God's servants.* "God hath given thee all them that sail with thee." Paul was the temporal saviour of all on board. The world is preserved for the sake of the good. Abraham is an example. Every righteous man is a bulwark to his city and his country. The history of six thousand years has illustrated this truth.

Acts 27:27-32

PAUL'S VOYAGE FROM CÆSAREA TO ROMF

3. *Selfishness*

" *But when the fourteenth night was come, as we were driven up and down in Adria, about midnight the shipmen deemed that they drew near to some country ; and sounded, and found it twenty fathoms : and when they had gone a little further, they sounded again, and found it fifteen fathoms. Then fearing lest we should have fallen upon rocks, they cast four anchors out of the stern, and wished for the day. And as the shipmen were about to flee out of the ship, when they had let down the boat into the sea, under colour as though they would have cast anchors*[1] *out of the foreship, Paul said to the centurion and to the soldiers, Except these abide in the ship, ye cannot be saved. Then the soldiers cut off the ropes of the boat, and let her fall off.*"

EMENDATIVE RENDERING.—(1.) Carried anchors.—ALF.

EXEGETICAL REMARKS.—" *But when the fourteenth night was come, as we were driven up and down in Adria.*" " The fourteenth night since the storm began. ' *Adria,*' *i.e.*, the Adriatic Sea, which then included, according to Strabo, Ptolemy, and other geographers, not only what is called the Adriatic Gulf, or the Gulf of Venice, but that portion of the Mediterranean lying between Greece, Africa, Sicily, and Italy, and sometimes called the Ionian Sea. This is evident from the situation of Melita, or Malta (chap. xxviii. 1), which lies south of Sicily." —LIV.

" *About midnight the shipmen deemed that they drew near to some country.*" " There are various signs addressed to eye, and ear, and smell, by which experienced mariners, even in the night, could discover their approach to land." The roar of the breakers would inform the veteran sailor that land was not far off.

" *And sounded, and found it twenty fathoms : and when they had gone a little further, they sounded again, and found it fifteen fathoms.*" The somewhat rapid approach to land, indicated by the sounding, started a new fear —the fear that the vessel would be dashed on the rock and struck to pieces.

" *Then fearing lest we should have fallen upon rocks, they cast four anchors out of the stern, and wished for the day.*" Though anchoring vessels by the *stern* is not, it would seem, usual, it is sometimes done. " So it was at the battle of the Nile. And when ships are about to attack batteries, it is customary for them to go into action prepared to anchor in this way. This was the case at Algiers. There is still greater interest in quoting the instance of Copenhagen, not only from the accounts we have of the precision with which each ship let go her anchors astern as she arrived nearly opposite her appointed station, but because it is said that Nelson stated after the battle that he had that morning been reading the 27th chapter of the Acts of the Apostles."

" *And as the shipmen were about to flee out of the ship,*" *&c.* The sailors, notwithstanding the anchorage, felt they were still in danger of being hurled on the rocks, and, utterly regardless of the lives of others, cunningly endeavoured to save themselves.

HOMILETICS.—This paragraph presents to us the subject of *selfishness*.

Observe three things—

I. THE HIDEOUS CHARACTER OF SELFISHNESS. See it in these "shipmen."

First, Here is its *cowardice*. They sought to flee out of the ship. Selfishness is essentially cowardly; disinterestedness is the soul of heroism.

Secondly, Here is its *cunning*. "Under colour," pretending "as though they would have cast anchors," they let down the boat into the sea, in order to escape the danger. Selfishness always works "*under colour*." It has always a guise. In all the trades, professions, and interests of life it works, but always under a hypocritic garb. It dares not show itself.

Thirdly, Here is its *cruelty*. All on board were in the same danger, but they only thought of themselves. What cared they though all perished, so long as they were saved? Self was everything. Selfishness is always ready to sacrifice others for its own ends.

II. THE MANLY EXPOSURE OF SELFISHNESS. "Except these abide in the ship ye cannot be saved." There was one on board whose keen eye penetrated the motives of these men, discovered and exposed their base conduct. Paul in this case is a type of those few men in every age to whom, through the purity of their own motives, and the clearness of their own moral intuitions, it is given to *discern spirits*. They see baseness, falseness, and self-seeking, under the garb of dignity, benevolence, truth. It would be well for selfish men to remember that there are men, few indeed in number, who can see through them, and estimate them at their true value.

III. THE ULTIMATE FRUSTRATION OF SELFISHNESS. "Then the soldiers cut off the ropes of the boat, and let her fall off." With that short sword with which the Roman legions cleft their way through every obstacle to universal victory, they "cut the ropes," and the boat fell off, and if not instantly swamped, drifted off to leeward into the darkness, and was dashed to pieces on the rocks. Thus they were frustrated, and thus all selfishness must ultimately be thwarted and confounded. "He that seeketh his life shall lose it."

Acts 27:33-37

PAUL'S VOYAGE FROM CÆSAREA TO ROME

4. *The leading attributes of a great character*

" *And while the day was coming on, Paul besought them all to take meat, saying, This day is the fourteenth day that ye have tarried and continued fasting, having taken nothing. Wherefore I pray you to take some meat; for this is for your health:*[1] *for there shall not an hair fall*[2] *from the head of any of you. And when he had thus spoken, he took bread, and gave thanks to God in presence of them all: and when he had broken it he began to eat. Then were they all of good cheer, and they also took some meat. And we were in all in the ship two hundred threescore and sixteen souls.*"

EMENDATIVE RENDERINGS.—(1.) Safety. (2.) Perish.—ALF.

EXEGETICAL REMARKS.—"*And while the day was coming on, Paul besought them all to take meat, saying, This day is the fourteenth day that ye have tarried and continued fasting, having taken nothing. Wherefore, I pray you to take some meat.*" The expression " having taken nothing" is not to be understood literally ; it means having taken nothing equal to their requirements.

" *Then were they all of good cheer, and they also took some meat.*" Paul had cheered them by assuring them that not a hair of theirs should be injured, and by imparting to them bread for the recruiting of their exhausted frames. He struck hope into their souls. With land not far distant, the vessel anchored. The sailors, being necessitated to stick to the ship, and with day approaching, notwithstanding the continual fury of the storm, there was some indication of improvement. The first grey beams of the morning dawn would do much to assuage the tempestuous anxieties and fears of all on board. Paul avails himself of this moment to raise the drooping spirits, and to strengthen the exhausted frames, of his fellow-passengers and the crew.

" *And we were in all in the ship two hundred threescore and sixteen souls.*" Josephus relates his being shipwrecked in the Adriatic Sea with six hundred men on board.

HOMILETICS.—This paragraph reveals to us *the leading attributes of a great character.*

I. SOCIAL CONSIDERATENESS. The emaciated appearance of all on board, through lack of food, touched Paul's generous heart. " And while the day was coming on, Paul besought them all to take meat, saying, Wherefore, I pray you to take some meat." The feelings of alarm and anxiety with which their souls had been flooded " for fourteen days and nights," had, according to a physiological law, deadened their appetite, and destroyed all their desire for food. Paul, with the tact of a practical philosopher, sought to resuscitate their inclination for food by allaying their fears : " For there shall not an

hair fall from the head of any of you." This social considerateness
Paul had often displayed before in his conduct, always inculcated
in his teaching ; and it is an essential attribute of that Christianity
in which he was a practical believer and a heroic apostle. We are
only great, only Christian, as we *bear one another's burdens*, and thus
"*fulfil* the law of Christ." Here is—

II. CALM SELF-CONTROL. He was in the midst of the most agi-
tating scenes. The boisterous billows—the furious hurricane—the
reeling, plunging, shattered ship—the two hundred threescore and
sixteen terror-stricken men, were confessedly scenes of terrible excitement ; yet how sublimely calm this man is ! " He took bread, and
gave thanks to God in the presence of them all : and when he had
broken it, he began to eat." A finer picture of moral majesty in man
can scarcely be conceived than this. The philosophy of his tranquillity we know. It was faith in that God whose he was and whom
he served. " None of these things move me," &c. Here is—

III. PRACTICAL RELIGIOUSNESS. " He gave thanks to God in
presence of them all." This was according to the Christian practice.
(Matt. xv. 36, xxvi. 27 ; John vi. 11–23 ; Rom. xiv. 6 ; 1 Cor. x. 13,
xi. 24, xiv. 17 ; Eph. v. 20 ; 1 Thess. v. 18.) This thanking God
before food, on Paul's part, was not a matter of fanaticism, form, or
parade ; it was an expression of the spirit of his life. Paul lived in
the divine ; religiousness was his moral heart. There is no moral
greatness apart from religion. Here is—

IV. COMMANDING INFLUENCE. What he said and what he did
struck new energy into the heart of all. " Then were they all of
good cheer, and they also took some meat." So inspiring were the
words and example of the apostle, that he re-animated all with the
energy of hope. A soul strong with goodness can energise others.
These features of his greatness will further appear under the heading, " Voyage of Life."

Acts 27:38-44

PAUL'S VOYAGE FROM CÆSAREA TO ROME

5. *The bad, the good, the divine, and human*

" *And when they had eaten enough, they lightened the ship, and cast* [1] *out the wheat into the sea. And when it was day, they knew not the land: but they discovered a certain creek with a shore, into the which they were minded, if it were possible, to thrust in the ship.* [2] *And when they had taken up the anchors, they committed themselves unto the sea,* [3] *and loosed the rudder bands, and hoised up the mainsail* [4] *to the wind, and made towards shore. And falling into a place where two seas met, they ran the ship aground ; and the forepart stuck fast, and remained unmoveable, but the hinder part was broken with the violence of the waves. And the soldiers' counsel was to kill the prisoners, lest any of them should swim out, and escape. But the centurion, willing to save Paul, kept them from their purpose ; and commanded that they which could swim should cast themselves first into the sea, and get to land : and the rest, some on boards, and some on broken pieces of the ship. And so it came to pass, that they escaped all safe to land.*"

EMENDATIVE RENDERINGS.—(1.) Casting. (2.) On which they were minded, if it were possible, to run the ship aground. (3.) And when they had cut off the anchors, they left them in the sea. (4.) Foresail.—ALF.

EXEGETICAL REMARKS.—" *And when they had eaten enough, they lightened the ship, and cast out the wheat into the sea.*" Having followed Paul's advice and example, and eaten enough of food, with revived spirits and reinvigorated frames, they put forth fresh efforts to reach the shore in safety. To relieve the still sinking vessel, they " cast out the wheat "—the remaining portion of the cargo—" into the sea."

"*And when it was day,*" &c. The day broke on them, and the land became visible ; but they knew not what land it was. So long had they been driven hither and thither in the tempest, that they were uncertain of their location.

" *They discovered a certain creek with a shore,*" &c. A bay or inlet, breaking up from the sea into the land, and they determined, if possible, to run the vessel ashore at that point. This was a terrible crisis. It was the last effort.

" *And when they had taken up the anchors,*" &c. The utmost caution was now required. They took up the anchors ; cutting them adrift, they let them fall into the sea.

" *They loosed the rudder bands,* and *hoised up the mainsail to the wind,* and *made toward shore.*" Dashed by the force of the tempest, the vessel is soon hurled thither.

" *And falling into a place where two seas met, they ran the ship aground ; and the forepart stuck fast, and remained unmoveable, but the hinder part was broken with the violence of the waves.*" Amid conflicting eddies "the forepart"—the bows or forecastle—"stuck fast," plunged into the sand, "and remained unmoveable." The stern, meanwhile, exposed to the fury of the breakers, is broken to pieces. Now it is a question of life or death—each man for himself.

" *And the soldiers' counsel was to kill the prisoners, lest any of them should swim out, and escape.*" Strange that any at that terrible moment should have thought of anything save their own preservation. But the soldiers thought of the prisoners, and desired to kill them. The strictness of the Roman discipline was such, that soldiers were held responsible for the escape of those under their keeping, and were visited with an equal punishment to that to which the prisoners themselves were exposed. Hence the counsel of these soldiers to kill the prisoners.

"*But the centurion, willing to save Paul, kept them from the purpose.*"

The centurion interposed to thwart this murderous project, and he does so for the sake of Paul, who was a prisoner, and who had saved the vessel.

"*And commanded that they which could swim should cast themselves first into the sea, and get to land: and the rest, some on boards, and some on broken pieces of the ship. And so it came to pass, that they escaped all safe to land.*" Thus all are rescued, and thus, according to the word of Paul, as given him by the angel, "there was no loss of any man's life, but of the ship."

HOMILETICS.—In this paragraph we discover—

I. THE BRUTALISING TENDENCY OF A MILITARY LIFE. One might have thought that the common trials of the perilous voyage, and the terrible shipwreck, would have made every heart soft with tender sympathies for his suffering companion. A common sorrow tends to a common sympathy; but these soldiers meditated the cold-blooded murder of men who had done them no harm, and who had participated in the same trials as themselves, and one of whom was the saver of their lives. Why was this? The soldiers were trained to bloody deeds. Human life to them was very cheap. We may learn from this—

II. THE SOCIAL VALUE OF A GOOD MAN. "The centurion, willing to save Paul, kept them from their purpose," &c. The salvation of passengers and crew must, under God, be ascribed to Paul, and the other prisoners were saved from the heartless massacre of the soldiers because of him. No one but God can tell the social value of one good man in a neighbourhood or in a nation. Ten righteous men would have saved Sodom, &c. We may learn from this—

III. THE FAITHFULNESS OF THE DIVINE WORD. God had said, through Paul, that no life should be lost, that they should be cast upon a certain island, and that the ship should be destroyed. And here, on the shores of Malta, is the fulfilment of that word. The floating wreck, the two hundred threescore and sixteen men standing on the shore, and the scene of the whole, were demonstrations of divine veracity. Ah! "Heaven and earth shall pass away," &c. We may learn from this—

IV. THE NECESSITY OF HUMAN EFFORT. Although the safety attained had been promised by God, yet the human agency employed seemed indispensable. This is further illustrated in the next article.

THE VOYAGE OF LIFE

We may profitably look at the whole chapter as illustrating the course of man's life through this world.

There are some events in history that throw much more light on human life than others. Some only throw a glimmering ray upon some one phase and sphere; others seem to light up the whole realm, and radiate on all sides. Such is Paul's stormy and perilous voyage over the Adriatic billows, as graphically portrayed in the chapter before us. Far indeed am I from a taste for, or a belief in, what is called the "spiritualising" method of treating God's book. I deprecate such a method as a sad and impious perversion; but to look upon its historic records in order to interpret life is, I think, both legitimate and wise. When I look upon Paul, with *two hundred and seventy-five* other men of various tribes, social grades, and religious sects, on board a frail barque, struggling through many cloudy days and starless nights in the fierce tempest, I discover much which throws light upon a whole generation of men. This globe is a ship crowded with passengers; all are battling with the fierce storms of time, as the ship bears them through seas of immeasurable space on their way to a destiny eternal.

Thus reviewing the whole chapter before us, I observe :—

I. THAT IN THE VOYAGE OF LIFE WE HAVE A GREAT VARIETY IN OUR CONTEMPORARIES. On board this vessel that was "*now driven up and down in Adria, exceedingly tossed with a tempest,*" there were no less than two hundred and seventy-five souls with Paul; and they were of a very mixed character. There were the rough, weather-beaten sailors, with might and main endeavouring to guide the barque, which bounded on the swelling billows like a maddened steed amidst moving mountains. There were merchants on their way from Egypt to Italy, some to buy, others to sell, and all in quest of gain. There were "prisoners" in the custody of the stern officers of Roman law, who had either been convicted of crime, and were on their way to execution, or were on the way to Rome to be tried at the tribunal of the emperor himself. There were soldiers, men trained for murder on a gigantic scale, and taught to regard a bloody crime as the most illustrious virtue. Luke, the physician, the evangelist, and historian was there; and so was Aristarchus, one of Paul's most faithful friends. Indeed, on board this storm-tossed barque you have a whole age, a whole generation in miniature. Almost all the social forces of an age are in that vessel. There is labour represented in the sailors, there is war in the soldiers, there is commerce in the merchants, there is law in the men who hold the prisoners in custody, there are literature and science in Luke, there is religion in Paul and Aristarchus, as well as Luke. So varied, indeed, were the companions of Paul in their tendencies, tastes, habits, and aims, that amidst the numbers there could, I think, be but little society. Though in close material contact, they lived in spiritual worlds remote from each other;—worlds lighted, warmed, and ruled by different centres.

In all this, you have a mirror of the human world at the present moment. In our voyage through time, we are thrown in the district in which our lot is cast, amongst contemporaries between whom there are such immense *accidental* differences, that instead of souls meeting and mingling together in sweet and harmonious intercourse, there are but few instances, comparatively, in which you have any spiritual contact. Each has his own little world and interests. Like Paul, we are thrown amongst numerous contemporaries, but there are only a few Lukes or Aristarchuses amongst them, with whom we can have much intercourse. If we are of the Christianly true, " The world knoweth us not." Our sphere of being as far transcends the ken of worldlings as planets that roll beyond telescopic vision. A man morally must *be* what he would understand. He must be a saint to understand a saint, a devil to understand a devil. The tyrant, the pope, the philanthropist, the Christian, are little else than sounds to men who have not the elements that form these characters in their own hearts. Morally, no man *can* be judged but by his own peers.

Now this immense spiritual variety amongst our fellow-voyagers, or, without trope, amongst our contemporaries in this life, is to a reflective mind suggestive of certain important considerations.

First, *It suggests a characteristic of human nature distinguished from all other terrestrial life.* Natural history shows that there is a perfect correspondence in the tastes, impulses, and habits, among all the members of any species of non-rational life. To understand one of the individuals is to understand the entire species. The same external influences produce on all the same results. Their *conscious* life is the same. They move within the same circle ; not one has power to take one step beyond the boundary line. Not so with man. Each individual has the power of striking out an orbit for himself ; an orbit in some respects different from that in which any one had ever moved before or will ever move again. Wonderful in this respect is the power of a moral creature. A self-determining, self-transfiguring power is his. All modes of life are possible to man. He can transmigrate into the grub, the seraph, or the fiend. That living soul which is breathed into our material frames at first may, through this sensuous body, work itself into a beast like Nebuchadnezzar, a devil like Herod, or an apostle like Paul.

Secondly, *It suggests that mankind are not now in their original condition.* The power to form different modes and spheres of life is confessedly a distinguishing gift of our being; but to use that power inconsistently with the royal law of benevolence is the essence of sin and the source of ruin. Power is the gift of God, and is a blessing; the employment of it is the prerogative of man, and may be either a virtue and a blessing, or a sin and a curse. It can never be that the God of love and order intended that our innate moral energy should be so employed as to create such an immense variety in the tastes, tendencies, and aims of our contemporaries as to render social intercourse and harmony impossible. The divine idea of humanity seems to me this, that all souls should have a common centre, and that in all their revolutions, their social radiations, borrowed from a common source, should genially and harmoniously blend, intermingle, and combine. Some great catastrophe has befallen man's social system;—a catastrophe which has hurled souls from the normal centre into regions of darkness and confusion. The Bible explains this.

Thirdly, *It suggests the probability of a future social classification.* Will such men as Paul, Luke, Aristarchus, be doomed for ever to live with mercenary merchants, besotted seamen, and bloody soldiers? Shall good men, whose deepest prayer is, " Gather not my soul with sinners, nor my life with bloody men," dwell for ever with such companions? Is the world to go on for ever thus? Are the Herods to continue kings, and the Johns prisoners? Are the Pauls ever to be at the mercy of centurions? Are the Jeffreys to be on the bench and the Baxters at the bar for ever? It cannot be. Man's deepest intuitions say it cannot be ; the prayers of the good say it cannot be, and the Bible says it shall not be. The tares and the wheat will one day be separated—the good and the bad one day divided. We are only mixed while on board this earth-ship : as soon as we touch the shores of the retributive and everlasting, we separate on the principles of moral character and spiritual affinities. Blessed be God! there is a world in which the " nations of them that are saved shall walk in the light of it : and the kings of the earth do bring their glory and honour into it;" and into which there shall " in no wise enter anything that defileth, neither whatsoever worketh abomination or maketh a lie; but they which are written in the Lamb's book of life : " a world outside of which will be " dogs and sorcerers, and whoremongers and murderers, and idolaters, and whosoever loveth and maketh a lie."

From this narrative I observe—

II. THAT IN THE VOYAGE OF LIFE THE SEVEREST TRIALS ARE COMMON TO ALL. The one trial common to all on board that barque was the danger of losing life. Luke's description of their common trial is very graphic. " And when neither sun nor stars in many days appeared, and no small tempest lay on us, all hope that we should be saved was then taken away." They tried every expedient, but all failed ; the lamp of hope for a time went out. Their souls were in despair ; as dark were they as those heavens that had not seen " sun nor stars for many days." Danger of life is universally felt to be the severest of trials. Death is "the king of terrors." It is that which gives terror to every other terror. And to this trial all are exposed in a thousand different ways every day. All the individuals, families, tribes, nations of the earth, at the present moment, are like Paul and his companions on an ever-surging sea, battling for life. The clouds of death darken every sky; its gales breathe about all. Some, it is true, are in more immediate and conscious contact with death than others, and their struggles are more severe. But all, every hour, are in danger, and all must one day, like Paul and his companions, feel "all hope" of being saved from death taken away. For a short time, in healthy youth and vigorous manhood, you may flow on propitiously like this vessel in the first stage of its voyage, when "the south wind blew softly." Gentle gales awhile, my brother, may fill thy sails, and flattering seas may smile: but farther on, the sea will rise to mountains and marshal its billows against thee; the winds will grow wild with fury, the sun will set, the moon go down, and every star disappear, and thou shall feel thyself only as a bubble on the breakers.

> "Sure a time will come
> For storms to try thee and strong blasts to rend
> Thy painted sails, and spread thy gold like chaff
> O'er the wild wave; and what a wreck—
> If judgment find thee unsustain'd by God!"

The scene suggests two thoughts concerning the common trials of men:—

First, *That they develop different dispositions.* How different were the feelings of Paul, Luke, and Aristarchus from the others. This storm blew open the doors of their hearts, and disclosed the moral stuff they were made of. In all, perhaps, on board, save Paul and his two spiritual brothers, there was a wild tempest of terrific emotion, of which the outward storm was not merely the passing occasion, but the material type. Fear had unmanned them all; so that for fourteen days they could eat nothing:—"they continued fasting." Even the brave sailors were at their wit's end;—they sought "to flee out of the ship." None of them thought of anything but their own safety. Selfishness, the source of all fear, and indeed evermore the source of all painful feeling, had in them risen to a passion. What cared the sailors now who perished, so long as they were saved? The soldiers, too, displayed their base and heartless selfishness; for they proposed to "kill the prisoners" rather than they should have the slightest chance of escape. In sublime contrast with all this was the spirit of Paul, and we presume of his two companions in the faith. None of these things seemed to have moved him. The whole of his conduct, as here recorded, during these fourteen eventful days, was characterised by a magnanimity which can only take its rise in a vital alliance with the Infinite, and a benevolent sympathy for mankind. His every word shows an unfaltering faith in Him to whom he had committed himself. His bearing, too, was calm and hope-inspiring. His great nature was taken up with the sufferings of his companions; he seemed to have no care for himself. "I pray you," said he, "take some meat, for this is for your health." Severe trials, especially those which powerfully threaten life, are sure to develop the moral dispositions of men. Never did the faithless, ungenerous, selfish, dastardly nature of the Jews, as a whole people, show itself so fully as when they stood in front of the Red Sea, with unscaleable heights on both sides, and the avenging Pharaoh and his host swiftly advancing in the rear. They said to Moses, their friend and temporal deliverer, "Because there were no graves in Egypt hast thou taken us away to die in the wilderness?" In this one utterance their base natures leap into daylight. So it ever is. The trials of life reveal the dispositions of the heart; they take off the mask, they strip off all shams, and show us to ourselves and the universe. Trials test our principles as fire tries the minerals.

Secondly, *That they develop the indifference of nature to social distinctions.* Nature cares nothing for any of the distinctions amongst men. The centurion and his subordinates, the prisoners and the officers, the Christians and heathens, were all treated alike on board this vessel. Old ocean cares no more for the boats with which Xerxes bridged the Hellespont than for any worthless log of timber. It heeds no more the voice of Canute than the cries of a pauper's babe. Nature knows nothing of your lords and kings. The ocean in her majesty of wrath cares nothing for your Cæsars. "Napoleon," says a modern author, "was once made to feel his littleness and impotence when at the height of his power and glory, in a storm at sea, off Boulogne. His mighty fleet lay before him, proudly riding at anchor. Wishing to review it in the open sea, he desired Admiral Bruyes to change the position of the ships. Foreseeing that a fearful storm was gathering, the admiral respectfully declined obedience to the Emperor's commands. The ominous stillness of the atmosphere, the darkening sky, the lowering clouds, the rumbling of distant thunder, fully justified the fears entertained by the admiral. But Napoleon, in a rage, peremptorily demanded obedience to his iron will. Vice-Admiral Magon obeyed the order. The threatening storm burst with terrible fury. Several gun sloops were wrecked, and above two hundred poor soldiers and sailors were plunged in the raging waves, very few of whom escaped. The Emperor instantly ordered the boats out to the rescue of the perishing crews. He was told, 'No boat could live in such a sea.' He then ordered a company of his grenadiers to man the boats, and as he sprang the first into a large boat, exclaimed, 'Follow me, my brave fellows!'" They had scarcely entered the boat, before a huge wave dashed over the Emperor, as he stood erect near the helmsman. 'Onward! onward!' he cried; his voice swelling above the tempest's roar. But the daring effort was vain; progress in such a sea was impossible. 'Push on! push on!' cried

Napoleon; 'do you not hear those cries? Oh this sea! this sea!' he exclaimed, clenching his hands; 'it rebels against our power, but it may be conquered!' At this moment a mighty billow struck the boat with tremendous force, and drove it back, quivering, to the shore. It seemed as though this were the ocean's answer; or rather the answer of the God of the ocean, to the proud monarch's boast! Napoleon was cast ashore by the spurning billows of the stormy sea, like a drifting fragment of dripping sea-weed."

Nature's indifference, however, to mere *secular* distinction is not so strange as her want of respect to the *moral*. She paid no deference to the good men now on board; she looked down as indignantly on Paul and his two Christian friends as on the rest. She hid her stars, and made her winds and waves dash with the same wild fury around the heads of all. Nature treats apostles and apostates alike. The sun shines alike, and the showers descend alike, upon the just and the unjust. Nature knows nothing here of moral retributions. Her fires will burn, her waters will drown, and her poisons destroy, the good as well as the bad. Our character and moral position in the universe are not to be estimated by nature's aspect towards us. "The tower of Siloam" may fall on the good as well as on the bad; children may be "born blind" of righteous parents as well as of wicked. The ground of wicked men may bring forth plenteously, while the soil of the good man be struck with barrenness. As far as the system of nature is concerned, "All things come alike to all: there is one end to the righteous and to the sinner, to the clean and to the unclean, to him that sacrificeth and to him that sacrificeth not." She has her own system of laws; he who attends to them most loyally, let him be vile as hell can make him, shall enjoy most of her bounties and smiles. In this respect she is an emblem of the moral system. Both are impartial. Both treat their subjects according to their conduct towards them, not according to their conduct towards anything else. Neither shows respect to any man's person. The great cardinal dictum of each is, "He that doeth the wrong shall suffer for the wrong."

From this narrative I observe—

III. THAT IN THE VOYAGE OF LIFE SPECIAL COMMUNICATIONS FROM GOD ARE MERCIFULLY VOUCHSAFED. "And now I exhort you to be of good cheer; for there shall be no loss of any man's life among you, but of the ship. For there stood by me this night the angel of God, whose I am, and whom I serve, saying, Fear not, Paul, thou must be brought before Cæsar; and, lo! God hath given thee all them that sail with thee." The great God knew the fearful situation of the vessel, the dire perils to which Paul and his companions were exposed, and mercifully interposed. It is even so with our world. He knows the moral difficulties and dangers to which we are subjected, through sin, on our voyage to eternity, and He has graciously vouchsafed the necessary communications for our relief. Between the divine communication vouchsafed to the men on board this vessel, and that which in the Bible God hath given this world, there are certain points of instructive resemblance.

First, *The divine communication to the men on board this vessel came through the best of the men.* Paul was the selected medium of communication. It was not one of the influential merchants, not the commander and owner of the ship, nor even the Roman centurion; but Paul, the prisoner, the heretic, the outcast. There was no man on board the ship, probably, in a more abject condition than he. Notwithstanding his secular abjectness, he was a *good* man. There was no one on board of such high spiritual excellence. He was God's: "Whose I am, and whom I serve." This was the reason for his selection as an organ of divine communication. God has ever spoke to the world through the best men. It matters not how poor they are, if good. He speaks to them, and makes them His messengers. "The secret of the Lord is with them that fear Him, and He will show them His covenant." What is the Bible but communications which God addresses to the world through holy men, "who spoke as they were moved by the Holy Ghost?" Moral goodness alone can qualify a man for this. The divine voice can only be heard by the holy; the carnal mind "discerneth not the things of the Spirit, neither can he know them, for they are spiritually discerned." "Blessed are the pure in heart, for they shall see God."

Secondly, *The divine communications which came to the men on board this vessel were the final and effective means of meeting the emergency.* The maritime genius and energy of all on board had been taxed to the utmost, and all in vain. Finding at the outset of the tempest that they could not direct the vessel through the full fury of the storm, they "let her drive," gave her as much sea room as possible, and yielded her up to the mercy of the elements. Then, having run under "a certain island," they used their best efforts to bind up the shattered ship. "When they had taken up the boat, they used helps, undergirding the ship; and fearing lest they should fall into the quicksands, they strake sail, and so were driven." They took down the sails, and, perhaps, the masts and yards, and bound the vessel round with ropes and cables. Still she was "exceedingly tossed." They then lightened her, committing to the waves part of her precious cargo. Still the tempest raged. Next and last they threw "the tacklings" overboard. "And when neither sun nor stars appeared for many days, and no small tempest lay on us, all hope that we should be saved was then taken away."

Now it was while in this hopeless state that the communication came. After human effort had exhausted its powers, then God interposed. It is so with the gospel. It was after human reason had tried every effort to solve the stormy problems of the conscience, and guide the soul into the haven of spiritual peace, that Christ came.

" You may see," says Culverwell, a writer whose thoughts are ever fresh, because always real and earnest, " Socrates in the twilight lamenting his obscure and benighted condition, and telling you that his lamp will show him nothing but his own darkness. You may see Plato sitting down by the water of Lethe, and weeping because he could not remember his former notions. You may hear Aristotle bewailing himself thus, that his ' potential reason' will so seldom come into act, that his ' blank sheet' has so few and such imperfect impressions upon it, that his intellectuals are at so low an ebb, as that the notions of Euripus will pose them. You may hear Zeno say that his ' porch' is dark ; and Epictetus confessing and complaining that he had not the right ' handle,' the true apprehension of things."

Thirdly, *The efficacy of these communications depended upon a practical attention to the directions.* " There shall be no loss of any man's life among you, but of the ship ; " yet, though this is the purpose, " unless these," the sailors, who understand how to manage the ship, " abide in the ship, ye cannot be saved."

The practical lesson I learn from this is, *that every promise which God makes to man should be regarded as conditional, unless a most unequivocal assurance is given to the contrary.* Paul regarded the promise, that all on board should be saved, as depending upon the right employment of the suitable means. Hence he captured by his orders the affrighted seamen as they were attempting to abandon the wrecking ship. " Unless these," these men, who alone amongst us understand nautical matters, " abide in the ship, ye cannot be saved." But what reason had Paul to regard the promise as *conditional?* There was no *if* in it ; it is most positive and unqualified : " There shall be no loss of any man's life among you, but of the ship." It does not contain, does not suggest, a hint about means. What reason had he therefore to understand the promise as conditional? Every reason. His natural instincts, his experience and observation, and all analogy, satisfied him that divine ends are always reached by means ; that God carries on His universe by an inviolable principle of connexion between means and ends. Unless, therefore, the great God who worketh all things, makes to man a promise of good with the most unequivocal and emphatic assurance that it will come without means, he sins against his own reason and against the established system of the universe in so interpreting it. Thus understanding His promises, they afford no pretext for a Calvinistic carelessness. Has God promised knowledge? It implies study. Has He promised salvation? It implies " repentance towards God, and faith in our Lord Jesus Christ."

From this narrative I observe—

IV. THAT IN THE VOYAGE OF LIFE ONE MORALLY GREAT MAN, HOWEVER POOR, IS OF IMMENSE SERVICE TO HIS CONTEMPORARIES. Let us notice two things—

First, *The characteristics of a truly great man as illustrated in Paul's history on board the vessel.* Observe his *forecast.* At the very outset he had a presentiment of the danger which awaited them. " Sirs," said he to the officers, " I perceive that this voyage will be with hurt and much damage, not only of the lading and ship, but also of our lives." But these men, " dressed in a little brief authority," paid, of course, no attention to the statement of a poor prisoner. " The centurion believed the master and the owner of the ship more than those things which Paul spoke." One can imagine the old captain looking with proud contempt at Paul, and saying, What does he know about nautical matters? he is one of those poor timid landsmen that we brave sailors often have to deal with on board. They see danger in every approaching wave ; in every turn of the vessel they fancy they are going down. Poor cowards ! I wish those timid landsmen would mind their own business. I know how to manage my gallant ship ; I have steered her through fiercer storms and more perilous waves than these. Hush, captain, that poor prisoner, Paul, has a *sensibility* which enables him to see nature, and interpret her as thou canst never do.

An *intense sympathy* with a man's principles and aims will enable me to foresee and predict much of his future conduct. *Godliness,* the soul of all moral greatness, is this sympathy. It is such a close and vital alliance with the Eternal Spirit as enables the soul to feel the very pulsations of the Divine Being, and to anticipate His doings. This sympathy with God is the prophetic eye. Give me this, and, like Isaiah, in some humble measure, I shall foretell the ages. This sympathy is a new faculty—a new eye to the soul. Because of this Paul saw what the captain could not. His heart was in such a contact with that Spirit which controls the winds and the waves that he felt that something terrible was about to transpire. The first motion, as it were, of the Great Spirit of nature, in waking this tempest, vibrated through his heart. Moral greatness, because it is godliness, has always forecast ; it " foreseeth the evil." Never let us disregard the warnings of a great and godly man.

Observe his *magnanimous calmness.* We have already referred to this. Paul displays no perturbation ; his spirit seems as unruffled by the storm as those stars that roll in placid brightness beyond the black tempestuous clouds—stars whose peaceful faces he had not seen " for many days." Indeed, he had such an exuberance of calm courage, that when the storm was at its height, he breathed a cheerful spirit into the agitated hearts of all, and got them to feast with him in the tempest : " They were all of good cheer, and they also took some meat." A man must be sublimely calm to breathe calmness into the agitated hearts of all these men in the fury of the tempest. Trust in God was the philosophy of his remarkable calmness. He could sing with David, " God is our refuge and strength, a very present help in trouble. Therefore will we not fear, though the earth be removed, and though the mountains be carried into the midst of the sea ; though the waters roar with the swelling thereof."

Observe his *self-obliviousness*. Whilst all others were struggling for themselves, he seemed only concerned for them; though, for the most part, they stood in an antagonistic position towards him. He was a prisoner in the custody of Roman officers. The vessel was bearing him, not to his home, not to a scene of friendship, but to that of punishment and death. He did not seem to think of this. His own trying circumstances did not appear to affect him ; he was careful for others ; he had the " charity that seeketh not her own."

Observe, moreover, his *religiousness*. "He took bread, and gave thanks to God in the presence of them all." This explains his greatness. He felt that God was with him. He saw God in the tempest and in the bread. He bowed in resignation to the one—he thanked Him for the other. Whilst his piety would not allow him to complain of the greatest trial, it prompted him gratefully and devoutly to acknowledge the smallest favour.

Secondly, *The service which he rendered was both direct* and *indirect*. The spirit of confidence which he breathed, the efforts he put forth, the directions he gave, were all direct. Then the *indirect* service was great. For the sake of Paul the prisoners were not killed. " And the soldiers' counsel was to kill the prisoners, lest any of them should swim out and escape. But the centurion, willing to save Paul, kept them from their purpose, and commanded that they which could swim should cast themselves first into the sea and get to land." One might have thought that the common trials which they had endured would have softened, in some measure, their brutal natures into genial sympathy. But as soldiers they had been trained to a reckless disregard of life, and to deeds of cruelty. By habits of carnage the spirit of humanity had been expelled from their breasts, and the tiger-nature had become theirs. The particular reason however for this bloodthirsty suggestion was, probably, the fear that, should they escape, they themselves would be charged either with unfaithfulness or negligence by the military authorities at Rome,— their masters. The poor prisoners, however, were saved from this fate for the sake of Paul. " The centurion, willing to save Paul, kept them from their purpose." The signal service which Paul had rendered conciliated the centurion. For Paul's sake the prisoners were saved. None but the Great One can tell the benefits, not only directly but *indirectly* that a *good* man confers upon his contemporaries. On the great day of account it will be found that many an obscure saint has conferred far greater service on the age in which he lived, and the race to which he belonged, than those illustrious generals, statesmen, poets, and sages who have won the acclamations of posterity. The world has yet to learn who are its true benefactors.

The service of a *good man is appreciated as trials increase*. In the first stage of the voyage, when "the south winds blew softly," Paul was nothing. When he uttered his impression of danger, he was treated, probably, if not with insolence, yet with indifference. "The centurion believed the master and the owner of the ship more than those things which were spoken by Paul." But as the storm advanced, Paul's influence increased. Like all truly great men he rose into more majestic attitude as difficulties thickened. The merchants, the soldiers, and the centurion, who were very great men, no doubt, in their way, and were conventionally regarded as great in their own departments on land; and who, perhaps, in their own circle would not condescend to speak to Paul, grew less and less as the tempest rose. Your conventionally great men are only great in fair weather; but the truly great become great in storms. Paul who, at the outset, when "the south winds blew softly," was nothing in that vessel, became the moral commander during the tempest. Amidst the wild roaring of the elements, the cries of his fellow-voyagers, the crashes of the plunging ship, the awful howl of death in all, he walked upon the cracking deck with a moral majesty, before which, captain, merchant, soldier, and centurion, bowed with loyal awe. So it has ever been; so it must ever be. The good show their greatness in trials; and in trials, the evil, however exalted their worldly position, are compelled to appreciate them. How often do the world's great men, on death-beds, seek the attendance, sympathies, counsel, and prayers of those godly ones whom they despised in health!

Brothers! we are on a voyage. Thank God! that whilst various worthless classes are sailing with us, and we are destined to meet with storms in which they can render us no help, yet in the Bible "the angel of God" hath appeared unto us, and hath given us a *conditional* promise that "there shall be no loss of any man's life." Let the fiercest tempest arise, let winds and waves dash about us with utmost fury, yet if we follow the counsels of this Angel-Book, and rightly employ the skill and energy we possess, we shall, though "on boards and broken pieces of the ship," escape "all safe to land."

> "Give thy mind sea-room, keep it wide of earth,
>   That rock of souls immortal; let loose thy cord;
>   Weigh anchor; spread thy sails; call every wind;
>   Eye thy great pole-star; make the land of life."

> "Land a-head: its fruits are waving
>   On the hills of fadeless green,
>   And the living waters laving
>   Shores where heavenly forms are seen."

Acts 28:1-6

1. *Good in heathendom*

" *And when they were escaped, then they knew that the island was called Melita. And the barbarous people* [1] *showed us no little* [2] *kindness : for they kindled a fire, and received us every one, because of the present rain, and because of the cold. And when Paul had gathered a bundle* [3] *of sticks, and laid them on the fire, there came a viper out of the heat, and fastened on his hand. And when the barbarians saw the venomous beast hang on his hand, they said among themselves, No doubt this man is a murderer, whom, though he hath escaped the sea, yet vengeance suffereth not to live. And he shook off the beast into the fire, and felt no harm. Howbeit they looked when he should have swollen or fallen down dead suddenly : but, after they had looked a great while,* [4] *and saw no harm come to him, they changed their minds, and said that he was a god.*"

EMENDATIVE RENDERINGS.—(1.) Barbarians. (2.) Common. (3.) A certain quantity. (4.) When they were long looking.—ALF.

EXEGETICAL REMARKS.—We have followed Paul in his journey to Rome through the terrific voyage " up and down Adria" until the vessel was dashed to pieces on the shores of Melita. He, with the "two hundred threescore and fifteen souls," who had shared with him the terrors and sufferings of that voyage, have " escaped all safe to land."

" *When they were escaped, then they knew that the island was called Melita.*" That this island is our modern Malta, is a point on which most of our acknowledged expositors are agreed. The place known as " the bay of St Paul," on the north-east coast of Malta, which tradition assigns as the scene of the shipwreck, presents *all* the features mentioned in this narrative. It is described as a " rocky shore, with creeks or inlets ; a place of two seas, both in the sense of a narrow channel and of a projecting point. It is a tenacious anchorage—beds of mud contiguous to banks of sand and clay. It has sound-

ings exactly answering to those recorded, and in the same relative position ; and in precisely such a coast as to shape, height, breakers, and currents, as would account for a shipwreck taking place just here."

" *And the barbarous people.*" The people who inhabited this island at that time are here called " barbarous," so named in order to distinguish them from Greeks and Romans, who regarded all nations as barbarians who did not speak their language. " Its population was of Phœnician origin, speaking a language which, as regards social intercourse, had the same relation to Latin and Greek which modern Maltese has to English and Latin."

" *And when Paul had gathered a bundle of sticks.*" The great apostle gathering " sticks." He was great because he could descend to such labours ; he shunned no labours, shrunk from no hardships, which served to help his fellow-men.

" *There came a viper out of the heat,*

and fastened on his hand." The venomous reptile, benumbed by the cold amongst the sticks collected by Paul, as soon as the fire touched it, sprang from its lurking-place, and "fastened on his hand."

" *No doubt this man is a murderer, whom, though he escaped the sea, yet vengeance suffereth not to live.*" "Vengeance" or justice—Nemesis,the goddess of recompense, ἡ δίκη. Retribution was shadowed forth in pagan mythology. "The rude and superstitious people of Malta were quick to interpret every event as some special sign, and to leap to the conclusion that Paul must be a very great criminal because he had been bitten by a serpent."

" *But after they had looked a great while, and saw no harm come to him, they changed their minds, and said that he was a god.*" This was but the same superstition under a new form : running first to one extreme, then to the other : now shuddering at the apostle as a murderer, and now revering him as a divinity. Milman justly remarks, that "in the barbarous Melita, as in the barbarous Lystra, the belief in gods under the human form had not yet given place to the incredulous spirit of the age."

HOMILETICS.—The character of the islanders is very strikingly revealed in the verses before us, and that character shows us the *good* that there is in the human heart where there is neither civilisation nor Christianity. It is common to regard all men outside of Christendom as utterly destitute of every element of goodness. Their kingdom of darkness is unrelieved by a single ray of *goodness*. They are the incarnations and instruments of evil, and evil only. This is untrue to fact, and a libel on human nature. Observe in these barbarians several good things.

I. A SYMPATHY WITH HUMAN SUFFERING. "And the barbarous people showed us *no little kindness,* for they kindled a fire, and received us every one, because of the present rain, and because of the cold." And then in the seventh verse we are told, "that the chief man in the island, whose name was Publius, received and lodged us three days courteously." The appearance of these shipwrecked men, destitute of food and raiment, shivering in the cold and the rain, stirred their hearts with commiseration, and they showed them "*no little kindness.*" They kindled a fire to warm their shivering frames, and no doubt prepared food to allay their hunger, and to recruit their exhausted natures. This *social love* dwells in men of every colour and every clime. It pulsates in all hearts. How can this be maintained, it may be said, in the presence of the fact that cannibalism and human sacrifices, and bloody wars, and nameless cruelties, prevail amongst many barbaric and heathen tribes ? My reply is— (1.) That these cruelties are perversions of this very social sympathy. (2.) That the very existence of tribes implies it ; men could not exist at all in unity without this social and kindly affection. (3.) That cruelties in the forms of oppression, murders, and wars, exist even in Christendom, where this goodness is patent to all. That this kindly sympathy does, as a rule, exist in all hearts, however deeply sunk in ignorance and depravity, is proved—

First, *By modern travellers.* Livingstone found it in those dark regions of South Africa which had never been visited by any European until he appeared. Everywhere he found hearts that could be touched with sympathy by the sight of suffering. It is proved also—

Secondly, *By the Bible.* The Bible is a revelation of love, and unless men have the element of love in them, they would be as incapable of understanding its meaning or feeling its power as the ravenous beast that prowls in the forest. What meaning, for example, would there be to a man who had no love in him in the tale of the Prodigal Son, in the story of Jesus and the family at Bethany and in the other sketches of love that make up the gospel history? Of what service, moreover, would it be to give a history of Christ's sufferings, to depict Him in agony on the cross, if humanity had no heart to be touched with sympathy at the sight of suffering? In fact, if the Bible is a book to be understood and felt by man the world over, man everywhere must have in him the element of love. You may as well bring the magnet to clay as take the gospel to men who have no love in them. Observe in these barbarians—

II. A SENSE OF RETRIBUTIVE PROVIDENCE. "And when Paul had gathered a bundle of sticks, and laid them on the fire, there came a viper out of the heat, and fastened on his hand. And when the barbarians saw the venomous beast hang on his hand, they said among themselves, No doubt this man is a murderer, whom, though he hath escaped the sea, yet vengeance suffereth not to live." Here is a fine subject for a picture. Artistic genius may get for itself immortal fame by transferring this scene with rigorous faithfulness to canvas: the great apostle gathering sticks and kindling a fire; a viper, which lay at first torpid in the cold faggots, springing into venomous activity and striking at the hand of Paul as the fire began to kindle. The barbaric Maltese looking on with horror and disappointment, feeling for the moment that the man towards whom they had shown "no little kindness" was a murderer "whom vengeance suffereth not to live." That viper seemed to them for the moment, Nemesis, the goddess of vindictive justice, avenging the cause of the innocent, and inflicting punishment upon the guilty.

This sense of the connexion between crime and punishment is so *universal* that it must be regarded as *instinctive.* It is a feeling that underlies all religions, and runs through all societies, barbaric as well as civilised. This sense led these people to associate crime with murder, and suffering with crime; so far they were correct, they were true in their theology. It is true that they made mistakes concerning retribution, but their mistakes have ever been too prevalent, even in circles professedly Christian. Their mistakes were—

First, That punishment for crime came in a material form. The sting of the viper they thought the punishment. It was a mere natural occurrence, this spring of the venomous reptile to Paul's hand. They thought it punishment. Men have ever thought punishment comes thus. The fall of the tower of Siloam was a natural occurrence, but some of the people of that day thought that it was a judgment upon those whom it destroyed. A crowded theatre is on fire, its tenants are destroyed in the conflagration; men say it is retribution to the votaries of theatrical amusements. Thus men are prone to regard some terrible occurrence in nature, as the avenger punishing crimes; whereas the fact is, that nature in her operations pays no attention to moral distinctions; her storms shall shipwreck a Paul as well as a Nero. Vipers will sting apostles as well as apostates; providence will pamper a Dives and starve a Lazarus. The other mistake which they made respecting retribution was—

Secondly, That it followed flagrant crimes only. "This man is a murderer," a tremendous criminal—and therefore he is punished. Men have the same idea now. Murder they think the greatest of crimes, and deserving the greatest punishment. But there is a spirit which often possesses men, that calls for greater punishment even than a material murder. "The truth is," says Frederick Robertson, in a masterly discourse on this subject, "we think much of crime, little of sin. There is many a murderer executed whose heart is pure and whose life is white compared with those of many a man who lives a respectable, and even honoured life. David was a murderer. The Pharisees had committed no crime : but their heart was rotten at the core. There was in it the sin which has no forgiveness. It is not a Christian but a barbarian estimate, which ranks crime above sin, and takes murder for the chief of sins, marked out for Heaven's vengeance." Observe in these barbarians—

III. A FAITH IN A SUPREME BEING. "And he shook off the beast into the fire, and felt no harm. Howbeit they looked when he should have swollen, or fallen down dead suddenly ; but after they had looked a great while, and saw no harm come to him, they changed their minds, and said that he was a god." The rapidity with which these men changed their opinion concerning Paul—passing from the notion that he was a flagrant criminal to the belief that he was a "*god*," is only an example of that instability and fickleness of soul which ever characterise the uncultured and the untaught. All souls who are not "rooted and grounded" in the true faith are as "unstable as water."

The point, however, which is most noteworthy here is, that that which brought up to them the idea of God, was that which they con-sidered the *marvellous*. They knew that the natural tendency of the viper's sting was to produce a swelling wound, if not instant death. Because in Paul's case it did not do so, they thought him "a god." They had the feeling that the laws of nature could only be counter-acted by God himself. It was in the *wonderful*, not in the *good*, that they saw God. Thus men generally feel. The idea of God comes up to them most powerfully, not in the calm goodness that is present in every part of the universe, but in strange and startling occurrences.

The good in them, however, was the natural *feeling* they had of a god, not their *conception* of Him. The feeling of God in the human soul is God's own implantation, and is good; the conception formed from it is man's, and may be good or evil. It is in every soul, this feeling. Livingstone says that "the existence of a God and of a future state has always been admitted by all the Bechuanas. Everything that cannot be accounted for by common causes is ascribed to the Deity, as creation, sudden death, &c. 'How curiously God made these things!' 'He was not killed by disease, he was killed by God,' are common expressions. And when speaking of the departed they say, 'He is gone to the gods!'" The Brahmins profess that nothing which appears sin to us ever appeared otherwise to them.

These three things, then, *sympathy with human suffering—a sense of retribution*—and a *faith in a Supreme Being,* constitute what I call *good* in heathens. Changeful, dark, and tempestuous as are the heavens of men with corruption and crime, these three things, like settled, calm, and bright stars, break ever through the gloom.

CONCLUSION. Several things may be fairly deduced from this subject:—

First, *The identity in authorship of human souls and divine revelation.* The grand rudimental subjects of the Bible are love, retribution, God; and these, as we have seen, are written in ineffaceable characters on the tables of the human heart everywhere. What Christ put into His book, He put first into the human soul, and thus *He* is "the Light that lighteth every man that cometh into the world."

Secondly, *The impossibility of atheism ever being established in the world.* Systems that are inconsistent with the intuitions of the human soul can never stand. They may be fabrics most logical in structure, gorgeous in aspect, but they are on the sand, and must fall. The human soul is essentially theistic and religious.

Thirdly, *The responsibility of man wherever he is found.* The heathens, with this inner light of goodness, are bound to walk according to their light. "The invisible things of him from the creation of the world are clearly seen, being understood by the things that are made, even his eternal power and godhead; so that they are without excuse."

Fourthly, *The duty of missionaries in propagating the gospel.* Let those who go forth to the heathen not ignore the good in the human heart on all shores and under all suns, but let them (1) *recognise* it, (2) *honour* it, (3) *appeal* to it, (4) *develope* it.

Acts 28:7-9

2. *Good in Christianity*

"In the same quarters were possessions of the chief man of the island, whose name was Publius; who received us, and lodged us three days courteously. And it came to pass, that the father of Publius lay sick of a fever and of a bloody flux: to whom Paul entered in, and prayed, and laid his hands on him, and healed him. So when this was done, others[1] also which had diseases in the island, came, and were healed."

EMENDATIVE RENDERING.—(1.) The rest.

EXEGETICAL REMARKS.—*" In the same quarters were possessions of the chief man of the island, whose name was Publius: who received us, and lodged us three days courteously."* This Publius was most probably the governor of the island. Heathen though he was, he had a heart that was touched into compassion at the suffering of Paul and his ship-wrecked companions. He received and lodged them "three days courteously." The word "courteously" means benevolently, or philanthropically. The father of this chief was the patient on whom the great apostle performed his miraculous operation.

" The father of Publius lay sick of a fever and of a bloody flux." It has been remarked, that no writer of the New Testament uses such exact technical expressions of diseases as Luke, who was trained as a physician. Formerly it was maintained that a dry climate, such as Malta, did not generate dysentery and inflammation of the lower bowels; but recently physicians resident in the islands have shown that these diseases are by no means uncommon at the present day.—HACKETT.

HOMILETICS.—We have seen that the conduct of the Maltese towards Paul manifested a certain kind and measure of *good* that is found even in the heathen world; and now the conduct of Paul toward the Maltese, recorded in these verses, gives us an insight into a *good* which is found only in Christendom—*the good of Christianity.* The service that the apostle renders the Maltese, here recorded, suggests that the good in Christianity is supernatural, restorative, and impartial.

I. HERE IS THE SUPERNATURAL. Paul performs a miracle upon the father of Publius. In the effectuation of this cure, Paul only did that which was a part of his great mission as an apostle of the new faith! "They shall take up serpents, and if they drink any deadly thing, it shall not hurt them; they shall lay hands on the sick, and they shall recover." Christianity is good in a *supernatural* form. It is a good, not naturally rising from the human heart, but supernaturally imported from heaven. The supernaturalness of Christianity may be argued—

First, *From the history of Christ and His apostles.*

Secondly, *From the manifest incapacity of human nature to evolve such a system.*

Thirdly, *From the utter insufficiency of good in any natural form to produce the results which Christianity has actually achieved.* There is good in human nature, even in its fallen state. This good has tried in all ages to regenerate mankind ; but has failed, signally failed. " The world by wisdom knew not God." Christianity is a stone cut out of the mountain " *without hands.*"

II. Here is the restorative. " Paul entered in and prayed, and laid his hands on him, and healed him." The supernatural power with which Paul, as the apostle of Christianity, was endowed, was not to inflict diseases, but to remove them, not to destroy men's lives, but to save them. Restoration is the great work of Christianity. In all the miracles of Christ there is only one connected with destruction, and that was on the fruitless fig-tree. Redemption is its mission.

First, *It redeems men from moral diseases.* From error, carnality, selfishness, impiety, guilt, &c.

Secondly, *By redeeming men from moral diseases it redeems them from all others,* corporeal, social, and political. Its grand consummation will be the redemption of the entire man, body and soul, from all evil.

III. Here is the universal. " So when this was done, others also which had diseases in the island, came and were healed." The healing of the father of Publius, their host, was the commencement of a series of miraculous cures. The afflicted from all parts of the island came to the messenger of Christianity, and he healed them. He treated all alike, he knew of no distinction of birth, influence, or position. They were human, and as such he sympathised with them and restored them. Christianity is no respecter of persons. It has the same message to all—barbarian, Scythian, bond, and free. It offers salvation to all. Such is a specimen of good in Christianity— *supernatural, restorative, universal.*

Acts 28:10-15

PAUL'S JOURNEY FROM MALTA TO ROME

" *Who also honoured us with many honours ; and when we departed, they laded us with such things as were necessary. And after three months we departed in a ship of Alexandria, which had wintered in the isle, whose sign was Castor and Pollux. And landing at Syracuse, we tarried there three days. And from thence we fetched a compass, and came to Rhegium : and after one day the south wind blew, and we came the next day to Puteoli ;*[1] *where we found brethren, and were desired to tarry with them seven days : and so we went toward Rome. And from thence, when the brethren heard of us,*[2] *they came to meet us as far as Appii forum, and The Three Taverns : whom when Paul saw, he thanked God, and took courage.*"

EMENDATIVE RENDERINGS.—(1.) The south wind sprung up, and we came the second day to Puteoli. (2.) The tidings concerning us.—ALF.

EXEGETICAL REMARKS. — These verses bring under our notice three things : Paul's departure from Malta ; his voyage to Puteoli ; his walk from Puteoli to Rome.

1. His departure from Malta.
" *Who also honoured us with many honours, and when we departed they laded us with such things as were necessary.*" The natives having received nothing but priceless gifts from the apostles, expressed their gratitude by presenting them with " many honours "— gifts, and also such things as were necessary in the voyage. The men who will present Christianity to heathens, as Paul presented it to them, will, instead of generating their suspicions and enmity, leave them with grateful memories and loving hearts. It is not in human nature to hate the good and kind.

" *After three months.*" All that we have recorded of Paul's doings there those three months are these few verses. We should like to have had a full history of his three months' labours and trials at Malta. We may rest assured that every day was spent in preaching Jesus of Nazareth.

" *We departed in a ship of Alexandria, which had wintered in the isle, whose sign was Castor and Pollux.*"

This vessel was, no doubt, like the one in which he had been wrecked, a corn ship from Egypt. She had " wintered in the isle." Her sign is given, " Castor and Pollux." The ancient ships, besides the sign of some tutelary god upon the stern, bore a carved or painted figure-head upon the prow, which gave name to the vessel ; but in some cases, and perhaps in this, the *insignia* and *tutelar* were the same, *Castor and Pollux,* literally *Diocini, i.e.,* the boys or sons of Jupiter (and Leda), regarded by the ancients as the gods of navigation and the guardians of seamen. This particular is mentioned, not to show the piety or superstition of the mariners, nor to show how Paul was brought into compulsory contact with heathenish corruptions, but as a lively reminiscence on the part of an eye-witness.

2. His voyage to Puteoli.
" *And landing at Syracuse, we tarried there three days.*" " *Syracuse* is the capital of Sicily, a town in the eastern part of the island, the birthplace of the famous mathematician and philosopher, Archimedes, and celebrated for its wealth, splendour, and arts. Its modern name is Syracusor ; it has a population of about

20,000."—Liv. The "three days'" residence here was probably for commercial purposes.

"*From thence we fetched a compass,*" that is, coasted round.

"*And came to Rhegium,*" the name of a town and promontory situated on the Italian coast, in Calabria, across the straits from Sicily. It was ruined by an earthquake in 1783.

"*And we came next day to Puteoli.*" "The port of Puteoli was, in the century before and in the century after Christ, the most famous in the western coast of Lower Italy, particularly for Eastern produce. Here the Egyptian corn-ships were accustomed to unload. It was the custom also to land here from Syria, and to proceed to Rome by land."—Lange. "The voyage from Syracuse to this port took them through the straits between Italy and Sicily, on the Italian side of which were the noted rocks called *Scylla*, and on the Sicilian the whirlpool called *Charybdis.*"

"*Where we found brethren, and were desired to tarry with them seven days.*" How the gospel reached this place, and who were the instruments of converting these men to Christianity, we are not told. Probably some of the disciples from Jerusalem, who had been scattered abroad in time of persecution, went through Italy preaching the gospel.

3. His walk from Puteoli to Rome. "*And so we went toward Rome. And from thence, when the brethren heard of us, they came to meet us as far as Appii Forum, and The Three Taverns: whom when Paul saw, he thanked God, and took courage.*" Tidings having gone from Puteoli to Rome of Paul's arrival, brethren from the imperial city hastened to meet him, and they meet at Appii Forum and the Three Taverns, two well-known stopping-places on the oldest and most famous Roman roads. "Appii Forum" was a market-place, and Tres Tabernæ a group of shops and inns; the former about forty miles from Rome, the latter ten miles nearer. The meeting of these brethren gave new inspiration to the apostle. "He thanked God, and took courage."

HOMILETICS.—Paul's journey from Malta to Rome reveals several subjects for homiletic thought.

I. THE FINDING OF GOOD MEN WHERE LEAST EXPECTED. Little, perhaps, did the apostle expect to find the disciples of Christ either at Puteoli or hastening to meet him from Rome. There is more goodness in this world than bigotry will admit, or even perhaps charity will venture to believe. Elijah once fancied that he was the only good man in Israel. "I am left alone," said he. But what was the answer of God unto him? "I have reserved unto myself seven thousand men who have not bowed the knee to the image of Baal." The journey reveals—

II. THE POWER OF THE GOSPEL TO FRATERNALISE MEN. The men found at Puteoli, and those who came from Rome, are both called "*brethren.*" Though Paul had never seen them before, though he belonged to a different class of men, Christianity had made these strangers brothers to each other and brothers to him. Sin has broken the brotherhood of humanity; Christianity restores it. It binds all the diverse races of mankind into a heavenly brotherhood of soul. It does this in two ways—

First, *It centres the affection upon a common Father.*

Secondly, *It enlists their energies in a common cause.* The journey reveals—

III. THE DIVINE PURPOSES REALISED UNDER IMMENSE IMPROBABILITIES. The Great God had revealed long before this to Paul that it was His purpose that he should visit Rome (Acts xxiii. 11), but how many circumstances on land and water intervened, suggesting the high improbability to all human thought of his ever seeing that great city! But he is in it now. Trust God. His word must come to pass, however improbable its fulfilment may seem to us. "Heaven and earth shall pass away," &c. Apply this to—

First, *The universal triumphs of the gospel.* How unlikely, at present, does the universal reign of truth appear ; yet it will come. Apply this to—

Secondly, *The universal resurrection of the dead.* How unlikely that all the buried myriads of the race shall rise from their graves. Yet it will be. The journey reveals—

IV. THE SPIRIT OF THE GODLY IN RELATION TO THEIR HISTORY. "He thanked God, and took courage."

First, *Gratitude for the past.* What a past was his !

Secondly, *Courage for the future.* What a future was before him ! Rome was now in the very zenith of its glory. It was the home of millions gathered from every corner of the earth. Its dominion was world-wide, its power irresistible. The capital, with her palaces, temples, columns, theatres, arches, baths, with the prowess of her arms, the vastness of her dominions, and the splendour of her arts, was the wonder and admiration of the world. Into this city, where the bloody Nero reigned, Paul was now entering, a poor prisoner, with the hope of striking a new life into its heart, and working out its spiritual reformation.

Acts 28:16-22

PAUL IN ROME.—I. HIS INTRODUCTORY MEETING

"*And when we came to Rome, the centurion delivered the prisoners to the captain of the guard : but Paul was suffered to dwell by himself with a soldier that kept him. And it came to pass, that after three days, Paul called the chief of the Jews together : and when they were come together, he said unto them, Men and brethren, though I have committed nothing against the people or customs of our fathers, yet was I delivered prisoner from*

Jerusalem into the hands of the Romans: who, when they had examined me, would have let me go, because there was no cause of death in me. But when the Jews spake against it, I was constrained to appeal unto Cæsar; not that I had ought to accuse my nation of. For this cause, therefore, have I called for you, to see you, and to speak with you: because that for the hope of Israel I am bound with this chain. And they said unto him, We neither received letters out of Judea concerning thee, neither any of the brethren that came shewed or spake any harm of thee. But we desire to hear of thee what thou thinkest: for as concerning this sect,[1] we know that every where it is spoken against.

EMENDATIVE RENDERING.—(1.) Heresy.

EXEGETICAL REMARKS.—Great had been Paul's anxiety to visit Rome (Acts xix. 21 ; Rom. i. 10, 15, xv. 22, 29). And now, through many perils, and by means altogether unexpected by him, he is conducted safely into the imperial city.

"*Paul was suffered to dwell by himself with a soldier," &c.* Though a prisoner, he is not treated with severity. He was not confined in the jail with the other prisoners. And for "two whole years he dwelt in his own hired house." Whether this "hired house" is the same that is referred to in ver. 23, is a question of no moment, and may remain a matter of uncertainty. The favour thus shown to Paul as a prisoner, in allowing him to live alone with the soldier to whom he was chained, would be owing probably to the information of him sent by the procurator Festus, and the personal intercession of the centurion Julius. He himself a shipwrecked man, a destitute prisoner, would have no private means by which to pay for his "hired house," and support himself for "two years" in Rome. But he had friends —friends hearty, and friends everywhere ; and in his letter to the Philippians (iv. 10–13), written from this city, we find him gratefully acknowledging their contributions towards his support. "I rejoiced in the Lord greatly, that now at the last, your care of me hath flourished again : wherein ye were also careful, but ye lacked opportunity. Not that I speak in respect of want, for I have learned, in whatsoever state I am, therewith to be content. I know both how to be abased and how to abound everywhere and in all things. I am instructed both to be full and to be hungry ; both to abound and to suffer need. I can do all things through Christ which strengtheneth me." The narrative before us gives an account of—*His introductory meeting there.* In three days after his arrival he began his work. Great must have been his physical exhaustion when he reached the city after his long imprisonment and trying journey and terrible privations. But his zeal would not allow him more than three days for recruiting his energy.

HOMILETICS.—His first introductory meeting, which he held in his own house, was a meeting of the "chief of the Jews," and which he himself convoked. How he called them together we are not told. Probably Luke, or Timotheus, or Demas, or some other of his companions who were not in bonds, went forth with invitations to "the chief Jews." At this first meeting two things are to be observed—

I. HIS ADDRESS. His address is essentially of a personal nature, and was designed to oppose the prejudices which the Roman Jews might have entertained against him, partly from his imprisonment, partly from the circumstance that he had appealed to Cæsar, and partly from the slanders which might have been brought from Judea. In justifying himself before them, he states four facts—

First, That his appearance before them as a prisoner was not occasioned by any crime either against the people of Israel or their religious customs.

Secondly, That he was compelled to appeal to Cæsar on account of the protest that had been entered on the part of the Jews against his liberation, whereas the Roman authorities judged his liberation to be just itself. "Yet was I delivered prisoner from Jerusalem into the hands of the Romans, who, when they had examined me, would have let me go, because there was no cause of death in me."

Thirdly, That his object in appealing to Cæsar was not to bring before him any accusation against his countrymen. "But when the Jews spake against it, I was constrained to appeal unto Cæsar ; not that I had ought to accuse my nation of." The meaning of this is : "I was forced to appeal to Cæsar for my own protection, not as having anything to charge my nation with at this tribunal." He does not say that he had no complaint against his nation ; that would have been an untruth, for his people had treated him not only unrighteously, but with a heartless cruelty. He asserts—

Fourthly, That it was only on account of the common Messianic hope of Israel that he was a prisoner, and wished to have an interview with them. "For this cause, therefore, have I called for you, to see you, and to speak with you : because that for the hope of Israel I am bound with this chain." By the "hope of Israel" he here means what he meant elsewhere—faith in the Messiah, as predicted in the Hebrew Scriptures. The other thing to be noticed in this first meeting is—

II. THEIR REPLY. In their reply two things are to be observed—
First, *Their avowal of their ignorance of the whole matter.* "And they said unto him, we neither received letters out of Judea concerning thee, neither any of the brethren that came shewed or spake any harm of thee." It may seem rather strange that tidings of the tremendous excitement that Paul's ministry had produced in Jerusalem, and everywhere amongst the Jews, should not have reached these Israelites in Rome, either through the Sanhedrim or some other channel. It must, however, be remembered that intercourse between Rome and Judea was not unfrequently interrupted by the disorders of the times. And then, too, the Jews, in all probability, dropped the persecution, and declined pressing it any further.

Secondly, *Their desire for information concerning the unpopular sect.* "But we desire to hear of thee what thou thinkest; for as concerning this sect, we know that everywhere it is spoken against." Justin Martyr says, "The Jews of Jerusalem sent messengers to prejudice their brethren in every part of the world against the disciples of Christ." These men had heard about the " sect," but every word that came to their ears was loaded with reproach. " It had come to this with the Jews," says Besser, "that after thirty years' gracious visitation they spoke everywhere against the gospel, and that the sign of Christ predicted by Simeon—'a sign that shall be spoken against'—was set up wherever the Jews dwelt, from Jerusalem even unto the ends of the earth."

Acts 28:23-28

PAUL IN ROME.—II. HIS SECOND INTRODUCTORY MEETING

" *And when they had appointed him a day, there came many to him into his lodging; to whom he expounded and testified the kingdom of God, persuading them concerning Jesus, both out of the law of Moses, and out of the prophets, from morning till evening. And some believed the things which were spoken, and some believed not. And when they agreed not among themselves, they departed, after that Paul had spoken one word, Well spake the Holy Ghost by Esaias the prophet unto our[1] fathers, saying, Go unto this people, and say, Hearing ye shall hear, and shall not understand; and seeing ye shall see, and not perceive: for the heart of this people is waxed gross, and their ears are dull of hearing, and their eyes have they closed: lest they should see with their eyes, and hear with their ears, and understand with their heart, and should be converted, and I should heal them. Be it known therefore unto you, that the[2] salvation of God is sent unto the Gentiles, and that they will hear it.*"

EMENDATIVE RENDERINGS.—(1.) Your. (2.) This.

EXEGETICAL REMARKS.—"*And when they agreed not among themselves, they departed, after that Paul had spoken one word, Well spake the Holy Ghost by Esaias the prophet unto our fathers, saying, Go unto this people, and say, Hearing ye shall hear, and shall not understand, and seeing, ye shall see, and not perceive, for the heart of this people is waxed gross, and their ears are dull of hearing, and their eyes have they closed; lest they should see with their eyes, and hear with their ears, and understand with their heart, and should be converted, and I should heal them. Be it known unto you, that the salvation of God is* sent unto the Gentiles, and that they will hear it." A terrible farewell address was this to the unbelievers as they departed. It sounds as the knell of doom. He peals into their ears the soul-startling words of Jehovah to the old prophet (Isa. vi. 9, 10). The prophet was ironically commanded to prosecute a ministry that should stupefy and blind the people. In the fearful process here indicated, "there are," says a modern critic, " three distinguishable agencies expressly or implicitly described—the ministerial agency of the prophet, the judicial agency of God, and the suicidal agency of the people themselves. The original passage makes the first of these most prominent : " Fatten the heart of this people, dull their ears, shut their eyes," &c. The quotation in John xii. 40 draws attention to the second : " He hath blinded their eyes, and hardened their heart." That in Matthew xiii. 15, like the one before us, dwells upon the third, and represents the people as destroyed by their own insensibility and unbelief. We have thus a striking and instructive instance of the way in which the same essential truth may be exhibited in different parts of Scripture, under several distinct aspects, or successive phases."—ALEXANDER.

HOMILETICS.—This second meeting is called by an appointment ; called for a special purpose, to receive information from Paul concerning that " sect " to which he belonged, and which was everywhere " spoken against." At this meeting, three things are to be noticed—

I. THE INTERESTING CHARACTER OF HIS PREACHING AT THIS MEETING.

First, *Evangelical.* His theme was the " kingdom of God "—the reign of the Messiah, as predicted by the prophets. Christ here, as everywhere, was his grand subject. Christ, as the predicted Messiah, the Son of God, the Saviour of the world.

Secondly, *Earnest.* He " expounded," he " testified," he " persuaded," and that " from morning till evening." The whole day was occupied, not probably in one formal discourse, but partly in familiar and colloquial discussion on the grand subject. At this meeting another thing to be noticed is—

II. THE EFFECTS OF HIS PREACHING AT THIS MEETING. The *effects* of the discourse upon his hearers were *different.* " And some believed the things that were spoken, and some believed them not." This is such a common occurrence that it excites no wonder, and seldom starts an inquiry into the cause. Perhaps no sermon ever produced the same effect upon all the assembled hearers. Even the discourses of Christ were far from commanding uniform impressions amongst his auditors. This *diversity* of result may be accounted for without calling in the unscriptural, though, alas ! somewhat popular doctrine, of the *partiality* of divine influence. Whilst it may be admitted as true, that where faith is, divine influence has been exerted, it does not follow that where faith is not, no such influence has been put forth. Man's power to think upon the subject presented to him or not, to think upon it in this aspect or that, with this intention or with that, is quite sufficient to account for the fact that the same discourse is believed by some and rejected by others. At this meeting the other thing to be noticed is—

III. THE TERRIBLE WARNING OF HIS PREACHING AT THIS MEETING. The language in no application must be regarded as teaching that God exerts any influence to morally blind and stupefy men. Such a work—

First, *Would be unnecessary.* Men are already in that condition.

Secondly, *Essentially incompatible with the Divine character.* His holiness and His love render such a work on His part an eternal impossibility.

Thirdly, *Opposed to the whole tenor of Scripture.* "Let no man say when he is tempted, he is tempted of God," &c.

Fourthly, *Denied by universal consciousness.* No sinner ever felt that the Creator exerted any influence in making him sinful. On the contrary, universal conscience charges sin on the sinner. All that the passage seems to teach is this—

(1.) That men may fall into an *unconvertible* moral condition. They may become so blind, insensitive, and obdurate, as to exclude all hope of recovery. A fearful truth this.

(2.) That the ministry of divine truth may promote this condition. The gospel hardens some men; it proves to be the savour of death unto death. As the heart of Pharaoh grew hard under the ministry of Moses, the hearts of thousands in every age are hardened under the ministry of gospel truth.

(3.) That a ministry that may fail with some will succeed with others. This comes out in Paul's warning, "Be it known unto you," &c.

Acts 28:29-31

PAUL IN ROME—III. HIS TWO YEARS' MINISTRY IN HIS "OWN HIRED HOUSE"

"*And when he had said these words, the Jews departed, and had great reasoning among themselves.*[1] *And Paul dwelt two whole years in his own hired house, and received all that came in unto him. Preaching the kingdom of God, and teaching those things which concern the Lord Jesus Christ, with all confidence, no man forbidding him.*"

EMENDATIVE RENDERING.—(1.) Omit this verse.

HOMILETICS.—This is the last account we have of the great apostle. His biographer takes leave of him here. Here the curtain falls and hides the greatest actor. The greatest lives have a close. We shall take the verses as suggesting—

I. THE ESSENCE OF CHRISTIANITY. What is it? "Things which concern the Lord Jesus Christ." Not the things which concern man's religious speculations or organisations, but the things which concern Christ. What are the things which concern Him? The verse itself suggests the best answer ; the things pertaining to the *reign of God over the human soul.* " Preaching the kingdom of God." The grand aim of Christ's mission to the world was to establish this reign of God, to bring human spirits, the world over, under the sovereign sway of divine truth and love. Nothing *concerned* Him more than this, nothing so near to His heart as this. This He urged in His appeals. " Seek ye first the kingdom," &c. This He illustrated in His teaching ; all his parables were about the kingdom of God ; for this He taught the world to pray, " Thy kingdom come," &c. ; for this He lived and died ; " To this end was I born, and for this cause came I unto the world," &c. ; for this He works now in heaven, and will work until the " kingdoms of this world shall be the kingdoms of our God." What is the end of Christianity ? To bring souls under the reign of God. And the things that most concern Christ are the things that He has designed and fitted to accomplish this. These things are the gospel. The verses suggest :—

II. THE TRIALS OF ITS DISCIPLES. Here we find one of its most faithful and illustrious disciples a prisoner in Rome. The apostle had escaped the malignant rage of the Jews by appealing from Felix, the Roman governor at Cæsarea, to Cæsar. This brought him to Rome as a prisoner. He was not, however, cast into the cell where prisoners were usually confined. Through the recommendation of Festus, on the intercession of the centurion, he was committed to the care of a soldier, and allowed to dwell " in his own hired house ;" though, according to Roman law, chained to his companion, and therefore subject to a thousand inconveniences and mortifications. The imprisonment of the apostle in Rome teaches us at least two useful lessons—

First, *That the best of men are not to expect exemption from trials.* Amongst the sons of men has there ever appeared a man more eminent in spiritual worth, more God-like than Paul ? And yet how tried he was ! " In perils often," &c. Let us not murmur in affliction—Paul felt that his was for his good. " Tribulation worketh patience," &c.

Secondly, *That the most useful minister is not essential to Christ.* He laboured more abundantly than they all, and more successfully too we think ; but now his activity is restrained ; he is not allowed to be at large, he is a prisoner. Let no man overrate his services ; Heaven can do without us. The verses suggest :—

III. THE MISSION OF ITS MINISTERS. What is that ? " Preaching the kingdom of God, and teaching those things which concern the Lord Jesus Christ."

First, *His preaching was teaching.* It was not empty declamation, nor a repetition of platitudes, however logically put or rhetorically arrayed. It was *teaching ;* imparting that to the intelligence of his hearers which they knew not before. Teaching implies *learning* on the part of the hearer, and *superior intelligence* on the part of the minister.

Secondly, *His teaching was the indoctrinating of men in Christian essentials :* "Things which concerned Christ and God's kingdom." He used all his knowledge, which was extensive, rich, and varied, to illustrate and enforce *these things.* He determined to know nothing amongst men but Jesus Christ and Him crucified; "He counted all things but loss," &c. The verses suggest :—

IV. THE FORCE OF ITS INFLUENCE.

First, *The force of its soul-sustaining influence.* "With all confidence;" with a fearless courage, here in Rome, in the midst of its enemies, this poor prisoner for two long years continued to preach the gospel. From other passages we learn, that during this time he did a great deal more than preach to them who came to hear him. He wrote numerous letters. According to Lardner he wrote his letter to the Ephesians, his second letter to Timothy, his letter to the Philippians, his letter to the Colossians, his letter to Philemon, and his letter to the Hebrews. How indefatigable he must have been in his work to have accomplished all this. He did this " with all confidence." He was afraid of no man. Sages, poets, artists, heroes, priests—he met them all " with all confidence."

Secondly, *The force of its aggressive influence.* Many, from time to time, of all classes, were drawn to the hired house of the poor prisoner, and not a few were converted. He tells us in his letter to the Philippians (i. 12–14), " that the things that had happened to him had fallen out rather unto the furtherance of the gospel, so that his bonds in Christ were manifested in all the palace, and in all other places ; and many of the brethren in the Lord, waxing confident by his bonds, were much more bold to speak the word without fear." Amongst the multitude he converted there, was Onesimus, a runaway slave (Phil. 10). The fact that the gospel was thus spread by Paul when a prisoner, shows its independency of all worldly power and wealth. It has won its most illustrious victories in direct opposition to the patronage, the power, and the authority of the world.

In addition to the very many important considerations which we have noted down on the whole account of Paul in Rome, as contained in the verses 16–31, there are others suggested which are worthy of our notice in conclusion.

I. THE ERAS OF A WONDERFUL HISTORY. The wonderful history is the history of the gospel. In looking at Paul in his " hired house" at Rome, we discover—

First, *The close of one chapter in church history.* This chapter records his travels, triumphs, defeats, from Jerusalem to Rome, from the metropolis of Judea to the seat of universal empire. The book began with Peter's sermon on the day of Pentecost, and now closes with Paul's ministry in Rome. What a marvellous history it is. "The course of the gospel from Jerusalem to Rome," says Lange, "is (1.) A painful course, full of shame and persecution ; (2.) A heroic course, full of the power of faith and love; (3.) A victorious course, full of mighty acts and divine wonders ; (4.) A blessed course, full of salvation and grace for 'the present and the future.'"

Secondly, *The beginning of a new chapter in church history.* From Rome the gospel starts on a new course. The Church which Paul established at Rome has been bearing the gospel through subsequent ages over various parts of the world. All Church history subsequent to the Acts of the Apostles begins at Rome. Paul in Rome, therefore, gives us the end of one chapter and the beginning of another in the glorious history of the gospel. We see in him there the virtual fulfilment of the promise : "He shall be my witness both in Jerusalem and in all Judea, and in Samaria, unto the uttermost part of the earth." Another thing suggested is—

II. THE MIGHTINESS OF A CHRIST-INSPIRED MAN. Who can read this account of Paul—read how this prisoner entered Rome, how unremittingly he toiled there, how heroically he declared his message there, how mightily he influenced many of its inhabitants, and even some of Cæsar's household, without feeling that he was animated by a spirit, not of earth, nor of any human school of religion or morals, but by the spirit of Him who gave his life a ransom to save the lost? It was the spirit of Christ in Paul that made him what he was. He felt this ; he acknowledged this. "The love of Christ constraineth me." "I live, yet not I, but Christ that liveth in me." By sin we have lost our manhood ; we are mean, and selfish, and cowardly. The spirit of Christ can alone restore to us the true heart of humanity.

III. THE MYSTERIOUS METHOD OF DIVINE WORKING. It was God's purpose that the gospel should be preached in Rome. But how was this purpose fulfilled?

First, By *one* man. One might have expected that the Eternal would have sent an army of messengers. Numbers, however, in moral campaigns, are secondary considerations. The one true man does the work.

Secondly, One man, who is a *prisoner.* One might have thought that the Almighty Master would have guarded his messenger from such evils, made his path straight and sunny. One might have thought that the man chosen of Heaven to bear the gospel to the very centre of worldly power, splendour, and influence, would go with an exultant heart, and with something of princely grandeur. But not so. What persecutions, perils, privations, disappointments, defeats, had Paul to experience in the way; and then he has to enter the imperial city a poor shipwrecked prisoner. His position seemed even to him a marvel, for he speaks of himself as "an ambassador *in bonds*." "God's ways are not our ways, nor his thoughts our thoughts."

IV. The fragmentary character of sacred history. Here the curtain drops upon the unfinished life of Paul. We read no more of him after this. He disappears for ever. It is true that tradition and certain references in one or two of his Epistles have led some to conclude that after this his first imprisonment in Rome, he was released, and returned to visit some of the Churches which he had planted. "It is very probable," says Howson, "that he went to Spain, and not improbable that he came to Brittany. The general impression is, that he was beheaded at Rome in the last year of the reign of Nero, when Peter was also crucified." All this, however, is at best conjecture; certainty ends with this verse. Curiosity craves for minute information concerning the closing scenes in the life of this wonderful man, but Scripture offers no gratification. Why this? Why is sacred history so fragmentary? There are, no doubt, good reasons. Fuller details are, indeed, unnecessary. Luke has given sufficient memoranda of this man's life to enable us to judge how sublimely he passed through the last scenes. The acts of a man's daily life, and not the details of his death-bed, are the best criteria of his soul-life. A fuller account, too, would, perhaps, have been inexpedient. God is as kind in concealing as He is in revealing. Were the Bible to give us a full account of all the men it refers to, it would be a volume of unreadable dimensions, and would rather pander to the curiosity than advance the culture of humanity.

Appendix

VARIOUS READINGS OF THE ACTS OF THE APOSTLES FROM THE
THREE MOST CELEBRATED MSS. OF THE ORIGINAL GREEK
TEXT, BY CONSTANTINE TISCHENDORF

THE following is Dr Tischendorf's account of the three famous
MSS. whose readings are given below :—

The *Codex Vaticanus* came first into the possession of learned Europe.
From what place it came into the Vatican Library is not known, but it is
entered in the very first catalogue of the collection, dating from 1475. It
contains the Old and New Testaments. Of the New it at present contains
the four Gospels, the Acts, the seven General Epistles, nine of St Paul's
Epistles, and that to the Hebrews as far as chap. ix. 14; but all that
followed this place is lost, namely, the last chapters of the Hebrews, the
two Epistles to Timòthy, the Epistles to Titus and Philemon, and the
Revelation. The text is written in three columns to a page. The peculiarity of the handwriting, the arrangement of the manuscript, and the
character of the text itself, more especially certain remarkable readings,
induce the opinion that the codex is to be referred to the fourth century,
and probably to about the middle of that century. During a long period
the Roman Court very seldom granted access to the manuscript for any
critical use of it; but in the year 1828, by the command of Leo the Twelfth,
the late Cardinal Angelo Mai undertook an edition of it. His edition first
appeared in 1857, three years after his death, and was found to be full of
mistakes. The writer of the present introduction corrected Mai's New
Testament in several hundreds of passages in his *Novum Testamentum
Vaticanum*, published in 1867. Still further corrections are supplied in
the fac-simile edition of 1868 by Vercellone and Cozzo ; inserted also in
the *Appendix Novi Testamenti Vaticani*, 1869.

The *Codex Alexandrinus* was, in 1628, sent as a present to King Charles
I. of England, from Cyril Lucar, patriarch of Constantinople. Cyril Lucar,
who had formerly been patriarch of Alexandria, brought it with him to

Constantinople; and this explains why it is called the Alexandrian Codex. It is written in two columns to a page, and contains the Old and New Testaments. It is imperfect in the New Testament, having lost Matt. i. 1 to xxv. 6; John vi. 50 to viii. 52; and 2 Cor. iv. 13 to xii. 6. It contains, however, the two epistles by Clement of Rome, which in it alone have descended to posterity; also an epistle of Athanasius, and a production by Eusebius on the Psalter. On palæographic and other grounds it is believed to have been written in the middle of the fifth century. The New Testament was edited in 1786 by C. G. Woide, and republished with corrections by B. Harris Cowper in an octavo edition issued in 1860.

The *Codex Sinaiticus* I was so happy as to discover in 1844 and 1859 in the monastery of St Katharine on Mount Sinai. In the year last named I was travelling in the East under the patronage of the Emperor Alexander the Second of Russia, and to him it was my good fortune to transfer the manuscript. It contains the Old and New Testaments, and is written with four columns to a page. The New Testament is perfect, not having been deprived of a single leaf. To the twenty-seven books of the New Testament are appended the Epistle of Barnabas complete, and part of the Shepherd of Hermas, which books, even at the beginning of the fourth century, were reckoned for Holy Scripture by a good many. We are led, by all the data upon which we calculate the antiquity of manuscripts, to assign the Codex Sinaiticus to the middle of the fourth century. The evidence in favour of so great an age is more certain in the case of the Sinaitic Codex than in that of the Vatican manuscript. It is even not impossible that the Sinaitic Codex,—we cannot say as much of the Vatican MS.,—formed one of the fifty copies of the Bible which in the year 331 the Emperor Constantine ordered to be executed for Constantinople under the direction of Eusebius, the bishop of Cæsarea, best known as a Church historian. In this case it must be understood that the Emperor Justinian, the founder of the Sinaitic monastery, sent it as a present from Constantinople to the monks at Sinai. The manuscript was edited by the discoverer in 1862 at the cost of the Russian Emperor Alexander II., in a form as literally exact as it was splendid; the New Testament of the same was reproduced for ordinary use in a cheaper form in 1863 and 1865.

From all that has been said it follows, that the first place for antiquity and extent, among the three chief manuscripts, belongs to the Sinaitic Codex, the second place belongs to the Vatican, and the third to the Alexandrian. This arrangement is altogether confirmed by the condition of the text of the manuscripts. That text is not only, in accordance with the writing of manuscripts in the fourth and fifth centuries, the same which was read in the East in precisely those centuries; but rather, for the most part it truly represents the text which was then copied from much earlier documents by Alexandrian scribes who knew very little of Greek, and, therefore, did not intentionally make the least alteration;— that is to say, the very text which, in the third and second centuries, was spread over a great part of Christendom. In further confirmation of this idea, we may refer to the agreement of our three ancient copies with the oldest translations,—the Latin, made in the second century in proconsular Africa; the Syriac versions of the Gospels made at the same time, and recently brought from the Nitrian desert in Egypt to the British Museum ; and the Coptic or Egyptian versions of the third century. The same opinion is also further confirmed by the agreements of the text of the three great MSS., with Irenæus, Clement of Alexandria, Origen, and others of the older Fathers of the Church. What we have been saying applies most of all to the Codex Sinaiticus, which, for example, is unapproachable in its close relation to the Latin version of the second century ; it applies in a lesser degree to the Vatican MS., and still less to the Alexandrian, which, however, is far preferable in the Acts, Epistles, and Revelation, to what it is in the Gospels.

The following are the explanations of the signs employed to distinguish the various readings :—

The letter S means the Sinaitic MS., V the Vatican, and A the Alexandrian. S*, V*, A* point out any reading of S, V, or A, which has been altered by some later hand ; though we give the original and not the altered reading in such cases. When we give an altered reading, it is marked S², V², or A² ; but as a rule, only original readings are noted, and reference is made but seldom to changes introduced by ancient correctors. The abbreviation " *om.*" signifies the omission of the word or words to which it refers ; " *adds* " or " *add*," point to the omission of a word or words in one or more of our MSS. If two or more notes belong to the same words of the Text, they are divided by a comma, and not by a semicolon. If words of the Text itself are quoted, they have after them the sign : , and then follow the readings of the Codices. Sundry manifest slips of the pen which occur in the MSS., especially in those of the Alexandrian scribes, have been passed over in silence. Yet there are some which have been noted which are to be regarded as erroneous, even if not pointed out by the words " *an error,*" or " *a mere error.*" I have no doubt that in the very earliest ages after our Holy Scriptures were written, and before the authority of the Church protected them, wilful alterations, and especially additions, were made in them. Many various readings consist only in the forms of words and their arrangement, and are of small import. Many others did not at all require to be noticed here, because they merely relate to the Greek idiom. In some cases I have allowed myself to indicate an inaccurate or unsuitable rendering of the Greek, prefixing " *translate* " or " *all MSS.*"

THE VARIOUS READINGS

Title.—S Acts, V Acts of Apostles.

Chap. I.—6. S *om.* together. 7. V *om.* And. 8. SVA my witnesses. 10. SVA in white garments. 13. SVA and John and James. 14. SVA *om.* and supplication ; SA and his brethren. 15. SVA in the midst of the brethren. 16. SVA the Scripture. 17. SVA among us. 18. A *om.* all. 19. S which also was known ; SV *om.* proper ; SA Acheldamach, V Aceldamach. 23. SVA Barsabbas. 25. VA take the place ; A to his just place. 26. SVA And they gave lots unto them.

Chap. II.—1. SVA they were all (S *om.* all) together in one place. 5. S *om.* Jews. 7. V *om.* all *before* amazed ; SVA *om.* one to another. 9. S *om.* and Elamites. 17. In the last days ; V after these things. 18. S and on my handmaidens and on my servants. 19. A *om.* above. 20. S *om.* and notable. 21. S* *om. this verse.* 22. SVA *om.* also. 23. SVA ye have by *the* hand of *the* wicked crucified. 25. S my Lord. 30. SVA that of the fruit of his loins should sit on his throne. 31. SVA that he was neither left in hell, nor his flesh. 33. SVA *om.* now ; V both see and hear. 37. S in their heart, saying unto Peter. 38. SVA *om.* said ; SA Repent, saith he,· and be ; SVA of your sins. 39. A whom the Lord. 40. SVA and exhort them. 41. SVA *om.* gladly ; SVA and in the same day. 42. SVA *om.* and *after* fellowship. 43. SA by the apostles in Jerusalem, and great fear was upon all. 44. V *were* together *and* had. 47. SVA added together daily such as were saved.

Chap. III.—1. SVA were going up into the temple. 6. SV *om.* rise up and. 7. SVA and lifted him up. 11. SVA And as he held Peter. 13. SA and the God of Isaac and the God of Jacob ; SVA *om.* him *after* denied. 18. SV of all the prophets ; SV. his Christ ; A *om.* that Christ should suffer. 20. SVA was appointed unto you. 21. SVA of his holy prophets. 22. SVA *om.* For ; SVA *om.* unto the fathers ; S the Lord our God ; V the Lord God. 25. VA of your fathers. 26. SV *om.* Jesus ; V from iniquities.

Chap. IV.—1. V the chief priests. 3. A and put them in hold. 4. A *om.* the word ; SA *om.* about. 8. SVA *om.* of Israel. 17. SVA *om.* straitly ; A *om.* henceforth. 18. SVA *om.* them *after* commanded. 24. SVA thou which hast made. 25. SVA by the mouth of our father thy servant David, by the Holy Ghost hast said. 27. together ; SVA *add* in this city. 28. VA* thy hand and counsel. 30. VA the hand. 33. SA of Jesus Christ the Lord. 36. SVA Joseph.

Chap. V.—5. SVA on all them that heard. 9. S How therefore is it ; A at the doors. 11. A and *upon* as many. 15. SA even into the streets. 16. SVA about Jerusalem. 18. SVA laid hands. 23. SVA *om.* truly ; SVA *om.* without ; SVA at the doors. 24. SVA Now when the captain of the temple. 25. SVA *om.* saying ; S are in the temple teaching. 28. SVA saying, We commanded you straitly. 30. SA Now the God. 32. SA And we are witnesses ; V And we are in him witnesses ; and so is also, *etc. ;* V and God hath given the Holy Ghost to them that obey him. 33. VA and desired to' slay them. 34. SVA to put the men forth. 36. A some great one. 37. SVA* drew away people after him. 38. S *om.* unto you. 39. SVA ye cannot (SV ye will not be able to) overthrow them. 40. SVA and let *them* go. 41. SVA for the name. 42. SVA Christ Jesus.

Chap. VI.—3. SV But brethren, A Now brethren ; S full of the spirit of wisdom. 7. Of the priests ; S of the Jews. 8. SVA full of grace and power. 9. SA of the synagogue of those who are called the Libertines ; A *om.* and of Asia. 11. SV men, saying ; S speak words of blasphemy against. 12. S *om.* and came upon him ; A and brought him. 13. S witnesses, saying ; SVA to speak words against the holy place. 15. S looking *at* him stedfastly.

Chap. VII.—6. S spake unto him, Thy seed shall—and they shall bring it—and entreat *it* evil. 8. S the seventh day. 10. SA and over all his house. 11. SVA over all Egypt. 13. SA and his kindred. 14. SVA and all *his* kindred. 15. V *om.* into Egypt. 16. SVA of Emmor in

Sychem. 17. SVA which God had promised. 18. SVA arose over Egypt.
19. SV the fathers. 20. SVA in *his* father's house. 22. SVA in his
words and deeds. 25. SV the brethren. 30. SVA *om.* of the Lord ; A
in a flaming fire. 31. A *om.* at the sight; SVA a voice from the Lord
came (*om.* unto him). 32. SVA and of Isaac and of Jacob. 35. S and a
judge over us ; S and a judge *instead of* and a deliverer ; VA with the
hand. 37. SA shall God raise ; S of *your* brethren ; SVA *om.* him shall
ye hear. 38. S *with* your fathers ; V who had chosen the ; S unto you.
40. S Moses the man which brought us. 42. V* *om.* in the wilderness.
43. S Romphan, V Rompha, A Rephan. 44. A Your fathers. 46. SV
for the house of Jacob. 48. SVA dwelleth not in what is made with
hands. 51. VA in hearts ; S in your hearts. 54. S When they heard.
55. S full of faith and of the Holy Ghost. 58. A and cast him out. 60.
S *om.* with a loud voice.

Chap. 8.—1. S *om.* and *before* they. 4. S *om.* everywhere. 6. SVA
Now the people. 8. SVA Now there was much joy. 10. SVA is the
power of God which is called great. 12. SVA preaching of the kingdom ;
S kingdom of the Lord ; A *om.* both. 14. S the word of Christ. 18. SV
the Spirit was given. 22. SVA and pray the Lord. 25. A the word of
God. 26. S unto the way called the going down. 27. SA of all her
treasure, had come. 28. SA and was returning ; V now he was returning ;
SVA the prophet Esaias. 30. SVA Esaias the prophet. 33. SVA in *his*
humiliation ; SVA *om.* and. 34. V* *om.* this. 37. SVA *om. this verse.*
39. A the holy Spirit of the Lord fell on the eunuch. But an angel of
the Lord caught away Philip.

Chap. IX.—1. S *om.* yet. 5. And the Lord said ; S And he said ; VA
And he *said;* A I am Jesus of Nazareth ; SVA *om.* it is hard for thee to
kick against the pricks. 6. SVA *om.* And he trembling—said unto him ;
SVA But arise. 8. SVA* he saw nothing. 12. SA *om.* in a vision; SA
his hands. 15. SA before both the Gentiles. 17. S* *om.* as thou camest.
18. SVA *om.* forthwith. 19. SVA Then he was certain days. 20. SVA
he preached Jesus. 24. SVA and they watched also the gates. 25. SVA
his disciples took *him* by night and let him down. 26. SVA Now when
he was come. 27. S *om.* and *before* how ; A in the name of the Lord.
28–29. SVA at Jerusalem, speaking boldly ; SVA *om.* Jesus. 30. A and
sent *him* forth. 31. SVA Then had the Church—and was edified—was
multiplied. 34. A the Lord Jesus Christ. 37. SA *whom* when they had
washed, they laid her ; V *whom* when they had washed, they laid *her.* 38.
SVA exhorting him, Delay not to come to us. .

Chap. X.—4. S *om.* for a memorial. 6. SVA *om.* he shall tell thee
what thou oughtest to do. 7. SVA which spake unto him ; SVA of the
household servants. 11. SVA *om.* unto him ; knit at the, *etc. ;* SVA let
down by the four corners to the earth. 12. *Translate* wherein were all
the fourfooted beasts ; SVA fourfooted beasts and creeping things of the
earth. 14. SVA that is common and unclean. 16. SVA was forthwith
received up into heaven. 19. V. *om* unto him. 21. SVA *om.* which were
sent unto him from Cornelius. 23. SVA on the morrow he arose and
went away. 30. SVA Four days ago until this hour I was at the ninth
hour praying in my house. 32. SVA *om.* who when he cometh, shall
speak unto thee. 33. SVA commanded thee of the Lord. 35. A shall be

accepted. 36. VA *God* sent the word unto. 38. S How he went about.
39. SV And we *are;* A And ye *are;* SVA whom also they slew. 45. As
many as; V which. 48. SVA in the name of Jesus Christ.

Chap. XI.—2. SVA But when Peter. 3. V saying that he went—
and did eat. 5. S *om.* praying. 7. SVA And I heard also. 8. SVA for
common or unclean hath not at any time entered. 9. SV *om.* me. 11.
SVA where we were. 13. SVA *om.* unto him; SVA *om.* men. 16. A
Then remembered we. 20. SVA spake also unto; A unto the Greeks.
22. SVA they sent forth Barnabas unto Antioch. 24. V* *om.* unto the
Lord. 25. SVA departed he to Tarsus; V to comfort Saul. 26. SVA
when he had found *him,* he brought *him;* SVA And it came to pass also.
28. SVA *om.* Cæsar.

Chap. XII.—1. S the king Herod. 3. SVA Now because he saw. 6.
A at the door. 9. SVA *om.* him; S by the angel: he thought he saw.
11. A *om.* of the people. 13. SVA And as he knocked; S came hearken-
ing. 17. A *om.* unto them *after* beckoning; SA *om.* unto them *after*
declared. 20. SVA And he was. 22. S and not of men. 24. V of the
Lord. 25. SV returned to Jerusalem.

Chap. XIII.—1. SVA *om.* certain. 6. SVA through all the isle; SVA
a certain man, a sorcerer *and* false prophet. 11. V (A* ?) there fell *on*
him. 17. V of the people. 18. Suffered he their manners; A bore he
as a nurse. 19–20. SVA he distributed their land to them for an inheritance, about four hundred and fifty years. And after that he gave *unto*
them judges until Sam. the prophet. 22. V the *son* of Jesse after. 23.
raised; SVA brought. 25. SVA What think ye. 26. V *om.* and *after*
Abraham; A among us; SVA to us is. 31. SA who are now. 33. SVA
unto our children; A² raised him up from the dead. 38. V that therefore is preached. 39. SA *om.* And *before* by him. 40. S *om.* upon you.
42. SVA And when they were gone out, they besought. 43. S was
broken up by them. 44. SA the word of the Lord. 45. SVA *om.* contradicting and. 46. SVA And Paul and Barnabas. 50. VA the devout
and honourable women; V out of the coasts. 51. SVA the dust of *their*
feet.

Chap. XIV.—1. S *om.* of the Jews *after* synagogue. 8. SVA *om.* being.
11. S they lifted up *their* voice. 13. SVA before the city. 15. *Translate*
men who suffer like things. 17. SV and gave you, A *om.* us; SV your
hearts. 21. SA and to Antioch. 25 SA the word of the Lord. 28. SVA
om. there.

Chap. XV.—2. SV Now when Paul. 4. S of the church, the. 5. A
certain men. 7. SVA among you. 8. SVA bare witness. 11. SVA *om.*
Christ. 17–18. SV saith the Lord, who made these things known from
the beginning; A *om.* all; A known unto the Lord *is* his work. 22. A
om. of their own company; SVA Barsabbas. 23. SVA *om.* after this
manner; SVA *om.* and *before* brethren. 24. SV certain from us; SVA
om. saying, Ye must be circumcised and keep the law. 28. A than the
things necessary. 32. S *om.* and confirmed them. 33. SVA unto those
who had sent them. 34. SVA *om. this verse.* 36. SVA visit the brethren.
37. SVA And Barn. would take with them also John. 39. SVA But the
contention. 40. SVA unto the grace of the Lord.

Chap. XVI.—1. VA also to Derbe; SVA and to Lystra; SVA of a

woman. 6. SVA Now they went. 7. SVA But after; SVA the Spirit of Jesus. 10. SVA that God had called; S *om.* us. 11. SA Now loosing from Troas. 13. SVA out of the gate; SVA where we supposed there was a meeting for prayer; S which resorted with us thither. 17. SV unto you. 26. V *om.* immediately. 31. SVA *om.* Christ. 32. SVA with all that were. 33. A he and all his family. 38. SVA but they feared.

Chap. XVII.—4. A of the devout and of Greeks. 5. SVA. *om.* which believed not. 10. A *om.* immediately; A *om.* by night. 13. SVA and stirred up and troubled the people. 14. SVA and Silas. 15. SVA brought *him* unto Athens. 16. S Now while he waited at Athens. 18. SVA Then also certain. 23. SVA* What therefore—that declare I. 26. SVA of one (*om.* blood); SVA *om.* before. 27. SVA seek God, if; A or find him; A* of you. 28. V of our own poets. 32. SVA also again.

Chap. XVIII.—1. SV he departed. 2. V that *he* had commanded. 5. SVA Paul was earnestly occupied with the word, testifying; A *om.* to the Jews. 7. A into the house of a certain Justus; SV named Titus (V Titius) Justus. 9. A *om.* in the night. 15. SVA if it be questions; SVA *om.* for. 17. SVA *om.* the Greeks. 20. SVA *om.* with them. 21. SV But bade *them* farewell and said; A But bidding *them* farewell and saying—if God will, he sailed; SVA *om.* I must by all means keep this feast that cometh in Jerusalem; but. 23. S and went also. 24. S named Apelles. 25. S and fervent in the spirit wherein he spake and taught; V and he spake; SVA the things of Jesus. 26. SVA Priscilla and Aquila.

Chap. XIX.—1. S Apelles; SVA came to Ephesus and found. 2. SVA and said unto; SVA And they *said* unto him. 3. SA But he said; SVA *om.* unto them. 4. SVA *om.* verily; SVA *om.* Christ. 9. SVA of Tyrannus. 10. SVA *om.* Jesus. 12. SVA *om.* of them. 13. SVA certain also of the; SVA I adjure you; S by the Lord Jesus. 14. SVA And certain men, seven sons of Sceva (V of one Sceva), a Jew and chief of the priests, were doing this. 15. SVA and said unto them. 16. SVA prevailed against both. 21. A purposed in the Spirit to pass through Mac. and Ach. *and* to go. 24. V made shrines; S made a silver shrine. 26. A but also almost; S *om.* persuaded and; S that gods are not made with hands. 27. S will be in danger; S *om.* but; A but also the temple—will be despised—will be destroyed. 29. SVA *om.* whole. 33. SVA And they thrust Alex. 34. V *repeats* Great is Diana of the Eph. 35. S Men *and* brethren; SVA who of men is there; S both of the great Diana; SVA *om.* goddess. 37. SVA of our goddess.

Chap. XX.—1. SVA and exhorted and embraced them. 4. SV *om.* into Asia; SVA Sopater *the son* of Pyrrhus of Berea. 5. SVA Now these. 7. SVA when we came together. 8. SVA where we were. 11. V *om.* and *after* again. 15. V and in the evening we arrived at Samos; SVA *om.* and tarried at Trogyllium. 18. A when they were come to him and they were together, he said. 19. SVA and with tears. 21. V *om.* Christ. 22. A that may befall me there. 23. SVA witnesseth to me. 24. SV But on no account do I hold my life dear unto myself, that I might finish my course (*om.* with joy); A neither hold I my life so precious to me as the finishing of my course and of the ministry. 25. SVA *om.* of God; S shall not see my face (*om.* more). 26. SV that I am pure. 28. SVA *om.* therefore; A the church of the Lord. 29. for I know; SA I know, V because

I know; SVA *om.* this. 30. V of you shall men arise. 32. SVA *om.* brethren; V I commend you to the Lord; SVA and to give an inheritance. 34. SVA *om.* Yea. 35. A *om.* Jesus.

Chap. XXI—3. *Translate* the ship unladed her burden. 4. SVA But finding; there: A with them. 5. A *om.* departed and; S *om.* till *we were.* 5–6. SVA and when we had knelt down on the shore and prayed, we took our leave—and entered into the ship. 8. SVA *om.* that were of Paul's company. 10. S And as they tarried there. 11. SV his own feet and hands. 13. SA answered and said; S *om.* to weep and. 16. V one Mnasus. 19. S among the Gentiles of his ministry. 20. SVA they glorified God; VA among the Jews; S *om.* of Jews. 21. S *om.* And *before* they; A *om.* all. 22. V What is it therefore? They will needs hear. 24. A but also *that* thou. 25. SVA *om.* that they observe no such thing, save only. 28. A and the law, and this holy place. 39. S to speak a word. 40. A in *their* own tongue.

Chap. XXII.—3. SVA *om.* verily. 5. V did bear. 8. S answered and said. 9. SVA *om.* and were afraid. 11 V I could see nothing. 12. A a man according (*om.* devout). 16. SVA calling on his name. 20. A *om.* Stephen; SVA *om.* unto his death. 26. SVA saying, What wilt thou do? for. 27. S Say, art thou. 28. A *om.* And; SV But the chief captain; S said, I was even. 30. SVA *om.* from his hands; SVA and all the council to come together.

Chap. XXIII.—2. S that stood by to. 6. SVA the son of Pharisees. 7. S between the Sadducees and Pharisees. 9. SV and certain of the scribes; A and certain of the Pharisees (*om.* the scribes) arose; S strove one with another saying; SVA *om.* let us not fight against God. 10. S *om.* from among them. 11. SVA *om.* Paul. 12. SVA the Jews *instead of* certain of the Jews. 15. SVA *om.* to-morrow. 16. A into the Synagogue (*a mere error*). 20. S as though it would enquire; VA as though thou wouldest enquire. 27. Having understood: *translate* perceiving. 28. A I brought *him.* 30. SA how that they laid wait; V how that wait was laid; SA *om.* straightway; V to speak before thee against him; SA to speak before thee (*om.* what they had against him); VA *om.* Farewell. 34. SVA And when he had read; S that he was of.

Chap. XXIV.—1. A after certain days; SVA with certain elders. 5. SVA of seditions. 6–8. SVA *om.* and would have judged—commanding his accusers to come unto thee. 8. A thou *for* thyself. 10. SVA I do cheerfully answer. 13. SVA can they prove to thee. 14. V believing the things. 15. SVA *om.* of the dead. 16. SVA Herein do I exercise also myself. 17. I came to bring; A I was about to bring. 20. SVA say, what evil they found, while. 22. SVA Now Felix having more perfect knowledge of that way, deferred them. 23. SVA to keep him; SVA *om.* or come. 24. VA his own wife; SV in Christ Jesus. 25. S of temperance and righteousness. 26. V *om.* him *after* given; SVA *om.* that he might loose him.

Chap. XXV.—2. SVA the chief priests. 5. *Translate* which among you are in authority. 6. SVA not more than eight or ten days. 7. SVA stood round about him; SVA *om.* against Paul. 8. SVA While Paul answered. 9. A Festus therefore. 11. SVA Therefore if I be. 16. SVA *om.* to die. 18. SVA of such evils as I supp. 19. A questions among them of.　22. SVA Then Agrippa *said;* SVA saith he.　25. V and that Paul himself.

Chap. XXVI—2. *Translate* accused of Jews.　3. A in customs; SVA wherefore I beseech to hear me patiently.　4. V all Jews.　7. SV. *om.* Agrippa; A *om.* king Agrippa; SVA accused of Jews.　9. V. *om.* verily. 10. V wherefore also I did *so* in Jer.　12. SVA of the chief priests.　14. SVA a voice saying unto me in the Hebrew tongue.　15. SVA And the Lord said.　17. SVA *om.* now.　21. SV *om.* the *before* Jews.　24. SVA Festus saith.　25. SVA But Paul saith.　26. V *om.* also.　28. SVA Then Agr. *said* unto Paul.　29. SVA And Paul *said.*　30. SVA *om.* when he had thus spoken.

Chap. XXVII.—2. SVA a ship of Adr., which was going to sail—of Asia, we launched.　3. A Julianus.　5. V we came to Myrra; SA we came to Lystra.　8. A the city of Alassa.　9. *Translate* the time of the fast 14. SVA called Euraquilon.　16. S²V called Cauda.　17. S help.　19. SVA they cast out with their own hands.　20. V *om.* then.　21. SVA And after.　34. V Wherefore also I pray; A for our health; SVA perish *for* fall.　37. V about *instead of* two hundred (*a mere error*); A fifteen. 39. A they wished.　41. SVA was broken by the violence (*om.* of the waves).

Chap. XXVIII.—1. SVA And when we were escaped, then we knew. 2. A *om.* every one.　3. A and Paul laid them.　5. S and felt nothing.　9. SVA But when; V *om.* also.　13. SV. we removed and came.　16. SVA And when we entered into Rome, Paul was suffered.　17. SVA he called; S he spake unto them saying.　18. S would have let me go.　21. S out of Judea against thee.　24. S And some therefore.　25. SVA unto your fathers.　27. S the heart of this people is overcharged; S *om.* and understand with their heart.　28. SVA this salvation of God.　29. SVA *om. this verse.*　30 SVA And he dwelt.　31. S *om.* Christ.